Winston
Graham
The Spanish
Armadas

Doubleday & Company, Inc. Garden City, New York

153574

To Luxton Arnold

AUTHOR'S NOTE. I would like to thank Miss Ann Hoffmann for her invaluable research assistance, my wife for much vital encouragement, Dr A. L. Rowse for helpful criticism and advice, Mr Wilfred Granville and Mr Robert Clark for generously reading the typescript, and Mr Lothar Mendes for some Spanish quotations. I would also thank Frances Partridge and Constable & Co Ltd for kind permission to use extracts from her translation of Captain de Cuellar's narrative, and Albert J. Loomie and the editor of *The Mariner's Mirror* for equally kind permission to use extracts from his translation of an Armada pilot's survey.

In 1582 Pope Gregory XIII introduced a new calendar, advancing the year by ten days. Continental Europe adopted it, but England for long clung to the old style. A historian of the sixteenth century may advance his dates – as Europe did – when the new calendar came in, and apply it to England. By doing this he alters all the dates which have been traditionally given to events in England by English historians. Or he may, as some English historians do, retain the old Julian calendar throughout, thereby distorting European dates. The only other method is to quote his dates with O.S. (Old System) or N.S. (New System) after each one to indicate his varying choice, a cumbersome and unattractive procedure. Readers of this book are therefore asked to assume that after 1582, where an event refers to the continent of Europe, the new calendar is used; where England, or a continental adventure seen through English eyes, the old. Fortunately the days of the week did not change. The Battle of Gravelines took place on a Monday both in English and Spanish eyes.

W. G.

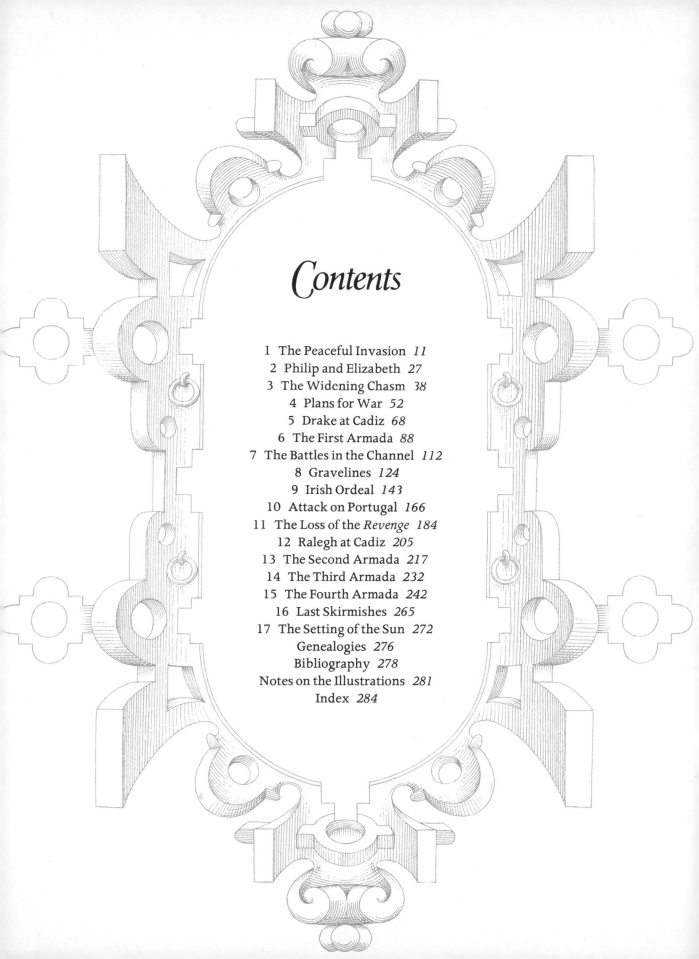

Contents

Colour Plates

1   *The Peaceful Invasion*

Late on Wednesday afternoon on the 18th July 1554, a Flemish squadron cruising in the English Channel off Portland Bill caught sight of a Spanish fleet moving east under full sail in a favourable breeze towards the Solent. The fleet consisted of about a hundred and thirty ships, some hundred of them substantial vessels, well equipped with bronze pieces, and carrying, aside from their crews, over eight thousand Spanish soldiers. A light rain was falling at the time, but the fleet as it approached land was in process of being dressed and beflagged; so the Flemish squadron dipped its flags in salute and fell in as escort. Near the Needles a dozen English naval sloops joined them, and by the morning of the 19th the whole armada was proceeding up the estuary of Southampton Water. It was four in the afternoon before all had dropped anchor under the eye of the castle.

The port of Southampton was flagged too and crowded for the occasion. Hardly one of its three hundred houses was not decorated, hardly one did not shelter some members of the English court, brilliant in velvet, gold chains and medals. Every hovel swarmed with servants, every stable and byre steamed with horses; carts and baggage jammed the greasy cobbled streets. For England, the southern part of a moderate-sized island on the periphery of Europe, was waiting to welcome the greatest prince in Christendom.

It was not difficult to pick out the Prince's ship among the newly arrived fleet, a Biscayan of nine hundred tons, the *Espiritu Santo*, because of the carved and gilded decorations on forecastle and poop. As soon as she came to anchor the bulwarks of this ship had been hung with heavy scarlet cloth; silk pennons fluttered in the damp, sultry breeze, and two royal standards, each ninety feet long, of crimson damask with the Prince's arms painted on them, hung from the mainmast and the mizzen. Three hundred sailors in crimson lined the decks.

Soon an ornamented barge left the quayside with a party of gaudy young English noblemen who had been chosen for their looks and their distinction

A 16th-century map depicting
Spain as the head of Europe

to welcome the Prince. Suspicious eyes from a hundred windows watched them go. Householders, lackeys, sailors, ostlers, rich merchants and fish-wives, urchins and beggars, all strained anxiously – and suspiciously – from vantage points to catch a first glimpse of visiting royalty. For he was a Spaniard, his name was Philip, and he had come to marry their Queen.

It had not been a good time, these last twenty years, for the people of England. The autumnal tyrannies of the Great King, his divorces, his quarrels with Rome, his suppression of the monasteries, his persecutions, clouded in people's minds the popularity and goodness of his earlier years. But the decade since Henry's death had been far worse than anything that had gone before. Ever higher prices, the infirmity of central government, the infiltration of the new rich everywhere, the enclosure of common land, the raising of rents and the turning out of long-rooted tenants, the disregard for public rights, the neglect of the fleet, and corruption and profiteering on a scale hitherto unknown even in sixteenth-century England, had led all men, or almost all men, to welcome the Queen when cold young Edward died. For years she had been neglected by her father, she had been persecuted by Anne Boleyn, she had been under constant pressure to change her religion, and she had been denied access to her mother, even when her mother lay dying; yet through it all she had retained the quiet loyalty of English people, who saw in her the only true heir and swiftly swept aside the pretensions of the Dudleys and Lady Jane Grey.

So, although she was the first queen the English had accepted for four hundred years, she had been crowned with great acclaim, and her early conduct and decrees had seemed conciliatory and clement and reasonable. She had even spared most of those who had conspired against her.

But now, within a year – exactly within a year of Edward's death – she was preparing to marry this foreign prince. The English have always been hypercritical and morbidly suspicious of foreign royalty who presume to marry their queens. They mistrust every gesture of friendship, analyse every public and private utterance he makes for signs of criticism or condescension, and see a plot for foreign domination under every secretary's cloak. It was her marriage to Geoffrey Plantagenet which made Matilda unacceptable in the twelfth century and finally lost her the throne. Mary's betrothal to Prince Philip had nearly done the same for her. Wyatt's formidable rebellion had been stopped only at the gates of London.

So Lady Jane Grey had finally gone to the block, but Mary had been unshaken in her resolve to pursue her marriage plans. Half Spanish herself, she saw nothing but good in a union with the future king of Spain. Spain and England had a long tradition of friendship. Henry's divorce of Catherine and England's subsequent apostasy had put some strain on that friendship, but now that England was returning to Catholicism such a union could only help to repair what had been damaged. It was true that Mary was now a virgin of thirty-eight and her husband a young widower of twenty-seven; it was true that they had never met or even corresponded, that all the courtship had been done on behalf of his son by Charles, Philip's father; it was true that Spain was at war with France and that an Anglo-Spanish marriage might drag England into the same war; but the advantages to Mary seemed far to outweigh all these objections.

Indeed, she might have argued – the later example of her half-sister not being available to her – what was a queen to do? Whomsoever she married she would offend someone. And it was essential for the continuance of the Tudor dynasty and the preservation of the Catholic faith that there should be an heir. Who more suitable to father one than a man who was heir to the Holy Roman Empire and who furthermore was a direct descendant of Edward III of England?

Philip II of Spain and Mary I of England on medallions struck in 1555, a year after their marriage

The watchers in the windows of all the little houses were not to see their new king that afternoon. Philip remained closely within the confines of his staterooms aboard the *Espiritu Santo* and slept aboard. It was not until the morning of the 20th that he stepped on to the splendid barge awaiting him and was rowed ashore surrounded by English and Spanish noblemen. On the barge the Earl of Arundel invested him with the Garter, and was in return presented with the wand of Chamberlain. The rain had temporarily eased when Prince Philip stepped ashore, so he was able to listen in more comfort to the Latin speech of welcome delivered by the enormous Sir Anthony Browne and to receive the gift of the white charger which the Queen had sent to him to greet him on arrival. The Prince said he would walk to the house prepared for him, but at this Sir Anthony demurred and 'took him up in his arms and put him on the saddle'. Thereupon, preceded by all the English and Spanish courtiers and nobles, he passed through the curious and mistrustful and largely silent crowd to the Church of the Holy Rood to return thanks for his safe arrival.

What sort of man did the English see? Clearly an impressive figure, despite his medium height and slight build, for he was in black and silver, hung with gold chains and glittering with jewels on coat and bonnet and breast. A quiet dignified young man – looking younger than his years – with a gracious manner and a charming, diffident smile. Titian's portrait of him painted about this time and now in the museum in Naples shows him to have a high forehead, strong up-growing rather short-cropped blond hair, firm winged eyebrows over heavy-lidded eyes, full lips, and a trace of a moustache and blond beard partly hiding the Hapsburg jaw. Not a young man, one would think, to whom women would be indifferent. Mary, when she met him, was not indifferent.

He had inherited considerable charm from his mother Isabella of Portugal, and he chose to exercise it upon the English. In the next weeks he was to need it all, not only to soften the distrust of the English but to allay the resentments of his own nobility who were to find themselves everywhere brusquely treated, and cheated and robbed at the slightest excuse. Of all the eight-thousand-odd Spanish soldiers, not one was allowed to land. The fleet was sent off to Portsmouth to revictual and the troops dispatched to the

Netherlands. The Spanish guard were kept in frustrated idleness on board one of the few ships remaining in Southampton Water, and attendance on the Prince was confined to Englishmen only. The noble Spanish watched in disgust at the — to their eyes — unrefined attempts of the English to wait upon their new master.

And it rained: how it rained! The weather in that century was nearly always on the side of the English, and now it weighed in with a commentary to suit the mood of the most convinced Lutheran. For all of the three days that Prince Philip remained in Southampton it rained so hard that the Spanish prince had to borrow a cape and hat to cross the street each day from his lodging to the church. When he eventually rode to Winchester for the wedding with an escort of three thousand nobles and retainers, halberdiers, archers and light horse, the weather was so bad that he was compelled to stop a mile from the city in the shelter of a recently dispossessed monastery to change his finery before entering the city.

Thereafter followed his welcome at the doors of the great cathedral by a sonority of mitred bishops, a procession to the high altar, sung Mass, and all the ceremonial by which God's annointed was greeted in a foreign but friendly land. This was Monday, and the wedding was not until Wednesday, but in the evening of Monday Queen Mary, unable longer to restrain her natural curiosity, sent secretly from the bishop's palace, saying she wished to meet him informally at ten o'clock that night and to bring only a select few of his retinue.

The events of their first meeting, as described by the Spaniards who accompanied the Prince, are in strange contrast with the reputation that Philip has been given by English, French and American historians of later centuries. It is hard to reconcile his behaviour with the picture of the monster many of them draw: the persecutor of the Netherlands, the bigot, the fanatic, the cold-blooded despot. Yet perhaps it is all — or nearly all — true. Perhaps age and authority changes men. Who, seeing Mary's father as the golden-haired boy coming to his throne and winning the hearts of his people at eighteen, could have foreseen the dangerous and unpredictable tyrant of his last years?

Prince Philip accepted the invitation of his future wife, but the 'select few' of his entourage amounted to more than twenty noblemen. On this point he was taking no risks. The whole party entered the bishop's palace by way of a back door and mounted a spiral stone staircase to the room where the Queen was waiting, attended only by Gardiner — the all-powerful Lord Chancellor and Bishop of Winchester, who had spent five years in the Tower for his religious principles — and by some dozen elderly noblemen and noblewomen. All women of her own age or younger Mary had excluded.

Tonight she was wearing a high-cut black velvet gown, a petticoat of frosted silver, a black velvet gold-trimmed wimple covering the head and sides of the face, and some of the finest diamonds at throat and waist that the English crown possessed. Mary at thirty-eight was a slim, rather small

The reredos,
Winchester Cathedral

In Winchester Cathedral:
Mary Tudor's chair

woman whose fair hair had become mousy in colour, and she seldom wore it about her face. Her eyes were grey and unwavering under sandy lashes and scarcely existent eyebrows. Her complexion, though naturally pale, was good and still youthful. She had a strong rather deep voice and a warmth and sincerity of manner that was not leavened by self-criticism or a sense of humour.

Philip at once bowed and went towards her, first accepting her hand and then kissing her full on the lips in what he said was 'the English manner'. It was a greeting that she clearly did not find distasteful; and she led him by the hand to two chairs placed under a brocade canopy where they sat talking in private for a long time. Presently the Prince asked if he might meet the Queen's ladies-in-waiting, and reluctantly she took him into the next room where they were all assembled, many of these being young and pretty girls. Philip kissed the lot. Again he claimed it was the English custom and no one denied him.

Afterwards Mary led him back into her private room and they chatted together for a further half hour. She was clearly captivated. It was now well after midnight and Philip rose to go, but said that he must first return to the ante-chamber to wish the ladies-in-waiting good night. How did one say this in English? The Queen taught him, and he started for the door, only to return laughing to say that he had forgotten already. Playfully she coached him again, and, repeating 'God ni hit' half under his breath, he returned to the ladies to salute them once more.

'Fickle Philip' he was sometimes called by his friends. It all seems a long way from 'the Spider of the Escorial'.

The wedding took place on the Wednesday, still in the pouring rain. Not for nothing had the cathedral been dedicated to St Swithin. But in its five hundred years of history there could never have been a more brilliant scene than this. Philip wore a white satin suit and a mantle of cloth of gold embroidered with jewels. The Queen again wore black velvet, but was so ablaze with precious stones that she seemed on fire. Her fifty ladies, according to the Spanish, 'looked more like celestial angels than mortal creatures'. The long ritual completed and the Mass done, the King of the Heralds, preceded by a blast of silver trumpets, proclaimed the titles of their majesties: 'Philip and Mary, by the grace of God King and Queen of England, France, Naples, Jerusalem and Ireland, Defenders of the Faith, Princes of Spain and Sicily, Archdukes of Austria, Dukes of Milan, Burgundy and Brabant, Counts of Hapsburg, Flanders and Tyrol.' It was a formidable list.

When the wedding was at last over, the King and Queen walked side by side to the palace through the crowd, which behaved with notable restraint. At the palace was a banquet for one hundred and fifty-eight, with four services of meat and fish, each service comprising thirty dishes, and endless toasts and more ceremonial, swords of state and ritual staffs and loving cups. The Spaniards noted that Mary was served on gold plate, Philip on silver; she, too, had the higher chair, was given precedence in everything.

The English were leaving them in no doubt as to how they saw the future. Only one Spaniard was allowed to serve the King at table, elsewhere ever since he landed his attendants had been English, the Spanish pushed out.

The meal lasted until six, then dancing until nine. Here there was difficulty, as the Spanish gentlemen and the English ladies did not know the same steps. Philip and Mary solved the problem by dancing in the German style. As night fell candles and torches lit the brilliant scene, but soon the King and Queen retired, not surprisingly after the fatigues and tensions of the arduous day. Mary's mother, so steadfast in her loyalty to the country of her birth and the faith of her ancestors, would have been happy to have seen that night. It looked as if friendship with Spain was restored and re-cemented and a permanent return to the Old Faith guaranteed.

What went wrong? Clearly Mary's inability to produce a child. Had a son been born it seems almost certain that the English, however much they hated the union which produced him, would have accepted him as their king. He would have been a male Tudor in direct descent from the two Henrys who had founded the line. The only other possible claimants were women.

The idea of Philip and Mary's union had originated with Philip's father, the Emperor Charles V, and had it succeeded it would have been a stroke of political statecraft of the first magnitude. In order to appreciate it one has to look at Philip's ancestry and at the map of Europe.

Philip's grandfather, Philip the Handsome, had married Joanna, daughter of Ferdinand of Aragon and Isabella of Castile, so combining the powerful houses of Hapsburg and Burgundy with the Spanish royal dynasty. Philip the Handsome died when Charles, Philip's father, was only six, and a succession of other deaths and misfortunes so struck the families with which he was connected that Charles before he was nineteen became master of a domain greater than Charlemagne's. To his possessions in the Low Countries and Spain were added Mexico, Peru, the Isthmus, the Caribbean Islands, Aragon, Catalonia, the Balearics, Naples and Sicily, Austria, Styria, Tyrol, Carinthia and Germany.

So the boy Charles became Charles V, Holy Roman Emperor. Born in 1500 in Ghent, Charles soon showed himself to be an able and autocratic ruler. A strong-willed, lusty and vigorous man, ever indulging his appetites, ever travelling about his domains, down-to-earth, practical, astute, gluttonous, he was both the savage persecutor of heretics and the brave defender of Christendom from the Turks. But the strain of kingship and the arduous life he lived wore down even his iron constitution, and by the time he was fifty-four he was an exhausted and sickly man. In 1540 he had created his son Duke of Milan, and, on his marriage to Mary of England, made over to him the Kingdom of Naples. With rare wisdom Charles had become convinced that the empire he had inherited was too unwieldy ever to be successfully governed by one man, and already he had given his brother

Ferdinand his Austrian possessions. For the rest he planned that Philip's son by his first wife, the infant Don Carlos, should succeed in Spain and that the child of Philip and Mary should inherit not only England but the Netherlands, thus taking the Low Countries away from Spain and giving them a strength and protection from across the Channel. One empire would become three kingdoms, each independent of the others, but all in friendly and fraternal alliance.

If Don Carlos died, Mary's child was to be King of Spain and of all Spain's vast possessions in the New World too. It is not surprising that Mary had so much to hope for.

And in those first weeks, despite the sullen looks of the English, all seemed well. It was true that the Duchess of Alva was highly offended at missing the wedding. She arrived from Southampton three days late, and even Mary's reception of her did not assuage her injured dignity. When she was presented, with splendid ceremonial, the Queen came to meet her and kissed her and, there being only one chair in the room, would not take precedence over her by sitting on it so suggested that they should both sit together on the floor. Not to be outdone in courtesy, the Duchess insisted that *she* only would sit on the floor. Mary therefore sent for two stools, and the comedy continued with first one on a stool and then both on the floor and then the other up and the first down, until at last they were seated side by side and talking amicably about something other than precedence. (The Duchess was offended all over again when the Earl of Derby tried to kiss *her* on the mouth. No one had had the impertinence to attempt such a thing ever before, and even though she was able to turn her cheek to him she could not contain her annoyance.)

The new and as yet uncrowned King of England used every grace and charm to engage the affections of his new subjects. He distributed gifts of silver to all the lords of the council and to many others besides. He promised pensions of thirty thousand ducats annually. He cancelled a debt of two and a quarter million ducats that his new wife had owed him. He treated everyone he met with the utmost courtesy, and scrupulously avoided any hint of interference in the affairs of the kingdom. Writing home to Spain a month after the wedding, one of his stewards, Don Pedro Enriquez, a nephew of the Duke of Alva, says:

> Their majesties are the happiest couple in the world, and are more in love with each other than I can say here. He never leaves her, and on the road is always by her side, lifting her into the saddle and helping her to dismount. He dines with her publicly sometimes, and they go to mass together on feast days.

By this date they were at Richmond on their way to Hampton Court. The great gatherings at Winchester and Southampton had mostly dispersed. Those of the English who were not in actual attendance on their majesties had galloped off home to their baronial estates. The Spanish were in less happy case. The Admiral of Spain was on his way back with part of his fleet to Coruña; the rest had convoyed the troops to Flanders. There still remained

The Tudor Mary I, whom Philip II of Spain, with a peaceful armada, arrived at Southampton to marry, hoping by this alliance to win England for Catholicism

some hundred noblemen with their servants, who had accompanied the Prince and who now in desultory fashion followed him to London.

Among them discontent at their early treatment had been succeeded by profound disillusion. The English were crude and ungentlemanly. And very unfriendly. There was no attempt on *their* part to hide their feelings. It was a barbaric country, full of heretics and renegades. The Spaniards found themselves jeered at in the streets, overcharged wherever they went, and actually attacked by vagabonds if they strayed far afield. Don Juan de Pacheco was robbed of a large sum of money and all his jewellery. The monks had to keep out of sight for fear of being set upon. Even such grandees as the Duke of Alva were given inferior lodgings on the way. When they reached London it was little better. There were constant quarrellings, and one week three English and one Spaniard were hanged for brawling. Two of the most distinguished of Philip's knights were set on in the streets by a raucous crowd who had taken offence at their costume and tried to strip it off their backs. What was worse, the political outcome of the marriage seemed likely to be far from what they had hoped. The Queen was surrounded by a group of powerful and suspicious councillors who would block as far as they could any Spanish influence over her decisions.

Soon the Spanish noblemen were craving their Prince's leave to go, and by late September all had slipped away except for Alva and four others and their personal servants. Thankfully the dukes and marquises, the counts and the knights took ship for home, bearing with them a memory of a land of uncivil and unpolished barbarians. But also a land of richness and plenty, the halls of the nobles doubly resplendent with the loot of the despoiled monasteries; a land of beautiful open harbours, of green fields and abundant flowers, of great flocks of sheep, of splendid palaces and churches and populous and prosperous villages and towns. They were memories that would linger long in the minds of the visitors. They had come to conquer in friendship. But they had received no friendship. The first Spanish invasion of England was nearly over.

Philip stayed a little over a year. During that time Mary fell completely in love with him, and she adored him for the rest of her short life.

In November Cardinal Pole returned from Rome to be made Archbishop of Canterbury, and was greeted with great joy by both Mary and Philip. On the 30th Pole solemnly absolved the Lords and Commons and the whole country from their apostasy and accepted England back into the Roman Catholic Church. At the end of the year the old heresy laws were revived, and the first Protestant was burned at the stake on the 4th February 1555.

It is difficult to apportion the blame for the reign of terror that spread through England, mainly in the south and east, for the next three and a half years. Pole certainly was the instrument of Rome; yet during his fourteen years of exile in Viterbo his rule was firm but mild: no record of the persecution of heretics. Gardiner was a controversial figure, deeply involved in

Painted by Titian, Charles v of Spain in the prime of his vigorous life, during which he ruled the largest and richest empire of his day

The burning of heretics and
unauthorized books in
the 16th century

many of the heresy trials; yet in his own diocese no victim suffered the fire until after his death. Bonner, Bishop of London, bears the stigma of the largest number of victims condemned in any diocese; but he was several times taken to task by the Privy Council for not being severe enough.

At the time, of course, the odium fell on Philip. The young man whose father had striven to root out heresy in his own kingdom wherever he found it and had burned the first Lutheran martyrs in Brussels in 1523, the young man who a few years later when attending a royal *Auto-da-fé* at Valladolid stated that 'if my own son was a heretic, I would carry wood to burn him myself', the young man who as he grew older grew steadily more fanatical in his hatred of Calvinism, would seem the natural instigator of the fires of Smithfield. Yet the evidence shows that he constantly urged moderation and clemency on his wife and her ministers. This may have been a piece of political calculation undertaken to endear him to his enemies. If so it failed. But if it were so it showed a degree of statecraft that would have served him well in later life. One can only conclude that at this date Mary was the more rigid sectarian, and that her charity towards her enemies – which she showed even to those who had tried to rob her of her throne – did not extend towards the enemies of her Catholic faith.

Of course some of the Protestants who burned did make things difficult for themselves. What could one do, for instance, with a preacher who on New Year's Eve 1555 offered up prayers from his pulpit for the Queen's death?

In November 1554 Mary announced that she was with child, and thanksgiving services were held in London churches. In March 1555 there were joustings, and the King and Queen spent Easter at Hampton Court. By May it became clear that Mary had been mistaken. In August Philip received word of his father's decision to abdicate in his favour, and on the 3rd September he left Dover to cross to Calais and ride to Brussels, where in the Hall of the Golden Fleece he formally accepted the sovereignty of the Netherlands. Early in the following year he became King of Spain.

Affairs of state, which were all-demanding, kept him away from England and his wife for eighteen months. When he returned in March 1557 and was reunited with Mary, it was to urge that England should honour her alliance with Spain and declare war on France. Easter they spent at Greenwich, together with the Duchess of Alva and the Duchess of Lorraine. But he was restive and unsettled and cold towards Mary. There are accounts of banquets and Garter processions and noble stag-hunts at Hampton Court in company with members of the Privy Council. On the 7th June England entered into a war for which she was completely unprepared, and soon after Philip announced his departure. On the 3rd July he and his Queen set out for Dover, spending a night at Sittingbourne. Mary was weak and ailing, and grieved at the thought of another separation. When he left her on the 5th July neither of them was to know that it was their last meeting. In sixteen months she was dead. Philip was never to visit England again.

One other event of great consequence occurred during Philip's visits to England. He met the tall, pale, slim, auburn-haired girl of twenty-one who was to succeed Mary and who was to be his adversary all his life.

At the end of April 1555 the Queen, still convinced that she was pregnant, went to Hampton Court to await her confinement, and, this being perhaps the happiest time in her rather joyless life, with Philip still beside her and the expectation of bearing his child, her feelings softened towards her half-sister. She had never forgotten the ignominy and humiliations thrust upon her and her mother by this girl's mother; yet although Elizabeth was kept in close confinement, Mary had been unable or unwilling to have her put to death, as she was often urged to do. Now in the warmth and burgeoning of her life (a fruitful marriage to a man she loved, a heart-warming return of England to the Old Faith) reconciliation and forgiveness were in the air. A modest forgiveness, anyhow. Elizabeth was summoned from Woodstock, but was allowed to bring only five servants and she rode under heavy guard. The journey took four days, and she entered Hampton Court by a back gate and was lodged in rooms recently vacated by the Duke of Alva.

This meant she was near the King, and it gives a ring of truth to the account given by Antoine de Noailles, the French Ambassador, and confirmed by Giovanni Michieli, the Venetian Ambassador, that Philip visited Elizabeth secretly, before his formal introduction to her in the presence of Mary. It would not be surprising if he was curious to meet this young woman, still a heretic, but known to be witty and popular wherever she went, the issue of that scandalous and adulterous union between Henry VIII and his so-called second wife. Recently suspected of complicity in plots to dethrone Mary, walking a tight-rope to save her life, living in a world where every innocent word had to be watched lest it smell of treason, yet firmly named by her father as the next successor to the throne – as if no question of her legitimacy had ever crossed his mind – Elizabeth was very clearly a person of the greatest interest to Mary's husband.

Later, when Mary at last consented to see Elizabeth and taxed her angrily with plotting against her throne, there is the well-known story that Philip hid behind the arras and listened – so far as he could follow it – to what was being said. Another account states that after the first formal meeting Mary sent Philip for a private conversation with Elizabeth to try to persuade her to confess her errors and throw herself on the mercy of the Queen.

In any event it is unquestionable that Philip and Elizabeth got on well together. Philip, at least until his middle years, always had an eye for a pretty girl, and Elizabeth, if not exactly pretty, had grace and vitality and charm and the ineffable glamour of youth – a very different person from the intent, plain, spinster-like, delicate woman who was his wife. As for Elizabeth, all her life she was susceptible, and Philip was not quite twenty-eight. He was a prince, had a charming courtesy of manner, and he was a potential ally. And she was most certainly a maiden in distress. More than ever in her life before or after, at that moment, she sorely needed an ally. Michieli, reporting later

Elizabeth I as a girl

to Venice, wrote: 'At the time of the Queen's pregnancy Lady Elizabeth contrived so to ingratiate herself with all the Spaniards and especially the King, that ever since no one has favoured her more than he does', and that 'the King had some particular design towards her.'

No doubt their friendship was politic on either side, but it was a genuine attraction too. Mary became jealous – it was the last emotion that Elizabeth would have wished to arouse – and Philip saw little more of her. But she was *preserved*. Philip pressed Mary to promise this before he left England. He also pressed it on various members of the Council and received an assurance from them. After being kept in close confinement at a house a few miles from Hampton Court, Elizabeth was permitted to see Philip off at Greenwich on his way to Dover at the end of August, though she was not allowed to take part in the state procession.

It is improbable that Philip saw Elizabeth on his second visit, for she was at Hatfield. There he sent the Duchess of Parma and the Duchess of Lorraine to press Elizabeth into a marriage with Emmanuel Philibert, Duke of Savoy. This would have meant that, if Mary died, the new Prince Consort would have been a devoted friend of Spain and an enemy of France. But Elizabeth, with that genius for dissimulation and delay she was to show so often, succeeded in putting off a decision until the crisis was past.

So Mary, after hoping a second time, though less publicly, that she was with child, slowly slid into her last illness and died, as sad a woman as she had lived, at the age of forty-two. When he knew of her grave illness King Philip pleaded pressure of business and sent Count de Feria to represent him. When Mary died de Feria made it known to the Privy Council that the King of Spain would support Elizabeth's claim to the throne.

Shortly after Elizabeth was crowned Count de Feria craved a private audience of the new Queen and there presented to her Philip's formal proposal of marriage. The proposal was couched in warmly diplomatic terms; but, being a Spanish prince, Philip forbade his ambassador to remind Elizabeth of any favour that she might owe him. It appears, however, that de Feria disobeyed his royal master, for Elizabeth's reply is documented in a manuscript still lying in the Spanish archives in Simancas. 'It is the people who have placed me in the position I at present hold as the declared successor to the Crown.'

2 *Philip and Elizabeth*

When in 1514 Louis XII of France lost his Queen, Anne of Brittany, Henry VIII of England proposed a marriage between Louis and his youngest sister Mary. Louis, who was fifty-two, agreed to the match. Mary was eighteen and passionately in love with the rich and charming Charles Brandon, later Duke of Suffolk. She stormed and raged and wept at her brother's decision, but finally had to surrender to it. When at last she sailed to meet her French husband in October of that year a splendid retinue accompanied her; among them a pretty little maid of honour called, in the *Cottonian MSS.*, Madamoyselle Boleyn.

The following January the narrow-shouldered and sickly Louis died – they said that his English wife danced him to death – and the young Queen contrived after some vicissitudes to marry her charming duke and retire to Suffolk, where in the due course of time she became the grandmother of Lady Jane Grey. Madamoyselle Boleyn, however, stayed on at the French court until 1522 when she returned to England, with consequences that we all know.

Madamoyselle Boleyn's daughter ascended the English throne in 1558. She had the disadvantage, like Mary, of being a woman, with the added drawback of being, in the eyes of many of her subjects, illegitimate. All Henry's thunderings and contrivings failed to convince the people that his true wife was not alive in the person of Catherine of Aragon when he married Anne Boleyn; and when Elizabeth was born the junketings and bonfires held throughout England were privately to celebrate that the child was but a girl and Henry had only got his just deserts.

Yet twenty-five years later England – which throughout its history had refused, often to its cost, to consider talented and brave royal bastards as having any claim to the throne at all – accepted this girl without hesitation, indeed with great rejoicing.

The reasons are numerous and quite clear. Henry VIII's will still counted for something in people's minds. And there was no alternative male of the

Tudor line. The only alternative, and legitimate, female was married to the Dauphin of France, which put her right out of the running. The majority of the country, although preferring the old forms of worship, did not like being under the tutelage of Rome. The new rich, although confirmed in some of their spoils by Mary, felt safer with a Protestant ruler. Everybody – except a crust of rigid fanatics – was disgusted and revolted by Mary's reign of terror. And Protestantism under persecution had increased rapidly through the country. These reasons, and a last personal one: Elizabeth was already popular and a convincing figure among those who knew her, and the word had spread.

Yet it was a sorely tried young woman who came to the throne. When one thinks of the abnormalities that psychiatrists today blame upon the relatively minor traumas of youth, Elizabeth's level head, emotional stability and unwavering judgment are qualities to be wondered at. No king's daughter of those days could have a simple and placid childhood, constantly, as they were, in the spotlight of court interest and an inevitable pawn in the matrimonial game of European power politics. But Elizabeth's mother had been beheaded for adultery when Elizabeth was two years and eight months old. Thereafter she was taught that her mother was an evil woman and that she was herself a bastard. When she was eight her stepmother and cousin, Katherine Howard, was executed for similar reasons. Fawned upon or ignored according to the whim of her father, she had endured the sexual attentions of one Seymour and the suspicions of another, had been the inevitable focus of plotting Protestantism under Mary and had been sent to the Tower, from which few royal personages ever safely emerged. Now at an age when most young women were happy to spend their time choosing a dress or a husband, she found herself on the lonely eminence of a throne, surrounded by advisers whose integrity she could only assess by her own fallible judgment, without a near relative on whom she could safely lean; and Queen of a country that was torn by religious bigotry, almost bankrupt, in the grip of inflation, the army defeated and the navy neglected, and at war with the French – who now had one foot in Calais and the other in Scotland.

It was a daunting prospect.

One of the most daunting features of it was the emergence from their holes in Germany and Switzerland of all those Protestant exiles and Calvinist fanatics who had fled the country during the Marian persecutions and who were now returning post-haste to exact their revenge and to scour out the kingdom and cleanse it of the last vile vestiges of Popery. And, only two weeks after Elizabeth's accession, news reached her that when the announcement of Mary's death reached France the King had proclaimed his daughter-in-law to be the true Queen of England; and from that time Mary Queen of Scots and her husband the Dauphin of France began to quarter the royal arms of England with their own.

In these conditions Count de Feria waited upon the young Queen and

OPPOSITE The main entrance of Hampton Court, Middlesex, where Philip II, on his visit in 1554 to marry Mary Tudor, met the future Queen Elizabeth for the first and only time

OVERLEAF An imaginative portrayal of Count Feria, Philip II's earliest ambassador to the English court

brought her news of Philip's proposal of marriage. She thanked him and said she would consider the matter.

It is quite possible that she did consider the matter. They had met and been attracted to each other. They were of suitable age – he only six years the elder. His attempts while in England to moderate Mary's persecution of the Protestants suggested that at heart he put politics above religion, as Elizabeth proposed to do. Further confirmation of this, as she would certainly see with her acute mind, lay in his preserving her and supporting her accession to the throne; for, apart from her desirability as a woman, he had no doubt concluded that it was better to have an independent Protestant on the English throne than a Catholic bound to France. Also Elizabeth knew of the inheritance promised to a child of Mary's marriage, and therefore one could assume the same for any child of hers if Philip were the father. It was not to be lightly dismissed.

Probably she toyed with it for a while, knowing in her heart that the bitterness which Mary had created in England towards Rome and Spain would make such a marriage virtually unworkable. A Catholic Elizabeth? They would not tolerate it. A Protestant Elizabeth with a Catholic husband? Balance and counterpoise. How better to preserve the country from the worst excesses of religious bigotry? It was just worth considering.

She was still considering some months later when she learned that Philip, despairing of an answer, had married the French princess, Elizabeth of Valois, instead. She said in annoyance to de Feria: 'Your master must have been *much* in love with me not to be able to wait four months!' Yet she continued to keep his portrait in her private cabinet all through the long years ahead, while friendly rivalry gave way to hostility and hostility at last to war.

The disruptive forces of the sixteenth century were too strong for all but the wisest and most cautious of rulers. Charles v, Philip's father, the last and one of the greatest of the Holy Roman Emperors, abdicated from his throne and his responsibilities and retired a broken man to the monastery of Yuste where he died in 1558, conscious that most of his ideals had come to nothing and that all his strivings and battles to preserve Christian unity had foundered. For they had come into conflict with intolerances worse than his own.

He was foredoomed to fail, as Philip failed after him. When Charles was born, Martin Luther was a chorister of seventeen waiting to read law at the university of Erfurt. Twenty-two years later, a noble and formerly dissolute Spaniard of thirty-one, Ignatius of Loyola, fasting in his cell in a Dominican convent and spending seven hours a day on his knees, began to have visions of the Virgin and her Blessed Son which led to the foundation of the Society of Jesus. At about the same date a Swiss boy, John Calvin by name, was sent by his parents to Paris to avoid the plague, and it was not many years before he too had a vision which convinced him that he alone

Philip II, the young but gravely responsible king, painted by Titian

The Inquisitor General of Spain, Tomas de Torquemada, with the young prince Don Juan

was the chosen voice of God. In 1480 the Inquisition had been instituted, primarily then as an anti-Jewish measure, by the chaplain to Queen Isabella, a Dominican friar called Tomas de Torquemada, and had spread throughout Spain. So the forces for Reformation and Counter-Reformation were poised. An emperor who sought to reconcile these forces, whether by reason or by arms, was trying to subdue an earthquake.

Because of this religious conflict the sixteenth became the bloodiest, bitterest century in Europe until the ignoble twentieth dawned. For, in whatever mood the Reformation was conceived, by the middle of the century its intolerance was as narrow, as cruel and as bigoted as the Catholic opposition. As John Buchan once said, there is no such disruptive force as a common creed held with a difference. Looking at the picture of devastation and persecution, particularly in France and the Low Countries, it is sometimes hard to believe that both sides could so completely have lost sight of the principles of the founder of their faith and of the tenets of tolerance, charity, loving kindness, humility and brotherly love that he preached. At least in the twentieth century some of the cleavages, some of the issues, seem to have been real. One believes that even when viewed from the perspective of four hundred years they may still appear to have been real. But in the sixteenth, both sides committed the atrocities they did carrying the same New Testament in their hands.

Yet as it happens most of the rulers of the day, excepting Philip, were humanists. Catherine de' Medici, although she bears the terrible stigma of the massacre of St Bartholomew, was no religious fanatic, and, so long as it ministered to the well-being of her house and children, she was all for moderation. William of Orange, though in a sense a willing prisoner of the Reformed Church, since it alone provided the dynamic of revolt, was personally a believer in freedom of conscience and worship for everyone. Henry of Navarre changed his religion twice – once to save his life and once to gain his kingdom. The rule of Mary Queen of Scots was perhaps too brief and stormy to assess, but her son James would certainly not have allowed a mere sectarianism to obstruct his view of the main chance, and it was he who shrewdly observed that 'one Puritan presbiter equals one Papist priest'.

The most successful of all these rulers was the one most successful in balancing the disruptive forces which threatened her kingdom, first from within and then from without. Elizabeth was fortunate in that the great mass of the people of her kingdom shared her views: they wanted the Anglicanism of Henry, not the fanatical Calvinism of Edward's time nor the savage Catholicism of Mary. They were fortunate in that they found in her the perfect expression of their will. Early in her reign she remarked that there was only one Jesus Christ and one faith, the rest was dispute over trifles.

In the destruction of the monasteries the bones of St Frideswide of Oxford, a holy woman who died in 735 after founding a nunnery on the site of the cathedral there, were cast out upon a dung heap, and the body of the wife of a Canon of Christ Church, a distinguished Protestant divine, was buried in their place. When Mary succeeded, the remains of the newly dead lady were thrown out too. On Elizabeth's accession a dispute arose among the Canons as to who should be reinterred in the place of honour in the cathedral. Elizabeth's reply was terse and to the point, and with great ceremony the bones of the two women were reburied together.

It was a portent of the new reign; and only the cold winds of bigotry from outside England, the revolt in the Netherlands, the bloody massacres in France, the anathemas of Rome, the claims of Mary of Scotland and the threat of invasion from Spain, forced Elizabeth and her Council into the narrowing restrictive measures of the 1580s.

Elizabeth and Philip corresponded from time to time in the early years of their reigns. Indeed both were assiduous correspondents and incredibly devoted workers at the tasks to which God had called them. Elizabeth, who spoke French and Italian fluently by the time she was eleven and could write to her brother in Latin at thirteen, dealt with visiting potentates without needing an interpreter and treated her Council early to the quality of her mind and tongue. Perhaps the most English of monarchs since Harold, she never left the country even to visit her grandfather's Wales.

Philip, although his mother was Portuguese and his father born in Ghent of Burgundian blood, was as true a Spaniard at heart as Elizabeth was English. After his return from England he travelled little and was only happy in Spain. And unlike his father, who was a big clumsy man of enormous appetites and popular appeal, Philip was reserved, dignified, quiet-mannered, proud, the perfect Spanish grandee. He became as well loved in Spain as Elizabeth did in England and gave expression to the Spanish will as truly as she did to the English.

The period following his marriage to Elizabeth of Valois was the happiest of his life. He fell in love with the fourteen-year-old princess, who was fresh and charming and appeared untouched by the corrupt French court in which she had been brought up. She bore him two daughters, who were always his favourite children, and died when she was twenty-three – almost inevitably – in childbirth. By this time Philip was forty-one and had shouldered the responsibilities of kingship for thirteen years. It had aged him, made him more cautious, more exacting, more set in his religious convictions and more prone to withdraw from court society. More than ever he sought not compromises but solutions to every problem. (Elizabeth of England, on the contrary, had realized that solutions are rare in politics; if one shelves a problem often enough it may in the end disappear. At least it is likely to be superseded by another more urgent!)

By this time Philip had just begun his life's monument by laying the foundation stone for his great palace-monastery of El Escorial, dedicated to St Lawrence the Martyr, whose convent in St Quentin had been burned by Spanish troops when taking the town from the French in 1557. Ever since,

Joanna of Austria, the sister of
Philip II and mother of
King Sebastian of Portugal

Philip, who had a special devotion to this saint, had been looking for a
suitable site to build a commemorative monastery near his new capital of
Madrid. From 1563 until 1584 the great project was in process of building,
employing three thousand workmen for over twenty-one years and costing
in all over three and a half million ducats. Whenever he could spare the
time in those early years Philip would go to a seat quarried out of rock at
the foot of the mountains called the Hermits to watch the work in progress.
The building was designed to the shape of an upturned gridiron, the instrument on which St Lawrence was put to death, and four great towers one
hundred and eighty feet high represented the feet of the gridiron. The
whole giant sombre building is six hundred and eighty-two feet long and
five hundred and eighty-one feet deep, and is settled on the south-western
slopes of the Guadarramas, with the gaunt and gloomy mountains rising
behind. Without shelter and exposed as it is to the searing heat of summer
and the blighting winds of winter, it has a loneliness and a harshness and a
dignity peculiarly in keeping with the nature of the King who conceived it.
Built of dark grey almost greenish granite, it has seven towers, fifteen gate-
ways and twelve thousand windows and doors, almost all of them small, and
within the building the great monastery church resembles St Peter's, Rome.

Yet, despite its forbidding appearance, the interior of the Escorial when it
was completed showed the rich garnerings of an Empire. White and
coloured marbles from the Apennines, green and black jaspers from
Granada, wrought bronze from Flanders, veined and spotted alabaster from
Tuscany, rose-coloured coral from Sardinia, delicate ironwork from Aragon,
all contributed to the magnificence. The new woods of the Indies had been
brought to combine with fine brocades from Florence, crystal chandeliers
from Venice and the silk damasks of Seville. Artists and sculptors had
worked for two decades decorating the walls and ceilings with carvings and
frescoes, statuary and paintings.

Even so, it is still more the pantheon than the palace, and here in due time
Philip brought many of his relatives to be reburied, including his father and
mother, Charles and Isabella; his aunts, Queen Leonore of Portugal and
Queen Mary of Hungary; his first wife Maria; his two brothers, Don
Fernando and Don Juan, who had died in infancy; his son Don Carlos; his
half-brother Don John of Austria; and his grandmother Joanna, who had
been insane for thirty-nine years before she died. Picturing this slightly-
built, humourless, deeply religious, self-contained man sitting with his
cloak wrapped round him to protect him from the winds of the Sierras,
watching the slow growth of his own monastery and his own tomb, one
thinks of the fourth dynasty Egyptians building their great pyramids at
Giza. Perhaps no one since the Pharaohs had been so preoccupied with
death. Perhaps no one since the Pharaohs had so closely intermarried as did
the Hapsburgs of Philip's time. The result was a strain of insanity running
through the family, together with hyperaesthesia and melancholia.

At the time of the death of Elizabeth of Valois, Philip's son, Don Carlos,

ABOVE The young prince
Don Carlos, whom his father,
Philip II, shut away because
of his insanity

LEFT Elizabeth of Valois,
the third wife of Philip II

also died, after being imprisoned in his rooms for six months hopelessly
insane. Six years earlier he had seriously injured his head in a fall and had
almost died; and some blame this fall for the deterioration which followed.
But the Venetian Ambassador, writing soon after the accident, says that for
three years already Don Carlos had 'suffered an alienation of the mind'. It
was the dread hereditary weakness claiming another victim.

These deaths left Philip without a wife and without a male heir, but
there is no record of his having approached Elizabeth again. In the ten years
since she came to the throne the two countries had drifted too far apart on
the tides of religious conflict. A political system in Europe which had
endured since the last decades of the fifteenth century was dissolving, and
no man knew how – or if ever – it would solidify again.

3 *The Widening Chasm*

For some seventy years the pattern of alignment in Europe had been relatively unchanged. On the one side was the Holy Roman Empire, a loosely associated group of nations and states, consisting of Spain, Germany, Italy and the Netherlands, to which, ever since Henry VII had concluded an alliance with Spain, England and the Tudors had adhered. Confronting this group, almost surrounded by it, and relatively smaller, but powerful, homogeneous and militant, was France, to which Scotland under the Stuarts was allied.

Now the explosion of the religious dynamic shattered these easily drawn frontiers. The revolt in the Netherlands gradually drew English sympathy towards the struggling co-religionists of the Low Countries and away altogether from Spain; and the rapid spread of Calvinism in Scotland meant an inevitable strain on her relations with a still Catholic France. And in countries unlike Spain (where Protestantism was early rooted out by the Inquisition), in countries where people of both creeds sought to live in peace, the demand by the fanatics was that religious loyalties should cut across national loyalty.

In its early days Calvinism was the religion of the opposition. Catholicism represented the older monarchies and the aristocratic and propertied families of the Middle Ages; Protestantism, though led by aristocrats, the thrusting new middle classes. The Protestant faith, by going back to the poverty and simplicity of the early Church, more closely resembled Christianity in its first days. But in the sixteenth century it was disfigured, as both extreme wings of religious belief were equally disfigured, by what D. M. Loades calls 'criminals whose anti-social neuroses were driven into religious channels by the atmosphere of the time'.

When Philip married his Elizabeth of Valois he was, apart from marrying a young girl whom he fancied, attempting a change of policy which would lead to Spanish friendship with France and would also, he hoped, help to combat the rise of Lutheranism there. But wedding celebrations in France that century had a way of going wrong. (It was another such event which sparked off the massacre of St Bartholomew.) On this occasion Elizabeth's father, Henry of France, a robust and vigorous man of forty who loved violent exercise, took part in the tournament celebrations, and after several passages at arms, wanted to break another lance before retiring and so commanded that the Count de Montgomery should be his opponent. Montgomery pleaded to be excused. The Queen told Henry that he was tired and should ride no more. Henry would have none of it and so the two men galloped towards each other and broke their lances after the approved style. But Montgomery forgot to release the broken end of the lance from his gloved fingers, and the splintered end entered the King's visor and pierced his eye. The King fell forward on the neck of his horse, which carried him with slowing pace to the end of the enclosure. In ten days he was dead.

The French King Henry II wounded to death while breaking a lance in a tournament, 1559

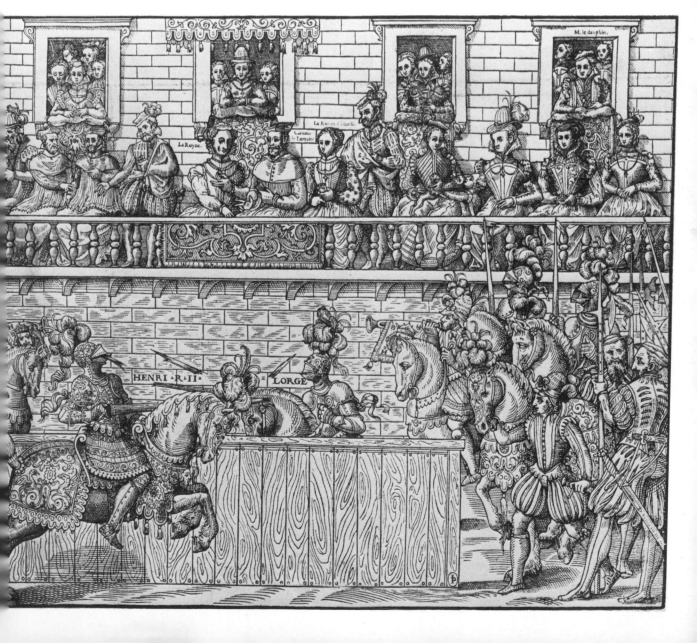

The King had been one of the most fanatical Catholics of his day, and as Henri Martin, the French historian, says: 'All Protestant Europe hailed the arm of the Almighty in this thunderbolt which had struck down the persecuting king in the midst of his impious festivities.'

Whether the reformers were right or wrong Henry's death, in the height of his vigour and authority, was a profound calamity for France and for his family, for it ushered in thirty years of bloody anarchy which saw towards its end the final disappearance of the house of Valois. At his bedside through his last days and when he died were two of the most famous women of the century. His young daughter-in-law, the Queen elect, was Mary, Queen of Scotland and the Isles. His wife was Catherine de' Medici.

It is generally overlooked that Mary Queen of Scots, although a Stuart by name, was by blood just as much a Tudor as a Stuart. Her grandparents were James Stewart, Margaret Tudor, Claude of Guise and Antoinette of Bourbon. Elizabeth was the granddaughter of Henry VII. Mary was his great-granddaughter.

Although her childhood was not as traumatic as Elizabeth's, it contained more than its share of tension, shock and high drama. She was born in December 1542, nine years later than her English cousin, and her father, James V of Scotland, died a week after her birth, at the age of thirty. She was not expected to live but she was crowned Queen when she was nine years old, and her mother, the French Mary of Lorraine, became Queen Regent. She did live, and, there being no question of her legitimacy, was quickly put on the marriage market as a political pawn of great importance. Before she was sixteen she married the Dauphin of France, and while she was yet sixteen she became Queen of France.

Mary of Guise and Lorraine, the second wife of James V of Scotland and mother of Mary Queen of Scots

After her shaky start in life Mary grew to be a tall girl, and a very attractive one, but her husband, the first of Catherine de' Medici's three sons to reign, was thin and undeveloped, small in stature and of low intelligence. During the short time that she was on the throne, Mary surrounded herself with courtiers, artists, musicians and poets, and gave herself over to the pleasure of being young and sought-after and gracious and charming; the affairs of the nation were left to her uncles, the Cardinal of Lorraine and Francis, Duke of Guise. It would have been virtually impossible for her to have done otherwise. Her husband was not yet sixteen, and of retarded development. Behind her two uncles, though not yet the formidable figure of later years, was her mother-in-law.

Mary might have developed into a considerable political force in France as she grew older and Francis grew older, for she already had almost complete dominance over him; but she was not given the chance. Francis reigned only sixteen months and then died from an abscess in the ear. Mary was left a beautiful young widow with no future at the French court. Her mother-in-law disliked her and was jealous of her, and schemed to take over the regency on behalf of the next of her sons, Charles, who was only ten. Mary hesitated for a while, surveying the European scene, and then proposed that she should next marry Don Carlos, the heir to the Spanish throne.

This proposition, coming from a glamorous, high-spirited girl in her teens, casts an interesting light on her character. Don Carlos was about the same age as herself, but was one of the most unprepossessing young men in Europe. Apologists of Mary have always argued that she eventually brought about her own ruin by allowing her heart to rule her head. Whatever happened later, on this occasion there was no sign of such a failing.

But the proposal was vetoed by Catherine de' Medici, who feared for her own daughter Elizabeth's precedence in Spain, and opposed by the other Elizabeth, who saw danger for England in such a marriage; so nothing came

The future second husband of
Mary Queen of Scots:
Lord Darnley, aged seventeen

of it. In August 1561 Mary accepted an invitation from the Scottish parliament to return to take up her crown, and arrived on the 19th of that month in Leith.

It could hardly have been a more unpropitious time, for religious war had only ceased the year before on the death of her mother, and in the interval the Scottish Protestants had embraced the doctrines of Calvin in their most extreme form. Mary was greeted apparently in expectation that she would instantly give up her Catholic faith, dropping it as it were overboard like an unwanted valise before she landed, and when she did not the fury of her parliament and council knew no bounds.

Nevertheless, in spite of her precarious hold on the country she imported courtiers, musicians and furnishings from France, gave balls, dinners and receptions of considerable taste, and, as a side issue, dispatched an envoy to the court of Elizabeth requesting that Elizabeth should recognize her as the next successor to the English throne. Elizabeth, while expressing the warmest sentiments, politely refused. 'Would you,' she asked, 'require me in my own life to set my winding sheet before my eyes? Princes cannot like their own children, those that should succeed them. How then shall I like my cousin being declared the Heir Apparent? I know the inconstancy of the people of England, how they ever mislike the present Government and have their eyes fixed upon that person that is next to succeed.'

Elizabeth at this stage, and all through the long quarter century ahead, was far more favourably disposed towards Mary than the English Privy Council or general public opinion. They would have had her blood long before. Mary indeed tried to arrange a meeting with Elizabeth, hoping not unreasonably that her charm would work towards a closer understanding of her rights to the succession; but one crisis after another supervened and it never took place.

Mary had still not abandoned the hope of marrying Don Carlos, and her envoy in England constantly treated with the Spanish Ambassador to this end. Perhaps to take Mary's mind off the more formidable power politics in which she was engaged, the young Lord Darnley was permitted to travel up to Scotland. Elizabeth 'allowed' it, rather in the way she allowed Drake and others to sail on their expeditions to the Spanish Main. Permission by absence of prohibition, while officially looking the other way, was a technique she brought to perfection in her long reign.

Mary met the handsome young man, for the first time in four years, at Wemyss Castle on the rocky coast of Fife, and this time instantly fell in love with him. In spite of 'official' opposition from England, they quickly married. Darnley was another great-grandchild of Henry VII, but his Tudor blood, like Mary's, was diluted with more feckless strains. Although their son eventually was the means of unifying England and Scotland, the marriage was an unmitigated disaster for both parents. Within four years Darnley had been found strangled in the garden of Kirk o'Field House, Mary had married Bothwell, who in the revolt which followed was forced to fly

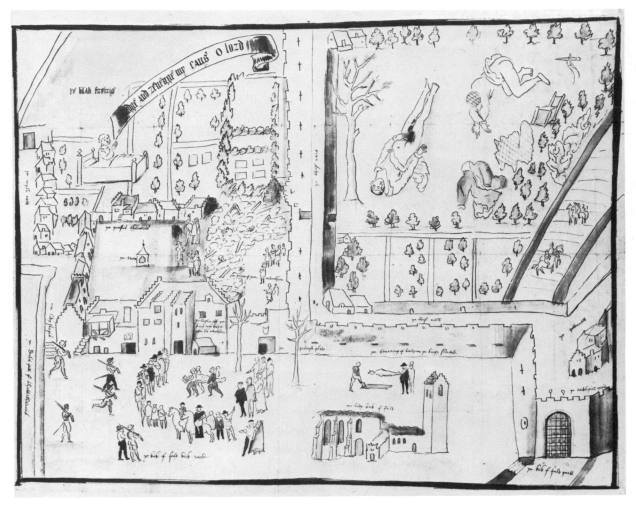

the country to save his life, and Mary, to save hers, had entered English territory and asked Elizabeth for sanctuary.

So began the long imprisonment – though imprisonment is a harsh word to describe a confinement in which Mary was throughout allowed an entourage of forty, and was permitted to hunt and to visit the local spa to take the waters. During it she never ceased to intrigue – or listen to intrigues – against Elizabeth's life and throne. This situation, which was dangerous to Elizabeth and frustrating and exasperating for Mary, persisted through two generations before it ended on a cold grey February morning in the great hall of Fotheringhay.

Elizabeth was no killer, especially not of another Queen, especially not one of Tudor blood. She resisted her Council to the very last, and then at the very last sought to evade the responsibility. Mary was not a compulsive martyr, not like Thomas à Becket, or her own grandson, Charles I. But, for all her many other qualities, she was a compulsive schemer and, in the context of the time, the outcome was bound in the end to be the same.

The scene, drawn by an English agent, at Kirk o' Field, Edinburgh, after the murder of Lord Darnley in 1567

43

During these two decades, geographically between Spain, which remained rigidly Catholic in the iron grasp of the Inquisition, and England, which, first from choice and then for self-preservation, became steadily more Protestant, religious war ravaged Europe. In the Netherlands, with Calvinism providing the explosive force, this became increasingly a nationalistic war to free the Low Countries from Spanish occupation. In France, under a succession of weak kings, it was always a dynastic conflict – at least at the top – with great Catholic families striving against great Protestant families to control the country.

The mother of the kings, Catherine de' Medici, was constantly struggling, scheming, working to preserve the Valois dynasty into which she had married. Despised by the French nobility, neglected during her husband's lifetime for his mistress Diane de Poitiers, without Elizabeth's intellect or royal blood, and lacking the charm of Mary Queen of Scots, she yet contrived to remain a power behind the throne and to perform an intricate *pas de deux* with each of her sons in turn, while she played off against one another the three great families of France : the Guises, the Bourbons and the Montmorencys.

The resultant civil war was not the consequence of her intrigues but the consequence of their failure. Time and again she conspired with one side or the other in an attempt to bring peace to France – while Huguenots stormed Catholic monasteries and compelled the monks to hang each other, while Catholics tore Huguenots to pieces and threw the pieces into the sewer, while whole villages and towns were put to the sword indiscriminately by either side.

The wedding of Henry of Navarre, a Protestant and a Bourbon, with the King's sister Marguerite, a Catholic and a Valois, was planned with a political reconciliation in mind – rather as Henry Tudor, a Lancastrian, had married Elizabeth of York. But Catherine de' Medici and her younger son the Duke of Anjou had long found Admiral Coligny's brusque influence over the King intolerable, and planned to have this leader of the Huguenots assassinated. The attempt failed and the twenty-two-year-old King Charles IX of France was then persuaded, after hours of resistance, to sanction a massacre in order, as he was told, to save his throne from the avenging Protestants.

So from the morning of the 24th August, with hysterical savagery the slaughter began, running its course for four days, spreading to the provinces, and not finally expending itself until mid-September, when the Protestant dead are likely to have numbered about thirty thousand men, women and children.

Such was the religious tolerance of the time that, when the news reached the Pope, he ordered that fireworks should be set off and bonfires lit for three nights to celebrate the deed and a commemorative medal struck. Pope Gregory further said that news of this slaughter was a hundred times more welcome than the news of the great naval battle of Lepanto in which the

On a tapestry, Catherine de' Medici with (centre) her favourite third son, the Duke of Anjou, later Henry III of France, and his younger brother François, Duke of Alençon

ABOVE Gaspard de Coligny,
Admiral of France and
a leader of the Protestants

RIGHT St Bartholomew's Day,
1572: the massacre, inspired
by Catherine de' Medici, of
the Protestant Huguenots

Christian navies had defeated the Turks. *Te Deums* were sung and a great number of little children danced in the streets 'blessing God and praising Our Lord who had inspired King Charles IX to so happy and holy an undertaking'. Some recent historians have sought to excuse the Catholic reaction by explaining that all these rejoicings were instituted as a thanksgiving that Charles had escaped a supposed attempt at assassination; but a study of the records of the time shows this to be completely untrue. It is an apologia dreamed up in more sensitive centuries.

In Madrid Philip was startled out of his customary melancholy dignity. When the news reached him he 'began to laugh' and demonstrated his extreme pleasure and content. Even his closest intimates were astounded at the extent of his joy. He wrote to Catherine congratulating her on possessing such a son and to Charles on possessing such a mother. But of course Philip, as was not unusual with him, was able to associate religious fervour with political gain.

In England news of the massacre and the arrival of a few terrified survivors brought a shock of dismay, an intense hardening of feeling against Rome and a cold anger which expressed itself as always through its Queen. A treaty had just been concluded with France and a marriage between Elizabeth and Catherine's favourite son, the Duke of Anjou, was in the air. (Never more than 'in the air' with Elizabeth, but now it was definitely out of the air.) For some days the Queen would not see La Mothe-Fénelon, the French Ambassador. When at length he was summoned to Richmond, he passed in utter silence through a court in which everyone was dressed in black, until he reached the person of the Queen. There he was told in undiplomatic language that this was 'a most horrible crime' . . . 'a deed of unexampled infamy'. Sir Thomas Smith wrote to Walsingham: 'Grant even that the Admiral and his friends were guilty of such a plot against the King's life, what did the innocent men, women and children at Lyons? What did the suckling children and their mothers at Rouen and Caen and elsewhere? Will God sleep?'

The Protestants all over Europe were determined that God must not be allowed to sleep.

Philip's satisfaction was understandable, for at a stroke Charles of France had not only destroyed the heretics but had made himself a prisoner of the Catholics at his court. Furthermore Admiral Coligny had been pressing Charles IX to furnish an army to go to the support of William of Orange; now the risk of Alva's Spanish army being trapped between two enemies was removed for good. Thirdly, the murder of so many of France's leading soldiers meant a weakening of her military strength for years to come.

Little wonder it was a happy day for him.

Now married, for the fourth time, to his niece Anne of Austria, he was finding his days increasingly preoccupied with the problems of his Netherlands possessions. The Duke of Alva, sent there to subjugate by terror, had succeeded only in setting all the provinces aflame. And it was not a matter of small concern, for, apart from the high cost of the war, this loose federation of small disparate states was the most densely populated trading centre in Europe; and the revenue from the taxes levied upon them was vital to the prosperity of Spain. No amount of treasure from the gold and silver mines of the New World was sufficient to make up for this loss. As fast as a victory against the rebels promised an end of the war, a new wave of revolt would break out. Massacring whole townships and burning the buildings to the ground so that nothing was left only served to harden the resistance and provoke reprisals. Even the Duke of Alva, who was now well into his sixties, was discouraged and suffering from ill-health and exposure to the cold and damp of campaigning.

What also galled Philip was the part his sister-in-law was playing. Troops in France not so long ago to aid the Protestants in the civil war there. A flow of volunteers in the Netherlands – whole regiments, in fact – discreet loans where most needed, protection for the rebel navies. During the years he had watched her somewhat shaky progress in her efforts to keep the English crown and the English religion on an even keel. He had seen her besieged by suitors – up to ten at one time – as quite the most eligible match in Christendom; but while she appeared to enjoy the courtship she did not seem able to surrender her person to a foreign prince. In a poem that she wrote herself she said:

> When I was fair and young, and favour graced me,
> Of many was I sought, their mistress for to be;
> But I did scorn them all, and answered them therefore,
> Go, go, go seek some otherwhere,
> Importune me no more!

As for the English suitors, they too were numerous; yet none of the successive Spanish ambassadors, who had paid spies close to the Queen, could find proof to confirm the rumours. Even the Venetians, who some-times leavened their perceptions with imagination, could not produce the evidence for which all the Catholic world waited.

It may of course be that Elizabeth was not highly sexed. A. L. Rowse has pointed out that all the Lancastrian kings, Henrys IV, V, VI, and VII, were singularly moral, being men of affairs rather than womanizers, and that Henry VIII took after his grandfather, the Yorkist Edward IV. Most historians have argued that a daughter of Henry VIII could not fail to be highly sexed; but it is very possible that in this respect she took after her Lancastrian forbears, and particularly her grandfather. Certainly she did not fall into the same trap as Mary Queen of Scots when she married Bothwell. Yet, only thirty-nine in the year of St Bartholomew, Elizabeth was still capable of marrying someone and bearing an heir to the throne; and she was under great pressure from her ministers and from Parliament to do so. If she died or was deposed, Catholic Mary was still the obvious successor, and a plot directed at marrying Mary to the Duke of Norfolk and putting them on the throne together had been formulated only the previous year by a Florentine banker called Ridolfi. The plot had collapsed, but it had received Spanish support, and as a consequence de Spes the Spanish Ambassador had been told to leave the country.

For fifteen years Philip had cautiously favoured Elizabeth's occupancy of the throne in preference to a queen of his own beliefs who had such close ties with France. Now he was gradually coming round to the view that, with France so riven by civil war and with England steadily gaining in strength and confidence, it was better to have a friend of the Valois on the throne of England than a friend of William of Orange.

Cumulatively events were pushing Philip and Elizabeth into opposition. But neither yet contemplated outright conflict. Elizabeth hated war: she felt that it seldom solved anything, and it *was* so expensive. Her incursions into France to help the Protestants had met with little success – or indeed thanks – and had cost her heavily in both money and men. Philip resented the slights and the insults put upon his countrymen from time to time, but he had his hands full in Europe and a vast empire to consider. Time would tell. He bided his time.

But other events apart from those in Europe were rubbing at the edges of patience and prudence. A new generation of English seamen was progressively challenging Spanish power wherever it was met. English ships, under new and ever more venturesome captains, were exploring the oceans for discovery, for trade, for plunder. Where one of their objectives failed they chose another, and since Spain and Portugal were the two great colonial powers, it was their property that usually came back to England in the holds of the little 60- to 100-ton barques and enriched the investors who sent them.

They went out too in a spirit of Evangelical fervour. To them the Scarlet Woman of Rome – who was indistinguishable anyhow from the imperial house of Spain – was the anti-Christ to be set upon and destroyed; and naturally if there was profit in the destruction who were they to complain? It is improbable that Elizabeth with her tolerant and humanist eye at all understood this fervour, or approved of it. Although there were notable exceptions, when she took the initiative, for the most part she was pulled along, following in the wake of her aggressively Protestant and self-reliant people, ever nearer to the abyss of war.

And of course Elizabeth could seldom resist the opportunity of making a little money. So she began to invest in the expeditions, which were launched exactly like joint-stock companies, with partners investing so much money and sharing proportionately in the dividends. Therefore as time went on it became increasingly difficult for the Queen to disown her famous sea captains. The best she could say to a protesting Spanish ambassador was that So-and-so had grossly exceeded his warrant and would be suitably punished. This really deceived no one, since the Queen pocketed her profit and the captain was rarely disciplined. And the depredations became steadily more daring and more successful.

On the 4th July, three years before St Bartholomew, the most successful of the captains, Francis Drake, was married to a girl called Mary Newman at St Budeaux church in south Devon. In the year of St Bartholomew, and in the month of the massacre, Drake landed on the isthmus of Panama near where the mule-trains carried their loads of precious metal across the narrow neck of land dividing the Pacific from the Caribbean. There with a total of seventy-three men he captured Nombre de Dios, a town the size of his native Plymouth. Seriously wounded, he failed this time in his objective, but the following year, having lurked in the vicinity during the intervening months, he attacked and took a mule-train and returned presently to Plymouth with £40,000 value in gold and silver booty.

It was this sort of activity, which went so far beyond the casual privateering raid, that Elizabeth found so difficult to explain away. It was this sort of activity which was earning England the reputation of being 'a nation of pirates'.

Sir Francis Drake:
a portrait preserved in
Plymouth

But of course the provocation was not on one side alone. English seamen were everywhere considered and treated as heretics when they happened by design or misfortune to land at Catholic ports. As early as 1561 a Bristol merchant had sailed to Cadiz and travelled overland from there to Malaga to buy wines. While he was absent, representatives of the Inquisition boarded his ship and searched it and, finding there books printed in English, assumed them to be blasphemous and arrested him on his return. He was flung into prison and three times racked and his ship and cargo and money seized. This was not an exceptional case.

Drake and Hawkins would ever bear with them the memory of San Juan de Ulua when the tiny English flotilla was set upon by the Spanish warships of the Flota, after having exchanged mutual guarantees of neutrality and safe conduct. While they barely escaped with their lives, many were killed and, of the seamen captured, four were burned at the stake and most of the others spent years in Spanish gaols. For this outrage Elizabeth seized Spanish gold on its way up the Channel to pay the army in the Netherlands.

Yet still both monarchs continued patiently to work for an avoidance of outright war. In 1573 indeed there was a *détente*, and Drake, arriving back with his booty from Nombre de Dios, was an embarrassment to the scene. He dutifully disappeared, and little was then heard of him until he undertook the voyage in the *Golden Hind* which ended in his circumnavigation of the world and earned him an immortality beyond the summits of war. By the time he returned to Plymouth it was September 1580; and by this time Philip, though he continued intermittently to work for peace with England, was toying with the idea of its possible destruction. He had also considered for some time the advantages which would accrue to him from Elizabeth's assassination.

4 *Plans for War*

The morale of political murder must be seen in its sixteenth-century context. In our century the assassination of kings or heads of state is usually left to the criminally unbalanced who hatch out their paranoiac hate-fantasies in private, or at most in concert with a few like-minded psychopaths. Four hundred years ago the deliberate assassination of a leader of an opposing faction was an act of power politics earning only one-sided opprobrium.

As early as 1570 the Papal Bull issued by Pius v declared all Elizabeth's subjects absolved from their oath of fealty, and was widely interpreted as meaning that her assassination would be considered lawful in the eyes of the church. When Gregory xiii succeeded him, the Cardinal Secretary at the Vatican informed two inquiring Englishmen that 'there is no doubt whatsoever that who sends that guilty woman of England out of the world with the pious intention of doing God's service, not only does not sin but gains merit.' Cardinal Allen writing a decade later urged all Englishmen to purge their souls by seeing to the death of Elizabeth.

The names of some of those who suffered assassination in this brief middle period of the century will show how often these attempts were successful. Francis, Duc de Guise, in 1563, by a Protestant. Lord Darnley, King of Scotland, in 1567, with the tacit connivance of his wife. The Earl of Moray, Regent of Scotland and half-brother of Mary Stuart, in 1570, by a Catholic Hamilton. The Earl of Lennox, another Regent of Scotland and Mary Stuart's father-in-law, in 1571, also probably by the Hamiltons. Admiral Coligny, in 1572, by order and in the presence of Henry Duc de Guise. William of Orange, after several previous attempts, in 1584 by a Catholic, under assignment from Philip ii. Henry Duc de Guise in 1588 by order and in the presence of Henry iii of France. Henry iii of France in 1589 by a young Dominican monk.

This list is not exhaustive, but it suggests that in this respect the Protestants were more sinned against than sinning.

It is not to be wondered at, therefore, that as Elizabeth passed out of the child-bearing age and so could not perpetuate her line, her Council and Parliament should be in ever greater concern to perpetuate her life. Mary remained in confinement, the continuing nucleus for Catholic discontent. It was true that her son James, whom she had not seen since he was ten months old, had been brought up a strict Protestant in Scotland and might eventually be a more suitable successor, but in 1580 he was only fourteen, and a backward, shambling, spavin-shanked fourteen at that.

So in England, as one assassination plot followed another, pressure grew to remove Mary, and tighter and stricter laws were introduced to compel Catholics to conform to the new religion. Walsingham, whose spies constantly preserved Elizabeth from death, was given greater liberty to enforce his secret decrees, and the 1580s became the decade of the dungeon and the rack. Elizabeth's great Summer Progresses through the land, which were often attended by a court and train of five hundred persons, were curtailed, and she seldom moved far from her palaces around London. Not that she took care for her own person. By her lack of simple safety precautions, by her confidence in the loyalty and good sense of her own people, she was a constant anxiety to her ministers and friends.

In 1577 Mary Queen of Scots made a will whereby she left all her rights in the English throne to Philip II of Spain. It was an open invitation to him to come and free her. The English Privy Council, and particularly the triumvirate of Cecil, Leicester and Walsingham, saw Mary's existence as the greatest single danger to the freedom and continued independence of England. Not only was she the magnet which lay at the source of all plots of assassination and invasion; she was also the stumbling-block to any *rapprochement* with France. There could hardly be an understanding between the two countries while an ex-Queen of France was held captive in England. Once she was gone, the sore place would heal.

But Elizabeth still would have none of it. Others could go to the block: not Mary, not a royal person.

Lest it should appear that Elizabeth was morally elevated above the other monarchs of the day, it should be mentioned that for two years before the St Bartholomew massacre, and in the year after, Sir Henry Killigrew, that cousin of the wild and lawless Cornish Killigrews but himself one of Elizabeth's most trusted and confidential servants, was up and down to Scotland with various secret and disreputable propositions to discuss with a succession of Regents: Moray, Lennox and Mar. The concept was that the English should release Mary and allow her to return to Scotland on condition that the Scots would guarantee to execute her as soon as she arrived. It was not at all a new idea to the Scots. Each of the Regents in turn was entirely agreeable to the proposal, indeed had assisted in its initiation, but each in turn, while haggling over the financial details of his reward, was overtaken by death.

After St Bartholomew feeling ran high in Scotland. Knox, in the last year

of his vehement life, thundered at the French Ambassador: 'Go tell your King that God's vengeance shall never depart from him nor from his house, and that his name shall remain an execration to posterity.' Many Scots blamed Mary for her French blood and more than ever would have been glad to see her disposed of; but Morton, succeeding to the regency in October 1572, though no more principled than his predecessors, was, in the words of a contemporary, 'too old a cat to draw such a straw as that after him'. He continued to negotiate with Killigrew but without any intention of concluding the sordid pact. If the English wanted to be rid of Mary, then let them bear the odium of the deed.

In 1580 Philip annexed Portugal. King Sebastian of Portugal, when only twenty-four, had been killed while fighting a religious crusade against the Moors, and he died without issue. Philip's mother had been sister to King João III, Sebastian's grandfather, and Philip's first wife had been sister to the Crown Prince João, Sebastian's father. The legitimacy of Philip's claim to the throne was supported by thirty thousand of the best soldiers in Europe, and the ill-organized resistance was brief. Don Antonio, the natural son of João III's brother, fled abroad; and in a stroke Philip had gained for himself a huge overseas empire second only to the Spanish, and an ocean-going fleet, a little run down but potentially as good as or better than his own. Additionally he had unified the Iberian Peninsula and had acquired in Lisbon and Oporto two fine ports on the Atlantic coast to match Cadiz.

As Elizabeth continued obdurately to hold out, to survive the secret infiltration of Jesuit priests, and to oppose him apologetically on all fronts, the idea of an actual open invasion of the island became more clearly the one ultimate sanction left. Pope Gregory had for some time been urging Philip to land in Ireland and build up a powerful force there before launching his attack on England. Don John of Austria, Philip's half-brother, had proposed to the Pope that he personally should lead an invasion across the narrow seas from the Netherlands. But Philip was slow to move. It was his nature. Also he knew England and knew Elizabeth and perhaps still had a grudging respect for the tall, slim, auburn-haired girl of his memory who had somehow survived and, ever protesting friendship, had defied him so long.

There had in fact already been landings on the Irish coast. In 1579 Papal volunteers under Dr Nicholas Sanders had arrived there, together with Spanish and Italian volunteers. A serious insurrection had developed, but it had been put down by the English in the following year.

In the meantime in the Low Countries, the Duke of Alva, whose savage tyranny had provoked the civil war it was designed to prevent, had been supplanted, after an intermediate period under Requesens and Don John, by Alexander Farnese, the greatest soldier of his day.

Farnese, who became Duke of Parma on his father's death in 1586, was the son of Ottavio Farnese and Margaret of Austria, the illegitimate daughter of the Emperor Charles. Philip II's father was therefore Parma's grandfather;

Alexander Farnese,
Duke of Parma,
the great Spanish general

and Farnese was eighteen years younger than Philip. Parma, a strategist and a tactician of the first order, was a man of great personal bravery, ruthless towards his enemies but tolerant and humane as an act of policy to those he conquered; and he very quickly perceived and took advantage of religious and political differences within the revolutionary states of the Netherlands and was able to split them. Where a swift and decisive use of his troops in battle was likely to achieve his end, no one was his equal in deploying and leading them. Where his charm or the offer of money or a title or an appeal to an old religious prejudice would do the work better, he used them.

For a time it seemed that this adroit combination of conquest, moderation and pacification would win the day, and that all, or nearly all, the revolting States would again come under the authority of Spain. Only the iron will and dedication and equally gifted diplomacy of one man appeared to prevent it. William Prince of Orange had begun life as a Lutheran and the son of Lutherans, but on the order of the Emperor Charles had been brought up a Catholic and had played his full part in the brilliant court life of Brussels. Until his mid-twenties he lived the easy-going extravagant life of a prince of the blood, and his splendid Nassau palace was the meeting place for gay and dissipated young noblemen like himself. In his youth William was a personal favourite of the Emperor, and at first was on terms of friendship with Philip too. But gradually as he perceived the tightness of the Spanish grip upon all aspects of life and administration and he witnessed the terrible persecution of the Protestants, his attitude changed and he found himself becoming an antagonist of Philip and of all Philip's policies in the Netherlands. After the judicial murder of Egmont and Hoorn, he became the principal antagonist and indeed the one figure around whom the forces of revolt and independence could centre. So his life changed, he left his palaces and his lands and his rich living and became the head of a forlorn but dedicated group of men and states determined to throw off the Spanish tyranny. He lived in the harsh world of soldiering, with the simplicity of a peasant, sometimes in want, always in danger. In 1582 he narrowly survived a first attempt at assassination when a pistol was fired into his head so close that the powder set fire to his hair and beard. In the following year four more attempts were made, and in 1584 a sixth was successful when he was shot dead in a disused convent known as the Prinsenhof which he was then using as his home. The assassin, a young clerk called Gérard, was tortured to death, and therefore could not receive the twenty-five thousand crowns Philip had offered as a reward for this 'laudable and generous deed'; so instead Gérard's parents were granted three seigniories in the Franche Comté and at once elevated to the landed aristocracy.

Well before William of Orange's death, Parma's brilliant combination of warfare and diplomacy had been regaining lost ground for Philip. One fortress after another had fallen and one town after another had been captured or gave way. Nowhere now was there sign of the 'Spanish fury'. Troops entering a town behaved with discipline and restraint; fair terms

Elizabeth I in the Rainbow Portrait, so called from its inscription meaning 'No rainbow without a sun', where fame is represented by the eyes and ears on the fold of the cloak, and wisdom by the serpent on the sleeve

INE SOLE

RIS.

were offered everywhere. Protestant worship was suppressed but Protestants were allowed to leave and given time to leave, and could take their goods with them. In many towns Catholics were in a large majority and had been themselves oppressed by fanatical Calvinists who had desecrated their churches and murdered their priests. So it was half a conquest, half a liberation.

Soon after William's death Ghent fell, and then Brussels. Bruges had already gone, and one could see that Antwerp was doomed. The Protestant secessionists were falling back everywhere leaderless and in disarray. It looked like the end of the war. Philip thought so. The States General in despair approached Henry III of France, offering him the crown in return for his aid. But Henry, who not infrequently dressed as a woman, loved to play with little dogs, and wore his hair in ruffles, was embroiled in the first stages of a civil war in which two other and altogether more formidable Henrys fought across his kingdom: Guise to try to drive the last Protestants from France, Navarre to try to prevent him and to survive as the heir to the throne. So Henry of Valois refused the honour. The States General thereupon offered it to Elizabeth.

She too refused. But now she offered more aid than she had ever done before, and of a different kind. Hitherto it had been money, reluctantly squeezed out, volunteer regiments led by gentlemen adventurers and soldiers of fortune, a trickle of supplies and some naval help. Now, after long negotiation, she signed a treaty in September 1585, by which she undertook to send an army of six thousand men, a thousand of them mounted; and their commander was to be her first and oldest favourite and close adviser, Robert Earl of Leicester. At the same time she published and had distributed an apologia, a justification, an announcement of her reasons for this action, which, in its statement of ideals and the ideals worth striving for, has been likened to the American Declaration of Independence. It was printed in English, French, Italian and Dutch, and she saw that Parma received a copy.

It was not a declaration of war but it was as near as Elizabeth was ever prepared to get. It was a declaration of intent; and it must have helped Philip to concentrate his mind wonderfully on the final issues which separated him and his sister-in-law.

The ultimate issue was whether she could be allowed to continue to attack and damage the priceless convoys bringing their treasure from the New World, and at the same time to prop up with her own army the rebels in the Low Countries. One of these activities could have been tolerated. Not both.

So Philip no longer continued to toy with the idea of invasion, to listen to other people's suggestions. He began to make his own plans.

Robert Dudley, Earl of Leicester, Elizabeth's closest and most enduring favourite

The early historians of the Great Armada, because most of them were Protestant, depicted a tiny England, with its simple godly seamen fighting David-like against the great Goliath that Spain launched upon her. Only

God, one felt, and the rightness of the Cause, and the splendid bravery and skill of the sailors enabled a few brilliantly handled but undersized warships to take on this great fleet and defeat it. The running battle up Channel, the fireships of Calais, the destructive in-fighting of Gravelines, and the great gales which followed, were all part of a divine pattern. Patriotism and religion triumphed together; great courage and simple faith walked hand in hand and the colossus was shattered.

Most later historians, suffering no doubt from the reaction from this medieval legend, have leaned in greater or less degree the other way, estimating that the fleets were roughly equal in size, with a great mobility and fire-power advantage to the English, depicting the Armada as a clumsy almost useless assembly of unseaworthy galleons, over-manned and under-gunned, herded together into a great unmanageable fleet and sent to keep an impossible rendezvous on the directions of an absolute monarch writing out his impractical orders from a cell in the Escorial.

Was it really like that at the time? Which is nearer the truth?

One tries to push the mists back another half millennium and wonder what would have happened if Harold had not had to fight Hardrada at Stamford Bridge and had come fresh to meet William at Hastings. If William had been defeated, as he probably would have been, there is no doubt that the Anglo-Saxon chroniclers would have hailed this as a victory for faith and English bravery and God. But it is not impossible to imagine later historians pointing out that from the beginning William's invasion plans were ill-organized and hopelessly optimistic and that from the beginning he hadn't stood a dog's chance.

A bastard Duke of Normandy with a tenuous claim to the English throne tries to enlist the help of his barons in making a piratical landing on the Sussex coast. At the great council of Lillebonne they turn his proposition down flat and he has to persuade them individually with bribes and threats. After his mass of tiny ships, laboriously built through the summer, have been held back for more than a month by contrary winds and storms, and many of them wrecked, there is sickness in his camp and many desertions among those of his troops who see that the hand of God is against them. Eventually he sails with his heterogeneous collection of fellow Normans, together with drop-outs and adventurers from Maine and Brittany, from Flanders, from Burgundy, from Aquitaine, from Piedmont, and from the Rhine: the idle, the unsuccessful, the unscrupulous, the dissipated, all looking for land and loot and easy plunder.

He sails thus, knowing that a large and active English fleet has been patrolling the Channel all through the summer waiting for just such an opportunity to attack him, and that all through the summer Harold has maintained a standing army in Sussex and Kent under his personal leadership, ready to do him battle. When he lands, if he lands, he is faced by a population comprehensively hostile, and united under a popular king.

No wonder he came to grief, the historians would say. For the enterprise was the dream of a desperate gambler, unaware of the strength of the forces that he challenged, an adventure badly thought out and clumsily executed. Even the blessing of the Pope could not help him. . . .

There were not people lacking with access to Philip who could urge him that *his* enterprise would be much more surely organized, with a far greater certainty of success than any of his predecessors had had. Among them the English Jesuit, Father Parsons, listed the times England had been invaded in the history of the island. The number was sixteen, of which all but two had been successful. It was a country with many good landfalls, with bays and harbours, and rivers easy of access, capable of taking large ships into the heart of the land. Most of Philip's advisers believed also that two-thirds of the English were still Catholic at heart (and perhaps they were not far wrong: you do not change a whole nation's religious beliefs in a few generations). The English had long had peace in their land, the castles were in decay, their swords and pikes rusty, their indiscipline a by-word.

No doubt someone also drew his attention to the fact that almost exactly one hundred years earlier the founder of the new Tudor dynasty, an exile and a fugitive for most of his life, a man described by Commines as 'without money, without power, without reputation and without right', had landed with a few supporters at Milford Haven, together with a band of three thousand Normans lent him by the King of France, and had marched to Bosworth and gained a crown. No seer was able to foretell to Philip that exactly one hundred years after the Armada another man, a Dutchman, was to land at Torbay and proceed without battle to London to turn the last of the Stuarts off the throne. But there were enough precedents without this.

For some time the Marquis of Santa Cruz, Spain's great veteran admiral, had been pressing his King to allow him to sail with his navy to invade England. Philip asked Santa Cruz for an estimate of what he would need.

When the estimate came it was a monumental one. The admiral said he would want five hundred and fifty-six ships of which one hundred and eighty were to be front-line galleons, with a total naval personnel of thirty thousand, and an army of sixty-five thousand men. There was also to be included two hundred flat-bottomed boats, to be carried in the larger ships, and a wealth of other provisions calculated to last eight months, which would cost in all nearly four million ducats. This equalled all the income Philip could expect to receive from his treasure house of the New World for about three and a half years. The King read it carefully and made his precise notations in the margins. It was an impossible demand. He filed the estimates away alongside Don John's plan to invade England across the Channel from the Low Countries, and various other ideas which had been put to him from time to time. Then early in 1586 a detailed scheme was submitted to him by the Duke of Parma, elaborating and yet simplifying Don John's plan. Parma's proposal was that he should launch his veteran army swiftly across the Channel in flat-bottomed boats in a single night. With the element of surprise and a screen of twenty-five warships, an army of thirty thousand men with five hundred cavalry could be thrown ashore in Kent or Essex, and the first crossings could be effected in eight or ten hours.

It was an exciting proposal, coming as it did from Europe's greatest soldier, and it would not be ruinously expensive, since the army was already in being. Philip reasoned, however, and noted so in the margin, that an element of surprise was not possible where the mustering of thirty thousand men was concerned, and only surprise could see them across without inviting weighty counter-attack at sea. Santa Cruz's plan, on the other hand, was entirely feasible, but there was not, and there never would be, the material or the financial resources to launch it.

Could not the two be combined? A naval force from Spain large enough to drive off or defeat the English warships. A military force under Parma ferried across the narrow waters and covered by the Spanish fleet. It was an idea with a good deal to commend it, since it integrated the suggestions of his two most brilliant captains. As the crisis deepened and the need for some military action became more imperative, Philip can hardly be blamed for seeing this combined offensive as a likely solution. It was to be an Enterprise, an *Empresa*. The Enterprise England, it would be called.

He directed Santa Cruz accordingly. And he directed Parma accordingly.

Whatever naval force Santa Cruz would be able eventually to assemble, Parma's army was already the most formidable in Europe. Indeed nothing like it had tramped across Europe since the Roman legions of the time of Christ.

It was a purely professional army, comprising men who had taken up soldiering as their career and expected to live as soldiers and die as veterans. They garrisoned frontier towns or fought where they were told to fight, seeing their enemy where they were instructed to see him. Their discipline in defence was only equalled by their *élan* in attack. The infantry regiments, which comprised a thousand to fifteen hundred men, were known as *tercios* from their custom of forming up into three ranks to do battle. In Spain, to become a military man was considered a thoroughly honourable vocation. Even the hidalgos and lesser nobility were proud to serve in the infantry – a very different matter from any form of manual labour or despicable trading. It matched their sense of heroism and their sense of dignity. The fields and vineyards of Spain went untended while the men who owned them fought in Brabant or in Brittany, in Lombardy or Peru.

But of course the Spanish army was a polyglot one, as befitted the army of a widespread empire. In April 1588 Parma's army of sixty thousand men was roughly divided in the proportion of 34 per cent German, 31 per cent Walloon, 18 per cent Spanish, 12 per cent Italian and 5 per cent of other nationalities. It also enjoyed a local autonomy, and at times its very discipline, as when turning to thoughts of mutiny for lack of pay, made it the harder to control. The 'Spanish Fury' of 1576, in which eight thousand men, women and children were savagely slaughtered in Antwerp and a thousand buildings burned – a blow from which the city never recovered – was not an act of policy like other, and lesser, massacres, it was an uncontrollable revolt, a mutinous outburst by an army shut up too long in its fortresses, unpaid and neglected. There had been other mutinies before and since, and at the taking of any city at any time the soldiers usually got out of hand; but under Parma the authority of the commanding officers had been restored, malcontents weeded out, and some of the back pay made up. Troops, particularly professional troops, will always give of their best for a brilliant and personally fearless general; they are quick to recognize the master touch.

If a force of thirty thousand such infantry could be landed in England, there was virtually nothing to stop them. A few miscellaneous, hastily gathered forces of militiamen, town trained bands and farmers who had been drilling once a week on coastal defence; these were the best that could be thrown up behind the dyke of forty miles of sea. The towns were undefended and ripe for the sacking. How many more Spanish Furies might there be?

Even the new English army now operating in the Netherlands had met with indifferent success. Although when they fought they did so with their customary obstinacy and refusal to retreat – a characteristic which resulted in Parma always ascertaining from his spies the proportion of English among the troops in any fort or strong point before he attacked it – Leicester himself had quarrelled with everyone, even with 'Black' Norris, England's ablest soldier, who had been in the Netherlands on and off for ten years and had forgotten far more than Leicester would ever know of war. The States General, from first greeting him as a saviour and a future sovereign, now saw him as a meddler, an incompetent and even, eventually, as a betrayer of their cause.

This last with some reason, for when returning to England in November, he left, in spite of the protests of his allies, two of the most important outposts in the hands of Catholic-English commanders. These were Sir William Stanley, in charge of the city of Deventer, which had recently been captured from Spain; and Rowland York, commanding the fort of Zutphen, overlooking the town of that name. Hardly was his back turned than both went over to the Spanish, Stanley taking twelve hundred Irish troops with him. Later the Scotsman, Pallot, did the same in Gelderland. The French historian Mariéjol says that Stanley was a former soldier of the Duke of Alva, and that, although he had three times sworn fidelity to Elizabeth, he was secretly under engagement to the King of Spain in the Low Countries. Whatever the truth of this, he was far too sincere a man to turn his coat for gain. He did so to serve God, as he understood it.

This, in January 1587, must have been a great encouragement to Philip to believe that there were many others of like mind and heart in England who were only waiting the opportunity to declare themselves. Let the

OVERLEAF The 'Spanish Fury': the sacking of Antwerp by the Spaniards in 1576

63

Catholic standard once be raised . . .

And now the English Lutherans shocked the civilized world by bringing Catholic Mary of Scotland at last to the block. The plot which finally resulted in her execution was led, if not engineered, by a wealthy young Derbyshire nobleman called Sir Anthony Babington, who had known and served Mary when he was a page to Lord Shrewsbury in the 1570s. It was coldly designed to accomplish the assassination of Elizabeth by six young Catholic friends of Babington, while Babington himself and a hundred others freed Mary and raised the standard of the new queen at Chartley.

In two decades of imprisonment Mary had outlived the obloquy of Darnley's murder and the Bothwell marriage and had become a heroine to many English and foreign Catholics, a romantic princess locked away in a tower. Certainly she was still this to Babington and his friends, though in fact she was now forty-five and her notable good looks had faded. An eye-witness at the time of her trial – possibly an unfriendly one – writes: 'She is of stature tall, of body corpulent, round shouldered, her face fat and broad, double chinned, with hazel eyes and borrowed hair.' When the Babington plot was uncovered she was so obviously incriminated that there was little chance for her this time. Indeed Burghley and Walsingham and others of the Council for their own sakes simply had to see Mary go to the block, for if Elizabeth died and Mary succeeded, their own heads would be the first to fall.

Mary was moved to Fotheringhay Castle in September 1586, and in October was brought to trial before thirty-six noblemen, privy councillors and judges of both religions. At first she refused to recognize the validity of the court, but later, encouraged by a curt note from Elizabeth holding out a bare hint of clemency, she appeared before her judges and defended herself ably for two days, until the trial was adjourned. When it was resumed at the Star Chamber, Westminster, two weeks later, Mary was not present, and the verdict was a foregone conclusion. Yet the signature of Elizabeth to the death warrant had still to be obtained. While she struggled with her agony of indecision Mary wrote – and was allowed to send – letters appealing for help to Pope Sixtus V, to the Duc de Guise, to Mendoza in Paris, to the Archbishop of Glasgow and others. She also wrote a dignified and touching letter to Elizabeth which made Elizabeth cry and no doubt added to her hesitations. The French and the Scots sent emissaries to the English court to appeal for clemency. Yet behind Elizabeth all the time was her formidable Council presenting to her the inescapable truth – which she herself fully recognized – that only Mary's death would now suffice.

There is no question that at this juncture Elizabeth would have been glad of four knights such as Henry II had had at court waiting to misunderstand his words and ride off to murder Thomas à Becket. Indeed, she more than hinted as much to Mary's jailers; but they were upright men as well as Protestants and gave her no help. So at last, four months after the trial and two after the verdict, she signed the warrant and later, in a tormented struggle to placate her own conscience and to evade responsibility in the eyes of the world, she tried to throw the final blame on one of her secretaries for having borne the document away without her permission.

When it was known that Mary's head had at last fallen, there was rejoicing in the streets of London and in many other parts of the country. To all English Protestants she had been the ever-present danger to their new and prosperous existence, a menace to their Queen's life, a possible successor of Mary Tudor's calibre and a threat to the whole future of the Reformed Church. Elizabeth had hesitated so long over the drastic decision that, now it had finally been taken, there was an overwhelming sense of relief in the country. The die was cast, the knot was cut, there was no going back even if the way forward might lead to outright war with Spain. It was what the country wanted and was psychologically prepared for. To her own great surprise, Elizabeth found her personal popularity increased.

In Scotland there was a brief national outcry in which James as briefly joined. But he had long since let it be secretly known that the execution of his mother would not be allowed to injure his own alliance with England, made in the hope of succeeding to the English throne. The news took several weeks to reach Paris. There the court went into deep mourning and a requiem Mass was held at Notre Dame attended by all the royal family. Henry III had lost a sister-in-law, the aged Catherine a daughter-in-law, the Guises a cousin. It was a dastardly act, but France, as ever in those days, was in too great a disarray to do more than protest.

In Rome the shrewd, vigorous, tactless, uneducated Sixtus had just succeeded his old enemy Gregory as Pope. He greeted the news of Mary's death with lamentation, but added in an aside about Elizabeth: 'What a valiant woman – she braves the two greatest kings by land and sea. A pity we cannot marry, she and I, for our children would have ruled the world!' To the Spanish Ambassador he repeated his promise to give Philip one million ducats as soon as Spanish soldiers landed on English soil, but would not advance a single one by way of a forward loan.

From Brussels Parma wrote to his King advising him not to break off peace negotiations with Elizabeth out of anger or shock but to continue them as a cloak for the preparations being made. 'One cannot help feeling,' he went on, 'and I for my part firmly believe, that this cruel act must be the last of many which she of England has performed, and that Our Lord will be served if she receives the punishment which she has deserved for so many years . . . For the reasons I have so often put before your Majesty we must be able to achieve our aims if we are called on to undertake any of the many parts which fall to us. Moreover, the aims of your Majesty as a most powerful and Christian king oblige you to try to end this affair as the service of God requires . . . Above all, I beg your Majesty that neither on this nor on other occasions will you relax in any way in regard to your preparations for the prosecution of this war and the *Empresa* which was conceived in Your Majesty's heart.'

The trial of Mary Queen of Scots at Fotheringhay Castle in 1586: a drawing found among the papers of Robert Beale, who bore the death warrant

5   *Drake at Cadiz*

Many reports had reached England during the last year or so of the preparations going ahead in the Spanish and Portuguese sea towns, and in Naples and Genoa too. Old galleons were being repaired, new ones laid down. Foreign ships were being commandeered, ships belonging to Danes and Germans, Neapolitans and Ragusans, some impounded, some chartered. The King's agents were out and about fixing up new contracts for cordage and sail, for biscuit and dried fish, for barrels and timber and tar. Galleys were being refurbished. New ships called galleasses, which attempted to make the best of both worlds by using wind and oar together, were being built in Naples. All Europe was being scoured for cannon and ball and shot. For first-quality Dutch guns the Spanish were paying as much as £22 a ton. A substantial quantity of arms was also bought in England, and Ralegh complained bitterly of this traffic. The Privy Council did its best, but the prohibitions were constantly evaded. Ralph Hogge, of Buxted in Sussex, who was the first man in England to cast iron and became the Queen's 'gonstone maker and gonfounder of yron', wrote to Walsingham in 1574: 'There is often complaints coming before your honours about the shipping and selling of ordnance and cast iron to strangers to carry over the seas, they say in such numbers that your enemy is better furnished with them than the ships of our own country are.' He then explained that no licence was needed for shipping guns from port to port along the English coast, and therefore it was perfectly easy for ships to load supposedly for another English port and then slip over to a foreign one.

As the demand increased, so did the price, and so did the flow of contraband. One Sussex ironmaster alone sold a hundred pieces of cannon to the Spaniards, and Bristol merchants sold them nine shiploads of culverins cast in the forest of Dean, together with powder, muskets and shot – all this during 1586 and 1587, and mainly routed through Naples.

With a military commitment in the Netherlands, however reluctantly maintained, and Mary executed, the forward party in the Council was in the ascendant. Drake had just returned from his great West Indies raid, during which he had first impudently called in and watered at Vigo, challenging the King of Spain to come and fight on his own doorstep, then had sailed to the Cape Verde Islands where he captured and burned Santiago and Porto Praya. Then he had crossed the Atlantic, and, although beset by sickness in his ships, had attacked and captured the supposedly impregnable city of San Domingo and lived there in luxury for a month with his crews before revictualling with Spanish stores and departing with additions to his fleet, two hundred and forty extra guns and a large number of freed galley-slaves, Turkish as well as Christian. From there he had sailed to Cartagena, the capital of the Spanish Main, which, being warned of his coming, had been heavily reinforced. But by a manoeuvre of sheer genius he had captured the place, had stayed there six weeks unmolested and had finally returned to England, after many other adventures, laden with spoil.

This voyage was in a real sense the one great setback to the Counter-Reformation in the years following the death of William of Orange, when all over Europe Spain and Rome seemed triumphant. It confirmed Drake as the foremost and only successful champion of the Protestant cause which everywhere else was in retreat. *'El Draque'* was famous throughout Spain, being at once dreaded and respected; and 'many princes of Italy, Germany and elsewhere, enemies as well as friends, desired his picture.' The moral effect of this great adventure was much greater than the immediate physical damage done. It struck at the empire from which Philip drew so much of his wealth and authority, it damaged Spanish credit by preventing the treasure ships from sailing and thus starved Parma of the money to pay his army; it was rumoured that the Bank of Seville would be broken and that Philip would become bankrupt.

But Philip survived and quietly went ahead with his preparations while Parma continued to negotiate with Elizabeth. Drake, in spite of the various dramatic proposals he put forward for his own employment, was kept on a leash after his return; and it was nearly a year before the forward party at court succeeded in persuading Elizabeth to let her lion free again.

On the 2nd April 1587 Drake sailed with a mixed fleet of sixteen ships and seven pinnaces to do mischief upon the Spanish ports. His instructions were 'to prevent or withstand such enterprises as might be attempted against her Highness's realm or dominion', and these instructions he proceeded joyfully to carry out. After reaching Lisbon on the 16th, he learned that there was a great concourse of shipping in Cadiz just getting ready to sail, so he fled south under all canvas, instructing his fleet to follow to the best of their sailing abilities. Arriving off Cadiz in the afternoon of the 19th, accompanied only by those few who were as fast as he, he called a council aboard his flagship, the *Elizabeth Bonaventure*, and announced his intention of sailing in and attacking the harbour at once – this in spite of the strong opposition of his vice-admiral, William Borough, who considered the defences of Cadiz too strong, with batteries commanding the narrow entrance to the harbour, and at least a dozen powerful galleys in harbour, and one or more galleons much larger than the English ships.

According to the orders laid down by Henry VIII, it was obligatory that an admiral in charge of a fleet should call a council-of-war and fully discuss policy and strategy with his captains before taking any such grave step as landing on enemy territory or forcing the entrance of an enemy harbour. But Drake's councils were always perfunctory. It was said of him by a friend that though he was a willing hearer of other men's opinions he was mainly a follower of his own. This time he barely listened. He gave his captains his instructions, and even Borough's urgent request that they should wait until nightfall – not an unreasonable one – was unregarded.

Even while the 'council' was in progress, the ships were nearing Cadiz, and, barely giving his captains time to leave, Drake stood in. The wind was favourable, the sky clear, the time four o'clock. The ancient town drowsed like a white cat in the afternoon sun. In the harbour was a scene of peaceful industry appropriate to a warm spring day. Something like a hundred ships, from small barques to armed merchantmen, were in port, of every type and nationality, loading up stores, being repaired, or ready and waiting orders to sail. Foreign ships which had been commandeered had no sails, for this was a useful way of ensuring that they should not slip away in the night. Others were without guns and some were without crews.

As soon as Drake's ships were sighted two galleys put out to challenge them, but these in the open spaces of the bay were driven off. Once in the harbour it might be different – this sort of combat in an enclosed space had never taken place before. Galleys, though lightly built and lightly armed, were swift and dangerous and could out-manoeuvre any sailing ship – they could turn on their axis in their own length – and they had been the traditional ships of war for three thousand years.

Elizabeth Bonaventure sailed in under the barking cannons of the Matagorda fort, followed by *Golden Lion*, *Rainbow* and *Dreadnought* – the four Queen's ships – and a group of armed merchantmen led by Captain Flick in *Merchant Royal*. In the port all now was sudden panic and chaos, as every ship that could move at all cut its cables and tried to find some sort of escape from the attack. Many collided, some went aground, a few smaller ones were able to retreat into water too shallow for the English ships to follow.

From opposite the town ten galleys appeared to attack the intruders. Drake ordered his armed merchantmen to deal with the panic-stricken ships in the harbour and turned the attention of the four Queen's ships to combat with the galleys. The galleys opened fire as they approached from the single gun platforms mounted forward. Drake, handling his five-hundred-ton warship like a skiff in the fresh breeze, came about and discharged broadsides of demi-cannon and culverin, the guns firing eight at a time, into the packed benches of oarsmen. As one galley fell away the others pressed in to the attack, and were met with the same devastating fire from the English warships. In fifteen minutes it was all over, and history

A map of Cadiz carried in his pocket by William Borough, Vice-Admiral to Drake, whom he tried to dissuade from attacking the town when they arrived off it in April 1587

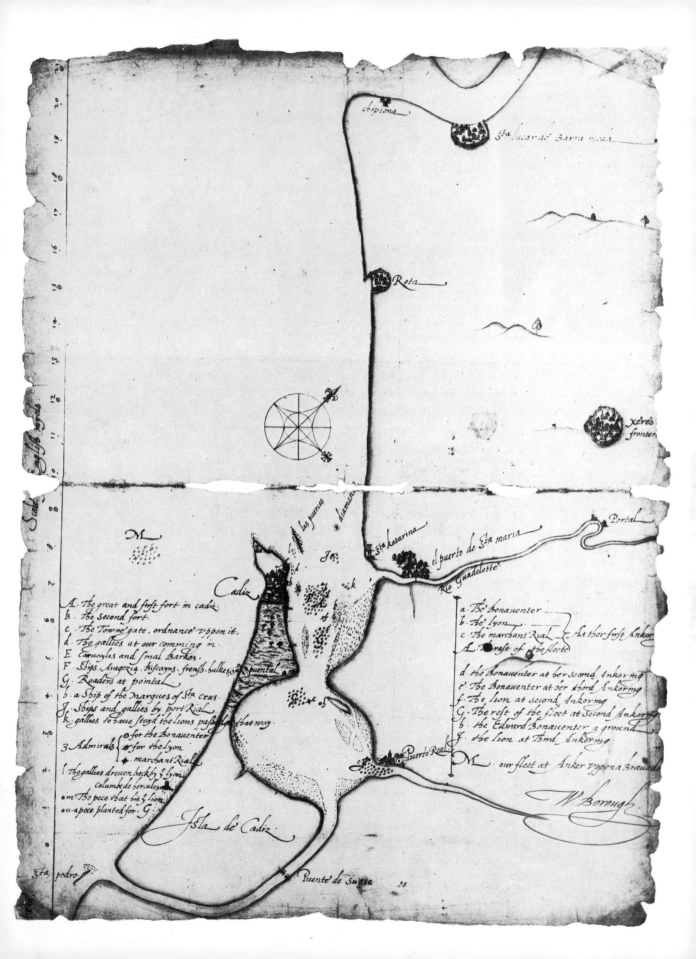

chipiona
Sta lucar de Barra neda
Rota
Xeres fronter

Las puercas
diamant...
Sta Lazarina
el puerto de Sta maria
Portal

M

Cadiz
Rio Guadelette
puental
Puerto Real
Isla de Caliz
Sta pedro
Puente de Suaca
20

A. The great and first fort in cadiz.
b. The second fort.
c. The Towne gate, ordnance vppon it.
d. The gallies at our comming in
E. Carrocyles and smal Barkes.
F. Ships Aragozia, Biscayns, frenss. bulkes ...
G. Roaders at pointal
h. a Ship of the Marques of Sta crus
J. Ships and gallies by port Rial
k. gallies to haue stayd the lions passage that way.
3 Admirals { for the Bonauenter / for the Lyon / marchant Rial }
l. The gallies dreuen backe by y lyon columbe de serules
m. The pece that hit y lion
n. a pece planted for G

a. The Bonauenter
b. The Lyon
c. The marchant Rial } At ther first Ankor
A. The rest of the fleete

d. the Bonauenter at her second Ankoring
e. The Bonauenter at her third Ankoring
f. The lion at second Ankoring
G. The rest of the fleet at Second Ankoring
h. the Edward Bonauenter a ground
J. the lion at third Ankoring

M. our fleet at Anker vppon a brauade

W Borough

Juan Martinez de Recalde,
the Spanish admiral second
only to the Marquis of
Santa Cruz

had been made. The long pre-eminence of the galley as a ship of war was ended. (Or at least the results of the very rare clashes between galleys and sailing ships during the last few years had been heavily and dramatically underscored.) One galley was sinking; the other nine retired under the shelter of the shore guns.

Of the many ships captured in the harbour, those with full equipment were taken as prizes, those without sail or otherwise thought unsuitable were set afire. As night fell Drake ordered his ships to anchor out of range of the town guns, which had been firing on him for three hours, and told his captains, who had come to consult him, that they must stay where they were until the morning. Vice-Admiral Borough, who was anxious to finish the work and move away from this land-trap while they were still free to do so, was not heeded.

At dawn, instead of making off with his prizes, Drake organized and personally led a flotilla of pinnaces into the inner harbour where he took and destroyed one of the largest Spanish galleons of the day, belonging to the Admiral, Santa Cruz, himself. In the meantime Borough, finding himself under fire from a shore gun, had edged further and further out of the harbour, until six galleys, seeing him separate from the rest, attacked him, and Drake had to send eight of his ships to the rescue. The galleys were beaten off, but Borough continued his slow retreat, taking with him the ships which had been sent to his aid, and finally anchored at the mouth of the harbour, where he could catch the fitful wind, and waited petulantly for Drake.

Drake was nearly ready. The galleon was burned down to the water line; thirty other ships had been destroyed and six captured; his own ships were laden with whatever could be seized from deck or quayside, and food and wine to last his fleet three months. His loss in ships was nil and in personnel quite small. By now more and more Spanish troops were arriving from the mainland and marching across the narrow isthmus into Cadiz: it was time to go. And at that moment the wind dropped.

It was an awkward situation. A sailing ship without wind is an unwieldy hulk which can only be moved laboriously by oarsmen in ship's boats straining to keep way on her. Or in shallow water anchors may be dropped and she can be warped forward or aft a few yards at a time. But her wings are suddenly clipped, and it is not comfortable at such a time to find oneself in an enemy harbour, almost surrounded by land which is rapidly being occupied by hostile troops. This was the time, too, for galleys to come into their own. Also it was known that somewhere not far away Juan Martinez de Recalde, after Santa Cruz the most experienced and notable Spanish admiral of his day, was abroad with a squadron of Biscayan galleons and might be nearing Cadiz. A calm, of course, is a calm; but there is more chance of light airs out at sea. There were also other squadrons about the coast, the main concentration being at Lisbon, where Santa Cruz, superintending the Armada preparations, now knew of Drake's presence on the coast and might be coming to seek him. Ill fortune could bring a sufficiency of ships to Cadiz to imprison Drake's fleet in the harbour and sink them.

It is not to be wondered if some of the English captains, and perhaps even Drake himself, watched the declining sun with an anxious eye. Borough was certainly in no doubts as to their danger, although his partial retreat had put him less at risk.

In the afternoon the Duke of Medina Sidonia reached Cadiz with another three thousand infantry and three hundred cavalry. The people of Cadiz, some of whom had trampled others to death in the panic of yesterday, breathed again, and began to help to manhandle new guns into position where their shot could reach the English ships. The galleys made another concerted onslaught on their now unwieldy adversaries. It was like dogs attacking a circle of bears. But by warping and paying out skilfully the English ships presented their broadsides constantly to the enemy, and the galleys after some hot exchanges again retired.

Then just before dark fire-ships were tried. These could have been disastrous, but they suffered from the prevailing lack of wind. They had to be towed in the direction of the English ships, and once they got within range they were necessarily abandoned, so the English small boats could take them in tow and beach them out of danger. About nine the galleys tried again, but again without success. Meanwhile the guns barked regularly, but only a few shots hit the English ships.

At midnight, just twelve hours after the wind dropped, a light breeze began to blow off shore, and Drake and his ships with flags flying, kettle-drums beating and trumpets strident, slipped out to sea.

The adventure was not over yet; for, after further brushes with the opposing galleys, Drake sailed back to Cape St Vincent, landed a force of a thousand men on a sandy beach nearby and at the second attempt captured the impregnable Sagres Castle, the fortified monastery of St Vincent, and Valliera Castle, together with all supplies and guns. These the English carried away after burning the forts. They also captured and destroyed over a hundred fishing boats and coastal barques, thereby ruining the Algarve tunny fishing industry, on which any Spanish armada had to rely for its salt fish, and at the same time destroying the seasoned barrel staves being carried by many of the coastal vessels. The navies of the world relied on such casks for storing water and wine and salt meat and biscuits, and the lack of good barrels to keep provisions sweet was one of the notable deficiencies in the Armada when it sailed in the following year.

Nor was this all. Having appeared next off Lisbon and vainly challenged Santa Cruz to come out to fight him, Drake then with a part of his fleet – Borough in the meantime having mutinously sailed for home – succeeded in capturing the *San Felipe*, a huge Portuguese carrack homeward bound from Goa, laden with spices, ivories, silk and gold to a value of £114,000.

The voyage was an astonishing achievement, a success in everything that it was sent out to do – in which it was so different from most enterprises of those years. It disrupted Spanish plans and communications – no one knew where Drake was going to turn up next – and no one dared to take a chance, so no one moved. It hit precisely at the weakest links in the Spanish preparations for the invasion of England – indeed it delayed the sailing of the First Armada for a year – it shook Spanish confidence and added to the legend of *El Draque*; and finally it made a thundering profit for the Queen. As model of its kind, as an example of how much a small fleet may achieve, if brilliantly handled, in breaking up the preparations and organization for war of a powerful nation, it has probably not been equalled in history.

The adventure has come to be known as 'Singeing the King of Spain's beard', from Drake's famous comment. Drake had all the arrogance of genius, but, as Mattingly has pointed out, this was not intended as a boastful remark. After the Spaniards with their allies defeated the Turks in the great battle of Lepanto in October 1571 the Sultan said. 'When the Venetians sank my fleet they only singed my beard. It will grow again. But when I captured Cyprus I cut off one of their arms.' Drake was claiming a small victory, not a large. He knew the danger and he had seen the preparations afoot. He was under no illusions about the danger to England. And his great concern over the next twelve months was to dispel the illusions that still lingered in England, especially at court.

He had returned reluctantly from patrolling off the coast of Spain; weather, lack of reinforcements, sickness in his crews, the desertion of Borough, and lastly the capture of the great treasure ship, had brought him home. He expected to be allowed to resume his commission as soon as he had refitted and refurbished his fleet. The overwhelming success spoke for itself; this was the one sure – and wonderfully economical – way of continuing to disrupt Spain's preparations. Indeed, with such tactics it seemed likely that an armada never *would* be got ready to sail against England. Although virtually an act of war, it made outright war less likely by preventing a confrontation. The Queen, of all people, must appreciate the brilliant logic of this.

But the Queen, influenced by Burghley, who had a temperamental antipathy to Drake and his bravado, was still intent on appeasing Philip rather than on fighting him. Whatever she may have felt privately, she hypocritically expressed strong displeasure to the Spanish at Drake's violation of their coast, and Drake found himself a national and international hero in temporary eclipse.

Then by October the pendulum swung again and the English fleet mobilized, expecting the Armada that autumn. In the week before Christmas Lord Howard of Effingham as Lord Admiral took command of the English Fleet, and two days later Drake became his vice-admiral and was given command of an independent fleet to be based on Plymouth. (In January the English again partly disbanded, mainly in the interests of economy, but with some regard too to the impracticability of keeping large groups of men

Sir Francis Drake, the sea-commander whom the Spaniards most feared, and who fought against their First Armada in the *Revenge*

cooped up for months without epidemics; and Drake's fleet did not materialize as promised but became a makeshift group that he assembled as and where he best could.)

Then on the 9th February 1588 the Marquis of Santa Cruz, Spain's great admiral, died, followed a few days later by his vice-admiral, the Duke of Paliano, and it seemed for a time that the whole armada project would be abandoned. At least Elizabeth, on false intelligence from Spain and from France, allowed herself to be persuaded so, and peace commissioners were sent to Flanders to discuss terms with Parma. At the same time Drake was forbidden to leave the English coast. Philip, however, never had the least intention of abandoning his Armada, now it was so far forward. Nor was he to be deterred then or later by complaints from his commanders that all was not at a peak of readiness for the great adventure. Precisely similar complaints had reached him before Lepanto, that other great and victorious crusade. Slow to make up his mind, he was not a man to change it because of a few setbacks. The young prince of Elizabeth's memory, cautious but statesmanlike, wise, and essentially a lover of peace, had long since been submerged by the years; and it was a cardinal error on her part – one of the few she had made – to think of him as unchanged. To Philip the sailing of the Armada had become as holy an enterprise as any crusade of the middle ages. Indeed at one time he had intended to sail in it himself, so that he could be on the spot to dictate terms when the English collapsed.

To many Spaniards, high born and low, it was the same. To join the Armada was to join the popular cause, to embark on a Crusade. To proceed against the Infidel and try to recapture Jerusalem was an undertaking no more blessed of God than one to reunite Christendom and bring all Europe back into the bosom of the Church of Christ. Indeed, the people they were to fight were more ignoble than infidels, for they were 'fallen angels'. Lutherans condemned the belief that one could pray to the Virgin and the saints to intercede for them with God. They condemned the worship of images and holy relics, and wherever they conquered they ruthlessly destroyed them. They condemned indulgences and a belief in purgatory. They condemned the confessional. They condemned almost everything that was fundamental to the Catholic religion. They were people who sinned not out of ignorance but who, having known the light, had set their face against it.

There were also of course the practical considerations mentioned already – and these were becoming more urgent with every year that passed. The Iberian mercantile economy would founder if a stop were not put to the depredations of the English pirates. The economy of Spain itself might collapse unless the Netherlands were regained. So Philip cast around among his distinguished admirals and his generals and his noblemen for the most suitable man to take the place of Santa Cruz.

Like Elizabeth – only even more so than Elizabeth – Philip was compelled to place an aristocrat of great distinction at the head of his fleet. Elizabeth

Portuguese carracks off a
fortified coast

was lucky in Howard, who had served at sea when his father was Lord High Admiral, whose family in the past had given four admirals to England in Tudor times alone, and who had had separate command of a squadron of ships as early as 1570. (As further recommendation, he was first cousin to Anne Boleyn.) The death of Santa Cruz deprived Philip of just such a man; one of unimpeachable nobility and of high enough birth to take precedence over all others, but born to the sea. After consideration Philip chose to succeed him Don Alonso Perez de Guzman, Seventh Duke of Medina Sidonia, Count of Nebla, Marquis of Casheshe in Africa, Lord of the City St Lucar, Captain General of Andalusia and Knight of the Honourable Order of the Golden Fleece.

It was a formidable title for a man of formidable means and position. But the Duke of Medina Sidonia – then aged thirty-seven – suffered all his life from one of the gravest and rarest afflictions known to man: he had a poor opinion of his own abilities. He was also more than a trifle melancholic. He underestimated himself; and his contemporaries and most of his successors have taken their cue from him – they always do. But lately some historians, notably Mattingly, have done something to rehabilitate his reputation.

He was a sturdily built, rather short man of fresh complexion, with brown hair and beard, and dark intent eyes which certainly did not lack determination, though they may have lacked the self-certainty of a leader. At the time of the Armada his reputation stood high. Not only was he the largest and richest feudal landowner in Spain, but his career up to this time showed him to be a man of ability and distinction. He had served in several military capacities, and had led troops into battle on two occasions – though the occasions as it happened had not resulted in much fighting. He had been responsible for fitting out the Spanish fleets which sailed to the Indies and the Magellan Straits; and for two years he had been active behind the scenes helping with preparations for the Armada. On many of the most vital questions of recruitment, provisioning and finance his advice had been constantly sought by the King and followed. He was probably the best administrator in the kingdom.

We know that other names were considered along with his, among them the Duke of Savoy and the Grand Duke of Tuscany. Juan Martinez de Recalde suggested his own appointment. In his well-known letter to Philip asking to be relieved of the honour of leading the Armada, Medina Sidonia, after listing the reasons for his own unworthiness, suggested as a substitute Don Martin de Padilla, Adelantado of Castile.

Padilla, who had been a group commander at Lepanto and had had a distinguished fighting career, was later chosen by Philip to lead the Second and the Third Armadas of 1596 and 1597. It is stated by Duro that he offered the King a thousand men for the First Armada, with wages paid for six months. But it is possible that in 1588 Padilla was under something of a cloud, for, although the actual commander of the galleys that fought Drake was Don Pedro de Acuña, Padilla was Captain-General of the galleys of Spain, and so bore over-all responsibility. It is usually the case, if some part of a nation's services fails, that the man in charge bears some of the odium, however little it may be deserved. So Padilla was left in the Mediterranean to keep an eye on the Turks.

I. A. I. Thompson has recently put forward some additional reasons for Philip's choice of Medina Sidonia in 1588. Portugal, only recently conquered, was growing very restive under the burden of the Armada preparations with its ruinous demands on their shipyards and their grain supplies. Whereas Santa Cruz was hated, Medina Sidonia was popular in Portugal, his wife being half Portuguese and his grandfather having been on terms of close friendship with the Portuguese royal family. The Duke was also known in England and had friends among the Catholics there, and if England should collapse it was essential to have someone apart from Parma to represent the King on the spot. The Duke was also a man of the highest reputation and honour, and with him as leader many would flock to follow him, not merely

his vassals and dependants but adherents and friends, and even strangers, knowing of his financial repute.

And of course there was the money. If one takes the value of the maravedi at this time as being roughly five hundred to the pound sterling, and multiplies by forty to bring nearer present-day standards, one can estimate that the Duke of Medina Sidonia contributed about £650,000 – or about $1,600,000 – to the cost of the Armada out of his own pocket. No other could have done so much.

Indeed, whatever he thought later, Philip may not have been too upset at the time in having to make this vital change in the leadership of the *Empresa*. Philip's dry comment when he heard that the Marquis of Santa Cruz had died was, 'God has shown me a favour by removing the Marquis now rather than when the Armada has put to sea.' He does not sound heart-broken or appalled. In fact from the inception of the Enterprise Philip had worked with two difficult yokefellows. His intention was, and he had made it plain all along, that the Armada's role should be mainly defensive and should be there only to defeat the English fleet if it attacked. Mainly its purpose was to serve as a massive covering force for the passage of his veteran soldiers under Parma into England. Parma was to take command. At the juncture of the two forces he was to become the supreme general.

But Parma of late had been dragging his feet. Enthusiasm had given way to caution. Philip had certain suspicions of Parma. Also Santa Cruz with his sea prestige and knowledge of war might react in some unpredictable way to a crisis which arose far out of reach of the Escorial. They might indeed quarrel, Parma and Santa Cruz, and endanger the success of the Enterprise.

Medina Sidonia was more to be trusted than either. He would obey Philip's orders; he would do exactly as he was told; at the juncture of the fleet and the army he would gladly and modestly surrender the supreme command to Parma. But if he carried secret instructions from Philip – as Philip determined that he should – then these too would be faithfully carried out if the need arose. It looked like a guarantee against failure. At least it was a guarantee against failure to obey instructions.

Perhaps Philip was looking for someone like Eisenhower in the Second World War – not the best general but the best generalissimo.

So the Duke – a home-loving man and a pessimist – protesting that he was unequal to the task, went down to Lisbon, where he found chaos. It was no wonder that the Armada had not sailed under Santa Cruz. It looked as if it never would have done under him. In four short months of toil Medina Sidonia composed jealousies, abolished the worst abuses, increased recruitment, stockpiled food and ammunition, and created a central administration and something like a fleet ready to sail against England.

Inset on a 16th-century map: an engraving of activity in the port of Cadiz

So as the spring of 1588 drew on, and the windy unseasonable summer broke, the portents of conflict threw deepening shadows across Europe. It was the year of ill-omen, predicted more than a century before by Regio-montanus, the great German astronomer and astrologer, who said that in 1588, if total catastrophe did not befall 'yet will the whole world suffer upheavals, empires will dwindle and from everywhere will be great lamentations'. These predictions had been confirmed by other learned philosophers since that time.

A Latin verse of the time, freely translated into English, runs:

> When after Christ's birth there be expired
> Of hundreds, fifteen year, eighty and eight,
> There comes the time of dangers to be feared
> And all mankind with dolors it shall fright.
> For if the world in that year do not fall,
> If sea and land then perish nor decay,
> Yet Empires all, and Kingdoms alter shall,
> And man to ease himself shall have no way.

If not the end of the world, was it to be the end of England? In the Low Countries Parma after a long and bitter siege had taken Sluys and had dug fifteen miles of new canals, making it possible to haul barges to the invasion coast at Nieuport. From there one could reach Dunkirk without exposing the barges to attack from the sea. Dunkirk to Deal is about forty miles – in good weather an easy night crossing. Parma's troops were slowly massing in that direction, and he was assembling and having built hundreds of flat-bottomed canal barges.

France, still ravaged by civil war, was for the time being too weak to take sides at all. Her Catholic nobles, financed by Spain, were now in control of Paris, and King Henry had fled to Blois. It meant that for the duration of the coming summer France would be completely neutralized. She could not menace Parma's flank if he crossed the Channel and left the Netherlands weakly guarded. Nor could she aid England, even if she wished, by sea.

As for Scotland, Parma had for two years been toying with the idea of an insurrection, led by the Earl of Morton and Colonel Semple, but this idea had been allowed to lapse. Nevertheless King James and his puritan ministers were in no position to help 'the Englishwoman'. Scotland, whatever her true feelings, would militarily be neutral. Denmark, the then naval power of the north, was highly apprehensive of a possible Spanish conquest of England; but her King had just died, the new King was ten years old; and her offer of help, if any, was likely to be too little and too late to sway the issue.

So it augured well for the crusade. In Lisbon the vast array of ships was weekly growing. All Europe was waiting for the coming trial of strength, and not many gave a great deal for England's chances. Pope Sixtus, chattering away in the Vatican, remarked that it was strange that a man who was emperor of half the world should be defied by a woman who was queen of half an island.

In that half island musters were being called and trained in villages and towns throughout the land. They were a motley lot, some armed with pikes and pitchforks, others with ancient swords or bows and arrows, all making do with what weapons they could find, like the Home Guard of 1940. Stow, in his *Chronicles of England*, speaks of 'certain gallant, active and forward citizens of London, merchants and others of like quality, to the number of three hundred, who voluntarily exercised themselves and trained others in the ready use of war'. They met every Tuesday.

From Gravesend to Tilbury Fort a chain and a bridge of boats was thrown to bar the enemy's passage up the river and to provide a ready communication from one bank to the other so that troops could move quickly to meet a threat to the north or south. Peter Pett, the engineer in charge of this operation, was still consulting with Leicester about completing the bridge when the Armada was off Torbay.

In the west country, where the main blow might come, five deputy lieutenants were appointed for Devon, two for Cornwall. Ralegh, as Lord Lieutenant of Cornwall, was much assisted by his cousin, Richard Grenville. Throughout England old forts were repaired as best they could be in a short time and field trenches were dug. Beacons were built all along the coast and far inland. A map of the beacons erected in Kent and Sussex shows that almost every high point was utilized, so that once the alarm was given the whole countryside would be alive with tiny fires spreading the alarm. A great wave of patriotism ran through England. High and low rushed to offer their arms to the Queen. Aged noblemen got out of their beds, put on armour and led their retainers to join the army camps. It was a bad time for aliens – of whom there were many in the City of London. Ubaldino says that it was 'easier to find flocks of white crows than one Englishman who loved a foreigner'.

An anonymous author lists the men available in each county in 1588, the numbers trained, the numbers untrained, the weapons available, the leaders of each regiment. In sum it looks a formidable total, but spread throughout the land it is wafer-thin, a paper-bag defence capable of being punctured at any point by a strong and resolute blow. Of course, once the Spanish landed, the country would have resisted to the last breath, but it is impossible to believe that the musters, however obstinate and bravely led, could have held out at a local level against disciplined and well-armed soldiers. So long as Spain retained the vital initiative she could strike anywhere along hundreds of miles of coastline.

The Queen was left in no doubt about the feelings of Drake. He besought her and her council in a stream of letters to allow him to descend again on the Spanish coast before it was too late. 'If there may be such a stay or stop made by any means of this fleet in Spain,' he wrote, 'so that they may not come through the seas as conquerors – which I assure myself they think to do – then shall the Prince of Parma have such a check thereby as were meet . . . My very good lords, next under God's mighty protection, the

Elizabeth I: an illustration to a contemporary manuscript

advantage again of time and place will be the only and chief means for our good; wherein I most humbly beseech your good Lordships to persevere as you have begun; for that with fifty sail of shipping we shall do more good upon their own coast than a great deal more will do here at home.'

This was in March. On the 13th April he wrote personally to the Queen: 'The advantage of time and place in all martial actions is half the victory, which being lost is irrecoverable. Wherefore, if your Majesty will command me away . . .' On the 28th April, again: 'Most renowned Prince, I beseech you to pardon my boldness in the discharge of my conscience, being burdened to signify unto your Highness the imminent dangers that in my simple opinion do hang over us . . . The promise of peace from the Prince of Parma and these mighty preparations in Spain agree not well together . . . these preparations may be speedily prevented by sending your forces to encounter them somewhat far off and more near to their own coasts, which will be cheaper for your Majesty and her people and much dearer for the enemy.'

Still Elizabeth hesitated. She was a woman born to hesitate and prevaricate, and thirty years on the throne had proved to her how often prevarication and delay had been her friend. There was another reason: the Queen was trying to buy Parma off by offering him the independent sovereignty of the Netherlands. It would have been a betrayal of her Dutch allies, and her Dutch allies suspected this; but it would have prevented an Anglo-Spanish conflict and would probably have terminated the war in the Netherlands, which, as it was, still had many bloody generations to run. But even if this offer failed – and she must have known that even with Parma's emotional commitment to the Netherlands it was likely to fail – she was not altogether won over by Drake's aggressive views. If the Armada did eventually sail, the seas were wide; might not Howard and Drake if cruising off the Spanish coast miss the Spanish fleet and allow it to reach an undefended England? (That this was not an academic objection was proved by the events of 1597, when this was precisely what happened.)

In May, however, Drake was able to leave Plymouth and visit the Queen at court. There, with all the ebullience and confidence of his genius, he was able to bring Elizabeth to his way of thinking, and Lord Admiral Howard, though unconvinced at first, also came to accept the aggressive ideas of his lieutenant. Howard was dispatched to Plymouth to take command of the much augmented fleet there, and he arrived on the 23rd May, Drake now becoming his second-in-command in fact, as he had been since December in name. It was a situation almost bound to lead to disharmony; but from the first they worked together without jealousy or ill-will.

Drake, throughout all the adventures which had made him the most famous commoner in the world, had *always* been his own supreme commander, yielding to no one, arrogant in his rightness because he had always proved to be right. Strict, religious, jolly, dynamic, beloved, he must have faced one of the sternest tasks of self-discipline to have accepted graciously

Lord Howard of Effingham, whom Drake won over to his plan for taking the initiative to defeat the First Armada

the arrival of a supreme commander to take charge of his fleet at this time of all times. Howard, born to the sea but knowing himself to be looked on by the fleet as something of a figurehead, knowing that throughout the world his name and his very real naval talents meant little enough; that the Spanish if they came would come to fight Drake and that if the English lost he would get the blame, while if they won Drake would get the credit; Howard, knowing this and knowing the explosive, prideful genius of his second-in-command, must equally have shown admirable tact and self-discipline in the weeks of inactivity that lay ahead.

For inactivity there still was, occasioned by a pitiful lack of all supplies, despite Howard's six-months-long campaign to get them; by atrocious weather that kept his ships storm-bound; by reports – true enough – that part of an Armada had been sighted off the Scillies and had been driven back by the great gales; by further impossible instructions from Elizabeth to beat up and down and try to protect the whole of the English coastline from invasion; by genuine uncertainty now as to the target the Spanish might aim at if they were already so near; and by further storms. The initiative, it seemed, was lost. Drake's offensive plans had been agreed to too late.

Then at last reliable information reached England that in fact the Armada had sailed, that parts of it had reached the Lizard and Mounts Bay and then all had been battered by the storm, and the great fleet was back in Coruña licking its wounds and replenishing its supplies. With the news came – wonder of wonders – permission from the Queen to move, so move they did, nearly a hundred ships, scantily provisioned, the men already having been on half rations for some time, but all so eager to be off before another countermanding order should reach them. They fled with a favourable wind, and in two days were within a hundred miles of the Spanish coast. Had the wind stayed fair there can be no doubt that there would have been a battle in or around the approaches to Coruña, for by now, after a period of depression and discouragement, the Armada and its captains had regained their resolution and were waiting a favourable wind to sail.

But at this point the wind backed right round to the south, and Howard and Drake, having gambled on picking up extra provisions from their raids in Spain, found themselves beating into the wind, making small progress, dangerously short of supplies, and all too aware that what was an adverse wind for them was ideal for the Spanish. They could do only one thing, and this they did, which was to turn about and return to Plymouth. As they reached Plymouth the Armada began to leave Coruña.

Froude writes: 'It was a treacherous interval of real summer. The early sun was lighting the long chain of the Galician mountains, marking with shadows the cleft defiles and shining softly on the white walls and vine-yards of Coruña. The wind was light and falling towards a calm. The great galleons drifted slowly with the tide on the purple water, the long streamers trailing from the trucks, the red crosses, the emblem of the crusade, showing bright upon the hanging sails. The fruit boats were bringing off the last fresh supplies and the pinnaces were hastening to the ships with the last loiterers on shore.'

That was on the 12th July. By the afternoon of Friday the 19th they were off the Lizard. At sight of land the Duke of Medina Sidonia ordered his great flag to be hoisted, showing the crucifixion, with the Virgin Mary and Mary Magdalene kneeling beside the cross. It was the banner which had been blessed by the Pope. On that same afternoon Captain Thomas Fleming in the *Golden Hind* (fifty tons, with a crew of thirty), one of the screen of barques keeping watch in the Channel, returned in haste to Plymouth with news

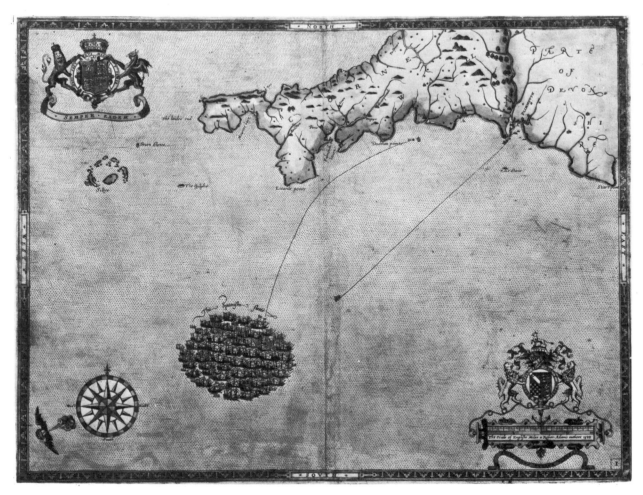

that the Armada, which was still thought to be in Coruña, was in fact in the Sleeve and advancing towards Plymouth.

Its arrival was a complete surprise – of the sort that Drake was fond of springing on his enemies – and it found the English fleet in the worst possible position: desperately low in all essential supplies, with the enemy to windward of them, themselves trapped in a harbour with an impossible south-west breeze blowing full into the port, and a neap tide flowing against them.

The story that Fleming found Howard and Drake playing bowls is substantiated by people who wrote within living memory of the occasion, and by the Spaniards themselves in 1624. Drake's comment, made before his superior officer could speak, that there was time to finish the game and beat the Spaniards after, accords with the nature of the man. A quick tongue is almost as much an essential of leadership as a cool head. It was precisely the right thing to say to avoid the risk of panic. And, as so often with Drake when he said things which did not conform to the normal run of probabilities, he was absolutely right.

Chart 1 from a contemporary volume. The arrival of the First Armada off the Lizard at 4 p.m. on Friday the 19th July 1588

6   The First Armada

The Christian Catholic crusading Armada was at last upon the English shores. All flags flying, bands playing, unscathed from its days at sea except for the four galleys, which had turned back, and one other ship, the *Santa Ana*, which had been unable to weather the storms of Wednesday. But otherwise intact, in good spirits and ready for battle. The *Empresa*, as Philip first called it. Then the *Felicisima Armada*. Then the *Armada Invencible* – a name later picked on by its foes and immortalized in much the way that one speaks of the Old Contemptibles.

What did this fleet, after all the early losses through storm and last minute additions, actually consist of? And who were the men, apart from the Duke, who commanded it?

The total of the fleet which eventually reached the Channel was about one hundred and thirty-seven, of which one hundred and nine were combat vessels, the others supply ships. The combat vessels varied from full war galleons of upwards of a thousand tons, with fifty guns and five hundred men; through ships of five hundred to eight hundred tons which were virtually converted merchantmen with rebuilt forecastles; to hulks – heavy built, slow-moving auxiliaries – and pataches and zabras, which were sloop-rigged, fast, and lightly armed.

This fleet was divided into nine squadrons. The first squadron under the direct command of the Duke of Medina Sidonia consisted of twelve ships: ten of the Royal Galleons of Portugal and two zabras. The Duke himself sailed in the *San Martin*, the fleet flagship, a vessel of one thousand tons with forty-eight guns and a complement of nearly five hundred men. The second was the Biscay Squadron of ten galleons (now reduced to nine) and four pataches, under the command of Admiral Juan Martinez de Recalde; the third consisted of the Galleons of Castile: fourteen fine ships, with two pataches, under Admiral Diego Flores de Valdes; the fourth was the Andalusian Squadron: two large ships, three galleons, five hulks and one patache under Admiral Pedro de Valdes; the fifth was the Guipuzcoan

Squadron of nine big ships, one hulk and two pataches, under Miguel de Oquendo; the sixth was the Levantine Squadron of ten big ships under Martin de Bertendona; the seventh was the fleet of hulks – twenty-three of them, ranging from two hundred to eight hundred tons under Juan Gomez de Medina; the eighth was a full squadron of zabras and pataches, twenty-two in·all, under Don Antonio de Mendoza; and the ninth was the four galleasses under Don Hugo de Moncada – these last each carried a mixed crew of around three hundred and fifty men, with three hundred galley slaves as oarsmen. The total tonnage of the fleet was about fifty-eight thousand – immeasurably the largest fleet that had ever sailed the seas – and it was manned by eight thousand sailors and nearly nineteen thousand soldiers. There were also some four thousand others aboard, of whom twelve hundred were the galley slaves in the galleasses, and the rest non-combatants of one sort or another: a hospital staff of sixty-two, one hundred and eighty monks, four hundred and fifty-six servants of the gentlemen adventurers – these adventurers including four English, one Irish and one German. (There were also among the salaried officers eighteen English or Irish and an Irish priest.) Many of the noblemen had long retinues of servants; the Duke of Medina Sidonia had fifty, the Prince of Ascoli – a natural son of Philip II – had thirty-nine, Don Alonso de Leyva had thirty-six, and so on down the list of diminishing nobility and importance.

And the men in command? For all Medina Sidonia's administrative ability, even Philip's commission could not make a seaman of him, so someone must stand at his side, someone who could support and guide him in the day to day conduct of the fleet at sea. For this post Philip had chosen Don Diego Flores de Valdes, the commander of the Galleons of Castile. Diego Flores was a very experienced officer (much older than the Duke) who had been responsible for the design of some of the latest galleons and who for more than twenty years had commanded the fleet known as the Indian Guard – that is the warships detailed to protect the treasure ships. He was also an expert on tides, seas and currents, and the choice so far seemed a good one. Yet his record was marred by a succession of quarrels with his brother officers, not least that one which had led to the failure of the expedition to the Straits of Magellan in 1581; and it is surprising that Philip did not know he was one of the most unpopular men in the fleet. He had a permanent feud with his cousin Pedro de Valdes, an equally distinguished officer, who commanded the Andalusian Squadron; and the King's choice meant that, standing next to the skilled administrator, the noble figure-head of Medina Sidonia, was this narrow-minded, acrimonious man who by his mere presence would automatically undo much of the conciliatory work of his chief. Most of the time Flores de Valdes sailed aboard the *San Martin* beside the Duke.

By the wording of this appointment Philip also took something from the authority of Medina Sidonia's second-in-command, who naturally was Recalde, Spain's greatest living sailor. Born in Bilbao in 1526, Recalde had

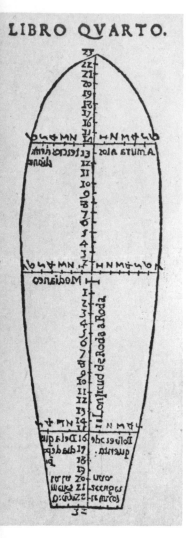

ABOVE AND OPPOSITE Three plans for shipbuilding, from the oldest Spanish work on navigation, published in 1587, a year before the sailing of the First Armada

been Superintendent of the Royal Dockyards, had been second-in-command to Santa Cruz and had also commanded the Indian Guard. In 1579 he had been the admiral in charge of landing a thousand Spaniards in Ireland, and after doing this he had reconnoitred the English coast before returning to Spain. He had had considerable other experience of the northern seas and the Channel. It was he whom Drake had missed near Cadiz. If one thinks of a better alternative to the chief commander one looks no further than Don Juan Martinez de Recalde, Knight of Santiago. It is a view with which Recalde himself would have agreed.

Recalde did not sail in a ship of his own squadron either but in the vice-flagship of the Duke's squadron, the *San Juan de Portugal*, a galleon of one thousand and fifty tons, with fifty guns and a crew of five hundred.

Pedro de Valdes, commanding the Andalusian Squadron, was also a seaman of long experience, having been in numerous fights against the French and the Portuguese, and having been seriously wounded in a grim little battle with two English ships which in 1580 took refuge in the estuary of Ferrol, near Coruña. He had had, however, one or two vicissitudes in his career, being imprisoned in 1582 on the King's orders, on the failure of his attempt to land in the Azores and his loss of a large part of the soldiers he landed there. He sailed now in the *Nuestra Señora del Rosario*, one of the largest and newest of the galleons of the fleet.

It would be incorrect to assume that Spain derived no benefit from Drake's raid on Cadiz. The fighting there finally demolished the belief that galleys could hold their own against sailing ships. Without that demonstration a considerable number of galleys would have certainly accompanied the Armada. (Santa Cruz had asked for forty.) With it, even the most conservative of naval men were constrained to see the light, and even the four that eventually were sent were turned back by Wednesday's storm. But a small squadron of four powerful galleasses accompanied the fleet, those oar and sail vessels which it was hoped would combine the best of both worlds, being heavily armed – as galleys could not be – and as manoeuvrable as galleys and independent of wind. This squadron was under Don Hugo de Moncada, a high-born veteran of the Netherlands campaign, with a long experience of galley warfare, sailing in his flagship, the *San Lorenzo*. But it was the *Gerona*, the third of these great ships, which was to make the saddest history for Spain.

Two other men had inevitably been appointed to high command. One, Don Miguel Oquendo, commanded the Guipuzcoan Squadron, sailing himself in his flagship, the *Santa Ana* (not the one that turned back). He was a sailor of great skill and dash, handling his ship, it is said, as if she were a light horse. In the battle of Terceira in 1582 he had fought beside Santa Cruz and had saved the Admiral from destruction by running his own ship under full sail between two of the enemy ships and boarding and capturing the French flagship, hoisting his own flag on her masthead above the smoke of the battle.

The other was Don Martin de Bertendona, commanding the Levantine Squadron, and sailing in his flagship *La Regazona*. The most gifted of the younger captains, his was a name which was to occur a number of times in English history. His father, an earlier Don Martin, had been in command of the Biscayan great ship which had brought Philip to England to marry Mary thirty-four years before. Three years hence, the younger de Bertendona was to take the leading part in the great fight off the Azores when Sir Richard Grenville in the *Revenge* took on the Spanish fleet single-handed and was at last overwhelmed. Between the first Armada of 1588 and the second and third of 1596 and 1597 a new generation of Spanish seamen grew up. De Bertendona is the only officer who commanded a squadron in all three armadas.

The last officer needing mention did not command a squadron but was in fact designated by Philip to take charge of the Armada if Medina Sidonia should die or be killed. This was the Lieutenant-General of the Fleet, a brilliant young soldier called Alonso de Leyva. A tall, slender, handsome man with a blond beard and smooth flaxen hair, he was a favourite at court, a hot-head, a dashing soldier; one thinks of him as the Spanish parallel to the Earl of Essex. De Leyva had already commanded the Sicilian Galleys, had been Captain-General of the Milanese Cavalry, and had resigned his high position in order to lead the army which was to sail in the Armada against England. His ship, the *Rata Encoronada* of eight hundred and twenty tons, complement four hundred and nineteen, was part of de Bertendona's squadron. In her sailed the flower of Spain's young noblemen.

Let us make no mistake: these men and the captains who sailed under them were not indolent gallants, not inefficient officers, not fair-weather sailors. It is true that they carried more than their share of 'passengers' — noblemen of high spirit but no knowledge of the sea; the servants of these dons; and a high proportion of trained and well-equipped soldiers who, because of the

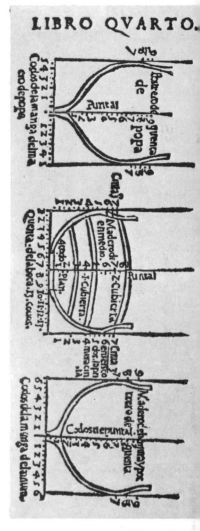

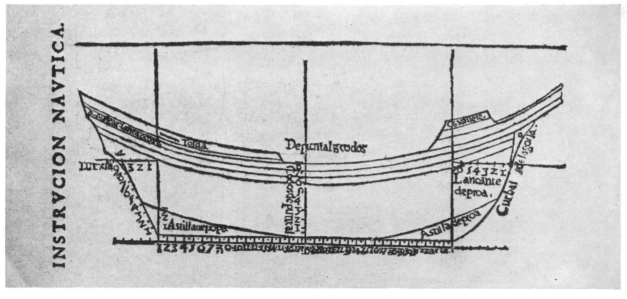

tactics of the English, were never to be utilized. It is also true that the sailors themselves were more used to the Mediterranean and the long runs with the trade winds to the West Indies and back. But anyone who supposes these waters are always calm can never have sailed on them. Mediterranean storms can be sudden and vicious; the Atlantic is the roughest ocean in the world; and the Bay of Biscay, which was home territory to the Spaniards, is as nasty as the English Channel any day. That a new style of sea warfare was in the process of being evolved and that their ships were ill-designed for this evolution is not a reflection on the people who manned them.

First among the admirals on the English side was the fifty-two-year-old Howard of Effingham, a personal friend as well as a cousin of the Queen's. As soon as Elizabeth came to the throne his good looks and ability, together with his kinship, had brought him advancement and high office. Ambassador to France at the age of twenty-three, General of Horse under the Earl of Warwick in putting down the northern rebellion, Member of Parliament for Surrey from 1563 to 1573, a Knight of the Garter, Lord Chamberlain of the Household, a commissioner at the trial of Mary Queen of Scots and one of the strongest advocates for her execution; a grandson of the second Duke of Norfolk, the victor of Flodden, he was, unlike many of the Howards, a staunch Protestant.

There was no doubt about the family religion of his vice-admiral. Born about 1545 at Crowndale Farm near Tavistock, Francis Drake was the eldest of twelve children whose father, Edmund, having become a passionate Lutheran, was too ardent in his advocacy of the New Religion during the Prayer Book Rebellion of 1548 and had to decamp with his family to the safer areas of eastern Kent. There, during the reign of Mary, he lived with his multiplying family in one of the hulks on the river, in considerable poverty – and no little danger, since he read prayers and preached religious sedition to the seamen in the Queen's ships. Young Francis was brought up in an aura of persecution where the identity of the persecutor was quite clearly the Scarlet Woman of Rome; and all through his life his utterances bore the mark of religious conviction and were adorned with the metaphors of the Reformed Church.

When only twenty-two he had sailed with his cousin John Hawkins on the voyage to the West Indies which ended in the disastrous events of San Juan de Ulua, where warships of Spain, under the direction of Don Martin Enriquez, the new Viceroy of Mexico, having first given the small English fleet a promise of safe conduct, treacherously set upon them; with the result that the English returned home with a hundred and fifty men alive of the six hundred who ventured, and about a quarter of their ships. From this point forward Spain became the practical enemy to Drake, 'the wolf with the privy paw', the embodiment of all that was worst in the Catholic faith. The results had since been plain for all to see. By nature an individualist, by necessity a privateer, Drake had so exercised his naval genius

ÆTATIS SVÆ LVIII
Ano Dni 1591

Sir John Hawkins, who as Treasurer of the Navy had supervised the building of the English ships before he commanded one of them, the *Victory*, against the First Armada in 1588

that the Spanish credited him with supernatural powers – powers of darkness of course – and felt they needed God's help when fighting him. It was a considerable moral disadvantage for them.

Of equal importance in the English fleet – some would even say greater – was John Hawkins. A man of fifty-six at the time of the Armada, Hawkins had been born in Plymouth of a prosperous ship-owning family, and, almost more than Drake's, the history of his career traces the burgeoning of English maritime enterprise in the sixteenth century. Always well dressed, unfathomable, courteous and charming, he claimed friendship with King Philip of Spain and argued that he was a loyal subject of Philip's, dating

OPPOSITE A contemporary illustration of 'Popish Plots and Treasons' in the reign of Elizabeth I, including a picture of the 'Inuincible Armado'

BELOW An English man-of-war in the year of the First Armada

from the time of the King's marriage to Mary. Directly involved in the Ridolfi plot of 1571, which was one to assassinate Elizabeth and put Mary Queen of Scots on the throne, in which he was to provide naval cover for an invasion of Spanish troops under Alva, Hawkins had contrived to keep Elizabeth and Cecil informed of every step and yet was adroit enough to avoid suspicion by the Spanish that he had betrayed them, even when the plot was uncovered and the main conspirators arrested.

Partly as a reward for these services, Elizabeth two years later had appointed him Treasurer of the Navy, and in this position not only was he able to attack the abuses and dishonesty that he found at every level but he was largely responsible for building the ships which these last tense months had floated in dockyard and harbour, half-crewed and ill-provisioned, awaiting their greatest test. However starved they were of men, rations, gunpowder and shot, these vessels were in design ahead of any others in the world.

Compared to those which preceded them, and to the Spanish ships they opposed, they were longer in relation to their breadth – a proportion of something like three to one – deeper in keel, and lying 'low and snug' in the water, with the forecastle and sterncastle greatly reduced and with the deep waist decked over. The mainmast was stepped further forward, the

A° ḋñi · 1577 ~
Ætatis svæ · 39 ~
· K · F ·

MARTIN FROBISER MILES
GVALTERI CHARLETON, M.D.

sails were flatter, and there was a reappearance of top gallants. Such ships could sail nearer the wind and were more manoeuvrable than any warships that had been built before. The English had not previously been renowned for original or creative ship design, and the predominant influence of sailors of great experience at the dockyards during this period of building and rebuilding was as vital to the survival of England as the development of the Spitfire three and a half centuries later.

Hawkins was fortunate, since he was able to take a prominent part in the battles in which his ships were put to the test. But perhaps too the spirit of Henry VIII breathed down over the scene. For it was Henry who introduced the broadside which so revolutionized war at sea; Henry who initiated the policy of putting guns of longer range into his ships so that future battles might be won by gunfire; and Henry who had laid down the dockyards without which it would have been impossible to build the ships of 1588.

The last of the great trio of seamen adventurers was also in his middle fifties at this time. Martin Frobisher was a Yorkshireman, though the family was originally Welsh. He had gone to sea as an orphan with Wyndham in 1553, and was one of only forty to survive the voyage. The following year, when with John Lok, he had been captured by Negroes and spent some months in a Portuguese gaol. When Queen Elizabeth came to the throne he was living as a merchant's factor in Morocco. There had been a smack of real piracy about his middle years, when he had used southern Ireland as a base of operations and combined with like-minded gentlemen of the sea issuing from the Cornish coves and creeks. In the 1570s he had made three voyages to the Arctic, where Frobisher's Bay is named after him, and he had sailed as Vice-Admiral under Drake, commanding the London merchant-man *Primrose*, on the great West Indian voyage of 1585–6. A tough, irritable, unruly man, he combined ill with Drake; but when the Armada came he commanded the largest English ship of the time, the *Triumph*, of eleven hundred tons with a crew of five hundred, and was always in the thick of the fight.

In the first stages of the battle the English did not divide into squadrons. Howard was aboard his flagship, the *Ark* – sometimes called the *Ark Ralegh* because she had been designed for Ralegh and sold by him to the Queen – a vessel of eight hundred tons with a crew of four hundred, and Drake sailed in the *Revenge*, of five hundred tons with a crew of two hundred and fifty. As against a Spanish total of one hundred and thirty-seven ships of all sizes, the English had, in the neighbourhood of Plymouth at the beginning of the fight, about sixty-four. (Another fleet of forty-odd vessels under Lord Henry Seymour was guarding the Thames and Dover against a surprise landing there.) But, in order to have such ships as he brought out of Plymouth fully manned, Howard had to strip some of his ships bare and leave them to be provisioned and crewed later, so that only a proportion of the sixty-four were at first in the battle. If, however, the total fleets of England and Spain confronted each other, as they did in the battle of

Sir Martin Frobisher, the Yorkshireman who, against the First Armada, commanded the most massive English ship, the *Triumph*

Gravelines, the Spanish still had a big advantage in fire power. The average Spanish ship had a broadside twice as heavy as the English, and while the English had many more smaller long-range pieces, the Spanish carried three times as many heavy cannon as the English and nearly eight times as many perrier types. So that at close quarters they had every chance of crippling the English ships and boarding them. Nor is there much to be said for the theory that the Spanish guns were inferior to the English. The Armada, as has been seen, carried a considerable proportion of English-made guns, and the rest came from the finest foundries in Europe. The Spanish personnel outnumbered the English by two to one, though the superiority lay in soldiers, who in the event were never used.

These comparisons are of the two fleets when both fully engaged. So it is clear that the Spanish superiority at the outset, when engaged by about half the English fleet, was overwhelming.

Not only were they superior but they had the English at the worst possible disadvantage, catching them in harbour while still re-provisioning after their own voyage, and embayed by wind and tide. It will be remembered what Drake did in a not altogether dissimilar situation outside Cadiz. Vice-Admiral Borough's concern as to the hazards of going straight in, and a plea that they should at least wait until dark, were blown away by the wind as *Elizabeth Bonaventure* cast off her captains one by one to return to their own ships and follow as best they could.

Medina Sidonia, when only ten miles off Plymouth, hove-to to allow his straggling fleet to close up. It was thirty-four years to the day since Philip had landed at Southampton to marry Mary. After prayers 'when all our people kneeled down, beseeching Our Lord to give us victory against the enemies of His holy faith', and while they could see the clouds of smoke blowing across the land as the beacons flared to give warning of their coming, the Duke called a council-of-war. It was an act of which Vice-Admiral Borough would have approved.

There are varying reports of what happened at that council, but the best founded is that de Leyva, the handsome young Lieutenant-General of the Fleet, supported by Recalde and Oquendo, the two most aggressive admirals, urged an instant attack on Plymouth. They were not absolutely certain that Drake was there, but their wide sweeping of the seas on their way from Spain had made no contact with English forces, so that it was a reasonable inference that he was in the port. If not he, certainly a substantial part of the English fleet. An attack pressed home now with fire-ships and a favourable wind might very well destroy that fleet and so provide a first resounding victory for Spain. Medina Sidonia – like Borough – saw danger in entering a fortified harbour which would only allow entry of three vessels abreast and an impossibility of retreat – with the present wind – if the attack did not prosper. Other admirals – including Pedro de Valdes – were against the venture; but the debate ended when the Duke told them of his personal instructions from the King. These instructions were to defeat the

enemy if or when he attacked or attempted to impede the progress of the
fleet, but not to seek him out – the overriding objective of the Armada
being to arrive off Margate intact and to make juncture with the Duke of
Parma to cover the landing of his troops.

As evening drew on and the Spanish council-of-war broke up, the
English fleet, in the eye of the damp wind, began to warp laboriously out of
Catwater. By dusk most of the big vessels were out and struggling close-
hauled to beat out of and down the Sound towards the comparative safety
of Rame Head. The decision not to attack Plymouth having been taken, the
Armada proceeded on its way, thus assisting the English in their efforts to
claw to windward of them. Dark fell and all the headlands were aflame with
their warning bonfires, spreading the alarm throughout England faster
than an express train. The Spanish were here at last. About one in the
morning a Spanish pinnace returned with captured fishermen who told that
Howard and Drake were now at sea, and the Duke decided to come to
anchor until morning, in the meantime dispatching orders to his great fleet
to close up into battle formation.

By dawn the wind had veered to west–north–west and the two fleets
sighted each other for the first time. The English fleet was now to windward,
having performed a feat of which the Spanish ships however handled
would have been quite incapable. This English fleet was still hastily
assembling, being joined from time to time by some of its larger ships which
were only now able to get free of the land. It was a straggling formation
stretching from north to south in a line of about nine miles, with some of

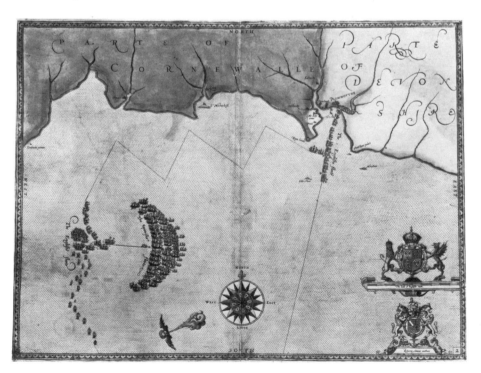

Chart 2. The First Armada off
Dodman Point, Cornwall,
from Saturday the 20th July
1588 pursued by the English
fleet, which left Plymouth,
tacked along the coast, and
got to windward

99

the largest warships nearest the land, a group of vessels of all types in the centre, and a wide screen of smaller ships, armed merchantmen, pinnaces and the like, sweeping south far beyond the enemy.

The Armada had already adopted its famous crescent formation, and, besides being so much more numerous and formidable to look at, was more closely concentrated, the bulge facing away from the English ships, and the tips of the crescent like the pincers of a crab about six miles apart and arching to close. Duro says that all the contemporary writers, especially the foreign ones, agree in describing the consternation of the English when they saw the mass of ships. He then goes on to quote the Italian, Bentivollo: 'You could hardly see the sea. The Spanish fleet was stretched out in the form of a half moon with an immense distance between its extremities. The masts and rigging, the towering sterns and prows which in height and number were so great that they dominated the whole naval concourse, caused horror mixed with wonder and gave rise to doubt whether that campaign was at sea or on land and whether one or the other element was the more splendid. It came on with a steady and deliberate movement, yet when it drew near in full sail it seemed almost that the waves groaned under its weight and the winds were made to obey it.'

This was a confrontation such as had never happened before in the history of the world. No such forces had ever faced each other; no rules or principles of attack or defence existed. Communication between one ship and another was by flag or by hailing trumpet; no opportunity existed for working out new tactics to counter the manoeuvres of one's foe or the accidents of war or weather; discipline in ships was good but between ships depended on the personality and impulses of the varying captains. Understanding on this score was better on the English side because it was a homogeneous fleet; the Spanish included various nationalities sailing with varying degrees of communication and conviction.

Yet at this stage the Spanish formation was the stronger and much the better controlled. It was slow moving but tightly knit, like a battle square on land; and equally hard to attack. In the most exposed positions at each end were some of its largest and best-gunned galleons; while no lighter fleet – or part of a fleet – would willingly attack the centre, for it could immediately be surrounded. The left end of the crescent – that is the one nearest the land – was defended by Recalde with his Biscayan squadron, with Pedro de Valdes in support. At the right end was Bertendona, with Oquendo in support, both officially under de Leyva in the *Rata Encoronada*.

The English without hesitation decided to attack both ends of the crescent, since these could be more easily isolated than the rest and because the wind would make them hardest to succour if they became so isolated. While Howard in the *Ark* led his ships into an attack on the right wing, Drake in the *Revenge*, followed by several others including Frobisher in the *Triumph*, attacked Recalde on the left. The two sorties met with very different results. Howard, the first to close, engaged in a furious cannonade

OPPOSITE Lord High Admiral Charles Howard of Effingham, First Earl of Nottingham, supreme commander of the English fleet against the First Armada

OVERLEAF The battle off Gravelines, Flanders, on Monday the 29th July 1588, when the First Armada was finally put to flight

with de Leyva's *Rata Encoronada*, Bertendona's *Regazona*, the *Lavia*, and the other seven ships of the Levantine squadron, which had come about to meet them. The thunder of the guns was carried widespread over the little flecking waves, to fishing smacks far out at sea, and to the land for miles around Plymouth, greeting the new ships as they beat out of the port to join Howard's fleet, telling the anxious watchers on beach and cliff that the battle was at last joined.

Sailing in line ahead, the English ships swept past the Spanish, but they did not attempt to close the distance, and even their own guns, lighter but of longer range, fell short, so that although the exchange was fierce no damage was done on either side. When the attack was made on the other wing, however, Recalde himself in the *San Juan de Portugal* came about to meet the English fire as the first wing had done, but only the *Gran Grin*, his vice-flagship, followed suit; the rest of his squadron sailed on leaving the two big galleons isolated and to be quickly surrounded. Various reasons have been given for this event: (*a*) that the rest of the captains panicked at the heavy firing of the English fleet, (*b*) that Recalde in the emergency of the moment failed to make the proper signal to his squadron. The first seems improbable, since the Biscayan squadron was one of the best in the fleet; the second quite impossible for a sailor of Recalde's eminence.

It has also been suggested that Recalde deliberately disobeyed the Duke's orders so as to create a *mêlée*. It is true that Recalde, of all the officers, had the least faith in the idea of joining up with the Duke of Parma; and yesterday he had been cheated of his chance of catching Howard and Drake embayed in Plymouth. With such a massive fleet it was probably intolerable for him to retreat slowly up Channel while the English dogs barked at his heels. And all the captains knew – even Philip II knew and had so written in his orders to Medina Sidonia – that the English would *try* to keep their distance, attacking from long range, refusing the invitation to board the enemy, doing what damage they could without being damaged themselves. Well, here was a chance to break the deadlock before the deadlock had begun to grip.

If this is a fair interpretation of Recalde's actions, it is worse than Nelson's blind eye, for by going contrary to the whole of the Armada strategy Recalde played directly into the hands of the English. But his was a bluff which might have succeeded. Two of the biggest galleons were an enormous prize: the sort of prize that Drake or Frobisher would be unable to resist. Let them but come within range and the fight would be on. Even if the galleons were heavily pounded, the English guns were not likely to be able to finish them off. To capture them they would have to be boarded, and the *San Juan* and the *Gran Grin* carried between them nearly six hundred trained soldiers. In the meantime other units of each fleet would be drawn in, and once locked in combat . . .

Whether this was his reasoning or not, or whether the rest of his captains did panic at a cannonade such as they had never heard at sea before, no

Alvaro de Bazan, First Marquis of Santa Cruz, Spain's great admiral who planned the Armada of 1588 but did not live to command it doubt the isolation of the two galleons did present a terrible temptation to Drake and Frobisher. But it was a temptation they resisted. They closed only to a range of about four hundred yards, where their fire could be effective and the Spanish fire would fall short. So for nearly two hours the *San Juan* and the *Gran Grin* were bombarded, and both were damaged, though this damage was largely to personnel and superstructure, for the English shot was not heavy enough to hole the enemy between wind and water. As soon as Medina Sidonia saw his rearguard in trouble he came about in his galleon the *San Martin* and, followed by his squadron, sailed to the rescue. But since he was well in the van of the whole Armada, it meant not merely beating back into the wind, a difficult enough operation in itself, but skirting the whole crescent front of the fleet in order to get to the southernmost tip.

When eventually about midday the *San Martin,* the *San Marcos*, the *San Felipe* and the *San Mateo* reached the battle area the English ships fought them for another two hours, but always giving sea room when they had to, never closing the range, ignoring the Spanish invitations to grapple and board, avoiding the rushes of the Spanish squadrons and snapping at their heels. But as more and more of the galleons arrived on the scene Howard gave orders to break off the engagement and to retire to a safe distance. Still needing reinforcements and still sounding out the strength of his opponent, Howard hesitated to commit himself further, and so the first clash came to an end. Recalde was gathered into the fold of the Armada, and the great fleet began slowly to re-form and move up channel again. But while the regrouping took place in a rising wind and sea, Pedro de Valdes in the *Rosario*, the flagship of the Andalusian squadron, making towards Recalde with the intention apparently of helping him, collided with another Biscayan ship and then, swinging round, fouled a galleon of his own squadron, the *Santa Catalina* of eight hundred and eighty-two tons, and lost his bowsprit and brought down the stay of his foremast.

For a while all was confusion; and almost before it could be sorted out there was a tremendous explosion aboard the *San Salvador*, which tore out her stern castle, splintered her masts and killed two hundred of her crew.

Many romantic stories have been told of the cause of this explosion, the most picturesque being Ubaldino's of a Flemish gunnery officer who took exception to an army captain making free with his wife, 'who was with him, as is the custom of the country'. The army captain ordered the Fleming to be beaten, whereupon, when he was released, the gunner plunged a lighted taper into a barrel of gunpowder and wrecked the ship. However, a more mundane explanation is far more likely, namely that the ship had been in action and a gunner's carelessness resulted in a spark reaching the gunpowder in the rear hold. Whatever the cause, the *San Salvador*, a vessel of nine hundred and fifty-eight tons with a crew of three hundred and ninety-six, belonging to Oquendo's squadron, became almost a total wreck, and in the confusion caused by the explosion and the flames, Howard saw another

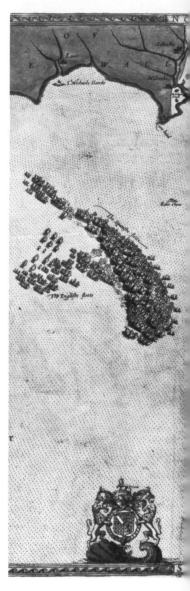

Chart 3. Sunday the 21st July 1588: off Plymouth, the English fleet engaging the Spanish crescent

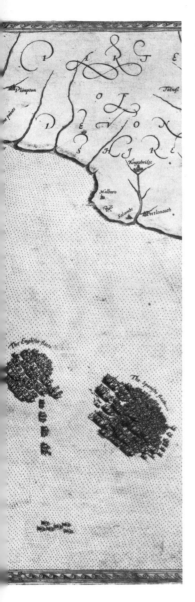

opportunity to attack, and led a dozen of his best ships back into action.

Once again the Duke and his squadron came to the rescue, driving away the English ships to a respectable distance and with the help of two galleasses, which could make greater headway into the wind, came up with the *San Salvador* and got a line aboard her and was able to salvage the bullion and put out the flames. In the growing sea the *Rosario* was in further trouble, for her foremast gave way at the hatches and fell on the main yard. The *San Martin* herself got a line aboard the *Rosario* and took her in tow. But the line parted; and now Diego Flores, appointed by Philip as Medina Sidonia's chief adviser, was at the Duke's side angrily reminding him that it was his duty to command the fleet, not to succour all its lame dogs, and that anyway the bulk of the Armada was now so far in advance of him that if he did not follow soon the fleet would be split in two, and that with dusk falling any attempt to recall the van of the Armada would fail.

The Duke, who had eaten nothing all day – the first of many such days to come – would not at first accept the advice of his chief of staff; but as the ships pitched ever more dangerously around the damaged *Rosario*, with an increasing risk of further collision, he sent word to Pedro de Valdes asking him to leave his ship and come aboard the *San Martin*. De Valdes vehemently rejected the invitation. At length, having appointed six smaller ships to attend the *Rosario*, the Duke gave the orders to follow the slow progress of the rest of the Armada eastward.

The first day's fighting had brought losses to the Spanish, but not from enemy action. It had brought some depression to the English. They could outsail the Armada but not outgun it, and the discipline of the Spaniards was impressive. Howard wrote to Walsingham: 'We durst not adventure to put in among them, their fleet being so strong. But there shall be nothing neglected or unhazarded that may work their overthrow.' Drake wrote to Admiral Lord Henry Seymour, chafing in the Narrow Seas on watch for Parma: 'The fleet of Spaniards is somewhat above a hundred sails, many great ships . . . as far as we perceive they are determined to sell their lives with blows.'

At least the danger to Plymouth was past, and the present course of the Armada did show that their objective was not to be Ireland or any of the extreme western ports. It might still be Torbay or the Isle of Wight or some other harbour along the south coast. By refusing battle on the advice of his more experienced captains, Howard had delayed the final clash at the expense of leaving the initiative with Spain. The English still retained the 'weather gage' – that is, they remained to windward of the enemy, and were therefore at a great advantage, being able to choose their time and place of attack – but this also meant that they could not prevent the Armada from assailing any English port or harbour it might choose. The question was, would the Spaniards dare to do this with the undefeated English fleet still at their heels? It was a possibility which had to be faced. Therefore above all things contact with the Armada must not be lost. There would be about six hours of darkness. After a council-of-war in the gathering windy dusk, with a short choppy north-westerly sea, and clouds obscuring the stars, each captain returned to his own ship with precise and absolute instructions as to his station and course. Drake had been appointed to lead the way, showing his big poop lantern to the ships astern for their guidance.

Yet by dawn, which was before four a.m. and further lightened by the rising gibbous moon, the English pursuit had completely broken up. Drake had quenched his light and had veered south in quest of some unknown and mysterious sails, had come with his usual astonishing nose

BELOW LEFT *Chart 4*. The Spanish crescent followed at a distance by English ships past Start Point, Devon

BOTTOM LEFT *Chart 5*. Spanish and English ships in close engagement off Portland Bill, Dorset, on Tuesday the 23rd July 1588

for a prize upon the crippled *Rosario* and had taken her and her commander Admiral Pedro de Valdes prisoner, with all crew, forty-six guns and fifty-five thousand gold ducats intact.

Most of the English fleet, missing his lantern, had heaved to or shortened sail, and so were far behind; but Howard in the *Ark*, accompanied by Lord Edmund Sheffield in the *White Bear* and Edmund Fenton in the *Mary Rose*, had closed with the Spanish fleet, in the dark mistaking their lights for the lights which Drake should still have been showing. At dawn they found themselves off Berry Head, near Brixham, and almost within the crescent of the Spanish fleet, certainly more part of that fleet than of the English, which

The English flagship, the *Ark Royal*, commanded by Lord Howard of Effingham against the Armada of 1588

was hull down on the brightening horizon. They had to go about sharply, into the slackening wind of dawn, to avoid being surrounded and attacked. Hugo de Moncada, commanding the galleasses, requested that he might pursue them, for he had a chance of overtaking them and holding them until the rest of the Spanish fleet closed in; but for some reason he was refused, and the three English ships escaped.

Drake's utter disregard of discipline, which would have ensured a court-martial in Nelson's time, was scarcely criticized then, and we have to see it in the context of its age. He was more envied for his uncanny ability to know where a rich prize was to be taken than blamed for breaking formation in the night. After all Howard himself in the final battle of Gravelines did nearly the same thing, though not with such profitable results.

But one thinks of Philip's written instructions to Medina Sidonia: 'You should see that your squadrons do not break battle formation and that their commanders, moved by greed, do not give pursuit to the enemy and take prizes.'

If Drake has been judged more harshly since by standards which did not altogether then apply, Pedro de Valdes's surrender was treated too kindly at the time and has been ever since. No doubt he was unlucky to lose his bowsprit and later his foremast when attempting to go to the help of another ship. No doubt he felt he had been unjustly deserted and left in the lurch as the rest of the Armada proceeded on its way. No doubt he was beside himself with anger that his cousin Diego Flores, with whom he had this continuing feud, should have been able to convince Medina Sidonia that his duty was to sail on. But about twelve hours passed between the loss of his mainmast and Drake's arrival; some sort of repair or jury rig must have been possible in the time. No account speaks of any being attempted. And the *Rosario* was eleven hundred and fifty tons, one of only six ships in the Armada over the thousand tonnage; she carried, as has been said, forty-six guns, many of them the biggest cannon, capable of firing fifty-pound cannon balls and holing an enemy ship or wreaking the greatest damage if she came within range. She had one hundred and eighteen sailors and three hundred and four soldiers aboard; she had so far fired few shots. She would not be easy to handle in a beam wind but she had suffered no other hurt. Her forecastle and poop were much higher out of the water than the English, which would have made boarding a murderous business.

Instead of fighting, Pedro de Valdes, when he found that Drake was his adversary, considered it proper that he might gracefully surrender to a man 'whose valour and felicity was so great that Mars and Neptune seemed to attend him'. It was a knightly act, a chivalrous and courteous yielding to superior forces, and Drake accorded his enemy all the honours of war, entertained him in his cabin to dinner and presently saw him given every comfort before being conveyed to an honourable internment in England.

Drake was always a man who believed in the full etiquette of war. When on his voyage round the globe Thomas Doughty rebelled against him and was condemned to death by Drake for mutiny, Drake took Communion with him and then entertained him to a good dinner before leading him out to the block to be executed.

More reason here for all possible chivalry. One of the greatest galleons, surrendered without a fight! No doubt they could have pounded her for ever from a distance, but would they have had time, with Howard calling for all aid and the Armada likely to land in Torbay? Could one have imagined Drake meekly surrendering if positions were reversed? Or Recalde? Or Oquendo? Or Medina Sidonia? One thinks of the traditions of the Spanish navy summarized nearly three hundred years later by Admiral Mendez Nunez off Callao: 'My country prefers honour without ships to ships without honour.' De Valdes should have hanged himself.

A map carried in his pocket by Sir Francis Drake and used for navigation

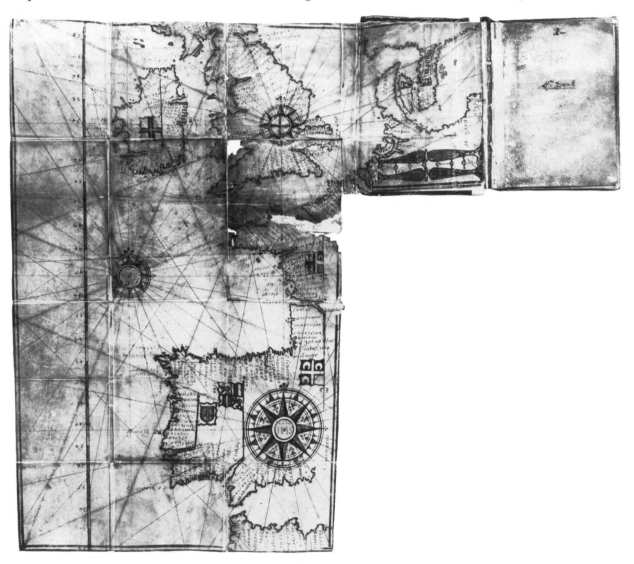

7 The Battles in the Channel

But the Armada was not going to land in Torbay. All day, the wind gradually dropping, it crawled across the smiling blue water of Lyme Bay towards Portland Bill, and the English fleet reassembled itself after the confusions of the night and followed.

In the afternoon Medina Sidonia called a council and appointed Don Diego Enriquez, son of the Viceroy of Peru, to command the Andalusian Squadron in place of Pedro de Valdes. He also appointed Alonso de Leyva commander of all the rearguard, which was to consist of forty-three of the best ships of war. Recalde, his galleon still being repaired, was to be sheltered until he was fighting fit again. Medina Sidonia, aware of the risk of panic among ships exposed for the first time to the violence and rapidity of the English fire and of the disorders of yesterday which had cost him two capital ships, issued new orders. If henceforward any ship broke formation the captain would be hanged immediately. The provost marshal and the necessary hangmen were appointed and three majors were told off to each squadron to carry out the order without delay. (This order ten days later accounted for the execution of Don Cristobal de Avila, and for the arrest and near execution of Captain de Cuellar of the *San Pedro*.) At this time the Duke was expecting a frontal attack from Lord Henry Seymour – actually far away off Margate – so he put himself and the rest of his best ships in the van. The hulks, the supply ships and the victuallers were thus as usual protected on all sides. By retaining so tight a formation Medina Sidonia made himself most difficult to attack; but he limited his progress to the speed of the slowest. So far, from the time they sighted the Lizard they had progressed at the rate of three knots. But this infinitely slow progress did mean that the galleons with any sort of favourable breeze at all could move backwards and forwards among their flock and go to the help of any in peril.

As Monday afternoon wore on the light airs dropped, the sails of the galleons flapped and hung motionless, flags drooped and the opposing flccts drifted gently with the tide. Only the galleasses had motive power, but Don Hugo de Moncada, smarting under his rebuff of the morning from Medina Sidonia, refused to use them in attack. It had been a brilliant day since noon, but in the long light evening a few clouds assembled to obscure the sunset and to promise a change on the morrow.

All night the dead calm persisted, and well on into dawn. As light grew the look-outs reported that the relative positions of the two fleets were unchanged. The Armada was just east of Portland Bill. But at five a.m. a breeze sprang up; and it blew from the north-east. The change provided the Spaniards with what for two days they had been seeking, the weather gage.

By minutes the English fleet was the first to move, and Howard swung north-west towards the land, hoping to outflank the Spanish. But this time Medina Sidonia was too quick for him and led his own squadron to intercept. Howard presently was forced to come about on the opposite tack, steering south-east, and tried instead to attack the southern wing of the Armada. Now the powerful Spanish rearguard took a hand. De Leyva in the *Rata*

Chart 6. Wednesday the 24th July 1588, between Portland Bill and the Isle of Wight: close action, in which the Spaniards suffered their greatest casualties so far

Encoronada, Bertendona in *La Regazona*, followed by their squadrons, with the wind in their favour, cut across the English path and fierce exchanges took place.

In the meantime a small part of Howard's fleet, Frobisher in the *Triumph*, together with five armed merchantmen, had mistaken or disobeyed Howard's orders and had come so close in to Portland Bill that they could not weather it and dropped anchor to avoid going aground; and there they were attacked by Hugo de Moncada and his four galleasses, coming into action at last. These ships in addition to their oar motive power were perhaps the best armed of any of the Spanish fleet, carrying over forty brass guns each, a large part of their armoury being fore and aft, but a considerable number of guns being mounted on the deck above the rowers, and a few even between the rowers.

While this was going on the main battle drifted back slowly westward into Lyme Bay. Here the greatest cannonade in naval history took place, with the more cumbersome and unwieldy Spanish ships straining every nerve and every sail to take advantage of the wind and close with their English opponents. Many times it looked as if individual English ships or groups of ships would be cut off in the *mêlée*, but every time their superior sailing qualities got them out of trouble.

And now the wind was beginning to hesitate and to veer. Drake, who so far had been disengaged, knew the likely properties of an easterly breeze at dawn and the likelihood of its veering later, and he had manoeuvred his squadron into a position where he could take advantage of the change. When it came he launched a sudden and fierce attack on the Armada's seaward wing. His ships, appearing out of the smoke of battle like a new fleet, broke up the seaward wing and turned the whole battle front.

As the wind picked up from the south-south-west the Armada began to re-form to meet this new attack. It had attempted two things – to isolate Frobisher and to bring Howard to battle. Now a third front had opened, and in the early exchanges many of the Spanish ships suffered. Recalde, who could not be kept out of any fight, again found himself isolated, and was surrounded by English ships which pumped shot into the *San Juan*. Medina Sidonia, who saw that Howard was going to take advantage of the change of wind to rescue Frobisher, now directed his Portuguese galleons and five others, himself in the van, to intercept this move; but, suddenly informed of Recalde's plight, and seeing that all except his own galleons were to leeward of Recalde and therefore unable to lend immediate aid, he instructed the whole of his squadron of fourteen large galleons to go to Recalde's aid, and alone in the *San Martin* continued on his course to intercept Howard. He thus presently found himself isolated from the rest of his fleet and bearing down alone upon the *Ark*, the *Elizabeth Jonas*, the *Leicester*, the *Golden Lion*, the *Victory*, the *Mary Rose*, the *Dreadnought*, and the *Swallow*. Although he saw himself likely to be surrounded, the Duke would not bear away and attempt to escape from a squadron flying the

Lord Admiral's flag, so he came up into the wind and backed his foretopsail, inviting the English to grapple and board.

It was the conventional, the knightly thing to do; but the day for such gestures was over. Howard came no nearer than to bring the galleon within the range of his guns, and as he passed he discharged broadsides into the *San Martin*. Again sailing in line – the new order which was to become the classic order for centuries to come – the rest of his squadron did the same. Then they wheeled about and came back. In the meantime, Drake, having withdrawn before the might of the Portuguese galleons coming to Recalde's aid, had doubled round them and he too came to attack the *San Martin*. The Spanish flagship was blazing away with all her forty-eight guns, but it was nearly an hour before she could be rescued, by which time the holy standard had been ripped in two, her masts were damaged, and torn rigging was hanging among the dead and wounded on her decks.

Long before the *San Martin* was finally extricated, Howard and his squadron had left her to Drake and had gone on to rescue Frobisher. How far Frobisher wanted to be rescued is a debatable point. He and his London merchantmen, after a fight, had finally dealt with the four big galleasses. The English shot was not sufficiently heavy to hole the galleasses, but their aim had been directed at the rowers, who had been cut down in swathes, and the galleasses had broken off the fight before Howard arrived.

If Medina Sidonia instead of attempting two objectives had swung round as soon as he saw Frobisher isolated, and, after leaving a screen to ward off Howard, had set about the destruction of the six embayed ships, there might have been a different story to tell, for Howard could hardly have kept his distance while the six ships were destroyed. But it has been suggested that Frobisher, hard-bitten, sea-wise and as pugnacious as Recalde, may just as deliberately have offered himself as a prize in order to lure the main Spanish fleet into the treacherous waters of the Portland Race and the

A playing card with Elizabeth I as the Queen of Diamonds, supported by naval forces under Sir Francis Drake

Shambles. Whatever his secret purposes, if any, in becoming so surrounded, his fight with the galleasses made him the hero of the day.

In the first light airs of Wednesday's dawn a Spanish straggler was discovered, the *Gran Grifon*, the flagship of the urcas, which during the night had drifted out of the protective range of the rest of the fleet. She was a ponderous, moderately powerful but slow-moving vessel; and she was immediately attacked by Drake, who had shown his usual ability to be in the right place at the right time. A considerable action blew up, with Recalde again in the fray, and Bertendona and Oquendo. After damage on both sides the *Gran Grifon* was eventually rescued by one of the galleasses which took her in tow, and Drake and Howard then withdrew before the approach of Medina Sidonia and his Portuguese galleons. Although the action lasted for less than two hours, it seems to have been at closer quarters than on Tuesday. The *Gran Grifon* was quite badly damaged, with forty of her crew killed and an unknown number wounded, and Drake lost his mainyard and a number of men.

(Perhaps it should be mentioned here that all through the Armada battles the English understated their losses in personnel, for the simple reason that if a ship reported, say, ten men killed, a due proportion of victuals and back pay was automatically deducted from the next meagre allowance.)

But, after that early morning battle, there was little further action on Wednesday. All day in light airs and fitful breezes, the Armada continued its slow, stately progress up channel towards the Isle of Wight. All day the English fleet shadowed it. Howard held a council-of-war in the afternoon, and for the first time divided his fleet properly into squadrons. Howard himself, Drake, Hawkins and Frobisher were the natural choice for command. Until now it had been something of a free-for-all on the English side; ships more or less followed whom they liked; Drake's friends kept close to him, and any others who saw Drake's flag and fancied his leadership did the same. Now the English had learned the value of grouping from the Spaniards, and some order began to appear in the fleet. They were coming bitterly to appreciate the fact that the better discipline of the Spaniards was preventing them from breaking up the Armada or indeed seriously damaging it. So far two vessels only had fallen out after all this fighting; and neither had been from enemy gunfire. The Armada was scarred but intact.

The English were almost out of shot, and still short of men and ordinary victuals. Howard in his *Relation of Proceedings* speaks of the enormous expenditure of great shot on the Tuesday and says that although the musketeers and the harquebusiers (who fired a heavier type of musket) were discharging their weapons as rapidly as they could, the sharper bark of the hand weapons could never be heard because of the rapid firing of the cannons and the culverins. Sir George Carey writing to the Earl of Sussex says: 'The shot continued so thick together that it might rather have been judged a skirmish with small shot on land than a fight with great shot on sea.' Both fleets indeed had blazed away in the heat of the first engagements as if ammunition were unlimited. 'We sent,' writes Howard, 'divers barques and pinnaces on to the shore for a new supply of such provisions.'

But a nation which had been at peace within its own boundaries for over a hundred years could not produce powder and shot anywhere for the asking. Some ammunition was ferried out from Portsmouth, Weymouth, and the little towns along the coast, but there was never enough, scarcely enough for another major engagement. Indeed without the ammunition salvaged from de Valdes's *Rosario* there might not have been enough to go round at all. Meanwhile Howard's fleet was constantly being reinforced by volunteer vessels which were emerging enthusiastically from all the little harbours. But their presence was an embarrassment rather than a help to the main fleet, which could really make no use of them in a fight against a close-knit and disciplined enemy who proceeded on his way and protected his weaker ships within a hard ring of galleons.

As for the Spaniards, they had been provided by Philip with one hundred and twenty-three thousand round shot of varying sizes and five hundred and seventeen thousand pounds of powder. It should have been enough for all emergencies. And they had ample yet. They were more than half way up the Channel; but these constant running fights were eating into their supply. And unlike the English they were on an unfriendly coast. As they neared the Isle of Wight Medina Sidonia sent off messages to Parma, telling him of his approach and requesting that new supplies of powder and shot should be made available to him when they linked up.

The Spanish even more than the English were guilty of firing too often while out of range. Most of the engagements so far had taken place at a range approximating to an average par-4 hole at golf. At this distance the English ships were just out of effective range of the heaviest fifty-pound balls that the Spanish guns could fire, and it would have been a great tactical stroke for the Spanish to have refrained from firing them, once it was seen that they were not reaching their mark. But it would have required a superhuman restraint which would have been psychologically impossible. To wait until you can see the whites of their eyes is good tactics when the other side is getting ever nearer. The English never got nearer. They continued to turn away and refuse all contest at close quarters.

But this very policy, well though it paid off in the end, meant that even the English gunfire was erratic and had the minimum of serious effect. It brought down a few spars and killed some men but it never completely disabled and it certainly did not sink. Something more had to be concerted to break up the Spanish discipline, to prevent them reaching their destination.

The gentlest of breezes persisted through Wednesday night, but dawn broke in a complete calm with the two fleets drifting a mile or two apart and about ten miles off the Needles, the westernmost tip of the Isle of Wight. Daylight showed a situation not unlike that of the day before. This time two Spanish ships had lagged behind: a Portuguese galleon, the *San Luis*, eight hundred and thirty tons, thirty-eight guns, and another hulk, the *Duquesa Santa Ana*, nine hundred tons, twenty-three guns. Nearest to them of the English fleet was the dreaded 'Juan Achines', as the Spaniards called him, commanding the *Victory*, of eight hundred tons and sixty-four guns. Thereupon began a battle in dead calm between ships dependent on wind for movement.

As soon as he saw game so near Hawkins put down boats, which began laboriously to tow him into range of the enemy. The rest of his squadron followed suit. Medina Sidonia at once countered by dispatching three of the four galleasses to the rescue, but, having noted how vulnerable the galleass, unsupported, was to saker and culverin fire directed at the banks of rowers, he had them tow along one of the great carracks to add to their firepower. This was de Leyva's *La Rata Encoronada*, in which so many of Spain's young noblemen sailed. It also, according to Artiñano, carried fifty-three guns and was 'the Spanish ship with the most artillery'.

The Duke, watching the considerable conflict which now developed between a few heavy ships of both sides while the rest of the fleets looked helplessly on, had something on his mind greater than the outcome of this immediate action. He had already during the night called and listened to one council-of-war. For this was the day to seize the Isle of Wight if it were to be done at all. In his letter to the King of last Saturday, before any of the fighting began, the Duke had expressed himself quite plainly as having no intention of proceeding further up the Channel than the Isle of Wight until he had made contact with the Duke of Parma. It made good sense. It was a reasonable precaution to wait here until he received a reply to the messages he had sent on ahead. So far he had preserved his fleet splendidly intact. He should know Parma's precise intentions before venturing into the narrows of the Channel, with no port of shelter or replenishment and the uncertain weather of the North Sea to face. Most of his officers were in favour of this plan.

But the Armada could not very well just anchor for several days in the Solent. The island could be captured, though at considerable cost, at considerable wastage of strength, especially with the English fleet still at large and undamaged. Yet, once the Isle of Wight *was* in his possession, the Armada had a sure base from which to emerge to meet Parma, a base to return to if things went wrong.

But the King's letters were on the table before him. One was headed: 'Secret Instructions for you, the Duke of Medina Sidonia, my cousin, my Captain General of the Ocean' and signed 'I, the King'. It said: 'If God gives the success which is desired, as it is hoped that He will, you are to follow strictly the order of my public instructions to you. If, however, through our sins it should fall out otherwise, and the Duke, my nephew, should not be

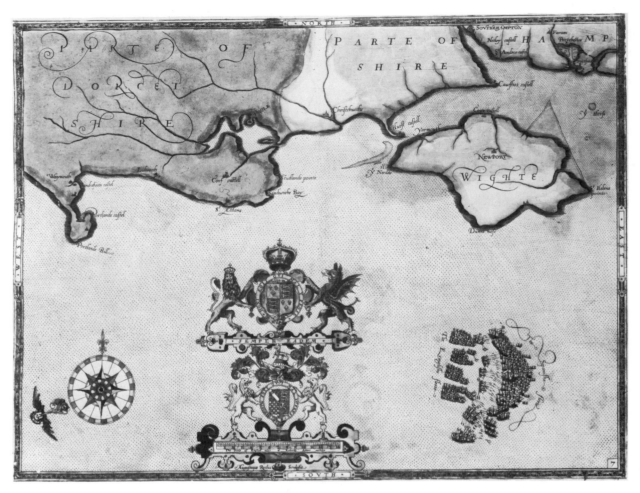

able to cross to England, nor you for that reason meet him, then, after communicating with him, you will see whether you are able to capture the Isle of Wight.' Philip then goes on to outline the advantages of having a secure base but concludes by saying emphatically: 'On no account should you try to capture the island on your journey eastwards without first having made a supreme effort to achieve success in the main task.'

So there it was – the precise instructions. So far the Duke had obeyed all his instructions, and had done so with complete success. Was he now to go against these instructions at the very last, and perhaps leave Parma high and dry, for lack of the courage to go on? All the King's advice so far had been good. His knowledge of the English coast had proved correct in every detail, so had his predictions as to the tactics of the English fleet. The sailors and soldiers of the Armada were clearly anxious about their position, but not in poor heart. The swiftness of movement of the English fleet dismayed them, but losses so far had been slight. The weather, after the appalling early summer, was seemingly set fair; so far nothing could have been more

Chart 7. The English squadrons harrying the Spanish crescent past the Isle of Wight on Thursday the 25th July 1588

119

favourable for their journey up the Channel. How many great military enterprises had failed for lack of resolution, from over-caution on the part of the commander-in-chief?

It is not clear what the Duke – or his council – would finally have decided, for the events of Thursday, operating on indecision, took the choice gradually out of their hands. The local battle in the calm of dawn gradually developed into a major clash. Hawkins, for a time outgunned by the arrival of *La Rata* and the three galleasses, was eventually supported by both Howard in the *Ark* and his cousin Lord Thomas Howard in the *Golden Lion*, who got themselves hauled by longboats into the battle area. Then the galleasses, in spite of English harassment, were able to get ropes aboard the two stranded ships and tow them away to safety, though not without damage to the galleasses. The *Gerona* was holed in the bows and had her lantern shot away, while the *San Lorenzo*, with Moncada aboard, again suffered heavy casualties.

The English were of course just as concerned as the Spanish about the Isle of Wight, and during the night Frobisher had edged himself so far forward in order to be between the Armada and the land that he found himself once again isolated and inshore, much as he had been off Portland yesterday. With no wind but a strong eastward current, the stronger the nearer it was to the land, he and a few supporting ships were only a mile or two off Ventnor and within range of the Spanish northern wing. He was quickly engaged by them and seemed in danger of being overwhelmed, so he dropped longboats, and others went to his assistance, there being in all eleven to take him in tow and drag him back out of range of the Spanish.

Then at last a light wind began to stir and, as movement in the fleets became possible, a confused battle developed. The breeze favoured the Spanish, and several of their galleons bore down on the *Triumph* again. But Frobisher's ship, though somewhat damaged, immediately shook off her tow and, although pursued by two of the swiftest galleons in the Spanish fleet, drew away so quickly that, in Calderon's words, 'our own ships seemed to be standing still'. Probably in this the *Triumph* was aided by the currents, which Frobisher knew how to utilize so well.

Meanwhile Medina Sidonia brought his main squadrons to bear on the English centre and in an hour's mixed fighting drove them back westward. Howard in the *Ark* got the worst of this, and Fenner in the *Nonpareil* and Fenton in the *Mary Rose* stood between him and Recalde in the *San Juan* and Oquendo in the *Santa Ana*, who were eager to press home their advantage. There was nothing now, if he so chose, to prevent the Duke from swinging northwards and entering the undefended eastern arm of the Solent – that recommended to him by the King – and seizing Spithead. But again following the pattern of the previous day, Drake, little engaged so far, had used the new wind to claw himself out to sea, and from there with his squadron he now launched a fierce attack on the southern wing of the Armada, where first the *San Mateo* and then the *Florencia* bore the brunt.

These ships retreated east and north towards the land, causing disarray in that wing of the Armada and bending the crescent so that its tip straightened and was in danger of breaking away.

There was still nothing to prevent Medina Sidonia from leading his biggest galleons straight up the Solent, but he would have done so at the risk of leaving the ships of his southern wing to fend for themselves and to see the defensive formation that he so much prized disintegrate under pressure. With so rigid a strategy there was really only one course open to him at this stage, and that was to re-group his ships back into their tight formation and sail to the rescue of his menaced southern wing. Once he had re-grouped he could then in theory turn if he so desired and sail up to Spithead.

When eventually the main Spanish fleet came up, Drake and Hawkins broke off the engagement. Their primary objective seems to have been to draw the Spanish fleet further from the mouth of the Solent and into a position where the flow of tide and current would make it difficult for them to turn and enter the estuary. In this they were successful. They may also, as has been suggested by many modern writers, have been trying to edge at least a part of the Spanish fleet on to the Owers Bank off the Bill of Selsey. If so, they failed in this, as they failed to disrupt the essential Armada formation.

There is no record, however, from any Spanish source that the Duke or his advisers had second thoughts about attempting to double back and take the Isle of Wight after all. We shall never know how far the scattered battles of Thursday, and especially Drake's fierce attack which ended them, influenced the Duke in his decision to continue on his way without news from Parma. He may always have intended to do so. At any rate he sailed on with his four pilots, his sailing master, Captain Marolin de Juan, his naval adviser, Diego Flores, and his military adviser, Don Francisco de Bobadilla, at his side, towards his destiny in the narrows of the Channel.

What that destiny was the English did not know any more than the Spanish. Again there had been a day's inconclusive fighting. Again the Armada proceeded on its way with a few ships damaged, a few hundred men dead and perhaps twice as many wounded. But still virtually untouched, considering its total size. Since the second day not a single ship had fallen out, not one prize for the English to claim. It was no story to tell the Queen.

Yet, rightly, the English celebrated Thursday as a great strategic victory, and on Friday Howard held a council-of-war at which he knighted Martin Frobisher, John Hawkins and several others. The Armada against all probabilities had forced its way up the Channel unbroken, but it was now past the last of the most suitable of invasion harbours and, although its attempted junction with Parma still remained a possibility, Howard knew that ahead of them was a new and unused English fleet under Lord Henry Seymour. This would be a reinforcement not of brave useless little fishing-boats armed with a pop-gun cannon apiece but of a powerful squadron of about twenty-four capital ships and eighteen others. None of these was large by Spanish standards or those of the *Triumph* or the *Bear*, but two at least were brand-new ships embodying the very latest principles of naval design, and all were fresh and fuming for a fight and might even conceivably carry some powder and shot to use in their guns.

Which Howard notably now had not. Friday was a superb day, brilliant and cloudless and hot; and not a shot was fired either then or on Saturday, when the weather clouded and there were a few showers. The only bombardment was Howard's upon the sea-coast towns: of pinnaces with urgent messages demanding from the Earl of Sussex, Sir George Carey and the captains of the forts and castles along the coast that at all costs they should send him food for his guns and victuals for his men. Quite clearly there would be another and perhaps final trial of strength somewhere off Margate or Dunkirk; for this he must have ammunition and men with food in their bellies.

And men who had had some rest. In none of the accounts of the Armada is mention made of the fatigue and strain that the commanders and men of both fleets must by now have been suffering. For the best part of six days the two great fleets had accompanied each other up channel, never out of sight of each other except at nightfall, when the chance of accidental encounter increased, and almost always in the day fighting or manoeuvring to fight. The opportunity for sleep or even rest for any of the commanders was minimal. Medina Sidonia, it has been said, hardly left the taffrail during the whole time, receiving up there such food as he would eat, constantly consulting his advisers, usually in the thick of the battle or directing his own galleon to steer to that part of his fleet most directly menaced, sometimes snatching a few hours rest at dusk and then up again and leaning over the stern through the night.

If the strain was perhaps greatest of all for him, it can hardly have been much less for Howard, with all England to lose; and so on down the fleets.

Twice a day Medina Sidonia now sent off fast pinnaces to Parma, but so far had received no reply.

Parma, indeed, who had blown hot and cold over the *Empresa* for the last twelve months, was in no position to answer Medina Sidonia as the Admiral wanted and hoped. After the failure of this Armada and its return to Spain much of the blame for the failure was put on Parma's shoulders for letting Medina Sidonia down. Indeed, from that time on Philip never really trusted him again. Later historians, studying the warnings that Parma had sent to Philip and the almost insuperable difficulties involved in ferrying the Spanish troops across the narrow seas with the obstacles that existed, have tended to absolve Parma of all blame.

Yet he must bear his full share of responsibility for what happened. Although others – like Alva and Don John of Austria – had thought of invading England from the Netherlands long before Parma suggested it, it was he who in the spring of 1586 first submitted his detailed scheme to Philip, outlining the possibility of a landing in Kent or Essex with thirty thousand infantrymen and five hundred cavalry, in flat-bottomed boats, screened by an escort of twenty-five warships. When later Philip decided to amalgamate this scheme with an Armada under Santa Cruz, Parma at first was in full agreement; and after the death of Mary Queen of Scots he wrote to Philip, as we have seen, assuming that the great *Empresa* would now go forward. Until March 1587, too, his own drive in the Netherlands had been northward; but from that time on he turned his eyes west, and the maps hanging in his headquarters in Brussels, instead of being of Leiden and Utrecht and Amsterdam, were of Flanders and the ports along its North Sea coast. After weeks of bloody and bitter fighting among the mud and tidal channels of Sluys he had at last forced the town into surrender – one of his dearest-bought victories. What could that victory be intended to further more certainly than the enterprise against England? After the capture of the town his troops began to dig the canals necessary to get the barges to Nieuport, so that from there they could be moved to Dunkirk while still under protection from the shore.

In November 1587 he wrote to Philip telling him that the barges – with fly-boats to escort them – were ready at Antwerp and Dunkirk, and that in two weeks he could launch the invasion – a palpable piece of wishful thinking if one does not use a harsher word. Then he moved his headquarters from Brussels to Bruges and discovered that his exits along the coast were all blockaded by Justin of Nassau, Admiral of Zeeland. He at once wrote to Philip, warning him of this and pointing out that Santa Cruz and the Armada would now necessarily have to clear a way for him before he could stir. He also later emphasized the extreme difficulty of the link-up, because galleons could not approach Dunkirk for lack of sea depth and Justin of Nassau could attack the troop-filled barges in the shallow water before they could gain the protection of the galleons.

Through the spring and summer many barges and fly-boats were certainly laid down at Dunkirk and Nieuport, but work on them proceeded with excruciating slowness. It is difficult to believe that Parma, who could achieve miracles of organization when he chose to, could not have hastened on this building programme. Yet he never appears to have let either Santa Cruz or Medina Sidonia know the true extent of his naval weakness. Certainly no general of Parma's experience would have considered launching his troops in defenceless flat-bottomed barges into a sea patrolled by enemy fly-boats – though he made a token effort to do this when it was too late. But no general of Parma's brilliance could not have advanced his preparations further than he did in the time at his disposal.

Engravings published in the year before the First Armada: *top* an arquebusier and *bottom* a musketeer

Perhaps he half thought the Armada would never come. (He did not know it had left Spain until it was off the Isle of Wight.) But in war you cannot afford to be caught in two minds. And it was Medina Sidonia who paid the price.

8   *Gravelines*

At its majestic crawl – about the speed of a rowing-boat – the Armada proceeded unharassed all through Friday and Saturday, and in the evening of the latter day it came to anchor off Calais, still unbroken, still in its strong defensive formation. The English fleet dropped anchor half a mile away. The fine week of summer seemed to be over, and a fresh westerly breeze was bringing lowering clouds and a threat of rain.

Before darkness fell the English fleet was reinforced by the arrival of the new squadron of Lord Henry Seymour who, disobeying the Queen's express instruction to continue his patrol duties off Dunkirk, gladly accepted Howard's summons to join him. This meant that the English fleet was now increased by about a third, and that its numbers were for the first time something like equal to the Spanish. At the same time Justin of Nassau took over the guard duties of Seymour; but with his fleet of small tough shallow-draught warships of fifty to one hundred and fifty tons each he was able to keep a closer watch on Nieuport and Dunkirk than Seymour had done.

The night passed quietly, and on Sunday morning both admirals held councils-of-war. They both had cause for anxiety, for Howard, though stronger than he had ever been before, was well aware that the two Dukes were now only twenty-five miles apart by sea and little more by land. He had no certain knowledge of what Parma had been able to build during the last months or how many fly-boats he might have accumulated. A juncture between the two forces was at hand and this must be challenged at all costs. The Spanish had anchored rather dangerously inshore; but they, the English, were only half a mile further out and might also be in difficulties if the weather broke. Monsieur Gourdan, the Governor of Calais, was a known Catholic and an adherent of the pro-Spanish Guises, and would no doubt give the Spaniards 'all help short of war'.

But Medina Sidonia's anxieties were far greater. At last he had heard from Parma – a message expressing his 'great joy' that the Armada had forced the

Channel passage and promising that his forces would be ready to take part in the invasion of England in about six days. But Don Rodrigo Tello de Guzman, Medina Sidonia's relative and envoy, had found Parma in Bruges, not in Dunkirk, and he had a most depressing story to tell of the extent of the unpreparedness he had seen in Nieuport and Dunkirk. His own view was that nothing would be likely to be ready for at least fourteen days.

A fourteen-day stay off Calais Roads – or even six – was an impossibility for the Armada. Indeed Gourdan, who yesterday had driven cheerfully down to the shore with his wife in his coach hoping to be able to watch an immediate battle, sent a message of friendly greeting to Medina Sidonia on Sunday morning, pointing out that his present anchorage just east of Calais cliffs was an extremely dangerous one, because of the strong cross currents at the mouth of the English Channel.

Medina Sidonia dispatched a further urgent message to Parma: 'I am anchored here two leagues from Calais with the enemy's fleet on my flank. They can cannonade me whenever they like, and I shall be unable to do them much harm in return. If you can send me forty or fifty fly-boats of your fleet I can, with their help, defend myself here until you are ready to come out.' Parma had in all fewer than twenty fly-boats, and some of those were not ready for sea.

Medina Sidonia also replied to the Governor of Calais, thanking him for his warning and for the present of fruit and fresh vegetables he had sent, and he requested that Monsieur Gourdan should sell them whatever powder and shot he could spare. Gourdan, sitting on the fence, refused this, but offered

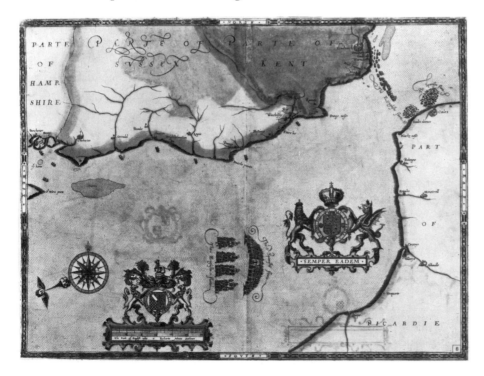

Chart 8. The Spanish fleet off Calais, Saturday the 27th July 1588

to sell them food or any other 'non-combatant' provisions they were short of. Stow in his *Chronicles of England* writes of that Sunday afternoon: 'The Flemings, Walloons and the French came thick and three-fold to behold the Spanish fleet, admiring the exceeding greatness of their ships, and warlike order: the greatest kept the outside next the enemy, like strong Castles fearing no assault, the lesser placed in the middle-ward. Fresh victuals straight were brought aboard; Captains and Cavaliers for their money might have what they would, and gave the French so liberally, as within twelve hours an egg was worth fivepence, besides thanks.'

The figure of five pence was about twenty-five times what an egg was fetching in London at that date, so one perceives that the French, as usual, were not averse from making a profit out of casual callers.

One can visualize the scene, people flocking on foot or by horse or cart or donkey from the town and the neighbouring villages; a fine Sunday afternoon with something to gaze at, as they would have come to stare at a wreck – only this was more dramatic, a real treat, tension growing – sitting on the edge of the cliffs, hurrying down to the beaches with their produce or standing in clumps gossiping and speculating on a possible battle while the little boats went speedily back and forth plying their profitable trade.

Stow goes on: 'Whilst this lusty Navie like a demi-Conqueror, rid thus at anchor, the Spanish faction in sundry nations had divulged that England was subdued, the Queen taken and sent prisoner over the Alps to Rome, where barefoot she should make her humble reconciliation.' The first of many such rumours that spread through Europe during the next few weeks.

Another rumour had spread around the Armada – or had been deliberately started – that Parma was coming out to join them tomorrow. It was perhaps a necessary lie to try to relieve long pent-up tensions and fears and to revive flagging spirits. For now the strain was making itself apparent in the whole Spanish fleet. Throughout the long week up the Channel most of the hulks, the supply ships and the smaller armed merchantmen – that centre core to the Armada – had not been in action at all. Like sheep they had continued on their slow and ponderous way while the ring of great galleons, like guard-dogs, had protected them against the wolves. But they had witnessed the battles, they had seen – and reluctantly admired – the speed and mobility of the English fleet, and their nerves were wearing thin. A considerable proportion of the masters and crews of these ships was not Spanish; they had no particular relish for a fight and, being good seamen themselves, they were not comfortable anchored so close to a lee shore. Already there had been one desertion to the English, of the hulk *San Pedro el Menor*, of five hundred tons, and that under Portuguese command. There might soon be others.

Nor was the depression and the tension confined to the weaker members of the fleet. The obvious sailing superiority of the English at all times, the complete failure of the galleons even to close and board one English ship, the English reinforcements, their menacing position now off the weather

Chart 9. Sunday the 28th July 1588: the Spanish and English fleets massed against each other in the Calais Roads

flank of the Armada, all added to the nervousness and the depression. The greatest single calamity, of course, after the failure of Parma to come out, was the shortage of shot. There was powder in plenty yet, but some of the ships had only shot enough left for one short action, particularly for the heavier cannon which had so far kept the English at a distance. Medina Sidonia had obeyed his instructions and achieved his objective with the maximum fidelity and the minimum loss. But what now? Parma was *not ready*, and Sidonia's pilots warned that to venture further out into the North Sea would be to add to the hazards of navigation.

It probably never entered Medina Sidonia's head to take Calais. It needed a later century for man to discover the considerable advantage of attacking neutrals. But if one deducts two thousand for sickness and casualties, the Duke still had some eighteen thousand trained soldiers in his fleet. It would not have been difficult to pick a quarrel with Monsieur Gourdan and force the town: the fighting might have been fierce but it would have been brief. Then he could have sailed into a safe harbour, linked with Parma on land, and restored and refurbished his fleet and picked his time for an invasion.

By Monday anyway it was too late for such perfidy, for on Sunday night the English launched the fire-ships.

There was nothing new or original about fire-ships, no stroke of inventive genius bearing the stamp of Drake or some other master mind. They were a common arm of naval warfare, far more lethal to stout wooden ships than the inaccurate cannon of the day. Fire-ships had been attempted against

127

Drake in Cadiz; the Spaniards had contemplated using them a week ago when considering an attack on the English fleet in Plymouth; Philip in one of his letters had expressly warned Medina Sidonia against the risks of such an attack. (He really did try to think of everything.)

The present situation was ideal for their use. A fresh breeze blowing steadily from the English fleet towards the Spanish, the Spaniards still in close defensive formation, a lee shore, the onset of night, and the turn of the tide at eleven p.m.

The decision to use the fire-ships had been taken at the council-of-war on board the *Ark* that morning. As soon as it was known that the Armada was succeeding in its attempt to force the Channel, Walsingham had given orders for a number of fishing-vessels to be requisitioned at Dover and laden with pitch and faggots, and immediately the decision was taken to use them Sir Henry Palmer was sent in a pinnace to bring them over. But the day wore on and evening came and there was no sign of Palmer, so it was decided to act without him while the best tidal conditions prevailed and to sacrifice some of the smaller ships of the fleet. Drake gave a two-hundred-ton vessel, the *Thomas*. Hawkins gave the *Bark Bond* of one hundred and fifty tons, and six others were contributed. These were all bigger than anything that had ever been used before; and as soon as darkness fell they were made ready for their work. An old Devonshire captain called John Young, one of Drake's men, was put in charge of the fire-ships, and his second-in-command was a Cornishman called Captain Prouse. All the masts and rigging were tarred, all the guns were left on board double-shotted to go off of their own accord when the fire reached them.

Medina Sidonia and his advisers were alert for some such attempt. With the tide and the wind as it was, a special risk must exist, and they made all the preparations they could to meet it. A screen of patrol boats equipped with grapnels was thrown out to cover the Spanish fleet from the seaward side, and one of the Duke's most trusted officers, Captain Serrano, was put in charge. At the same time the Duke sent a message to every ship in the fleet that an attack by fire-ships might well occur that night. If such an attack came the fleet was not to panic, for the screen of patrol-boats would protect them; and if by any chance a fire-ship should get through they must have their own boats ready lowered to fend it off. Supposing even this failed they were to slip their cables, marking the position with buoys, and stand out to sea, then return to station and to pick up their cables once the fire-ships were past. The Duke could have done no more.

Unfortunately something worse than fire-ships was feared by the anxious captains receiving this message. Three years before at the siege of Antwerp an Italian engineer called Giambelli had devised ships called hell-burners which, when the fire reached the powder within them, had exploded and killed a thousand men, flinging the blazing wreckage of boats and bridges over a square mile of the city. It was the most destructive weapon that had ever been seen by man. And Giambelli, it was known, was in England and

Sir Francis Walsingham, the head of Elizabeth I's secret service

working for the Queen. (In fact he was in London and working innocently on its defences, but no one was to know that.)

Soon after midnight, with the tide racing, the eight ships were lit up and sent away. Almost immediately they were seen by the Armada and the alarm given. The eight ships were sailing in line abreast, and they bore down on the Spanish fleet with the flames already leaping and crackling all over them. Their very size was more than the Spaniards had ever reckoned with. A two-hundred-ton barque, with the wind and the current behind her, and manned by determined men until the last moment, is a very hard obstacle to stop. The Spanish patrol-boats had no motors to aid them, only sail and oar against the wind and the tide, and eight ships to deal with at once, all much larger than they were themselves. They got hawsers aboard one at either end of the line and pulled them off course. An attempt was made in the middle, but the fire on the blazing ships had now reached the guns which began exploding in every direction. This convinced the Spanish that they had not to deal with ordinary fire-ships but with the dreaded hell-burners all over again.

The defences of London, improved in 1588 by the Italian engineer Giambelli, who also invented 'hell-burners', the elaborated fire-ships used at Antwerp

129

As the six ships came on, Medina Sidonia fired a warning gun and slipped his cables and luffed up close-hauled against the wind. A few others of his squadron did the same. But for the rest the long-imposed discipline at last broke. They did not wait to slip anchors; they cut them and shook out their sails and went with wind and tide, drifting past Calais out towards the North Sea and the low coastline of Dunkirk. In the confusion ship collided with ship and it was every man for himself. The fire-ships in fact did no material damage of themselves at all; they drifted harmlessly on to the beach to burn down to the water-line; but they had achieved what the English fleet in six days of fighting had failed to do, they had broken the disciplined defensive formation of the Armada, and it was never to be recovered.

As soon as he saw the fire-ships safely past, Medina Sidonia in the *San Martin* brought his ship back again to near his original anchorage, put out a sheet anchor and fired a gun to direct the rest of his fleet to follow suit. But very few did. The *San Marcos*, with the Marquis de Penafiel on board. The *San Juan* with Recalde. The *Santa Ana* with Oquendo. Two or three others. The rest had scattered over several square miles of water and most could not anchor if they would; they had had two anchors out against the swift-running tide and had cut both away in the panic. If they possessed a spare anchor it was stowed away and could not immediately be brought into use.

A gusty dawn showed a half dozen of the great galleons riding at anchor where dusk had left them and the other one-hundred-and-thirty-odd ships strung out eastwards towards the Dunkirk sandbanks. The big galleass *San Lorenzo*, with Hugo de Moncada on board, had fouled her rudder in a collision with the *San Juan de Sicilia* and had then run into another ship, with the result that she was now crawling in a crippled fashion just off the French coast and dangerously far in. The English fleet, of course, had not shifted.

With the first light there was instant activity. The Duke, knowing that the tight defensive grouping had so far been his salvation and that if his fleet were to survive it must at all costs reassemble before the English attacked, had sent off fast pinnaces during the night to make contact with the scattered ships and to order them to reassemble around him. But the dawn showed them still far scattered and a south-westerly wind blowing, which would make their return a difficult and lengthy matter. So the Duke, with the wind in his favour, weighed anchor to catch them up and try to regain formation somewhere off Dunkirk. And with the light the English, seeing for the first time the success that their fire-ships had achieved, at once attacked.

Thereupon began what has been described as one of the great decisive battles of the world. The English order of battle was never put to paper but was agreed orally among the commanders. However, it seems that they attacked by squadrons more or less abreast – with Drake, who had as usual contrived his anchorage nearest to the enemy, slightly in the van. The

Duke's small squadron of galleons, seeing themselves being overhauled by the English and perceiving that if they could hold the enemy here it would give time for the scattered Armada to reassemble, came about and formed line abreast also to meet the attack. In the meantime Howard, the commander of the whole English fleet, seeing the great galleass *San Lorenzo* in trouble near the Calais beach, allowed himself to be diverted from his main task of destroying the Armada by the lure of a rich prize and sailed with his whole squadron to attack the *San Lorenzo*. Both he and Drake – on different days – thus conducted themselves in a way which would have led to an instant court-martial in later times.

The injured galleass, crowded with three hundred and twelve oarsmen, one hundred and thirty-four sailors and two hundred and thirty-five soldiers, strained like an injured beetle to gain Calais harbour but ran aground on the bar and heeled over in the surf, pointing a host of slender oars to the sky. The water was too shoal for the *Ark* or any of her companions to reach her, so Howard launched his longboat with sixty men, many of these gentlemen adventurers hot for spoil and to prove their courage. Soon a dozen other small ships were following, including the two-hundred-ton London ship the *Margaret and John*, Captain John Fisher, which had been in the thick of the fighting throughout the week. This time, however, Fisher overplayed his luck and his ship went aground too, not far from the stranded galleass. Since the tide was still falling they could do nothing yet to refloat her, so half of her ninety crew piled into the boats to make a boarding-party.

In the galleass pandemonium reigned, with the galley-slaves fighting to get free, some of the soldiers and sailors leaping overboard and struggling through the surf to the safety of the beach, while Hugo de Moncada and his officers rallied the rest to resist attack. The English boats in the last fifty yards were fine targets in the bright morning light, and dozens of men were killed and wounded by small-arms fire. Richard Tomson, Lieutenant of the *Margaret and John*, says: 'We continued a pretty skirmish with our small shot against theirs, they being ensconced within their ship and very high over us, we in our open pinnaces and far under them having nothing to shroud and cover us.' After a bitter fight Moncada himself was killed outright by a musket-shot between the eyes, and after that resistance collapsed.

Moncada was the first of the high-born Spanish admirals to lose his life.

The English, about two hundred in number, having accepted the surrender of the remaining officers, proceeded to loot the ship and would have taken the ship as well had not the French, who had been watching the whole bloody battle with detached interest from the shore, now put in a claim that the ship was in French territorial waters and ship and guns at least belonged to them. The English, whose temper was up, were prepared to dispute this with their arms, but Monsieur Gourdan reinforced his rights with such accurate gunfire from Calais Castle and the ramparts above the beach that the raiders had to withdraw in haste. Howard now at last

A combined axe and pistol of the 16th century

directed his squadron towards the main battle. In capturing this one ship he had kept a dozen of the best English ships out of the decisive struggle for more than three hours.

The shape of the great battle of Gravelines is hard to determine from contemporary accounts. Indeed the one fact which emerges is that, after the first hour, it had no shape at all. This was the battle in which the English were determined at all costs to destroy the Spanish fleet. For a week they had been frustrated, knowing themselves more seaworthy but able to turn this to no advantage. Frustrated, aware that they had done nothing that had been so confidently expected of them at home, for ever up against the defensive wall and the Spanish challenge to 'come and board us', they now saw for the first time the Armada scattered and in disarray. Now in these next hours, before it could reassemble, they must tear it to pieces. And this is what they proceeded to do.

Drake in the *Revenge* was the first to close Medina Sidonia in the *San Martin*. It was a meeting of admirals, but this time there was no long-range firing. Drake had to get in to kill and Medina Sidonia was on his last supply of heavy shot. So when they did fire it was at close range, and in the thunderous cannonade which followed heavy damage was done to both ships. Drake's ship was 'pierced through by heavy cannon-balls of all sizes which were flying everywhere between the two fleets, and was riddled with every kind of shot'. Twice Drake's cabin was pierced by cannon-balls, and rigging was brought down on the heads of the sailors. No sooner was the *Revenge* past than Thomas Fenner in the *Nonpareil* took his place. And then Lord Edmund Sheffield in the *White Bear*, and so on down the line while the *San Martin* fought each one in turn. Soon her decks were a shambles and she was holed both above and below the water-line. The *San Juan* and the *San Marcos* also became closely involved.

But this time Drake was not to be caught by the lure of a prize, even the prize of the ship bearing the Armada's supreme commander. Already in answer to Medina Sidonia's commands the Spanish ships were regrouping, forming that hard outer shell of the old crescent behind which the weaker ships could shelter. It was a notable feat in the conditions of the morning and, although never completed, was partially carried out in spite of the English challenge. Drake remained no longer fighting the first line of galleons but by-passed them and drove in to cut up the assembling groups

The cannon known as Queen Elizabeth's Gun, installed at Dover

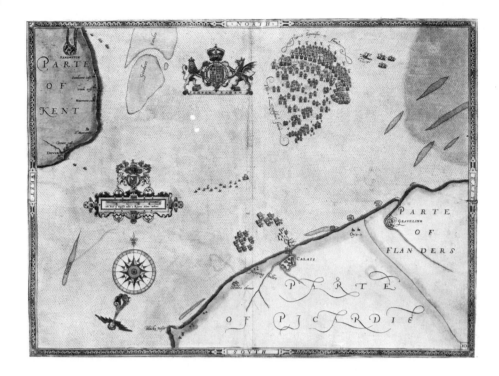

behind. Frobisher, fuming with annoyance at this, took up the battle with the front-line ships, and behind him came Hawkins in the *Victory*, Edward Fenton, his brother-in-law, in the *Mary Rose*, Sir George Beeston in the *Dreadnought*, Hawkins's son in the *Swallow* and a host of others, outnumbering the effective Spanish ships now by four to one.

The bitter confusion of the fight is perhaps best described by an eyewitness, Calderon, who was on board the *San Salvador*, a ship of seven hundred and fifty tons attached to Oquendo's squadron.

The enemy opened a heavy artillery fire on our flagship at seven o'clock in the morning, which was continued for nine hours. So tremendous was the fire that over 200 balls struck the sails and hull of the flagship on the starboard side, killing and wounding many men, disabling and dismounting guns and destroying much rigging. The holes made in the hull between wind and water caused so great a leakage that two divers had as much as they could do to stop them with tow and lead plates working all day.

The galleon *San Felipe* of Portugal was surrounded by 17 of the enemy's ships, which directed against her heavy fire on both sides and on her stern. The enemy approached so close that the muskets and the harquebusses of the galleon were brought into service, killing a large number of men on the enemy ships. They did not dare, however, to come to close quarters [i.e. to board], but kept up a hot artillery fire from a distance, disabling the rudder, breaking the foremast and killing over 200 men in the galleon. This being noticed by the captain of the *San Mateo*, he brought his galleon to the wind and bravely went to the rescue. Then some of the enemy's ships attacked him and inflicted much damage upon him.

One of the enemy's ships came alongside the galleon and an Englishman jumped on board, but our men cut him to bits instantly.

In the interim the Duke's flagship, the *San Martin*, and the *San Salvador* luffed up as close as possible and went to the aid of the galleon. The *San Salvador* engaged an admiral's and a commodore's flagships, her bows, side, and half her poop being exposed for four hours to the enemy's fire, during which she had a larger number of men killed and wounded, and her hull, her sails and rigging were much damaged. She leaked greatly through shot holes, and finally the *Rata Encoronada*, under Don Alonso de Leyva, came to her assistance, distinguishing herself greatly. On board the *Rata* there fell Don Pedro de Mendoza and other persons. They had to defend themselves against three flagships, a vice-flagship and ten or twelve other war vessels. This engagement lasted until four o'clock in the afternoon, the *San Juan* and the *San Marcos* suffering very severely. Don Felipe de Cordoba, son of Don Diego, his Majesty's Master of the Horse, had his head shot off.

The Duke's flagship lost 40 soldiers, and Sergeant Juan Carrasco, Alonso de Orozco and others. Diego Enriquez, who succeeded to the command of Pedro de Valdes' squadron, also fought bravely in this engagement, and his ship suffered to such an extent that every one of his sails were destroyed. Don Pedro Enriquez had a hand shot away in this fight, and the ship's company generally behaved with great gallantry.

We sailed between Dover and Calais in the direction of Norway with a W.N.W. wind. The enemy inflicted great damage on the galleons *San Mateo* and *San Felipe*, the latter having five of her starboard guns dismounted. In view of this, and that his upper deck was destroyed, both his pumps broken, his rigging in shreds and his ship almost a wreck, Don Francisco de Toledo ordered the grappling hooks to be brought out and shouted to the enemy to come to close quarters. They replied, summoning him to surrender in fair fight; and one Englishman, standing in the maintop with his sword and buckler, called out: 'Good soldiers that ye are, surrender to the fair terms we offer ye.' But the only answer he got was a gunshot, which brought him down in the sight of everyone, and the Maestro de Campo then ordered the muskets and harquebusses to be brought into action. The enemy thereupon retired, whilst our men shouted out to them that they were cowards, and with opprobrious words reproached them for their want of spirit, calling them Lutheran hens and daring them to return to the fight.

At seven o'clock in the evening, having lost 60 soldiers killed and 200 wounded, the *San Felipe* fired shots for aid to be sent her, and the hulk *Doncella* went to her. She found the galleon sinking and took on board 300 of her men. Captain Juan Poza, who was with them, said he believed that the hulk too was going down. The Maestro de Campo then replied that if that were the case they had better be drowned in the galleon than in the hulk, and they both went back to her. *San Mateo* had her hull so riddled that she was also in a sinking condition, the pumps being powerless to diminish the water. She came alongside the flagship and asked for help. The Duke sent a diver who stopped some of the leaks, but in the end the galleon was obliged to drop astern with the *San Felipe* and their subsequent fate is unknown; but it is said that they ran aground on the banks.

(In fact both ships did drift helplessly into the shore between Nieuport and Dunkirk where they were attacked by three Dutch fly-boats and after a three-hour battle were totally destroyed.)

This is a corner of the great battle, the corner of a page turned up and illumined by a narrator who survived. All over the area of sea between Gravelines and Dunkirk equally bitter fights were taking place, in a free-for-all in which the Spaniards were gradually shot to pieces, fighting almost everywhere with great courage but now without formation, in many cases after the first hours their big guns falling silent for lack of shot.

All the time too the English were edging the Spanish fleet nearer to the sandbanks of Dunkirk, the Spanish, under the leadership of Medina Sidonia and Diego Flores, luffing up into the wind and trying to edge further north.

When Howard himself came on the scene with his dozen fresh ships he charged at once into the *mêlée*. Seymour in the *Rainbow* with Wynter beside him in the *Vanguard* had attacked the enemy's starboard, or inshore, wing – in so far as it remained a wing; and there had done battle with Oquendo in the *Santa Ana* and de Leyva in the *Rata*. The *San Juan de Sicilia*, one of the Levantine squadron, was so badly mauled that half her crew were dead, and eye-witnesses say that 'her port holes were all full of blood'; yet she would not give ground and remained fighting on for three more hours. Martin de Bertendona in his flagship *La Regazona* was engaged alongside, but eventually her battery guns fell silent too as she ran out of shot. With blood spilling from her scuppers she refused to fall out of line but continued to fight with musketeers in her tops and crouching among the dead and the dying on her decks.

As the long day wore on, so the superiority of the English became more manifest. With rare self-control, after the mistake of boarding the galleass in the morning, they made no attempt to capture, or indeed to sink, individual ships; but once they had pounded them into semi-wrecks they moved on to the next target.

By four in the afternoon the battle had almost worn itself out. The English now as well as the Spanish were out of shot. The great Armada galleons were scattered, sometimes in groups of two or three, sometimes alone. For a time the *San Martin* herself was behind the English fleet, and it is said that Medina Sidonia, although wounded in the leg, climbed to the trees to discern for himself what was happening through the clouds of drifting smoke.

It still seemed likely that a total destruction of the Spanish fleet might be achieved, but a heavy squall about six accompanied by blinding rain forced both fleets to look to their sea safety; and when it was past the Armada by running before the wind had got itself temporarily out of range, and a little freer of the menace of the sandbanks. They had also miraculously contrived to re-form, so that once again they were steering in a fairly compact mass, and indeed Sidonia had the courage to shorten sail and wait for another English attack. Howard, however, did not attempt to close again but ordered his ships to shadow the Spanish fleet, of which one after another appeared to be in sinking condition.

Just before sunset the *Maria Juan*, six hundred and sixty-five tons, of Recalde's squadron, which had had a long encounter with Captain Crosse in the *Hope*, signalled for help – she was going down. Somehow the Duke with his battered *San Martin* was still able to put on sail and go to her assistance. But it was too late. He was able to take off one boatload of her men and then she heeled over and sank, carrying with her two hundred and fifty-five men and her captain, Pedro de Ugarte.

So night fell, and the sea rose and the damaged leaking defeated fleet drifted parallel with the coast, putting its dead overboard, trying to minister to its many wounded, mopping the blood from its decks, replacing or patching its tattered sails, repairing rudders, stopping and caulking leaks, its unwounded sailors and soldiers in utter exhaustion, trying between tasks to eat such food as there was – much of it rotten biscuit – and drink the sour water.

No sleep for any, least of all for its commanders, with the English fleet close behind them (and preparing, for all they knew, a new attack at dawn) and the dreaded Dutch-occupied beaches on their starboard wing. It was a prospect which would have daunted any man.

As for the English, they were conscious of winning but not yet that they had won. They knew they had done great damage but only a half dozen of the enemy had gone down. Sir William Wynter, Seymour's second-in-command, wrote to Walsingham: 'Great was the spoil and harm that was done unto them . . . Out of my ship there was shot 500 shot . . . [my ship] was never out of harquebus shot of theirs and most often within speech of one another . . . no doubt the slaughter and hurt was great, as time will discover it; and every man was weary with labour and our cartridges spent and our munitions expended.'

Howard wrote cautiously to Walsingham: 'I will not write unto her Majesty until more be done. Their force is wonderful great and strong; and yet we pluck their feathers by little and little.'

Drake wrote: 'God hath given us so good a day in forcing the enemy so far to leeward, as I hope in God the Duke of Parma and the Duke of Sidonia shall not shake hands this few days; and whensoever they shall meet, I believe neither of them will greatly rejoice of this day's service . . . There must be great care taken to send us munitions and victuals whithersoever the enemy goeth.'

Hawkins wrote: 'All that day Monday we followed the Spaniards with a long and great fight, wherein there was great valour showed generally by our company . . . In this fight there was some hurt done among the Spaniards . . . Our ships, God be thanked, have received little hurt . . . Now their fleet is here, and very forcible, it must be waited upon with all our force, which is little enough. There should be an infinite quantity of powder and shot provided . . . The men have long been unpaid and need relief.'

Richard Tomson wrote: 'At this instant we are as far to the eastward as

OPPOSITE William Cecil, Lord Burghley, Elizabeth I's chief adviser at the time of the Armadas

OVERLEAF The launching, by the English fleet, of fire-ships with doubly loaded cannon that exploded themselves, against the First Armada in the Calais Roads about midnight on Sunday the 28th July 1588

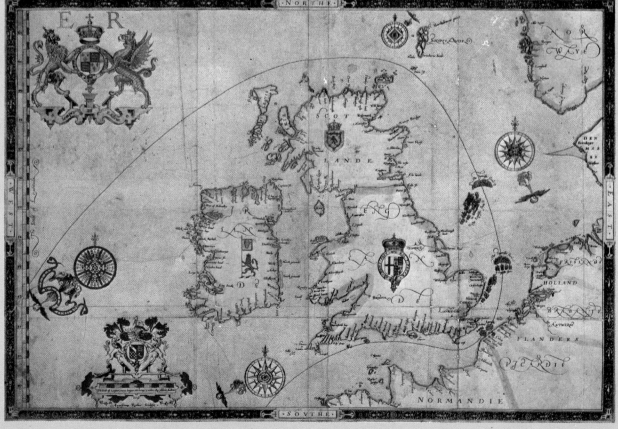

the Isle of Walcheren, wherein Flushing doth stand, and the wind hanging westerly, we drive our enemies apace to the eastward, much marvelling if the wind continue in what port they will direct themselves. Some imagine the river of Hamburg . . . There is want of powder and shot and victual among us which causeth that we cannot so daily assault them as we would.'

When dawn broke on a blustery and showery Tuesday morning, total destruction did indeed face the Spanish fleet. Overnight the wind had come north-west, and with the daylight it was seen that the shore of Zeeland was very close. And not only the shore; for everyone knew that, lurking among the banks and shoals, negotiating them with the familiarity of long experience, was a fleet of fly-boats under Justin of Nassau, whose policy towards the Spaniards – as theirs to him – was one not of ordinary war but of complete extermination.[1]

Behind them, scarcely two miles to windward, were the white sails and bobbing masts of the English fleet.

At the rearguard of the Armada, in the place of greatest danger, ready to meet the first shock of the expected new English attack, were as usual the relatively few fighting ships which had borne the brunt of the battle ever since the first clash at Plymouth: Medina Sidonia and Diego Flores in the *San Martin*, Recalde in the *San Juan*, de Leyva in the *Rata Encoronada*, Oquendo in the *Santa Ana*, de Bertendona in *La Regazona* and about two dozen others. With them were the three surviving galleasses, *Napolitana*, *Gerona* and *Zuniga*. The rest of the fleet struggled ahead under light sail, falling off to leeward ever nearer the shore.

Howard did not attack for the simple reason that he was saving what little shot he had scraped together for the final catastrophe when the Armada took the ground.

The *San Martin* was 'sailing abaft of the rearguard, in consequence of having one of her anchors down, her lead having only reached seven fathoms and she being near the banks'. Various officers now came to Medina Sidonia and besought him to take one of the pinnaces and the much-torn Holy Banner and make for the safety of Spanish-held Dunkirk, but he refused. 'Having confessed himself with his officers he prepared to die like a Christian soldier.' Presently Oquendo in the *Santa Ana* came up and the Duke shouted to him: 'We are lost. What shall we do?' Oquendo said: 'Ask Diego Flores. As for me I am going to fight and die like a man. Send me a supply of shot.'

The lead said six fathoms and then five. The pilots insisted they were helpless; with the wind as it was shipwreck was a matter of minutes. It was just a question of which ships would strike first.

---

[1] It must be said, however, in effect that the Dutch were not as merciless as they perhaps had reason to be; from the two big galleons which drifted ashore on the Monday some four hundred prisoners were taken. These of course included the high-born officers, who could be ransomed, but also many ordinary sailors and soldiers as well.

Then occurred what appeared as a miracle to the Spaniards; the wind hesitated, gusted for a few moments, and began to back. From north-west it became south-west, and within what must have been only yards from shipwreck the Armada shook out its tattered sails and began to move out of danger towards the safer reaches of the North Sea. 'God succoured us in our distress, as He always does,' wrote Calderon. 'We were saved by God's mercy,' said the Duke. What the English thought has never been recorded. A simple change of wind deprived them by a matter of half an hour of that complete victory which the day before they had gone so far to earn. They were powerless to attack again, they could only fall in and shadow. Even the harassing tactics of the Channel were not possible.

As a result of this, no one knew for many weeks whether the threat to England was really over. And for the Spaniards that God-given change of wind meant the difference between annihilation on the Flanders sandbanks and the long-drawn-out agony of a return round the British Isles to Spain.

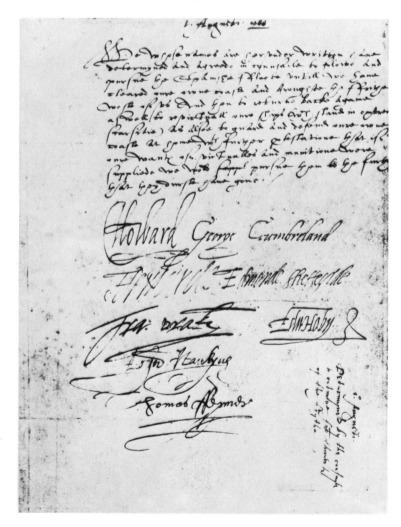

A resolution signed by the English naval commanders, including Lord Howard of Effingham, Sir Francis Drake, and Sir John Hawkins, on the 1st August 1588 after defeating the First Armada off Gravelines, 'to folowe and pursue the Spanishe Fleete vntill we haue cleared oure owne coaste'

9 *Irish Ordeal*

For long the myth was fostered that the Armada was destroyed not by the English but by the storms of August and September. On the Spanish side it was a better excuse than to admit they had been defeated in battle. On the English side it was preferable to believe that winds provided by God in a righteous cause were more potent than the guns and ships provided by man. Yet the myth really did no honour to either side; neither to the seamanship of the Spaniards nor the gunnery and tactics of the English – nor to the bravery of both. In fact the Spanish were comprehensively defeated in the Battle of Gravelines, shot through, decimated, all but completely destroyed. It was this more than any storms which sank them on the way home.

Another myth is that the Armada was blown relentlessly north by an unceasing south-west wind and could not have returned to the Channel if it would. The wind remained roughly south-south-west from the Tuesday afternoon until Friday. Late on Friday it veered round to the north-west again and presented the Spanish with a favourable opportunity of retracing their course, indeed making it difficult for them not do do so. They did not do so.

On the Tuesday evening before sunset the Duke had summoned his generals and advisers for a council-of-war, and they had discussed the future. It cannot have been a cheerful gathering, and harsh words flew. Diego Flores was for returning as soon as the wind changed and making one more attempt to link up with Parma; but the majority was against him – as indeed was common sense. Without ammunition, and with no friendly port in which to rest and re-arm and re-equip, the move would have been suicidal. But perhaps, like Oquendo earlier in the day, the mood of some of the captains *was* suicidal. Better death in the jaws of the enemy than a long and dishonourable retreat.

But saner councils prevailed, and the pilots were called in. Theirs was not a hopeful outlook. It would be a long and laborious trek home, fifteen hundred to eighteen hundred miles, days and weeks sailing in possibly stormy seas in that treacherous summer, in waters known only to a few of them, almost every ship damaged, every ship full of wounded men, the whole fleet desperately short of food and water and medical supplies: this prospect was almost as daunting as the first. But it was chosen; there was no other alternative but to surrender, and that course, in spite of the early example of Pedro de Valdes, was not even discussed. So they sailed on ever north and ever shadowed by ninety ships of the English fleet. When the wind changed on the Friday the English took advantage of it and, out of food and water themselves, ran for home, leaving only two pinnaces, one belonging to Drake, to continue to follow the enemy as far as the Northern Islands.

The Spanish made no such change of course. Sharing supplies among themselves, for some ships were better off than others, limiting the thousands of men, wounded and fit alike, to eight ounces of bread, half a pint of wine and a pint of water daily, they beat on slowly – at the speed of the slowest – up into the north.

There was no conviction in England that the danger was past. The very caution and modesty of the dispatches and letters sent by the English captains told against them. The Armada was still in being, and few realized how mortally it had been wounded. The English fleet had parted with the enemy off Newcastle, and there were three dangers still very much in English minds: (1) a return of the Spanish fleet to try again to link up with Parma, (2) a landing in the Firth of Forth, with Protestant James not so sure of the loyalty of his Catholics as Elizabeth had been of hers, or (3) a landing in Ireland, where a Catholic and rebellious population would be waiting to welcome them as friends and liberators.

It took the English fleet several days to reach home, for they ran into a westerly gale, which scattered them along the coast from Harwich and Margate to the Downs. Although casualties had been light – though not so light as was claimed – sickness had spread throughout the ships, and they arrived in their various ports exhausted and undermanned. Drake thought that possibly a fourth choice existed and that the Spaniards on the wings of the westerly gale might have made for Denmark. 'If they should go to the King of Denmark and there have his friendship and help for all their reliefs, none can better help their wants in all these parts than he; for that he is a prince of great shipping.' Drake perhaps more than anyone had seen at close quarters the devastation wrought in the Spanish ships, and he thought it unlikely that Medina Sidonia would dare to attempt the long northern route home without first trying to recover and refit.

Elizabeth's first letter to Howard, sent to greet him as soon as he reached port, asked as many detailed questions as any modern civil service could devise – most of them unanswerable – about the condition and numbers of her fleet, the amount of powder and shot used and the casualties suffered. It also inquired pointedly what Spanish ships and prisoners had been taken, also what treasure, and why the Spanish ships had not been boarded by the English – at least if the largest galleons were too big, why not some of the smaller ones?

It is plain from the wording of this letter that neither the Queen nor any of her ministers had even begun to understand the strategy adopted by her fleet in this running battle. The last two great naval battles before 1588, those at Lepanto and Terceira, had both seen a grappling of ship with ship and a fight to the finish between boarding parties; and the Queen and her council had clearly expected the same now. (Oddly, Philip had appreciated the probable English tactics better, although he had assumed they could be overcome.)

Ralegh in his *History of the World*, written twenty years later, does not mince his words on this point:

> He that will happily perform a fight at sea must believe that there is more belonging to a good man of war upon the waters than great daring, and must know there is a great deal of difference between fighting loose and grappling. To clap ships together without consideration belongs rather to a madman than to a ship of war; for by such an ignorant bravery was Peter Strozzi lost at the Azores when he fought against the Marquis of Santa Cruz. In like sort had the Lord Charles Howard, Admiral of England, been lost in the year 1588 if he had not been better advised than a great many malignant fools were who found fault with his behaviour.

If one were seeking an example to illustrate 'Gloriana's' meanness, one would look no further than this letter to the battle-worn yet victorious Howard. But in her defence it could be argued that throughout nearly two decades she had grown accustomed to her captains returning with prizes from their private wars with Spain and she had shared in the spoils. It is not perhaps to be wondered at that, not understanding the strategy of the battle, she should expect greater prizes from a national war in which she had sunk so much of her scanty revenues, and one in which clearly there were enormous pickings to be had both in bullion and in ransomable grandees. (Nor, in this climate of opinion, is it altogether surprising that Drake broke line to capture the *Rosario* and Howard to try to take the *San Lorenzo*.)

For Elizabeth the safety of her realm was paramount; but she did not see at first why her commanders had only been able to ensure this by adopting a policy without profit to her.

In the meantime, though Elizabeth was anxious to take the risk of disbanding her fleet in order to save the expense of keeping it together, her council and her admirals argued hotly against it. While the Armada was in being they could not relax. So the battle-worn ships lay in the little ports, and men died on them from typhus at the rate of a hundred a day. 'They sicken one day and die the next,' Howard told the Queen.

The hideous conditions in which men lived aboard made the spread of disease inevitable if the voyage or the time were long. Because of the com-

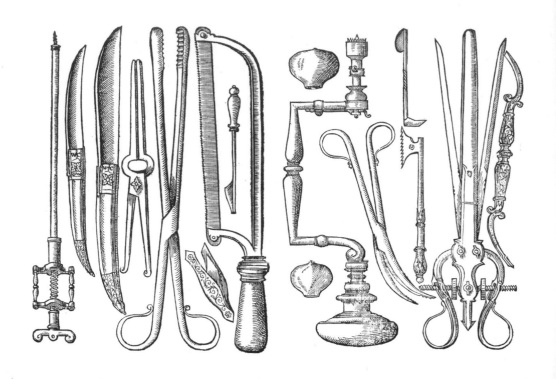

FELIX·QVEM
FACIVNT·
ALIENA·
PERICVLA·
CAVTVM

MENDAX·

TOP Surgical instruments
of the 16th century for use in
treating gunshot wounds

BOTTOM A 16th-century
quack with his patients

plete lack of sanitary arrangements it was practically impossible to keep food and cooking uncontaminated; and when in port this was made worse because so-called fresh water, often itself bad in cask, was kept solely for drinking, and all other water used was drawn up from the harbour, which was filthy with excrement and even corpses.

Disease now spread so sharply that it converted the admirals half way to Elizabeth's line of thought, and it was decided to disband the auxiliaries and split the main fleet into two divisions, one in the Downs[1] and the other at Margate. Rumour flew throughout the Continent that Drake was captured, that Medina Sidonia was in London, that the Queen had been dethroned. Rumour in England told that the Armada had landed in Ireland, in Scotland, or was returning, miraculously refreshed, down the English coast to challenge Howard again.

Then towards the end of August definite news filtered through that Parma at least had accepted defeat. He had ordered his men to return to Bruges, the victuals on board his fleet of barges and fly-boats to be un-shipped, and the sails to be taken from the yards. Shortly following this, an English pinnace commanded by a man called Anthony Potts reported having sighted the great Armada sailing westward of the Orkney Islands. All immediate danger did at last seem to be truly over.

So the Queen had her way, and most of the fleet was disbanded, with the result that the seaport towns of the south-east were swamped with sick and disabled and starving men begging for food and shelter. West Country ships were packed off home, unpaid and half manned, with sick and dying crews and one day's supply of victuals aboard.

Howard was absolutely furious. 'It is a most pitiful sight to see, here at Margate, how the men, having no place to receive them into here, die in the streets. I am driven myself, of force, to come a-land, to see them bestowed in some lodging; and the best I can get is barns and outhouses. It would grieve any man's heart to see them that have served so valiantly to die so miserably.' He paid some of the seamen out of his own pocket. Greatly daring, he paid more of them out of the treasure found aboard de Valde's *Rosario*. He pawned his own plate and spent his last guinea to keep the dying sailors alive, while now, all over the land, the victory, seen at last as a victory, was being celebrated with bonfires and processions and the ring of bells.

Elizabeth has been much criticized for this disgraceful neglect of the men who had saved England; and, although in actual fact it was nothing directly to do with her, the payment being sanctioned by the Council and issued at the order of the Lord Treasurer, one cannot but be aware that a sharp intervention by her would have made all the difference. Her care for her homecoming sailors was so much less generous than Philip's.

[1] The Downs is that roadstead off Deal and between the North and South Foreland which is protected from bad weather on two sides by the curve of the coast and from the east by the Goodwin Sands.

Yet such was the scarcity of money at this time that she like Howard might have had to pawn her plate to pay them. Philip had nearly bankrupted himself to launch the Armada; Elizabeth with all her cheeseparing had come near to bankrupting England to defeat it. Philip had a wide empire to draw on for his revenue; Elizabeth had much smaller resources and she had no private fortune. She could not compel her people to pay their taxes – at least, not the rich ones – it was done on a semi-voluntary basis. A few years later Francis Bacon was to write: 'He that shall look into other countries and consider the taxes and tallages and impositions and assizes and the like that are everywhere in use, will find that the Englishman is most master of his own valuation and the least bitten in purse of any nation in Europe.' In fact in 1588 by exceptional methods which could hardly be repeated Elizabeth had been able to raise her revenue for the year to £392,000. Her expenses in the Netherlands alone that year amounted to £120,000 and the cost of the Navy was £153,000. This left her about £120,000 for all other calls on her purse: the court, the army, the Yeomen of the Guard, the royal residences, the mews with its three hundred horses and one hundred and thirty grooms, the ambassadors, Walsingham's spies, subsidies, rewards for faithful service, the hundreds of incidental expenses falling upon even the most careful monarch.

It was of course not nearly enough. But during the pre-war years when the risk of war was monthly growing, the Queen and Burghley had adopted a policy of frugality and retrenchment; the repair of the royal palaces was postponed, players and musicians at the court were dispensed with, the royal progresses through the land abandoned or curtailed, every detail of expenditure watched, so that by 1588 Elizabeth had built up a reserve fortune of about £300,000. This too went, and by the end of her forty-five years on the throne she had been compelled to sell nearly £900,000 worth of Crown lands to pay her way. Over all, her reign does not look like the reign of a mean woman but of a wise one who knew how to husband her resources and not oppress her subjects.

So while responsibility lies on her for the unnecessary suffering of so many good men – immensely more died than were killed by the Spanish – it is a responsibility which everyone in the Council must share.

In August there had been the great procession of the Queen to Tilbury with her review of the troops and her marvellous speech to them. There has probably never been another monarch with such a command of words, and few commoners: one thinks of Ralegh and Lincoln and Churchill. In November came the service at St Paul's. It was another magnificent occasion; but whereas Tilbury had been a promenade of defiance, a splendid appearance before her people in their hour of greatest peril, this procession was before a victorious people who were joining with her in thanksgiving.

She drove from Somerset House to the City in a chariot drawn by two white horses. Above the chariot was a canopy topped by an imperial crown, and a gold lion and dragon flanked the coach. With her were the

Elizabeth I at Tilbury in August 1588, when the fate of the First Armada was not yet certain, addressing her troops in one of the most eloquent speeches ever made by a monarch

Blessed be the great
God of my salvation

2.Kings.6:16.

Hollanders

...AND FOR THE KINGDONE I HAVE BEENE YOVR QVEENE IN ... NOW FOR
... AND NEITHER WILL I BID YOU GOE AND FIGHT. BVT COM AND I WILL
FIGHT THE BATTELL OF THE LORDE· FOR WHAT AR THES PROVD PHILISTINES THAT
THEY SHOVLD REVALE THE HOST OF THE LIVING GOD· IT MAY BE THEY WILL CHALLENGE MY
... THAT AM I WOMAN SO HAD I CHARGE ... MOVTE OR THAT IS ...
... BREATH IS IN THIRE NOSTRELLS AND IF GOD DOE NOT CHANGE
ENGLAND WITH THE SINNES OF ENGLAND WE SHALL NOT NEEDE TO FEARE WHAT
ROME OR SPAYNE CAN DOE AGAINST VS. WI ... WISOME IS BVT AN ARME OF FLESH
WHERE AS WITH VS IS THE LORD OVR GOD TO FIGHT OVR BATTELLS AND TO HELPE
... WITH VS YT SKILLS NOT GREATELY IF ALL THE DEVILS IN HELL BE AGAINST VS·
SING VNTO THE LOD A NEW SONG FOR HE HATH DONE MARVELOVS THINGES HIS RIGHT HAND AND HIS HOLY ARME HATH
GOTTEN HIM THE VICTORY AND ALL THE ENDS OF THE EARTH HAVE SEENE THE SALVATION OF OVR GOD· Selah

Privy Council, most of her notable lords and the judges of the realm, the admirals who had won the victory, and heralds and trumpeters, all on horseback. The Earl of Essex, Master of the Horse, rode directly behind her, and he was followed by all the Queen's ladies of honour. The streets were gay with blue streamers, and at the gate of the Temple the Lord Mayor and aldermen in scarlet robes were waiting to greet her and hand her the sceptre. Then with the City Livery Companies added to the procession she was drawn to St Paul's, where at the great west door she knelt a time in prayer on the steps. Dr Pierce, Bishop of Salisbury, preached the sermon, and afterwards she dined in the bishop's palace, and then returned in the falling November dusk in a torchlight procession to Somerset House. She was in truth Gloriana to everyone who saw her at that time. It was thirty years since her accession, and this might have been her jubilee.

Earlier in the month she had with her usual aplomb and versatility composed a poem for the occasion, and this was sung at St Paul's during the service of thanksgiving.

> Look and bow down thine ear, oh Lord,
> From thy bright sphere behold and see
> Thy handmaid and thy handiwork;
> Amongst thy priests offering to thee
> Zeal for incense reaching the skies
> My self and sceptre sacrifice.

> My soul ascend to holy place,
> Ascribe Him strength and sing Him praise
> For he refraineth Prince's spirits,
> And hath done wonders in my days.
> He made the winds and waters rise
> To scatter all mine enemies.

> This Joseph's lord and Israel's god,
> The fiery pillar and day's cloud,
> That saved his saints from wicked men
> And drenched the honour of the proud,
> And hath preserved in tender love
> The spirit of his Turtle dove.

Before His Turtle Dove could quite relax there had been one more alarm for the English. The Armada had disappeared into the northern seas, no one knew whither. No one at that time could safely calculate that it would return home without a further attempt to justify its coming out. After it had been sighted off the Orkney Islands there was clearly little risk to the Channel ports. But England has a long and vulnerable seaboard. And there was still Scotland with its dissident Catholics. And there was still Ireland, passionately Catholic and already in semi-revolt.

When therefore the news first reached England that great numbers of the enemy fleet were off Ireland, it was thought that the Spanish were about to land their troops there and begin a large-scale invasion. Twenty, forty,

The rocky coast of Ireland, on which many ships of the First Armada were thrown sixty ships, many of them still crammed with trained soldiers: it was a likely enough event. Only after a few days, as more messages came through, did it become clear that these were ships in distress seeking only succour. Some of the ships were already wrecked among the treacherous rocks off the Dingle and Donegal coasts. Some came in seeking food and water. Some were in a sinking condition and were just making landfall in time.

It is clear that many of these ships had suffered from the rough weather, but it is not clear how rough the weather really was. What is evident is that crews and ships together had been so maltreated at Gravelines that they were in a condition to succumb to the first gale they met. Medina Sidonia's orders, given to the fleet when north-east of Scotland and later taken from one of the wrecked vessels, ran:

> The course that is first to be held is to the north-north-east, until you be found under 61 degrees-and-a-half; and then to take heed lest you fall upon the Island of Ireland, for fear of the harm that may happen unto you upon that coast.
>
> Then parting from those Islands, and doubling the Cape in 61 degrees-and-a-half, you shall run west-south-west until you be found under 58 degrees; and from thence to the south-west to the height of 53 degrees; and then to the south-south-west, making to the Cape Finisterre, and so to procure your entrance into the Groyne or to Ferol, or to any other port of the coast of Galicia.

The last direction is a mistake: south-south-west should have been south-east; but any ships which followed the instructions that far were not likely to fall into error.

In the cold northern waters between the Faroes and Ireland, some two hundred and fifty miles north of the northernmost tip of Scotland, the limping damaged fleet was finally split by storm and it never came together again. Medina Sidonia's *San Martin*, which, whatever the Duke's detractors may say, had been in the thick of every fight since the beginning and the special target of the English whenever they could attack her, kept to the prescribed course, and those who stayed with her and followed her reached Spain safely again, albeit in however terrible a condition. Perhaps she was the strongest-built ship in the whole Armada; we do not know. (In fact, about the 4th September, Diego Flores transferred from the *San Martin* to another galleon, the *San Juan de Avendano*, and took Medina Sidonia with him: this because of the typhus and dysentery raging aboard the *San Martin*.) But at least they all arrived home together and apparently only had two days of storm, although the weather was constantly rough and blustery, with south-west winds prevailing.

Whatever the cause, it is hardly Spanish seamanship that was at fault, though often their charts were inaccurate, and of course nine out of ten were sailing in waters they had never been in before. Some sixty-odd ships splintered from the main body of the fleet and drifted or were blown towards that island against which the Duke had expressly warned them. They came in 'like flocks of starlings', were wrecked or fought for their lives or were slaughtered as they struggled ashore. Most of them were killed by – or on the orders of – the English.

The arrival of floods of Spanish soldiers – in whatever straits – upon the shores of this conquered but rebellious island threw the English on the spot into an understandable panic. They had fewer than two thousand troops in the whole of Ireland at the time, many of them half-trained, and with ancient muskets and rusty cannon, and gun carriages 'rotting for want of men to maintain them' and the universal and inevitable shortage of powder and shot. This force had to keep the peace in a country thirty-two thousand square miles in area, a country full of mountains, wild moors, lakes and treacherous bogs, and populated by about a million temperamental and quarrelsome Gaels who hated the Anglo-Saxons and all they stood for.

The Lord Deputy Fitz William, writing on the 22nd September, paints an even gloomier picture: 'There are not 750 foot in bands in the whole realm. We cannot impress the few soldiers for the shoeing of their horses. We feel rather to be overrun by the Spaniards than otherwise.'

An engraving, published in 1581, of Irish peasants setting fire to a village

England was at war with Spain. These were invaders, in whatever guise they came. If the position had been reversed English survivors would certainly have fared no better at the hands of the Spanish. What does stain the record is that the English on several occasions accepted the surrender of the Spanish survivors on fair terms, and then proceeded to hang them just the same. Of course the Spanish so far outnumbered their captors and there were so few stockades or keeps in which they could be safely imprisoned that their being merely alive was a menace to the security of the country. So at least argued – however inexcusably – Fitz William, Bingham and the rest; though Christopher Calleil was a noted and humane exception.

It was fashionable for many years to put all the blame for the slaughter on the wild Irish who were said to have killed and robbed the Spanish as they came ashore. Now it is as fashionable to put all the blame on the English, where in truth most of it rests. But the accounts of the few Spanish survivors who have left their stories do not leave the Irish blameless – though essentially the natives mostly wanted Spanish clothes and gold and ornaments more than they wanted Spanish blood. All through these accounts the Spaniards refer to the native Irish not as potential allies but as 'the savages', much as a shipwrecked sailor would write of being cast away on the coast of Borneo. *The Calendar of State Papers (Ireland)* records the claim of one Melaghlin M'Cabb who stated that he killed eighty Spaniards with his galloglass axe.

Among the commanders of the Armada, Bertendona followed the Duke, as did Oquendo, though Oquendo died of typhus soon after he reached Spain. Diego Flores was of course with the Duke and was tried and imprisoned in Spain for the 'bad advice' that he had given Medina Sidonia.

The veteran Recalde was one of those who lost touch with the Duke and, in company with two other ships, found himself off the dreaded Blasket Islands at the jagged tip of the Dingle Peninsula, the westernmost point in Europe. His ship, the *San Juan*, like the *San Martin*, had been in the thick of the fighting all through and appears to have suffered more. Calderon says: 'He was dreadfully in need of everything and his ship was in a very injured state.' It is at least fairly to be assumed that Recalde would not have put in to the Irish coast willingly or unless driven by sickness or shortage of supplies.

Of the two ships with him one was a Castilian galleon, the *San Juan Bautista*, of seven hundred and fifty tons, with a complement of two hundred and forty-three men. On board her was the Paymaster and Controller of the galleons of Castile, Marcos de Arumburu, who survived to give an account of his adventures and also ultimately to command a Spanish squadron in the Armadas of 1596 and 1597. The second ship was the *San Pedro el Mayor*, a vessel of five hundred and forty-one tons and a complement of two hundred and forty men: one of the only two hospital ships in the Armada. No doubt at this date she was crowded to the ports with sick and wounded men. The two ships had sighted the *San Juan de Portugal* through the driving mists of a windy September morning and had attached themselves to her, recognizing Recalde's ship and knowing his reputation for seamanship.

At first Recalde anchored between the Great Blasket and the shore, but this was no place to stop. In Irish waters the long Atlantic swells often run counter to the winds ruffling the surface, and this made navigation for sixteenth-century sailing-ships a matter of peculiar peril, even when in the peak of condition. Now Recalde, after edging his galleon closer to the inhospitable cliffs, veered away and approached the island of Inishvickillane, which is a smaller island than the Great Blasket about three miles to the south-west. This has a tiny rock-bound harbour big enough to take fishing-boats. In Arumburu's words, Recalde ran into the port of Inishvickillane 'through an entrance between low rocks, about as wide as the length of a ship, and so anchored. We came in behind her, and after us the tender . . . This day we saw another ship to leeward close to hand.'

It was a superb piece of seamanship performed with a badly damaged vessel and a half dying crew. How far an anonymous Scottish pilot was responsible, how far Recalde himself – who knew the coast – we can never be sure. Recalde at once sent a longboat to the mainland several miles distant with eight men under a Biscayan officer called Licornio to reconnoitre the situation. They were captured and after being questioned were executed by the small band of English soldiers guarding the coast. After waiting vainly for their return Recalde sent a bigger boat containing fifty arquebusiers, and these men, outnumbering the English, proceeded to spend three days ashore, obtaining fresh water and what little else might be gleaned of the bleak countryside. The English and the Irish watched them in enmity but did not attack.

There then blew up one of the worst winds of that windy month, and the two *San Juans* dragged their anchors in the tiny harbour and collided, doing each other further damage. On the wings of this storm the galleon *Santa Maria de la Rosa*, vice-flagship of Oquendo's squadron, drifted in, her sails in ribbons, and sank before their eyes with the loss of the entire crew except for one man. Following her came yet another *San Juan*, which tried to anchor in the shelter of the island while the last of her tattered rigging blew to shreds. Presently, in spite of Recalde's efforts to save her, she too went down with most of her crew.

As soon as the wind blew itself out Recalde, who was now almost too ill to rise from his bed, gave orders to set sail, and the three remaining vessels, still in bad condition but at least re-watered and their crews rested, crept out of the narrow harbour in the dark and began the next leg of their long journey home.

It was each one for himself. The *San Juan Bautista* after a hazardous and sickly voyage was the first to make port. Recalde and his *San Juan de Portugal* reached Coruña on the 7th October, one of the very last to come home; but Recalde was so far spent that he died four days after his return. So disgusted and humiliated was he at the fate of the great Armada that he

OVERLEAF The Cliffs of Moher, Liscannor, western Ireland, originally considered a suitable landing place for an armada invasion, but faced by the Spanish in 1588 when straggling home

did not wish to see even his family and friends before he died. The *San Pedro el Mayor* was even less fortunate. She was blown by contrary winds back into the English Channel and wrecked in Hope Cove, off Salcombe. Some of her crew and patients were drowned but the majority got ashore. Although not important enough to be ransomable, none was slain: they were hauled out of the water by the sturdy Devonshire villagers and were fed, albeit scantily, by the local magistrate, George Cary, at his own expense until the country took them over.

Higher up the Irish coast, in Clare, in Galway, in Sligo and in Donegal, the other Spanish ships had drifted in in their dozens, a few to shelter and to water and to be off again, but the vast majority to founder, with the whole of their crews either drowned or killed as they came ashore or hanged after capture. Among these ships was the *Rata Encoronada*, with de Leyva aboard and his cargo of dashing young men. De Leyva, like Recalde, and Medina Sidonia, had all the time been in the thick of the battle, and his great carrack, less stoutly built than the Portuguese galleons, had suffered the more. Separated from the main body of the fleet, he led three other ships to an anchorage in Blacksod Bay in Galway, far to the north of Recalde. It is a wild coast, smiling and green in fair weather, grim and deadly in bad, and for some reason he chose an exposed anchorage off Ballycroy.

De Leyva, like Recalde, sent a boat ashore to reconnoitre, and these men were set upon by one of the petty chiefs, Richard Burke, who robbed and maltreated them. A gusty wind and a heavy tide meanwhile snapped the hempen rope of the one serviceable anchor and the *Rata* drifted on to the beach. Almost all her crew landed safely, and with them brought such possessions as they could carry: plate, money, clothing, some armour, but precious little food. They camped one night on the beach and then took possession of a ruined hill-fort, called Doona, from which they began to scour the countryside for food and water. Presently scouts brought news of another Spanish ship, that hulk of Andalusia, the *Duquesa Santa Ana* of nine hundred tons, anchored beyond the next headland. This was the ship which on the Thursday morning of the Channel fight, together with the *San Luis*, had drifted out of the protective range of the rest of the fleet and had had to be rescued from the clutches of John Hawkins by three of the galleasses and the *Rata Encoronada*. Perhaps it was fitting that she should now offer hope of escape to the *Rata's* distinguished company. De Leyva marched his men across and found the *Santa Ana* in fair condition but with already more than her full complement of men, for she had saved some from another sinking ship.

A council-of-war was held, at which the captains of both ships and the pilots were of the opinion that to attempt to sail to Spain with eight hundred men aboard and scanty provisions, and with the prevailing headwinds, would mean certain disaster. De Leyva therefore decided to sail *north* again, to skirt the savage Irish headlands and try to land on the west coast of Scotland. This being a neutral country, if not actually a friendly one, there was a good chance of making one's way in due course to Flanders and thence back to Spain.

So at the first favourable wind the hulk weighed anchor and began to creep up the coast. Past Annagh Head and Erris Head and Benwee Head, each one as dangerous as the last, and then across the fifty-mile gaping mouth of Donegal Bay to Rossan Point, about a hundred miles in all, before another strong wind coming up out of the north-west drove the ailing *Santa Ana* on the rocks of Loughros More Bay.

This was a nastier shipwreck than the last: rocks, not a sandy beach; some were drowned and de Leyva himself 'was hurt in the leg by the capstan of the ship in such sort as he was able neither to go nor ride'. But some of their arms were ferried ashore, and most of the men survived and once again made some sort of camp in the rainy September twilight and committed their souls to God.

The next morning the usual scouts were sent out. This force under de Leyva was the most dangerous to England of any that landed or attempted to land. Not only did it still contain all the vigorous and enterprising young noblemen but, in spite of its sore straits, it was the only one, because of de Leyva's guidance, that kept a degree of cohesion and discipline; and if it were allowed to consolidate itself it could well become the nucleus of a major revolt. But the English, although aware of its existence, had not yet located it, and de Leyva was able to send his scouts out without hindrance. Once again there was a convenient ruin near, and the great mass of men set about converting it into a defensive position, de Leyva being carried about in a chair and directing operations. The neighbouring Irish, those who were friendly, gave what help they dared.

So they stayed for eight days until an Irishman brought information that just south of them across the mountains of the Malin Mor peninsula in

The rocks of the Giant's Causeway, County Antrim, on which, during the retreat of the First Armada, the *Gerona* foundered

Donegal Bay was the *Gerona*, one of the galleasses, not too badly damaged and with a complement of crew and galley-slaves. The following day de Leyva struck camp and made a forced march in rain over the steep pass of Ardara to Killibegs with his seven-hundred-odd men, he being carried in a chair by relays of four soldiers at a time.

When they arrived they found the *Gerona* in a poor condition and most of her crew camping on the beach beside her. Near them were the remains of yet another Spanish ship, and de Leyva at once ordered his men to strip her of everything useful to their purpose and with the timbers and ironwork and ropes to set about repairing the *Gerona* and making her ready for sea. His position here was eased by his making contact with the local chieftain, one of the O'Neils, who offered de Leyva the hospitality of his home. This de Leyva refused, on the grounds that when he was gone his host would suffer at the hands of the English; but he gladly accepted supplies, and after fourteen days of hard work the galleass was repaired and declared fit for sea.

By now the English were in full alarm, and the Lord Deputy Fitz William was directing as large a force as he could muster to attack them. So on the 14th October de Leyva put to sea again, this time in an even more over-crowded ship, there being eleven or twelve hundred men in all. This time in addition to his patched-up sails he had the oars to propel him and not more than three hundred miles to go.

But the galleass, heavy with fore and aft superstructure and weak in fundamental design, particularly of the rudder, was the prey to every wind, and they made but slow progress, inching north and east day by day. Then in the dark of the night, when they were past almost all the worst hazards and only about forty miles from Scotland, the rudder broke in a sudden squall and the great ship drifted on the rocks near the Giant's Causeway. In the shadow of Dunluce Castle the ship broke to pieces and all but nine

Dunluce Castle, a short way from where the *Gerona* finally broke up

common soldiers of her enormous crew were drowned. Hardly a noble house in Spain did not lose a son or a nephew or a cousin in this great disaster. Philip, brooding over his defeat in the Escorial, said when the news was brought to him that the loss of Alonso de Leyva meant more to him than the loss of all the Armada.

One other story of the shipwrecks concerns Captain Francisco de Cuellar, captain of the galleon *San Pedro*. During the retreat from the English fleet in the North Sea, his and another ship disobeyed the explicit instructions of Medina Sidonia and broke line by sailing ahead of the others. He was brought before that harsh and hated disciplinarian General Bobadilla, who sentenced him to be hanged. This was repealed by Medina Sidonia, but de Cuellar was relieved of his command and transferred under open arrest to the Levantine vice-flagship *La Lavia*.

Nearly a month later, in company with two other ships, *La Lavia* found herself unable to make headway against the southerly winds so put into the Irish coast near Sligo Bay and dropped anchor off Streedagh Strand, a five-mile stretch of pale sand flanked by cliffs. There she stayed about a mile off-shore for four days, hoping for better weather but with the surf too heavy for anyone to land. On the fifth day, instead of the wind abating, it grew worse and broke the frail cables which held the ships. With the sea 'as high as heaven' all three ships were driven ashore, and in an hour were broken into gaunt pieces by the thunderous surf. More than eleven hundred men were drowned and something fewer than three hundred reached the shore alive.

Diego Enriquez, the Camp Master aboard *La Lavia*, and a half dozen aristocrats carrying sixteen thousand ducats worth of jewels and coin, took to the ship's tender, which had a covered deck, and ordered the hatch to be battened down and caulked behind them. This was done, but as usual in the panic more than seventy men clambered aboard hoping to reach the shore, with the result that the tender capsized and all were drowned. Later when she drifted ashore the Irish seized her and began to break her up for the sake of the nails and the ironwork, when they discovered not only the drowned men inside but the treasure. Joyfully they stripped everything and left the corpses unburied on the sand, anxious to get away before someone surprised them in their rich find.

As for Cuellar himself, he could not swim, but clung to the poop watching others drown around him, saw them clinging to rafts, hatches, spars, barrels, anything that would float, and saw the few who were lucky enough to reach the shore being set on by a horde of two hundred hungry Irish, dancing and leaping with delight, who knocked them down as soon as they reached shallow water and stripped them naked. Presently with the Judge Advocate beside him – that Judge whose prisoner he still officially was – he found a hatchway as big as a table, and between them they contrived to float themselves away on it. On the way ashore the Judge was washed off and, weighted down as he was with crown pieces sewn into his doublet and hose, was instantly drowned. But somehow Cuellar kept afloat, though by now his legs were crushed and bleeding from collision with a piece of wreckage.

When he landed on the beach, gasping and half drowned, there were so many others coming in around him that he was ignored by the 'savages' for more promising prey, and he was able to crawl away through his naked and groaning countrymen and find shelter among some rushes growing in the sandhills near a stream. He stayed there until dark, when he was joined by a young Spaniard, naked and shivering with the cold. Together the two crouched there, half dead with pain and hunger, while they heard a search in progress. A small English garrison at nearby Grange had now taken charge and was rounding up such of the enemy as were left alive.

After about half an hour the two Spaniards were discovered by a couple of villainous-looking Irishmen, one with a captured sword, the other with a great iron axe. They stared at each other in the light of a lantern for a few seconds, and then the savage with the sword swung it to cut down the rushes. These, with grass and reeds from near by, they piled on top of the two fugitives until they were hidden from sight; then they passed on.

All night lights flickered and horses neighed and there were the shouts of men and the crash of axes as the great crowd on the beach broke up and dragged away whatever was left of value on the wrecks. Cuellar at last fell asleep, and when he woke at dawn he saw that the young man beside him had died in the night. The beach was still occupied with a few scavengers picking among the remnants, but the great crowd had gone. The only other population was the hundreds of dead and naked bodies piled in heaps waiting for the ravens and the wolves.

He crawled away and began to limp inland, searching for some monastery or Catholic retreat where he might hope for succour. Two miles inland was Staad Abbey, a small monastic church, and Cuellar saw its grey stone walls through the misty sunlight and hastened towards it, hoping to find at least one kind monk to help him. When he pushed open the door he saw the inside of the church had been wrecked, images destroyed and crosses broken, and hanging from the iron grilles of the church were the bodies of twelve Spaniards.

In sick despair he fled from the place and began to make his way back to the beach in the hope that now it would be quite empty and there might be biscuits or bread being washed up by the tide. As he neared the shipwrecks he met two more Spaniards and together they returned to the beach. Here Cuellar came upon and recognized the body of Diego Enriquez, and he and his new companions made an attempt to bury their noble commander. While doing this they were surrounded by Irishmen who did not molest them, being chiefly interested in their occupation; but later in the day Cuellar was robbed of his clothes and the money that he had carefully secreted about himself: forty-five crown pieces and a gold chain worth a thousand reals. Then, through the intervention of a 'beautiful girl of about twenty', some of his clothes were restored to him, and he was at last given a piece of oaten bread to eat with butter and milk, and his wounds were dressed.

> I set about putting on my doublet and coat again, but they had taken away my shirt and also some precious relics that I was carrying in a little vestment of the order of the Holy Trinity. The young savage woman had taken these and hung them round her neck, making signs to me that she wished to keep them, and telling me that she was a Christian, though she was no more a Christian than Mahomet was.

The following night he was given shelter in a hut by some men, one of whom was able to talk to him in Latin, and in the morning he was lent a horse and boy to guide him on his way. The road was so bad that there was 'mud up to the girths'. But they had gone no distance before they had first to hide from a troop of English searchers, and then were discovered and surrounded by 'forty savages on foot' who wanted to hack him to pieces. The boy's intervention saved his life but did not prevent him from being beaten with sticks and robbed of every stitch of clothing. After they had gone he found a piece of old matting and some bracken to try to protect himself from the cold, and went on alone.

All day he made north-east for the Darty Mountains and finally came on a lake, Lough Glenade, where he found thirty huts, all of which were empty except for three naked men who, after the initial alarm, embraced him as another shipwrecked Spaniard. For supper they ate blackberries and watercress and then bedded down together in the straw, burying themselves in it to keep out the cold.

In the dawn however the 'heretic savages' returned to work in the fields about the huts, and the four Spaniards lay hidden in the straw all day, unable to stir, while men came in and out of the hut. At nightfall, as the moon rose, they wrapped themselves in the straw and slipped away, and after another long trek during which they were at their 'last gasp for thirst and hunger and pain', they found a village belonging to Señor de Ruerque (Sir Brian O'Rourke) where they were given shelter at last. O'Rourke was away fighting the English, but Cuellar was given 'a rotten old blanket swarming with lice, and I covered myself with it and somewhat relieved my plight'. There were in fact already seventy Spaniards in the village, many wounded and all semi-naked, so it is not to be wondered at that supplies of clothing ran short.

News reached the village next day that a Spanish ship lay offshore and she was waiting to pick up fugitives; so Cuellar and twenty others set off to join her. But Cuellar's leg, once injured and once wounded, let him down and he lagged behind, and when he got to the shore the other nineteen men had embarked and the ship, fearful of attack from the land, had sailed. Cuellar's utter despair later turned to thanksgiving when he learned that the

An Irish feast in the 16th century, with a bard, accompanied by his harpist, declaiming the country's legends

ship had been wrecked further along the coast and those not drowned in her had been slaughtered by the English.

A chance meeting with a monk directed him to a village and castle belonging to a native chieftain, one M'Glannagh, eighteen miles distant. There at last he was well treated – 'the womenfolk wept to see me so ill used' – and there he stayed three months, living as one of them.

> It is the custom of these savages to live like wild beasts in the mountains. They live in huts made of straw; they . . . eat only once a day and that at nightfall, their usual food being oaten bread and butter. They drink sour milk for lack of anything else; water they do not drink, though theirs is the best in the world. On feast days it is their custom to eat some half-cooked meat without bread or salt. The men dress in tight hose and short coats of coarse goat's hair; over this they wear a blanket, and their hair falls low over their eyes . . . Their great desire is to be thieves and plunder one another, so that hardly a day passes without a

call to arms among them, for as soon as the men of one village discover that there are cattle or anything else in another village they come armed by night and attack and kill each other. The English garrisons get to know who has rounded up and stolen most cattle and at once fall upon them and take away their spoils . . .

They sleep on the ground on freshly cut rushes, full of water and ice. Most of the women are very beautiful but poorly dressed; they wear nothing but a smock covered with a blanket, and a linen kerchief folded tightly round their heads and fastened in front . . . These savages liked us Spaniards well . . . indeed if they had not taken as much care of us as they did of themselves not one of us would still be alive. We were grateful to them for this, although they had been the first to rob and strip naked any man cast alive upon their shores, from whom these savages gained great wealth in jewels and money.

After Cuellar had been living in the town for three months, news reached M'Glannagh that a force of English infantry was advancing on them, and the Irish chief decided to evacuate the castle and take to the mountains where he and his family and his people and their cattle could hide until the English had retired again; but Captain Cuellar and eight other Spaniards refused to leave and said they were prepared to defend the place with their lives. The keep was in fact in an extremely defensible position, being on an island in the middle of a deep lake about two miles across and ten long, with an outlet to the sea. The Irish chief agreed to their remaining, and they were left with six muskets, six arquebuses and enough food to last them for a prolonged siege.

When the English arrived they sacked the village and encamped before the castle for seventeen days but could not take it; then December storms and a heavy fall of snow decided them to return to winter quarters. The Irish reappeared and M'Glannagh in his gratitude offered Cuellar one of his sisters in marriage. Cuellar tactfully refused, but asked instead for a guide to take him and his compatriots across the mountains to some port where he could take sail for Scotland. M'Glannagh returned an evasive answer, having by now decided that his Spanish allies were too valuable to release.

So once again it meant a secret departure, stealing away at dead of night in company with the only four of his compatriots who would accompany him, and putting as big a distance as they could behind them before their escape was discovered. They left shortly after Christmas Day 1588–9 and for twenty days fought their way across the savage mountains of Tyrone and Londonderry to reach one of the tiny villages at the extreme north-east of Ireland, from which it is only a matter of twenty-five miles to the Mull of Kintyre in Scotland.

Missing one boat by a day, and losing his companions, who could walk faster, Cuellar was befriended first by some 'exceedingly beautiful girls', who hid him in the huts of their families for a month and a half, and then by a bishop, who, living in disguise, was sheltering twelve other Spaniards. Through him at last a boat was found, probably something like a ship's longboat, and eighteen people embarked in it. First they were blown to

Shetland, their boat waterlogged and their sail torn, and then venturing again they reached Scotland after three more days. 'Blessed be God who delivered us from so many and such sore trials.'

Captain Cuellar was disappointed in the reception he received in the 'neutral' country. He lived in Scotland for six months, destitute and begging for food and shelter. 'The King of Scotland is of no account, nor has he the authority or dignity of a king, and he takes no step nor eats a single mouthful except by order of the Queen.' However, eventually contact was made with the Duke of Parma, who had offered to pay a Scottish merchant five ducats per head to ship Spanish refugees to Flanders. A large party of Spaniards sailed in four separate ships, which had apparently received a safe conduct from the English, for the ships called at English ports and left unmolested.

But whether by a deliberate act of perfidy on the part of the English, as Cuellar thought, or whether Parma could make no such bargain with his more hated enemies, the Dutch fly-boats were patrolling off Dunkirk and instantly attacked the four Scottish ships. Two ran aground, and Cuellar again found himself clinging to a spar in the pounding surf and being washed up on a beach while the Dutch guns cannonaded the fugitives and all who tried to rescue them.

Almost in front of our eyes the Dutch were cutting to pieces two hundred and seventy Spaniards arriving in the boat which had brought us to Dunkirk, and leaving no more than three alive. This deed they are now paying for, as more than four hundred Dutchmen taken prisoner since then have been beheaded. I desire to write to you concerning these things.

From the city of Antwerp, 4th October, 1589

10 *Attack on Portugal*

An English spy called Anthony Copley wrote an account of what happened when Philip was told of his total defeat.

> When news of the disgrace of the King's late Armada was brought unto him, being at Mass at that very time in his Chapel, he sware (after Mass was done) a great Oath, that he would waste and consume his Crown, even to the value of a [last] Candlestick (which he pointed to standing upon the Altar) but either he would utterly ruin her Majesty and England, or else himself and all Spain become Tributary to her. Whereby it was most evident that his Desire for Revenge was extreme and implacable towards England.

This account is at variance with other reports which describe Philip as accepting the disaster calmly and sadly and ascribing it all to the will of God. Yet Copley's version does seem to accord better with later events.

It must have been an excessive humiliation for Philip, more especially because for a month and more after the sailing of the Armada all Europe echoed with reports of its victories. The Queen was deposed. Drake was captured while trying to board Medina Sidonia's flagship. Mendoza, the Spanish Ambassador in Paris, had publicly announced this and lit bonfires to celebrate the victory. The Ambassador in Prague ordered a Te Deum Mass to be held at the cathedral in celebration. The Ambassador in Rome went to see the Pope and requested a similar Mass in St Peter's, together with the first part of the million gold ducats Sixtus had promised to pay Spain as soon as Spanish troops landed in England. The Pope, according to the Ambassador, 'heard me out without interruption, although he writhed about a good deal with inward impatience; but when I finished his anger leapt out, and he replied that he told me now, as he had told me before, that he would more than fulfil all he had promised, but I was not to worry him any more about the matter until positive news of the Armada was received.' But all the sad English exiles in Rome, led by Cardinal Allen and Father Parsons, accepted the tidings as true and prepared joyfully to return.

TOP English shipwrights of the 16th century at work

BOTTOM A 16th-century drawing for the construction of an English ship

60
24
40
880
200

A shipp being 24 foot brod to byt he kell 12 foot depe syde borne an good 200 tonns in the making of rigging
tymber & masts spent in tymber of all sorte being reasonabel to answere frome hyon 112 Lodd so put to the lod
this lodd 6 Lodd in euery plank 4000 in my plank 8000 in my plank 1200 in ij yere 3000
in yere 6 Lab 3500 lab carpenters 16000 to vvork euery shipt will make a shypp grand that from hyon auto &c
hym shall 24 tiʒ to byt he kell iʒ te[ ] good vvisdom in my yere plank & tre good vvisat vvill supp
asking of 32 foot brod 42 feet by te kell and 15 foot depe maferyly tis ij Couerd as Prim to be
brod & tis gone to 40 foot depe & tys send 16 2 944 vvhse tyn bylyyg vvst to the eryswark tht in

By now, however, the English had already held their own first thanksgiving service in St Paul's – this was in September, not the big November one – and twelve captured flags and banners had been paraded through the streets. There were circumstantial reports from Holland and from England about the prisoners held. And Medina Sidonia's emissary had reached the King. Then came the battered fleet, drifting in all along the west Spanish coast like ghost ships, full of sick and dying men.

For weeks the people of Spain could hardly accept the reality and the extent of the defeat. They had been accustomed for so long to war in the form of religious crusades which they had almost invariably won. It was a blow to national pride, to religious belief, to historical precedent and to reason.

The actual losses sustained by Spain in the first Armada are difficult to estimate. Something like fifty-five ships never returned, but of the eighty which did come home many were in such a condition that they were past repair. Of the thirty thousand men who sailed about ten thousand survived. Of the twenty thousand lost, possibly half were killed in battle or were drowned, the other half died from typhus, dysentery, scurvy or sheer privation.

It was a stunning loss, but Philip refused to be stunned. When the starving, dying men drifted in at every port, where there were no medical supplies to deal with them, the King assumed full responsibility for all relief work. He had no word of rebuke for Medina Sidonia, or for anyone except Diego Flores. When the Duke came to see him to explain the disaster, the King said: 'I sent you to fight against men, not against God.' He issued orders that there was to be no mourning 'for heroes who had died gloriously in the defence of religion'. Quietly he docketed the fact that the Duke of Parma had let him down, and resolved only to make use of him so long as he could find no substitute in the Netherlands. Quietly he absorbed the lessons of the defeat. Because of his sins and the sins of the nation, God had not been on their side. But Philip, as well as being deeply religious, was also essentially practical. God might have been more favourably disposed had there been a Spanish-controlled deep-sea port – such as Calais – available for his fleet. God would certainly have been better pleased with him if his ships had been built on the lines of the English.

There was only one way to remedy these defects – not by acquiescing in a position where the heretics ruled all the seas, but by striving more vigorously than ever to redeem the situation and by coming to a bitter, dedicated resolve that next time would be different. By the end of the year timber as far afield as the Adriatic was being felled for the construction of new galleons in the shipyards of Lisbon, Cadiz, Santander and San Sebastian.

The brilliant soldier who took part in the naval attacks on Lisbon and Cadiz: Robert Devereux, Second Earl of Essex

In this, as in many other matters, he expressed the sentiments of the Spanish nation. The cities voted immediate extra money for his military and naval use: Castile eight million ducats, Toledo one hundred thousand; even Milan a quarter of a million. Too often it is implied that Philip, the

absolute monarch, made his own decisions as it were in a vacuum and the Spanish people suffered for them. His popularity in Spain – which survived even this defeat – shows that he acted more often than not as his people wanted. In this case they united behind him in a determination not to accept defeat.

The Spanish downfall was greeted with an enormous wave of relief in the Protestant countries of Europe. The collapse of the Huguenots in France, and Parma's victories in the Netherlands, followed by and following the assassination of William of Orange, had dismayed dissenters everywhere; Drake's West Indian and Spanish victories had been a single sharp flame of defiance in a dark world. But the defeat of the whole might of the Spanish fleet was an achievement which altered men's thinking overnight. Men saw that God was not necessarily on the side of the powerful and the mighty; indeed in a religious age it proved to many that God was a Protestant too. The victory put new heart into the hard-tried defenders of the Netherlands, into the war-torn French Protestants, into the Danes and the Germans and the Swiss; and it raised Elizabeth's prestige to dizzy heights. It was the apogee of her reign – a triumph blighted for her only by the sudden death of Leicester, the one man in her life who was quite irreplaceable. Bereaved and sad at heart, she gathered the plaudits of the world and of her people; but at their best they were comforting embers at which to warm her hands and keep away the sudden chill of age. Essex was young and dashing and handsome and temporarily made one forget the passing of the years; but he was headstrong, conceited and frequently – almost invariably – took too much on himself. Ralegh was by turns brilliant and sombre; but as Aubrey says, 'he had that awfulness and ascendancy in his Aspect over other mortals', which perhaps was what prevented the growth of true warmth between himself and the Queen. Others about her grew old and grey in her service; trusted men, dedicated men; but she had loved none of them.

Even some of the Catholic countries took Spain's defeat philosophically. Elizabeth's religion was deeply offensive to Pope Sixtus, but he admired her courage and intellect. Philip II was his brother in religion, but a personal antipathy existed between the two men that a common cause could not bridge. The failure saved the Papacy a million ducats, shook Spanish hegemony in Europe and a general wish on Spain's part to dictate Catholic thought and policy from Madrid.

In Italy generally, and especially in the Venetian republic, which had always been too civilized to become deeply involved in religious wars, it looked like a welcome shift in the balance of power; and possibly, it was reasoned, this in the end would lead to a return to the older and more subtle political power diplomacy which all Italians understood.

In France a profound change took place. Henry III had recently made Henry of Guise his Lieutenant-General and had been forced to declare all Protestants incapable of trust, office or employment; but as news of the defeat of the Spanish fleet came in he began to reassert himself. This was of

Henry III of France, who struggled to throw off the influence of his Lieutenant-General, Henry of Guise, an adviser supported by Spain

Henry, Duke of Guise,
whose assassination was
instigated by Henry III
of France

course a struggle between two Catholics, but Guise was subsidized by Spain, while Henry III, though a weakling, strove for national independence and a united France. In October he dismissed all his ministers and threw off finally the influence of his too oppressive mother, who had come to favour Henry of Guise more than she did her own son. In December, still struggling to free himself from the dominance of a man so much stronger than himself, the King arranged for and superintended the assassination in his own bed-chamber of his great rival. Then in January 1589 Catherine de' Medici died, leaving the King apparent master of France. But the murder of Guise, who was widely popular throughout France, left Henry III even less master of the realm than he had been before. As James Stephen has said: 'Heaven and earth rose against the murder of Blois.' Just as sixteen years before the massacre of the Huguenots virtually left his brother a prisoner of the Spanish-dominated Catholic League, so Henry found himself now forced into the hands of the Huguenots, who alone could help him to preserve a part of his violently erupting kingdom. It paved the way for friendship with Elizabeth and for the succession of the Protestant Henry of Navarre.

There are various reports about Philip's health at this time. Some say that the last blond streaks disappeared from his beard and hair, that this beard grew untidy, that he was ill from the shock of all the bad news. Yet he does not seem to have suffered from anything worse than a return attack of gout in his right hand. His fourth wife had been dead eight years, and all the children of their marriage had died except young Philip, the heir to the throne. Catherine, the younger of Philip's two daughters of whom he was so fond, was married and gone, so he was much alone except for his confessor and his secretaries. When he went to Aranjuez early in 1589 one of his doctors asked him why he insisted on going there. 'For companionship,' was the reply. It was the companionship of memories. He drove around the ponds in a small carriage, did a little shooting, sniffed the orange blossom and the spring flowers. Back in Madrid he spent a while adding to his vast collection of paintings, visited the Academy of Architecture which he had founded six years earlier, attended a concert given by the choir of picked singers he had recruited from the Netherlands, inspected the illuminated manuscripts created for him by the monks for the new church of San Felipe el Real in the Puerta del Sol. At the Escorial for Easter, he washed and kissed the feet of twelve beggars on Maundy Thursday, and afterwards waited on them at table.

After Easter he returned more fully to considering preparations necessary to meet the expected English invasion of Portugal that summer. Mendoza in Paris had written as early as the previous November to warn him that it was coming.

Don Antonio of Crato, the claimant to the Portuguese throne, now a man of fifty-seven, had been in England for some time, having been compelled to leave France because of Philip II's attempts to have him assassinated. He had become friendly with Drake and had stayed at Drake's home in Devon. For years Don Antonio had been urging that the English should land him in Portugal with a supporting army, and claiming that the Portuguese were only waiting for his arrival to rise and overthrow their Spanish conquerors. As long ago as 1581 he and Drake had made plans to seize the Azores; later he had attempted it with the assistance of a French fleet under Admiral Strozzi and had been comprehensively defeated; but all through the years he had kept his claim alive.

Now with the Spanish fleet out of action the time seemed ripe for a really serious attempt to install him. With the jewellery and gold he had brought with him when he left Portugal he had been able to maintain spies working for him in the Iberian Peninsula and elsewhere for nearly a decade, and they reported now on the great discontent in Lisbon and Oporto. Two of these spies incidentally, de Escobar and de Endrada, worked both for him and for Philip II, but were so skilled that though they often met they never suspected each other, nor did either employer suspect that their men were receiving money from the other side. Contrary to what is generally believed, the age of the double-spy did not begin in the present century.

The front door of Buckland Abbey, Tavistock, Sir Francis Drake's home in Devon

Don Antonio's offer to Elizabeth was that two months after his attaining the throne he would defray the full cost of the expedition and would pay England a further three hundred thousand ducats annually, and that he would give England full trade privileges in Portugal and her possessions. It was enough to tempt anyone as near bankruptcy as Elizabeth.

But the possibility of recreating an independent and friendly Portugal was not the only issue at stake. At this moment the Spanish fleet was knocked out and the Spanish coast defenceless. In various Atlantic and Biscayan ports, in varying degrees of mutilation and unseaworthiness, were the remains of that fleet: galleons, great ships, carracks, armed merchantmen, galleasses, pataches, zabras. In spite of the havoc wrought off Gravelines and the even more disastrous wrecks off the Irish coast, a surprisingly large number of the great fleet had somehow drifted home: seven out of the ten galleons of Portugal, six of Recalde's Biscayan great ships, half of Pedro de Valdes's Andalusians, more than half of Diego Flores's Castilians, seven of Oquendo's, two of Bertendona's Levantines. These were the capital ships; no one could be sure how many of them could be repaired, or how quickly. But at the moment they were virtually defenceless in ill-defended seaports. Drake had demonstrated only eighteen months ago what he could do in Cadiz. A bigger raid now – indeed something of a small armada in reverse – could wipe out these ships and so make absolutely complete the victory of last year. Drake put this to the Queen – in company with Sir John Norris, England's most accomplished and experienced soldier. It was all, for once, very much to Elizabeth's way of thinking, and she agreed in principle to the proposal within three weeks of its being put to her.

There was another idea too in the minds of the planners. It was to seize the Azores and establish a regular blockade of the treasure flota sailing to Spain from the Indies. Hawkins had put forward this proposal in December 1587 after Drake's successful raid on Cadiz; it had been impracticable then because of the existence of the Spanish fleet. Now, especially if it were preceded by the destruction of the remnants of that fleet, it was a very feasible proposition and, combined with his loss of control in the Netherlands, would be likely to force Philip to sue for peace. So it was agreed that the enterprise should be put in hand: another *empresa* but with smaller resources and having three objectives instead of one.

It was floated as a joint stock company, with a capital of about £80,000. One quarter was to come from the Queen, one half from private adventurers, including merchants and nobility, one eighth in kind from the City of London and one eighth in kind from the Dutch. The Queen has come in for bitter condemnation from historians for allowing this to become a commercial enterprise, in which almost inevitably the aims became blurred; but in fact she had little choice.

As we have seen earlier in explaining if not excusing her neglect of her victorious sailors, she was on the verge of insolvency. By Christmas 1588 she had about £55,000 left. One half of what she could expect to receive in the following year from ordinary revenues she was pledged to pay towards helping her Dutch allies, under the treaty of 1585. Money was needed urgently in Ireland. James still expected his subsidy in Scotland. And if Henry of Navarre was to help Henry III to survive in France, he too was likely to need more financial help before the year was far gone. None of these calls on her purse was concerned with the ordinary expenses of English civil or military life. In 1588 Burghley had tried to borrow £50,000 abroad at 10 per cent interest. In early 1589 she tried and failed to raise £100,000 in Germany. By November of that year she was reduced to the straits of selling crown lands.

The Queen promised £20,000 towards the cost of the expedition to Portugal; it was the most she could do; and as a pledge of her intentions she advanced most of the money before the rest had been subscribed. London merchants, who had slid off into the country in 1588 in order to avoid paying the forced loans imposed then, now vied with each other in putting money into what so clearly was to be a profit-making venture. With the national hero, Drake, in command and 'Black' Norris at his side, one could hardly go wrong.

The assent and cooperation of the Dutch took longer to obtain. Parma, swinging his troops away from the invasion ports, had laid siege to Bergen-op-Zoom. Thanks largely to English help, the attempt to capture the town failed, but with Parma only hibernating for the winter months and clearly anxious to restore his lost credit in the eyes of Philip, it was not the most propitious time to ask the Dutch to release three thousand troops and six siege-guns with the necessary transports and ten hulks for carrying horses. They were seven weeks making up their minds, but eventually they agreed

Mortars used as siege
weapons in the 16th century

to send fifteen hundred of their own troops with ten warships, and they also agreed to the withdrawal of three thousand of the English troops to join the enterprise, provided that all their own men should be back by June.

Speed was of the essence, for winter had brought almost all the fighting in Europe to a standstill, and this was the moment when troops and money could best be spared. Unhappily a quarrel broke out with the Dutch, in which the English appear to have been to blame, about the number and manner of the withdrawal of the English troops. This was further aggravated by Lord Willoughby's jealousy of Norris and Drake and by a general reluctance of the English commanders to release trained veteran troops from their armies and have them replaced by raw country levies, so that other men should have the glory of leading them on a wildcat invasion of Portugal. One thinks of the Dardanelles.

So the expedition, instead of sailing for Portugal on the 1st February, did not reach Plymouth until the 19th March and was then held back by persistent south-westerly winds for another month. When it sailed it was in a much depleted condition compared to the original plan. Not one of the Dutch warships had arrived and only a few of their transports. The cavalry did not exist and the seasoned troops only numbered eighteen hundred. On the other hand the expedition was swollen by inexperienced volunteers who, flocking in to Plymouth to follow Drake anywhere, increased the total number of soldiers from a planned ten thousand to around nineteen thousand. At the same time the long delay in Portsmouth consumed something like one-third of the total victuals laid on for the voyage.

At the last the Queen, who previously had been unwavering in her support of the expedition, began to have doubts about its success, for by now the winter was past and all the forecasts of the pessimists were coming true. Geertruidenberg, one of the key positions in the Netherlands, had fallen; Henry III's ineptitude in France put the Channel ports in peril, and he had sent a desperate appeal for a loan of £27,000 to hire an army of German mercenaries; while James of Scotland was asking for a subsidy to keep down his Catholic nobles. Elizabeth's attitude was also exasperated by the escape of young Essex who, having distinguished himself in the fighting in Holland, now disobeyed her express instructions to stay at court and rode down to Plymouth in time to sail in the company of the famous Welsh soldier, Sir Roger Williams. She dispatched message after message recalling him, and pinnaces to search the Channel. Eventually one of her darkest messages was sent winging in pursuit of Drake. 'Sir Roger Williams' offence,' she wrote, 'is in so high a degree that the same deserveth to be punished by death . . . If Essex be now come into the company of the fleet, we straightly charge you that you do forthwith cause him to be sent hither in safe manner. Which if you do not, you shall look to answer for the same at your own smart; for these be no childish actions . . . As we have authority to rule so we look to be obeyed.' (Happily for Essex's ambitions, this stern order did not reach the fleet until most of the land fighting was done.)

The English Armada which sailed with such high hopes and with so many diverse ambitions was, though much watered down from the original outline, still a considerable force. Its chief lack was siege-guns and cavalry, both of which had been included in the preliminary plan. For the first time, like the Spanish Armada, soldiers greatly outnumbered sailors, the numbers who finally embarked being approximately seventeen thousand of the former and four thousand of the latter, besides about fifteen hundred officers and gentlemen adventurers. Six royal galleons, sixty English armed merchantmen of displacements varying from four hundred tons to eighty tons, sixty tough little Dutch flyboats of around one hundred and fifty to two hundred tons and a score or more of pinnaces. Nevertheless, even as a naval force, it was far from being an all-out effort, as Spain's had been. Most of the latest and finest of the royal ships were laid up at Chatham; Frobisher with three royal ships and three pinnaces was patrolling the Straits to prevent war material reaching Spain from the north; Sir George Beeston had a similar squadron in the North Sea protecting English sea trade with Germany; and the Earl of Cumberland was fitting out the *Victory* and six other ships at his own expense for raiding the Spanish sea routes.

Having learned the value of formation fighting from the Spanish, Drake had divided his fleet into five squadrons, each led by a Queen's ship: himself, again in the *Revenge*, in the first, Sir John Norris in *Nonpareil* in the second, Vice-Admiral Thomas Fenner in *Dreadnought* in the third, Sir Roger Williams (with the rebellious Essex) in *Swiftsure* in the fourth, and Sir Edward Norris in *Foresight* in the fifth. The first two were of five hundred

tons each, the second two of four hundred tons, the fifth of three hundred.

Both Drake and Norris, much taken with Don Antonio and the thought of liberating Portugal, would have liked to attack Lisbon at once; but the 'Instructions' with which they were issued made the destruction of the Spanish fleet the first objective. This was a vital order of priorities; but unfortunately, although a few of the smaller Armada ships were sheltering in the west-facing Spanish and Portuguese ports, the majority, indeed more than fifty of the biggest ships, were in harbour in the northern ports: forty of them in Santander and twelve in San Sebastian. To attack these ships meant taking the whole fleet far to the leeward of the prevailing winds and alerting all Spain to the presence of the raiding force; and, once in this corner of Biscay, the fleet might find itself embayed.

Here was a strong conflict of interest: the national interest which dictated that the damaged galleons must be destroyed before anything else at all was attempted; and an interest which could be of great national advantage but which also promised much private profit for the investors. Two separate fleets could have attended to two such different objectives, but the existing fleet was not strong enough to divide.

Instead, as so often happens, a fatal compromise was attempted. Hearing that a large concentration of shipping was 'in the Groyne', they attacked Coruña instead. Here they found only one of the Armada galleons, the *San Juan* of one thousand and fifty tons, two greatships, two galleys and a hulk. Drake landed Norris to take the town, and after much confused fighting in the dark and the rain, which in those days rendered muskets useless, the lower town was taken with a minimum of loss. Young Admiral Martin de Bertendona, not long recovered from commanding the worst hit of all the Armada squadrons, had to set fire to the *San Juan* to save her from being captured. (Little wonder that two years later he enjoyed attacking the *Revenge*.) About five hundred Spaniards were caught and killed and Don Juan de Luna, the military commandant of the town, was taken prisoner. But part of the garrison contrived to retire into the higher town, from which they were able during the next few days to harass the English with gunfire.

The shipping burned, the scanty provisions of the fleet replenished, the remaining victuals in the town destroyed, there was nothing to keep the English fleet. But in the darkness and confusion of the first victory great wine barrels had been discovered, and most of the soldiers who had landed drank themselves into insensibility after sacking the town. Many of them were immediately ill, and dysentery was widespread. In the meantime an attempt was made to mine the fortress of the upper town, but this failed. Then an Italian came in with news that an army of eight thousand Spaniards was approaching to relieve the town.

Immediately Sir John Norris and his brother Sir Edward led nine regiments of pikemen and musketeers to intercept them. In the battle which followed, both Norrises behaved with that kind of mad, inspired gallantry which characterized the most successful generals of the sixteenth century, each in turn leading the way across a narrow two-hundred-yard-long bridge spanning a river, under a hail of musket-fire and into a barricade at the other end. Sir John did not even bother to put on his armour and escaped without a scratch; Sir Edward received a sword slash on his head. The Spanish were put to flight with about a thousand dead, and the country around was laid waste by the victorious infantry. The battle of El Burgo Bridge occurred not very far from where Sir John Moore, fighting *for* the Spanish, was to die two hundred and twenty years later.

By now the expeditionary force had been in Coruña two weeks and, apart from some not very valuable booty, they had little to show for the exploit. Their duty now lay, as it had always lain, two hundred and fifty miles west, where the bulk of the shattered Armada awaited them. But Sir

The likeness and signature of Sir John Norris, the soldier who, with Sir Francis Drake, commanded the expedition to the coast of Spain in 1589

Cardinal Archduke Albert, Governor of Lisbon in 1589 when it was besieged by the forces of Sir Francis Drake and Sir John Norris

John Norris now said he was doubtful of the ability to 'distress a fleet' while it was guarded by the guns of a town, and doubtful of his ability to take the town without the siege guns that he had been promised but notably lacked. Also the captains and shipmasters of the Queen's ships reiterated their opinion that with the prevailing westerly winds it was dangerous to take the fleet so far into the Bay.

There is no reason to doubt the sincerity of the second opinion, but the first, coming from, of all people, such men as Norris and Drake, sounds a trifle disingenuous. (Drake, with his notorious entry into Cadiz and a dozen other miraculous exploits; Norris with all his iron experience of campaigning in the Netherlands.) The truth is surely that they saw little prospect of profit in it for the investors. Also their clash with Spanish forces at El Burgo Bridge had convinced them that they could land where they chose in Spain and none to stop them. 'An army of 10,000 good soldiers may pass through the whole realm without great danger,' wrote the Queen's agent, Anthony Ashley, to the Council on the 7th May.

So, with full apologies and explanations sent hastening homewards, they deliberately disobeyed the Queen's instructions and sailed, as they had always wanted to, for Lisbon.

The Queen when she received the dispatches had no doubt in her mind as to what had happened. 'They go to places more for profit than for service,' she commented bleakly. The leaders of the fleet beating southwards towards Lisbon can hardly have been unaware that only a resounding success in Portugal could now make their homecoming a happy one.

Spanish spies, with unerring skill, had reported that when the English fleet arrived off Lisbon it was likely to land a force near Peniche, fifty miles north of the city; and this was what happened. Led by Sir Roger Williams, with Essex recklessly courageous beside him, several regiments succeeded in getting ashore through the surf, and after a brisk bloody encounter the defending forces retreated and the open town surrendered. The same night the castle overlooking the town surrendered to Don Antonio.

It was a propitious start. The rest of the fourteen regiments were landed safely, and the following day the two forces split: the army proposed to march to Lisbon overland while the whole countryside flocked to Don Antonio's standard; the fleet was to sail to Lisbon and intimidate the capital city from the sea.

That Lisbon was intimidated when it became known that *El Draque* was in the Tagus there can be no doubt. The little fortified town of Cascaes, sixteen miles from Lisbon at the mouth of the Tagus, surrendered precipitately, and there was a panic flight of the population from Lisbon despite all efforts of the Spanish governor, the young Cardinal Archduke Albert, to halt it.

For once in his life Drake did not commit his ships to an all-out attack on the city. Perhaps the consciousness of having so flagrantly disobeyed the

Queen hung heavy on him; perhaps he had been overborne by his military advisers to allow them first to attack from the land; certainly he overestimated the extent to which the Spanish, obviously warned of his coming, had been able to add to their garrison and fortify the town. There were in fact rather less than seven thousand troops in all available for the defence, and many of these were Portuguese with no stomach to fight on behalf of their conquerors. All that the Archduke Albert could do was initiate a reign of terror in the city, in which anyone suspected of having sympathy for the claims of Don Antonio was at once executed.

In 1580 when the Spanish took Portugal, Santa Cruz had landed the Duke of Alva with his seasoned Spanish veterans at Cascaes, and, while the troops marched on Lisbon, Santa Cruz had sailed his fleet up the Tagus, the two forces never losing contact with each other. Had this plan been followed now it would surely have succeeded again. Instead Drake waited for the Portuguese to rise and for news of Norris who, lacking cavalry or even enough horse for the transport of baggage, marched his troops in great heat across the peninsula. Many of the men were already sick from seaboard infections or from their excesses at Coruña.

The port and city of Lisbon in 1580

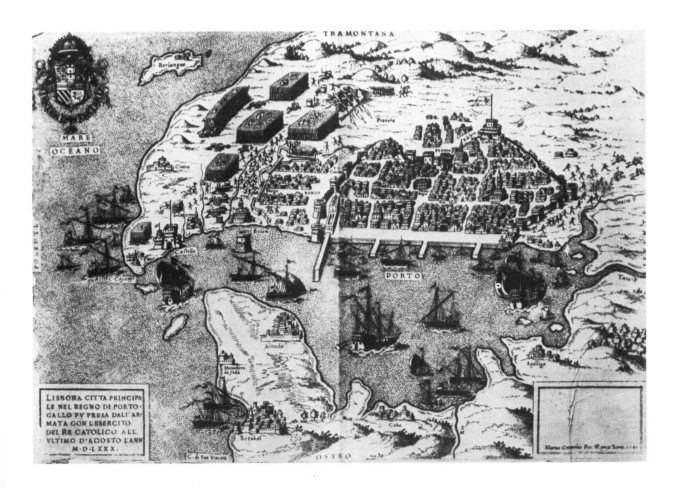

181

Don Antonio, as well as being illegitimate, was also half Jewish, and this did not endear him to some of the great Portuguese families; but he had always claimed that the general population would immediately rise at his name. In Lisbon the Portuguese, intimidated and decimated by the Archduke's ruthlessness, could hardly have done more than wait and see. But in the countryside the response to the arrival of their 'rightful king' was dismally negative. Only about two hundred joined the English army, and those, according to Sir Roger Williams, were 'the greatest cowards that I ever saw'. Considering what they put at stake by joining at all, it seems an unfair description.

There was at first no fighting, for the Spanish withdrew before the advancing army, who by the 25th May were in the suburbs of Lisbon. Here, after firing the storehouses to prevent their falling into English hands, the Spanish launched a powerful counter-attack; but it was repulsed with heavy casualties and they then retreated within the walls of the city.

For three days Norris lay encamped outside the city, expecting Drake. Of his force of about nine thousand men more than three thousand were now too ill to be anything but a liability. He was running short of ammunition and he had no siege-guns. In this situation he could only wait for the Portuguese to rise, while in their situation the Portuguese could only wait for him to take the city. Had Drake come up the Tagus it might have turned the scales, but he, like Norris, was expecting the Portuguese revolt that did not come. One cannot imagine him being intimidated by the forty cannon of Fort St Julian which guarded the narrow entrance, though he claims this was a deterrent. Probably he was already turning his eyes on the third objective of the expedition, the treasure ships likely to be coming in from the Azores.

On the 28th Norris gave Don Antonio one more day in which to rally his supporters. When they did not come he struck camp and marched with his whole army to Cascaes. Because they had the Portuguese Prince with them, looting in the suburbs of Lisbon had been rigorously forbidden, otherwise, wrote Captain Richard Wingfield regretfully, 'we had been the richest army that ever went out of England'. Before they left Lisbon Essex, tall and splendid in his full armour, walked up alone to one of the gates of the city and thrust his sword into the wood, crying in a carrying voice if any 'Spaniard mewed therein durst adventure forth in favour of my mistress to break a lance'. No Spaniard adventured forth.

When the army reached Cascaes, siege was already being laid to the castle there by Drake's men, and the arrival of the army settled the issue. But now there were repeated councils-of-war and mutual recriminations. Norris was not an easy man to get along with at the best of times, and here, justifiably, he had cause for complaint.

While they were so in angry conference the only piece of luck of the whole expedition befell them. A big fleet of Hanseatic ships sailed into the Tagus unsuspecting and, apart from a few escorting ships which made their escape, all were captured. The Hanseatic League, which was composed of the Baltic and north German cities, did not approve of the English blockade of their trade with Spain, and this fleet, carrying grain and valuable war commodities, had dodged both Sir Martin Frobisher's and Sir George Beeston's patrolling squadrons by sailing all round the north of Scotland, like the retreating Armada of the year before. Some of the ships were newly built and intended for Spanish use, and all were seized. It added sixty sail to the English fleet and new hope to their flagging spirits. At this stage the squadron of Dutch flyboats was given permission to return home.

Now supplies arrived from England – with that sulphurous letter from the Queen which hastened the departure of my Lord of Essex – and with news that Drake's vice-admiral and Ralegh's friend, Captain Robert Crosse, was off Cadiz with another squadron of supply ships. So the troops were re-embarked and the fleet abandoned Lisbon and sailed south. One spares a moment of sympathy for the broken hopes of Don Antonio, who had seen so much begun and then it all fail from the use of half measures.

After the juncture with Crosse they proceeded to try to accomplish the third object of their mission, or at least, in Drake's words, 'to find some comfortable little dew of Heaven', which would increase the profit of the venture. But now Heaven, or at any rate the weather, turned foul on them and they were beaten back to the Bayona Islands near Vigo. Here they again landed, one party led by Sir Roger Williams, the other by Drake in person, and captured and burned Vigo and laid waste the settlements and villages around. Here Rear-Admiral William Fenner, commanding the sixth Queen's ship, the *Aid*, died of wounds. By now there were scarcely two thousand fit men who could be mustered, and a number of the ships had been badly used by the storm, so it was clearly futile to attempt anything against the Azores in this condition. Drake therefore took the pick of the men and ships that were left – twenty ships in all – while Norris turned for home with the sick and the wounded.

But for once Drake's uncanny ability to conjure victory out of defeat, his knack of being in the right place to seize at least one rich prize, this time failed him. His luck would not turn for him, perhaps because for once he had hesitated to trust to it. A violent storm struck his ships and scattered them before they could reach the Azores, and the *Revenge* sprang a dangerous leak that could not be repaired at sea. Robert Crosse and Thomas Fenner with a few other ships did in fact reach Madeira and landed at Puerto Santa and captured and plundered the port. But they entirely missed the treasure fleet.

And Drake led the remnants of his own fleet home. The *Revenge*, nearly foundering, reached Plymouth just in time. The only prizes of substantial value gained out of the expedition were the sixty Hanseatic vessels and their contents seized in the Tagus, which later were sold for £30,000. Apart from this, like Norris, he only had excuses with which to attempt to placate Elizabeth.

Captain Robert Crosse, who commanded a squadron of supply ships for Sir Francis Drake in the 1589 expedition against Spain

11 The Loss of the Revenge

A comparison of the expedition of 1589 with the Spanish Armada of the previous year is hardly valid. The Lisbon expedition was never an all-out effort, and if every ship had sunk it would not have crippled the Queen's navy. In fact no ship was sunk. Yet, while no really reliable estimates exist as to the number of men who came home, it seems probable that about half of those who sailed were lost – a couple of thousand perhaps by enemy action, the rest victims of that other and more deadly and more thoroughly impartial enemy: General Disease. Ralegh, whose estimate is likely to be better than most, reckoned the total loss at eight thousand men.

By less demanding standards than those expected of it, the expedition could have been considered a modest success. It had landed in both Spain and Portugal and had marched with impunity about the countryside. It had diverted regiments intended for the Netherlands and caused the Spanish to recruit new ones. It had destroyed the granaries round Lisbon and had captured a whole fleet of grain and supply ships arriving to help the Spanish food and naval shortage. It had delayed the treasure ships, and a revolt in the Netherlands army in the following August for back pay can be traced to their late arrival. As Norris said: 'If the enemy had done so much upon us, his party would have made bonfires in most parts of Christendom.'

The narrowness of the margin by which they missed taking Lisbon is emphasized by historians who, unlike the commanders of the time, have the advantage of hindsight. But neither Norris nor Drake could have known by how much their attack on Lisbon, although long heralded, was a complete surprise when it occurred, by what a thin and to some extent disaffected garrison the city was held, and by what terrorist measures the Archduke Albert just prevented any sign of an uprising.

What reflects worst on the expedition is that they had no naval opposition to overcome. The Armada had to face a fleet as numerous if not as heavy as itself, much more mobile and fighting in home waters. One wonders what Medina Sidonia would have achieved if there had been no English fleet.

Drake and Norris in 1589 sailed where they would and landed where they pleased, and made little enough of it.

Elizabeth, of course, with her usual grasp of essentials, knew exactly what had gone wrong, and she never forgave Drake. Pushed inch by reluctant inch and year by year into an outright war with Spain which Philip at last had made unavoidable, she was well aware of the temporary advantage she held after the defeat of the Armada, and, having come to war, she was willing to wage war. Even as early as August 1588, while reports of the full extent of the Spanish disaster were by no means complete, she had personally initiated discussions on how best to capitalize on the victory. Never as enamoured as Drake and others were of Don Antonio's chances of raising a full-scale revolt in Portugal, she had kept always before her the primary purpose for which an expedition must be launched: the destruction of what was left of the Spanish fleet.

These had been her instructions. If they had been followed, the loss of men could hardly have been greater than in the half-measure landings which were undertaken, and forty or fifty of Spain's remaining galleons lying in varying stages of repair and disrepair would have been destroyed – all those ships which had so narrowly got home from the disaster, all those ships which otherwise could be repaired to form the nucleus of a new fleet, all those ships which as soon as repaired would be at sea again to guard the treasure fleets. 'If,' wrote a correspondent from nearby St Jean de Luz, 'Sir Francis had gone to Santander as he went to the Groyne he had done such a service as never subject had done before, for with 12 ships he might have destroyed all the forces which the Spaniards had there, which was the whole strength of the country by sea. There they did ride all unrigged and their ordnance on the shore and some 20 men to a ship only to keep them.'

So Elizabeth's explicit instructions had been disobeyed, and perhaps more clearly than anyone at that time, unless it was Burghley, she saw that the one chance of ending the war quickly was lost. Of course she was only the principal shareholder in a joint stock company which was not this time declaring a dividend. She made no public complaint about the outcome of the expedition; formally if icily she thanked her captains and men, as befitted a sovereign served loyally but inefficiently. Privately Drake and Norris were called upon to answer articles charging them with disobeying their instructions and other matters.

In the meantime England's correspondent in St Jean de Luz reported that in addition to the fifty-odd ships of the old Armada being repaired in the northern ports, nine new galleons were being built in Portugal, and twelve others designed on the English model – later to be known as the Twelve Apostles – had been laid down in various Biscayan ports. The hour of danger for Spain was passing.

A month after the return of Drake and Norris the face of Europe was convulsed by another event. A monk called Jacques Clément, encouraged by

the Duchess of Montpensier, sister of the recently murdered Duc de Guise, gained an audience of Henry III and, while the king was reading his petition, drew a dagger and stabbed him in the belly. So, less than eight months after the assassination of Guise, and only seven after the death of the woman who had schemed and contrived all her life for the preservation and perpetuation of her line, the last of her sons passed from the scene. He was also the last of the house of Valois which had given thirteen kings to France in the space of two and a half centuries.

It seems improbable that Elizabeth, whose great-great-grandmother was a Valois, shed any tears at the passing of the house.

The King did not die immediately, and to the many people crowding into his chamber in his last hours he left no doubt as to his will – that his cousin and brother-in-law and most recent ally, Henry of Navarre, should succeed to the throne of France. Thus the paradox emerged that the fanatic Clément had murdered a Catholic in order that he should be succeeded by a Huguenot.

But it was a murder as much of revenge as of religion. All the Guises went frantic with joy, and Catholic Paris set up tables in the streets and held mid-day banquets and midnight bonfires. Clément, who had been immediately killed by the King's attendants, was 'honoured in the pulpits, sung in the streets, invoked as a saint'. Pope Sixtus proclaimed him a new martyr.

The position of the new King, Henry of Navarre, was precarious in the extreme. Not only was the whole of the Spanish-dominated Catholic League against him, but half the supporters of the previous king were riven with religious scruples as to whether they could continue to serve a Protestant. Some continued to do so because they preferred a French King on the throne to a Spanish Infanta; and the Venetian Republic infuriated its co-religionists by immediately – and for the same reason – recognizing Henry. The Pope by his own famous Bull of Deprivation of September 1585 had declared Henry of Navarre forfeit of all his rights to the throne of France, so now, though as anxious as anyone that France should retain her independence, he could do no more than privately urge Henry to change his religion. Under much pressure from his French friends too, Henry could only reply that he had been born a Catholic, reared as a Calvinist by his mother, become converted to Catholicism to save his life at the St Bartholomew massacre and reverted to Protestantism as soon as he was free again. 'You require a change in me which would argue no sincerity either in one faith or the other.'

He appealed to Elizabeth for help, and Elizabeth, fearing once again for the safety of the Channel ports, was compelled to give it him. She was now drawn more and more into a military struggle in Europe, to the consequent neglect of her navy. As the years progressed, she found herself with troops dotted along the Channel coast or in adjacent regions supporting the Dutch and the French everywhere against the common enemy.

In March 1590 with a mixed army of French, English, Germans and Swiss, some of them quite unable to understand each other's languages, Henry IV comprehensively defeated the Catholic Leaguers under the Duc de Mayenne.

Henry of Navarre, who became Henry IV of France

This was at Ivry, now known as Ivry-la-Bataille, between Mantes and Dreux. It followed up his other two successes at Coutras and Arques, and had been confidently forecast by the incorrigible Pope Sixtus, who remarked that Henry of Navarre spent less time in bed than his opponents did at their food. The succession of victories marked Henry as a soldier of eminence, and there was a noticeable shift in general public opinion towards him. He had also that other gift of leadership, an ability for uttering the memorable sentence at the most suitable moment. It endeared him to his new subjects as much as Elizabeth's did to the English.

In May 1590 Henry laid siege to Paris, which remained recalcitrantly opposed to a Protestant King. It was a strange siege, for Henry had thirteen thousand soldiers in all and the city a quarter of a million inhabitants. But the young governor, the Duke of Nemours, was overawed by the successes Henry had achieved in the field and he did not trust the fifty thousand amateurs that he could command, so the city suffered all the horrors of a three-month siege. In the first month alone thirteen thousand died of hunger and about thirty thousand of fever. Hideous practices were resorted to within the city in order to keep starvation at bay.

What was Philip to do? The unification of France under a strong Huguenot king, the conquest of the pro-Spanish Catholics, the complete collapse of his influence in the country and the virtual isolation of his forces in the Netherlands: could these be tolerated? Better to seize all France. And more tempting. He still had far the most powerful army in Europe. He wrote to Parma, instructing him to march to the relief of Paris. Parma vehemently protested. Slowly, inexorably, he was advancing again to squeeze the United Provinces into surrender. To take off the pressure now might undo all the dearly won victories of the last two years. The Armada had failed but not Spanish military power. With the forces that he now possessed, the Dutch, even with Elizabeth's aid, must soon find their backs to the sea.

Paris in the late 16th century

Philip's reply was peremptory: 'If Flanders is lost,' he wrote, 'it is mine to lose.' Parma must relieve Paris.

Parma was slow in moving, but this time he could not be blamed for the delay. The English raid on Lisbon and the Azores which had delayed the silver fleet from the Indies had deprived Parma of the money to pay his long-deprived troops, and there was a mutiny. He put it down as only he could, but had to pledge his own jewellery as surety for his promises.

In Paris by August, with people dying in their tens of thousands, there was great pressure within the city to surrender. This was chiefly resisted by the Archbishop of Lyons and by Mendoza, the Spanish Ambassador. 'I am here serving you as best I can,' old Mendoza wrote racily to Philip, 'but wherever I am there is sure to be a storm, and I am running under close-reefed topsails fore and aft.' When emissaries of surrender were just about to leave the capital, news came that Parma had joined the Duc de Mayenne at Meaux, only twenty-five miles east of Paris. Henry raised the siege and faced the relieving army, but Parma out-manoeuvred and out-flanked him, and the inconclusive clashes which occurred could not hide the fact that Parma with an apparently inadequate army of veterans was still master of the field wherever he chose to fight. Henry was driven from Paris, the city relieved and the pro-Spanish faction encouraged.

By the autumn a Spanish army three thousand strong, under Don Juan de Aguila, had landed on the coast of Brittany, to support the League there and to secure a base at the western end of the Channel. This gravely alarmed England, and the council sent Norris off with three thousand troops, half of them veterans, to oppose the landing. Henry contributed a small local force but nothing else, since Parma's presence was a menace to his whole kingdom. The situation in France at this stage posed as many dangers for England as those of the Armada year, because only Henry and his supporters stood between them and a Spanish occupation of the Channel coastline. Had France fallen then, it is unlikely that the Netherlands could have held out.

In November, however, Parma, conscious of a rapid deterioration of the situation in the Netherlands under his deputy, the Count of Mansfeld, disengaged himself in France and, although harassed all the way by French cavalry under Henry, retreated in perfect order and without loss; another notable feat of arms, though it was not appreciated by Philip who wished him to stay and by his continuing presence assist the Spanish Infanta's claim under Salic law to the French throne. (She was of course the daughter of Henry III's sister.)

Information reaching Spain that Sixtus was willing to recognize Henry IV if only, or as soon as, he turned Catholic, led to a dramatic scene in the Vatican, where the new Spanish Ambassador, the Duke of Sesa, delivered a curt message from Philip declaring it intolerable that the Papacy should even be considering a reconciliation with a man who in Spain would have been 'burned a thousand times already' for his relapses; and stating that if Sixtus persisted in this conduct Philip would demand a National Council (at which Sixtus might be deposed). The Pope thereupon uttered words which were not far from anathema upon Philip and all Spaniards and strode from the room, leaving his Cardinals trembling. Sesa, white with anger himself, then turned to the Cardinals and told them that if they trifled with his master he 'would drop a brick on them', and he too stamped out.

Whether or not consumed by his own choler, the sagacious, eccentric Sixtus V died shortly after this, whereby Philip lost an enemy and the world an utterer of outrageous but brilliant *bons mots*. Philip declared himself *'muy contento'* with the Pope's death.

Thereafter followed a succession so rapid that the Papal chair might have been electric: Sixtus in August 1590, Urban VII in October 1590, Gregory XIV in 1591, and Innocent IX in 1592, Clement VIII thereafter. But none of them, willing or unwilling, could or would help Philip to marry his much loved daughter to the new Duc de Guise and put her on the French throne.

Henry IV, deprived of Paris, was encouraged by Elizabeth and Burghley to lay siege to Rouen. Almost all the great towns of northern France were staunchly Catholic, and without their revenues he was poverty stricken. In one year alone Elizabeth had to advance him £60,000 apart from material help, which consisted of an army in the field. For this latest continental adventure Elizabeth, after Essex had spent two hours on his knees before her on three separate occasions, was persuaded to let him lead the English army, which was to consist of four thousand foot soldiers and appropriate cavalry. Cautiously and hoping for the best, she appointed his old friend and mentor, Sir Roger Williams, to be his chief of staff. Williams, hard-bitten, scarred and worldly-wise, is thought by many to be the original of Shakespeare's Fluellen.

Essex was twenty-four, and, while conducting his part of the campaign on the best soldierly lines, yet contrived to give it all a flavour of twelfth-century chivalry. As soon as he landed he led a dangerous cavalry dash through enemy-held territory to link up with his hero, the French King; and the foot soldiers under Sir Roger Williams followed him, a notable march

made without loss. A French writer describes Essex's arrival in Compiègne: 'Nothing more magnificent could possibly be seen. Six pages preceded him mounted on chargers and dressed in orange velvet embroidered with gold. He himself had a military cloak of orange velvet all covered with jewels. His dress and the furniture of his horse alone were worth sixty thousand crowns. He had twelve tall body-squires and six trumpeters sounding before him.'

So the campaign for all its dour purpose took on a gayer air. At a dinner-party given by Essex the three Swiss colonels present could not stay the course and collapsed under the table, but Essex and his friends and the French officers present rode riotously out, shouting and singing right up to the gates of Rouen. When nearly there they met the Governor of Rouen out on a reconnaissance. Essex at once challenged him to a duel. The Governor's only reply was a volley of shot from his escort of musketeers.

Nevertheless the siege failed, and for the same reason as the siege of Paris.

Maurice of Nassau, Stadholder of the Dutch Republic, a great military commander who retook several major cities from the invading Spaniards

The campaign had dragged on all winter and Essex had returned to England, when Parma once again suddenly appeared with his army only ten miles from the city. Reluctantly, under orders from his King, he had again withdrawn from his campaign against Maurice of Nassau and marched his men through the spring muds of Flanders to relieve yet another Catholic city. But at Caudebec, on the Seine west of Rouen, he received a wound in the hand which was eventually to prove fatal. The greatest general of his age died in Arras in December of that year, not long before the letter arrived from Philip which was to relieve him of his command.

Parma's absence with part of his troops from the Netherlands had already opened the way to a Dutch revival. Though only twenty-four, Maurice of Nassau, William of Orange's son by his second wife, Anna of Saxony, had inherited his father's military talents, and in the space of five months he recaptured Breda, Zutphen, Deventer and three other vital forts, by the conquest of the last of which, Nijmegen, he was able to gain control of the whole of Gelderland. Surviving the customary attempts at assassination, he reorganized the army of the Netherlands, instituting a high level of training and discipline which matched the Spanish, and introducing many new ideas, such as arming his cavalry with carbines instead of with swords. Behind the army Jan Oldenbarneveldt was organizing the rebel provinces into a unit of great economic strength. Indeed the contrast between the southern provinces, which, under Spanish rule, were declining into poverty and banditry, and those northern provinces comprising the Union of Utrecht, which prospered in conditions of war, was yearly more marked. Antwerp, occupied and blockaded, lost its great position as the trading centre of Europe. Amsterdam, free and thriving, took its place.

Nor by sacrificing such advantages as his great general had gained in the Low Countries did Philip advance his cause in France. The Duc de Mayenne permitted twelve hundred Spanish troops to be garrisoned in Paris; but the Spaniard had by now become more unpopular in France even than the Englishman. If Spain sent money the French accepted it but derided the Spanish for sending it; if they sent troops it was a greater offence. It is not an unfamiliar pattern.

In January 1593, Mayenne summoned the States General and received the Spanish Ambassador with regal honours. The Count de Feria reminded the French of all the favours they had received and the six million gold ducats Philip had spent. He urged the assembly not to disperse until they had elected a truly Catholic King – or preferably Queen.

But even this gun was in process of being spiked. Convinced at last by the Spanish armies of Parma and the obduracy of his own people that there could never be peace in France with a Protestant on the throne, Henry IV changed his religion for the last time. In his famous words, he had decided that 'Paris was worth a Mass'. Elizabeth, shocked and indignant, sent him several strongly worded letters on the theme of 'what shall it profit a man'.

Henry replied that his change of religion would not affect his friendship towards England. Nor did it. As François Guizot later wrote: 'He became a Catholic of France without ceasing to be the prop of the Protestants in Europe.' But for many earnest Protestants in England and elsewhere it was a bitter disillusion.

In consequence of his apostasy Henry was able to enter Paris without a shot fired and, from a window in the Port St Denis, to watch the Spanish garrison marching out. 'Commend me to your master,' he said, 'but do not return.'

If Philip had been giving ground on the military front he had been recouping it on the naval. By 1590 there had been a complete reorganization of the defences in the Caribbean. All the ports, such as St Domingo and Cartagena, and those in the Canaries and Azores too, had been greatly strengthened to resist surprise attack, and at most of these places frigates and other small but fast warships were now stationed to be on hand if the Flotas were attacked. A system of communication had been established by means of pinnaces which could make the passage across the Atlantic in twenty-eight days and carry advance news of hostile squadrons approaching. More important, Pero Menendez Marquez in Havana developed a new type of warship of about two hundred tons burden which he called galleyzabras – on the same principle as the galleass but of quite different proportions and seaworthiness. Built like galleys but mainly propelled by sail, they were sufficiently heavily armed to outfight anything of their own size and too fast to be caught by anything bigger. (One thinks of Admiral Fisher's dicta in the First World War, of the birth of the battle-cruiser, and, later, of the German pocket-battleships.)

But these ships were not just for war: they were to take over the carrying of the silver bullion and other treasure from the old conventional slow-moving carracks. Merchants were compelled to unload at Havana and have their valuables refreighted in the galleyzabras. There were not nearly enough of these ships yet to take over from the East India carracks, and they for the time being still had to take their chance. Towards the end of 1589 both the Earl of Cumberland and Sir Martin Frobisher seized prizes of great value on the trade routes; but this sort of raid was to become more difficult with each year that passed.

Hawkins had a more methodical plan, which was the establishment of a regular blockade off the Azores, maintained by a squadron of English warships four months at a stretch, each squadron to be relieved by another, so that at no time throughout the year would the treasure-ships be free to sail through. It was a plan he had advocated before the Armada, but then the menace to England was too great to see it implemented. The year 1590 was the big opportunity, and although like most such schemes of the time it failed to be efficient for the half measures employed to furnish it, the fact of its presence, plus the remarkable depredations of a leading city merchant,

Alderman John Watt, and other privateers in the Caribbean, caused Philip to send word that the treasure-ships were not to risk the Atlantic crossing that year.

As soon as this was learned in England it was resolved to fit out a squadron of warships to intercept the treasure-fleet in the spring of 1591. Drake remained in eclipse, though busying himself reorganizing the defences of Plymouth; neither Hawkins nor Frobisher had particularly distinguished himself in the Queen's eyes in last year's blockade – that is they had brought nothing of value home; Lord Admiral Howard's was rather too big a name to command this light compact squadron. So Elizabeth chose Lord Thomas Howard, the Lord Admiral's young cousin, with Sir Walter Ralegh as second-in-command. Lord Thomas Howard, who was thirty, had commanded the *Golden Lion* against the Armada and had handled his ship like a master; but his other sea experience was slight. Ralegh, now thirty-nine, had had a lifetime's experience of soldiering but relatively little naval experience, though as an empire builder he had already set down one colony of settlers in Virginia.

However, at the last moment the Queen, who seldom liked her favourites to stray far from court – and just then Ralegh was back in favour – forbade him to go. She may also have realized that the Howards as a family no more liked Ralegh than he liked them. They looked on him as an arrogant upstart living on the Queen's favour. He looked on them as his mental inferiors, which, not unnaturally, they were.

Probably on Ralegh's initiative, the Queen appointed his cousin, Sir Richard Grenville, to sail in his place. The outcome is both history and legend. The squadron that sailed was small but well found. Howard in the *Defiance*, Grenville in the *Revenge*, were accompanied by two comparable Queen's ships, the *Bonaventure*, Captain Robert Crosse, and the *Nonpareil*, Sir Edward Denny, of around five hundred tons each with crews of two hundred and fifty and about forty guns. The *Crane*, a ship of half that size, a half dozen well-armed London merchantmen, and about eight pinnaces, made up the fleet. Before they had been at sea more than a month news reached London that a Spanish fleet of remarkable size and power was abroad: about fifty sail, of which thirty were galleons, including six of the new 'Apostles' of fifteen hundred tons each. They were under the command of Don Alonso de Bazan, younger brother to the dead Santa Cruz; and immediately this news reached Ralegh he sent off a fast pinnace to warn the English. At the same time strenuous efforts were made to reinforce Howard's fleet. Thomas Vavasour in the *Foresight* and George Fenner in the *Lion*, with seven more armed merchantmen, were hurried off towards the rendezvous that Howard had left, an area a little to the west of the island of Flores.

In mid-August the Spanish fleet reached Terceira, the main naval base in the Azores, and shortly afterwards news of the English took them to Flores. By this time the English squadron had been at sea nearly four months, had captured little and were heartily tired of waiting for the treasure-fleet. As

Lord Thomas Howard, who with Sir Richard Grenville commanded the raiding expedition to the Azores in 1591

NON QVO SED QVOMODO

TOTI' ANG: THESAVRARI ET CO: SVFFOLCIÆ ET HONORATISS: D⁰: THOMAS HOWARI

The
righte Honourable THOMAS:
HOWARD Earle of Suffolke. Lorde Walden
and Lorde Treasurer of England and one of his

usual they were beset by sickness, and when Captain Middleton, who had been dispatched by the Earl of Cumberland, arrived in a pinnace to warn them of the approach of a Spanish fleet, most of the ships' companies were ashore. Ralegh in his famous *Report* writes: 'Some were providing ballast for their ships; others filling of water and refreshing themselves from the land with such things as they could either for money or by force recover . . . one half part of the men of every ship were sick . . . in the *Revenge* there were ninety diseased.'

The Spanish admiral had so divided his fleet that the English would be surrounded and attacked from all sides; and, but for Cumberland's warning pinnace, the plan would have been entirely successful. As it was, Howard had less than an hour in which to recover his crews from the land before, at around four in the afternoon, the first squadron of the Spanish fleet under Marcos de Arumburu – that Paymaster of the Castilean galleons who was so nearly wrecked off the Blasket Islands – came round the corner of the island and was upon him. So close was it that several of the English ships had to slip their cables in order to be away in time; and then it was touch and go whether they could gain the weather gage and so make out to sea. One indeed, the *Revenge*, did not.

Sir Richard Grenville is one of the strangest, fiercest, most heroic figures of all that fierce, heroic age. Obstinate, of an inflammable temper, a man of action, always at war either on land or sea and a natural leader, his reputation in Spain was nothing like Drake's, but it was a darker one. '*Ricardo de Campo Verde gran cossario.*' A great pirate. He took a pride in his grim reputation. The legend was current at the time, and for long after his death, that when Grenville took prisoners he would have them to dine and would chew and swallow glass till the blood ran from his mouth. Returning from Virginia in 1585 he had come on a Spanish ship containing treasure and, having no small boat to board her, had used an old ship's chest which floated him and his men across and sank as they sprang aboard the Spaniard. Not a man to turn his back on the enemy however much common sense demanded it.

By turning tail and running back before the wind the *Revenge* almost certainly could have got clear. Instead, while Arumburu and Howard exchanged broadsides, Grenville decided to force his way right through the Spanish fleet, obliging the big galleons of Seville to give way before him. Naturally they did no such thing. The *San Felipe* first got a grappling-line aboard, but this parted, being of rope, and the *Revenge* 'discharged her lower tier loaded with cross-bar shot and forced her to fall away and stop her leaks'. But so big was the *San Felipe* beside the *Revenge* that she becalmed the sails of the English ship, and after a succession of further broadsides Martin de Bertendona, thirsting to repay all the defeats he had suffered, came up on the other side in the *San Barnabas*, and was able to grapple more securely.

'The Spanish ships,' says Ralegh, who got it all direct from survivors, 'were filled with companies of soldiers, in some two hundred besides the

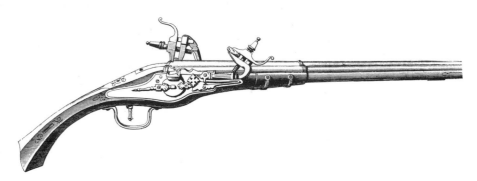

mariners . . . In ours there was none at all beside the mariners but the servants of the commanders and some few voluntary gentlemen. After many interchanged volleys of great ordnance and small shot, the Spaniards deliberated to enter the *Revenge*, and made divers attempts, hoping to force her by the multitudes of their armed soldiers and musketeers, but were still repulsed again and again, and at all times beaten back, into their own ships or into the seas.'

One English ship only turned back to help, the *George Noble*, an armed London victualler of one hundred and fifty tons, which sailed recklessly into the fighting zone and put herself under Grenville's command. Grenville's order was to save herself before she was shot to pieces.

In the meantime Arumburu had crashed into the poop of the *Revenge* and got some men aboard, who fought their way as far as the mainmast and captured the ship's ensign; but he had so damaged his own galleon in the collision that she had to disengage and request aid from others of the fleet. His place was immediately taken by Don Pedro Manrique in the *Ascension* and behind him came Don Luis Cuitiño who put his flagship alongside the *Ascension* and ran his men across her decks. Then the *San Andrea* forced her way in near the bows.

By now night had fallen, but the fight went on in the dark unabated. Grenville was everywhere, wolfishly encouraging his men and directing them, and somehow he bore a charmed life in all the slaughter about him. The *Revenge's* upper works were completely torn to pieces and many of the crew who had taken to the tops for better aim had died. At eleven Grenville at last was seriously wounded in the side, and had to retire behind a splintered bulwark while his surgeon attempted to dress the wound. While fastening the bandages the surgeon was shot dead and Grenville again wounded, this time in the head.

The commander of the Spanish fleet, Alonso de Bazan, having very narrowly missed catching and boarding Howard and having lost the other English in the dark, returned and circled helplessly round this bitter and bloody battle in which one lone Queen's ship was locked inextricably with fifteen of his own, like a fox among a pack of hounds. About three in the morning the galleon *Ascension* began to sink, and her crew were taken off by other vessels. Later, as the *Ascension* went to the bottom, Don Luis Cuitiño's flagship was found to be fatally holed, and this too was abandoned, to sink soon after dawn. Two others were so damaged that they foundered later.

But there were always more eager for the kill. And Bertendona's *San Barnabas* was still locked to the *Revenge's* larboard side in a grip that could only end in death.

At dawn the fighting almost stopped. No Spaniard lived on the decks of the *Revenge*, but few English either. All the upper works had been shot away down to the main deck. Not a mast or a spar was standing. English and Spanish dead and dying lay heaped together in the scuppers. Not a pike remained unbroken. All powder was spent. The Spaniards surrounded her still, but they had fired something like eight hundred rounds of heavy shot, had lost nearly four hundred men killed, including two captains, and they waited for her surrender to save more bloodshed. Out of the morning mists another English ship, the *Pilgrim*, under Captain Whiddon of Plymouth, having hovered in the area all night listening to the battle, put in a brief appearance, but a dozen Spanish ships closed on her and she slipped hastily away.

Meanwhile Grenville, dying in his cabin, gave orders to the master gunner to split and sink the *Revenge* so that she should not fall into enemy hands. The gunner and others were willing but were stayed by Captain Langhorne and the Master, who argued that the *Revenge* was already so badly holed that if surrendered now it was unlikely anyone would ever get her safe to port, and it was not dishonourable to save themselves and those others not mortally wounded to fight another day.

While some pleaded with Grenville, the Master, who had 'at least ten or twelve wounds in his head or on his body,' – and was to die of them later – hastened to be conveyed aboard the *San Pablo* where he met Don Alonso de Bazan and demanded generous terms if they were to yield. The terms were willingly granted, and the great fight was over. 'When the answer was returned and that safety of life was promised, the common sort being now at the end of their peril, the most drew back from Sir Richard and the master gunner, it being no hard matter to dissuade men from death to life. The master-gunner, finding himself and Sir Richard thus prevented and mastered by the greater number, would have slain himself with a sword, had he not been by force withheld and locked in his cabin . . . Sir Richard thus overmatched, was sent unto by Alonso Bazan to remove out of the *Revenge*, the ship being marvellous unsavoury, filled with blood and the bodies of dead and wounded men like a slaughter-house.'

Sir Richard Grenville died two days later on board the *San Pablo*. Shortly afterwards a storm of hurricane force from the west and north-west scattered and sank many of the Spanish ships. With them went the *Revenge*. So many ships were wrecked and so many thousands of bodies were cast up on the islands that, according to a Dutch merchant called Van Linschoten, the islanders began to doubt the power of God. 'So soon as they had thrown overboard the dead body of Vice-Admiral Sir Richard Grenville, they verily thought that, as he had a devilish faith and religion and therefore the devils loved him, so he presently sank into the bottom of the sea and down into hell, where he raised up all the devils to the revenge of his death. Such and the like blasphemies against God they ceased not openly to utter, without being reproved by any man.'

Lord Thomas Howard was much criticized at the time for leaving the *Revenge* to her fate, rather as Medina Sidonia was for leaving Pedro de Valdes in the *Rosario*. Although the behaviour of the two captains thus left behind is so opposite as to belong to different worlds, the action of the admirals has a similarity in that it was dictated by larger considerations than the safety of one ship. Medina Sidonia by staying with the *Rosario* would have split his Armada. Howard by returning to fight alongside the obstinate commander of the *Revenge* would probably have lost his squadron. Also to stay to grapple or be grappled would have been contrary to all the precepts of the Armada battle. It was precisely this that the Spaniards wanted, precisely this that the English had learned to avoid.

But Howard, it is argued, might have stayed near, harrying and biting at the edges of the Spanish fleet and distracting them from their attack on the *Revenge*. This presupposes that the English ships were still much faster and more manoeuvrable than the Spanish. But the Spanish ships, or the majority of them, had been built in the last four years on lessons learned in the Armada battle; the English were the same ones and had been at sea four months. It is doubtful if Howard could have harried the Spanish ships and yet maintained his distance. Indeed the Spaniards claimed that had night not fallen, they would have overtaken several of the English ships, certainly the *Defiance*, which was the slowest of the royal vessels.

The news of the capture of the *Revenge* and the scattering of the English fleet was brought in to Lisbon by one of the Apostle galleons, the *San Andrea*, which had been in the thick of the fight, with all her flags and banners flying. This was the first and only English capital ship captured throughout the war, and efforts were made in Spain to make the most of it and to hide the cost in Spanish ships and the disaster of the gale which followed. In England the death and defeat of Grenville was accompanied by wild rumours which only the publication of Ralegh's *Report* helped to stifle. The Queen privately was upset and offended by the manner of Grenville's death. The ultimate realist, she saw no point in sacrificing a valuable and famous warship and a valuable and brave commander and crew for the sake of an immortal gesture. Pedro de Valdes, safe in comfortable captivity in England, would no doubt have agreed with her.

But the last fight of the *Revenge* has become a legend in men's minds that defies rational assessment. In Froude's memorable words: 'As the most glorious actions, set like jewels in the history of mankind, are weighed one against the other in the balance, hardly will those three hundred Spartans who in the summer morning sat combing their long hair for death in the passes of Thermopylae have earned a more lofty estimate for themselves than this one crew of modern Englishmen.'

In 1590 the Earl of Essex married Frances, the widow of Sir Philip Sidney. Her Majesty was furious but quickly forgave him. Late in 1591 Sir Walter Ralegh secretly married Elizabeth Throckmorton, one of her ladies-in-waiting, and when it was all discovered the following year they found themselves both in the Tower – in separate cells, as Ralegh's numerous enemies were amused to point out. Even when released, Sir Walter was banished from court, and it took him years to regain a partial return to favour.

Elizabeth was as conscious as most of her court that she alone had raised Ralegh to great eminence. Essex, on the other hand, had royal blood in his veins. Through Thomas of Woodstock, Duke of Gloucester, he traced his ancestry from Edward III. An ancestor, Eleanor de Bohun, had been the sister of Mary, wife of Henry IV. Another, Anne Woodville, had been the sister of Elizabeth, wife of Edward IV. His grandmother had been Anne Boleyn's sister. There was almost too much royal blood in his veins, as Elizabeth was to decide later. But for the moment it counted in his favour. And his choice, though perhaps it aligned him too closely with the Walsingham faction, was otherwise a highly respectable one. Whereas Ralegh had married one of her ladies-in-waiting – this was the unforgivable sin: a breach of his oath as Captain of the Guard, and of the girl's oath too. It was a direct affront to the Queen; and even when it was discovered there seems to have been no full submission or apology.

When it came to recovering the Queen's favour, Essex had the additional advantage of being thirteen years younger – and so handsome and chivalrous and so much the popular hero. And it may have been that for all Ralegh's loyalty – and this never wavered towards the Queen, terribly to his detriment in the last two years of her life – the dark, haughty brilliance of his mind was a challenge to hers, as other men's were not, and that, although at first fascinated, almost hypnotized by it, she later, when the spell began to wear off, unconsciously resented the challenge.

Just before his disgrace, Ralegh had the mortification once again of mounting a naval expedition in which he was to play the leading part, this time in company with Sir John Borough, and once again of being recalled to court, while Sir Martin Frobisher was appointed in his place. But neither Borough nor Robert Crosse, Ralegh's vice-admiral, would serve under Frobisher; so the expedition broke up and went its several ways, Frobisher to sail to Cape St Vincent, only to feel the full weight of Spain's new naval power and be forced to run for cover. Borough and Crosse, however, succeeded in capturing the seven-deck, two-thousand-ton *Madre de Dios*, the richest prize of all the war, and bringing her into Dartmouth. Here scenes of pillage and looting took place which were so uncontrollable that Elizabeth, who had only just consigned Ralegh to the Tower, was forced much against her will to release him in company with a gaoler to try to restore order. This he quickly did, since he was as popular with his sailors and Devonshire country folk as he was unpopular with the courtiers of Westminster and the citizens of London.

Sir Richard Grenville, the commander of the *Revenge* off the Azores in 1591, who died after fighting a prolonged battle against fifteen Spanish ships

AN· DÑI ·1571·
ÆTATIS·SVÆ
·29·

For a time these and smaller raiding successes, which helped to disrupt the Spanish trade routes, disguised the lack of purpose in English naval policy. It looked for a time as if Philip did not intend another Armada, but planned instead to establish a naval base somewhere along the Channel coast so as to harass English shipping at its source. So England's chief energies were still directed to helping Henry IV in France and Maurice of Nassau in the Netherlands. Between 1589 and 1595 Elizabeth sent five armies to France in support of Henry, and by the latter year Henry could call himself King in more than name, in spite of individual pockets of League resistance and in spite of an attempt on his life by a Jesuit youth. Guise was made governor of Provence in an attempt to heal the schism, and Henry, to fulfil his obligations to his chief ally, declared war on Spain in January 1595. By the Edict of Nantes full rights, religious and civil, were granted to Protestants and Catholics alike.

In the Netherlands a new English commander, Sir Francis Vere, proved to be the most successful ever sent, both as a soldier and as a friend of the Dutch. And for the first time the two nations fought together and worked together in complete harmony. Parma's successor in the Low Countries, the Count of Fuentes, a Portuguese of noble birth, was another very able commander who, taking over after a brief interim period, soon brought the Spanish troops up to their old level of efficiency and discipline and was a combatant to be respected by both Maurice of Nassau and Henry of France. Indeed, he besieged and took Doullens, only forty miles from the French coast south of Boulogne, and then swung east and took Cambrai too. In the meantime the Spanish penetration of the Brittany peninsula went on – indeed it sometimes seemed that Henry, preoccupied with emergencies nearer his capital, left the defence of Brittany entirely to Elizabeth – and in 1594 the Spaniards, having been able to land strong support for their troops at Blavet, opposite Lorient, marched across country and seized and fortified Crozon, a rocky promontory overlooking Brest harbour. Quite clearly their next move would be to take the city and so obtain a near-Channel port.

This was not to be tolerated, so a joint expedition under the two veterans, Sir John Norris and Sir Martin Frobisher, was launched with a substantial army and a fleet of eighty sail, and after weeks of sporadic but bitter fighting the Crozon fort was captured and the remains of its garrison put to the sword. Leading his sailors up a ladder over a wall, Frobisher was shot in the thigh. So close was the gun discharged that wadding entered the wound. It was allowed to remain and caused blood poisoning, from which the tough, quarrelsome, courageous old sailor eventually died.

So went the first, if the least, of the great triumvirate of sea captains and strategists who had fought against Medina Sidonia in 1588. In England at this time the other two were making ambitious plans which were to lead equally to their own end.

12 *Ralegh at Cadiz*

By 1592 Philip II was sixty-five, and he was ageing quickly. Gout and arthritis constantly plagued him, and he had withdrawn more and more into the monastic life of the Escorial. When in that year there was an insurrection in Aragon he made the long and difficult journey across the mountains to Segovia, Valladolid, Burgos, Logrono and Tarazona, where the Cortes was waiting for him, and received its expressions of loyalty and a grant of six hundred thousand ducats towards his expenses of war. On his return to Madrid he was thought to be a dying man. The doctors warned him that unless he reduced the amount of work and took more regular and prolonged rest he could not hope to survive.

The famous *Junta de Noche* had been in existence since 1588, whereby a few intimate counsellors worked far into the night with the King, formulating policy and carrying out his secret instructions; but from 1592 it became still more exclusive, the King's closest advisers being Don Cristoval de Moura, who was a Portuguese, and Don Juan de Idiaquez, a Basque; and it was seldom that directives were not signed by Idiaquez on behalf of the King. Philip also recalled the Cardinal Archduke Albert from Portugal to act as Regent if he were to die while Philip, his sole surviving son, was only fifteen. The thirty-three-year-old Albert was the son of the late Maximilian II, the enlightened ruler of Austria and Germany, and therefore Philip's second cousin. He was also Philip's nephew and brother-in-law, and, in the almost incestuous way of the time, was in a few years to become his son-in-law, when he married the Infanta Isabella, Philip's beloved daughter.

The following year the King's health improved again, and he was able to bend all his considerable energies once more to the prosecution of the war. Setbacks in the Netherlands and in France, induced at least partly by English support, convinced him that his only hope of military success was by way of naval supremacy. His spies reported that Drake was emerging from the eclipse he had suffered and was much at court now; and there were rumours that he would soon be let loose again. In the Parliament

Isabel Clara Eugenia, the elder daughter of Philip II and his third wife, Elizabeth of Valois

Godolphin House, Helston, Cornwall, the home of Sir Francis Godolphin, who opposed a small landing of Spaniards at Mousehole in July 1595

which met in February 1593 both Drake and Ralegh had argued for a new and aggressive naval policy against Spain. Ralegh had also been active in planning a new adventure to Guiana, and in 1594 sent out his emissary, a Devonshire captain called Whiddon, on a reconnaisance to the Orinoco. All this trespassed on the King's domains.

Where, however, when it was assembled, should the next Armada be directed to land? Ireland was, as always, in a state of smouldering rebellion, and a landing there with several thousand troops could set the whole country aflame. Then a bargain might be struck that Spain would only withdraw from Ireland if the English agreed to withdraw from the Continent. Or another descent on the Isle of Wight, this time to capture it and possibly to parley with Elizabeth from there. To attempt any ferrying of troops from the Netherlands was clearly impracticable without a French port. But Philip as always was reluctant to land in support of the Irish; and in any event an occurrence in 1595 had the effect of turning his attention elsewhere.

In July of that year the aristocratic Don Carlos de Amesquita, commanding a squadron of four Spanish galleys with their accompanying small craft on a routine cruise, raided a fishing-village in Brittany and then was blown by adverse winds across towards the Scillies. Running short of water, he decided to put in on the Cornish coast and get water and to see what was to be found. It was not of course unusual for Spanish warships to be about in those waters. In May of that year a shallop from Blavet had captured a St Keverne fishing-boat in Falmouth Bay and taken its crew prisoner; a month later there had been galleys close in to the savage cliffs of St Eval on the north coast; following that there were twenty enemy sail sighted off the Manacles. The English coastal towns, particularly the west-country towns, lived ever on the *qui vive*. What was exceptional about this was that the Spanish captain dared to land. But Captain Amesquita had aboard with him at the time a noted English renegade called Captain Richard Burley, who knew the coast well and no doubt directed the landing at Mousehole.

It was a startling success. The population fled in panic and Amesquita landed two hundred men, pikes and musketeers, and burned the village, then sent pickets up the hill and they burned Paul Church and several hamlets around. Sir Francis Godolphin rushed an urgent message to Plymouth for help, supposing this to be the opening move of a full-scale invasion; but the Spaniards returned to their ships, rowed two miles across Mount's Bay and landed again at Penzance, which they fired also. Godolphin tried to rally opposition here, but apart from his servants none would stay with him, and the Spaniards, four hundred of them now, celebrated Mass on the western hill and took an oath to build a friary on the spot after they had conquered England. Then, learning of the nearness of a fleet under Drake and Hawkins, they took advantage of a favourable wind and made off for Brittany.

It was the first time Spanish soldiers had ever landed on English soil, and the weakness of the opposition was something that Philip was not to forget.

If the galleys had not left when they did they would in fact have been trapped by Drake, who at last had received a commission to go to sea again. It was tardy and reluctant when it came, and the Queen, no longer sure of her old hero, appointed the even older Hawkins to sail with him as joint commander. No doubt she felt that in sudden crisis or emergency the sager counsels of Hawkins would keep Drake in check. Hawkins was by now sixty-three, a tired man who had spent much of his life in the service of his country, who was unwell and had no desire to go to sea again; but he accepted the commission as an order from the Queen. Drake was only just turned fifty and was itching to resume his role as England's greatest sailor. But neither of them quite appreciated the change in sea power which had taken place in the six years of their retirement.

In any event the shared command soon proved to be a grave error – as shared commands always do. Their fleet, though small, was well found, with six of the Queen's ships and twenty-one other warships of varying sizes. It carried as colonel-general of the army Sir Francis Baskerville, another of the new officers, who had so distinguished himself against Parma that, in a brief period of truce, Parma had embraced him and told him that there was no braver soldier alive.

Four days out of Plymouth Hawkins discovered that Drake was carrying three hundred men more than he had provisions for – they had so flocked in he had not had the heart to turn them away – and proposed to raid the Canaries first to levy a ransom of new supplies. There was a quarrel between the two captains which Baskerville attempted to heal by appealing to Hawkins's good nature. In the end this early diversion was agreed to.

Partly because of these dissensions, they just missed a fleet of thirty carracks carrying something like ten million ducats' worth of treasure. Drake was bitter about this, but had they met them they would also have encountered twelve of Spain's best galleons which sailed as escort, so the misfortune might have cut both ways. Then when they reached Las Palmas they found the fortifications of the town so strong and newly developed that they had to call off the attack and sail for the Indies, having watered on the other side of the island but without further provisions.

It was the end of October before they reached Guadeloupe, and there they lost one of their smaller ships, the *Francis*, which had been lagging behind and was captured by five of the new fast and well armed galleyzabras. News of Drake's coming therefore preceded him to Porto Rico, where an attempt to land failed with the loss of many men and several of his best officers. At the same time Sir John Hawkins, who had been a sad man and failing throughout the voyage, died; and this cast a deep gloom over an expedition which was as thoroughly pursued by bad luck as so many of Drake's earlier enterprises had been by good.

Leaving Porto Rico, the fleet now made a succession of other raids on the

The city of Panama, unsuccessfully approached in a raid by Sir Francis Baskerville and a land party during the expedition made by Sir Francis Drake and Sir John Hawkins in 1595

way to Panama; some modestly successful, some repulsed by the new defences. Where they were not repulsed, a scorched earth policy deprived them of most of the booty. Unimpeded by any Spanish fleet attack, for his name was still dreaded everywhere, Drake at last reached Nombre de Dios, where the fort was taken, the town burned and the shipping seized. Baskerville was sent overland with seven hundred and fifty men on the old Panama road, but after three days in constant wet weather, which ruined his supplies and rendered his muskets useless, he came on hills and a ravine heavily defended by Spanish troops and knew his march to be useless. He could only retire to the ships, which he did by the 2nd January and so ended yet one more of Drake's hopes.

There was nothing now to do but go on and try to find some treasure somewhere to carry home, but at Escuda de Veraqua, an island near the coast, so many of the crews were ill with dysentery that barely enough were left to man the ships. Then Drake took it, and, in order to find healthier air, the defeated fleet again put to sea. At sea on the night of the 27th January 1596, Sir Francis Drake died. He was buried three miles off the town of Puerto Bello, and so many others were sick or dead that his prizes and two of his own ships had to be sunk over his grave so that enough sailors were left to man the rest home.

It is probably true that Elizabeth never fully forgave Drake for his failure to destroy the remnants of the first Armada in Santander in 1589, for, although she allowed him to go on this final raiding venture and provided him with some of her excellent smaller ships, she did not reserve him to lead or assist in the much bigger venture which was being planned for 1596. This had not, of course, been approved when Drake sailed. In typical Elizabeth fashion it was not approved until the last minute, though it had been in the air long enough and indeed in preparation.

What brought it to sudden implementation was the turn of events in France. Henry IV was now king in more than name, and his war against Spain had prospered to the extent that only in Brittany and Picardy and parts of Normandy were the Spanish still established. But there were endless disagreements between the Allies, and the French people were impoverished and heartily sick of war. There was talk of the Pope mediating and negotiating a separate peace between France and Spain. Into this situation came the Archduke Albert, fresh from Philip's council and the strongest man in Spain. Injecting new life into the Spanish army of the Netherlands, he began to move towards the Channel ports. This caused alarm both in France and in England; but in reply to Henry's urgent request for more English help, Elizabeth said that she could only do this if in return the French would give Calais into English keeping. It was an answer which bitterly annoyed Henry. 'I would as lief be bitten by a dog as scratched by a cat,' he observed.

As indeed he was, for while both countries were hanging back waiting for the other, quietly confident anyway that Calais was in no immediate danger, the Archduke switched his direction and sent a flying column north under de Rosne. Calais was quite unprepared for the attack, its fortifications almost in ruins and its garrison inadequate. By the 17th April the Spanish were in the city, and a week later they took the citadel and massacred its defenders. Later they fanned out south, taking Ardres and Guisnes. This brilliant coup struck dismay into all three of the allies, but particularly into England; for Spain at last had its Channel port available for a future Armada.

At first it seemed probable that the projected fleet being made ready to attack Spain on her own coasts would be cancelled; but on the 24th May, Elizabeth signed a new treaty with Henry, and from then on, saving the customary vacillation, there was no pause until the fleet sailed.

This was another 'joint' command, the Lord Admiral Howard himself sharing it with Lord Essex. There was a slight but wise division of responsibility in that the former was given precedence at sea and the latter on land. The fleet consisted of forty-eight fighting vessels, including some of the finest warships, and eighty transports and victuallers. It was divided into five squadrons: the first under Howard, again in the *Ark Royal* of eight hundred tons; the second under Essex, in the *Due Repulse*; the third under Lord Thomas Howard in the *Mere Honour* of nine hundred tons; the fourth under Sir Walter Ralegh in the *Warspite*; the fifth, a Dutch squadron under Admiral Van Duyvenvoord, Lord of Warmond, in the *Neptune*. It will be noticed that the names of ships built since the Armada were beginning to appear on the English side too. Both *Due Repulse* and *Warspite* were brand-new ships, launched only that year and the last to be laid down in Elizabeth's day. The tonnage of the *Due Repulse* was seven hundred and seventy-seven and of the *Warspite* six hundred and forty-eight. About six thousand five hundred troops sailed under Sir Francis Vere, two thousand of them veterans from the Netherlands. There were nearly a thousand gentlemen adventurers, many of them titled youths seeking fame more than fortune.

Just before the expedition was due to leave, Sir Francis Baskerville arrived off the Scillies with the remnants of Drake and Hawkins's fleet, having fought a successful engagement on the way home with the fleet sent out by Spain to intercept him. Barely four hundred of his men were left alive. Thrilling rumours of Drake's successes had been reaching England over the last few months, and this crushing news of the total failure of the voyage, coupled with the death of both Drake and Hawkins, was a terrible blow to English morale. This later and stronger expedition had been partly organized to cover Drake's return.

News of Drake's death had been greeted in Spain with overwhelming joy. Lope de Vega, who had sailed and suffered with the First Armada, wrote a poem of praise and thanksgiving; and to many a devout Spaniard it seemed that the sins they had had to expiate were now at last forgiven them. But the news had the mistaken effect of persuading the Spanish that any proposed English raid on their coasts would certainly now be cancelled, what with the death of their two greatest seamen and the threat of a Spanish-occupied Calais.

By the united persuasions of Essex, the Howards and Ralegh, and by that of Maurice of Nassau, who had a true conception of the strategy of war, Elizabeth did not change her mind, and the fleet left England on the 3rd June and in just over two weeks was off Cadiz.

It was a moment of pent-up passion for the English leaders. The triumph of 1588 was eight years behind them – already a part of history. Since then, apart from numerous successful minor ventures, the picture had been a dismal one. The utter failure of the Lisbon expedition to fulfil its primary purpose. Grenville's death and the capture of the *Revenge*. Howard's flight. Drake's defeat and death. Hawkins's defeat and death. A Spanish garrison seven leagues from Dover. Another one in Brittany. Spanish galleys off the Cornish coast landing with impunity and burning villages and churches and saying Mass. Another Armada partly built.

At daybreak on the brilliantly clear morning of the 18th June, while the fleet was thirty miles off Cadiz, Howard captured an Irish barque bound for Waterford and learned that in the harbour were twenty galleys and sixty ships, among them four of the Apostle galleons, the *San Andrea*, the *San Felipe*, the *San Tomas* and the *San Mateo*. It was an opportunity not to be missed.

The reconciliation between Essex and Ralegh, fresh from his tremendous adventure in search of El Dorado, had been begun last year, and this year it had warmed to sincere friendship. It was fortunate that this was so, for the exigencies of the next hours was to put a strain upon tact and understanding. On the Friday Ralegh, much against his own wishes, was ordered away to try to cut off an argosy of ten ships which the Waterford captain reported had just left Cadiz for Lisbon. He returned on Monday, having run one of his quarry aground but lost the rest in fog, to find that he had not as he feared missed the attempt on Cadiz, but that it was about to begin, in a way which offended all his best tactical instincts.

Lacking the genius and the splendid arrogance of Drake, Howard and Essex had held a number of councils at which differing views had successively prevailed; then the weather had turned adverse; and now Essex was committing himself to a frontal attack with soldiers on the sea side of Cadiz where a creek called the Caleta ran into the sea. With the surf rough, all advantage of surprise lost, and four galleys drawn up inshore to oppose the landing, this was an attempt bound to result in enormous casualties among the landing troops – they were in full armour and when spilled into the sea sank like stones; and Ralegh rushed aboard the *Due Repulse* to try to stop the landing before the assault troops were too far committed.

It was a difficult meeting, at which Ralegh did not mince his words, and Essex at first haughtily refused to alter his dispositions, declaring it was all the fault of the Lord Admiral for refusing to force the bay until Cadiz was

MEDIO ET TEMPORE

S.r Francis Vere

Sir Francis Vere, who commanded the *Rainbow* in Sir Walter Ralegh's attack on Cadiz in 1596

taken. Eventually however the vehement arguments of the older man took effect, and Essex agreed to call off the assault if Howard would admit the error of his own arguments. At once Ralegh swung down into his pinnace and was rowed across to the *Ark Royal* where Howard standing stiffly at the taffrail awaited him.

We do not know what charm Ralegh used on the essentially reasonable old admiral, but presently Howard agreed to a complete reversal of the order of assault, and Ralegh was back in his pinnace calling to Essex as he slid past '*Entramos! Entramos!* we're going in!' Essex threw his hat in the air, and a burst of cheering broke out along the bulwarks of the *Due Repulse*, to be caught up by sailors on all the nearby ships. They were going in as Drake had gone in. What had been done before could be done again.

But reorganization of the ships, and re-embarking of the soldiers already in the boats, took several hours; and they missed the tide. Ralegh, having saved the precipitate and foolhardy landing, now counselled caution; there could be no surprise; then let all be got ready for the following dawn.

At ten that night in the great cabin of the *Ark Royal*, with the yellow lanterns gently swaying, and all the captains, generals and admirals present in their gold braid and rich velvets, Ralegh put forward his plan of attack, as if he had quietly insinuated himself into a position of supreme command. And when all had agreed his plan, the position of honour, the privilege of leading the attack, was accorded him in the *Warspite*.

So at first light of dawn next morning the attack began. During the night the Spanish galleons, which had been drawn up in defensive formation opposite Fort St Philip, had retired a mile or so more into the neck of the inner harbour, with the intention of blocking the entry at its narrowest point where the two pincers of land were less than a mile apart. To reach the Spanish ships the English therefore had to run the gauntlet of shore fire from Fort St Philip and from the town. The *Rainbow*, under Sir Francis Vere, trying to catch the wind nearer the Cadiz shore and so steal ahead of her larger rivals, was the first to come under fire, and she had her sails shot to ribbons. *Warspite* was the next to receive attention, but the range was greater and she suffered no hurt. Ralegh ordered his trumpeters to blow a triumphant blast on their trumpets every time the batteries fired.

It would be satisfactory to record that some of the naval discipline reluctantly adopted by the English captains during the later stages of the Armada fight remained with them in 1596; but in fact each captain was so eager to get at the enemy that he looked on every other captain with a sort of angry rivalry. These were huntsmen, leaping every fence, taking every risk, and jostling each other dangerously to be in at the kill.

The fair channel at its narrowest point between Puntal and Matagorda was almost blocked by the four Apostle galleons, anchored head to stern across the passage, and behind these were two Portuguese galleons, three Italian armed merchant ships and a group of Levanters. Three of the galleyzabras – out of their element in a battle in such a confined space – were

in the shallower water of St Mary Port, and a group of galleys lurked under the protection of Fort St Philip. Into this defensive formation the whole weight of the English fleet crashed: Ralegh in the lead by half a ship's length in *Warspite* from Lord Thomas now in *Nonpareil*, Sir George Carew in *Mary Rose*, Sir Robert Southwell in the *Lion* and Sir Conyers Clifford in the *Dreadnought*. Ralegh made first for the *San Felipe*, 'being resolved,' as he wrote later, 'to be revenged for the *Revenge* or to second her with mine own life'.

Like the others, Ralegh had been forbidden to hazard a Queen's ship by boarding – this was to be left to fly-boats later – but after a heavy exchange of broadsides lasting two hours Ralegh stormed across to see Essex, demanding that this prohibition should be lifted. Essex agreed and said he would go in with him. But in the twenty minutes Ralegh had been away his rivals had stolen up on him. Vere, coming up in the tattered *Rainbow*, had slid around ahead of the *Warspite*; also Lord Thomas Howard in *Nonpareil*. So Ralegh ordered Captain Oakes to up anchor and seize the initiative again, even at the risk of going aground and losing his ship. Then *Due Repulse*, forcing a way in, collided with *Dreadnought*, and both ships were out of the fight for half an hour. In the confusion Ralegh dropped his anchors again so that he swung athwart the tide and so sheltered the others from the fight, but

213

Rainbow and *Nonpareil* threw lines aboard him and warped themselves into the front line again. 'The shooting of the ordnance was great,' wrote Vere, 'and they held us good talk by reason their ships lay athwart with their broadsides towards us, and most of us right ahead, so that we could use but our chasing pieces.'

In the three-hour battle *Warspite* suffered the most of the English ships, but the Spanish were in much worse shape. All had been holed repeatedly and many of their guns fell silent, either put out of action or for lack of crews. As the English edged nearer, the Spanish galleons at last slipped their cables and began to drift further inshore. Within a matter of minutes both the *San Felipe* and the *San Mateo* had grounded, 'tumbling into the sea heaps of soldiers,' wrote Ralegh, 'so thick as if coals had been poured out of a sack in many portholes at once; some drowned and some sticking in the mud.' Both these fine galleons were fired by their captains to avoid capture, and presently blew up: ' . . . many Spanish drowned themselves; many, half burnt, leapt into the water; very many hanging by the ropes' ends by the ships' sides, under the water, even to the lips; many swimming with grievous wounds, stricken under water and put out of their pain, and withal so huge a fire and such tearing of the ordnance in the Great Philip . . . if any man had a desire to see Hell itself, it was there most lively figured.'

This was virtually the end of the sea fight, but in the last minutes of it Ralegh was wounded in his leg, which was 'interlaced and deformed with splinters' – and would limp from it for the rest of his life – so he took no part in the storming of the city of Cadiz: a wonderful but bloody exploit in which Essex, Vere, Bagnal, Savage, Morgan and others performed prodigies of valour. Sir John Wingfield, one of the most daring of the leaders, was killed as the last of the resistance was collapsing. But many of the inhabitants fought bitterly from house to house – one of the most ruinous of all forms of war. One enormous Franciscan friar killed nine Englishmen before being overwhelmed. Orders had been given by Essex that there was to be no burning of the city, and although a few soldiers inevitably got out of hand on the first night, this was brought under control, and two men were hanged for molesting a woman. Priests and churches were spared and fifteen hundred nuns were permitted to leave – even politely assisted to. 'Such a gentleman,' said Philip when he heard, 'has not been seen before among heretics.'

On the night of the conquest Ralegh had himself conveyed by his men into the city. All along he alone of the commanders was concerned with the treasure-fleet, which had retreated into the Port Royal basin. He tried to find Howard to convince him of the necessity of seizing the ships at once, but Howard would not split his forces, and since there was no way out of the harbour except past the narrow entrance where the English ships and the Spanish wrecks lay, he felt they could wait. While the flota was being bargained for on the following day the Spaniards fired the fleet. Thirty-six vessels were destroyed and treasure valued at twelve million ducats was

John Donne, the poet and divine, who sailed with the 1596 expedition against Cadiz

lost. The loot of Cadiz, enormous though that was, was trifling compared to this. It was a tragic loss to England, a supreme sacrifice on Spain's part. The King approved it but the merchants concerned were bitterly antagonized: they would rather have paid the ransom.

The English remained in full possession of Cadiz for two weeks, debating whether to stay in permanent occupation or to go. They buried Sir John Wingfield with full military honours in the cathedral, while the whole fleet fired guns and dipped flags in salute. John Donne, who was with the expedition, wrote a poem on Wingfield's gallant death. The following day they held a state banquet in the Friary of St Francis, and in Stow's words: 'After dinner they made a great many knights, even all almost that did deserve it or affect it or not neglect or refuse it (as some did).' In all sixty-four officers were knighted. In the Armada Howard had knighted only five. Essex's prodigality in honouring his friends was a continuous source of irritation to Elizabeth.

In the end the invaders left Cadiz, for disease was spreading again and they had great quantities of booty to carry away. At the last, through a misunderstanding, most of the churches were fired and the city left in utter ruin. It was a fitting overplus revenge for the burning of one small church in Cornwall. On the way home the English landed at Faro, sacked the town and made off with the library belonging to Bishop Osorius. This became part of the Bodleian Library at Oxford.

They missed, however, by a matter of two days the great West Indian convoys which reached Lisbon safely in late July.

The shock to Spanish pride and Spanish finance by this invasion was enormous. Drake's raid in 1587 was puny by comparison. They had lost the whole of the treasure-flota, plus one hundred and twenty thousand ducats in ransom money; four of the fine new Apostles (*San Felipe* and *San Tomas* sunk, the *San Andrea* and the *San Mateo* captured and taken to England), five Biscayans, four Levanters, two galleasses, three galleyzabras, and three Italian ships laden with stores and artillery for the Low Countries, plus a host of small ships. It was an Armada in itself. As a result of this defeat and the financial loss entailed, Philip had to default on the payment of the whole of the bills of the Archduke Albert in the Netherlands: about one and a half million ducats; and on his own loans he offered only 45 per cent payment. Banks and commercial houses went into liquidation and there was a panic on the exchanges.

But its effect on the King's health was remarkable. He had been seriously ill again at Easter, but the news of the shattering defeat at Cadiz was like a shower of cold water on him. He began to move more quickly, his red-rimmed eyes grew bright and alert, his capacity for work returned.

In his reaction to the loss of Cadiz, as in so much, he reflected the feelings of the Spanish people. They were tired of war, lethargic, financially impoverished, disunited; but the events of Cadiz galvanized them and brought them together again with one common purpose. Money flowed in from the Church, from the Cortes, even from the provincial towns. The court, the petty noblemen who proliferated throughout Spain, the clergy, the peasants, all were demanding that now, at whatever cost, the Second Armada must sail. Whatever the cost in money and lives, Cadiz must be avenged.

13 *The Second Armada*

The man chosen to command the new Armada was Don Martin de Padilla Manrique, Adelantado Mayor of Castile, Count of Santa Gadea and Knight of the Order of Alcantara; in fact the man the Duke of Medina Sidonia had suggested should take his place in 1588.

At least ten years older than Medina Sidonia, Padilla had had a long and continuous experience of war, having received his baptism as a junior officer at St Quentin in 1557. Nine years later he was made commander of four galleys of Sicily, and the next year led eight hundred sailors against the Moors of Granada. In the great battle of Lepanto in 1571, 'the new Salamis', he sank four Turkish ships. In 1585 he was Captain General of the galleys of Spain, but did not take part in the Armada of '88, possibly for the reasons already stated. In 1589 he was concerned in the defence of Lisbon against Drake and Norris. In 1591 he captured three English and twenty Dutch vessels in the Gulf of Almeria, east of Malaga, and had generally been the scourge of Anglo-Dutch trade in the Mediterranean.

This hardy and experienced fighter, now about fifty-six, was appointed *Primer General de la Armada del Oceano* and instructed to lead a fleet against England that year. He protested – as most admirals appointed by Philip seemed doomed to protest – for the fleet was far from ready and the great blow struck at Cadiz had seriously weakened its fighting power. Nor can it have been easy to have followed in Medina Sidonia's wake, knowing in full the disaster of '88 and the obloquy heaped on the Duke's head. Any captain facing the same enemy in the same waters would be doubly concerned to avoid a similar catastrophe.

Of course in some ways circumstances had altered much for the better. The Spanish galleon was a greatly improved fighting vessel; many of them were recently built and most of their captains were of a new generation and spoiling for a chance to wipe out the stain of their predecessors' defeat. Nor, with Blavet and Calais in Spanish hands at either end of the Channel, was there any risk of a similar kind of disaster. True, Archduke Albert, between the two fires of a resurgent Netherlands and a hostile France, could hardly commit his army to an invasion of England as Parma could have done. But although Philip knew that Henry had entered into an agreement with Elizabeth that neither should make peace with Spain without the other, there were signs that Henry was wavering. If he could be detached . . .

And England itself still appeared to be militarily undefended – just as she had been in 1588: militia, trained bands, raw farmhands brandishing pikes, gentlemen on horseback with swords but no armour. The professional regiments of England were quite different; no one could fail to respect them; the reports of Parma, Mansfeld, Fuentes, and Albert were plain to read, and Philip was not so foolish as to disregard them. But nearly all England's professional soldiers were in the Netherlands or Brittany. England lay unguarded except for her navy. For instance Falmouth: as fine a natural harbour as you could find in the world, yet little better defended than Penzance where Don Carlos de Amesquita had landed with such success. The renegade, Richard Burley, reported to the King that for the defence of Pendennis Castle at the entrance to Falmouth harbour the Captain, John Killigrew, had only himself, a deputy captain, a master gunner, two other gunners and a porter, and the 'trained' bands of Budock to call on in need. And, by way of arms, some old cannon, two lasts of powder and forty muskets.

It was a great temptation; but all through 1596 Philip had been beset by letters from Hugh O'Neill, Earl of Tyrone, appealing for his help in saving Catholic Ireland from the English. Tyrone was a master of diplomatic intrigue and quite brilliant at playing friend to both sides; but in 1595 he was forced into open rebellion, and by 1596 his need of Spanish help was urgent. Not only had he and O'Donnell and Maguire and MacWilliam Burke written repeatedly and separately to Philip begging for an army to help them to preserve the Catholic faith; but when none came Tyrone and O'Donnell sent a joint letter to Prince Philip asking him to intercede on their behalf with his father. They asked that the King might be persuaded to help 'this most excellent and just cause, that of assisting Catholic liberty and of freeing the country from the rod of tyrannical evil, and that, with the help of the Divine Majesty, he may win for Christ an infinite number of souls, snatching them from the jaws of hell, and may wholly destroy or compel to return to reason the ministers of satanic fury and the impious disturbers of the Christian state.'

It was an appeal that was difficult to ignore. Two Spanish officers had brought back a precise statement of what Tyrone wanted. He had men, already far more than the English; but most were untrained and nearly all lacked arms. A stiffening of Spanish troops would set the country aflame.

One can picture the long sessions of the night during which this matter was debated by the *Junta de Noche* in Philip's simple study in the Escorial. The flickering candles, the windows open to the soft September night, the old King crouched behind his desk fingering his crucifix, one foot up on the

Tiles showing famous Spanish soldiers, at the Palace of Viso del Marques, once the residence of the Marquis of Santa Cruz but now a naval and military museum, near Almuradiel

THE MARINERS MIRROVR

Wherin may playnly be seen the courses, heights, distances, depths, soundings, flouds and ebs, risings of lands, rocks, sands and shoalds, with the marks for thentrings of the Harbouroughs, Havens and Ports of the greatest part of Europe: their seueral traficks and commodities. Together with the Rules and instrumēts of NAVIGATION.

First made & set fourth in diuers exact Sea Charts, by that famous Nauigator Luke Wagenar of Enchuisen. And now fitted with necessarie additions for the use of Englishmen by ANTHONY ASHLEY.

Heerin also may be understood the exploits lately atchiued by the right Honorable the L. Admirall of England, with his Maiesties Nauie and some former seruices don by that worthy Knight S. Francis Drake.

stool to ease his gout; his close advisers seated in stiff wooden armchairs around the desk, two or three personal secretaries hovering in the shadows, the crackle of parchment, the scratch of quill, the dry murmur of responsible voices, a shaft or two of moonlight, colder than the candles, falling on the blue Talavera tiles.

In that room, after much weighing of the risks and opportunities, the decision was made that this time the Second Armada should indeed sail to Ireland. It was not an unwise decision, if the Armada had to sail that year at all; for the maximum embarrassment would be caused to the Protestant cause at the minimum risk. It was unlikely that there would be a fleet action of any sort, so if the fleet sailed in an incomplete condition the consequences need not be so serious. Troops and supplies the Irish wanted. A single voyage of the fleet to Sligo or Galway would carry a sufficient army with all provisions for a campaign and land it on friendly soil. The Armada would then return to Spain, and during the winter regular supplies could be ferried up from Coruña and Blavet. By the summer of '97 another armada could be got ready to invade England.

So with remarkable speed for those days a scratch armada was assembled in San Lucar and in Lisbon and made ready to sail in October. It was to consist of over one hundred ships, with some thirty galleons including the remaining eight 'Apostles'; and picked regiments of soldiers were withdrawn from Flanders and Spain to man it. The number sailing was nine thousand Spanish and three thousand Portuguese, and it was arranged that more soldiers should join it from Brittany. New galleons were being built in most of the Biscay ports, but these would not be ready in time. Pedro de Valdes, newly released from his long exile in England, where he said there was much war-weariness and desire for peace, requested that he might go as vice-admiral, but this post, not unnaturally, was refused him. Only de Bertendona and Arumburu of the former officers were given important commands.

Even for this, the smallest of the three main armadas, the preparations were immense, the provisioning a mountainous achievement of the Spanish commissariat. A list of provisions shipped – published by the Spanish Ministry in October – includes 12,837 barrels of biscuits, 696 skins of wine, 1,498 barrels of salt pork, 1,031 barrels of fish, 6,082 barrels of cheese, 2,858 barrels of vegetables, 2,900 barrels of oil, 850 barrels of vinegar, 2,274 barrels of water, 631 barrels of rice; this apart from the requirements of war such as 1,200 barrels of powder, 30,000 cannon balls, 1,300 bullets, 700 cables, 200 wheels, and 50 wagons.

In England, which had as excellent a spy system as Spain, news of the coming reprisal was soon received. For all the striking success of the capture of Cadiz, the financial gain to England – as against the loss to Spain – had been small, and Elizabeth had been bitterly disappointed, for she too desperately needed the money for survival. So the fleet had once again been laid up at Chatham, the soldiers disbanded; Vere had been sent back to the

221

Netherlands with the crack regiments, and England again lay relatively undefended. Nor were Pedro de Valdes's reports of war-weariness so wide of the mark. From 1594 onwards had been years of great rainfall in England, with corn rotting in the fields and grain at famine prices. 'Our July is like to February,' people said. In Devon in midsummer 1596 wheat was nine shillings a bushel, which one might multiply forty times to arrive at a modern equivalent. Although there was undiminished loyalty to the Queen and great pride in such adventures as that at Cadiz, this was matched by wide discontent throughout the country over the conditions of day to day living, with dispossessed farmers, ruined smallholders, and crime and vagabondage everywhere. Areas of the country were becoming waste land for lack of cultivation, villages were emptying and falling into ruin, beggars were crowding into the coastal towns. Justices of the Peace were urged to go back and live in their country houses and to care for the poor of their own parishes; but they themselves were hard hit by the double subsidies imposed by parliament, by having to pay for the musters and trained bands of their parishes, by trying to enforce unenforceable laws in dealing with desperate and starving men.

But once more the cumbersome and hideously expensive processes of mobilization had to be gone through to try to avert the threatened invasion. Two thousand veteran soldiers bound for Picardy under Sir Thomas Baskerville were halted at Dover, Sir Samuel Bagnal was posted to defend the Isle of Wight, Ralegh hastened down to Cornwall, ten of the best of the bigger warships were recommissioned, and relays of dispatch boats were kept at sea to give warning of the enemy's approach.

The problem was, as in 1588, that no one knew where the blow would fall. At a council-of-war summoned by the Queen, Essex said he expected the Spaniards once again to attempt the Isle of Wight or the Margate coast. Lord Burghley thought they would attack Falmouth. Willoughby thought it would be Ireland, Lord North thought the Isle of Wight, Sir William Knollys said Plymouth, Ralegh said the Thames, Carew agreed with Essex. So all through a wild November the country was on the alert. The weather at times was so bad that even the screen of scouting vessels could not get out of port, and they the most weatherly of ships.

In fact by then, though no one knew it, the danger for that year was past. On the 24th October the Adelantado had set sail from Lisbon with his unfinished but still formidable Armada. In vain he had protested to the King that the season was already too late: no ships in those days, not even the English, made war in November. It was inviting disaster. But the King would brook no delay so the fleet sailed, and four days out disaster duly struck. Off the north Portuguese coast a storm, violent even for that month of storms, blew in from the west. It was worse than anything in 1588, and in a matter of days the Armada was destroyed. Seven galleons were wrecked between Finisterre and Santander, and twenty-five armed merchant ships and forty other vessels. Three thousand men were drowned, among them

Sir Walter Ralegh's study at his home, Sherborne Castle, Dorset, which he built in 1594

many Irish, Catholic English, friars and Jesuit priests.

It was the end of the King's hopes, of Spain's hopes, and indeed of Tyrone's hopes, for another year. The Protestant God was still looking after the heretics.

As 1597 dawned it became clear that both countries, though weary and impoverished by the long war, were building up for a final trial of strength. The destruction of the Second Armada had not in any way weakened Philip's resolution, nor, for that matter, that of his ministers and intimates. The Adelantado himself saw this year as the one in which the errors and shortcomings of last year should be repaired. In the spring the Third Armada would begin to assemble in Lisbon and in Coruña and this time it would all be ordered differently. Early in the year an expert pilot was dispatched in a vessel trading under the French flag to make a new and full survey of the English coast. When completed the report filled eighteen sheets of parchment and covered all the most useful harbours from Liverpool in the north-west, through Chester, Milford Haven and Bristol, right round the coast to Scarborough, Newcastle and Berwick in the north-east.

Liverpool is described as 'a good harbour after entering within, broad and deep, but the entry is dangerous and to be approached by soundings; it is encircled by sand banks. There are many Catholics in this region . . . The mouth of the harbour at low water has six fathoms and four within. There is room for 300 ships. The land is inhabited but there is no fortress there. There is water, meat, bread, an abundant countryside and everything is priced cheaply.'

North of Milford Haven 'is a bad coastline, and on this account every year many of those fishing for herring are lost. Milford is the finest port in England; sixteen fathoms at the mouth and within there are seven or eight fathoms . . . There is no fortress and but one tower at the entrance. On the right side it usually has two pieces of artillery, but these cannot prevent an entry. It is six leagues to the head of the river. There is an open village, with water, meat and grain in abundance. There are many Catholics and the people are the natural enemies of the English and do not speak their language.'

The document was sent to Philip, who consulted with his ministers but for the present kept his own counsel. He had ideas for the Third Armada as definite as for the First, for he had not forgotten the outstanding success of the galleys at Mousehole and Penzance. So that part of the pilots' report which privately he must have studied most closely ran as follows:

From Cape Lizard to Falmouth is eight leagues. At the fourth league care must be paid to the rocks which are called Manacles, which are on the shore side.

On the left side before entering Falmouth there is a harbour called Helford. At low water there is six foot at the mouth and at high tide twenty-four feet; within at low water there is four fathoms. The harbour has room for 200 ships. The port

is a haven for the corsairs and robbers of England, for there is not any fortress to restrain them.

In the middle of Falmouth harbour there is a rock named Falmouth which can be passed on one side or the other. There are four fathoms at the mouth at low water, and, within, it is eighteen fathoms. It will hold any number of ships. At the two points of the harbour there are two castles, one on each shore, with much artillery. On the right side it is flat, but both reach to the middle of the channel. Care must be had of some shoals on the right side after passing the isle. Almost all the artillery is emplaced outside of the two castles together with their gabions. They can be taken by land with a small party of men. There is a large population, but it is not warlike. There is water, meat and grain.

Queen Elizabeth was now sixty-four – and a vigorous and healthy sixty-four at that. Paul Hentzer, a foreign traveller in England, writes of a visit he paid to her that year at Greenwich. He was met at the door of the hall by a gentleman 'dressed in velvet, with a gold chain, whose office was to introduce people to the Queen'. In the hall were a large number of people, including the Archbishop of Canterbury, the Bishop of London, most of the Privy Counsellors, and officers of the Crown and other gentlemen. When the

Pendennis Castle, Falmouth, described to Philip II as guarding the harbour with strong artillery

English costumes of the
16th century

Queen came in she was attended by 'Barons, Earls, Knights of the Garter, all richly dressed and bareheaded, followed by the Lord High Chancellor of England with two other gentlemen, one carrying the royal sceptre, the other the sword of state in a red scabbard studded with fleur-de-lys'. The Queen, he says, was 'very majestic, her face oblong, fair but wrinkled, her eyes small, jet black and pleasant, her nose a little hooked, her lips narrow, her teeth black'. She had two pearls in her ears, an auburn wig set with a small crown, her bosom was uncovered, as was the English fashion with all ladies until they married, she was of medium height, her hands slender, her fingers long. She was 'dressed in white silk bordered with pearls the size of beans, with a mantle of black silk shot with silver threads, her train was long and borne by a marchioness'. She spoke very graciously as she went along, in English, French and Italian. 'Whoever she speaks to is kneeling, unless she raises them up. Sometimes she pulls off her glove as a special favour for her hand to be kissed; then it is seen to be sparkling with rings and jewels.' Wherever she turned her face they fell on their knees, saying: 'God save the Queen!' To which she replied: 'I thank you, my good people.'

At dinner that afternoon – the Queen now having retired – a gentleman came in bearing a rod, and another carried a tablecloth and spread this upon the table with great veneration and then retreated. Two others followed, one again with a rod, the other with a salt-cellar and plate and bread. Then 'a beautiful young lady (a countess) and another older woman' came with a tasting fork and rubbed the plates with bread and salt with 'as much reverence as if the Queen were there'. Then the Yeomen of the Guard came in, a hundred of the biggest men in England, bearing in at each turn a course of twenty-four dishes, served on silver-gilt. These were received by one of the first gentlmen and put on the table, where 'a Lady tastes a mouthful of each dish that be brought, for fear of poison. During all this, twelve trumpets and two kettledrums make the hall ring for half an hour'. At the end of this a number of the Ladies in Waiting appeared to convey the food to the Queen's inner chamber for her to make her choice. The rest of the food went to the ladies of the court. 'The Queen dines alone with very few attendants.'

Round the Queen at this time, among her counsellors, an unusual and unexpected harmony prevailed, particularly with regard to England's foreign policy. Burghley and his second son, Robert Cecil – recently created Secretary of State – though seeing peace with Spain as their ultimate objective, sided for once with the two fire-eaters: Essex, soon to be Earl Marshal of England, and Ralegh, just restored to his old post as Captain of the Queen's guard. The latter two wanted to defeat Spain; the first two thought that one more blow now would bring an ultimate reconciliation nearer.

It is also possible that the quietly calculating Robert Cecil knew that naval adventures abroad involved not only physical hazard for the leaders but also – if they failed – damaged prestige. His position close to the Queen could hardly fail to become closer while her two favourites were off fighting the country's wars.

So unanimity of counsel persuaded the Queen to sanction another expedition similar to last year's. But its destination this year must be Ferrol, where the bulk of the new armada was assembling. After that the intention was to seize Terceira in the Azores and cut off the year's treasure-flota. When this was planned it was also intended that a strategic reserve of some of the most powerful warships should be kept ready at Chatham, as in 1588, as a second guard against the Armada; but sheer lack of money and supplies prevented these ships from being commissioned. Indeed, a request made to the City of London – usually the most willing of donors – for a squadron to augment the royal fleet was met with an apologetic excuse and a plea of complete impoverishment.

This time, the Lord Admiral Howard pleading his age not to go, the expedition was to be led by Essex in undivided command, with Lord Thomas Howard as Vice-Admiral, Ralegh as Rear-Admiral and Admiral Van Duyvenvoord again leading a Dutch squadron. Although Sir Francis Vere went as Marshal, the military command was given, much to Vere's chagrin, to Lord Mountjoy, one of Elizabeth's younger favourites.

In France in March the Spanish under Archduke Albert took Amiens, and Henry IV's position was materially weakened. Then the Spanish turned and

Robert Cecil, First Earl of Salisbury and Secretary of State, who supported the plans of the Earl of Essex and Sir Walter Ralegh, made late in Elizabeth's reign, to overcome Spain by war

227

threatened Boulogne. There was a partial mobilization in England to meet the new threat, and for a time it seemed that the old familiar counterstresses of the long war would prevent the naval expedition from sailing. But as in the previous year the English refused to be diverted and the fleet preparations went ahead. Seventeen royal warships – of which two were the Spanish 'Apostles' captured at Cadiz and modified to meet English ideas – twenty-four Dutch warships, a similar number of transports and supply ships and various ancillary vessels, made a total of ninety-eight, carrying six thousand soldiers and five thousand sailors.

It was the objective of both Philip and Elizabeth to be the first to strike; and news of the assembling fleet reached Coruña in May where the Adelantado was struggling to get the Third Armada into shape. But the Groyne, though an admirable harbour, was too distant from the centres of Spanish administration, and the accumulation of supplies went on with desperate slowness, for as soon as they were assembled they were consumed. Sailors deserted even faster than they did in England, and too many already lived in too confined a space, so that disease was endemic. About the bare hillsides the soldiers camped in tents, talking in a half dozen languages and dialects, spending their leisure dicing or sleeping, swearing or drinking or whoring, while the priests kept their temporary chapels open for Mass all day long, the militia patrolled, and the white dust settled over all.

The harbour of Ferrol, which is twelve miles from Coruña, is approached through a narrow channel that can be guarded from the rocks on either side, and it is even more defensible than Cadiz. When the news reached Padilla that the English fleet would be ready well before his own, he put out a screen of guard-boats, manned mainly by Ragusans – for he was desperately short of good Spanish sailors – and stationed four of his oldest and biggest merchant-ships ready to block the harbour entrance in case of surprise.

The transport of heavy artillery by the Spanish in the 16th century

Ferrol was not of course to provide the fleet, but it was to be the assembly point and the nucleus. The galleys of Genoa were to make their way there under Prince Andrea Doria; also a strong Andalusian squadron under Don Marcos de Arumburu, with smaller contingents from Naples, Guipuzcoa, Vizcaya and Vigo. In the meantime the main fleet, under the supreme direction of the Adelantado, was to be led by Don Diego Brochero, Knight of the Order of St John of Jerusalem, and a man who in vigour and experience matched the Recalde of 1588. About forty-eight at this time, he had had a chequered career, having at one time served a prison sentence for privateering with his own galleon in the Mediterranean. An energetic advocate of reform in the Spanish navy, he was known as a leader of great courage and resource.

Below him, after Bertendona, were the new men: Urquiola, Oliste, Villaviciosa and Zubiaur. The last of these, a hardy and adventurous Basque of fifty-five, had been at sea since he was sixteen, but had interspersed his maritime life with periods spent in England. Coming first in 1580, as 'a merchant of Seville', overtly to negotiate the restoration of, or compensation for, some of the plunder brought to England by Drake, Zubiaur in fact had remained as a spy, reporting direct to Philip and by-passing Mendoza, the then Spanish Ambassador. Implicated in one of the unsuccessful attempts to assassinate William of Orange, he had been in and out of English prisons during the next few years, and in 1585 had been sent to the Tower for being involved in a plot to seize Flushing (from the early days one of the centres of Dutch resistance) and other activities directed against the state. After two years, during which he was tortured, he had been exchanged for English prisoners, and at the time of the First Armada was in Flanders. After he made his way home, and after the Spanish landing in Brittany, he had been put in charge of the Biscayan galleys which with notable success had for five years

ferried supplies and reinforcements up to Blavet from the Spanish ports.

And behind the scenes of the Third Armada was the influential Captain Pedro Lopez de Soto, the newly appointed Secretary to the Adelantado, a fanatic to get to sea and a man in constant personal touch with the King. Indeed, such were his activities, that he might almost be looked on as approximating to the dark-suited man in the modern police state sitting behind the commander to see that he keeps up to scratch and toes the party line. In his confidential letters to the King de Soto frequently remarks that the Adelantado's complaints about lack of supplies and the unreadiness of the fleet are exaggerated and defeatist and should be ignored.

In the first week of July the English fleet, which had been pinned in Dover and Chatham by contrary and violent winds for nearly a month, at last managed to get as far as Weymouth, where it picked up reinforcements and supplies before moving on to Plymouth. It left Plymouth for Spain on the Sunday afternoon of the 10th July, but almost immediately was scattered by a short but violent storm, and each squadron became separated from the others. There was a brief interval of good weather and then a worse gale than ever blew up from the south-west and almost destroyed the English fleet. John Donne, who had again sailed hoping to find his fortune, found instead scope for his descriptive pen.

> Then note they the ship's sicknesses, the mast
> Shaked with this ague, and the hold and waste
> With a salt dropsy clogged, and all our tacklings
> Snapping, like too high stretched treble strings;
> And from our tattered sails, rags drop down so
> As from one hanged in chains a year ago.

Ralegh was blown back into Plymouth, trying successfully to save the two ex-Spanish galleons which stood the gale even less well than the English ships. Essex, after a contest lasting a day longer, put into Falmouth with his *Merhonour* sinking under him. Van Duyvenvoord lost touch with his own squadron trying to keep company with the damaged *Merhonour*, and returned to port with Essex. Thomas Howard and his squadron missed the absolute worst of the storm and arrived off Ferrol as arranged; he cruised up and down for several days, putting the Spanish defences into a panic, before despairing of his comrades and returning to England.

This storm, which seemed to suggest that after all God might be impartial, was a signal respite to the Spanish, for several of the English ships needed extensive repairs – the *Merhonour* in particular – before they could be considered seaworthy again; and the raw 'pressed' English seamen ran through the fingers like sand, as Ralegh put it. Many of the gentlemen adventurers went home too.

Howard's parade off Ferrol also lulled the English into a false sense of security. If the Adelantado could not come out to fight a half dozen English warships challenging him on his own doorstep – and this in July – there seemed little chance of his being ready to do anything offensive this year at all. So the leaders began to think less seriously of their original mission of attacking the assembling Armada, and more of capturing the treasure fleet again, or even of a West Indies raid in the old style of Drake. Even the news that the now famous Captain Pedro de Zubiaur had moved out of Ferrol and sailed along the Biscay coast to Blavet with seven galleys, some supply ships, and two thousand veteran soldiers did not seem to disturb them greatly, though the west country defences were strengthened against the possibility of another galley raid like last year's.

When the English fleet at last got to sea again in mid-August it was much more a naval adventure than the month previous; but Elizabeth had left her commanders in no doubt that they were still expected to attempt Ferrol before they went off on any adventures in search of treasure fleets. She also insisted that Essex must not hazard his life in attacking the port, a prohibition which meant that Essex immediately lost interest in the attempt; and when transports were not ready to accompany the fleet, and there was a favourable wind, he insisted on sailing without them. It seems clear that despite the lack of success which had attended Drake's Lisbon voyage of 1589, the leaders were bent on following in his footsteps, and if at all possible they intended to find an excuse to disobey the Queen.

Again the weather was unseasonably violent and the fleet was scattered. Ralegh's *Warspite* lost a mainyard, the *Repulse*, with Essex in her now, was leaking badly, and the two ex-Spanish galleons were so damaged that they were only saved from wreck by taking refuge in La Rochelle. Then while the scattered ships were reassembling off Finisterre the wind set strongly east, making an attempt to beat back to Ferrol a long and difficult process. This was the excuse Essex needed, and after a brief consultation he followed Ralegh and Howard to Lisbon.

Cruising off there, attempting to catch one of the small Lisbon carvels to pick up information, they stopped instead an English barque which told them that Ferrol was in fact empty of their prey and that the Adelantado and most of his Armada were in the Azores to cover the return of the treasure-fleet. Whether the captain of the barque was misinformed or whether he was one of the renegades such as Burley and Elliot, deliberately sent out to spread false news, it is impossible to tell. But the news so exactly suited the commanders of the English fleet that they immediately and gladly acted on it. By the time the various units reached the Azores and assembled there it was the 18th September.

14 The Third Armada

It did not seem to occur to anyone in the English fleet that the reason the Adelantado did not respond to Lord Thomas Howard's challenge was that he would not hazard some of his ships in a small and indecisive action off his own coast, nor did he wish to betray his strength or preparedness – or lack of it – to a scouting squadron of the enemy. The English assumed his weakness – and later his absence.

And the English at home felt equally secure, waiting for news of some great feat of arms from their own fleet, not at all worried, as they had been last year, about a possible visit from the Spanish. Sir Henry Palmer in charge of a small Channel squadron – the only defensive squadron at sea – was ill, and his place had been taken by Sir John Gilbert. The rest of the Queen's ships were out of commission at Chatham. The military defences of the country, though in a far better state of organization than in 1588, were not on the alert.

In 1588 every Englishman knew that the great Spanish *Empresa* was coming to attack them. It was common knowledge throughout Europe, and everyone in England was at the stretch to meet the threat. Bonfires were tended and beacons manned day and night. The whole English fleet was either mobilized or on the verge of mobilization. In 1597 no one suspected or feared an imminent attack. If surprise is half the battle, then the Adelantado had a battle half won.

But in spite of an urgent command from Philip, who saw the possibilities plain, Padilla took his time. He still did not know his destination. No one in the fleet did – it was a matter on which even de Soto bitterly complained to the King. But intensive preparations were still going ahead. Every ship had been issued with an English flag, and all carried English-speaking personnel. The Proclamation still exists which was printed for the Adelantado for distribution and exhibition when he landed in England. It is the first printing ever done in Portugal in the English language, and the text was obtained some time later by a Cornishman, one John Billett, master of a trading vessel,

Prepared by the Spaniards for bringing to England by the Third Armada, a proclamation in English reproduced here from the copy smuggled out of Coruña by a Cornish sea-captain in his shoe

ONSIDERINGE The obligation, vuhich his catholike magestye my lord and master hathe receaued of gode almighty forto defend and protect his holy faythe ant the Apostolical Romane churche: he hathe procured by the best meanes he could for to reduce vnto the auncient Cartreuue religion the kingdomes of Inglaud and Ierland as muche as possibilly hathe beyn in his pouer: and all hahe not beyn sufficient to take auuay the offensis doun agaynst god, in domage of the selfe same kingdomes vuith teaidall of vuholl cristianity: eye rather abusinge the clemency anel benignity et his catholike magesty: the heade and chiff of the heretikes vuith littill feare of god haue taken corage for to extende theyr euell doctrine vuith the oppresinge of catholikes, mattering them, and by diuers vuayes and meanes taken from them theyr liues and goods, forsinge them by violence to folloue theyr damnable sects and errors, tho vuhich they haue doun vuith the loos of many soules. The vuhich cosilered his catholike magesty is determined to fauor and protect thos catholikes, vuhich cooragiously haue defended the catholike faithe, and not only thes, but also thos vuho for pusillanimity and humayne respects haue condescended vnto them, forced theyr vntethoroue the hard and cruell dealinges of the sayd heretikes. And for the execution of this his holy zeale, he hathe commaunded me, that vuith the forcis of sea and land, vuhich be and shalbe at my charge, to procure all meanes necessary for the reduction of the sayd Kngdomes vnto the obedience of the holy catholike Romane churche. In compliment of the vuhich i declare and protest that ne sayd forces only shalbe imployed for to execut this holy intet of his catholike magesty directed only to the common good of the treuu religio, and catholikes of the saydKingdomes, as vuell thos vuhich be already declared catholikes, as others vuho vuill declare them selfes for suche, for all shalbe vuell receaued and admitted by me in his riall name, mich shall soperat and apart them selfes fro the herretikes and furdermore they shalbe restored into theyr honors, dignityes and possessions, vuhich hearetofore they haue ben depriued of. Morouer euery one shalbe reuuardad accordinge vnto the demonstratioes aud seats vuhich he shall shoue in this godly interprise: and he vuho shall procead vuith most valor, more largly and amply shalbe remunerated vuith the goods of the obst ia theretiKes. Vuhearfor seinge god almighty doothe present vnto his elected so good an occasion: that vuith liberty and in publiKe they may confess the treuue religion: let not pass and escap so fitt an opportunity, seing they can not excuse them selfes et her before god or man: ether before god or man: ether can they lament of any body, but of them selfes. Aud for theyr more segurity i ordeare and commaund the captaynes Generals of horse and artillary, the master General of the fild, as also other masters of the fild, the Captaynes of companyes of horse and foot, and all other officers greater and lesser and men of vuar: the Admiral General, Genera Captaynes of squadrones, and the reast of the Captaynes and officers of the Army, that as vuell in land as in sea, they vse uue l and receaue vuith all curtesy the catholiKes of the sayd Kngidomes, vuho shal come to defend the catholiKe cause vuith arms or vuitout them: for i commaund the General of the Artillary that he prouidethem of vuepones vuhich shallbringe none. Also i ordeine and streatly commaund that they haue particular respect vnto the houses and familyes of the sayd CatholiKes, not toucking (as muche as is possible) any thinge of theyrs but only thos vuhich vuill obstinatly folloue the part of the heretiKes: in doing of the vuhich, they be alto gether vnuuorthy of thos fauors, vuhich be heare graunted vnto the good, vuho vuill declare them selfes for treuue catholiKes, and as suche shall taKe armes in hand or at least seperat them selfes fro the heretiKes, agaynst vuhom and theyr fauorers all this vu ar is directed in defence of the honor of god, and good of the sayd Kingdomes: trustinge in gods diuine mercy, tha they shall recouer agayne the catholiKe religione so longe ago lost, returne to theyr auncient quietnes aud felicity, and to the diuu obedience of the holy Romane churche norouer the sayd King domes shall inioy theyr former immunithys and priuilegis vuith increase of many other for the tyme to come, in great frendshipp, confederation and traffic vuith the Kingdomes of his catholiKe nagesty, vuhich in tymes past they vueare vuount to haue for the vniuersall good of al Christianiry. And that this be putt in execition, i exhort all the faythfull to the fulfilliug of that vuhich is heare conteaned, vuarranting them vpon my vuord (the vuhich i gue in the name of the catholiKe Knge my lord and master) that all shalbe obserued vuhich heare is promised. And thus i dicharge my selfe vuith the losses and domages, vuhich shall fall vpon thos, vuho vuill folloue the contrary vuay vuith the ruyn of theyr sooules, he good of theyr ouune country, and that vuhich is more the honor and glory of god almighty. And he vuhich can not taKe presently armes in hand, nor declare him selfe by reasone of the tiranny of the sayd heretiKes shalbe admitted, if being in the enemges canp, shall pass vnto the catholiKe part in some serimishe or battell, or if he can not pass, should fly, before vue shall come to the last incounters. In testimouy of all the vuhich i haue commaunded to dispache this present, firmed vuith my ouuen had, aud sealed vuith the seale of my armes, aud resirmed by the secretary vnderuuritten.

The great Adelantado of Castilla earle of sant Gadea and of Bundia commendador of Salamea Captayne General of the gallyes and army of the occan sea, and of the catholiKe camp.

who called in at Coruña and brought the paper away hidden in his shoe. The Proclamation promises freedom and fair treatment for Catholics and for all who turn Catholic and calls on them to rally to the support of the Spanish invaders.

The reason for the Adelantado's delay in sailing in September is one of the most vital questions of the whole Anglo-Spanish war, and no absolute or single explanation can be given. For instance on the 4th July de Soto, writing one of his private letters to the King, says the fleet should be ready to sail by the middle of August with an effective landing in England on the 8th September. He gives the details of the ships available then: twenty-three large galleons, twenty-five smaller galleons, twenty-six supply boats, a number of galleyzabras and about seventy pinnaces to land soldiers rapidly – the force to consist of twenty thousand soldiers and four thousand sailors. And de Soto was on the spot in the midst of all the preparations, not writing airily from Madrid.

Yet in mid-September, when the greatest opportunity of the war presented itself, the fleet still remained in port. The reasons for the delay can only be speculatively listed: (1) The Adelantado was not only dealing with pressed men, as the English were, but with impounded ships and pressed captains. Whatever the hard core of Spanish fighting ships wanted to do, the Flemish and German hulks, the Italian and Ragusan supply ships, were not at all anxious to sail into those enemy waters where others of their kin had perished nine years ago. It is not easy to get a mixed fleet ready to sail as a unit when considerable parts of the unit are seeking cause for delay. (2) After a sudden and astonishing return to health during the summer, when he went hunting and had a wild boar turned loose for his own entertainment, the seventy-year-old Philip was taken seriously ill in early September; and as always happens when one hand alone holds all the power, the reins fell loose at a most crucial stage. (3) The appearance of the English fleet off Lisbon had put Portugal in a panic, and at least until news was confirmed that the English had actually been decoyed to the Azores, Arumburu and his Andalusian squadron of eleven fine galleons dared not leave Lisbon undefended. Then contrary winds kept them embayed. (4) Rumours were widespread in Spain that England had sent ambassadors to Turkey attempting to form an alliance against Spain (a heretic banding with an infidel against the true faith), and in August it became known that thirty-four ships under Mami Pasha had left Constantinople and were cruising in the Mediterranean. This menace, combined with a sudden attack of French Protestants, who had advanced across the eastern Pyrenees into Catalonia, caused Prince Andrea Doria with his squadron of ships and three whole *tercios* of Italian veteran soldiers to halt at Lisbon and come no further; and presently indeed he returned to the Mediterranean.

The Adelantado, not unnaturally at first, waited for his expected reinforcements to come up: it is not in many admirals to want to sail with two-thirds of a fleet. But Philip as soon as he recovered sent an urgent messenger spurring across the dusty Sierras and the mountains of Galicia to instruct Padilla not to delay a moment longer but to leave at once. So embarkation began on the 25th September.

This took two days, and it was late in the morning of the 27th before the first galleon was able to make sail and be under way out of the narrow jaws of the harbour. The fleet had orders to assemble in Betanzos Bay, fifteen miles from Ferrol, and this took another thirty hours to complete in gusty and none too favourable weather. But there they at last were assembled in six lines, each line consisting of ten galleons of varying sizes and fourteen other ships, hulks, transports and flyboats; and there they were inspected by the Adelantado from a decorated barge rowed by twenty-four crimson-clad oarsmen. His own personal standard, an enormous swallow-tailed flag in green silk, fluttered and dipped from the maintop of the *San Pablo* of twelve hundred tons. The whole fleet was dressed with flags and standards, and the men lined the decks and cheered and guns were fired as the supreme commander passed. According to Agostino Nani, the Venetian Ambassador, the fleet consisted of forty-four Royal galleons, sixteen private galleons and fifty-two urcas or hulks, of a total tonnage of thirty-five thousand. In addition there were seventy-six smaller ships, and the complement was four thousand sailors and eight thousand six hundred and thirty-four soldiers, besides three hundred horses, together with mules, carts, mills, field artillery and siege material. Some historians put the final muster even higher than this. In Cheyney's words, it was 'scarcely less in strength than the Armada of 1588'.

Even then there was a hesitation before sailing, for the weather was poor and the winds threatening, and they awaited a flyboat from the Azores confirming the position of the English fleet. This arrived on the same day as a further message from Philip, now completely recovered. He promised that Arumburu and his Andalusian squadron would follow the Armada within a few days, but that in the meantime the Adelantado must brook no further delay, and any captain who created difficulties was to be hanged at once from his own yard-arm.

Man proposes, but in the days of sail even a threatened admiral could not defy the winds, and that night a gale blew up that pinned the fleet within Betanzos Bay for six more days, and it was the 9th October before at last the weather set fair and they were able to get away.

And at last the Adelantado was permitted to open his sealed orders.

He was to proceed to Falmouth and land his troops there. It was perhaps the best kept secret of the sixteenth century, and only perhaps four men apart from Philip had known what was in the sealed letter before it was opened. Once he had gained possession of Falmouth and left eight thousand troops in occupation of the peninsula, Padilla was to return to the Scillies and catch the English fleet on its way home, since he was enormously more powerful than they. But he was given freedom of action in this, depending on weather conditions, the success of the landing at Falmouth and what naval opposition, if any, he encountered in the Channel.

The fleet went on its way now with high hopes and in fine favourable weather. The first squadron was led by Don Martin de Padilla himself flying his green cleft pennant; the second by his vice-admiral, Don Diego Brochero in the *San Pedro*, of one thousand tons, with a yellow flag; the third by Don Martin de Bertendona, with a red flag, in the new *San Mateo*, of twelve hundred tons, just launched from the shipyards of Renteria to replace the one taken by the English at Cadiz. Orders were given that at sunset all ships of the fleet were to pass by the admiral's ship and to shout three times and sound their trumpets. Each ship as it passed was to ask the watchword for the night and what course to steer, and then to drop astern into its allotted position. The evening hymn to Our Lady, with her image held high, was to be followed by all lights out except those in the cabins of gentlemen, who had had their lamps trimmed with water covered with oil to combat the lurching of the ship; but no candles were permitted for fear of fire. At the stern of the *San Pablo* a cresset with flaming combustibles was to burn so that everyone knew the Adelantado's ship and could follow. When the wind was too strong for the cresset, a large lantern with four lamps in it was to be used instead. Each sunrise there was a fanfare of trumpets, and the ships came up to salute again, the *San Pablo* keeping under easy sail until this was done. Then a *Missa Sicca* (dry Mass without consecration) was celebrated before the Armada proceeded on its way.

Fine weather and favourable winds took the fleet quickly to Blavet, where Captain Zubiaur was waiting with his seven galleys, his extra supply ships and his two thousand picked infantry. In easterly winds the fleet then made for the Scillies, and after assembling there and a final council-of-war, Don Diego Brochero led his squadron as the advance guard against Falmouth. With him was the eager Captain de Soto in command of the *Espiritu Santo*, one of the new galleyzabras of three hundred and fifty tons, three other galleons, three of the Zubiaur galleys, twelve flyboats and a half dozen supply ships.

At this stage nobody in England knew anything about a possible Spanish Armada being out and almost on their coasts. The Lord Admiral Howard was about to be made Earl of Nottingham in reward for his distinguished services against the First Armada of 1588 and Cadiz last year. Parliament was meeting in leisurely session, and one of the subjects up for discussion was defence measures to be taken in the event of a Spanish attack the following year.

The security of that autumn in England is in the strangest contrast with the almost constant *qui vive* in which the country had lived for more than a decade. As will be remembered, only the year before there had been partial mobilization and a recommissioning of the fleet against the Second Armada. Almost all through 1598 there was acute apprehension; and in 1599 came the famous and most complete mobilization of all, when, as it turned out, no fleet sailed against England at all. On every other occasion throughout the long war Spanish preparations had been carefully observed and prepared

Plymouth in the 16th century

against. Spies had brought news, fly-boats had scurried home. Drake was waiting on the Hoe playing his immortal game of bowls. The fine ships built by Hawkins were waiting to warp out into the Channel to attack the oncoming enemy.

Not so this time. Sir Ferdinando Gorges was in command at Plymouth, but he had no warships at all to send out to battle. Those that were not laid up in Chatham were, apart from the small squadron patrolling off North Foreland, far out with Essex in the Atlantic returning from the Azores after yet one more unsuccessful attempt on the treasure-flota.

But after all the Protestant winds came just in time to save the country. The weather steadily worsened during the last day of the Armada's advance from the Scillies, and, when only twenty miles off the Lizard, a violent north-easterly storm broke in the Channel and the flagship of the advance guard, the *San Pedro*, was so badly damaged that she had to drop out of station and run before the wind. This at once robbed the enterprise of its most aggressive admiral; though Brochero, as soon as his ship was in a Biscay port, put to sea again in a flyboat to try to rejoin the Armada. At the same time the Adelantado, half a day behind with the main fleet, tried to ride out the storm. But the storm would not relent. It blew unabated from the worst possible quarter for three days, and one by one the Spanish galleons however hard they fought were broken and had to give up the unequal struggle. The Adelantado hung on and refused to give way until of all his great fleet only four other ships remained with him; then he had no recourse but to return to Spain empty-handed, as he had the year before, defeated not by the enemy but by the autumnal storms.

A few of the advance squadron, however, rendezvoused off Falmouth, as they had been instructed to do if scattered, and the appearance of these ships was the first notification the English had of the peril in which they stood. At least two of the contemporary foreign accounts say that the Spanish landed seven hundred soldiers near Falmouth, and these threw up defences, held them for a day or so; then when the rest of their fleet did not come they withdrew again. No English account mentions this, and it seems very improbable that there would not be some record of it if it had occurred. It is possible that some Spanish troops may have briefly landed at Helford, that 'haven of corsairs and robbers', as the Spanish pilot calls it. There are also stories of a landing on the north Devon coast.

Whatever the case, panic prevailed in England. Parliament was prorogued, all English troops in France were recalled, mobilization of the western countries was decreed and the Lord Chamberlain, the second Lord Hunsdon, posted down to organize the levies there; the big warships in Chatham were ordered into commission, Sir Robert Crosse rushed to take command of the Channel squadron. It was a tremendous shock, a tremendous blow to confidence, that this emergency should occur when the whole of the commissioned English fleet was at sea and England daily expecting news of some great and glorious exploit off the Azores. It was exactly what Elizabeth had feared when listening to Drake's 'forward' policy in 1587 and 1588.

It is interesting to speculate what might have happened if, instead of the bitter and seemingly endless gale, there had been a couple of weeks of golden autumnal weather to aid the Adelantado in his plans. Certainly he would have landed at Falmouth and thrown ashore six or eight thousand troops with minimal or no loss. The captain of Pendennis Castle at the time, John Killigrew, though of a staunchly Protestant family, had lived a rake's progress for twelve years, getting even deeper in debt than his father, similarly bent, had left him. As the *Salisbury MS.* puts it:

> Having brought himself into desperate case, he lived chiefly by oppressing his tenants, being a landlord in name only, by robbery of strangers in harbour there, by cosening his friends and neighbours, by selling her Majesty's provision of the Castle, by receiving of stolen goods, by consorting with pirates and abuse of his place and command.

The same MS. accuses him of treacherously conniving with the Spanish, a charge which, not unnaturally, he strenuously denies. In an MS. written some years after his death he is referred to as the man 'who sold his castle to the King of Spain'. Certainly the Spaniards looked on him as a friend; but, since his loyalty was never put to the final test, there is no proof of what his ultimate choice would have been. No charge was preferred against him in England, but as soon as the emergency was over he was called to London and imprisoned for the rest of his life, ostensibly for debt. In May 1598 he was writing that he had now been three months in the Gatehouse 'without knowing my offence'.

Whatever John Killigrew's choice, it could not have affected more than temporarily the Spanish landing, and, although the local population would no doubt have resisted where they could, there was no force in the west remotely capable of withstanding veteran troops skilfully deployed. In the meantime the English fleet was returning from the Azores with, apart from a brilliant feat of arms by Ralegh in capturing Fayal, nothing to show for its long and arduous voyage. The commanders were by now at bitter odds with each other; the ships were making for home anyhow, as best they could, in ones and twos and in haphazard groups; sickness was rampant among the crews after so long at sea, and many ships were short-handed. Most of the battleships had stowed away their big guns in the hold to ease the strained timbers after all the storms. Certainly the straggling, disorderly squadrons were in no condition to fight a fleet action.

That English command of the narrow seas would have been quite soon re-established there seems no doubt. With the Channel squadron reinforced by the great ships hastily recommissioning at Chatham, and a Dutch squadron to assist, the Spanish fleet could hardly have maintained its temporary supremacy. But how soon the Spanish in Cornwall could have been dislodged is an open question. It would have been no more difficult to supply the forces in Cornwall by sea than it was those in the Low Countries; and the Genoese, Frederico Spinola, was to demonstrate in 1599 how that could be achieved by his masterly use of that outdated warship, the galley.

Conceivably the Spanish would have been content with a short occupation of a piece of England in retaliation for the seizure of Cadiz. Conceivably they would have attempted to hold it permanently as a forward base for the harassment of English trade. Or they might have used it as a bargaining counter to force an English withdrawal from the Continent. At the best they were still hoping, of course, for a Catholic rising which would put all England in their hands. But most English Catholics had made their choice in 1588, and the militant Romanists – those who would actually have taken up arms to fight for a foreign power – were probably few. In fact England in the last two decades had become rapidly more Protestant in thought and sympathy. Those with Heaven to gain combined with those with property to lose, and the union had been fused in the heat and peril of the Spanish war.

But the value to England of the storms which wrote off so many of the already defeated Armada of 1588 was as nothing compared to the great north-easterly gale of October 1597, which in fact sank only one galleon, the *San Bartolomeo*, but which alone protected the West Country from suffering the horrors of a full-scale Spanish invasion.

The returning English fleet came back by instalments at the height of the scare. They had entirely missed contact with the Spanish in the wild waters of the Channel. Mountjoy was the first to come in at Plymouth on a change of wind with four of the Queen's galleons. They were all hardly used and the crews in a poor way, but their appearance caused an acute alarm. Soldiers rushed to the fortifications, people began to barricade their houses and prepared to fight as the Spanish had done at Cadiz. Not even the English flags fluttering at the mastheads could at first reassure them. On hearing of the emergency Mountjoy ordered the four ships to turn about and ride in the

The only 16th-century model of a Spanish galleon extant in Spain

Hamoaze, to be able to put to sea again at once to meet the Adelantado if he came in. Essex, arriving the following day, sailed incautiously right up the Catwater, so was caught and could not get out again. Ralegh with part of his squadron put in at St Ives on the opposite coast; and on hearing of the emergency he landed and galloped overland to take charge of the defences of Cornwall. Lord Thomas Howard arrived at Plymouth, and other ships of the returning fleet were blown in at various south coast ports. Here and there a Spanish ship appeared, giving fight to small English coasters or themselves surrendering.

Essex was in his usual fever of impatience to be at the enemy's throat, and wrote an emotional letter to the Queen in which he offered to eat ropes' ends and drink nothing but rainwater until they were at sea again and able to destroy the entire Armada that threatened them. The Queen was not assuaged. Indeed she was bitterly angry, for all that she had so often feared had happened – she had been right and her blundering war-advisers had been wrong. The English fleet had cost an enormous amount to fit out, and it had achieved nothing, nothing. What was infinitely worse, its absence had deeply imperilled the kingdom. She swore to old Burghley that she would never again let a fleet out of home waters, and she did not.

She wrote to Essex: 'Seeing already by your late leaving the coast upon an uncertain probability that no army would come forth from Ferrol until March, you have given the enemy leisure and courage to attempt us.' She then charged him not to leave the coasts again on any pretext, 'whereby our own kingdom may lie open to serious dangers; but that you do proceed in this great affair according to the rules of advised deliberation as well as affection of zeal and diligence. For treasure, for victual, and what may be fit for us to send, you shall find that you serve a prince neither void of care nor judgment what to do that is fit in cases of this consequence.'

It was a dignified letter worthy of a great Queen, and when Essex posted up to court to explain his actions and to enumerate his needs he was greeted with an icy disapproval, which upset him deeply. After the emergency was seen to be fully past, he withdrew to nurse his injured dignity at Wanstead. It was the beginning of another break between them; each one cut deeper than the last and left a more memorable scar. Essex was growing out of the brilliant and impulsive boy, handsome, charmingly wayward, ineffably brave and gallant, the idol of the unthinking crowd; middle age was turning his impulsiveness into obstinacy, his high spirits into arrogance; his popularity with the crowd gave him delusions of greatness beyond even his attainment. The Queen was as astute as ever beneath her feminine fads, as clear-sighted as she had been when she came to the throne; but in her last years there were hints of that sombre unpredictability of mood with which her father had made his courtiers tremble for their lives half a century ago. Less than ever now was she a woman to be trifled with, and in Essex's underestimation of her – as he underestimated everybody but himself – lay the seeds of his eventual downfall.

15 *The Fourth Armada*

In February 1598 Martin de Bertendona, the most successful of all the Spanish admirals in their war against England, sailed up the Channel with twenty-eight ships of varying size and power and a complement of four thousand troops. They were destined for Calais, and they reached there unchallenged and for most of the voyage as unannounced as the Adelantado's great Armada of the previous October. When news of this fleet reached England there was another emergency. Essex and Ralegh went hurriedly down to the south coast. The Earl of Cumberland, who was just off on a privateering raid with a small but sturdy squadron, was ordered to reinforce the Channel Guard.

But a landing was not attempted. The troops were intended as a reinforcement not only of the Calais garrison but of the bargaining power of Philip in his new negotiations with Henry of France – a show of the iron hand still available if Henry were not amenable to the velvet glove. And, like the escape of the German warships, the *Goeben* and the *Breslau*, into Turkish waters in 1914, the success of the stroke served to upset the whole delicate balance of power. France was half seduced, half intimidated into signing a peace treaty with her old enemy. Cecil, who had been about to sail to bolster up the weakening resolves of Henry with more promises of English and Dutch support, and was delayed by the advent of Bertendona, arrived in Paris too late to prevent the collapse of the old alliance. The Peace of Vervins was signed in late April.

When Elizabeth heard of it she called Henry, whom she had supported for so many years, 'the Antichrist of Ingratitude'.

But at Vervins in 1598 Henry gained almost as much by changing friends as in 1593 he had gained by changing religions. Both were primarily political moves to gain great objectives – they would have been betrayals of principle only in a more principled man. In 1596 Henry wrote: 'I have hardly a horse on which I can fight. My doublets have holes at the elbows and my pot is often empty.' A contemporary estimated that in the twenty years up to

1598 nearly a million French had died in wars and massacres; nine cities had been completely destroyed, two hundred and fifty villages burned, one hundred and fifty thousand houses reduced to rubble. It was a situation which Henry was determined to redeem or perish. By the Edict of Nantes he had already granted a large measure of tolerance and freedom to both religions in France, thereby reducing the likelihood of a return to the bloody civil wars. Now by the Treaty of Vervins the Spanish agreed to evacuate Picardy and Calais, to leave Brittany, to give up Blavet, to recognize Henry as legitimate King of France; and received in return only a recognition of their own rights in Burgundy, which, however, they promised not to assert by force of arms. For Spain it was a great strategic withdrawal, partly balanced by a diplomatic success. For France it was a major victory on all counts.

It removed from England the most obvious danger of a fourth Spanish Armada, but it deprived England for ever of the return of Calais, something dear to the hearts of most sixteenth-century Englishmen; and it marked the re-emergence of a strong and no longer necessarily friendly France. In justice to Henry it must be said that he had made some half-hearted efforts to include his old allies, but Spanish terms for the Dutch provinces were still unacceptable to the Dutch, and England would not desert the Netherlands.

Nor now would the Netherlands desert England. In the last few years, so rapid had been the expansion, commercially and militarily, of the United Provinces that an Anglo-Dutch alliance, instead of being the greater supporting the weaker, was becoming an association of equals. Within months of the Franco-Spanish peace, the English and the Dutch signed a new treaty whereby the Dutch agreed to repay the Queen by large instalments all the money loaned them and also all the expenses incurred in their defence over the years. If the Spanish fleet were to attack England the Dutch undertook to supply forty warships for its defence, and, if the Spanish landed, five thousand infantry and five hundred cavalry, all at Holland's own expense. Moreover, if the Queen wished to send another expedition against Spain the Netherlands promised to contribute an equal number of ships and men. It was a striking proclamation of the growth of Dutch power, which in the next century was to make Holland one of the most prosperous countries in the world and was to see the founding of the Dutch East India Company and the establishment of the great empire in the Netherlands Indies.

On the 4th August Lord Burghley, Elizabeth's oldest and most trusted counsellor, died at the age of seventy-eight. Her Spirit, she had always called him; and at the last, trying to rally him, she fed him with her own hand. With old adversaries and old friends dying about her, the Queen must have felt more than ever her lonely eminence. It was not now just a regal eminence but one which comes to all who live beyond their generation. So many had gone from around her: her beloved Robert Leicester, embittering the triumph of the Armada year; then Walsingham and Warwick, Frobisher and Drake and Hawkins, Hatton and Shrewsbury and the elder Hunsdon.

Sir Christopher Hatton, who was known as the 'Dancing Chancellor' because he had first won the approval of Elizabeth I at a court masque, and who served her as Lord Chancellor from the year before the First Armada till he died in 1591

Now Burghley. All about her were younger people, eager, thrusting, loyal, but *younger*, belonging inevitably to another world, without her *memories*. Who but she could remember her father, his later wives, her brother, her sister? There was none she could talk to in the old way, except Lady Warwick and old Lady Nottingham, the Lord Admiral's wife. Before this sort of loneliness even the disaster of war loses its importance.

Yet the responsibilities of kingship must go on, so long as life lasted, and she was giving up none of them. In her grief she found time to write James of Scotland a stinging letter rebuking him for having had the impertinence to send envoys to Europe asserting his reversionary rights. Let him beware, or the English crown could still be snatched from his feeble grasp. Then, only ten days after Burghley's death, news reached the English court of a great defeat in Ireland, one of the gravest ever suffered. Sir Henry Bagnal, marching with four thousand men to the relief of a besieged fort on the Blackwater, had been utterly defeated by Tyrone in a pitched battle, with the resulting death of Bagnal himself, thirteen other officers and about fifteen hundred men. With this victory resounding through Ireland a rebellion at once broke out, and, according to the *Annals of the Four Masters*, within seventeen days 'there was not an Anglo-Saxon left alive in all the Desmond domains'.

It was a situation which must be redeemed as quickly as possible by the dispatch of fresh troops; for such open rebellion as now existed was the perfect opportunity for Spanish intervention. (Just as Elizabeth had intervened in the Netherlands in 1585.)

Philip did in fact send a hearty message of congratulation to the triumphant Tyrone; even the Pope sent a crown of peacock's feathers; but unfortunately for the Irish earl Philip II was at last dying.

He had spent the winter in Madrid, still, with the help of his few intimates, holding tight to the reins of his great empire. He had had the Adelantado before him to make a full report on the failure of the Third Armada and to receive instructions for the preparation of a fourth, to sail in the coming summer. But when spring came he was so ill that his doctors would not allow him to return to the Escorial. At the end of June he defied them and announced his intention of going there to die, 'to lay my bones in my own house'.

So he was carried on a litter in great pain, it taking six days to cover the thirty-one miles. He now had four suppurating sores on the fingers of his right hand, another on his foot and an abscess on his right knee, from which could be pressed great quantities of foul smelling matter 'as thick as plaster of Paris'. He could not sleep or eat and his stomach was distended with dropsy. In this condition he remained for fifty-three days. After a while it became impossible to change the bed-clothes or his night-robe, and, following the purges given by his doctors, he lay for the last days in his own excrement, surrounded by swarms of flies and overrun with vermin, his eyes fixed on the high altar in the great church, thanking God for the pain and the

OPPOSITE Catherine, the younger daughter of Philip II and his third wife, Elizabeth of Valois

OVERLEAF In the Escorial, the palace and monastery built by Philip II between 1563 and 1584: the Pantheon, where he and his family are buried

humiliations. 'Look at me,' he said to his son. 'This is what the world and all kingdoms amount to in the end.' Dr Affaro who attended him, and the thirty-year-old Infanta, about to marry the Archduke Albert, were both taken ill from the insufferable stench in the sick-room. He died, holding a crucifix firmly in his hands, exactly at dawn on the 13th September 1598.

So died the first of the two great monarchs who had confronted each other across a war-torn Europe for exactly forty years, and who for the last ten had themselves been in open conflict. It is almost impossible to summarize the character of Philip. To the Protestant world he was a monster of evil, cold-blooded, vengeful, cruel, spinning his intolerable webs, a symbol of the Inquisition and the *Auto-da-Fé*, the 'Spanish fury' and the iron hand of oppression. In the Catholic world outside his own country he had always been unpopular, representing the slow-moving but irresistible colossus, the enemy of small freedoms as well as large, the military dictator, the religious bigot who yet used religion for the aggrandizement of his own state.

Nevertheless in Spain itself he was esteemed and popular and held in warm affection by his subjects. He represented so much that the Spanish people revered and prized, and under his rule they remained a united nation proud of their eminence as the masters of Europe. Yet even in his own country his reign was riddled with contradictions. When he came to the throne his father was already heavily in debt, so he put up titles for sale at five thousand ducats a head and in this way added a thousand petty new noblemen to the many who had already existed. The building of the Escorial cost three million five hundred thousand ducats over two decades; in it he assembled one of the finest libraries and one of the greatest art collections in the world. Under him poetry, literature, music and art flourished, and the golden age of Spanish painting began. Yet, although he commissioned Titian to paint a series of religious masterpieces for the Escorial, Titian complained to the end of his long life that he had not been fully paid for them. And when Titian's favourite pupil, the Cretan Domenicos Theotocopoulos, moved to Spain and settled in Toledo, there to become known simply as The Greek, or El Greco, Philip first commissioned him to paint exclusively for the Escorial, and then, not liking the first two paintings, cold-shouldered him and gave the work to a relative nonentity.

Philip converted Madrid, an old fortified town standing on a spur of rising ground at the foot of the Guadarrama Mountains high above the sea, into his new capital city, and largely rebuilt it. He fought an interminable war, lost his battles against the Protestants, unified the Iberian peninsula, saved the Mediterranean countries from the Turk. He gave his name to the Philippine Islands, where the Spanish conquest and rule was unusually mild and beneficient. He devotedly loved his children; yet when his eldest son began to show signs of the family insanity, he had him shut up in a room from which the young man never emerged alive.

Philip II in old age

Personally fastidious, quiet and modest, by turns kindly and cruel, forgiving and revengeful, he would not allow anyone to write his biography because he thought this an evidence of worldly vanity. Yet in the midst of all his war expenditure, when Spain was twice bankrupt, it never occurred to him to cut down on the vast cost of his own household, which absorbed over seven per cent of the total income of the nation and comprised more than fifteen hundred persons. Under his paternal rule for forty-three years Spain suffered no serious invasion, no rebellions – except one Moorish one – within its own frontiers, no religious schisms. Yet everyone in the country groaned under taxes or the results of taxes; men went overseas to fight or for conquest and the fields they left behind grew rank and untended. The King planted twenty thousand trees, but they were intended only for timber for his galleons. During his reign the population fell from ten million to eight million. The condition of the countryside is not exaggerated in *Don Quixote*. Although the monasteries and convents prospered, the inns were in ruin, so that travellers could hardly find a bed to rest in; roads, such as there had been, became rutted tracks, rivers were silted up.

A lover of flowers and music and dancing, Philip lived much of his life in a gloomy austerity that could hardly have failed to satisfy the most convinced Calvinist. A personal renunciation of the world within his palace doors went hand in hand with a rigid, fanatical determination to continue to control every aspect of the world outside. In his later years in particular, he lived in absolute piety, and once, it is said, spent three consecutive days making his confession. He died full of self-contrition for his sins against God but without a trace of self-doubt about any sin against man. It was a source of genuine remorse to him that he had frequently not carried out God's will with sufficient fervour. It did not occur to him ever to wonder if sometimes he might be confusing God's will with his own.

The war did not end with Philip. Elizabeth said of his son: 'I am not afraid of a King of Spain who has been up to the age of twelve learning his alphabet', but, after an initial period of paralysis, reports began to come in of a new vigour being injected into Spain's military and naval plans by Philip III's advisers. Indeed, the Adelantado, who had suffered a great deal of both frustration and intimidation from the old king, remarked that the world would now see what Spaniards could do when they were no longer subject to a ruler who thought he knew everything and treated everyone else as a blockhead.

In England strenuous efforts were being made to retrieve the situation in Ireland. By the end of March 1599 Essex, chosen after much ill-tempered discussion and intrigue to lead the relief troops, was in Dublin with the largest expeditionary force ever to leave England in Elizabeth's lifetime: seventeen thousand infantry and thirteen hundred cavalry. Part of the fleet, ten of its largest ships, were commissioned to protect the transportation of

Philip III, the son of Philip II and his fourth wife, Anne of Austria

Cahir Castle taken by the Earle of Essex in anno 1599

Cahir Castle, taken by the
Second Earl of Essex during
his expedition to Ireland
in 1599

so important an army; but it was not used, for the Dutch informed Elizabeth that they were sending a separate fleet of seventy ships against Spain to attack Coruña. This was partly provoked by new measures in Spain putting an end to the commercial trade between Spain and the Netherlands which Philip II had wisely tolerated; but the fact that Holland could now mount such a naval offensive was a mark of her rapid emergence as a power in her own right. The attack on Coruña was a failure, but the English rightly reasoned that with the Dutch fleet at sea Spain would be too busy to launch another armada against England.

So Essex transported his troops in safety and misused them so badly that by September he was back in England, to be cast into prison in the penultimate act of his life's tragedy. And his friend Mountjoy took his place and was as startlingly successful as Essex – and many others before him – had been a failure.

By July 1599 the Adelantado under his new master had concentrated once again a force of ships and armoury at Coruña. Thirty-eight galleons and great ships, fifty supply vessels, eight thousand troops, twenty-three galleys, again commanded by the seasoned admirals of the '96 and '97 Armadas: Brochero, Zubiaur, Bertendona, Villaviciosa and Oliste. News of these intensive preparations reached England at the same time as word of the complete failure of the Dutch fleet to damage the port, and in the middle of the month Captain George Fenner, perhaps the most distinguished seaman England had left, sailing in the *Dreadnought*, with Captain Matthew Bredgate in the *Swiftsure*, returned to Plymouth from a cruise in Biscayan waters with the news that the Adelantado was about to sail. His numbers were exaggerated to one hundred warships, seventy galleys and fifteen thousand troops.

The English council ordered instant mobilization, and for a while panic ran through the country. By the first week in August much of the English fleet was ready for sea and troops were pouring into the old Armada camp at Tilbury. On the rumour that the Spanish had already landed, chains were strung across the streets in London and coast towns, men barricaded their houses, levies rushed to their stations. Ralegh and Howard, Carew and Greville worked night and day to bring the country to a state of preparedness, and thirty thousand troops were concentrated on London; the whole of the south of England was on its feet. It was said that Philip III had himself sailed with his Armada and that he had vowed that he would 'make his finger heavier for England than his father's whole body'.

Rumour and counter-rumour flew, and Howard put to sea with twelve of the Queen's largest warships, fourteen of the new smaller vessels called 'crompsters', and a dozen armed merchantmen. In the Downs he was joined by the Channel squadron under Sir Richard Leveson and by a Dutch squadron of twelve ships with a promise of sixteen more under Justin of Nassau. It was nevertheless a puny force to pit against the reported fleet which had set out from Spain.

But the Armada never came; nor did it ever approach the Channel. Six Spanish galleys only appeared; but more probably it was the returning Dutch fleet – worn out with months at sea and decimated by disease – which, seen through the Channel mists, gave rise to the rumour that the Spanish had already arrived. In fact the Dutch, although they had failed at Coruña, had succeeded in diverting the Spaniards by sailing on to the Canaries and capturing Las Palmas. From there it was likely that they would attempt the Azores and the treasure-fleets, so the Adelantado, ready to sail for England, at the last moment had his orders countermanded and was directed to the Azores instead.

It seems certain that the excessive sensitiveness of the English in 1599 was caused by the near miss of the 1597 Armada – they must never, they knew, be so caught again. It was an enormous expense to counter a false alarm, and people murmured and bitterly complained; but at least it was a full-dress rehearsal if the play were ever to be put on, and it did prove not only to themselves but to Spain and all Europe how vastly the organization of mobilizing England's strength had improved since 1588.

The six galleys which had appeared in the Channel were no part of the Adelantado's fleet at all but were commanded by the young Genoese Frederico Spinola, who had fitted out the galleys at his own expense and during the next few years was to light up the last days of those outdated warships with a startling brilliance. The twenty-eight-year-old Spinola, Duke of Santa Severina, who had served his apprenticeship with his fellow Italian Parma in the Netherlands, had proposed to Philip II shortly before he died that by establishing a squadron of galleys in one of the Spanish-held ports on the North Sea it would be possible to help break the stranglehold on Spanish relief supplies to Flanders and at the same time interrupt the Dutch maritime trade on which they depended for so much of their growing wealth. Philip, now thoroughly disillusioned with the value of galleys as against sailing-ships, especially in northern seas, had given a grudging and qualified approval so long as it cost him nothing; and on this Spinola had acted.

Now, just as Bertendona had done the year before, the Genoese began to work his way up the coast, from Santander to Conquet near Brest, from Conquet to Le Havre, from Le Havre to Dunkirk. Unfortunately, unlike Bertendona, who had the good fortune to make his passage unobserved, Spinola's progress was spotted early on, and English and Dutch warships were sent out to destroy him. At each port where he put in officers deserted him, preferring to face possible charges rather than the certain death he offered. However, by stratagems, using his oars to better the winds, with clever seamanship and great courage, he completely outwitted the warships sent to intercept him. He eventually arrived in Dunkirk, his ships laden with treasure to finance the Archduke Albert's armies, and full of shipwrights and industrious Italian workers, who proceeded to dig out the harbour so that it was suitable for galleys to use, and built there, right under the noses of the enemy, new galleys and several small warships to harass their shipping. Spinola had only been in harbour a day before he slid out with two galleys and captured a Dutch ship and brought her in as a prize.

It was an augury of things to come. For three and a half years he maintained his position against the united attempts of both enemies to dislodge him, and continued to menace and raid English and Dutch shipping – indeed to take on their warships when the odds were not too great. So impressive were his successes that both the English and the Dutch were constrained to put the clock back and lay down galleys in an attempt to beat him at his own game – an extraordinary backward step in naval development which should have made Drake turn over in his West Indian sea-grave. Four were actually built by England, two being completed in 1600 and two in 1601. Meanwhile the Dutch built three: the 'Black Galley' of Dordrecht, which was to spend most of its time watching for Spinola to come out – 'a great ship

Dutch ships of the 16th century

254

H· Cock ex

to lie like a bulwark in the channel before Sluys' – and two lighter galleys for patrol work.

It was an expensive resort for the northern allies, for they had to pay their galley 'slaves'. Spinola ran through hundreds a year from combat or disease, but he always succeeded in getting more from Spain.

Archduke Albert, now married to the Infanta and recently created independent sovereign of the loyal provinces of the Netherlands, opened peace negotiations with England and the rebel states on behalf of the young King of Spain; but these progressed no further than what we should now call discussions for the agenda before they broke down. Yet for the time being active combat between the two sides died away. Great epidemics were decimating the Spanish sea towns and dockyards. The Dutch, using their new-found strength, were taking care of the Narrow Seas and trying to contain Spinola and the Dunkirk pirates. England was preoccupied with the Irish problem.

Kings are notoriously bad at picking favourites: history is littered with the debris of their extravagances and their mistakes. But Elizabeth, even with her favourites, had a pretty shrewd eye for a man's worth under his gallant manner and handsome face. Essex was her worst error, yet even he, before he developed delusions of semi-kingship, was a tireless and fearless soldier with a splendid gift for leadership. As for the others: Leicester, Ralegh, Hatton, Mountjoy and the rest, they were all men of parts.

Charles Blount, Lord Mountjoy, came of an old but impoverished family, and had intended to study law; but an appearance at court and a marked talent in the tilt-yard brought him into prominence and an entirely un-merited command over his elders and betters in the Azores expedition of 1597. Since then, and before then, being refused permission to leave the court and get himself killed 'like that inconsiderate fellow Sidney', he had spent most of his spare time studying the art of war. When he reached Ireland after his friend's disastrous failure he proceeded to put his book learning into practice.

By the judicious combination of sea and land power, and with Sir George Carew as his experienced right-hand man, he so overcame the Irish that by the beginning of 1601 Desmond was a fugitive, McCarty was trying to change sides, and many of Tyrone's followers were giving up the struggle.

Now, too late by a couple of years for the most favourable circumstances, Spain chose to intervene. It was known all through the spring and early summer that yet another Armada was assembling in Lisbon in spite of lack of money, discouragement and rampant disease. Don Diego Brochero and Pedro de Zubiaur were to command it, and, though by early standards it was small, it still consisted of about twenty galleons and twenty other ships, carrying four thousand five hundred of Spain's best soldiers, a quantity of siege equipment and a mass of military stores.

As always (except in 1597) the English were well alerted to its approach, but as always, being on the defensive, they had no certainty as to the objec-

tive in mind. Ireland was certainly considered, but an attack on the West Country could not be ruled out. Nor, in spite of a lack now of Channel ports, could there be ruled out a possible attempt to link up with the Archduke Albert, who was at present laying siege to Ostend. The English commissioned a new squadron under Sir Henry Palmer to meet the threat, but in September news reached Plymouth that the whole Spanish fleet of some forty or fifty ships had been seen on a northerly course clearly bound for Ireland.

The Spanish fleet carried with it as commander of the military the sturdy Don Juan de Aguila who had been landed in Brittany in 1590, had remained there in spite of all Anglo-French efforts to drive him out, and had only been compelled to relinquish his position there under the terms of the peace treaty of Vervins. Now it was the Spanish intention to inject him and his *tercios* into Ireland, where they could, if successful, join up with Tyrone and the other Irish rebels and take the whole island or, if unsuccessful, remain like an unassimilable foreign body in possession of a part of the coast where they could be most nuisance to the English. It was not the intention of the Spanish to keep a fleet in being off Ireland; their aim was to land troops and from time to time furnish it with supplies and more troops, just as Zubiaur had so successfully done for so many years in Britanny.

Inevitably the weather intervened in these plans. A storm struck the Armada and it was split into three parts. Zubiaur to his fury was driven back into Coruña. With him were nine ships, eight hundred of the soldiers and most of the stores. A large transport in considerable distress was captured by an English privateer. Three ships under the command of Don Alonso del Campo reached and seized Baltimore on the southern coast of Ireland. The main fleet under Brochero arrived off the mouth of Cork harbour and were about to attempt to take the town when the wind changed, making their entry up the river impossible. They therefore sailed west and took Kinsale instead – another fine harbour but a less important base. Here they encountered no resistance; the people opened the gates of the little walled town and welcomed them in as friends and deliverers. Brochero, not wanting to stay in harbour a moment longer than he need – for if the wind changed he might find himself pinned there until an English fleet arrived – disembarked his three thousand army veterans, their equipment and supplies, and put out to sea again.

Aguila knew that most of the Irish rebels were far in the north, so he set about making the place as defensible as possible to await their arrival. He put a garrison in Castle Park on the Bandon River and another on the opposite bank in Rincurren. There were, however, no horses to be found in the vicinity of Kinsale, and this greatly reduced the Spanish mobility.

With the troops was Mathew de Oviedo, the Spanish-appointed Archbishop of Dublin, and he issued a proclamation stating that Queen Elizabeth had been dethroned by the Pope and therefore Irishmen were relieved of their allegiance, and to fight for Spain was to fight for the Pope and the only true religion. The proclamation fell flat, for there was an unexpected English army just arrived near Cork, and the ordinary folk of the district did not yet feel like committing themselves.

As soon as the news reached him that the Spaniards were coming to Ireland, Carew had been convinced that they would try to take Cork; he had moved quickly south and there he had been joined by Mountjoy, who had ridden down from Dublin with only one hundred men as escort. The presence of the Lord Deputy in their midst had a steadying effect in Munster, but neither English nor Spanish were yet in sufficient force to risk a major encounter. Mountjoy had sent urgent messages to England for reinforcements and awaited them and the rest of his troops from Dublin. Aguila waited the arrival of Tyrone and O'Donnell.

Weather and problems of organization caused delays on all fronts, but by the end of October Mountjoy had built up a force of about six thousand infantry and six hundred horse, and with these he moved in to invest Kinsale. On the 1st November, after a bitter struggle during which Aguila tried repeatedly to relieve them, the hundred and fifty Spaniards in Rincurren surrendered.

In the wild north-west the Irish earls were also, though more slowly, on the move. O'Donnell, Lord of Tirconnel, gathered together an army of three thousand men in Sligo, ferried them across the upper reaches of the Shannon and then stayed three weeks in Tipperary waiting for Tyrone. While waiting he ravaged and plundered the countryside for miles around, even though the victims were Irish Catholics like himself — presumably on the excuse that those who were not for him were against him. On hearing of his approach, Mountjoy decided to take the risk of splitting his own army, and sent Carew north with twelve hundred foot soldiers and two hundred and fifty cavalry to intercept O'Donnell before he could join forces or coordinate with the Spanish.

As Tyrone had still not arrived, O'Donnell eventually moved on again and came upon Carew's army straddling the only road south. It was an impasse. O'Donnell did not want a trial of strength against regulars who had the choice of position. Carew did not want to attack an army which could melt at will into the bogs and the forests. Then occurred that extreme rarity in Ireland, a sharp November frost. Immediately and successfully O'Donnell led his army across the temporarily frozen quagmire of the Slievefelim Mountains and so gave Carew the slip. By dawn Carew knew what had happened and turned about and led his troops back by forced marches, hoping to rejoin Mountjoy in Kinsale in time.

He succeeded, for O'Donnell, having come to within thirty miles of Kinsale, once again sat down and waited for Tyrone. In the meantime Aguila inside Kinsale had not been idle, and Mountjoy with his depleted force had had several bloody encounters with the Spanish. At this stage the army investing Kinsale was fewer in number than the army defending it.

But now the forces began to build up on both sides for a final trial of strength. Zubiaur, back in Coruña, had forced repairs through at a great rate and soon sailed again with ten ships, nine hundred soldiers and quantities of provisions and powder and shot. With him sailed the secretary to the Adelantado, Pedro Lopez de Soto — two fire-eaters together — and although the usual storm split the squadron, they arrived in Castlehaven — near Roaring Water Bay and thirty miles west of Kinsale — with seven of their ships intact and proceeded to land men and stores there.

News of their arrival was a welcome fillip to the spirits of the Spaniards beleaguered in Kinsale, and this, together with the rumoured approach of Tyrone, gave rise to the first dangerous signs in Munster of Irish support for the invaders. The castle at Castlehaven and two overlooking the entrance to Baltimore were handed over without a shot being fired, as a few days later was the important castle of Dunboy, which has a valuable small harbour overlooking Bantry Bay. All these strategic points were quickly garrisoned by Spaniards, and soon they joined forces with O'Donnell and with the Spanish in Baltimore. It was an explosive situation.

In the meantime the Earl of Thomond arrived in Kinsale Harbour with English reinforcements of sixteen hundred men and one hundred horse, and three days later Sir Richard Leveson put in at last with his strong fleet of *Warspite, Garland, Defiance, Swiftsure, Crane* and *Refusal*, together with seven supporting ships and two thousand very raw, very seasick troops, whom he proceeded to land. The stage was all set and waiting only for Tyrone.

Leveson, on landing his men, learned of the arrival of Zubiaur in Castlehaven, and at once split his force and warped his part of it laboriously out of the harbour in the teeth of the wind to try to attack Zubiaur before he could establish himself. He took with him *Warspite, Defiance, Swiftsure, Crane* and three supporting ships and by the following morning was off Castlehaven.

Zubiaur however had already firmly established himself, not only in the castle but in entrenchments along the beach, now manned by musketeers, and eight guns were just being hauled up to cover the narrow entrance of the harbour. Leveson did not pause for a council-of-war but, like Drake at Cadiz fourteen years before, burst straight in. Zubiaur had two galleons of about five hundred tons each, as against the heavily armed *Warspite* of six hundred and fifty tons and the lesser English warships (the other Spanish ships were transports); but with the guns and soldiers ashore the prospects for an attack could hardly have been less favourable. But in a battle lasting five hours Leveson sank Zubiaur's flagship and three other ships and left a fifth burning.

In spite of this signal victory he could not hope to dislodge the Spanish soldiers from the shore and now, again like Drake at Cadiz, he found himself unable to retreat, for the wind was adverse. He stayed there two more days waiting a change that would let him out, and in the meantime was the target of Spanish gunnery. It is said that the *Warspite* was hit three hundred times by shot. When he was finally able to leave, he was soon followed out of the harbour by Zubiaur, who took the remnants of his battered fleet back to Spain. Pedro Lopez de Soto remained behind to command the Spanish infantry.

Now at last the slow-moving Tyrone was almost on the scene – not without his own record of burning and pillaging on the way; but at the sound of his name all Munster, which had hardly lifted a finger for the Spaniards, was ready to rise. He made contact with the Spaniards at Castlehaven, and a contingent of two hundred of them joined him. Then he linked up with O'Donnell and advanced on Kinsale. Between them the Irish alone had about seven thousand men.

A 16th-century Spanish
vessel riding at anchor

It was a nasty position for the English. Mountjoy with all his reinforcements from England had at one time commanded twelve thousand troops;
but, thanks to the problems of bringing raw recruits from England, some of
whom even died on the way, the enormous number of desertions which
followed (hundreds at a time), and the long siege of Kinsale with its routine
casualties from disease and warfare, his active force was now down to
about six thousand. All were on short rations, the horses were starving and
he had none too much powder and shot. Furthermore, although he was
officially investing Kinsale, he was now in fact between two armies whose
total force was fifty per cent greater than his own. The Spanish were
veterans. And Tyrone had shown what he could do to the English on the
Blackwater.

It was a suitable moment to lift the siege and evacuate his army as best he could – by ship to Cork, since he was cut off by land. Instead he remained obstinately where he was and continued to bombard Kinsale in the hope that it would provoke an attack. The Spaniards within the walls were in none too good a state either, being reduced to eating rice and stale biscuits, and Aguila wrote in some irritation to Tyrone proposing an immediate joint assault upon the English from front and rear. Tyrone, whose policy of masterly inactivity had been producing desirable results, was reluctantly persuaded by O'Donnell to agree, and the time of the attack was fixed for dawn on Christmas Eve.

Betrayals through the centuries have taken many peculiar shapes, but few perhaps have been quite so bizarre as that of Brian MacHugh Oge MacMahon on the 23rd December 1601. One of the chiefs close to Tyrone, he found himself short of whiskey. There was none in the camp, nor was any to be obtained in the villages round. It was an acute crisis; so, very thirsty, and friendly as you please, he sent off a boy to the English camp to ask Sir George Carew if he could possibly be letting him have a bottle for the old times' sake. (MacMahon's son had once been a page to Carew.) The Englishman, not to be outdone in the courtesies, at once sent him a bottle. MacMahon could well have sent the boy back with a note of thanks. Instead he sent, along with his love, a warning to Carew to be on his guard against a surprise attack on the following day at dawn, with details of the dispositions.

People betray for money, for power, for religion, for vengeance. Surely only an Irishman could betray out of sheer goodness of heart.

The battle began in a thunderstorm just before daybreak and lasted for three hours. Warned in advance, the English, though outnumbered, could concentrate their best troops in the most threatened places. The Irish advanced in three main armies: Tyrone and his men from Tyrone and Londonderry, O'Donnell leading the regiments of Tyrconnell and Connaught; while the third army consisted of some of the best troops in Ireland under Tyrrell, a mixture of Munster volunteers and the small Spanish contingent under Alonso del Campo himself. These last were on the Irish right and their task was to establish contact with the beleaguered Spanish in Kinsale.

But no sooner did they probe forward than they met strongly posted English forces barring the way. As day broke del Campo, seeing the thin lines of the English slowly advancing to meet the Irish main armies, pressed Tyrone to attack them at once; but instead Tyrone, fresh from a quarrel with O'Donnell over precedence, ordered a retreat. His aim was to immobilize the English cavalry by retreating behind a bog; but the partly untrained Irish did not know how to retreat in good order and Mountjoy, seizing the moment while it was there, ordered a general attack. Sir Edward Wingfield with two hundred and fifty cavalry charged a force of eighteen hundred

The Irish town of Kinsale, where the Spaniards were besieged by the English under Lord Mountjoy in 1601

The Castle of Rincrone

THE KINSALE OF

E · W
N · S

An entrenchement where S. Gerret Kar:

The Last entrenchment

HARBROWE

Castle ny Parke placed & taken
The Enimy at Castle ny Parke

nd takinge
astle by
dent

S. Richard Leueson Admirall of her Mat Fleet

The Admirall & vice Admirall playinge vppon y towne

The Admirall Second battry

The Earle of Thomonds Second Campe.

The Skirmishe the last of october wherin the Enimy was beaten

Stakes pitched to gale the Enimies Horse

The entrenchment where 6. Peeces of ordinance were planted to beat into y Towne & vppon the North gate Here the Enimy Sallied w 2500: men, and were repulsed w the losse of 300: of there best men & 6 Capteines

The first Approche on the Comandinge ground.

The Earle of Clanrickard goinge to the rescue of the entrenchment entred by the Enimy

The Spittle hill where y Lo: Deputie & Lo: President encamped.

The stone mille

The Lord Deputies first Campe.

Her Maᵗᵗ forces marchinge towards the Enimye the 21: of December

Here the Spaniards and the Rebells first presented themselues the 21: of December pikemen, who stood firm and repulsed him. But then, reinforced by regiments under Sir Henry Danvers, he swung off to the right and attacked the Irish cavalry. These were no match for the English and scattered widely; and the Irish pikemen, seeing their own people fleeing towards them, parted ranks to let them through and could not reassemble in time to keep out the English cavalry.

So a rout began. Brian MacHugh Oge MacMahon, fighting valiantly be it noted, was severely wounded in the fight. In a short time the only Irish standing firm were Tyrrell's vanguard, which resisted for a while and then also fled, leaving del Campo and his Spanish contingent standing alone. Though now hopelessly outnumbered the Spaniards fought on, giving no ground, until of the original two hundred only del Campo, two other officers and forty-seven soldiers were left alive. Then they surrendered. The Irish loss in the battle was perhaps twelve hundred, though on their return northwards many hundreds more were set upon and killed by the other Irish they had despoiled on the way south. A favourite way of killing them was throwing them into a bog and then treading them down.

Having never received the prearranged signal from del Campo, Aguila and the Kinsale garrison did not make a sally until the fighting was virtually over, and then they were sharply rebuffed.

Through the next week they continued to make sorties but to no avail. It was a stalemate, for an English attempt to take the fortress would have been a desperate and bloody business. Then on the 31st December Aguila offered to parley. Mountjoy gratefully accepted the invitation and sent his Cornish friend Sir William Godolphin to open negotiations. The bargaining was hard on both sides, but, since Mountjoy only had six days food left for his troops and most of his guns were out of action, he felt justified in agreeing generous terms.

So presently English and Spanish officers were dining amicably together, and even Captain Robert Harvey, who was sent to Castlehaven to accept its surrender under the terms of the general agreement, was greeted and entertained to dinner by Pedro Lopez de Soto. Indeed de Soto, arch apostle all his life of the war against England, as he became friendly with Harvey during the next weeks, allowed it to be seen that his mind was changing. Why could there not be peace between England and Spain? he asked. Who was benefiting from this dreary and bloodthirsty war?

16 *Last Skirmishes*

Aguila, do Soto, del Campo and three thousand six hundred Spanish officers and men were duly repatriated to Spain, without ransoms, without massacre. This was of course contained in the terms of the agreement, but all the same it speaks a new spirit.

For the failure to exploit the last Armada, the Spaniards blamed the Irish, the Irish blamed the Spaniards. Feeling was very bitter. Aguila said that when Satan showed Christ all the kingdoms of the earth he withheld Ireland as being fit only for himself.

The Spanish had a lot to complain of, for they had landed as promised with a large contingent of troops, had subsisted there for nearly three months without any help at all, when they had been promised assistance 'within days'. Then when the Irish army did eventually come it had 'been broken by a handful of men and blown asunder'. They had done their share and been abysmally let down.

This was true enough; but considerable lack of judgment, or lack of local knowledge, had been shown by the places at which they landed. Munster was peaceful: no chief or earl raised his standard of rebellion there. If the Spanish had sailed to Sligo it would have been different. As it was, the two great northern earls had had to make a trek of more than two hundred miles across wild and mountainous country, with all the difficulties of ordnance and supply that that entailed. To help a rebellion in Lisbon, would you land troops in Coruña?

The man who came out of it with an enormously heightened reputation was of course Mountjoy. Throughout the whole emergency he had contrived to do the right thing at the right time. Always with inadequate forces and poor supplies, he had deployed his resources notably and had achieved one of the outstanding tactical victories of the sixteenth century.

Almost as important as his defeat of the Irish armies was his creation of conditions around Kinsale such as to induce Aguila to parley. It had been very much the intention of the Spanish to retain Kinsale permanently and

The 7 of Iune the Army lodged here Opposit to Dunboy

Beare Haven

The Castle of Dunboy taken by assault the 17 and 18. of Iune 1602 blowne uppe with powder the 22 of the monthe afore said

Part of the great Iland where ye Erle of Thomond spake with Richard McGoghagan

THE SI IDGE OF DUNBOY

The Marlin

The Spanish Bay

Here and ates transpor ge of the dinance

Here were twoe Minnions planted

The Batterye plan ted the 16 of Iune

The 10 Iune ye Campe Was quartred and entrenched on the n.th

Here ye Ordin ance Landed ye 10.th of Iune.

The Bridge

A Smal Sconce betwene the Campe and the Bridge

PART

OF

THE

CONTRYE

OF   BEARE

THE WEST OCEAN

to use it as a forward base against England. A considerable fleet could lie at anchor there. It could be a place from which it was possible to harry enemy shipping with far greater impunity than Spinola could employ from Sluys. Whatever the initial failure to rouse them, it would gradually have become a focal point for the rebellious Irish, who would be sure of sanctuary there. And as Spanish-Irish power grew, it could spread along the coast and take a firmer grip inland. It would lock up or preoccupy a sizable proportion of Elizabeth's army and navy.

Don Martin de Bertendona had been about to sail with more troops and supplies when news reached Madrid of Aguila's surrender. When Aguila reached Spain he was placed under house arrest; but before he could answer the charges against him he was taken ill and died. One of his last acts was to send off a crate of wine and oranges and lemons to his late captor, Sir George Carew.

So the long war was petering out at last – partly from exhaustion, partly from a growing mutual respect.

Of course there were still some flickers of the flame. The Spaniards, keeping to their terms of surrender, gave up Dunboy Castle too, but it was at once seized by O'Sullivan Bere who owned the castle, who claimed descent from the Spanish and who now proposed to hold it in the name of King Philip III. It was a difficult place for the English to tackle, and so it remained as a thorn in the English flesh. O'Donnell of Tirconnell after his defeat went to Spain and there was received at court with every honour; so Dunboy would prove to be a most useful harbour if Bertendona came out with his fleet, as he seemed disposed to do.

At the same time the active Frederico Spinola had been back in Madrid pressing the young King for reinforcements to improve on his recent successes. His brother, the Marquis of Spinola, was willing to raise five thousand infantry and one thousand cavalry in Italy if Philip would match it with eight more galleys and two thousand Spanish veterans. Then they would sail back to Dunkirk and have a force there ready to disrupt Channel shipping and even seize an English port. Young Philip, beset by failure elsewhere, readily agreed.

In England Elizabeth's veto on large overseas expeditions still remained, but the sore memories of 1597 were now five years old. Leveson, though elevated in the first place through marriage and not merit, had now established himself as one of the outstanding admirals of the day; and he was permitted to take a fleet of eight galleons on a tour of the Spanish coast to see what mischief they could wreak. He took with him, apart from a few auxiliaries, the *Repulse*, *Warspite*, *Defiance*, *Nonpareil*, *Mary Rose*, *Dreadnought*, *Garland* and *Adventure*; and as his vice-admiral he was given the thirty-three-year-old Sir William Monson, who as a young lieutenant of seventeen had fought against the first Armada in the frigate *Charles*, had commanded the *Repulse* at the taking of Cadiz and been knighted in the

Dunboy Castle, Ireland, surrendered by the Spaniards to the English in 1602 but taken over by an Irishman, O'Sullivan Bere, in the name of Philip III general euphoria following that event. He had made three voyages with the Earl of Cumberland, and in 1591 had been taken prisoner by the Spaniards while manning a recaptured prize and had served some time as a galley slave, so he had old scores to settle.

It was a fleet big enough to disrupt trade but not big enough to try conclusions with a Spanish fleet, as Leveson found to his cost when, sailing some days ahead of Monson with four of his ships, he intercepted the Spanish treasure-fleet – the failed dream of so many of his distinguished predecessors. He took one prize and then found his small squadron surrounded by thirty-eight Spanish ships-of-war. He could have died like Grenville but he preferred to live like Leveson, and, abandoning his prize, he found a gap in the closing fleet just in time.

Thereafter, joined by Monson, he cruised up and down the Spanish coast for several weeks with nothing to report but the usual decay of his crews. Then in early June, off Lisbon, he learned that one of the great Portuguese carracks, laden as always with the treasure of the Indies, was sheltering just inside the mouth of the Tagus under the guns of Cezimbra castle. She had been two years on the voyage, her crew of six hundred reduced to thirty by sickness and privation, and she had just made the shelter of the river at her last gasp.

Already help for her was on its way from Lisbon. The governor had sent out four hundred men to supplement the exhausted crew, and Spinola, just ready with his eight new galleys and one thousand trained soldiers to begin his dash north, was diverted to protect the carrack. Three other galleys under the new Marquis of Santa Cruz kept him company. By the time Leveson looked in it was a formidable sight, for he faced the guns of the fort, the big forward-firing guns of the galleys, and cannon and infantry camped on the hillsides. Riding at anchor towered the great carrack with her seven decks, being rapidly unloaded. Leveson and Monson had five warships with them, but the captains of all the ships protested that to go in meant suicide, and it took the two commanders all their persuasion and authority to force them to attack.

Thereafter followed five hours of battle during which in spite of their choice of stations the galleys suffered the more. Indeed Santa Cruz and his three Lisbon galleys had had enough by noon and would have fled, but Spinola held his ground and the others would not be shamed into admitting defeat before he did. However by two p.m. Santa Cruz had been seriously wounded and his crews decimated and Spinola's fine new galleys were all badly damaged. Monson wrote later of 'watching the slaves forsaking them and everything in confusion amongst them'. Two galleys surrendered – one, to Monson's understandable glee, the galley in which he had been chained – and in the end even Spinola had to make off to save what was left of his fleet.

Then, after long parleying, the carrack itself surrendered, the Portuguese captain and officers were entertained to dinner and music aboard the *Garland* before being set ashore, and next morning the English sailed away with their monstrous capture while thousands of Spanish and Portuguese soldiers watched helplessly from the shore.

It was an epic worthy of Drake and deserves more honour than it has received in English naval annals.

The indefatigable Spinola was not yet beaten. With his usual consuming energy he set about repairing his battered flotilla, and within two months was ready for sea again. He sailed direct for Santander with fifteen hundred slaves as motive power and one thousand troops. His own galley had five slaves to an oar instead of the usual four, to give him extra speed when necessary. Monson, who was on the prowl again, this time with flag command, missed him altogether; but the Dutch were able to send a warning, so by mid-September all possible dispositions had been made to welcome Spinola in the Channel.

The English Channel Guard at this time consisted of three ships only under Sir Robert Mansell, the *Hope*, the *Adventure* and the *Answer*, but it was supplemented by four Dutch warships under Admiral Cant; and of course there were the two usual Dutch blockading squadrons outside Dunkirk and Sluys, making it almost impossible to enter or leave the ports. Spinola decided this time he would change his tactics and hug the English coast instead of the French; but Anglo-Dutch reasoning had anticipated this, and Spinola and his galleys were first spotted by two Dutch fly-boats as he was running before a stiff south-westerly breeze off Dungeness. They gave chase.

He kept his distance well throughout the night, but at dawn he found he was being carefully headed towards the English flagship, which lay waiting for him. It was not his purpose at present to try conclusions with a warship of the size of the *Hope*, so he struck sail and took to the oars, heading back athwart the wind. So began, during most of a fine September day, a battle of manoeuvre between three sailing-ships and six depending on sail and oar. Not once during it did the Anglo-Dutch squadron come within firing distance of the galleys, and the day's end saw the galleys slip through a gap their brilliant navigation had created and make off up Channel with their opponents crowding on sail to try to keep them in sight.

But Mansell was not done yet, for the north-easterly course the Spaniards were taking would bring them close by the South Foreland and almost into the waiting arms of the rest of his squadron headed by Admiral Jan Cant in the *Moon*. Mansell therefore veered east-north-east, away from Spinola in anticipation that, when the Italian saw his way blocked by Cant, he would swing his squadron south-east and make directly for Dunkirk: then Mansell would be between him and his home ports.

It happened as Mansell foresaw. So close did Spinola come to the coast that people ran along the cliff watching him, and Dover Castle sounded an alarm gun. The sight of the white cliffs was too much for three English slaves and they jumped overboard and swam ashore at St Margaret's Bay.

Carefully Mansell kept the galleys just in sight, but well to the south of them, shepherding them towards the Goodwins. Then just as dusk fell the leading galleys saw three warships in their path. It was the *Moon*, the *Sampson* and the *Answer*, completely blocking the way ahead. Behind Spinola were the two Dutch frigates, and on his starboard quarter but on the seaward side of the Goodwins, Mansell waited in the *Hope*. It looked like a fair capture.

Spinola, of course, had chosen a moonless night, but now fortunately for him cloud came up too, blotting out the stars, and for an hour after dusk the wind dropped. So it was a game of blind man's buff with only the galleys capable of movement and the dangerous Goodwins never far away. Spinola had turned about as soon as darkness fell and had made for the southern end of the Goodwins; but as he reached them the breeze sprang up again, this time from the north-west.

Mansell for the second time had guessed right and suddenly loomed up among the galleys. There was an explosion of broadsides and sixty-pounders. In a violent ten minutes of blind fighting one of the galleys was severely damaged, and then Mansell himself hauled away in the freshening breeze. With galleys all around him he was enormously outnumbered and might

Dover Castle, Kent, from which an alarm signal was fired when a Spanish fleet under the Italian commander Frederico Spinola passed dangerously close in 1602

have been boarded and quickly overrun. So Spinola once more continued on his way, with apparently only the Dutch blockading squadron now between himself and safety.

But he was still pursued by the six Anglo-Dutch vessels he had eluded, and his rowers after twelve hours of stroke and counter-stroke were near the end of their endurance. Also one of his galleys was partly disabled and Spinola would not desert her. So as the wind freshened on that last thirty endless miles from the Goodwins to Gravelines the sailing warships began to catch up.

Mansell, at last guessing wrong, made for Sluys and took Captain Bredgate in the *Answer* and Captain Jonas in the *Advantage* with him. The Dutch held on for Dunkirk, and it was they who began to overhaul the galleys in the dark of the night. First the damaged galley was caught and raked with broadsides until she was a wreck; then Captain Sael in the *Sampson* rammed another and bombarded her until she sank, forty only of a complement of four hundred and fifty being picked up. Then Vice-Admiral Cant overran a third in the dark and shot her to pieces, so that eventually she drifted upon Calais beach and was wrecked.

The cannonade had attracted a swarm of blockaders, who, having already been forewarned, were out in extra strength, and the three remaining galleys could not avoid running into them. In the ensuing fight two of the galleys were badly damaged and captured, the third with Spinola on board and its extra turn of speed, reached the shoals of Dunkirk beach. Here, pursued only by boats of the shallowest draught, he had everything possible flung overboard to lighten his craft, and promised the galley slaves freedom if they made the harbour. Somehow he avoided taking the ground and entered Dunkirk with his own ship and his treasure intact.

One would have thought that the lessons of Lisbon and the Channel would have convinced even the bravest of men. Or the most obstinate. Spinola continued undeterred, and throughout the winter his galley and those he commanded were a continuing menace to shipping in the vicinity of Dunkirk. But like Grenville and others in that strange heroic century, he seemed to have a death wish, or at least a wish to triumph over quite insuperable odds. By May 1603 there were dissensions among the Archduke and the officers he commanded, and Spinola had angry exchanges with the Governor of Sluys who he thought was impeding him at every turn. Gathering his eight remaining galleys and four frigates, he sailed out of the harbour to attack the island of Walcheren, and so deliberately challenged the blockading squadron of four ships under Vice-Admiral Joost de Moor. The battle began at daybreak and went on all through the morning until Spinola had his right arm blown off by gunfire. He died an hour later, and the galleys, damaged and outgunned, retreated into Sluys harbour, never to emerge again.

Spinola was twenty-eight, and had he lived might have matched his elder brother's later military fame with an even greater renown at sea.

17 *The Setting of the Sun*

In the last year of her life Queen Elizabeth finished her translation of Horace's *Art of Poetry*. She entranced the Commons with two of the finest speeches from the throne to be heard even in her reign. She welcomed the Venetian Envoy in fluent Italian and told him it was a pity the Republic had waited forty-five years before venturing to appoint a full diplomatic representative. She made another of her 'progresses', and once or twice rode horseback to the chase and to the other field-sports. Sometimes the palace at Westminster still rang with her hearty laughter.

But these were flickers of a flame that otherwise burned low. Luckier than her Spanish brother-in-law, she did not suffer from diabetic gangrene – nor indeed from any other apparently incurable complaint. It was just age bearing her down: old age, fatigue, loneliness and a sad heart. Most old people not weeded out by one of the killer diseases suffer the same way, and it is as much a matter of mental stamina as of physical how long they survive.

Elizabeth's stamina was notorious, but seventy was a great age in the sixteenth century, and she never had the same spirits after Essex had gone to the block. 'She disregardeth every costly dish that cometh to the table,' Harrington wrote, 'and taketh little but manchet and succory pottage. Every new message from the City doth disturb her, and she frowns on all the ladies.' When he tried to entertain her by reading her some of his witty verses she said : 'When thou dost feel creeping age at thy gate, these fooleries will please thee less.' Harington thought her 'in a most pitiable state'.

She had made a new favourite of the young Earl of Clanricarde, but sometimes his marked resemblance to Essex distressed her as much as it pleased her. She told the new French Ambassador, Count Harlay de Beaumont, that she 'was tired of life, for nothing new contenteth my spirit or giveth me any enjoyment'. Her days became as substantially peopled by ghosts as by the faces and figures of the middle-aged courtiers around her who had not been born when she came to the throne. Even her old friend Lady Nottingham had just passed away and so had moved over the far side of the arras where lurked the whispering faces and forms of all the other dead.

Just after Christmas the Queen was well enough to attend several state banquets, but at one of these she caught cold, and so shortly moved to Richmond, where the air was less dank from river mists. There she began to fail more rapidly, and she sat for long hours in silence 'with the dulness and frowardness familiar to old age'. She had always had a distaste for the ministrations of her doctors, a fact which had contributed materially to the length of her life; but now she would not let them even come near her; nor after a while would she eat or drink. Feeling the end approaching, she rose from her chair and stood beside it, refusing now even to sit lest she should never rise again. So she stood for fifteen hours while her court watched from the shadows and waited in awe for the end.

Many of her courtiers posted back to Whitehall, preparing for the change. Orders were issued to transport to Holland all vagrants and unknown persons found in London or Westminster; numerous gentlemen who it was thought were likely to cause trouble were arrested and put in the Tower, to be on the safe side. Arms and ammunition were supplied to the court, an armed guard put on the exchequer. The fleet was ordered to sea. All that could be put in readiness was put in readiness.

At last the Queen was forced to sink back upon some cushions, which had been spread around her, and there lay unspeaking for four more days, her finger in her mouth. Music was played to her, and this seemed to bring a little pleasure to the old eyes. More than did Archbishop Whitgift's prayers, though he prayed unceasingly at her side. Unlike Philip, religion had never been a dominating influence in her life; this had enabled her to rise above the prevailing passions; now it provided her with small succour at the end.

From her only relative of near contemporary age, the old Lord Admiral Howard, now Lord Nottingham, she accepted one bowl of soup. To him she complained that she was tied with an iron collar about her neck. He tried to reassure her but she said: 'No, I am tied, and the case is altered with me.'

To the last she would not name her successor, though those about her thought she nodded once at the King of Scotland's name. Towards the evening of the 23rd she allowed the Archbishop to examine her in her faith; she replied only by nods or a raising of the hand. Then he prayed at her bedside until late in the night, when she fell asleep. At three o'clock in the morning the courtiers remaining around her couch noticed a change in her and saw that she was dead. She had passed away 'as the most resplendent sun setteth at last in a western cloud'.

Fate sometimes has a way of staging the sorry anti-climax, and one scarcely more painful could have been arranged than the succession of King James. In place of the dead Queen with her great authority, with the aura of forty-five years as a monarch, with her talent for majestic eloquence, her wit, her coarse dynamic vitality, her legendary prestige, there came a thin-shanked, pot-bellied little man, wearing a bonnet awry upon his head and clothes so

TOP Sir John Harington, who, having vainly attempted to reconcile the Second Earl of Essex and Elizabeth I, wrote of the dispirited abstemiousness she showed in her old age

BOTTOM Archbishop John Whitgift, who attended Elizabeth when she was preparing for death

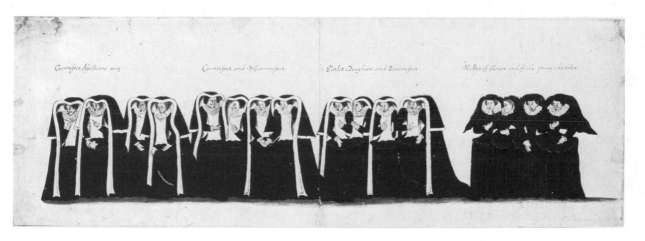

Countesses Assistans xiiij   Countesses and Viscountesses   Earles Doughters and Baronesses   Maides of Honor and of the privy chamber

ABOVE Ladies of the court
mourning the death of
Elizabeth I

OPPOSITE James VI of
Scotland, who succeeded
Elizabeth I to become also
James I of England

thickly padded to protect him from possible dagger thrusts that he looked like Humpty Dumpty; a man who could only sit a horse if it were saddled like an armchair, whose fingers were ever fumbling with his codpiece, whose tongue was too large for his mouth, whose eyes were large and watery and his beard thin and straggling. It is extraordinary that two such handsome creatures as Mary and Darnley could ever have produced so unhandsome a son.

But underneath his shambling, drooling exterior he had a good deal of shrewd wisdom and a clear eye for the practical realities of a situation. And the situation regarding Spain was to him perfectly straightforward. As King of Scotland he never *had* been at war with Spain; why should he now be in his larger domain? He saw himself as the Peacemaker, and on the whole his new subjects were ready enough to accept his point of view. France was already at peace with Spain. Holland was virtually independent. It was time for England to come to terms with her old enemy.

This James did on England's behalf very quickly, and by 1604 peace was formally signed. The terms of the peace were unsatisfactory to the adventurous and burgeoning spirit of maritime England, and could only lead – as they did – to a renewal of the struggle later in the century; but for the time the treaty sufficed. It sufficed too to see the end of the great Spanish fleets built regularly in the Atlantic ports to be launched against a heretic England. Though religious divisions were to remain as acute for another hundred years, it was the end of Spanish hegemony in Europe and Spanish monopoly in the Caribbean. Though frequently at war with England, or near war with England, Spain never again considered, or was in a position to consider, conquest. It was never again between the two countries a war *à outrance*.

The last of the Spanish Armadas had sailed. For two centuries England was to be free from the threat of invasion.

Tudor and Stuart Succession

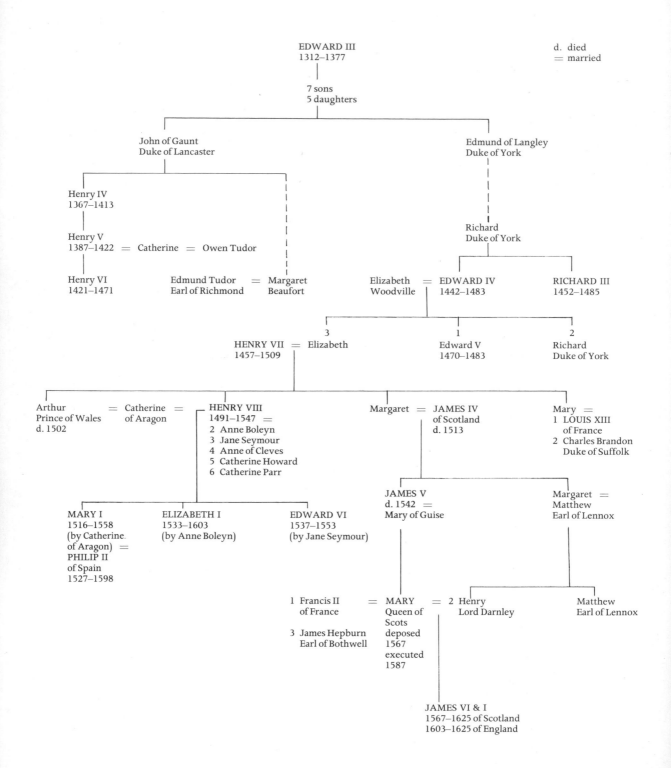

EDWARD III
1312–1377

d. died
= married

7 sons
5 daughters

John of Gaunt
Duke of Lancaster

Edmund of Langley
Duke of York

Henry IV
1367–1413

Henry V
1387–1422 = Catherine = Owen Tudor

Richard
Duke of York

Henry VI
1421–1471

Edmund Tudor
Earl of Richmond = Margaret
Beaufort

Elizabeth
Woodville = EDWARD IV
1442–1483

RICHARD III
1452–1485

3
HENRY VII = Elizabeth
1457–1509

1
Edward V
1470–1483

2
Richard
Duke of York

Arthur
Prince of Wales
d. 1502 = Catherine =
of Aragon

HENRY VIII
1491–1547 =
2 Anne Boleyn
3 Jane Seymour
4 Anne of Cleves
5 Catherine Howard
6 Catherine Parr

Margaret = JAMES IV
of Scotland
d. 1513

Mary =
1 LOUIS XIII
of France
2 Charles Brandon
Duke of Suffolk

MARY I
1516–1558
(by Catherine
of Aragon) =
PHILIP II
of Spain
1527–1598

ELIZABETH I
1533–1603
(by Anne Boleyn)

EDWARD VI
1537–1553
(by Jane Seymour)

JAMES V
d. 1542 =
Mary of Guise

Margaret =
Matthew
Earl of Lennox

1 Francis II
of France

3 James Hepburn
Earl of Bothwell

= MARY
Queen of
Scots
deposed
1567
executed
1587

= 2 Henry
Lord Darnley

Matthew
Earl of Lennox

JAMES VI & I
1567–1625 of Scotland
1603–1625 of England

The Spanish Hapsburgs to Philip III

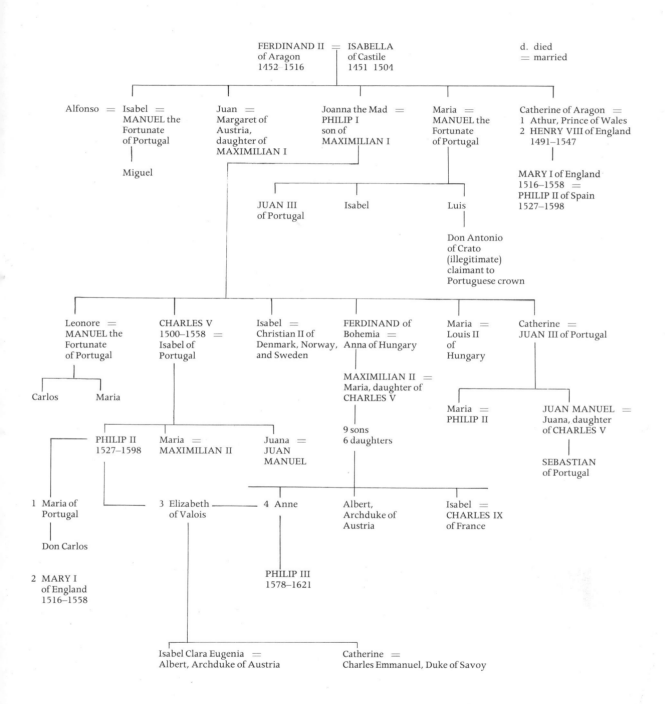

Bibliography

This is not the kind of book in which source notes at the bottom of the page are appropriate; in any case they disfigure the page and distract the reader. A full bibliography is therefore the more essential. Clearly all the books listed here are not of equal importance; from some only a few facts have been gleaned, to others my debt is considerable. Yet for the student who wishes to go to source material it is probably more helpful to list the lot, so that he may pick and choose as he wishes.

Allingham, Hugh. *Captain Cuellar's Adventures in Connaught and Ulster, 1588*. London, 1897.

Andrews, K. R. *Drake's Voyages*. London, 1967.

Aramburu, Marcos de, account of (translated by W. Spotswood-Green), in *Proceedings of the Royal Irish Academy*, Vol. XXVII. Dublin and London, 1908–9.

Artiñano, G. de. *La Arquitectura Naval Española*. Madrid, 1920.

Aubrey, John. *Brief Lives*. Edited by Oliver Lawson Dick. London, 1949.

Bagwell, Richard. *Ireland under the Tudors*. 3 vols. London, 1885–90.

Baldwin Smith, Lacey. *The Elizabethan Epic*. London, 1966.

Calderon, Pedro Coco, account of, in *Calendar of State Papers (Spanish)*, Vol. IV.

Calendar of State Papers, Domestic Series: Mary and Elizabeth.

Calendar of State Papers, Foreign Series: Elizabeth.

Calendar of State Papers (Holland and Flanders), 1586–8.

Calendar of State Papers (Ireland), 1586–1603.

Calendar of State Papers (Scotland), 1547–1603.

Calendar of State Papers (Spanish), 1580–1603.

Calendar of State Papers (Venetian), 1558–1603.

Camden, William. *Annales . . . Elizabetha*. Edited by T. Hearne. 3 vols. London, 1717.

Chamberlin, Frederick. *The Sayings of Queen Elizabeth*. London, 1923.

Cheyney, E. P. *A History of England, from the Defeat of the Armada to the Death of Elizabeth*. 2 vols. London, 1914.

Commines, Philippe de. *Mémoires*. Translated by A. R. Scoble. 2 vols. London, 1855–6.

Copies de Simancas, Vol. 18: *Archives Générales Royales*. Brussels.

Corbett, Julian S. *Drake and the Tudor Navy*. 2 vols. London, 1898.

Corbett, Julian S. *Papers relating to the Navy during the Spanish War 1585–7*, Vol. XII. Navy Records Society. London, 1898.

Corbett, Julian S. *The Successors of Drake*. London, 1900.

Cottonian MSS.

Cuellar, Francisco de, narrative letter (translated by Frances Partridge), in *Survivors of the Armada* by E. Hardy. London, 1966.

Drummond, Humphrey. *Our Man in Scotland*. London, 1969.

Duro, C. Fernández. *Armada Española*. 9 vols. Madrid, 1877.

Duro, C. Fernández. *La Armada Invencible*. 2 vols. Madrid, 1884–5.

Edwards, Edward. *The Life of Sir Walter Ralegh*. 2 vols. London, 1868.

England, Sylvia L. *The Massacre of Saint Bartholomew*. London, 1938.

Erlanger, Philippe. *St Bartholomew's Night*. Translated by P. O'Brian. London, 1962.

Essen, Leon van der. *Alexandre Farnèse*. 5 vols. Brussels, 1933–7.

Falls, Cyril. *Elizabeth's Irish Wars*. London, 1950.

The Four Masters, Annals of Ireland.

Edited by J. O'Donovan. Dublin, 1851.

Fox, John. *Actes and Monuments.* London, 1576.

Fraser, Lady Antonia. *Mary Queen of Scots.* London, 1969.

Froude, James Anthony. *History of England.* London, 1868.

Froude, James Anthony. *English Seamen in the Sixteenth Century.* London, 1895.

Glasgow, Tom, Jr. 'The Shape of Ships that defeated the Spanish Armada' in *Mariner's Mirror*, No. 50, August 1964.

Grierson, Edward. *The Fatal Inheritance.* London, 1969.

Guizot, François. *Histoire de France.* Paris, 1835.

Hardy, Evelyn. *Survivors of the Armada.* London, 1966.

Harleian Miscellany, Vol. I. London, 1808.

Hentzner, Paul. *Travels in England during the Reign of Queen Elizabeth.* Translated by R. Bentley. London, 1894.

Hilton, Ronald. 'The Marriage of Queen Mary and Philip of Spain' in *Papers and Proceedings of the Hampshire Field Club and Archaeological Society*, Vol. XIV, Part I. 1940.

History of the Spanish Armada . . . for the Invasion and Conquest of England . . . 1588. London, 1759.

Hogg, O. F. G. 'England's War Effort against the Spanish Armada' in *Society for Army Historical Research Journal*, No. 44. March 1966.

Howard, Charles, 1st Earl of Nottingham. 'Relation of Proceedings' in *The Defeat of the Spanish Armada* by J. K. Laughton. Navy Records Society. London, 1894.

Hume, Martin A. S. 'The Visit of Philip II' in *English Historical Review*, Vol. VII. 1892.

Hume, Martin A. S. *Two English Queens and Philip.* London, 1908.

Hume, Martin A. S. Introductions to the *Calendar of Letters and State Papers relating to English Affairs, preserved principally in the Archives of Simancas*, Vols. I–IV.

A Journal of all the Particularities that fell out in the voyage of two Lord Generals . . . [to Cadiz, 1596]. *Lambeth Palace MSS.*, No. 250.

Keightley, Thomas. *History of England.* London, 1839.

Laughton, J. K., editor. *Papers relating to the Defeat of the Spanish Armada*, Vols. I and II. Navy Records Society. London, 1894.

Lewis, Michael. *The Spanish Armada.* London, 1960.

Lewis, Michael. *Armada Guns.* London, 1961.

Loades, D. M. *The Oxford Martyrs.* London, 1971.

Loomie, Albert J. 'An Armada pilot's survey of the English coastline October 1597' in *Mariner's Mirror*, No. 49. November 1963.

Machyn, Henry. *Diary 1550–1563.* Edited by John Gough Nicols. London, 1848.

McKee, Alexander. *From Merciless Invaders.* London, 1963.

Mariéjol, Jean H. *Master of the Armada.* Translated by W. B. Wells. London, 1933.

Martin, B. L. Henri. *Histoire de France.* Paris, 1860.

Mattingly, Garrett H. *The Defeat of the Spanish Armada.* London, 1959.

Miller, Amos C. *Sir Henry Killigrew.* London, 1963.

Motley, J. L. *The Rise of the Dutch Republic.* 3 vols. London, 1855.

Motley, J. L. *History of the United Netherlands.* 4 vols. London, 1869.

Mumby, Frank A. *The Girlhood of Queen Elizabeth: A Narrative in Contemporary Letters.* London, 1909.

Naish, G. P. B. 'Documents illustrating the History of the Spanish Armada' in *The Naval Miscellany*, Vol. IV. Navy Records Society. London, 1952.

Noble, T. C. *An Historical Essay on the Rise and Fall of the Spanish Armada AD 1588.* London, 1886.

Petrie, Sir Charles. *Philip of Spain.* London, 1961.

Ralegh, Sir Walter. *A Report of the*

Truth of the Fight about the Isles of Azores. London, 1591.

Ralegh, Sir Walter. *History of the World.* London, 1614.

Rowse, A. L. *Sir Richard Grenville.* London, 1937.

Rowse, A. L. *Tudor Cornwall.* London, 1941.

Rowse, A. L. *The Expansion of Elizabethan England.* London, 1955.

Rowse, A. L. *Bosworth Field.* London, 1966.

Salisbury MSS.

Sitwell, Edith. *Fanfare for Elizabeth.* London, 1946.

Stephen, Sir James. *Lectures on the History of France.* London, 1851.

Stow, John. *The Annales or Generall Chronicles of England.* London, 1615.

Strachey, Lytton. *Elizabeth and Essex.* London, 1928.

Straker, Ernest. *Wealden Iron.* London, 1931.

Strickland, Agnes. *Life of Mary Queen of Scots.* 2 vols. London, 1837.

Strype, John. *Annals of Queen Elizabeth's Reign.* 4 vols. London, 1725–1731.

Thompson, I. A. A. 'The Armada and administrative reform: the Spanish council of war in the reign of Philip II' in *English Historical Review*, No. 82. October 1967.

Thompson, I. A. A. 'The Appointment of the Duke of Medina Sidonia to the Command of the Spanish Armada' in *Historical Journal*, Vol. 12. 1969.

Ubaldino, Petruccio, *A Discourse concerning the Spanish fleete invadinge Englande in the yeare 1588* (translated by Dr Magri-Mahon and Miss Painter and edited by G. P. B. Naish) in *Naval Miscellany*, Vol. IV. Navy Records Society. London, 1952.

Vandenesse, J. de. *Journal des Voyages de Philippe II*, Vol. 4. Brussels, 1882.

Waldman, Milton. *Elizabeth and Leicester.* London, 1946.

Wallace, Willard M. *Sir Walter Ralegh.* London, 1959.

Walsh, William T. *Philip II.* New York, 1937.

Wernham, R. B. 'Queen Elizabeth and the Portugal Expedition of 1589' in *English Historical Review*, No. CCLVIII. January 1951.

White, Henry. *The Massacre of St Bartholomew.* London, 1868.

Wiesener, Louis. *The Youth of Queen Elizabeth 1533–1558.* Translated by Charlotte M. Yonge. London, 1879.

Williams, Neville. *Contraband Cargoes.* London, 1959.

Williams, Neville. *Elizabeth Queen of England.* London, 1967.

Williamson, James A. *Age of Drake.* London, 1946.

Williamson, James A. *Hawkins of Plymouth.* London, 1949.

Notes on the Illustrations

Where the following abbreviations appear in the notes, they are intended to indicate the locations of pictures, and to acknowledge permission to reproduce photographs that the museums, art galleries and other institutions (or specifically their governing bodies) have granted in cases where they hold the copyright.

ACL: Institut Royal du Patrimoine Artistique, Brussels.   BM: The Trustees of the British Museum, London.   BN: Bibliothèque Nationale, Paris.   Bodleian: The Curators of the Bodleian Library, Oxford.   Edistudio: Instituto de Estudios Editoriales, Barcelona.   HMSO: Controller, Her Majesty's Stationery Office, London.   Mansell: The Mansell Collection, London.   ME: Mary Evans Picture Library, London.   NMM: National Maritime Museum, London.   NPG: National Portrait Gallery, London.   Prado: Museo del Prado, Madrid.   PRO: Public Record Office, London.   RTH: Radio Times Hulton Picture Library.

Page numbers in **bold** type indicate colour plates.

Jacket Design: Ronald Clark. Photo of pikes: Chris Ridley.

Reverse of frontispiece Medallion, 1588. NMM. Photo: Derrick Witty.

Frontispiece Design for a tapestry by an unknown artist, 1588. NMM.

page

10 Engraving from *Cosmography* by Sebastian Münster, c. 1527. BN.

13 Medallions by Jacopo da Trezzo, 1555. NPG.

15 By permission of the Dean and Chapter of Winchester Cathedral. Photo: A. F. Kersting.

16 By permission of the Dean and Chapter of Winchester Cathedral.

19 Oil painting by Antonio Moro, 1554. Prado. Photo: David Manso.

20 Oil painting by Titian, c. 1534. Prado. Photo: David Manso.

22 Engraving from *The Book of Martyrs* by John Foxe, first edition 1563. Mansell.

25 Oil painting by an unknown artist, c. 1542–7. Windsor Castle. Copyright reserved: reproduced by gracious permission of Her Majesty the Queen.

29 Photo: Michael Holford Library.

30 Oil painting by Vincencio Carducho, 1633.
–1 Prado. Photo: David Manso.

32 Oil painting by Titian, 1551. Prado. Photo: David Manso.

34 Oil painting by an unknown artist, 16th cent. Prado. Photo: David Manso.

36 Oil painting by Antonio Moro, c. 1560–70. Prado. Photo: David Manso.

37 (left) Copy by Pantoja of a painting by Sánchez Coello. Prado. Photo: MAS. (right) Oil painting by Sánchez Coello, c. 1560. Prado. Photo: David Manso.

38 Engraving by U. Perrissin and J. Tortorel,
–9 1559. BN. Photo: Giraudon.

40 Drawing by F. Clouet, c. 1560. BN.

41 Oil painting in the style of Corneille de Lyon, 16th cent. Scottish National Portrait Gallery, Edinburgh.

42 Detail from an oil painting by Hans Eworth, 1563. Holyroodhouse, Edinburgh. British Crown Copyright: reproduced by gracious permission of Her Majesty the Queen.

43 Drawing, 10th February 1567. HMSO.

45 Tapestry, 16th cent. Uffizzi Gallery, Florence.

46 Drawing by F. Clouet. BN. Photo: Giraudon.

46 Engraving, 1572. BN, Cabinet des Estampes.
–7 Photo: Giraudon.

51 Detail from a copy of an oil painting possibly by William Segar and now lost, c. 1590. City Art Gallery, Plymouth.

54 Oil painting by Otto Van Veen, 16th cent. Musée Royal des Beaux-Arts, Brussels. Photo: ACL.

57 Oil painting by ?Isaac Oliver, c. 1600. Hatfield House, Hertfordshire. By permission of the Marquess of Salisbury.

58 Oil painting, possibly by Steven van der Muelen, c. 1565–70. Private collection.

64 Oil painting by local master, 16th cent.
–5 Konknklijk Museum voor Schone Kunsten, Anvers. Photo: ACL.

67 Drawing from the papers of Robert Beale, 1587. Mansell.

71 Map, 1587. HMSO.

72 Oil painting by Alcalá Galiano. Photo: MAS.

75 Detail from an oil painting by Marcus Gheeraerts the Younger, 1594. Bodorgan, Anglesey. By permission of Lieutenant-Colonel Sir George Tapps-Gervis-Meyrick.

76 Oil painting by Cornelius Anthoniszoon, 16th cent. NMM.

78 Oil painting, 16th cent. Photo: Thomson Newspapers Ltd.

80 Detail from an engraving in *Civitates Orbis*

Terrarum, 1572. Biblioteca Nacionale, Madrid. Photo: Edistudio.

83 Woodcut, 16th cent. Photo: John Freeman.

85 Engraving, late 16th cent. Mansell.

87 Engraving by A. Ryther from plate drawn by R. Adams, in P. Ubaldino's *Expeditionis Hispanorum*, 1588. BM. Photo: John Freeman.

90 Plans from *Coleccion de Incunables Ameri-*
–1 *canos, Siglo XVI*; Vol. VIII, 'Instruccion Nautica para Navegar', by Dr Diego Garcia de Palacio, 1587. Museo Naval, Madrid.

93 Oil painting by Federigo Zuccaro, 1591. City Art Gallery, Plymouth.

94 Engraving, early 17th cent. Mansell.

95 Engraving, 16th cent. Mansell.

96 Detail from an oil painting by Cornelius Ketal, 1577. Bodleian.

99 See note for page 87.

101 Oil painting by an unknown artist, said to be a 17th- or early 18th-cent. copy of a lost painting. NPG.

102 Detail from an oil painting by an unknown
–3 artist. By permission of the Worshipful Society of Apothecaries. Photo: Derrick Witty.

104 Oil painting by an unknown artist, 16th cent. Museo Naval, Madrid. Photo: David Manso.

106 See note for page 87.

108 See note for page 87.

108 Engraving from a 16th-cent. woodcut.
–9 Mansell.

111 Map, 16th cent. By permission of the Master and Fellows of Magdalene College, Cambridge. Photo: Edward Leigh.

113 See note for page 87.

115 Engraving by Callot from the *Life of Ferdinand I de Medicis*. BM. Photo: John Freeman.

116 Playing card, late 16th cent. RTH.

119 See note for page 87.

123 Engravings by Jacob de Ghenn after Heinrich Goltzius, 1587. Photos: John Freeman.

125 See note for page 87.

127 See note for page 87.

128 Oil painting by John de Critz the Elder, *c.* 1585. NPG.

129 Engraving, late 16th cent. Photo: John Freeman.

131 Engraving of a late 16th-cent. weapon. Mansell.

132 Engraving of a 16th-cent. cannon. ME.

133 See note for page 87.

137 Oil painting by an unknown artist, *c.* 1575. Bodleian. Photo: Nicholas Servian, Woodmansterne.

138 Oil painting by an unknown artist, 1588.
–9 NMM.

140 (top) Spanish chart, c. 1550–60. NMM. (bottom) Chart by Auguste Ryther, 1588. NMM.

142 Document, '1st August' (11th August, New System) 1588. BM. Photo: John Freeman.

146 (left) Engraving from *Profitable and necessarie book of Observations* by William Clowes, 1596. The Trustees of the Wellcome Historical and Medical Museum, London. (right) Engraving from *A briefe and necessarie treatise* . . . by William Clowes, 1585. The Trustees of the Wellcome Historical and Medical Museum, London.

149 Oil painting by an unknown artist, 16th cent. Said to be painted on wood from an Armada ship. By permission of St Faith's Church, Gaywood, King's Lynn. Photo: C. J. Nicholas.

150 Photo: J. Allan Cash.

153 Engraving from *The Image of Ireland* by John Derrick, 1581. BM. Photo: John Freeman.

156 Photo: Edwin Smith.

158 British Travel and Holiday Association.

159 British Travel and Holiday Association.

163 Engraving from *The Image of Ireland* by John Derrick, 1581. BM. Photo: John Freeman.

167 Engravings from *Fragments of Ancient Shipwrightry* by Matthew Baker, 16th cent. By permission of the Master and Fellows of Magdalene College, Cambridge. Photo: Edward Leigh.

168 Oil painting by William Segar, 1590. National Gallery of Ireland.

170 Oil painting by an unknown artist, 16th cent. Louvre, Paris. Photo: Giraudon.

172 Oil painting, 16th cent. Musée de Versailles. Photo: Giraudon.

173 Plymouth Corporation.

175 Engraving from *Kriegsbuch* by Fronsperger, 1575. Mansell.

177 Oil painting after Nicholas Hilliard, 1588. NPG.

178 Autograph, 1575. RTH.

179 Engraving after an oil painting by Frederico Zuccaro. RTH.

180 Detail from an oil painting by Peter Paul Rubens, late 16th cent. Musée Royal des Beaux-Arts, Brussels. Edistudio.

181 Map, 1580. Edistudio.

183 Detail from an engraving of a Pine tapestry. RTH.

186 Oil painting, early 17th cent. Musée de Versailles. Photo: Giraudon.

188 Engraving by Matthaeus Merian, early 17th cent. Mansell.

191 Oil painting attributed to John Bettes II, *c.* 1585–90. NPG.

192 Oil painting, 16th cent. Musée Royal des

Beaux-Arts, Brussels. Photo: ACL.

195 Engraving by R. Elstracke, 16th cent. RTH.

197 Engraving of a 16th-cent. weapon. ME.

201 Oil painting by an unknown artist, 1571. NPG.

202 Oil painting by an unknown artist, 1602. NPG.

204 Oil painting by a disciple of Sánchez Coello. Prado. Photo: David Manso.

206 By permission of Sydney Schofield, Esq. Photo: J. Crampton.

208 Engraving, 16th cent. Mansell.

212 Engraving, 16th cent. RTH.

213 Engraving, c. 1596. BM. Photo: John Freeman.

215 Oil painting by an unknown artist, c. 1595. Monteviot, Jedburgh, Roxburghshire. By permission of the Marquess of Lothian. Photo: Scottish National Portrait Gallery.

219 Glazed tiles at Palacio Viso del Marques, early 17th cent. Edistudio.

220 Title page from *The Mariner's Mirrour*, 1588. Folger Shakespeare Library, Washington, DC.

223 Sherborne Castle, Dorset. By permission of Simon Wingfield Digby, Esq. Photo: J. Crampton.

225 Photo: J. Crampton.

226 Engraving, 16th cent. Photo: John Freeman.

227 Oil painting by Marcus Gheeraerts the Younger, 1608. Hatfield House, Hertfordshire. By permission of the Marquess of Salisbury. Photo: Courtauld Institute.

228 Engraving, 16th cent. Biblioteca National, –9 Madrid. Edistudio.

233 Document, 1597. PRO.

237 Drawing, 16th cent. BM. Photo: John Freeman.

240 Model, 1540. Museo Naval, Madrid.

243 Detail from an oil painting by an unknown artist, 1589. NPG.

245 Oil painting by Sánchez Coello, c. 1585. Prado. Photo: David Manso.

246 Photo: Michael Holford Library. –7

248 Oil painting by Juan Pantoja de la Cruz, ?1598. El Escorial. Photo: MAS.

251 Oil painting by Justus Tilens, c. 1593. Prado. Photo: David Manso.

252 Engraving from *Hibernia Pacata*, 1633. RTH.

255 Engraving by H. Cock after Brueghel. Mansell.

257 Engraving after Juan Pantoxa, 1606, ME.

261 Engraving by Visscher, 16th cent. ME.

263 Engraving from *Hibernia Pacata*, 1633. RTH.

266 Engraving from *Hibernia Pacata*, 1633. RTH.

270 Photo: J. Allan Cash.

273 (top) Oil painting by an unknown artist, c. 1583. By permission of the Archbishop of Canterbury. Copyright reserved by the Courtauld Institute and the Church Commissioners. (bottom) Oil painting attributed to Hieronimo Custodis, c. 1590–5. NPG.

274 Oil painting by Daniel Mytens, 1621. NPG.

275 From a series of drawings, probably by William Camden, early 17th cent. BM. Photo: John Freeman.

Index

Page numbers in **bold** type refer to colour plates; page numbers in *italics*, to black-and-white illustrations.

Due 14 Days From Latest Date

AUG 20 1984	DEC 30 1985		
SEP 4 1984	JUL 0 2 2004		
SEP 15 1984			
SEP 24 1984			
OCT 26 1984			
FEB 2 1985	WITHDRAWN		
MAR 22 1985			
MAY 17 1985			
OCT 19 1985			

Feast from the Mideast

Also by Faye Levy

Jewish Cooking for Dummies

1,000 Jewish Recipes

Classic Cooking Techniques

The New Casserole

Faye Levy's International Vegetable Cookbook

Faye Levy's International Chicken Cookbook

Faye Levy's International Jewish Cookbook

Sensational Pasta

Fresh from France: Vegetable Creations

Chocolate Sensations

Feast from the Mideast

Mideast

250 Sun-Drenched Dishes

from the Lands of the Bible

FAYE LEVY

HarperCollins*Publishers*

HarperCollins books may be purchased for educational, business, or sales promotional use. For information, please write: Special Markets Department, HarperCollins Publishers Inc., 10 East 53rd Street, New York, NY 10022.

FIRST EDITION

Designed by Cassandra J. Pappas

Printed on acid-free paper

Library of Congress Cataloging-in-Publication Data
Levy, Faye.
Feast from the Mideast: 250 sun-drenched dishes from the lands of the Bible / Faye Levy.—1st ed.
p. cm.
Includes bibliographical references and index.
ISBN 0-06-009361-7
1. Cookery, Middle Eastern. I. Title.
TX725.M628L48 2003
641.5956—dc21   2003042329

03 04 05 06 07 ❖/ RRD 10 9 8 7 6 5 4 3 2 1

In memory of
Rachel and Zechariah Levy,
my parents-in-law,
for their Middle Eastern cooking,
culture, and hospitality.

Acknowledgments

First, I would like to thank Yakir, my husband, who was born and raised in the Mideast, and has helped make our last thirty-four years such an exciting culinary adventure. With his affinity for Middle Eastern people, culture, and food, he has contributed a great deal to my research, writing, and tasting. Indeed, this book is the fruit of the effort of the two of us.

Yakir's parents, Rachel and Zechariah Levy, taught me as much about the culture of their native Yemen as about its cuisine. So did many Middle Eastern members of our extended family, notably his aunt, Mazal Cohen.

During the last three decades I have learned from my Middle Eastern family about numerous aspects of the region's food. My sisters-in-law have joined me at Israel's outdoor souks in search of the best produce and the most delicious, fresh-baked flatbreads, and have cooked many family recipes so I could enjoy them. I truly appreciate all I discovered about Yemenite food from my sister-in-law Hedva Cohen, and about Middle Eastern food and culture from my brothers-in-law Yahalom and Prachya Levy, Avi Levi, and David Cohen. Thanks also to my sisters-in-law Mati Kahn and Ety Levy, for their wonderful vegetable and lentil dishes and their insights on the uses of fresh spices, and Nirit Levy, for her delicious spicy Yemenite soup and her advice on making many savory Israeli dishes.

Thanks also to my mother, Pauline Kahn Luria, and my brother, Tzvi Kahn, both Jerusalemites for decades, for sharing their experiences as Americans adopting Middle Eastern culture and cuisine, for introducing me to great local markets and eateries, and for their wholehearted support.

Over the years many friends, neighbors, colleagues, and casual acquaintances have freely given their time to tell me about their favorite foods and how they cook them. It's impossible to mention everyone. I am especially grateful to my good friend, cookbook author Ronnie Venezia of Jerusalem, for teaching me about Lebanese and Israeli food; and to her mother, Lebanese-born Suzanne Elmaleh, who taught me to make kibbe, *ma'amoul*, and other Middle Eastern delights. Thanks to my friend Lior Moore in Givatayim, Israel, for valuable information about Middle Eastern ingredients and Iraqi specialties; and to Said and Manar Oorabi of Akko, for the warm welcome to their home and the tasty tour of their city and for their tips on preparing Palestinian Arab specialties.

Thanks to Dogan Ozcan of Istanbul, for introducing Yakir and me to the food culture of his city and for showing us wonderful markets, pastry shops, and other eateries; to my friend Samir Abdullah of Alexandria, Egypt, editor in chief of *Arab World* newspaper, for information about Egyptian cooking; to my friends Valerie and Hayim Alon and to Yakir's cousin Orit Levi, for their tasty Middle Eastern and Israeli dishes and tips on ingredients; to my friends and former neighbors Treaty and Kaikoo Zartoshty, for their delicious Iranian home cooking at their lavish family parties; and to my friend Shahrouz Zandi, for sharing information about Persian culture and cuisine over the years.

Thanks so much to Middle Eastern culinary expert and historian Charles Perry of the *Los Angeles Times*, for inviting us to his home for a memorable Middle Eastern feast he cooked himself. We have treasured his friendship for two decades. We benefited from his advice on finding the ingredients for Middle Eastern cooking and the most interesting restaurants, bakeries, and markets, whether in California or in Turkey or elsewhere in the Mideast. His wonderful articles on the subject have been priceless.

I appreciate the tips I gleaned from Lebanese chefs Sameer Eid of Phoenicia restaurant in Birmingham, Michigan, and Mohammed Hachem of Oasis Restaurant in Walled Lake, Michigan; from Turkish chef Esin Denktas; from Malek of Ta'ami Mid-east Food Market in Garden Grove, California; and from Norik Shahbazian of Panos Pastry in Hollywood, California.

Over the years many books and articles have brought foods to life even before I could taste them. To benefit from exploring the Middle Eastern foods in my own area I have especially enjoyed articles on markets and restaurants written by Linda Burum, Jonathan Gold, Barbara Hansen, and Max Jacobson.

I value the support I received from the editors of my own articles, most recently Connie Pollock of the Los Angeles Times Syndicate, Russ Parsons and Jennifer Lowe of the *Los Angeles Times*, and Michal Meyers of the *Jerusalem Post*. By publishing my stories, each enabled me to research recipes and subjects close to my heart.

Thanks so much to my editor, Susan Friedland, for her creative ideas and for making the process of turning my manuscript into a book smooth and enjoyable. Her appreciation of fine food, her high standards, and her thorough knowledge of cooking made the book much better. I also appreciate the quality editorial work of Califia Suntree, as well as Carrie Bachman's and Beth Tarson's work in promoting the book. Thanks to my agent, Jane Dystel, for enthusiastically and efficiently helping to bring my ideas to light.

Contents

Introduction

I was seventeen years old when I visited the Middle East for the first time. On a trip to discover the legendary land of "milk and honey" of my ancestors, I found a sunny world of olive trees, grape arbors, citrus groves, friendly people, and bold flavors. I loved it so much that a year later I moved to Jerusalem from my birthplace, Washington, D.C. Living in this part of the globe proved to be an incredible cultural adventure. Marrying a Middle Eastern man—Yakir Levy—the next year and becoming a part of his family awakened my passion for cooking and was the genesis of my life's work.

You could say that my introduction to the Middle Eastern kitchen was anything but auspicious. It came as an admonition from Yakir's mother: "How can I accept that my son marry someone who does not know how to cook?" Where she came from, a traditional society on the southwest coast of the Arabian Peninsula, a primary role of a wife was to cook for her husband.

I figured it wouldn't hurt to find out how to prepare a few dishes. I began to cook with neighbors, friends, and family members. As I learned to prepare the region's repertoire of dishes, I gained a new perspective on flavor from their fresh, mouthwatering specialties: stuffed vegetables, tempting rice pilafs, roasted vegetable appetizers, spicy meat soups, peppery fish stews, hearty bean casseroles, and delectable savory and sweet pastries.

Delving into this cuisine proved so fascinating that I decided to pursue a career in the culinary field. For over three decades I have been learning, cooking, refining, and teaching the recipes of my second homeland. I enjoy sharing my firsthand knowledge of this wonderful, delicious cooking style and its many time-tested, flavor-rich formulas with my friends, readers, and students. I like to focus on Middle Eastern foods that are a pleasure to prepare, serve, and eat in America today.

The Middle East is the meeting place of three continents—Asia, Africa, and Europe—and the birthplace of three major world religions—Judaism, Christianity, and Islam. The region stretches from the Indian Ocean to the Mediterranean and encompasses terrains ranging from mountains to deserts to fertile coastal plains. Its population exceeds that of the United States and its area is nearly as large.

In spite of the vast contribution of the Middle East to our cultural heritage, many of the region's food specialties have yet to be discovered by most Americans.

The Middle East has had an immense impact on our food fundamentals. Agriculture itself is said to have begun in the area. There is evidence that some of our most basic foodstuffs—cultivated wheat, yeast-risen bread, cheese, and wine—were first produced in the region.

This is a personal book about the cuisine I have embraced and my joy in discovering this delightful way of cooking. My entertaining has gained a new dimension of color and flavor from the astounding array of Middle Eastern appetizers. My celebrations are enhanced by tender grilled meats like savory kabobs and citrus-marinated chicken, great grain dishes like saffron rice pilaf studded with toasted almonds, and exotic sweets like walnut phyllo fingers with orange-flower water and cinnamon. There's plenty to enliven simple everyday meals too, from refreshing salads to aromatic, fast-grilled fish to satisfying whole-meal soups.

Food lovers ask me about dishes that are low in fat and high in taste. When they sample the fragrant Middle Eastern dishes, they become immediate fans. Like the Mediterranean diet, the Middle Eastern manner of preparing food is perfect for our time and corresponds to contemporary nutritionists' guidelines for healthful dining.

The nations of the Middle East share many food customs that are worth emulating in our own kitchens for reasons of taste, health, simplicity, and variety. A popular practice is beginning the meal with a bite of freshness—whether it's an Israeli-Lebanese diced salad of tomatoes, cucumbers, and onions; a profusion of herbs rolled up in lavash flatbread with a little feta cheese in the Persian manner; or a selection of fresh and grilled vegetable meze. To enrich vegetables and to moisten their bread, people often opt for olive oil rather than butter or animal fats.

In this book you will find dishes that will enable you and your family to enjoy meat in the frugal, healthy Middle Eastern manner by using a small quantity to accent a generous portion of vegetables or legumes. You will savor gently stewed dishes in which the flavors of meats and vegetables mingle.

Living in the Middle East gave me the finest introduction I could wish for to its civilization and cuisine. I communicated with people every day and grew to understand their culture. From my college education in the region, at the Hebrew University in Jerusalem and Tel Aviv University, I acquired an academic understanding of Middle Eastern society as well by majoring in sociology and anthropology.

I also discovered how much fun it is to learn about cooking by simply talking to people. With a notebook in my hand, I asked everyone how he or she cooked—fellow students, friends, neighbors, colleagues at work, and people I met on the bus and at the store. Although some found my enthusiasm amusing, they were friendly and always glad to talk about their favorite meals.

Living at the western end of the Mediterranean, in France, home to Europe's largest Arab community, enabled Yakir and me to further explore North African and Lebanese cuisines. Six years of culinary education in the French capital at La Varenne Cooking School gave me an overview of culinary styles and methods and an essential understanding of food, from the market to the table.

Because of my Jewish heritage, I was drawn to the Middle East in my youth in search of my cultural roots. My husband, his siblings, and nearly all of our extended family are natives of the Middle East, as were their parents and grandparents, whose origins were in Yemen, Iraq, or Morocco. My mother and brother have also made the Middle East their home and have lived in Jerusalem for the last thirty-four years. We have a close connection with the region. We return regularly to visit our family and friends in Israel and they come to vacation with us in our home in Los Angeles. Our relatives and many of our friends around the globe are also Middle Eastern, and the region's traditions lend a lively flavor to our get-togethers on holidays and special occasions.

Los Angeles, with its Mediterranean climate, attracted us, like many other people from the Middle East. Indeed, southern California has the largest Middle Eastern population in the country and many of our neighbors are from that part of the world. Our area has the largest Persian community outside Iran, the greatest Armenian population outside Armenia and a substantial number of Israelis. Here, we continue to pursue our passion. At our favorite food markets, many of the shoppers share our culinary culture, and we frequently engage them in conversations about our favorite subject. But there are many other areas in North America with considerable Middle Eastern communities and the ingredients for these recipes are therefore easy to find.

I have chosen recipes that are best suited to American ingredients, kitchens, and inclinations to prepare certain kinds of dishes. I have included plenty of quick entrées, as well as homey casseroles that simmer unattended on a low flame, which are great for make-ahead meals. Whenever possible, I have streamlined recipes to save time and effort.

To best represent Middle Eastern cuisine, I have tried to develop modern, enticing recipes and menus that are tempting to Americans and that suit our lifestyles while remaining true to their sources. Most of them feature ingredients that are readily available in our markets, as many Middle Eastern ingredients and dishes have become mainstream in our country. Also included here are tips I have learned from Middle Easterners who cook in the United States, as well as tricks I have discovered over the years in my own cooking.

These recipes range from unhurried, slow-simmered meat, vegetable, and bean casseroles enlivened with spice, to rapid renditions of certain dishes using good-quality, timesaving ingredients. If a traditional dish is high in fat, I try to suggest healthier ways to enjoy it, with, for example, vegetable variations of some meat dishes.

In perusing the recipes, you will find some exotic tastes as well as new versions of familiar favorites. If you're a chicken soup aficionado, you may enjoy the way the broth's flavor is transformed by my Middle Eastern mother-in-law's spice mix of cumin, turmeric, and pepper, as I did when I first tasted it. Lively Turkish rice pilaf accented with garlic, tomatoes, and cilantro makes a wonderfully savory bed for backyard barbecue favorites.

Middle Eastern cooking is a relaxing cuisine, full of convenient dishes created in simple kitchens. For this style of cooking, you don't need much culinary expertise. The recipes in this book are casual and down-to-earth and I hope they will make you want to go straight into the kitchen to start cooking. I hope you will find the book a pleasure to use and that you will enjoy these delightful dishes from the lands of the Hebrew and Christian Bibles and of the Koran.

The Distinctive Cooking
Styles of the Peoples
of the Middle East

People in many parts of the Middle East have similar kitchen customs. Food fusion, a modern concept to many of us, has been happening here for millennia as a result of commerce, conquests, and the movements of tribes and ethnic groups.

Some experts define the boundaries of the Middle East culturally, others politically, still others historically. All agree on one point: In the heart of the area lie the biblical lands—Egypt, Israel, Lebanon, Syria, and Iraq. Like its civilization, the region's vibrant culinary culture developed across a much broader territory— the area stretching from Iran in the east to Turkey and North Africa in the west. In this book I focus on the cooking of Egypt, Israel, Syria, Jordan, Lebanon, Turkey, Cyprus, Iraq, Iran, Yemen, Saudi Arabia, and the Gulf States, following the most common definition of the Middle East, also called the Mideast.

The Middle East is a bridge between three continents and was one of the chief cradles of civilization. At its heart is the Fertile Crescent, an ancient agricultural region extending from the Tigris and Euphrates basin in Iraq to the Mediterranean coast and the Nile River valley. Throughout history the region was crossed by traders and migrating peoples, which created a mosaic of many small groups with distinctive identities. Dishes were modified based on the availability of spices imported by Arab merchants, who also spread their culture and cuisine.

The ancient empires that ruled the area, such as the Assyrians, Babylonians, and Persians, each had their impact on the people and their food. In more recent history, the Ottoman Empire led to a broadening of the region's recipe repertoire by bringing together people and foodstuffs from the far corners of its territory, which stretched from the Balkans to North Africa to Iraq. The Ottomans encouraged trade, and their markets, such as the still-popular Egyptian Spice Bazaar in Istanbul, boasted a great variety of foods from near and far. Because the sultans enjoyed fine cuisine, they brought cooks from around the empire to create banquets in their palace kitchens. Many of their recipes later spread throughout the area. For this reason, the countries of the Middle East and some beyond its borders share many culinary elements.

In addition to climate, available foods, and history, religion has affected the development of certain dishes and dietary practices. Observant Muslims and Jews prohibit pork from their tables. Muslims also avoid wine, while Jews do not eat shellfish. On the calendar of Middle Eastern Christians there are numerous meatless days, which has led to an extensive repertoire of vegetarian entrées.

With its rich history, broad geographic expanse, and demographic diversity, Middle Eastern cuisine developed a tremendous number of lively dishes. The liberal use of robust ingredients—garlic, onions, peppers, tomatoes, olive oil, fresh herbs, and a wide spectrum of spices—makes this style irresistible.

Lovers of Mediterranean cooking will enjoy these foods too. Because the Middle East overlaps the Eastern Mediterranean, their cuisines share certain qualities. In both regions good ingredients are treated simply. For example, a plate of cooked fava beans drizzled with extra-virgin olive oil, accompanied by a few fine olives or a small piece of pungent cheese and some fresh flatbread, easily fits the bill as a light supper in either cuisine.

Yet these two major culinary styles are not the same. Mideast cooks emphasize different foods than do those in the Mediterranean countries most familiar to us—Italy, France, and Spain. Menus in the Mideast tend to include more vegetables, legumes, and grains and less meat, and call for lamb rather than pork. Like the Greeks, people in the Mideast have a predilection for plain yogurt, flatbreads, and bulgur wheat but flavor their food with more spices and less cheese than their Hellenic neighbors.

Entrées in the Mideast are flavored more often with cilantro or mint than with basil, and often feature sesame, cumin, cinnamon, and allspice, which are used infrequently west of Greece. Although not all Middle Eastern food is spicy, black and red pepper and chilies are often used with a more liberal hand. The variety of spices used is a legacy of the period when the spice caravans passed through the area. Cooks in the region do not shy away from bold flavors and exuberantly use fresh garlic and raw green onions in generous quantities.

Tart foods are valued for the liveliness they add to sauces. In much of the Mideast lemons are often on the table, not just to accompany fish, but to squeeze over everything from salads to soups to stews. In addition to vinegar, lemons, and limes, other tart flavors might come from pomegranate or tamarind pastes, which provide their sour accents to stews and braised dishes. Sumac, a tart purple powder made from dried berries, is sprinkled over kabobs and salads and added to salad dressings and herb blends. These accents balance rich foods or are used to create sweet-and-sour or spicy-and-sour dishes.

As in next-door India, ghee, or clarified butter, is used in many dishes, including cakes, pastries, and cookies. Nuts, notably pistachios, pine nuts, almonds, and walnuts, occupy a prominent place in the kitchen, not just as snacks and for sweets but as the basis for creamy sauces.

Locals love grapes but do not usually cook with wine. Instead, they use pomegranate, citrus, and other fruit juices, as well as dried fruit like raisins and dried apricots, to give a tangy sweetness to their entrées. They also use treasured fruits, such as dates and figs, to sweeten the daily diet and make desserts.

Flatbreads are the primary staple, some made with yeast and some unleavened. Wheat in other forms, both whole and cracked, appears in many dishes from appetizers, to meat and fish entrées called kibbe, to desserts. In much of the area rice is served every day but it is especially important for festive occasions. Around the Mideast, legumes are central to the diet and are used in some surprising ways—as breakfast dishes, roasted snacks, and sweets, for example.

Floral extracts of orange blossoms and roses lend their exotic perfumes to desserts and pastries, which are often sweetened with syrups. Although people from this area came up with the technique of making sugar from sugarcane, they remain faithful to the more ancient sweetener, honey. This biblical symbol of good living, which was also said to be a favorite of the Prophet Muhammad, is used in a variety of sweets. Indeed, natives sometimes refer to the syrups they prepare for moistening desserts as honey, whether or not it contains any.

It's good to keep in mind that the cooking ingredients of the region have changed considerably since biblical times. Middle Eastern cuisine would be hard to recognize without tomatoes and hot peppers, which originated in the New World.

Regional Differences

From a culinary standpoint, the Middle East can be divided into three areas: 1) The Eastern Mediterranean, 2) the Arabian Peninsula and Iraq, and 3) Iran. Differences between the cuisines are sometimes subtle. People use many similar spices, herbs, and flavorings and the distinctions are mostly a matter of degree. Some areas have a preference for peppery food, while others like milder cooking, but this also depends on individual taste.

The availability of ingredients also determines the style of cooking. Coastal inhabitants have a long tradition of eating fish, while among those inland the fruits of the sea simply have not had time to become part of those communities' culinary heritage. Even though seafood is available at their markets, many simply may not be tempted by it.

National borders are not culinary boundaries and many tastes spill over into other regions. The Mideast is a mosaic of peoples, with various ethnic groups living in several countries. Kurdish people, for example, live in Turkey and Iran as well as Iraq. Armenians reside in several eastern Mediterranean countries. Iraqi Assyrians living in North America cook spicier food than those whose families come from Iran. The Middle Eastern cooking at restaurants in America and the selection of breads, cakes, and ingredients in grocery stores depends on where the local population originated. Following the neighborhood's makeup, in Los Angeles there are Persian influences in some markets and Armenian ones in others. (See "Middle Eastern Marketing," page 22). Although there are exceptions to every generalization, here are a few broad guidelines to the taste and food habits of each area.

The Eastern Mediterranean—
Turkey, Cyprus, Syria, Lebanon, Israel, Jordan, and Egypt

Olives are central to this area's culinary style. The olive is native to the eastern Mediterranean and is among the world's oldest known cultivated trees. Turkish, Lebanese, and Israeli olive oil are exported to the west and found in specialty shops. Extra-virgin olive oil is prized, and used generously in fine vegetable dishes.

Lebanese families enjoy an aromatic, light cuisine, with plenty of fresh salads. To flavor sauces and stews, cooks rely on liberal amounts of fresh garlic, lemon juice, and herbs like flat-leaf parsley, dill, mint, and cilantro (fresh coriander) rather than pepper and other pungent spices. For seasoning meats they like sweet spices, such as cinnamon, cloves, and allspice. Creamy sesame tahini is the favorite sauce. Such tastes are loved in Syria, too, with the addition of red Aleppo pepper, which is not as searing as cayenne and gives food a pleasing warmth.

Turkish and Cypriot cooks also use these flavors in their food. In addition, they like luscious sauces made with walnuts, hazelnuts, or almonds with their chicken and meat. Many add a pinch of sugar to tomato sauces and to vegetable dishes to give them a subtle hint of sweetness. Inspired by the opulent palace cuisine of the Ottoman Empire, sumptuous pilafs and elaborate pastries also became part of Turkish cuisine, as well as a rich repertoire of desserts.

Flavors similar to those favored in Lebanon, Syria, and Turkey are prized by cooks in Israel, Palestine, Jordan, and Egypt, who also like cumin for seasoning their chicken and meats. Among Egyptian cooks coriander seed is a great favorite for a broad range of vegetable and meat dishes. Cardamom seeds enter many soup pots in the land of the Nile, and often mastic as well (page 11).

The Arabian Peninsula and Iraq

Pepper rules in this region, which includes Yemen, Saudi Arabia, the United Arab Emirates, Kuwait, Bahrain, and Qatar, and the cuisine is hearty and simple. Black pepper is used generously, as are hot red pepper and fresh and dried chilies. Pepper is often paired with garlic to make spicy stews, soups, and relishes. Cumin as well as turmeric lend a currylike aroma to these dishes, while cilantro is the favorite herb. Instead of olive oil, people cook with vegetable oil or clarified butter.

People from Iraq also flavor their stews with cumin and turmeric. *Baharat*, a mixture of mainly sweet spices (page 13), is another popular seasoning, primarily for meat dishes. These seasonings are also used in Saudi Arabia and the Persian Gulf States, sometimes combined with gingerroot, resulting in sauces that somewhat resemble those of their neighbor across the Arabian Sea, India.

Iran

Unlike people in other regions of the Mideast, Persians do not like peppery or highly garlicky food, and olive oil is not an important part of their culinary tradition. Instead, they accent their foods with a profusion of herbs, beginning meals with an assortment of fresh herb sprigs and using many cooked ones as a flavoring base for stews and soups. Favorite herbs include tarragon, cilantro, mint, chives, parsley, garlic chives, and fenugreek.

A variety of sour elements lend a tart taste to some Iranian sauces, including the juice of sour pomegranates or of unripe grapes. Limes are another favorite (our common limes, by the way, are known as Persian limes). The tart seasonings are used subtly so the dishes are not aggressively acidic. Sometimes dried fruit is added to sauces as well for a sweet-and-sour flavor.

Some Iranian foods are flavored with turmeric but the most-loved spice is saffron, used in numerous rice dishes, of which the Persians are particularly fond, and in marinades for grilled meats and many sauces as well. Saffron even flavors ice cream and other desserts.

Beyond the Borders:
The Influences of
Middle Eastern Cooking

Positioned at the crossroads of Asia, Europe, and Africa, the Middle East has long been a territory of trade and travel. Throughout history, different peoples have come here for many reasons, taking ingredients back to their land of origin and often exchanging foodstuffs and ideas with the natives of the area.

With the far-reaching influence of the ancient Persian, Roman, and Ottoman empires, among others, the Middle East found itself associated with other regions under a single rule. Over time, this also led to common culinary customs and tastes, sometimes among areas that are quite far from each other. Morocco, for example, shares with Iran a love of fruit simmered with poultry and meat for main courses to give the sauces a sweet accent. Moroccans call these stews tagines and Iranians call them *khoreshes.*

Couscous, Morocco's famous pasta, is valued in Egypt and some other Middle Eastern countries. Many of North Africa's savory and sweet pastries resemble those of the Middle East, from Turkey to Iran. They might have different names, and their presentation might be given a different twist, but the similarities are striking. For example, Tunisians transform Turkish *beurreks* into fried pastries called *briks*. In most of North Africa, rich date-filled Middle Eastern cookies are also popular, as are phyllo-dough desserts sweetened with syrup.

Northern Mediterranean countries west of Turkey also share many characteristics with the cuisine of the Mideast. The resemblance is greatest with Greek cooking, which recalls the Turkish style in many ways. Like the cooks of the Mideast, Greeks often prepare meatless meals based on oil-enriched vegetables and serve them with flatbreads or with rice. Greek bakers have become renowned for their baklava and other Middle Eastern sweets, such as buttery shortbread cookies called *graybeh* (or, in Greek, kourabiedes) and Noah's pudding made of wheat, fruits, and nuts. Yet Greek food tends to be seasoned differently, as it is less likely to contain cilantro, cumin, turmeric, and hot pepper than Mideastern dishes. There are numerous Middle Eastern influences in other Mediterranean countries as well, notably in Sicily, where cooks have a predilection for pairing pine nuts and currants in a variety of dishes.

Certain peoples, such as the Assyrians and the Armenians, are indigenous to the Mideast and thus they share much of its culinary culture. So do the countries of the Balkan Peninsula, which were ruled by the Ottoman Empire and exchanged many dishes with the inhabitants of Turkey. Similarly, the Caucasus countries relish several dishes that are prized in Turkey and Iran.

To the east of the region, Afghan cooking has much in common with the Persian style. Such dishes as yogurt-topped fried eggplant slices are loved by natives of both lands, although Afghanis tend to make theirs more peppery and, in general, enjoy hotter spices than do Iranians.

Still farther east, in India and Pakistan, nan, the region's signature flatbread, is said to have come from the Mideast perhaps via Iran, where the same word is used for flatbread. When the Arabs ruled the area, they brought their domed clay ovens, and these became the famed Indian tandoori ovens. In turn, the Indian Peninsula had a great influence on the flavor of Mideast food. The prized spices of India came to the Mideast through the spice route and by sea. The currylike Yemenite soup spice and the *baharat* blends of sweet spices and pepper used in Iraq, Saudi Arabia, and the United Arab Emirates have their roots in these spices.

You can even find Middle Eastern influence as far away as Mexico, which received its cumin and cilantro from the Mideast when the Spanish brought them, and contributed its peppers and tomatoes, a barter that immeasurably enriched both regions' repertoires. Thai restaurants have a delicious curry they call "Muslim curry," which they developed as a result of trade with Persia.

The Mideast's tradition of trade with other regions has become accelerated in modern times and has made many Middle Eastern foods familiar around the world. Americans can now buy fine pastries from Syria and Saudi Arabia at Middle Eastern markets, even though they were baked halfway around the globe.

The Mideast Pantry for the American Kitchen

Certain key ingredients, such as fava beans, pomegranate paste, *baharat* spice mix, *halloumi* cheese, and lavash flatbread, give dishes their Mideast identity. Here is a brief overview of the Mideastern pantry that can help serve as a guide to shopping and to getting to know special ingredients that may not be familiar from other cuisines. Additional information about specific foods can be found throughout the book.

Shopping

With the growing interest in Mediterranean and Middle Eastern cooking, you can find many ingredients at the supermarket. Quite a few have become part of the mainstream and are displayed with other similar American ingredients—hummus with the deli foods, for example. Others may be grouped in the ethnic, gourmet, kosher, or health food aisles. Because many ingredients for Mideastern cooking appeal to health-conscious cooks and to adventurous ones, there's often a wider choice in natural food stores and gourmet shops than in supermarkets.

You can find the most extensive selection in Mediterranean and Middle Eastern markets, which vary somewhat depending on your neighborhood. In my area many are Persian, Armenian, or Israeli, while in the Dearborn, Michigan, area near Detroit more of the markets are Chaldean or Lebanese. Greeks share a fondness for many of the same foods and this is evident from their grocery stores.

The recipes in this book almost always suggest substitutions, but if you don't find a special ingredient and would like to try it, you can get it by mail-order or on-line.

If you happen to pass a grocery store that might be Middle Eastern, one hint is a storefront sign relating to meat. A notice that the store has *hallal* meat or kosher meat is often a key that Middle Eastern foods can be found there too. Kosher meat has been prepared according to Jewish dietary regulations, while *hallal* meat conforms to Muslim ones.

Spices, Herbs, and Flavorings

People in the region have long enjoyed a variety of flavorings, such as olives, which have been cultivated in the Eastern Mediterranean since ancient times, and the native cumin and garlic. Thanks to the age-old spice trade with the Far East, Middle Eastern cooks have had more than a millennium to experiment with cinnamon, ginger, turmeric, and cardamom. Mediterranean herbs grow in the Mideast as well and are popular in the kitchen. Flat-leaf, or Italian, parsley, and thyme are especially loved. Cilantro (fresh coriander), which is native to the Middle East, dill, and mint are used by many cooks as well.

The freshness of spices and dried herbs is important for flavorful results. Buy them in a shop that has good turnover. Store them in tightly covered jars or airtight containers in a cool, dry, dark cupboard.

Following are some unique spices and herbs and a few useful spice blends that will lend their special flavor to specific dishes.

Spices

Aleppo pepper is a celebrated red spice you'll find at Mideastern grocery stores. It adds a gentle heat, more than paprika but much less than cayenne. Recently some prominent American chefs began featuring it on trendy menus. The usual substitute is paprika with a few pinches of cayenne.

Cardamom pods are popular in the Mideast for both savory dishes and desserts. You can buy whole pods or use only the seeds.

Mastic, a spice that looks like little pearls, is an aromatic resin from a Mediterranean tree in the cashew family called *Pistacia lentiscus.* The spice is used around the region in ice creams and, in Egypt, to flavor soups. It imparts a refreshing, woodsy aroma that recalls rosemary. Mastic is usually crushed, put in cheesecloth, or infused in a liquid and strained.

Saffron is native to the Mideast and is widely used in the region in rice dishes, marinades, stews, and, in Persian kitchens, in desserts as well. For more information, see page 15.

Sumac is a tart, reddish-purple spice ground from dried sumac berries. It gives foods a lemony flavor and is popular in salad dressings and for sprinkling on grilled meats. Often it is mixed with finely sliced onions, as an accompaniment for meat.

HERBS

Purslane is a succulent herb with tender, oval leaves used in salads in eastern Mediterranean countries. Like watercress, it is highly perishable and should be used within two days of purchase. It's called *verdolagas* in Spanish and is also available in Latino markets.

Fenugreek greens have attractive oval leaves and a bitter flavor. In the Persian kitchen, they are cooked with leeks and other herbs to flavor stews.

Garlic chives are served whole in the Persian kitchen on appetizer platters, along with other herbs.

Spice and Herb Blends

As in neighboring India, many cooks in the Mideast prepare spice blends at home, buying whole spices and pounding them in a mortar with pestle. To save time, you can use a spice grinder or coffee grinder (a separate one from the one you use for coffee). You'll find many spice blends at Middle Eastern shops, some for general uses and others for specific dishes like grilled meats or fish.

Seven Spices

Seven Spices, sometimes labeled Lebanese Seven Spices, is a popular blend for seasoning meats but is good with vegetables as well. Most formulas contain sweet spices, notably cinnamon and cloves, as well as black pepper. It may include ginger, nutmeg, cardamom, coriander, cumin, paprika, a small amount of cayenne, hot red chili powder, or allspice. A simpler three-spice blend used by some Lebanese cooks consists of paprika, cinnamon, and a little cayenne.

The usual alternative to Seven Spices is allspice, sometimes mixed with cinnamon. I occasionally substitute an Indian spice blend, garam masala, which generally contains sweet spices and black pepper and is available at many supermarkets. You can also use Quatre Epices, or Four Spices, a French blend of sweet spices.

To make your own Seven Spices blend, start with fresh spices. Mix together 1 tablespoon freshly ground black pepper, 1 tablespoon ground cinnamon, 1 tablespoon ground ginger, and 1 tablespoon ground cardamom. Add three of the following: 1 tablespoon paprika, ground coriander, ground cumin, or allspice, 1½ teaspoons freshly grated or ground nutmeg, or 1 teaspoon chili powder or ground cloves. Use this as an easy starting point, then increase the proportions of some of the spices if you like.

Baharat

Baharat is a spice blend favored in many Persian Gulf countries. Cardamom is an important flavor in this mix. Its other components resemble those in Seven Spices and they can be used interchangeably.

Soup Spice or Yemenite Soup Spice

Soup spice is a currylike, yellow-orange blend of cumin, turmeric, black pepper, and sometimes cardamom. It's used not only for soups but for stews, vegetable dishes, and in rubs for grilled meats.

To make your own Soup Spice: Grind ⅓ cup whole cumin seeds. Mix them with 4 to 5 teaspoons ground turmeric and 4 to 5 teaspoons freshly ground black pepper.

ZAHTAR

Zahtar is a blend of herbs and often sesame seeds popular in eastern Mediterranean countries. The term also refers to a specific wild herb called wild marjoram, Syrian marjoram, or hyssop. Others use the word zahtar to mean thyme, savory, or oregano.

The blend's usual components are dried thyme, marjoram, summer savory, or a mixture of herbs, combined with toasted sesame seeds, ground sumac, or both. Ground toasted chickpeas or toasted nuts may also be included.

Traditionally, zahtar is sprinkled over cheeses and accompanies breads. In Lebanese and Palestinian kitchens, zahtar mixed with olive oil is a favorite topping for bread dough, which is then baked as a pizzalike snack (see Sesame Herb Bread, page 319). The zahtar-olive oil blend is also used as a dip and, like pesto, is delicious in salads, dressings, pastas, and sprinkled over egg dishes.

Formulas vary greatly. Some have lots of sesame and very little thyme and sumac, others the opposite. To make your own, start with these amounts and adjust to your taste.

> ¼ cup sesame seeds, toasted (see "Basics," page 369),
> cooled completely, and ground
>
> 1 tablespoon dried thyme
>
> 1½ teaspoons dried oregano
>
> 1½ teaspoons dried marjoram
>
> 1½ teaspoons savory (optional)
>
> 1½ teaspoons to 1 tablespoon sumac (optional)
>
> Salt to taste (optional)

You can grind the sesame seeds with all the leaves to a fine powder, or keep the leaves and seeds whole.

If you'd rather use just one herb, use 2 or 3 tablespoons dried thyme with the same amounts of sesame seeds and sumac.

SAFFRON SCENTS: SAVORY AND SWEET SPECIALTIES

The word saffron comes from the Arabic *za'fran*, which means yellow. This intensely fragrant spice, with its unique taste sometimes called earthy or honeylike, is best known to many Americans as the signature flavor of Italian risotto Milanese, French bouillabaisse, and Spanish paella, but it reigns in a wealth of Mediterranean dishes. It originated in the Middle East and is said to have traveled westward with Phoenician traders. Esteemed far beyond its birthplace, for centuries it has been perfuming pots simmering in kitchens from Morocco to India.

In Lebanon, Egypt, and neighboring countries, saffron rice is a favorite for its wonderful flavor and festive orange-yellow hue. Often it is a simple pilaf served as a partner for fish or a stuffing for chicken or lamb. Faster and easier to prepare than risotto or paella, it's perfect when you want a special dish but time is short.

In the Maghreb and Egypt, saffron is married with sumptuous meat and poultry stews called tagines. Some, like lamb tagine with prunes, honey, and cinnamon, are both savory and sweet.

Perhaps the greatest saffron lovers are the Persians, who now are the world's major producers of the spice. My former next-door neighbor, Treaty Zartoshty, who was born in Iran, buys her saffron in tins holding over twenty times as much as the tiny vials of one gram or less sold in supermarkets and gourmet shops.

Iranians use saffron in many rice dishes, as well as mashed-potato cakes, flat herb omelettes, and meatballs, and baste kabobs with saffron butter. They even use saffron in desserts, and sometimes Turks do, too. Saffron enhances Persian puddings, pastries, and candies, as it does in India. To my astonishment, the bright yellow saffron ice cream I tasted at a friend's party turned out to be irresistible.

Because saffron is known as the world's most expensive spice, some shops keep it locked in a cabinet. The reason for the cost is that saffron, the stigma or female part of a crocus flower, must be hand-harvested. Each flower has only three and it takes nearly a hundred thousand to make a pound. Still, a small vial of saffron doesn't cost much more than two average spice bottles. And, you need only a pinch or two for most recipes for four portions. Although turmeric is commonly used as an inexpensive substitute, as it also dyes foods orange, its flavor is completely different.

Buying saffron in filaments is the best bet because the powdered form can be easily adulterated by the packager. The finest-quality saffron threads are bright red and impart more taste, aroma, and color than paler versions. If stored in a dark, cool dry place, saffron keeps for a year or longer.

Ghormeh Sabzi and Other Persian Herb Blends

Persian blends for stews, such as a *ghormeh sabzi* blend, a mixture of sautéed leeks, fenugreek, and other herbs, can be purchased frozen, dried, and, sometimes, fresh at markets with Iranian customers. Cooks often use them for convenience when making traditional dishes that call for several herbs, but I also use the frozen blends in nontraditional ways, such as heated and tossed with pasta.

Special Flavorings

Tahini, or sesame paste, is used to make creamy sauces and dips and to enhance savory dishes. Like peanut butter, it's used in sweet foods as well—in sweet spreads, Armenian and Turkish flatbreads, and cookies. For more on tahini, see page 32.

Pomegranate paste or pomegranate molasses is popular in much of the region for the pleasing tartness it contributes to foods along with a hint of sweetness. Cooks use it to flavor sauces and meat fillings for pastries. The paste has become fashionable among some American chefs and is becoming easier to find in a variety of markets.

Tamarind gives a tart flavor to sauces and is used to make refreshing drinks. It comes from an Arabic word meaning "Indian date" and is available as whole pods, in blocks, and as a paste, which is the easiest form to use. You'll find it in Middle Eastern, East Asian, and Latino markets.

Dairy Foods

Dairy foods have long played an important part in the Mideast diet. They are made not only from cows' milk but from that of goats and sheep as well, which thrive more easily than cows in much of the region.

Many traditional forms of dairy foods arose from the need to store milk without refrigeration. Therefore, milk and cream were made into yogurt and cheese. To store yogurt even longer, it was even dried in powder or cake form. Butter could keep for much longer by being cooked, or clarified. People developed a taste for these foods and they remain popular. To find special cheeses and other Middle Eastern dairy products, and for a greater selection of yogurt and feta cheese than in the supermarket, go to a Greek or Middle Eastern market.

Yogurt is popular throughout the Mideast and is made from cows', goats', and sheeps' milk, each of which imparts a distinctive flavor. You can find tangy goat's-milk yogurt in natural food stores. Sheep's-milk yogurt, which is rich, luscious, and mild tasting, is much harder to find. In North America it's available only in certain regions and by mail order.

Kashk is a Persian form of dried whey that does wonders to enliven the flavor of soups and appetizers (such as eggplant, page 42). It is found reconstituted in jars in the market's refrigerator section. *Kishk,* or yogurt dried with bulgur wheat or flour, is found in bags with the grains, and is used to make soups (page 92). *Jameed,* or cakes of dried yogurt, are best loved for the Bedouin lamb stew called *mansaf* (page 202), but I also like to add it to vegetable and legume soups.

Clarified butter is known from the shores of the Arabian Sea in Yemen to the Atlantic coast of Morocco as *samnah* or *smen* and is similar to Indian ghee. It is used for sautéing and to flavor pastries. People often make it at home, sometimes adding a flavoring such as the fenugreek seeds added by Yemenites for their pleasing aroma. You can buy ghee in Indian grocery stores and natural food stores.

To make your own *samnah:* Cut 8 ounces of butter or margarine, or 4 ounces of each, in cubes and put them in a heavy saucepan. If you want to flavor it, lightly toast ½ teaspoon ground fenugreek in a small skillet over low heat just until aromatic; remove from heat, add one of the butter cubes to dissolve it, then transfer it to the saucepan of butter. Heat the butter mixture over low heat until melted, stirring occasionally. Continue cooking over very low heat for 15 minutes. Cool completely. Transfer to jars and keep in the refrigerator. Makes about ¾ cup.

Eshta or *kaymak* is a particularly rich form of sweet cream and is served with desserts. See page 337.

Cheeses

Feta is often made from sheep's milk in the Mideast and sometimes from mixtures of sheep's and goat's milk, but there are also plenty of cows'-milk feta cheeses.

Labneh is a rich dairy product often called kefir cheese or yogurt cheese and is used as an appetizer or spread for bread. Its texture varies from that of sour cream to Italian mascarpone to soft cream cheese, but *labneh* has a slight tang. To make your own, see Thick Yogurt and Yogurt Cheese (page 125). *Labneh* is also made into cheese balls, which are packed with olive oil in jars.

Ackawi, one of the most popular of Middle Eastern cheeses, is a smooth, semi-soft slicing cheese that tends to be milder than feta. It is used as a table cheese, in sandwiches, and in fillings for savory pastries or, after being soaked in water to remove the salt, in sweet ones as well.

Braided string cheese, sometimes labeled Armenian or Syrian cheese, is widely available at a variety of markets. This tasty, mild cheese is great in sandwiches or as a snack. It comes plain or flavored with nigella (black caraway) seeds.

Shanklish, or **shinglish,** is a firm, salty, spicy cheese shaped like a half globe and coated with Mediterranean herbs. Sometimes it's sold packed in olive oil. It's popular in diced vegetable salads and is good with green ones too, like the spinach salad on page 64.

Halloumi is a semihard white cheese made in Cyprus from sheep's milk and mint. It is increasingly available in supermarkets and is used in salads and sandwiches, and is especially enjoyed grilled and panfried. Instead of melting when cooked, it softens and browns lightly. Some brands are quite salty.

Sweet cheese isn't really sweet. It's a slicing cheese that's less salty than others and is used to fill sweet pastries, notably the syrup-moistened *kunafe,* which is made from semolina dough or from the shredded phyllo dough called *kadaif.*

Kashkaval is a savory, slightly tangy cheese often made from sheep's milk. It's firm enough to grate but soft enough to slice easily and is popular in sandwiches and toppings for hot dishes. Many brands come from eastern European countries, such as Hungary and Slovenia. It's also made in Israel. Similar cheeses are made in Turkey.

Most Mideast pantry staples, like the prized basmati rice, can be found at well-stocked supermarkets but in the specialty markets you'll find a greater variety. Following are a few special items.

Wheat:

Bulgur wheat is used extensively in Middle Eastern cooking. At some markets you will find it in four sizes, which have different uses. The two finest ones are for making kibbe. The medium and large sizes are for pilafs, soups, and desserts.

Whole wheat berries are popular in several dishes, as are special forms, notably peeled wheat and green wheat. For more information on them, see pages 261 and 278.

Pasta:

Pearl-shaped pasta or large couscous, sometimes called *mugrabiya* or Israeli couscous, is used in Lebanese and Israeli cooking.

Toasted noodles that look like tan linguine and have a slightly nutty flavor are used in some Persian dishes.

Legumes:

Fava beans, fresh, frozen, dried, and canned, are available at some supermarkets and natural food markets, as well as Middle Eastern, Mediterranean, and Latino markets. At some markets you can find frozen peeled fava beans, which shorten the preparation and cooking time. You'll find fresh favas at farmers' markets.

Lentils: Green or brown lentils are easy to find at supermarkets. To find red lentils used in some soups, look in Mediterranean, Middle Eastern, and Indian markets and in health food stores. There you will also find canned lentils, which you can use in soups and stews to save time.

Breads

Flatbreads are the most common types of Middle Eastern breads. Pita bread with a pocket is a favorite for holding sandwich fillings and accompanying dips. You'll find the widest and best selection of pitas if you buy it fresh baked from a Mideastern or Mediterranean market or bakery. Their quality is much better than the thin, flimsy ones you find in some supermarkets, which can be as tasteless as cardboard.

Pita bread varies from one bakery to another. It differs in thickness and in size, from mini to large, and may be white, whole wheat, or sesame flavored. Not all pita bread has a pocket. In some markets you can find partly baked pocketless pita, ready for you to finish at home to have fresh-baked bread in a few minutes.

Large, thin, soft lavash is also popular both for scooping and for wrapping, and there's a crisp version, too, that's often labeled cracker bread. For more on lavash and pita bread, see page 317.

At Middle Eastern bakeries you can also find thicker flatbreads like stone bread, which is traditionally baked on stones and is about as thick as Italian focaccia. Persian bakeries make long ridged barbary bread, which has a tasty, attractive crust. Similar breads are available from Afghan bakeries and shorter, rounder versions called *matnakash* at Armenian ones. Middle Eastern bakeries and markets also carry breakfast breads, such as spiral-shaped tahini bread, a slightly sweet Armenian bread called *choereg* spiced with *mahleb,* and rich *gata,* which has a butter-and-sugar filling layered with the dough.

Prepared Foods

The prepared foods section of the market gives you a picture of the range of cooked dishes and relishes enjoyed in the Mideast and offers plenty of tempting tastes as well. Shopping at the deli counter and the preserved food aisles is a good way to familiarize yourself with the cuisine.

Sauces, Soups, and Spreads

Instead of making their own relishes and hot sauces, such as the fiery Yemenite *zehug* (page 307), many cooks save time by purchasing them. The freshest of these condiments are in the refrigerator case.

The sauces, soups, and appetizers available in jars and cans can introduce you to the flavors of certain dishes. Naturally, their quality varies and they are not the same as the dish is when prepared by a fine cook, but I've found quite a few of them, notably eggplant purees and Persian cooking sauces, pleasant to use.

Relishes and Condiments

At fine Mediterranean and Middle Eastern markets, you'll find an impressive array of olives, in bulk at the deli counter and on the shelves in jars and in cans. Some are oil- or salt-cured like the Niçoise type, others are flavored with herbs and spices. Olives are used in cooking, but most of all they act as a starter and a garnish for appetizers and salads.

Pickles of many varieties are basic items on Middle Eastern tables and you'll find them made from a profusion of vegetables. I like the tarragon-scented pickled cucumbers prized by the Persians, which remind me of French cornichons. Cooks from Iraq prefer spicy mango pickles. Some pickles are mostly salty, while others are very hot, vinegary, or both peppery and vinegary.

Ready to Eat Meats, Prepared Foods, and Snacks

Depending on the market, you'll discover different kinds of specialty meats. Two popular ones in Lebanese, Armenian, and Turkish groceries are *basterma*, a spicy, garlic-flavored dried cured beef, and *soujouk*, a similarly flavored beef sausage. These tasty meats are served as appetizers, in sandwiches, and in egg dishes.

You can purchase ready-to-eat specialties, such as spinach-filled phyllo *beurreks*, pizzalike flatbreads with savory toppings, and crunchy meat-stuffed bulgur croquettes called kibbe, from the freezer or refrigerator case at well-stocked Middle Eastern markets. Stuffed vegetables and spreads are often available at the deli counter.

Toasted seeds and nuts are popular snacks, along with dried fruits, and are often prominently displayed in a wide array at Mideast grocery shops. In the Middle East they are sold in nut shops, where the aroma of the roasting nuts is irresistible. Chickpeas also come roasted, either plain, salted, or spiced, and resemble soy nuts at natural food stores. They are a satisfying, healthy snack to keep on hand in the pantry.

One of the reasons I find shopping for food so delightful is the fascinating people I meet. Thanks to the contact with other customers who prize these fine ingredients, I gain a new appreciation of foods and enrich my knowledge of ethnic cooking and culture.

At one market, for example, we encountered a friendly man in the condiments section carrying a container of peeled garlic. Of Armenian descent, he talked with fervor about the virtues of yogurt, which he called a super food. Like my husband, he also loves red pepper and his favorite spice is cumin. Both men agreed they like to toast the whole cumin seeds in a skillet and then to crush them.

Our new acquaintance talked fondly of what he called "the Armenian Foursome"— onions, garlic, peppers, and tomatoes. "Without these," he said, "you cannot cook." He added that sometimes this group of four becomes five, with the addition of parsley or mint, and that's what he uses to flavor his *lahmajune,* or Armenian/Lebanese pizza (page 322).

I learned that this classic Armenian seasoning mixture accents dishes ranging from meat stews to vegetable casseroles to rice pilafs. It is the Armenian equivalent of the essential aromatic mixtures of other cuisines— the French mirepoix of onion and carrot; the Cajun trinity of onions, peppers, and celery; and the Chinese trio of ginger, garlic, and green onion.

His flavoring formula proved to be useful for quick cooking. By adding this combo, it's easy to turn one or two ingredients into a fine entrée. You can cook a tasty pilaf of rice or bulgur wheat by sautéing diced onion and bell peppers with garlic, then adding the grain, with tomato sauce and water. For a satisfying bean dish, add frozen lima beans or canned garbanzo beans instead of the rice or along with it. In fact, you can follow this technique to make an interesting accompaniment from green beans, zucchini, cauliflower, or your favorite frozen vegetable mixture. Season any of these dishes with cumin, paprika, cayenne pepper, and, if you like, Italian parsley or mint. Or cook the "Armenian foursome" to a sauce to spoon over grilled fish, chicken, or steak.

You can find the ingredients for most Middle Eastern desserts at the supermarket. Following are a few special foods to look for at ethnic markets. You'll find more information on them in "Cakes, Cookies, and Desserts," page 334.

Baking Ingredients

Phyllo dough can be found frozen and sometimes fresh. At some well-stocked Greek and other Mediterranean markets, there's also pistachio- and chocolate-flavored phyllo. Some stores carry *yufka*, a Turkish dough similar to phyllo that is made in round sheets instead of oblong ones and used to make *beurreks*.

Rose Water and Orange-blossom Water

These floral essences are used in a great variety of desserts, from fruit salads to elaborate pastries.

Coffee Spice Mix

Made of such sweet spices as cinnamon, cloves, ginger, cardamom, and, sometimes, nutmeg, coffee spice mix flavors black Middle Eastern coffee as well as tea. You can buy it as a mix or make your own.

At home people often pound the whole spices; if you've seen dried ginger in slices at a Mideast market, this is a favorite use for them. In my family's mix, the ginger taste tends to dominate, but people like the spices in different proportions. Some use equal amounts of all the spices, except for the cloves, which is added in smaller amounts. For an easy recipe, see page 365.

Salep Powder

Found in the market as a prepared mix that also contains sugar, salep powder is made from an orchid, like vanilla. The mix is used primarily to make warm drinks and to flavor ice creams and puddings.

Jams

Cooks in the Mideast make jams and preserves from many foods. Some interesting ones to try are fig jam flavored with sesame and anise seeds, quince preserves, and rose-petal jam.

Syrups

Sweet syrups are used as sauces, to make sweet spreads for breads, and to flavor desserts.

Date syrup is a dark syrup popular in Lebanon, Iraq, and Israel, for sweets as well as savory sauces.

Carob syrup is also rich, thick, and sweet. It is sometimes combined with tahini for spreading on bread. I find it's also a good alternative to chocolate sauce for accompanying ice cream.

Grape molasses is a similar thick, sweet syrup found in some markets.

Prepared Sweets

Although baklava is available at all kinds of stores, you'll find a greater range of these phyllo pastries and other cakes from the region at a good Middle Eastern market. Best of all, go to a bakery where they are made fresh. Their flavor and texture differ, depending on the clientele's origins. Persian baklava, for example, unlike the flaky, multilayered Turkish-style pastry, has a thick layer of cardamom-scented almond filling between two pastry layers.

Sweet snacks, such as candied nuts, are popular items at bakeries as well as markets. One of the favorites is aromatic candied almonds, coated with a white, fondantlike sugar glaze that may be flavored with rose water and cardamom. Chickpeas come candied this way, and are also made by the Persians into cookies.

Halvah made of sesame seeds and flavored with pistachios, vanilla, or chocolate, is a beloved treat on its own and is also used to make desserts. You can buy it in bulk at the deli counter or in packages.

Keeping Healthy the Mideastern Way

Eating the Middle Eastern way regularly has been the key to helping me arrive at and maintain my ideal weight. The Middle Eastern menu has the same nutritious characteristics as the Mediterranean diet.

The healthful aspects of Mediterranean meals came to the nutrition community's notice as a result of a landmark study of the eating habits in seven countries in different parts of the world over fifteen years. The research found less chronic disease and the highest life-expectancy rates in southern Italy, Greece, and, notably, the island of Crete, which had the lowest heart disease rates of all, and attributed the good health of these populations to their diet. Crete is the gateway to the Middle East and its people share many of the eating patterns of the other eastern Mediterranean countries. The region had an impact on Crete's culture and its cooking, due to the island's proximity to Turkey and its having been for centuries under the control of Middle Eastern powers, mainly the Ottoman Empire and, briefly, Egypt.

It's no coincidence that many of the Middle Eastern foods best known in America—hummus, tahini, tabbouleh, couscous, and pita bread—were available in health food stores before becoming common in mainstream supermarkets. They still can be found in an even broader array in natural food markets. The growing awareness of the healthful qualities of the Mediterranean and Middle Eastern ingredients during the last two decades has contributed to an impressive increase in the consumption of olive oil in the United States.

Produce is prominent in Mideastern menus, from an array of herb and vegetable appetizers to hearty soups of greens and beans to fresh fruit for dessert. A colorful salad of fresh diced vegetables with a very light dressing is a menu standard, enjoyed at everyday meals as well as festive celebrations. Appetizer spreads and snacks are often based on beans, eggplant, or yogurt rather than butter or cream cheese. Olive oil or vegetable oil, rather than butter or animal fat, usually flavors vegetables and grains, and mayonnaise is rarely used.

In coastal regions fish is a favorite, and chicken is enjoyed everywhere. For everyday meals these lean, healthful protein foods are prepared simply, often as stews. Lamb and beef are the best-loved meats and are a highlight of celebrations but do not appear on the table on a daily basis. Grilling is a preferred technique for fish, poultry, and meat, especially for festive meals, and is a healthful way of cooking.

For the main course, a whole-meal soup made from meat or poultry with plenty of vegetables is the norm at countless family dinners. With their liquid component, soups are filling and often lower in calories and saturated fat than other entrées.

Meat often serves primarily as a flavoring for vegetables and grains. There are meat stews containing three to five times more vegetables than meat. Stuffed vegetables, popular for festive occasions, may include a little meat or none at all.

Avoiding the overconsumption of meat is built into many of the area's cultures through custom-hallowed meatless days and guidelines about what kinds of meats to eat. The warm climate as well as frugality also promoted the extensive use of vegetables. Over the centuries an extensive repertoire of vegetarian dishes has developed.

Since ancient times Middle Eastern people have been great lovers of legumes. They use them creatively throughout the meal, from appetizers to main courses to sweets. The ancients may not have been aware of why they found legumes so satisfying but today we know they are powerhouses of nutrients. With legumes we get plenty of protein, fiber, vitamins, and minerals and very little fat and no cholesterol.

From the shores of the Mediterranean to the Persian Gulf, including legumes in tasty meat casseroles and soups has long been the custom. It's a practice worth emulating in all sorts of entrées.

Some people in the region, notably in Egypt, even serve beans in the morning, together with fresh vegetables. Most nutritionists would certainly find this a more healthful breakfast than one with bacon and sausages.

Some of the classics of the Middle Eastern kitchen, such as chickpeas with rice or lentil *majadra*, are composed of legumes and grains. They have been the model for vegetarians for creating meals of complementary proteins. Whole grains, prized by nutritionists, play a role in traditional Mideast menus as well.

Middle Eastern sauces are not usually made of cream, butter, or cheese. Instead, they are formed from the meat's natural juices and might be thickened lightly with a slurry of cornstarch or rice flour. Rich creamy sauces, as well as many desserts, are based on nuts or sesame seeds instead of dairy products. The fat of nuts is largely monounsaturated and therefore is much more healthful than butterfat.

Whether people like spicy Yemenite dishes or herb-scented Persian ones, seasoning dishes well is another good practice of Middle Eastern cooks that enables you to lower the fat and calories in menus and still enjoy the food. Even without the benefits of today's science, the ancients realized the importance of onions and garlic in the diet and to this day use them with gusto, another beneficial tradition.

The popular regional practice of cooking vegetables directly in a soup or sauce tends to conserve nutrients. My mother-in-law, for example, who lived her whole life in the Mideast—in Yemen and Israel—frowned on blanching vegetables: "You're throwing away the vegetable's strength," she objected when she saw me doing this with green beans. Only later I learned there was merit to her comment because many of the vegetable vitamins dissolve into the water, and I began saving my liquid to use as vegetable broth.

To end a meal, opting for seasonal fruit most of the time and reserving desserts for special occasions, as is the custom in the Mideast, is another healthful habit to follow. I also find it useful to serve desserts in small portions, garnished with fresh fruit.

In many Mideast homes the heartiest meal is served at midday, and a lighter supper in the evening. Quite a few nutritionists recommend this mode of eating, as there is more time left in the day to expend energy and make use of the calories consumed.

Naturally, modern cooks in the Mideast, as well as those originating in the region who live in other parts of the world, take today's nutritional knowledge into account in planning their menus. When a traditional dish is high in fat, health-conscious cooks find lighter ways to enjoy it; you will see examples throughout the book.

Appetizers, an Array of Fresh Temptations

Tahini Dip/Sauce • *T'hina*

Classic Hummus • *Hummus*

Egyptian Fava Bean Dip with Garlic and Coriander • *Bussara*

Soybean Hummus • *Mimrah Soya Dmuy Hummus*

Turkish Tomato and Onion Dip • *Acili Domates Ezmesi*

Red Pepper Walnut Dip • *Mohammara*

Grilled Eggplant Sesame Dip • *Baba Ghanoush; Mutabbal*

Israeli Eggplant Dip with Garlic Mayonnaise • *Salat Hatzilim im Mayonez*

Creamy Persian Eggplant • *Kashk-e Baadenjaan*

Cilantro-Garlic Eggplant on Pita Crisps with Roasted Peppers • *Bittingan Be Salsat Kosbarah*

Garlic Marinated Eggplant • *Bittingan Bel Khal Wal Tom*

Sweet-and-Spicy Marinated Grilled Peppers • *Fleifle Mechwie*

Roasted Pepper and Tomato Salad/Dip • *Salat Matbuha*

Asparagus with Egyptian Takliah Dressing • *Halyun Bel Takliah*

Chicken Pecan Bulgur Cakes with Cilantro Pesto • *Kibbit Djaj*

Chicken in Walnut Garlic Sauce • *Cerkez Tavugu*

Grape Leaves with Aromatic Rice Stuffing • *Mahshy Waraq Eynab*

Yogurt Cheese Balls in Herb Oil • *Labneh Makbus*

One of the glories of the Mideast table is an assortment of appealing appetizers, which together are often called meze, or *maza*. They consist of a colorful medley of dips, spreads, and salads and might include a few turnover-like pastries. Fresh breads are their essential accompaniment.

Humble foods like beans and eggplants form the basis of a good number of the items in this impressive array. For special occasions meat or poultry might become part of savory starters, like the celebrated cold Circassian chicken with its luscious walnut dressing beloved in Turkish homes or the rolled rice-and-meat-filled grape leaves popular throughout the region.

You can make a whole meal out of meze. For a festive summertime buffet lunch, serve a selection of cold meze. They are certainly worth getting to know, as many are easy to prepare, convenient to serve, and keep well. Some elements of the meze table involve almost no effort at all—you simply set out dishes of several kinds of good-quality olives, pickles, and perhaps some fresh small radishes, green onions, and sliced sweet peppers. You can present them as nibbles on their own or use them as components of a larger meze.

Although the Mideast kitchen is famous for lavish meze tables, grand displays are reserved for special occasions and holidays. For a casual gathering meze may be very simple indeed. Families from Iran enjoy starting meals with a platter of fresh herb sprigs, such as chives, mint, tarragon, and watercress, a plate of feta-type cheese, and a basket of fresh lavash-type flatbread. And Irani-

ans should know about meze. This Turkish word, widely used in other Mideastern countries as well, comes from a Persian word meaning to taste or relish.

Some of the best-known meze are luscious dips or spreads. Americans are familiar with hummus and baba ghanoush but there are many more. There might be a smooth dip with an intriguing smoky aroma achieved by grilling a vegetable, like Persian eggplant flavored with the tangy, yogurtlike *kashk*, or Israeli Eggplant Dip with Garlic Mayonnaise. If you like a touch of heat, try a fiery and fragrant chili paste like Yemenite *zehug* (page 307) or a rich and spicy bright red nut spread like Syrian Red Pepper Walnut Dip, or *mohammara* (page 39).

Be sure to have fresh, good quality pita or other Middle Eastern flatbreads to scoop up these delectable dips. You can warm the bread very briefly but keep it soft. Homemade Pita Crisps (page 332) also make a pleasing, albeit nontraditional, partner for the saucelike spreads.

If you fancy light appetizers, try a flavorful vegetable one, such as Roasted Pepper and Tomato Salad, or Asparagus with Egyptian Takliah Dressing with coriander and garlic, or peppery Turkish Tomato and Onion Dip. For a more substantial selection, you might like to include pizza-like pastries such as Lebanese *Lahmajune* (page 322), crunchy meat-filled kibbe balls, or Chicken Pecan Bulgur Cakes with Cilantro Pesto (page 48), Grape Leaves with Aromatic Rice Stuffing (page 50), or, of course, falafel (page 215). Small portions of any of the dishes in the salad chapter also are perfect candidates for the meze table.

TAHINI—MIDEASTERN MAYONNAISE

Many of us first encounter tahini as a pale sauce drizzled over our falafel. But tahini has many more uses. For many people in the Middle East, this creamy sesame sauce is indispensable.

The peoples of the eastern Mediterranean enjoy it often as a savory sesame dip for pita bread. They incorporate it into other dips and spreads, notably hummus and baba ghanoush. In fact, you could consider tahini the mayonnaise of the Middle East. It has one obvious advantage over classic mayonnaise—it is cholesterol free.

Tahini is used as a dressing for the favorite Middle Eastern salad of diced tomatoes, cucumbers, and onions, as a sauce for fish, an accompaniment for kabobs, and as a dunking sauce for hors d'oeuvres. The Lebanese spoon tahini sauce over potatoes, cooked greens, cauliflower, and beets. It's also good with salads of lettuce, spinach, and pasta. Some people bake sesame paste into cookies and other sweets.

For cooks in a hurry, tahini is one of the easiest sauces to make. You simply blend sesame paste with water, lemon juice, garlic, and salt. Sesame paste is a convenient pantry item, ready when you want it.

The Chinese make sesame paste too, but they first toast the sesame seeds until they are very aromatic, as they do for Chinese sesame oil. This gives their sesame paste a dark brown color and a different flavor from tahini.

Tahini can also be regarded as the peanut butter of the Middle East. Indeed, some American producers label their tahini "sesame butter" and recommend it as a spread for bread. For most palates, however, tahini straight from the jar is an acquired taste because of the sesame seeds' characteristic bitterness.

The word tahini comes from an Arabic word meaning "to grind." Jars of tahini are also labeled tehinah, tehineh, sesame paste, or sesame sauce. Some jars might contain ready-made sauce, but homemade tahini sauce has a fresher, much more lively taste. To make your own sauce you need the pure paste. To avoid confusion, check the label: It should contain only one ingredient—sesame seeds. If it's an already made sauce, the label will also list water, seasonings, and probably citric acid. In my area the Middle Eastern brands cost substantially less than the American ones.

Tahini sauce is rich and creamy without needing any dairy products. It has some protein, good amounts of iron and calcium, and a calorie content similar to that of peanut butter. Like all nut and seed butters, tahini is high in fat, but, fortunately, most of it is unsaturated. Enjoying tahini the Middle Eastern way makes sense nutritionally; since the paste is diluted with water and lemon juice, each tablespoon contains much less fat.

Whenever you use mayonnaise, a Tel Aviv friend of mine insists, tahini sauce is even better. I love it in all sorts of sandwiches, especially with roasted peppers, grilled eggplant, or grilled mushrooms. It's great on chicken, tuna, and hard-boiled eggs. For a tasty new twist on beef burgers, slip your patty into pita bread and spoon in a little tahini sauce to moisten it. You'll find this exotic sauce from the East a surprisingly good partner for the American classic.

Tahini Dip/Sauce

t'hina

Serve tahini, which some call *tarator*, as a dip with fresh pita bread or use it as a salad dressing or a sauce. The Lebanese especially love it as all-purpose sauce with fish, meat, and vegetables. (See "Tahini—Mideastern Mayonnaise," page 32.)

Middle Easterners like the zip of fresh lemon juice in their tahini and are generous when adding it. Lemon juice and salt provide the perfect balance for the taste of the sesame paste. Be sure to use fresh garlic and to mince it fine. If you're serving the tahini as a sauce or dressing, or if it thickens on standing, make it thinner by gradually stirring in more lemon juice or water.

When serving tahini as a dip, some add fresh flat-leaf parsley to make green tahini (see variations) or a dash of hot sauce to make peppery tahini. In summertime I make a nontraditional tomato basil tahini. Use this lighter dressing to enhance salads of raw or cooked vegetables, and to accompany grilled or fried eggplant or zucchini.

When you open the jar of tahini paste, in many brands you'll see oil on top of a firm layer. As in natural peanut butter, the oil separates from the sesame seeds on standing and must be stirred in before you use the tahini. I like to make tahini dip or sauce an hour or two ahead so its taste mellows. Refrigerate it in a covered container until ready to serve.

◆ MAKES ABOUT I CUP, 4 TO 6 SERVINGS.

½ cup tahini paste

2 to 4 tablespoons strained, fresh-squeezed lemon juice

6 to 8 tablespoons water

2 large garlic cloves, minced (2 teaspoons)

Salt to taste

In medium bowl, stir tahini to blend in its oil. Stir in 2 tablespoons lemon juice, 6 tablespoons water, garlic, and salt. If sauce is too thick, gradually stir in more lemon juice or water, depending on how tart you would like the tahini. Taste, and add more salt or lemon juice if desired.

To serve as a dip, spoon tahini onto a plate and spread it in a thick layer. To serve as a sauce, add enough water or lemon juice to make it thin enough to be spooned or ladled over the food; serve it from a bowl or saucedish.

Green Tahini

Add ¼ to ⅓ cup finely chopped Italian parsley to the tahini mixture. For a smooth, green hue, puree the parsley with the tahini in a blender.

Peppery Tahini

Add ½ to 1 teaspoon *zehug* (page 307), or hot sauce or cayenne pepper to taste.

Tomato Basil Tahini

Stir tahini paste with 4 tablespoons water, ¼ cup tomato juice, preferably fresh, 1 tablespoon lemon juice, garlic, and salt, pepper, and cayenne or hot sauce to taste. Adjust consistency with water or lemon juice. A short time before serving, stir in ¾ to 1 cup finely diced tomatoes and 2 to 3 tablespoons thin strips fresh basil.

Classic Hummus

hummus

It's amazing how quickly this golden chickpea spread has become familiar in Europe and North America. Growing up in Washington, D.C., I never heard of it until I encountered it in my early college years in Jerusalem. Now it can be found just about everywhere in the United States.

First the spread appeared in Middle Eastern markets and restaurants. As a tasty, nutritious alternative to butter, cream cheese, and mayonnaise, it became a staple on the tables of American vegans and health-conscious eaters. Its appeal quickly broadened and hummus spread from natural food stores to gourmet and mainstream markets.

Homemade hummus is much more delicious and fresh tasting than store-bought. When you have time to cook dried chickpeas, the chickpeas' cooking liquid enhances the hummus's flavor. The best hummus we've had, made by Israeli Arabs in Akko, near Haifa, was made with coarsely chopped chickpeas and served still warm.

A drizzle of olive oil, a little parsley, and a sprinkling of finely ground red pepper are the usual garnishes, plus a few cooked chickpeas or sometimes toasted pine nuts or sautéed ground beef or lamb. Some sprinkle tart sumac powder instead of red pepper. A favorite Lebanese accompaniment is a plate of radishes, green onions, and pickles.

In North America we have become so

fond of hummus that we have developed an endless array of variations unknown in traditional Middle Eastern cooking. At delis and markets I've seen tomato basil hummus, sun-dried tomato hummus, roasted red pepper hummus, black olive hummus, cucumber dill hummus, spicy walnut hummus, chipotle hummus, and even French onion hummus. You'll find hummus easy to prepare, and very quick if you use canned chickpeas. Be sure to serve it with good-quality pita bread or, for an American-style hummus partner, Sesame Pita Crisps (page 332).

♦ MAKES ABOUT 8 SERVINGS.

½ pound dried chickpeas (garbanzo beans) (about 1¼ cups), or two 15-ounce cans chickpeas, drained

2 large garlic cloves, minced

¼ cup tahini (sesame paste), stirred to blend before being measured

⅓ cup strained fresh-squeezed lemon juice

1 teaspoon ground cumin (optional)

½ cup chickpea cooking liquid or water

Salt to taste

1 to 2 tablespoons extra-virgin olive oil (for drizzling)

Aleppo pepper, paprika, or cayenne pepper (for sprinkling)

Italian parsley sprigs (for garnish)

Pick over chickpeas, discarding any pebbles and broken or discolored peas. Rinse well. If you like, soak chickpeas 8 hours or overnight in water to cover generously; this cuts their cooking time slightly and helps improve the texture if the peas are old. Drain soaked chickpeas and rinse.

Put chickpeas in large saucepan and add about 5 cups water. Bring to a simmer. Cover and cook over low heat for 1½ hours, or until very tender. Drain well, reserving cooking liquid. Cool slightly.

Chop chickpeas in food processor. Add garlic, tahini, lemon juice, cumin, and ¼ cup chickpea cooking liquid (or water, if using canned ones) and puree until blended. Transfer to bowl. Gradually stir in more chickpea cooking liquid or water until the puree is the consistency of a smooth spread. Season with salt to taste. Refrigerate in a covered container until ready to serve.

To serve, spoon hummus onto a serving plate and spread it so edges are thicker than center. Drizzle center with olive oil and sprinkle very lightly with Aleppo pepper. Put a few parsley sprigs on the edges of the hummus.

Herbed Hummus

In food processor, chop ¼ cup small Italian parsley sprigs with ¼ cup cilantro sprigs or additional parsley sprigs, 1 tablespoon fresh oregano or ½ teaspoon dried, and 2 teaspoons fresh thyme or ¾ teaspoon dried. Add garlic and chickpeas and process to chop. Add tahini or 2 to 3 tablespoons extra-virgin olive oil, ¼ cup lemon juice, 2 teaspoons finely grated lemon zest, and ¼ cup chickpea cooking liquid or water and puree until blended. Stir in 2 minced green onions (white and green parts).

Hot Pepper Hummus

To make very fast chili hummus, you can simply stir hot sauce into classic hummus, but homemade grilled peppers make a much more delicious version. Broil or grill and peel 1 large red bell pepper and, if you like, 3 red or green jalapeño peppers (page 370). Finely dice half the bell pepper. Mince half the jalapeño peppers. Put rest of bell pepper and jalapeño in food processor, add garlic, and process to chop. Add chickpeas and remaining ingredients and make hummus as above. Stir in diced red peppers and remaining minced jalapeño, or add 1 to 2 teaspoons *zehug* (page 307), *harissa*, or other hot sauce to taste, and cayenne if you like.

Egyptian Fava Bean Dip with Garlic and Coriander

bussara

Like hummus, this dip/spread is made with a famous bean of the Mideast—fava beans. It is a signature dish on Egyptian tables, garnished most often with cilantro and parsley or occasionally with toasted pine nuts and sautéed ground meat.

To make *bussara*, the dried fava beans are cooked until they become a puree, then blended with sautéed onions, garlic, cumin, dried mint, and, sometimes, hot red pepper or paprika. Alternative flavorings are parsley, dill, ground coriander, and dried *meloukhiya*, an Egyptian green (page 88). Serve the dip as an appetizer with pita bread or an accompaniment for meats. If you like, garnish it with fresh mint leaves or Italian parsley sprigs.

Use split peeled fava beans that are pale or white inside. If you can find only the large brown ones, which still have their skins, soak them for one or two days in water in the refrigerator, then remove the skins.

◆ MAKES 4 TO 6 SERVINGS.

> 8 ounces split, peeled dried fava beans (broad beans)
> 1 celery rib, chopped
> 3 onions, chopped
> 2 tablespoons olive oil, vegetable oil, or butter
> 4 large garlic cloves, chopped
> Pinch paprika or hot red pepper (optional)
> 1 teaspoon dried mint
> 1 teaspoon ground cumin
> Salt and freshly ground black pepper

Soak beans in bowl of water to generously cover for 8 hours or overnight. Drain beans and rinse them. Put them in saucepan with celery, two-thirds of the chopped onion, and water to cover. Bring to a boil and skim foam. Reduce heat, cover, and cook over medium-low heat for 1½ hours, or until tender and falling apart.

Heat oil in skillet. Add remaining chopped onion and sauté until deep golden brown. Add garlic and sauté 1 minute. Add paprika and stir a few seconds over heat to blend. Reserve half of mixture for garnish.

With slotted spoon, transfer bean mixture to food processor, reserving liquid. Puree beans with remaining onion mixture, mint, cumin, salt, pepper, and enough of bean cooking liquid to make a creamy puree. Taste and adjust seasoning. Serve cold or at room temperature, garnished with reserved sautéed onion mixture.

Soybean Hummus

mimrah soya dmuy hummus

Inspired by traditional hummus made from chickpeas, I like to make a spread from soybeans, which share similar properties. Both legumes are flavorful and have a satisfying, meaty texture.

Soybeans are rich tasting because of their natural fat and therefore are perfect for creamy spreads like this one. Sometimes I make a double-soy spread, enriching my puree of yellow soybeans with soy nut butter, both of which are available at natural food stores. Buy dried soybeans, or, for a quicker alternative, substitute canned ones.

For another time-saver, instead of dried soybeans use 3 cups shelled fresh green soybeans, or Japanese edamame, which are available frozen at natural food and Asian stores. These delicious beans cook in only 5 minutes and will give your spread a pale-green tint.

Soy nut butter is made of toasted soybeans blended with soybean oil and is roughly similar in texture to tahini and to peanut butter. If you want a spread that's more similar to Middle Eastern hummus, use tahini. Serve the spread with your favorite fresh flatbread.

◆ MAKES ABOUT 8 SERVINGS.

1¼ cups dried yellow soybeans, or two 15-ounce cans soybeans, drained

2 large garlic cloves, minced

¼ cup soy nut butter or tahini (sesame paste), stirred to blend before being measured, or 2 to 3 tablespoons extra-virgin olive oil

¼ cup strained fresh-squeezed lemon juice, or more to taste

½ cup soybean cooking liquid or water

Salt and freshly ground black pepper to taste

Pick over dried soybeans, discarding any pebbles and broken or discolored beans. Rinse well. Soak beans 8 hours or overnight in water to cover generously. Or quick-soak: Cover beans with 5 cups water in saucepan, bring to a boil, and boil for 2 minutes, then let stand, covered, for 1 hour.

Drain beans and rinse. Put them in large

saucepan and add 6 cups water. Bring to a simmer. Cover and cook over low heat for 2½ to 3 hours, or until very tender. Drain well, reserving cooking liquid. Cool slightly.

Chop beans in food processor. Add garlic, soy nut butter, lemon juice, and ¼ cup bean cooking liquid (or water, if using canned beans) and puree until finely blended. Transfer to bowl. Gradually stir in more bean cooking liquid or water to give the puree the consistency of a smooth spread. Season with salt and pepper to taste. Refrigerate in a covered container. Serve cold or at room temperature as an appetizer or spread.

Turkish Tomato and Onion Dip

acili domates ezmesi

This bright red, spicy dip from eastern Turkey is also popular in Israel, where it is known as *salat Toorki,* or Turkish salad. Often it is seasoned with a copious amount of Middle Eastern red pepper, such as Aleppo pepper, or with cayenne. The chef of Tempo, a Mediterranean restaurant in Encino, California, adds extra punch to his version with hot red chilies.

The thick, slightly chunky dip can be a simple mixture of tomato paste, onions, and spice or a more elaborate blend that includes fresh tomatoes, green peppers, cucumber, garlic, and herbs. Favorite flavorings are coriander, cumin, parsley, dill, and mint. It's a completely casual recipe with almost no need to measure; the proportions are up to each family's taste. For a tasty variation, stir in a few tablespoons of diced green olives, as does my friend and mentor, cookbook author Ruth Sirkis, the Julia Child of Israel.

Many cooks leave the vegetables raw but some sauté their onions so they'll be less pungent. I decide according to my onions— I add mild sweet ones raw; I salt and rinse medium-strong ones to tone them down; and I sauté the ones that have a lot of bite. I judge their strength by their smell and by how quickly the tears come as I cut them!

Often this bright red dip is served with paler ones, such as grilled eggplant salad or hummus, served with warm pita. It also makes a good accompaniment for meat, as a sort of hot homemade ketchup.

◆ MAKES 4 TO 6 SERVINGS.

1 medium onion, preferably mild, chopped

¼ cup small flat-leaf parsley sprigs

2 large ripe tomatoes, peeled and cut in chunks (see Note)

½ cup tomato paste

1 teaspoon ground coriander

1 teaspoon paprika

½ teaspoon Aleppo pepper, or ¼ teaspoon cayenne, or more to taste

2 tablespoons extra-virgin olive oil

1 tablespoon vinegar (optional)

Salt and freshly ground pepper to taste

If onion is too pungent, put it in a colander, sprinkle it with salt, and let stand for 10 minutes; rinse and drain. Combine onion, parsley, and tomatoes in food processor and chop until fine but not pureed. Transfer to bowl and stir in tomato paste, coriander, paprika, Aleppo pepper, and oil. Add vinegar if you like and salt and pepper to taste. Mixture should be a thick dip but if it's too thick, stir in 2 tablespoons water. Refrigerate 1 hour so flavors blend. You can keep it for one day but if you keep it longer than that, the onion flavor may get too strong.

NOTE You can omit the step of peeling the tomatoes if the skins don't bother you; or you can grate them on a coarse grater and most of the skins will stay behind.

Red Pepper Walnut Dip

mohammara

This delectable walnut spread from Aleppo in northern Syria, which is also loved in Lebanon and Turkey, is spiced liberally with red pepper to give it plenty of heat. When I tasted it at an Istanbul restaurant called Develi that specializes in southeast Anatolian cooking, I was immediately taken with the spread's rich texture and spicy flavor. Pomegranate molasses, olive oil, and cumin provide background flavors to balance the pungency. Some people make it with half pine nuts and half walnuts, and some add garlic or sweet red peppers. Be sure the walnuts you use are fresh.

The dip is easy to make—simply blend all the ingredients in a food processor. It's a tasty hors d'oeuvre with fresh pita bread or pita crisps and is also a delicious sauce for grilled fish, roast chicken, or kabobs. I also toss it with pasta as a pestolike sauce.

The dip should be deep red, so add some paprika if you don't want a large amount of hot red pepper. If you can find Aleppo pepper or Turkish Maraş pepper, it adds a pleasant heat and is much less fiery than cayenne. When fresh red chilies such as red jalapeños are in season, add one or two for a good fresh touch instead of or in addition to the cayenne.

◆ MAKES 4 SERVINGS.

1 cup walnuts

⅓ cup bread crumbs

1 tablespoon olive oil

1 tablespoon pomegranate molasses or fresh-squeezed lemon juice

1 teaspoon sugar

½ teaspoon ground cumin

1 tablespoon paprika

½ teaspoon salt, or to taste

1½ teaspoons Aleppo pepper, or ½ teaspoon cayenne pepper, or to taste

Grind walnuts and bread crumbs in food processor. Add oil, pomegranate molasses, sugar, cumin, and paprika and process to a slightly chunky paste. If it is too thick, add 1 or 2 tablespoons water. Transfer to bowl. Season to taste with salt and Aleppo pepper or cayenne, adding enough to make it hot.

Grilled Eggplant Sesame Dip

baba ghanoush; mutabbal

Eggplant becomes exciting in this rich, cream-colored dip because of the bold flavors—rich tahini, pungent garlic, and sparkling fresh lemon juice—matched with the smoky taste of the grilled eggplant. A good flavor balance is the secret to this appetizer's perennial popularity throughout the Middle East, and achieving it is the cook's challenge.

Some cooks feel that the best way to grill the eggplant is over a wood fire. A barbecue is also good, but the oven broiler works fine.

To vary the salad, add minced white, yellow, or green onions, diced roasted bell peppers or minced hot peppers. The usual garnish is a drizzle of olive oil, a sprinkling of red pepper, and a little flat-leaf parsley. For a festive presentation you can strew pomegranate seeds or toasted pine nuts over the top.

Pita bread is the accompaniment de rigueur. Try to buy fresh, fine quality loaves from a Mideast market or bakery. Other flatbreads like fresh lavash are also good.

◆ MAKES 6 TO 8 SERVINGS.

2 medium eggplants (total about 2½ pounds)

¼ cup pine nuts (optional)

3 large garlic cloves, minced

6 to 8 tablespoons tahini (sesame paste), stirred until blended

4 to 6 tablespoons strained fresh-squeezed lemon juice

1 to 2 tablespoons water

Salt and freshly ground black pepper

Aleppo pepper, paprika, or cayenne (garnish)

Extra-virgin olive oil (for sprinkling)

¼ cup pomegranate seeds (optional; see "Basics," page 374)

2 tablespoons minced Italian parsley, or a few whole fresh mint leaves

Grill or broil eggplants, then peel them (see "Basics," page 371).

To toast pine nuts in oven or toaster oven, preheat it to 350°F. Put nuts on baking sheet and toast in oven for 3 minutes, or until lightly browned. Or toast them in dry skillet over medium-low heat, tossing them often, for 2 to 3 minutes. Watch so they don't burn. Immediately transfer them to a plate.

Chop eggplant with a knife to a slightly chunky puree. Transfer to bowl. Add garlic and mix well.

Spoon tahini paste into medium-size bowl. Gradually stir in 4 tablespoons lemon juice and 1 tablespoon water. Add to eggplant and mix well. Season generously with salt, then add pepper to taste and more lemon juice for a sharper taste, or water for a milder taste or thinner dip.

At serving time, spread eggplant in a thick layer on a platter or plate. Sprinkle with Aleppo pepper, drizzle center lightly with olive oil, then sprinkle with pine nuts and pomegranate seeds. Garnish edges with parsley or mint.

Israeli Eggplant Dip with Garlic Mayonnaise

salat hatzilim im mayonez

This creamy dip was my first taste of eggplant and I have been fond of it ever since. The dip is ubiquitous in Israel, where it is sold in delis alongside eggplant with tahini. It is known in Jordan as well but is not common in the rest of the Mideast.

For a colorful variation, stir in some finely diced cucumber and tomato a short time before serving. I often add hard-boiled eggs because I like the taste and texture they contribute. Serve the dip with any kind of fresh bread you like: baguette, sesame bread, sourdough bread, whole-wheat bread, rye bread, or pita, or with Sesame Pita Crisps (page 332).

For a tasty sandwich, spread this eggplant dip on a whole-wheat roll and top with slices of smoked turkey, *kashkaval* cheese, or one of each.

♦ MAKES 6 TO 8 SERVINGS.

    2 medium eggplants (total 2 to 2½ pounds)
    2 large fresh garlic cloves, minced
    2 tablespoons minced green onion or mild onion (optional)
    ⅓ to ½ cup mayonnaise
    2 to 4 teaspoons strained fresh-squeezed lemon juice, or to taste
    Salt and freshly ground black pepper
    1 or 2 hard-boiled eggs (optional), coarsely grated
    ½ cup finely diced cucumber (optional)
    ¾ cup finely diced tomato (optional)

Roast, broil, or grill eggplants, then peel them (see "Basics," page 371). Chop eggplant pulp fine with knife or in food processor.

Transfer eggplant to bowl. Add garlic, green onion, and mayonnaise and mix well. Stir in lemon juice, salt, and pepper to taste; mixture should be generously seasoned. Lightly stir in eggs and taste again. Refrigerate in covered container at least 30 minutes to blend flavors.

A short time before serving, fold in diced cucumber and tomato. Serve cold in a shallow bowl.

Creamy Persian Eggplant

kashk-e baadenjaan

This eggplant appetizer is flavored with kashk, a creamy dairy product made of dried whey mixed with a little water. The ancient process of preserving milk by drying it is common in much of the Mideast. Popular in Persian cooking, you can find kashk in jars in the dairy case of Mideast markets with an Iranian clientele. Some companies label it kishk but in most of the Mideast kishk is a different product of grains and dairy; if the jar's label lists whey, salt, and water but no other ingredients, you have the right thing for this recipe. Kashk has the texture of very thick sour cream but has a more tangy, concentrated flavor and is lower in fat. If you happen to find kashk, try it; its intense flavor gives the tastiest result.

To replace kashk, I find goat's-milk yogurt, sheep's-milk yogurt, or a Bulgarian-style or other tangy cow's-milk yogurt is a good substitute. Although some form of dairy product is the essence of this dip, the combination of the other flavors— sautéed onion, garlic, and mint—makes the eggplant taste good even when left milk free.

You'll often find this specialty at Persian restaurants, where it's sometimes made of fried eggplant topped with the onion mix- ture and the kashk. Here is the simplest way to prepare the dish, which keeps well in the refrigerator. For garnish, my husband likes it topped with toasted pine nuts. Serve the dip with lavash, the flatbread favored by many Persians.

◆ MAKES 4 SERVINGS.

1 medium eggplant (1 pound)
2 tablespoons vegetable oil
1 onion, chopped
2 garlic cloves, chopped
1 teaspoon dried mint
4 tablespoons kashk (liquefied dried whey), yogurt, or Thick Yogurt (page 125)
Salt and freshly ground black pepper

Grill, broil, or roast eggplant, then peel it (see "Basics," page 371).

Chop eggplant with knife to a chunky puree. Transfer to bowl.

Heat oil in large skillet. Add onion and sauté over medium heat for 10 minutes, or until tender and golden brown. Add garlic and sauté for 30 seconds, then add dried mint and sauté for a few more seconds. Reserve 3 tablespoons of the mixture as a topping. Add the rest to the eggplant and mix well.

If substituting yogurt for kashk, drain off any liquid before measuring it. Add 3 table- spoons kashk to the eggplant and season to taste with salt and pepper.

Serve the eggplant at room temperature. To serve, spread eggplant dip in a dish or a shallow bowl. To finish, if using *kashk*, mix 1 tablespoon of it with about ½ tablespoon water to a thick sauce and pour it over the center. If using yogurt, simply spoon a dollop over the eggplant. Sprinkle with the reserved onion mixture.

Cilantro-Garlic Eggplant on Pita Crisps with Roasted Peppers

bittingan be salsat kosbarah

This Egyptian-style eggplant is one of my favorite appetizers. When I'm barbecuing, I usually put some eggplants on the grill to keep for the next day, so that eggplant starters like this are unbelievably easy to prepare. You simply chop some grilled or broiled eggplant and sauté it briefly with garlic and spices. The technique is similar to the one used for eggplant *bharta*, a popular item in Indian and Pakistani restaurants.

Most people use whole eggplants to make this appetizer, but if you have some grilled slices on hand they'll work well too. Serve the savory puree as a dip or spread it on pita toasts or crisps or on fresh pita wedges for tempting hors d'oeuvres. If you prefer, serve platefuls of the eggplant as an accompaniment to rice pilaf, meat, or vegetable entrées. For a lighter appetizer, you can stir in yogurt.

◆ MAKES 8 SERVINGS AS AN HORS D'OEUVRE OR 4 AS A SIDE DISH.

2¼ to 2½ pounds eggplant (2 medium)

3 to 5 tablespoons olive oil

6 large garlic cloves, finely chopped

1½ teaspoons ground coriander

½ to 1 teaspoon ground cumin

½ teaspoon Aleppo pepper, or cayenne pepper to taste

Salt and freshly ground black pepper

3 tablespoons chopped cilantro

½ cup plain yogurt (optional, if serving cold)

2 red bell peppers, grilled and peeled (page 370)

4 to 8 pita breads, fresh, made into crisps (page 332) or split and lightly toasted

Grill, broil, or roast eggplant, then peel them (see "Basics," page 371). Chop eggplant fine with a knife.

Heat oil in large heavy skillet. Add garlic and sauté over low heat, stirring, for 1 minute. Stir in coriander and cumin. Add eggplant, Aleppo pepper, salt, and pepper and mix well. Add 2 tablespoons of the cilantro. Cook for 4 to 5 minutes, or until eggplant becomes a thick, chunky puree. If serving eggplant cold, let cool and, if you like, stir in yogurt. Taste and adjust seasoning; eggplant is best flavored generously with salt and pepper.

Cut red pepper in thin strips. To serve, spread eggplant on pita crisps and garnish with pepper strips and with remaining I tablespoon cilantro.

NOTE The eggplant tastes best grilled or broiled, but if you prefer you can roast it in the oven instead.

Garlic Marinated Eggplant

bittingan bel khal wal tom

Around the Middle East marinated eggplant is a popular appetizer, with the vinegar balancing the richness of the fried vegetable. Garlic is the favorite seasoning for the marinade, and is often used in generous amounts. According to the cook's taste, the garlic might be sautéed lightly or simply crushed and mixed with the vinegar. Serve the marinated slices as an appetizer with pita or crusty French or sourdough bread or as an accompaniment to grilled meat or poultry.

◆ MAKES 4 TO 6 SERVINGS.

2 medium eggplants (2 pounds), unpeeled
2 teaspoons salt
About ¾ cup olive oil or vegetable oil
1 medium-size green bell pepper (optional), cut in wide strips
3 large garlic cloves, finely minced
¼ cup white vinegar
2 tablespoons finely chopped Italian parsley
Pinch salt
Black pepper to taste

Cut eggplants in ¾-inch-thick slices lengthwise, discarding ends. Arrange slices in I layer on a rack set over a tray. Sprinkle each side evenly with about I teaspoon salt. Let slices drain for I hour, turning them over after 30 minutes. Pat them dry very thoroughly with paper towels.

In large heavy skillet, heat 3 tablespoons oil over medium heat. Quickly add enough eggplant slices to make a single layer. Sauté eggplant about 2½ minutes on each side, or until it is tender when pierced with a fork. Transfer slices to a plate lined with paper towels. Add 3 tablespoons oil to skillet, heat oil, and sauté remaining eggplant in batches, adding remaining oil between batches as necessary.

If using pepper strips, add to skillet and sauté about 5 minutes, or until crisp-tender. Transfer to a plate.

Heat I tablespoon oil in small saucepan, add garlic, and cook over low heat for 30 seconds, or until beginning to turn golden. Add vinegar and bring to a boil. Simmer over low heat for I minute. Remove marinade from heat. Cool and add parsley and a pinch of salt.

Transfer eggplant to large shallow serving

dish. Spoon marinade evenly over eggplant slices and sprinkle them with black pepper to taste. Turn slices over to coat with marinade. Top with pepper strips. Let stand at room temperature for 30 minutes or refrigerate overnight before serving. Serve cold or at room temperature.

Sweet-and-Spicy Marinated Grilled Peppers

fleifle mechwie

Grilled sweet peppers marinated in olive oil and garlic are popular meal starters in eastern Mediterranean countries and appear on the tables of Egyptian, Israeli, Palestinian, Lebanese, and Turkish families. Red peppers tend to be the first choice but adding some green ones, which have a more herbaceous flavor, provides a nice balance.

Some cooks prepare semihot and hot peppers this way too. You can use jalapeño or poblano peppers or the long, mild Anaheim chilies or other peppers that catch your attention at the market. For this appetizer I combine sweet and hot peppers. I like to dice the chilies and mix them with the sweet peppers so they flavor the dish throughout. If you're serving them to people who may not like chilies, marinate the

sweet and hot peppers in separate dishes, adding some of the garlic to each one. Either cut the sweet peppers in strips so they marinate faster or leave them whole or in halves to keep them longer or for a different presentation. Serve a little of the marinade, which gains flavor from the peppers, as a dressing.

Serve the grilled peppers as a colorful, festive item on a buffet table, add them to a relish plate with olives and pickles, or use them to garnish. You'll find them a delicious addition to salads, eggplant dips, and rice dishes. Try them sliced or chopped as a topping for baked fish, or tuck some into a pita with grilled chicken for a savory sandwich. You can keep them for three days in a covered container in the refrigerator.

Be sure the garlic is fresh. Leave the cloves whole or halved to slowly permeate the marinade, or chop them to give the dressing a more pronounced taste, and in a shorter time.

◆ MAKES 4 TO 6 SERVINGS.

> 4 whole red bell peppers, with core and stems still on, or 2 red and 2 green bell peppers
>
> 2 Anaheim or poblano chilies (called pasilla in California), or 2 to 4 jalapeño peppers
>
> 3 garlic cloves, peeled and halved
>
> ¼ cup extra-virgin olive oil
>
> Salt and freshly ground black pepper
>
> 1 or 2 tablespoons fresh-squeezed lemon juice or vinegar (optional)
>
> 1 garlic clove, minced (optional)

Broil and peel bell peppers and chilies (see "Basics," page 370).

Put halved garlic cloves in bowl and add peppers. Add oil, turning peppers to lightly coat them. Cover and marinate for 2 or 3 hours at room temperature on a cool day or at least 4 hours or overnight in the refrigerator, turning them over once or twice.

To serve, cut sweet peppers in strips. Flavor marinade with salt, pepper, and, if you like, lemon juice. Spoon 2 or 3 tablespoons of the marinade over the peppers. Add the chilies whole or cut in strips or small dice. Add minced garlic, if desired, salt, and pepper. Serve at room temperature.

Roasted Pepper and Tomato Salad/Dip

salat matbuha

This chunky medley of grilled peppers simmered with tomatoes is a staple in the kitchens of Israeli Jews and Arabs and is also a popular deli item. Many call it simply "cooked salad." My sister-in-law Hedva Cohen makes it often, following her family's preference, from fresh tomatoes, sweet red peppers, and sweet paprika. Others mix red and green peppers and many add a few chopped roasted chilies, hot paprika, or cayenne.

Serve this salad on its own to begin a meal, as a dip with fresh pita bread, or as an accompaniment for grilled chicken or meat. You can keep it for three days in the refrigerator, or you can freeze it.

◆ MAKES 6 TO 8 SERVINGS.

4 large red bell peppers
2 or 3 tablespoons olive oil
4 large garlic cloves, chopped
1½ pounds ripe tomatoes, peeled, seeded, and coarsely chopped, or one 28-ounce can diced tomatoes, drained
2 teaspoons paprika
Salt and freshly ground black pepper

Broil and peel bell peppers (see "Basics," page 370).

Dice peppers. Heat oil in large skillet. Add garlic and sauté over medium-low heat for 30 seconds. Add peppers and stir briefly over heat. Add tomatoes, paprika, salt, and pepper. Cook uncovered, stirring often, until mixture is thick, about 15 to 20 minutes if using fresh tomatoes or about 10 minutes if using canned ones. Taste and adjust seasoning. Serve in shallow bowl, cold or at room temperature.

Asparagus with Egyptian Takliah Dressing

halyun bel takliah

To give stewed vegetables and soups a punch of flavor, Egyptians are fond of a quick garlic condiment called *takliah* or *ta'liya*. *Takliah* means frying, and this sauce has one main component—sautéed garlic, and often plenty of it. The garlic is partnered with ground coriander, or occasionally fresh cilantro, cayenne pepper, crushed chilies, or paprika. To sauté the garlic, use either vegetable or olive oil, butter, or ghee. *Takliah* is a traditional flavoring for beans, greens, okra, eggplant, and tomato sauce but I find it also enhances asparagus, pasta, and rice.

Serve the asparagus as an appetizer or with grilled salmon for an elegant springtime dinner. It's also delicious with scrambled eggs or omelettes for brunch or tossed with sautéed chicken strips. For a colorful variation, I sometimes use equal amounts of asparagus pieces and carrots cut in sticks.

♦ MAKES 4 SERVINGS.

1 pound asparagus, peeled if over
   ¼ inch thick

2 tablespoons vegetable oil or olive oil

6 large garlic cloves, minced

2 teaspoons ground coriander

Salt and freshly ground black pepper
   to taste

Cayenne pepper to taste (optional)

1 tablespoon fresh-squeezed lemon juice,
   or lemon wedges for serving
   (optional)

Cut asparagus tips from stems. Cut stems in 2 or 3 pieces, discarding tough ends (about ½ inch from end). Put the asparagus in medium saucepan containing enough boiling salted water to cover it. Boil, uncovered, for 2 or 3 minutes, or until asparagus is just tender when pierced with a small sharp knife. Drain, reserving 2 tablespoons cooking liquid. If cooking the asparagus ahead, rinse with cold running water until cool and drain well.

Heat oil in very small skillet, add garlic, and cook over low heat about 1 minute, until light brown. Add coriander, salt, pepper, and, if you like, cayenne and stir over low heat 15 seconds to blend. Immediately toss with asparagus, in the skillet or in a shallow bowl. Transfer to serving dish. Add reserved cooking liquid to skillet, swirl briefly over heat to blend in any remaining garlic, and pour over asparagus. Add lemon juice and toss again. Taste and adjust seasoning. Serve hot or warm, with lemon wedges, if desired.

Chicken Pecan Bulgur Cakes with Cilantro Pesto

kibbit djaj

Savory patties like this are a frequent choice for a hearty appetizer or party hors d'oeuvre. These are somewhat similar to kibbe, the famous Middle Eastern croquettes, but are lighter and much faster and easier to make than Crunchy Lamb Kibbe with Cinnamon and Cloves (page 204). These crunchy chicken cakes are tempting on their own but are even more fun to eat with a dip. Instead of the cilantro-flavored pecan pesto, you can serve them with Green Tahini (page 34) or Red Pepper Walnut Dip (page 39). If you don't have fine-ground bulgur, use the medium size, which is more widely available.

◆ MAKES 6 TO 8 SERVINGS.

1½ onions

4 to 6 tablespoons olive oil

⅔ cup bulgur wheat, preferably finest grind

⅓ cup parsley sprigs

12 ounces ground chicken (about 1½ cups)

1 teaspoon salt

¼ to ½ teaspoon freshly ground black pepper

1 teaspoon paprika

½ teaspoon ground cinnamon

¼ teaspoon cayenne pepper

3 tablespoons cold water

⅓ cup pecans, chopped

Cilantro Pesto (page 310)

Chop 1 onion. Heat 1 to 2 tablespoons oil in skillet. Add chopped onion and sauté over medium heat for 5 minutes, or until beginning to turn golden. Transfer to plate and cool.

Pour 3 cups cold water over bulgur wheat. Refrigerate and let soak for 10 minutes; if using medium bulgur, soak it for 15 or 20 minutes. Drain in a strainer and squeeze out excess liquid. Put in large bowl.

Cut remaining ½ onion in large dice, put in food processor with parsley sprigs, and chop them fine. Add chicken, salt, pepper, paprika, cinnamon, and cayenne and process until well blended. Add 3 tablespoons cold water and process briefly. Transfer to bowl of bulgur wheat and mix well with your hands. Add pecans and cooled sautéed onion and mix again. Broil or microwave a teaspoon of mixture and taste it for seasoning. Cover and refrigerate for 30 minutes.

Shape mixture in small round cakes, using ¼ cup mixture for each, and flatten them.

Heat 3 tablespoons oil in large heavy skillet. Add enough cakes to make one layer without crowding. Sauté over medium heat for 3 or 4 minutes per side, or until golden brown and cooked through; use two slotted spatulas to turn them carefully. Transfer to paper towels to drain. Keep finished cakes warm on a baking sheet in a 250°F oven. Sauté remaining mixture, adding oil to skillet if necessary and heating it before adding more cakes.

Serve hot or warm. Top each with a spoonful of Cilantro Pesto or serve it as a dipping sauce on the side.

Chicken in Walnut Garlic Sauce

cerkez tavugu

If you like chicken salad, try this luxurious appetizer, which is a sumptuous version. It is especially popular in Turkey, where it is known as Circassian chicken, or *cerkez tavugu,* and is served at weddings and other festive occasions. The Circassians are originally from the Caucasus area of Russia but many left that area in the mid-nineteenth century and today are found in larger groups in Turkey, Jordan, and Syria.

The lavish walnut sauce is a marvelous match for chicken. It consists mainly of ground nuts pureed with the bird's cooking broth to a creamy consistency. How assertive the garlic accent should be depends on the cook. When I tasted the dish at

Dervish, a Turkish restaurant in New York, there was only a hint of garlic. I too like to make the sauce delicate to complement the subtle taste of the poached chicken.

Usually this salad is served cold but some like it warm. For embellishment and a final fillip of flavor, red pepper oil is drizzled over the top, made with paprika or with hot or medium-hot red pepper.

◆ MAKES 6 TO 8 APPETIZER SERVINGS.

1 onion, cut in thick chunks
1 large carrot, sliced
2 garlic cloves
Salt and freshly ground black pepper
About 1 quart water
2½ to 3 pounds chicken pieces
2 slices white bread, crusts removed
1⅓ cups walnut pieces
1 tablespoon walnut, olive, or vegetable oil
1 teaspoon paprika
Pinch cayenne or Aleppo pepper
  (optional)

Combine onion, carrot, 1 garlic clove, salt, and pepper in a stew pan with 3 cups water. Bring to a simmer. Add chicken and more water if needed so chicken is just covered. Return to a simmer. Cover and cook over low heat for about 45 minutes, or until chicken is tender. Remove chicken, reserving broth, and let cool. Remove skin. Either leave chicken as whole pieces or shred it in bite-size chunks, removing bones.

Strain 2 cups chicken broth for sauce.

Chop remaining garlic clove. Soak bread in ½ cup broth. Remove, squeeze dry, and break into pieces.

Puree walnuts in food processor until finely ground. Add bread and chopped garlic and process again. With blades turning, gradually add I cup chicken broth. Add more broth if necessary, so sauce has a thick coating consistency. Season to taste with salt and pepper.

If you are serving the chicken in pieces, put them on a platter and spoon the sauce over them. If you have shredded the chicken, mix it with enough sauce to moisten it, spoon onto a serving dish, and spoon the rest of the sauce on top.

Serve chicken cold or at room temperature. A short time before serving, heat oil with paprika and cayenne in very small saucepan over low heat for I minute. Drizzle over the chicken.

NOTE If you prefer to further soften the flavor of both the walnuts and the garlic, soak the bread in milk.

Grape Leaves with Aromatic Rice Stuffing

mahshy waraq eynab

Grapes have been treasured in the Mideast since biblical times and people make use of their leaves as well as the fruit. In kitchens throughout the region, people lovingly fill the leaves with savory mixtures. Making these small tidbits takes patience and they are reserved for special occasions.

My neighbor in California, Valerie Alon, who is married to a Middle Eastern man, likes stuffed grape leaves so much that she planted grapevines primarily to have fresh leaves for stuffing. At Mediterranean and Middle Eastern shops you can occasionally buy fresh grape leaves, which have a sorrel-like flavor and a crisp-tender texture. When they are not available, most cooks use those that come in jars, which are easy to find. They're quicker to use because you can skip the step of blanching, needed to soften fresh leaves so they can be rolled.

The two most popular stuffings include seasoned rice, either meatless as in this recipe or with ground lamb or beef mixed in. Lebanese cooks often add chickpeas to their vegetarian version. Meat-based and meatless stuffings generally have the same seasoning, of sautéed or raw onions and parsley, and often mint or dill as well as tomatoes in some form—fresh, as sauce or as paste. Egyptians like sweet spices—allspice, cinnamon, or nutmeg—while Turks take the sweet effect a step further by adding currants and a pinch of sugar, and sometimes pine nuts. The rice might be rinsed, soaked to soften slightly, or boiled. In Turkey, where the dish is known as *yaprak sarma*, people often prepare the rice as pilaf, which I find especially good in meatless versions like this one. A common technique is to place a plate on top of the stuffed leaves as a weight so they won't unroll as they simmer. If you like, serve the stuffed grape leaves with velvety Lemon Egg Sauce (page 306).

◆ MAKES ABOUT 8 SERVINGS.

5 to 6 tablespoons extra-virgin olive oil, plus more for serving

2 large onions, chopped

Salt and freshly ground black pepper to taste

1 cup white rice, short or long grain

¾ teaspoon ground allspice

⅓ cup chopped walnuts or pine nuts

⅓ cup chopped Italian parsley

2 tablespoons minced fresh dill, or 2 teaspoons dried dill

¼ cup currants or raisins (optional)

⅓ cup finely chopped peeled, seeded fresh tomatoes or canned tomatoes

2 to 3 tablespoons fresh-squeezed lemon juice

12 to 16 ounces fresh grape leaves, or one 1-pound jar preserved grape leaves

Lemon wedges

To prepare filling: Heat 3 or 4 tablespoons oil in skillet or shallow saucepan. Add onions and sauté over medium-low heat for 12 minutes, or until tender and light golden. Season to taste with salt and pepper. Remove 1⅓ cups of onions and reserve. Add rice to pan and stir over low heat for 2 minutes, or until grains turn milky white. Add 1 cup hot water, ¾ teaspoon salt, ½ teaspoon pepper, and allspice and return to a boil. Cover and simmer over very low heat for 5 minutes; rice will be partially cooked. Stir in walnuts, parsley, dill, and, if you like, currants. Return reserved onions to mixture. Add tomatoes and 1 to 2 tablespoons lemon juice. Taste and adjust seasoning.

If using fresh grape leaves, rinse them well and arrange them in piles of 15 or 20 leaves. If you like, tie each pile in a bundle with string for easy removal from blanching water. Add to a saucepan of boiling salted water and submerge them in the water. Cook for 1 or 2 minutes, or until limp. Remove very carefully with slotted spoon and drain in a strainer.

If using preserved leaves, rinse them to remove excess salt. If they still taste too salty, soak them in hot water for 10 minutes, drain, then soak briefly in cold water. Taste again and repeat soaking if necessary.

Put leaves on work surface with their smooth, shiny side down and their rough side (with veins of leaves) facing upward. Spread each leaf out carefully and pat dry. Cut off stems and reserve. Put a heaping teaspoon of filling on a leaf near its stem end, or 2 heaping teaspoons if leaf is large, arranging filling in a row across bottom of leaf, not quite to edges. Fold stem end over filling, then fold left and right sides of leaf inward. If necessary, trim excess from edges of leaf, so there is enough leaf to hold filling but not too much overlap. Roll up leaf in a finger shape, pressing well but not too tightly to allow rice room to expand.

Put reserved stems and remaining leaves in stew pan or deep sauté pan. Arrange the stuffed leaves on top in a compact layer with their pointed ends facing down so they won't unroll; they should fit neatly but should have a little room. Put the next layer of leaves on top at a 90-degree angle to the first layer. Add enough water to cover leaves. Add a pinch of salt, 1 to 2 tablespoons oil, and 1 to 2 tablespoons lemon juice. Cover leaves with a plate slightly smaller than diameter of pan to keep them from unrolling. Bring to a boil, cover pan with lid, and cook over low heat for 45 minutes, or until rice is tender, adding water in small amounts if needed so leaves don't become dry.

With slotted spoon, gently remove stuffed leaves. Discard stems and unstuffed leaves. Serve leaves warm, at room temperature, or cold, drizzled with olive oil and garnished with lemon wedges.

Yogurt Cheese Balls in Herb Oil

labneh makbus

When visiting the Middle East, I love to buy rounds of cheese packed in jars of olive oil. Originally, this technique developed as a way to store cheese without refrigeration. The cheese balls were first thoroughly dried and then kept in the oil for up to a year. Now people eat them because they taste so good.

It's easy to make your own marinated cheese balls from purchased *labneh* (kefir cheese) or from homemade yogurt cheese. If you will be serving the cheese balls within a few days, you don't have to cover them completely with oil; just drizzle on the amount you'd like for flavor. Pour on enough oil to cover them if you want to keep them longer.

Serve the yogurt cheese balls with pita bread or lavash. Serve olives and raw vegetables or Middle Eastern Diced Salad (page 58) at the same time.

♦ MAKES 4 TO 6 APPETIZER SERVINGS.

1½ cups Yogurt Cheese (page 125) or packaged *labneh*

½ teaspoon salt, or to taste (optional)

½ to ¾ cup extra-virgin olive oil, or more if needed

4 garlic cloves, peeled and halved

2 to 3 teaspoons chopped fresh thyme,
   or 1 teaspoon dried thyme

Freshly ground black pepper to taste

Middle Eastern red pepper such as Aleppo
   pepper, paprika, or cayenne pepper
   to taste

Zahtar herb-sesame blend (page 14)
   (optional)

Be sure your yogurt cheese has drained until very thick, enough to form balls; it usually needs a few hours longer for shaping balls than for spreading. Packaged *labneh* is usually thick enough so it doesn't need draining.

Add salt to the yogurt cheese and mix well; purchased *labneh* is usually salty enough.

Roll cheese into 1-inch balls. Set them on a plate and refrigerate overnight.

Pour a little olive oil into jar or glass container large enough to contain the cheese balls. Add a few cheese balls at a time and pour more oil over them. When all the cheese is in the jar, add enough oil to just cover, if you want the cheese to keep for longer. Add garlic and thyme to the oil. Cover and refrigerate for at least 4 hours or overnight.

Serve cheese balls with a little of their oil spooned over them; you can use any extra oil for salads. Sprinkle them with black and red peppers and with zahtar.

Salads from Sunny Soils

Middle Eastern Diced Salad ♦ *Salata Khodra*

Mideast-California Diced Salad ♦ *Salat Mizrah Tihoni B'signon California*

Turkish Shepherd's Salad ♦ *Çoban Salatasi*

Diced Vegetable Salad with Garlic-Mint Dressing and Toasted Pita ♦ *Fattoush*

Spinach and Vegetable Salad with Feta Cheese ♦ *Ispanak Salatasi*

Simple Tomato Salad ♦ *Slatat al-Banadura*

Summer Purslane and Tomato Salad ♦ *Slatat al-Baqli Ma'Banadura*

Grated Vegetable Salad with Pistachios, Raisins, and Yogurt ♦ *Mast-o Kheeyar*

Green Salad with Herbs and Radishes ♦ *Marul Salatasi*

Cucumber Salad with Green Olives ♦ *Kheyaar Bi Zaytun*

Classic Cucumber Salad with Yogurt, Garlic, and Mint ♦ *Cacik*

Tangy Two-way Coleslaw ♦ *Salatet Malfouf*

Warm Carrot Salad with Lemon, Garlic, and Mint • *Jazar Bi Zayt*

Eastern Mediterranean Potato Salad • *Batata Mtabbli*

Egyptian-Style Potato and Green Bean Salad • *Batata Mtabbli Ma' Lubyi*

Tangy Beet Salad • *Pancar Salatasi*

Fava and Fennel Salad, Cypriot Style • *Salata Koukia Freska*

Three-Bean Salad with Tomatoes, Olives, and Cilantro • *Fassoulia Salata*

Classic White Bean Salad • *Piyaz*

Lemony Parsley and Bulgur Salad with Mint • *Tabbouleh*

Whole-wheat Couscous Salad with Pistachios, Chickpeas, and Corn •
Salat Couscous im Fistookim v'Hummus

Yellow Rice Salad with Red Peppers, Beans, and Dill •
Salat Orez Tzahov im Pilpelim v'Shi'ou'it

Persian Peach Pilaf Salad with Toasted Almonds • *Salade-e-berenj-Ba Hulu*

In homes around the Middle East, a salad of fresh vegetables is an essential part of every meal. A simple supper is incomplete without one. Even for breakfast, if someone is eating an omelette, there has to be a salad on the plate alongside it. Indeed, this custom is one of the most healthful aspects of the Mediterranean and Middle Eastern diets.

The most frequently prepared salad is what we call a "chopped salad," a colorful mix of cubed tomatoes, cucumbers, and onions. To many natives of the region it's important that these cubes be tiny, and friends don't hesitate to remind me if mine get too big.

Such a salad often accompanies the entrée, whether it's a grilled steak or a bowl of lentils. It can also be an appetizer or a partner for other starters, like falafel or eggplant dip. Diced salad is a standard sandwich component too, tucked into a pita pocket.

This is just the beginning of the salad story. There are several other classic medleys, such as tabbouleh, a parsley and vegetable salad with bulgur wheat, and *fattoush,* made of diced fresh vegetables tossed with toasted pita and a lively sumac dressing.

In addition to such mixed salads, the region's culinary repertoire includes a great selection of salads made of just one or two vegetables—some raw and others grilled, roasted, or boiled. In many Mideast cultures a sumptuous spread of salads is a major part of the meze that begins every celebratory feast. (For more on meze, see "Appetizers," page 28.)

Some of my favorites are: Cilantro-Garlic Eggplant on Pita Crisps with Roasted Peppers; Warm Carrot Salad with Lemon, Garlic, and Mint; Beet Borani Salad (page 257); and Eastern Mediterranean Potato Salad accented with capers, tomatoes, herbs, and lemon juice. Bean salads, such as one from Cyprus in which fava beans and fennel gain punch from black olives, are ideal for a light summer entrée. Pungent cheeses are a popular enhancement for greens, as in Spinach and Vegetable Salad with Feta Cheese (page 64), and for diced salads as well.

Refreshing dressings of fresh lemon juice, extra-virgin olive oil, and herbs enliven the vegetables, as do garlic and fresh onions. Unlike classic French vinaigrettes that feature three tablespoons oil for every tablespoon of vinegar, Middle Eastern dressings often have equal or nearly equal amounts of both. The result is a sharper dressing that wakes up your taste buds.

Many salads feature an interesting interplay of sweet-and-sour flavors, pairing sweet vegetables like carrots or beets with yogurt, lemon, or sumac. To make creamy dressings, mayonnaise is occasionally used (see Israeli Eggplant Dip with Garlic Mayonnaise, page 41) but more often the cook opts for tahini.

Middle Eastern Diced Salad

salata khodra

This lively, colorful blend of finely diced cucumbers, tomatoes, and onion is the most frequently prepared salad in the Mideast. It is known among my relatives as Israeli salad and among my Lebanese friends as Lebanese salad. My Iranian neighbors see it as their own as well. To them it is Shirazi salad, named for Shiraz in southwestern Iran. All around the region people love it and if they ask for salad, this is what they mean. It's served as an appetizer, often together with other salads, or as an accompaniment for any main course.

The salad is most delicious with its traditional dressing of olive or vegetable oil and fresh lemon juice. It's so good when made with quality vegetables that you can get by with very little dressing, or even, for days after too much feasting, none at all. The salad is at its best and prettiest if you cut the cucumbers and tomatoes in small cubes, preferably three eighths inch and no larger than half inch. Usually the cucumbers are peeled, but I don't peel the thin-skinned Middle Eastern variety.

For the salad's onion component, I like those that are not too sharp, like red or green onions. Sweet white and yellow onions, often available in the spring and summer, are best. If the onions are strong, I chop them and soak them for a few minutes in cold water.

You can make the salad a few hours ahead and keep it in the refrigerator. If you're making it in advance, the vegetables keep their texture better if you don't add the salt or lemon juice until right before serving.

The cucumber-tomato-onion trio is standard, usually with Italian parsley added, but there are variations. Lebanese and Armenian cooks like mint or purslane. Some cooks flavor their dressing with garlic. One of our Yemenite relatives adds a teaspoonful of her fiery green *zehug*, or Yemenite hot sauce. Israelis and Palestinians might sprinkle the salad with zahtar (see variation below). For a creamy dressing, some people use yogurt or tahini.

Depending on the season, radishes, sweet red, green, or yellow peppers, mild Anaheim chilies, romaine strips, or shredded green or red cabbage might be added. Sometimes the salad is enriched with cubes of feta cheese or crumbled spicy *shanklish* cheese (see "The Mideast Pantry," page 10) or a few flavorful black or green olives.

♦ MAKES 4 SERVINGS.

3 Middle Eastern or pickling (Kirby)
    cucumbers, ½ hothouse cucumber,
    or 1 Japanese or American cucumber

⅓ to ½ cup finely chopped onion

8 ripe but firm plum tomatoes, or 4 medium
    tomatoes, cut in small dice

3 to 4 tablespoons chopped Italian parsley

2 tablespoons extra-virgin olive oil or
vegetable oil

1 to 2 tablespoons strained fresh-squeezed
lemon or lime juice

Salt and freshly ground black pepper

Peel cucumbers if you like and cut in small dice, no larger than ½ inch. If using yellow or white onion and it smells very strong, rinse the chopped onion with cold water, drain, and pat it dry.

In glass bowl, mix together diced cucumbers, tomato, onion, and parsley. Add oil, lemon juice, and salt and pepper to taste. Refrigerate until ready to serve.

Israeli Salad with Zahtar

Sprinkle the salad with 2 to 3 teaspoons zahtar, the herb-and-sesame seed blend that you can purchase at Middle Eastern shops. If you don't have it, toast 2 teaspoons sesame seeds (see "Basics," page 369) and let cool. Mix with 1 teaspoon dried thyme and sprinkle the mixture over the salad.

DICED SALAD

A salad of the traditional tomato-cucumber-onion trio in small dice is a staple on the Mideast table. Everyone knows that the quality of the tomatoes is of great importance to this Mediterranean salad. But this is also true of the cucumber. It may not seem like an exciting vegetable if you've tasted only the standard supermarket type, but there are cucumbers and then there are cucumbers.

Get into a discussion of cucumbers with people from the Mideast, and they become passionate. "American cucumbers are inedible," they say, referring to the common fat cucumbers. They will acknowledge that the long, hothouse cucumbers and the slim Japanese cucumbers sometimes available are an im-

provement. But their favorite type is what gardening catalogs call Middle Eastern cucumbers. In my neighborhood they are sold in produce markets and farmers' markets as Persian cucumbers. In other parts of the country they might be called Israeli or Arabic cucumbers. I prefer these small, thin cucumbers. They are crisp, delicately sweet, and have tender skin with no trace of bitterness. If you don't have these cucumbers, use pickling cucumbers or fresh, slim supermarket cucumbers.

Any variety of tomato works for salads but they must be aromatic and ripe but firm. Very large, juicy ones make the salad wet, but if you have tasty heirloom tomatoes, they will make a delicious salad.

Mideast-California Diced Salad

salat mizrah tihoni b'signon california

California chefs have made what they called "chopped salads" famous by adding a great variety of ingredients, from sautéed artichoke hearts to blanched carrots, raw corn, radicchio, and Parmesan cheese. I keep my salads simple and stick to the principle of using only raw ones, but I often include a few elements that are rare in Mideast versions. In springtime I toss in thin slices of uncooked tender asparagus and in winter, bean sprouts. I flavor the dressing for my summertime salad with basil and might even slip in a little fruit from the garden, such as plums, nectarines, or tart summer apples. I got the idea of adding pine nuts and avocado from my sister-in-law, Monica Levi, who lives in Los Angeles.

My favorite nontraditional addition is jicama, which is unknown in the Middle East. The first time I added jicama was by chance, when I was short on cucumbers. Since Yakir, my husband, grew up in the Mideast eating the traditional salad, I wondered how he would react. He was delighted with the new salad and so was I—the jicama's subtle sweetness complemented the other ingredients and the lemon juice dressing perfectly. Yet like cucumbers, it has a pleasing crispness and a delicate sweetness. I now add jicama to the Old World recipe often, occasionally with a little cilantro or

jalapeño too (see the variation). I find the best jicamas at Mexican markets.

This colorful medley makes a tasty appetizer or accompaniment to any main course, from roast chicken to grilled tofu.

◆ MAKES 4 SERVINGS.

½ hothouse or Japanese cucumber, 4 Middle Eastern cucumbers, 2 pickling (Kirby) cucumbers, or 1 medium American cucumber, peeled and cut in small dice

8 plum tomatoes, or 4 medium tomatoes, cut in small dice

½ cup chopped red or sweet onion

1 red, orange, or yellow bell pepper, cut in small dice

½ cup bean sprouts (optional), or 5-ounce piece of jicama, peeled, cut in small dice (about 1 cup)

2 tablespoons extra-virgin olive oil

2 tablespoons strained fresh-squeezed lemon juice

Salt and freshly ground black pepper to taste

Hot sauce to taste

1 small ripe avocado, preferably Hass

3 tablespoons chopped fresh basil

3 tablespoons pine nuts, lightly toasted

Mix together diced cucumbers, tomatoes, onion, peppers, and, if you like, bean sprouts. Add oil, lemon juice, and salt, pepper, and hot sauce to taste.

Just before serving, peel and dice avocado and fold it gently into salad. Add basil. Taste and adjust seasoning. Serve cold or at room temperature, sprinkled with pine nuts.

Mediterranean-Mexican Diced Salad

Omit the bell pepper, bean sprouts, basil, pine nuts, and avocado. Peel and dice a 10-ounce piece of jicama (about 2 cups). Mix with the cucumbers and tomatoes. Substitute 6 tablespoons chopped green onion, white and green parts, for the red onion. If you like, substitute lime juice for the lemon juice and add 2 tablespoons chopped cilantro and 1 seeded minced fresh jalapeño pepper or hot sauce to taste.

Turkish Shepherd's Salad

çoban salatasi

This salad, a mixture of lettuce and raw vegetables garnished with olives, undoubtedly had humble beginnings and contained whatever shepherds happened to find growing in the countryside. Today many Turks consider it an indispensable partner for their preferred entrées, such as kabobs or grilled chicken. Often the vegetables are sliced but some cube them, as for the standard Middle Eastern diced salad.

◆ MAKES 4 TO 6 SERVINGS.

½ a mild yellow, white, or red onion

1 mild chili, such as Anaheim, sliced, or 1 to 2 hot chilies such as jalapeño, chopped (optional)

4 cups wide strips of romaine or other lettuce

½ green and ½ yellow bell pepper, cored, seeded, and cut in thin strips

½ hothouse cucumber, cut in thin half slices

4 radishes, sliced thin (optional)

⅓ to ½ cup coarsely chopped fresh parsley

1 to 2 tablespoons chopped fresh dill (optional)

2 to 3 green onions, sliced (optional)

4 ripe tomatoes, halved and sliced

1 tablespoon wine vinegar

1 to 2 tablespoons fresh-squeezed lemon juice

Salt and freshly ground black pepper

2 to 4 tablespoons extra-virgin olive oil

Cayenne pepper to taste (optional)

8 to 12 Mediterranean-style green or black olives

Halve the onion half and thinly slice each quarter. If the onion tastes strong, rinse the slices with cold water and pat dry.

Combine onion, mild chili, romaine, bell pepper, cucumber, radishes, parsley, dill, and green onions in shallow bowl and toss. Add tomato slices and lightly toss again.

To make the dressing, whisk vinegar with lemon juice, salt, and pepper in small bowl. Whisk in oil. Season to taste with cayenne. If using a hot chili (not a mild one), add it to dressing. Pour dressing over salad and toss gently. Taste and adjust seasoning. Garnish with olives and serve.

FATTOUSH AND PANZANELLA:
THE MEDITERRANEAN CONNECTION

When I was growing up, bread was revered as holy, and throwing any out was practically a sin. My parents' sentiment was not unique. Beliefs like this and a sense of thriftiness have long driven cooks to develop ways to utilize bread that is no longer fresh. Over the ages, Mediterranean and Mideastern cooks have come up with a simple solution—they turn the bread into a satisfying salad. Most notable are the *fattoush* of Lebanon and the panzanella of Italy.

Calling these dishes bread salads might give the impression that they are dense and heavy. Yet the opposite is true—they should be fresh, light, and colorful, graced with ripe vegetables, and redolent with herbs. The soul of these salads comes from both regions' venerated olive trees. Panzanella, of Tuscan origin, makes liberal use of the area's celebrated oil, with the occasional addition of a drizzle of wine vinegar. The Lebanese are equally passionate about olive oil but balance its richness with a generous squeeze of lemon juice and often with tangy sumac as well.

The other signature element in the two salads is the tomato, a New World ingredient now closely associated with Mediterranean cooking. Onions and flat-leaf parsley are also common additions. Lebanese cooks wake up the diners' palates with garlic and mint rather than opting for the Italians' choice, basil. *Fattoush* always includes cucumbers. Depending on the season, it might contain romaine lettuce, sweet peppers, radishes, or purslane.

Old-fashioned *fattoush* formulas for preparing the bread are similar to Italian ones, although the thinner pita bread does not need soaking and squeezing, as does hearty Italian bread. Dry pita pieces are sprinkled with water or simply moistened by the dressing.

Another way of preparing these salads, preferred by many today, is to use crunchy bread. Restaurant chefs in America and the Mideast and many home cooks toast, grill, or fry the bread and add it at the last moment like croutons. Perfect for the cook in a hurry, these salads are not only colorful and tasty, they're healthful and easy to make.

Diced Vegetable Salad with Garlic-Mint Dressing and Toasted Pita

fattoush

Fattoush is a diced salad with bits of crunchy pita that play the role of croutons. When I have extra pita or Italian bread, I bake it until crisp, so the bread part of my salad is ready when I need it. Slowly baking the pita dries it well so it keeps; if you're using the bread right away, simply toast it.

Like Lebanese cooks, I flavor my dressing with a combination of garlic, parsley, and mint. Dried mint works fine if you don't have fresh; unlike other tender herbs, mint's flavor holds up well when dried. I prefer a full-flavored extra-virgin olive oil from Crete, Tuscany, or southern Spain.

You can purchase the ingredients for this salad in just about any supermarket, but if you'd like to give it a special character, visit a Middle Eastern market, where you will find sumac and, in summertime, purslane, which can also be found in Latino markets. For more color and flavor, add a diced red or yellow bell pepper or four to six thin-sliced small radishes.

◆ MAKES 6 SERVINGS.

1 small fresh garlic clove, pressed or finely minced

2 to 3 tablespoons fresh-squeezed lemon juice, or more to taste

2 to 3 tablespoons extra-virgin olive oil, or more to taste

Salt and freshly ground black pepper

3 tablespoons coarsely chopped fresh mint, or 2 teaspoons dried mint

1 teaspoon ground sumac, or to taste (optional)

8 ripe plum tomatoes, or 3 medium or large tomatoes

3 Middle Eastern or 1 hothouse cucumber, unpeeled, or 2 pickling or 1 common cucumber, peeled

2 green onions, white and green parts, or ¼ to ½ sweet white onion, minced

¼ cup chopped Italian parsley

1½ cups diced romaine lettuce

1 cup purslane leaves (optional)

2 or 3 pita breads, toasted and broken into bite-size pieces, or Pita Crisps (page 332)

Combine garlic, lemon juice, oil, salt, pepper, dried mint (but not fresh), and, if desired, ½ teaspoon sumac in small bowl.

Cut tomatoes and cucumbers in ½-inch dice and put them in large bowl. Add onions, parsley, fresh mint, romaine, and, if you like, purslane. Add dressing and toss. Add half the toasted pita and toss again. Taste, adjust seasoning, and add more olive oil and lemon juice if you like. You can serve the salad at once or let it stand for 30 minutes to allow flavors to blend. Serve sprinkled with remaining sumac, if you like. Garnish with a few pieces of pita and serve the rest separately.

Spinach and Vegetable Salad with Feta Cheese

ispanak salatasi

From Turkey to Iran, feta and similar cheeses are among the most popular, not only to fill pastries, but as table cheeses as well. Cooks often crumble it over salads of leafy greens or of diced tomatoes and cucumbers. The rich, salty cheese is an ideal complement to the cool, refreshing vegetables.

Adding a tasty cheese is a quick, easy way to turn a simple salad like this one into a festive dish. You only need a little feta for accent. You'll need even less if you use another Middle Eastern cheese instead—the spicy, herb-seasoned Lebanese cheese called *shanklish,* which is even more crumbly than feta. This pungent cheese is best as a seasoning for greens and vegetables, which balance its assertive taste. Another flavorful cheese you can add in thin strips is Cypriot *halloumi* cheese. (See "The Mideast Pantry," page 10, for more on Middle Eastern cheeses.) Incorporating cheeses in salads like this one is a healthful way to enjoy their flavor because a little goes a long way.

◆ MAKES 4 SERVINGS.

One 10-ounce bag cleaned spinach, or a ¾-pound bunch, stems removed, leaves rinsed and dried

2 medium tomatoes, sliced

1 cup thinly sliced cucumber

1 small red or green bell pepper, cored, seeded, and cut in strips

2 green onions, sliced thin

2 teaspoons chopped fresh mint, or ½ teaspoon dried mint

3 or 4 tablespoons extra-virgin olive oil

2 tablespoons fresh-squeezed lemon juice, strained

Salt and freshly ground black pepper

Aleppo pepper or pinch cayenne pepper (optional)

½ cup crumbled feta cheese

Tear any large spinach leaves in two or three pieces. Toss spinach in large shallow bowl with tomatoes, cucumber, pepper, onions, and mint.

Whisk olive oil with lemon juice in small bowl. Season lightly with salt, and add pepper and, if you like, Aleppo pepper to taste.

A short time before serving, pour dressing over salad, then sprinkle it with feta cheese.

Simple Tomato Salad

slatat al-banadura

Like the French, the Italians, and other Mediterranean people, Middle Easterners love tomatoes and often eat them alone, with little embellishment. A tomato salad may be enhanced with a simple dressing of olive oil, lemon juice, and salt, with perhaps a little onion, a touch of garlic, or a sprinkling of herbs. Some garnish the salad with black or green olives or a few anchovies.

It's the quality of the luscious tomatoes that makes such a salad great. If you have heirloom tomatoes of different colors, this is a good way to highlight their beauty and character. Use tomatoes that are ripe but firm. If you like, substitute a very fresh minced garlic clove for the onions.

◆ MAKES 4 SERVINGS.

  ½ sweet red or white onion, or 3 or 4 green
    onions
  4 tomatoes, sliced or cut in large cubes
  ¼ cup chopped Italian parsley,
    or 2 tablespoons chopped fresh mint
    (optional)
  3 tablespoons extra-virgin olive oil
  1 to 2 tablespoons fresh-squeezed lemon
    juice or vinegar
  Salt to taste
  Freshly ground black pepper (optional)

Chop onion half or cut it in half lengthwise, then slice the two quarters thin and separate them into slivers. If the onions are strong, put them in strainer and rinse them with cold water; drain and pat dry. If using green onions, chop them or slice them thin.

Gently mix the tomatoes, onion, and, if you like, parsley. Add olive oil, lemon juice, salt, and, if desired, pepper. Mix gently. Serve cold or at room temperature.

Summer Purslane and Tomato Salad

slatat al-baqli ma' banadura

I first tasted purslane, a succulent, slightly tart herb with large round leaves, at a fancy restaurant in southern France. A few leaves garnished our appetizer plates, and I was struck by their smooth, rich texture. Ever since I found purslane in ethnic markets in my Los Angeles neighborhood, I've been adding it to my salads regularly.

Purslane is one of the few plant sources of omega-3 fatty acids, a beneficial nutrient found in certain fish. In spring and summer you can find purslane in the fresh herb display at Middle Eastern produce shops as well as at Mexican markets, where it's called *verdolaga*. Like watercress, it's very perishable and should be used within two days.

This healthful herb appears as an appetizer salad on Turkish, Lebanese, and Armenian tables, either on its own or in simple vegetable mixtures like this one. Some people use only the purslane leaves but, like many Mideastern cooks, I use the tender, thin stems as well. Some blanch the purslane for a minute or two, but I like the texture of the raw herb. If you don't have purslane and would like to prepare this salad, substitute 2½ cups baby spinach mixed with ½ cup sorrel, watercress, or arugula. The taste will be different but it will be a good salad.

◆ MAKES 3 OR 4 SERVINGS.

1 small garlic clove, finely minced
or pressed

1 tablespoon fresh-squeezed lemon juice

Salt and freshly ground black pepper

2 or 3 tablespoons extra-virgin olive oil

2½ to 3 cups purslane sprigs and leaves

2 large or 4 medium tomatoes, ripe but firm,
cut in bite-size pieces

3 Middle Eastern or 2 slim pickling
cucumbers, thinly sliced

Combine garlic, lemon juice, salt, pepper, and 2 tablespoons oil in small bowl. Whisk to blend.

Cut purslane in 1-inch pieces. Mix with tomatoes and cucumbers. Add dressing and toss gently. Taste, adjust seasoning, and add remaining olive oil if you like.

Grated Vegetable Salad with Pistachios, Raisins, and Yogurt

mast-o kheeyar

Toasted pistachios and raisins lend a festive look to this salad, which is both creamy and crunchy. It is my take on a Persian yogurt-dressed salad of cucumbers, walnuts, and raisins, which is also loved in neighboring Afghanistan.

In the Mideast, cooks often use rich, whole-milk yogurt or *labneh* (see "The Mideast Pantry," page 10) for salads like this. Use all yogurt or a combination of yogurt and sour cream of any degree of richness to make the creamy dressing as luscious or as lean as you like. Goat's-milk yogurt gives the salad an intriguing tang, and rich sheep's-milk yogurt is a terrific choice if you can find it, but plain cow's-milk yogurt is fine too.

If your raisins are not moist, soak them in hot water for a few minutes until they soften, then drain them before adding them to the salad.

◆ MAKES 3 OR 4 SERVINGS.

1½ cups coarsely grated peeled cucumber
(from about 2 pickling cucumbers,
total 6 ounces)

1 cup plain yogurt

1½ cups coarsely grated peeled carrot or
jicama

3 tablespoons chopped green onions,
green and white parts

1 tablespoon chopped fresh dill,
or 1 teaspoon dried dill

3 tablespoons chopped Italian parsley

¼ cup moist dark raisins

¼ cup toasted pistachios, coarsely
chopped

Salt and freshly ground black pepper

Drain grated cucumber in strainer for 5 minutes. If there is water in the yogurt, pour it out.

Lightly mix cucumber with carrot, green onions, and dill with fork. Reserve 1 tablespoon parsley, 2 tablespoons raisins, and 2 tablespoons pistachios for garnish. Gently stir remaining parsley, raisins, and pistachios into vegetable mixture. Lightly stir in yogurt. Season to taste with salt and pepper. Serve cold in shallow bowl. At serving time, sprinkle with reserved parsley, raisins, and pistachios.

Green Salad with Herbs and Radishes

marul salatasi

Although green salads are not as common in the Middle East as salads of diced vegetables, they are valued in the Turkish, Armenian, and Lebanese culinary repertoires. Cooks use a variety of greens, from peppery watercress and arugula to delicate purslane, each on its own or in a mixture like this one. Some season the greens with only olive oil and lemon juice but like many cooks, I add sliced green onions, or sometimes minced garlic, for a little extra punch. Salads of finely shredded cabbage are prepared the same way.

If you like, garnish this salad with toasted pine nuts or slivered almonds instead of olives. Serve it along with other vegetable appetizers or to accompany roast chicken or grilled meats.

To serve this salad the Iranian way, instead of tossing the ingredients, arrange the greens and vegetables on a platter, keeping each type separate and leaving the herbs in sprigs. Either make the dressing or set out cruets of oil and vinegar. Serve the vegetables with lavash, feta cheese, and walnuts.

◆ MAKES 4 SERVINGS.

> 5 to 6 cups bite-size pieces romaine lettuce, or one 10-ounce package romaine
>
> ¾ to 1 cup coarsely chopped arugula or watercress (optional)
>
> 6 small red radishes, sliced
>
> 2 green onions, sliced thin
>
> ¼ cup chopped Italian parsley
>
> 2 tablespoons chopped fresh dill or mint
>
> 2 tablespoons fresh-squeezed lemon juice or white- or red-wine vinegar
>
> 2 to 3 tablespoons extra-virgin olive oil
>
> Salt and freshly ground black pepper
>
> ⅓ cup good-quality black olives, such as kalamata (optional)

Toss lettuce with arugula, radishes, green onions, parsley, and dill in bowl.

Whisk lemon juice with oil, salt, and pepper in small bowl. Pour over salad and toss lightly. Taste and adjust seasoning. Serve garnished with olives.

Cucumber Salad with Green Olives

kheyaar bi zaytun

Sweet peppers, jicama, and mint enliven this light, refreshing salad. With its tart dressing, it is a wonderful partner for broiled salmon steaks or grilled lamb chops. For best results, use flavorful Greek, Syrian, or Israeli olives.

Although jicama is not found in the Middle East, I find it's a good complement to the other flavors in this salad. Kohlrabi, which is somewhat similar, is easy to find in Israel and is well liked in salads.

♦ MAKES 6 SERVINGS.

  1 pound cucumbers (4 pickling or 1 hot-house), cut in thin sticks (about 4 cups)

  1 pound jicama, peeled and cut in thin sticks (about 4 cups)

  2 small red, yellow, orange, or green bell peppers, halved, cored, seeded, and cut in thin strips (about 2 cups)

  2/3 cup pitted green olives, halved

  1/4 cup extra-virgin olive oil

  3 tablespoons white-wine vinegar

  Salt to taste

  Cayenne pepper to taste

  2 to 3 tablespoons chopped fresh mint or cilantro, or equal parts of both

Combine cucumber, jicama, pepper strips, and olives in large shallow serving bowl. Mix gently.

In small bowl, whisk oil with vinegar, salt, and cayenne. Add to salad and mix. Add mint and toss lightly. Taste and adjust seasoning.

Classic Cucumber Salad with Yogurt, Garlic, and Mint

cacik

If you yawn at the thought of a cucumber and yogurt salad, this one, called *cacik* in Turkish and *khyar bi laban* in Arabic, will wake you up with its garlic and mint accents. Be sure to use good-quality yogurt. The tangy taste of goat's-milk yogurt is great with the cucumbers, as is luscious sheep's-milk yogurt. Another wonderful option, popular in Lebanon, is *labneh*, or kefir cheese, which you can find at Middle Eastern markets; because it's so thick, it needs to first be thinned with a little cold water. You'll also have tasty results with Bulgarian-style yogurt, which is available at many supermarkets, or other whole cow's-milk yogurt. For lean days, low-fat or even nonfat yogurt is tasty when used this way.

Throughout the Eastern Mediterranean this refreshing combination is especially welcome during the hot summers, not only as an appetizer but as a cooling complement

68 ♦ FEAST FROM THE MIDEAST

for spicy stews. It can also be served as a dip with pita crisps or raw vegetables, as a crunchy spread for bread, or as a sandwich filling in a pita with roasted vegetables or grilled meats.

The proportions of cucumber to yogurt are up to you. Many people add plenty of yogurt, sometimes diluted with water to make a cold soup. Some like the texture of cucumber rounds or half slices, while others prefer the finer consistency of diced or grated cucumbers, which makes this salad more like a dip. Other good additions are mild radishes and sweet tomatoes.

◆ MAKES 4 SERVINGS.

    1 or 2 small fresh garlic cloves, minced
    Salt to taste
    2 tablespoons chopped fresh mint,
        or 2 teaspoons dried mint
    2½ to 3 cups Thick Yogurt (page 125)
        or plain yogurt, or 2 cups kefir cheese
        (*labneh*)
    4 Middle Eastern, 2 Japanese, or 1 hothouse
        cucumber
    1 to 1½ cups diced tomatoes or red bell
        peppers, or 1 cup thinly sliced radishes
        (optional)
    Pinch cayenne pepper (optional)

Mash garlic with pinch of salt in bowl, using back of spoon. Add 1½ tablespoons fresh or 1½ teaspoons dried mint and all but ½ cup of the yogurt or cheese. Blend well, thoroughly mixing in garlic mixture.

Peel cucumbers if you like. Halve them lengthwise and slice them thin or grate them on large holes of grater. Fold cucumbers gently into yogurt mixture. Add remaining yogurt if desired. If using kefir cheese and the mixture is too thick, gradually stir in a few tablespoons very cold water.

Fold in tomatoes if you like. Taste for seasoning, adding enough salt so the salad won't be bland; if using kefir cheese, the salad might not need more salt. Add cayenne to taste, if desired. Refrigerate at least 30 minutes before serving. Serve sprinkled with remaining mint.

Tangy Two-way Coleslaw

salatet malfouf

You can make this light, dill-accented salad with one kind of cabbage but the prettiest presentation is to serve it as two salads side by side—one with red and one with green cabbage. In Jerusalem I learned the trick to making red cabbage bright red: you pour hot vinegar over it. The salad is also delicious topped with crumbled feta or goat cheese.

If you're in a rush, buy shredded cabbage or coleslaw mix; you will need about 8 cups.

◆ MAKES 8 SERVINGS.

¾ to 1 pound green cabbage and ¾ pound
red cabbage (½ small head of each),
or 1½ pounds green or red cabbage
(1 small head)

¼ cup plus 2 tablespoons white-wine
vinegar

Salt and freshly ground black pepper

½ to ¾ cup olive oil or vegetable oil

1 or 2 large carrots, grated (optional)

⅓ cup chopped green onion

3 tablespoons chopped fresh dill

2 tablespoons chopped fresh mint,
or 2 teaspoons dried mint

½ cup toasted walnuts (optional)

Cut each cabbage half in two pieces and cut
out core. Cut each type of cabbage in very
thin strips with sharp, heavy knife or shred
each cabbage in food processor fitted with
shredding disk. Transfer each to separate
large bowl.

Bring ¼ cup vinegar to a boil in small
saucepan. Pour it over red cabbage and toss
quickly until mixed well.

Whisk remaining 2 tablespoons vinegar
with salt and pepper in medium bowl.
Whisk in ½ cup oil.

To each bowl of cabbage, add half of the
grated carrot, if using. Add 5 tablespoons
dressing gradually to each bowl of cabbage,
tossing. Add remaining dressing if needed.
If either salad is too tart, add more oil. Add
half of the green onion, dill, and mint to
each one. Keep the two salads separate or
toss them together. Taste and adjust seasoning. Serve sprinkled with toasted walnuts.

Warm Carrot Salad with Lemon, Garlic, and Mint

jazar bi zayt

When it comes to carrot salads, many people in the Middle East have a different
approach than Americans and Europeans
do. Instead of adding sugar or raisins, many
use savory seasonings.

Yogurt's tang makes it a good complement for carrots. On Turkish tables you'll
find sautéed carrots coated with garlic-
scented yogurt. Persians also pair carrots
with yogurt, or cook them with saffron and
red kidney beans.

Lemon is frequently matched with carrots in the Mideast. Tender carrots sauced
with lemon juice and olive oil are popular
in Kurdish homes. An Armenian carrot
salad features a similar dressing along with
sautéed onions and dill. The Lebanese relish
pungent and tart tastes, enriching cooked
carrot coins with garlic oil and mint as in
this salad, then squeezing lemon juice over
them at the table for the freshest taste and
aroma. Some of my Israeli friends enjoy carrots with vinegar, cilantro, cumin, and hot
pepper. Somehow, the sour note makes carrots' natural sweetness seem to shine even
more brightly.

Serve this salad warm as an appetizer
or a vegetable accompaniment. When the
weather gets hot, the salad can be served

cold, sprinkled with chopped Italian parsley, or garnished with sprigs of fresh mint.

Be sure the garlic you use is fresh because you're using it raw. For a more muted garlic taste, cook the whole garlic cloves in the water along with the carrots, then chop them and add them to the dressing.

♦ MAKES 4 SERVINGS.

  1 pound carrots, sliced diagonally or in
    rounds about ⅓ inch thick
  Salt to taste
  1 small garlic clove, peeled
  2 tablespoons extra-virgin olive oil
  1 tablespoon strained fresh-squeezed
    lemon juice
  1 teaspoon dried mint
  Pinch cayenne pepper
  Quartered lemons

Put carrots in saucepan with water to cover. Add salt and bring to a boil. Cover and simmer over medium-low heat for 6 minutes, or until carrots are just tender. With slotted spoon, transfer carrots to shallow bowl. (You can save the cooking liquid for soups or stews.)

For the dressing, crush garlic with a pinch of salt and chop it very fine. Put garlic in bowl and gradually whisk in oil. Whisk in lemon juice and add mint. Season dressing lightly with cayenne pepper. Add dressing to carrots and mix gently. Taste and adjust seasoning. Mix gently just before serving. Serve warm or at room temperature, with quartered lemons.

Eastern Mediterranean Potato Salad

batata mtabbli

When it comes to potato salad, lighter is better. Like Mediterranean cooks, Mideast ones love certain basic seasonings—extra-virgin olive oil, lemon juice, salt, and pepper. Instead of heavy salads laden with mayo, in these sunny lands many want their potato salads to be refreshing. Most add garlic or onions—red, white, or green—and throw in flat-leaf parsley by the handful. Lebanese and Egyptian cooks also like mint. Use the proportions of oil and lemon juice/vinegar to your taste. Many in the Mideast go for equal amounts, rather than following the French preference for three times as much oil as vinegar.

You can get good results with new potatoes, white- or red-skinned boiling potatoes, or the yellow-fleshed Yukon Gold variety. Avoid russets or baking potatoes, as they tend to fall apart. For embellishment, add pungent olives or capers to give your potatoes punch, and grilled red peppers or diced ripe tomatoes for a colorful, summery accent.

Potato salad does not benefit from prolonged chilling, because cold dressing can congeal and make the potatoes seem dry. Using a mayonnaise-free dressing allows you to serve the salad at room temperature.

♦ MAKES 4 SERVINGS.

2 pounds boiling potatoes, scrubbed but not peeled

2 to 3 tablespoons strained fresh-squeezed lemon juice

Salt and freshly ground black pepper

Cayenne pepper to taste

3 to 5 tablespoons extra-virgin olive oil

⅓ cup finely chopped red onions

4 plum tomatoes (optional)

½ cup flavorful black olives, such as kalamata, pitted

⅓ cup chopped Italian parsley

2 teaspoons capers, drained (optional)

To speed up the cooking, cut any large potatoes in half. Put potatoes in large saucepan, cover with water, and add salt. Bring to a boil. Cover and simmer over medium-low heat until a knife can pierce center of largest potato easily and potato falls from knife when lifted, about 25 minutes.

Meanwhile prepare dressing: Whisk 2 tablespoons lemon juice with a pinch of salt, pepper, and cayenne pepper in small bowl. Add 3 tablespoons olive oil and whisk again.

Drain potatoes in a colander, rinse them briefly, and leave just until cool enough to handle. Peel them if you like; do it quickly so they won't get cold. Cut them into 1-inch cubes. Put them in a large bowl and add the onions, 3 tablespoons of the dressing, and a sprinkling of salt and pepper. With rubber spatula, fold together gently so you don't mash the potatoes, but be sure the seasonings are mixed in thoroughly. Let cool to room temperature.

Dice the tomatoes to add them to the salad, or cut them in thick wedges to use as garnish. Dice half the olives. Whisk the remaining dressing, pour it over the potatoes, and fold it in. Add the parsley, capers, diced olives, and diced tomatoes to the potatoes and fold together lightly. Taste, adjust seasoning, and add more lemon juice and olive oil if needed. Serve at room temperature, garnished with tomato wedges, if you like.

Egyptian-Style Potato and Green Bean Salad

batata mtabbli ma' lubyi

Fresh mint and green onions do wonders to lift the flavor of cooked vegetable salads like this one. Diced carrot provides bright color and a pleasant sweetness to balance the tart garlic-lemon dressing. If you prefer, use a roasted sweet red pepper instead of the carrot. You might also like to garnish this savory salad with quartered hard-boiled eggs and black or green olives, following the custom in the region.

For a spicy variation, omit the oil, lemon juice, and herbs and flavor the salad with Fresh Chili Vinaigrette (page 308).

◆ MAKES 4 SERVINGS.

2 pounds boiling potatoes, scrubbed but not peeled, halved if large

Salt and freshly ground black pepper

1 or 2 garlic cloves, very finely minced

3 to 4 tablespoons strained fresh-squeezed lemon juice

4 to 6 tablespoons extra-virgin olive oil

Cayenne pepper to taste (optional)

1 carrot, diced (optional)

½ pound green beans, ends trimmed, broken in 3 pieces

⅓ to ½ cup chopped green onions

3 tablespoons chopped fresh mint

2 tablespoons chopped Italian parsley (optional)

2 hard-boiled eggs, quartered (optional)

Black or green olives (optional)

Put the potatoes in large saucepan, cover them with water, and add salt. Bring to a boil. Cover and simmer over medium-low heat until a knife can pierce the center of the largest potato easily and the potato falls from the knife when lifted, about 25 minutes.

Combine minced garlic with a pinch of salt and mash with the back of spoon in small bowl. Whisk in 3 tablespoons lemon juice. Add 4 tablespoons olive oil, black pepper, and, if desired, cayenne pepper and whisk again.

Drain the potatoes in a colander, rinse them briefly, and leave just until cool enough to handle. Peel them if you like, cut them in half, and slice them about ½ inch thick. Put them in large bowl and add 3 tablespoons dressing and a sprinkling of salt and pepper. With rubber spatula, fold together gently but thoroughly. Let potatoes cool to room temperature.

Put the carrot in saucepan of water, add salt, and bring to a boil. Cover and simmer for 3 minutes. Add green beans and cook uncovered over medium-high heat for 5 minutes, or until vegetables are just tender. Drain, rinse with cold water, and drain thoroughly in a strainer. Add to bowl of potatoes.

Whisk the remaining dressing, pour it over the salad, and fold it in. Add the green onions, mint, and parsley and fold together lightly. Taste, adjust seasoning, and add more lemon juice and olive oil if needed. Garnish with quartered hard-boiled eggs and, if you like, olives. Serve at room temperature.

Tangy Beet Salad

pancar salatasi

Beets are traditional fare in much of the Mideast, from Turkey and Egypt to Iran. Cooks in the region realize that freshly cooked beets taste so good that they don't need to be fussed with very much. Usually they turn the beets into simple appetizer salads like this one, flavored only with lemon juice or vinegar to complement the beets' sweetness, along with a touch of salt and little or no oil. Garlic is another favorite seasoning, and occasionally green onions.

Some serve the salad on a bed of lettuce or enhance it with walnuts or a sprinkling of sesame seeds.

Beets are easy to peel after they are cooked. Simply rinse off their skins under cold water.

◆ MAKES 4 TO 6 SERVINGS.

2 bunches of beets, or 10 small beets
    (about 1½ inches in diameter)
Salt
1 to 3 fresh garlic cloves, pressed or very
    finely minced
2 tablespoons fresh-squeezed lemon juice
    or vinegar
Pepper to taste
1 or 2 tablespoons olive oil (optional)
Leaves of tender lettuce, such as butter
    lettuce or green-leaf lettuce (optional)
1 tablespoon chopped Italian parsley
¼ cup walnuts, lightly toasted (optional)

Rinse beets. Put them in pan, cover with water, and bring to a boil. Add a pinch of salt. Cover and simmer over low heat 35 to 40 minutes, or until tender. Let cool. Run beets under cold water and slip off the skins.

Mix garlic with salt in small bowl, mashing garlic against side of bowl. Add lemon juice, pepper, and oil if you like.

Slice or dice beets. Put them in bowl and add dressing. Mix gently. Taste and adjust seasoning. Cover and refrigerate for 1 hour or overnight. To serve, leave salad in its bowl, or spoon it onto a bed of lettuce on a plate. Sprinkle with parsley and walnuts.

Fava and Fennel Salad, Cypriot Style

salata koukia freska

In this simple salad, fennel lends a refreshing note to the beans. I like to marinate the fennel briefly in the dressing to soften it slightly.

Fresh fava beans are delicious but time-consuming to prepare. To save time, I sometimes use frozen shelled ones from my Middle Eastern market. If you don't have fava beans, make the salad with fresh or frozen lima beans. I sometimes opt for a rich-flavored legume from the other end of Asia—Japanese green soybeans, or edamame, which need only a few minutes of simmering. For extra color and flavor, I occasionally add red bell peppers along with the traditional garnish of black olives.

◆ MAKES 4 TO 6 SERVINGS.

½ medium or large fennel
3 to 4 tablespoons extra-virgin olive oil
1½ to 2 tablespoons white-wine vinegar
Salt and freshly ground black pepper
2 pounds fresh fava or other shell beans,
    shelled, or 2 cups frozen fava or
    lima beans, or shelled green soybeans
    (edamame)
1 red bell pepper (optional)
2 or 3 garlic cloves, minced
12 kalamata olives

Remove outer layer from fennel bulbs. Chop 1 tablespoon fennel fronds. Cut off stalks; reserve them for soups and stews. Halve fennel bulb, put it cut side down, and cut each half into very thin slices. Separate them in half rings. Soak fennel in cold water to cover 15 minutes. Drain well. Put in bowl.

Sprinkle fennel rings with 2 tablespoons oil, 1 tablespoon vinegar, salt, and pepper. Marinate at room temperature for 15 to 30 minutes.

If using fresh or unpeeled frozen fava beans, cook them in saucepan of boiling salted water uncovered over high heat for 7 to 10 minutes, or until just tender. Remove from heat, drain, and press each bean to remove the thick skins, in order to have bright green beans. If leaving skins on, cook a few minutes longer so they will be more tender, and drain well. With other shell beans and peeled frozen favas, the cooking time may be different; taste occasionally as they cook. There's no need to peel them. If using frozen lima beans or green soybeans, cook according to package directions or until done to taste, and drain.

Add cooked beans to bowl of fennel. If using red pepper, cut in thin strips and add to bowl.

Whisk garlic with remaining oil, vinegar, salt, and pepper in small bowl. Add to salad and mix well. Taste and adjust seasoning. Serve at room temperature or cold, garnished with olives.

Three-Bean Salad with Tomatoes, Olives, and Cilantro

fassoulia salata

Instead of the mushy, sugary three-bean salads I've sometimes encountered at potlucks, I make this lively Middle Eastern version. I came up with it by using seasonings popular in bean stews—onions, tomatoes, garlic, cumin, hot pepper, and cilantro—which also make delicious accents for bean salads. Following the custom in the eastern Mediterranean, I dress my salad with almost as much lemon juice as oil.

For optimum color, don't let green beans sit very long in an acid mixture. If you would like to keep the salad's vivid hues, add the lemon juice just before serving. If you're making the salad in advance, add the diced tomatoes at most four hours ahead, so they don't become watery. Finish seasoning your salad a short time before you bring it to the table. This salad will brighten your next barbecue and is perfect for bringing to friends for a shared supper.

◆ MAKES 4 SERVINGS.

1½ cups fresh shelled or frozen fava beans, frozen lima beans, or green soybeans (edamame)

12 ounces green beans, ends removed, broken in half; or half green beans and half yellow (wax) beans

One 15-ounce can chickpeas (garbanzo
   beans), drained

⅓ to ½ cup black olives such as kalamata,
   halved and pitted

3 or 4 tablespoons olive oil

1 small onion, halved, cut in thin slices,
   and separated in half-moons

¼ to ½ teaspoon ground cumin

Salt and freshly ground black pepper

Cayenne pepper to taste

8 to 12 ounces ripe tomatoes, diced

3 tablespoons strained fresh-squeezed
   lemon juice

2 tablespoons coarsely chopped cilantro

If using fresh or unpeeled frozen fava beans, cook them, uncovered, in saucepan of boiling salted water over high heat for 7 to 10 minutes, or until just tender. Drain beans well. Press each fava bean to remove it from thick skin if you like. If using other frozen beans or peeled favas, cook according to package directions or until done to taste, and drain.

Cook green beans, uncovered, in large saucepan of boiling salted water over high heat for 5 minutes, or until crisp-tender. Drain, rinse with cold water, and drain well.

Combine fava beans, green beans, chickpeas, and olives in glass bowl and toss lightly. Heat 1 tablespoon oil in small skillet. Add half the onion and sauté over medium heat for 3 minutes, or until slightly softened. Add cumin and cook for ½ minute, stirring, to toast. Add mixture to salad. Add remaining onion, 2 tablespoons oil, salt, pepper, and cayenne and toss. Add tomatoes and toss again.

A short time before serving, add lemon juice and half the cilantro. Taste and adjust seasoning. Add more olive oil if desired. Serve salad at room temperature, sprinkled with remaining cilantro.

Classic White Bean Salad

piyaz

Sure, you can make this with canned beans. But the charm of this simple eastern Mediterranean salad, especially loved in Turkey, where it is called *piyaz*, and in Lebanon, where it is known as *fassoulia salata*, lies in its small number of fine-quality ingredients. It's outstanding when the beans are freshly cooked so they are tender but pleasantly firm and not mushy, then enriched with fruity olive oil and brightened with fresh onions, garlic, parsley, and lemon juice. I like the beans while they're still a little warm, but they're also tasty when cold after marinating in the dressing. If you prefer spicy beans, dress them with Fresh Chili Vinaigrette (page 308) instead of the oil and lemon juice here.

◆ MAKES 6 TO 8 SERVINGS.

1 pound dried white beans, such as
   Great Northern (2¼ to 2½ cups),
   sorted and rinsed

Salt and freshly ground black pepper

3 to 4 tablespoons extra-virgin olive oil

2 to 4 tablespoons strained fresh-squeezed
   lemon juice

2 garlic cloves, minced

1 medium or ½ large fresh onion, sweet,
   red, or white, halved and sliced thin

⅓ cup chopped Italian parsley

¾ teaspoon Aleppo pepper, or ½ teaspoon
   paprika and ¼ teaspoon cayenne pepper,
   or to taste

Put beans in large saucepan and add 7 cups water. Bring to a boil. Cover and cook over low heat for 45 minutes. Add salt and simmer for 30 to 45 more minutes, or until tender but not falling apart. Drain beans; you can reserve their cooking liquid for making soups.

Combine 3 tablespoons oil, 2 tablespoons lemon juice, garlic, salt and pepper in large bowl, and whisk to blend. Separate onion slices into half-moons, add to dressing, and stir to blend. Add beans and parsley and mix well. Add Aleppo pepper and more oil and lemon juice if you like. Serve lukewarm or at room temperature.

Lemony Parsley and Bulgur Salad with Mint

tabbouleh

No wonder this delicious salad has caught on so well as a mainstream appetizer in North America and Europe. It's fresh, colorful, satisfying, and healthful too. To Westerners, tabbouleh has become so emblematic of Middle Eastern cooking that Charles Perry, one of our country's top experts on the subject, dubbed Anaheim's Middle Eastern district "Tabbouleh Town."

When a Jerusalemite friend of Lebanese descent, Ronnie Venezia, first showed me how to make this Middle Eastern standard, I was surprised at the handfuls of herbs she added. Like many Americans, I had thought it was a bulgur wheat salad with parsley but, she advised me, it's a parsley salad with a little bulgur wheat. She was generous with the green onions and the fresh-squeezed lemon juice, and the result was delicious.

Ronnie adds cucumbers as well, which I include when I have some of top quality, such as the Middle Eastern or Japanese variety. Most people prefer fine bulgur wheat, but if your market carries only the medium type, it works well, too. Soaking the bulgur wheat in cold water gives it the best texture but to save time you can use the quick method in the note following the recipe. Chop the parsley and mint in the food processor if you like, but slice the green onions with a knife for good texture.

A popular way to serve tabbouleh is with tender leaves of romaine lettuce for scooping it up. That's how my friends Said and Manar Oorabi presented it in Akko (also called Acre), near Haifa, when they invited our family for a cultural and culinary tour of the Old City and prepared some popular Arab specialties. In Lebanon people use fresh young grape leaves, which contribute a refreshing tartness.

When the weather is hot, prepare a summery main course of chicken tabbouleh, following the variation, and serve it as part of a buffet lunch or supper. If you don't have bulgur wheat, you can make it with cooked brown rice, couscous, or barley.

◆ MAKES 6 TO 8 SERVINGS.

1 cup fine bulgur wheat

4 plum tomatoes

3 small Middle Eastern cucumbers,
　1 Japanese cucumber, or ½ hothouse
　cucumber, peeled if desired (optional)

4 green onions, white and green parts,
　sliced thin

¾ cup finely chopped Italian parsley

½ cup finely chopped fresh mint

Salt and freshly ground black pepper

6 to 8 tablespoons extra-virgin olive oil

¼ cup strained fresh-squeezed lemon juice,
　or more to taste

Small or medium-size romaine leaves
　(optional)

Soak bulgur wheat in 3½ cups cold water for 2 to 4 hours or longer, until it is tender;

taste it to check. Or, for a more speedy method, see Note below.

Transfer bulgur to a colander and drain. Squeeze wheat dry and transfer to large bowl.

Dice tomatoes and cucumbers very small. Mix diced vegetables with onions, parsley, mint, and bulgur wheat. Add salt, pepper, oil, and lemon juice to taste; salad should be fairly tart. Serve cold or at cool room temperature, with romaine leaves.

NOTE To quick-soak the bulgur wheat: Pour hot water over the bulgur wheat instead of cold water. Soak it until it is completely cool and tender.

Chicken Tabbouleh Salad
Add 2½ to 3 cups diced grilled or roast chicken to the salad. Substitute 1 diced red or yellow bell pepper for the cucumbers.

Whole-Wheat Couscous Salad with Pistachios, Chickpeas, and Corn

salat couscous im fistookim v'hummus

This is my twist on a Mideast bulgur wheat and chickpea salad known in Lebanon as *safsouf*. To enliven the basic duo and its olive oil and lemon juice dressing, I add colorful vegetables and a sprinkling of toasted pistachios. It's good with bulgur wheat (see Note), but I often use whole-wheat couscous, which approximates bulgur's taste and tan hue, cooks even faster, and, in many areas, is more widely available. You can find it in a natural food store, or substitute plain couscous.

Some say the salad developed as a quick, easy rendition of meatless stuffed grape leaves. Instead of rolling the bulgur and chickpea filling inside the grape leaves and simmering them, cooks turned the stuffing into a salad. They accompany it with young, tender fresh grape leaves so the diners can do the work instead. Another popular way to present the salad is with romaine leaves, which is more practical if you don't have a grapevine.

◆ MADE ABOUT 6 SIDE-DISH OR 3 OR 4 MAIN-DISH SERVINGS.

3 to 4 tablespoons extra-virgin olive oil
1 onion, minced
½ large zucchini, diced
Salt and freshly ground black pepper
1½ cups water
½ carrot, finely diced
1 cup whole-wheat couscous
2 to 4 tablespoons fresh-squeezed lemon juice
2 small garlic cloves, minced (optional)
Pinch cayenne pepper
1 teaspoon dried mint (optional)
1 cup cooked or canned corn kernels, drained

1½ to 1¾ cups cooked chickpeas (garbanzo beans) (see "Basics," page 374), or one 15-ounce can chickpeas, drained
⅓ cup salted pistachios, toasted

Heat I tablespoon oil in medium saucepan. Add onion and sauté over medium heat for 3 minutes. Add zucchini, salt, and pepper and sauté for I minute. Cover and cook for I more minute. Remove vegetables to bowl.

Add water, carrot, and a pinch salt to saucepan and bring to a boil. Cover and simmer for 2 minutes. Add couscous and bring to a boil. Remove from heat, cover, and let stand for 7 minutes.

Lightly spoon couscous mixture into large bowl and fluff with a fork. Add remaining oil, lemon juice, garlic, salt, pepper, cayenne, and mint, and mix lightly. Add corn, chickpeas, and sautéed zucchini mixture and toss lightly. Taste and adjust seasoning. Serve salad warm, cold, or at room temperature, sprinkled with pistachios.

ΠΟΤ℮ To make the salad with bulgur wheat, use I cup medium-size bulgur and increase the water to 2 cups. Cook carrot for 5 minutes, remove it with a slotted spoon, and add bulgur. Cover and simmer it for 10 to 15 minutes, or until tender. Add carrots to salad with remaining ingredients.

Yellow Rice Salad with Red Peppers, Beans, and Dill

salat orez tzahov im pilpelim v'shi'ou'it

Hot sauce, olives, and capers enhance this multicolored salad, which makes a fine appetizer, side dish, or light entrée. It's based on Yemenite yellow rice, which is seasoned with cumin and turmeric instead of the saffron used in other parts of the Mideast. If you prefer to serve it as a hot side dish, omit the vinegar or lemon juice. Instead of black beans, you can make it with white or red beans or baby lima beans.

♦ MAKES 6 SERVINGS.

3 to 4 tablespoons olive oil or vegetable oil

1 large onion, halved lengthwise and sliced thin

1 small or ½ large red bell pepper, halved, cored, seeded, and diced small

2 small zucchini or pale-green-skinned summer squash (½ pound)

Salt and freshly ground black pepper

1¼ cups long-grain white rice

1 teaspoon ground cumin

¼ teaspoon turmeric

2½ cups hot water

2 small carrots, diced

1 to 1½ cups cooked or canned black beans, drained and rinsed

2 to 3 tablespoons chopped fresh dill

1 to 2 tablespoons tarragon vinegar, rice vinegar, or fresh-squeezed lemon juice

2 to 3 teaspoons Hedva's Hot Pepper Relish (page 307) or other hot sauce, or to taste

½ cup green olives, pitted and halved

2 teaspoons capers, drained (optional)

Heat 2 tablespoons oil in large sauté pan. Add onion and cook over medium-low heat for 7 minutes, or until soft but not brown. Remove from pan. Add 1 tablespoon oil and heat it. Add red pepper and zucchini, sprinkle with salt and pepper, and sauté over medium heat for 3 minutes, or until crisp-tender. Remove from heat.

Return ⅓ of the onions to pan and heat them. Add rice and sauté over medium-low heat, stirring, for 3 minutes or until grains turn white. Add cumin, turmeric, ¾ teaspoon salt, and scant ½ teaspoon pepper. Pour hot water over rice and stir once. Bring to a boil. Reduce heat to very low, cover tightly, and simmer for 7 minutes. Scatter diced carrots over rice, without stirring. Cover and cook for 7 minutes. Scatter remaining sautéed onions over the top. Cover and cook for 2 to 3 minutes, or until rice is tender.

With a fork, fluff rice lightly and transfer to bowl. Lightly fold in beans, red pepper, squash, and dill. Let cool completely. Fold in vinegar, hot sauce, olives, and 1 tablespoon oil, or to taste. Taste and adjust seasoning. Serve at room temperature, garnished with capers if you like.

Persian Peach Pilaf Salad with Toasted Almonds

salade-e-berenj ba hulu

The ancient Persians loved peaches and introduced them to the western world. In Iran, peaches, like other fruits, are used in savory dishes because people enjoy the interplay of sweet-and-sour tastes. Often cooks highlight or balance the fruit's flavor with sugar or with tart seasonings like lime or sour pomegranate juice. Persians especially like fruit with rice, studding pilaf with fruit and nuts or turning the fruit into a savory sauce to spoon over the top.

These types of dishes are the inspiration for this colorful, fresh-tasting rice salad. I use it as a blueprint for making salads from my garden, with peaches, white nectarines, or plums and a generous accent of just-picked chives. I flavor the dressing with the juice of my Meyer lemons, which are slightly sweet, but the lime juice typical of Persian dressings also complements the salad well.

◆ MAKES 6 TO 8 SERVINGS.

    3 tablespoons vegetable oil
    1 large onion, finely chopped
    1 carrot, diced
    1 celery rib, diced
    1½ cups long-grain white rice
    3 cups hot water
    Salt and freshly ground black pepper to taste

1 teaspoon dried mint

1 teaspoon dried dill

1 cup cooked or canned chickpeas (garbanzo beans)

1 cup cooked or canned corn kernels

1 pound peaches or nectarines

2 tablespoons fresh-squeezed lime or lemon juice

3 tablespoons chopped fresh chives

⅓ cup whole unpeeled almonds, toasted (page 369)

Heat 2 tablespoons oil in large deep sauté pan or shallow stew pan. Add onion and sauté over medium heat for 8 minutes, or until tender and golden. Remove half of onion.

Add remaining oil to onion in pan and heat until sizzling. Add carrot and celery and sauté over medium-low heat for 1 minute. Add rice and sauté, stirring, about 2 minutes, until the grains turn milky white and are coated. Add the hot water, 1 teaspoon salt, and pinch of pepper. Stir once and cover. Cook over low heat, without stirring, until rice is just tender, about 18 minutes; taste a few grains to check.

With a fork, fluff rice lightly and transfer to bowl. Lightly fold in reserved onions, mint, dill, chickpeas, and corn. Let cool completely.

Dice the peaches; you will need about 3 cups. Gently fold in lime juice, peaches, and 2 tablespoons chopped chives. Taste and adjust seasoning. Serve at room temperature, garnished with remaining chives and toasted almonds.

Soups, Savory and Spicy

Chicken Noodle Soup with Tomatoes and Cilantro • *Shorbet Shareeya*

Hearty Chicken Chickpea Soup with Green Beans and Ginger •
Shorbet Feraakh bel Hommos

Chicken and Mung Bean Soup with Herbs • *Sholeh Mash*

Egyptian Green Soup with Garlic and Coriander • *Meloukhiya*

Sweet-and-Sour Turkey Soup with Dried Fruit • *Ash-e Torsh*

Aromatic Beef Soup with Bulgur Wheat • *Chorbet Burgul*

Beef and Winter Vegetable Soup with Rosemary and Cardamom •
Shorbet Lahm bel Khodar

Yemenite Beef Soup with Curry Spices and Potatoes • *Marak Basar Teimani*

Meatball Soup with Orzo, Mint, and Dill • *Chorbet Ima*

Spiced Lamb and Spinach Soup with Rice • *Shourbet Sbaanegh*

Lebanese Fish Soup with Linguine · *Chorbet Samak*

Mideast Minestrone · *Shurbat al-Khudar*

Spicy Lentil Soup with Dill and Cumin · *Shorbet Addss Balady*

Lebanese Lentil and Chard Soup · *Chorbet Adass bi Hamod*

White Bean Soup with Garlic and Hot Pepper · *Shouraba Lubee*

Split Pea Soup with Vegetables, Rice, and Mint · *Ash-e Lapeh*

Tomato Barley Soup with Peppers · *Hasa'a al-Habea*

Hot-and-Sour Summer Squash Soup · *Maradj Kar'a Hamiz*

Wintertime Wheat and Lentil Soup with Turnips and Garlic · *Masheh b'Shargomeh*

Cool Pumpkin Borani Soup · *Mast-o-Kadu Zard*

A hearty lunchtime soup every day is a custom in many Middle Eastern homes and the variations are countless. These traditional meal-in-one-pot soups are just as practical today for our contemporary lifestyles.

From my Yemenite family's table, it became clear to me that soups were the mainstay of meals. Every day when my father-in-law came home at midday, the family sat down to a bowl of soup. Even in summer, a hot soup at midday remained the daily tradition. This soup was invariably a beef or chicken soup with chunks of meat and a few vegetables. Aromatic and flavorful from the warm spices of cumin, turmeric, and plenty of black pepper, we savored it with generous quantities of home-baked pita or slices of dark bread.

The Bible's lentil pottage may be the most famous soup in history, and this ancient dish has remained a great favorite in the land of its birthplace. It illustrates the importance of legume-based soups on the Mideast menu. Fava bean soup is a staple on the Egyptian table and is also loved in Lebanon and around the region. Chickpea soups are popular as well, and, in Persian homes, mung bean and split-pea pottages. In many kitchens, especially those of Iran, a mixture of several legumes may be combined in a single soup.

Vegetable soups in the Mideast might be smooth and creamy with yogurt or thick with barley or rice. More often these soups are chunky and contain a variety of diced vegetables, as in Mideast minestrone, which is redolent of sautéed onions and leeks and enhanced with cumin and other spices. Greens are prevalent in the soup repertoire everywhere, often paired with beans or other legumes, as in Lebanese Lentil and Chard Soup.

Chicken Noodle Soup with Tomatoes and Cilantro

shorbet shareeya

In the Mideast hearty whole-meal chicken soups with plenty of noodles or rice appear often at family meals, especially in winter. For first courses, delicate chicken noodle soups thickened with egg and accented with lemon juice are also common, especially in Turkey and Egypt. Choose very fine, short egg noodles, or break spaghetti or vermicelli into short lengths.

Cilantro is much loved as a soup seasoning but flat-leaf, or Italian, parsley is no less popular and you can substitute it if you prefer. To season their chicken and meat soups, Egyptians like cardamom and mastic (see "The Mideast Pantry," page 11), Iraqis like turmeric, and Yemenis like cumin. Saudi noodle soup is spicy, calling for fresh chilies and plenty of black pepper as well as cardamom. Throughout much of the region cinnamon and allspice are favorite soup seasonings, especially among the Lebanese, Syrians, and Palestinians. Some put cinnamon on the table for each person to add to taste instead of simmering it in the soup.

♦ MAKES 6 TO 8 FIRST-COURSE OR 4 OR 5 MAIN-COURSE SERVINGS.

2 tablespoons olive oil or vegetable oil
1 large onion, chopped
2 pounds chicken pieces
Salt and freshly ground black pepper
8 ounces ripe tomatoes, peeled and diced, or one 14-ounce can diced tomatoes with their juice
1 carrot, diced (optional)
2 celery stalks, sliced
3 garlic cloves, chopped (optional)
7 cups water
1 cinnamon stick, or ¼ teaspoon ground cinnamon, or to taste
¼ teaspoon ground allspice or to taste
1⅓ cups very fine noodles (soup noodles)
⅓ cup chopped cilantro or Italian parsley

Heat oil in large heavy saucepan or stew pan. Add onion and sauté over medium heat until golden, about 7 minutes. Add chicken, sprinkle with salt and pepper, and sauté for 7 minutes. Add tomatoes and sauté lightly. Add carrot, if using, celery, garlic, if you like, and enough water to generously cover chicken and bring to a simmer. Skim foam from surface. Add cinnamon and allspice. Cover and simmer for 50 to 60 minutes, or until chicken is very tender and soup is well flavored, skimming fat occasionally.

Cook noodles, uncovered, in large saucepan of boiling salted water for 7 minutes, or until just tender. Drain well.

Discard cinnamon stick. Add half of cilantro or parsley to soup.

For a main course, either serve chicken pieces in soup, or remove bones and skin and return meat to pot. To serve soup as an appetizer, reserve most or all of the chicken for other dishes. Taste soup and adjust seasoning. Add noodles to each bowl of hot soup and sprinkle with remaining cilantro or parsley.

Hearty Chicken Chickpea Soup with Green Beans and Ginger

shorbet feraakh bel hommos

This spicy soup is accented with gingerroot. The fresh root is used, along with chilies and other spices often found in Indian curries, in the United Arab Emirates and nearby Persian Gulf States, where there is a pronounced Indian influence on the cooking. In the rest of the Mideast, ginger is more often used in its ground form, either combined with other spices like cinnamon or coriander as a seasoning for meat (see *baharat* in "The Mideast Pantry," page 13) or mixed with sweet spices—notably cinnamon, cloves, and cardamom—to flavor coffee and desserts.

♦ MAKES 3 OR 4 MAIN-COURSE SERVINGS.

⅔ cup dried chickpeas (garbanzo beans), sorted and rinsed, or one 15-ounce can chickpeas, drained

About 6 cups water (for soup), plus 3 cups for dried chickpeas

Salt and freshly ground black pepper to taste

2½ pounds chicken legs or thighs

2 medium onions, chopped

1 tablespoon chopped peeled gingerroot

4 large garlic cloves, minced

1 jalapeño pepper, seeded if desired, chopped, or 2 small dried chilies such as chiles de arbol

2 teaspoons ground cumin

1 teaspoon ground coriander

½ teaspoon turmeric

¼ to ½ teaspoon ground cinnamon

4 ounces green beans, ends removed, broken into 1-inch pieces

Pinch cayenne pepper

3 tablespoons chopped cilantro or parsley

If using dried chickpeas, put them in saucepan, add 3 cups water, and bring to a boil. Cover and simmer 1 hour, adding hot water occasionally to keep them covered with water. Add a pinch of salt and continue simmering 30 to 45 minutes more, or until tender.

Put chicken pieces in large stew pan or soup pot. Add onions, ginger, garlic, jalapeño, and enough water to cover the ingredients by about 1 inch. Bring to a boil, skimming foam from top. Add cumin, coriander, turmeric, cinnamon, salt, and pepper. Cover and cook over low heat for 45 minutes, occasionally skimming off the foam and fat.

Add cooked or canned chickpeas and green beans and bring to a simmer. Cover and cook over low heat for 10 minutes, or until chicken and vegetables are tender. Discard dried chilies. Remove chicken pieces and discard their skin. Leave pieces whole or remove meat from bones, discarding them. Return chicken to soup, reserving part of it for other uses if desired. Stir in cayenne pepper and cilantro. Taste and adjust seasoning. Serve hot.

Chicken and Mung Bean Soup with Herbs

sholeh mash

Mung bean soup is popular among Iranians. They prefer to use whole mung beans, which have dark green skins, rather than the yellow Indian moong dal, which are split and skinless. You can find the whole ones in Middle Eastern and Indian grocery stores. They're the same beans used to make Chinese bean sprouts.

When you cook mung beans, they thicken the liquid considerably. Their skins come off as they cook, and some cooks remove them from the soup with a slotted spoon. Many simmer the mung beans with rice and often with other legumes, notably kidney beans, black-eyed peas, and lentils. Some add vegetables as well, such as kohlrabi, turnips, pumpkin, or spinach.

Browning the onion in oil or butter is the usual way to begin cooking mung bean soup, but I find the chicken gives enough richness to the broth and so I consider this step optional. This soup is thick, almost like a stew, and is enlivened in the Persian fashion with a profusion of herbs. Traditionally the herbs simmer at length in the soup, but I add part of them at the end for a lively flavor. Fresh flatbread is the usual accompaniment.

◆ MAKES 5 OR 6 FIRST-COURSE SERVINGS.

1 large onion, sliced

1 to 2 tablespoons vegetable oil or butter (optional)

1½ pounds chicken drumsticks or thighs

¾ cup whole mung beans, sorted and rinsed

3 large garlic cloves, chopped

8 to 10 cups water

Salt and freshly ground black pepper

2 large carrots, sliced (optional)

1 teaspoon turmeric

½ cup white rice, long or short grain

⅓ cup chopped green onions

½ cup chopped Italian parsley

½ cup chopped cilantro

2 tablespoons chopped fresh dill or mint

If you'd like to brown the onion, heat oil in large saucepan, add the onion, and sauté over medium heat until it begins to brown. Add chicken, mung beans, garlic, and 8 cups water. Add a pinch of salt and bring to a boil. Cover and simmer for 45 minutes, adding water if soup becomes too thick.

Add carrots, turmeric, rice, salt, pepper,

green onions, ¼ cup parsley, ¼ cup cilantro, and I tablespoon dill. Cover and simmer for 20 minutes, or until mung beans, rice, and chicken are tender.

Skim fat from soup. Remove chicken pieces and discard skin and bones. Cut meat in strips and return to soup. Stir in remaining parsley, cilantro, and dill. Taste and adjust seasoning. Serve hot.

Egyptian Green Soup with Garlic and Coriander

meloukhiya

In the land of the Nile, soup made of *meloukhiya* greens is one of the most popular entrées. The greens are chopped and cook very quickly, like spinach, and the soup is finished with a lively sauté of garlic with coriander and, sometimes, cumin. The soup is an ancient specialty that some say has been prepared the same way since the time of the Pharaohs.

Fresh *meloukhiya* greens are available in the summer in some Middle Eastern shops, where you can also find frozen or dried *meloukhiya.* Plant dictionaries sometimes refer to these greens as Jew's mallow. In some markets they're labeled okra leaves, though they're not related to the okra plant; rather, they are from the jute family. The reason for the name is that *meloukhiya* has a sticky quality similar to that of okra, which helps it thicken the soup. This attribute makes these greens an acquired taste.

For best results, chop *meloukhiya* like fresh basil, keeping the leaves, the knife, and the board dry. The leaves turn bright green when you cook them. Some people substitute spinach or chard when *meloukhiya* is not available, or use one of those greens combined with dried *meloukhiya,* as in the variation below. Spinach and chard don't have the same flavor but still make a tasty soup (though it can't be called *meloukhiya*). Indeed, you can make this soup with all sorts of greens, including kale and collard greens.

Egyptians season their chicken soups with mastic (see "The Mideast Pantry," page 12). Cardamom is sometimes used instead, or both are combined in the soup pot. Flavoring the soup with onions, then mashing them and returning them to the broth is a common technique.

The first time I tried the soup, made by an Egyptian-born chef, it was quite rich, and I found it delicious. He cooked the greens in a rich chicken broth and enhanced them with plenty of garlic sautéed in butter; fruity olive oil and ghee are other popular choices in the Mideast.

The chicken used to make the broth is either served on the side, added to the soup, or reserved for another meal. Cooked rice, pita bread, or both always come with the soup, as well as fresh lemon wedges. Some

MIDDLE EASTERN GREEN SOUPS

Middle Eastern cooks, from the Mediterranean to the Arabian Sea, have a flair for turning humble greens into the highlight of a meal. The high proportion of greens and other vegetables on eastern Mediterranean menus is probably the primary reason behind that diet's renowned healthfulness.

Most striking is the variety of main-course soups that feature greens. Lebanese cooks simmer spinach in lamb and rice soup, then flavor it with fried onions, cilantro, and, sometimes, bulgur wheat dumplings made of a mixture similar to the one in Chicken Pecan Bulgar Cakes with Cilantro Pesto (page 48). A substantial Turkish pottage features collard greens in beef broth with white beans, orzo, and tomatoes. To turn chard or spinach soups into a tasty meatless meal, eastern Mediterranean cooks simmer the leaves with lentils (see Lebanese Lentil and Chard Soup, page 101) and, sometimes, potatoes, noodles, or eggplant, then accent them with browned onions, garlic, and cumin.

A hearty soup of greens is a weekday staple in many homes in Egypt. Occasionally the soup is composed of spinach, chickpeas, and tomatoes, but most often it's a green soup called *meloukhiya,* made from a leafy vegetable of the same name that's plentiful in Egypt. When cooked, the leaves have a sticky texture that challenged cooks to develop an appealing recipe to offset it. They came up with a two-step solution. First, they cook the *meloukhiya* in a flavorful, cardamom-scented meat broth. At the last minute they stir generous amounts of spiced sautéed garlic into the greens, so the garlic retains most of its power.

My husband and I feasted on this time-honored specialty with our friend Samir Abdullah, a newspaper editor and food lover from the Mediterranean seaport of Alexandria. He told us that chicken is the most popular choice for the soup, but beef, rabbit, and even fish are used. To ensure a satisfying entrée, the soup of garlicky greens is served with ample amounts of fresh flatbread or rice pilaf.

This southeast Mediterranean method for making savory soups from native leafy vegetables became popular in much of the Middle East. It's a technique that works well with all greens, and is useful to remember when you want to introduce your family to new nutritious vegetables.

For any of these soups, you can use familiar greens like spinach and chard, but you might also like to try kale, mustard greens, collard greens, or leaves that you find in Asian markets. To save time, buy packaged rinsed leaves rather than whole bunches. More and more markets display ready-cleaned greens of several varieties in addition to spinach. You can also use frozen greens.

serve *meloukhiya* as a saucelike side dish instead of as a soup, for spooning over poached chicken or meat.

♦ MAKES 4 MAIN-COURSE SERVINGS.

One 3- or 4-pound chicken, with neck and gizzard if desired, fat removed

2 medium onions, whole

Salt and freshly ground black pepper

About 2 quarts water

5 cardamom pods (optional), cracked or crushed

8 mastic pods (optional)

1 pound fresh *meloukhiya* ("okra leaves"), spinach, or chard, or ½ pound frozen

2 tablespoons butter, ghee, extra-virgin olive oil, or vegetable oil

6 to 8 large garlic cloves, minced

2 teaspoons ground coriander

Hot cooked rice

Lemon wedges

In large stew pan, combine chicken, onions, salt, pepper, and enough water to barely cover. Bring to a boil. Skim foam from surface. Add cardamom, if desired. If adding mastic, you can tie it in cheesecloth along with the cardamom, or simply crush it and add it directly to the soup. Cover and cook over low heat for 1½ hours, or until chicken is tender and broth is well flavored, skimming occasionally. Remove onions; chop finely in food processor and return to broth, or discard if you prefer. Discard cardamom pods if you like, as well as cheesecloth bag, chicken neck, and gizzard.

Remove chicken from soup and cut it in portions, discarding skin; or slice meat, discarding bones. Measure 6 cups broth and ladle into a large saucepan for cooking greens. Return chicken to stew pan and heat through, adding a little hot water if there's not enough broth in pan. Cover and keep warm.

Meanwhile, rinse fresh *meloukhiya* and discard stems. Spread out leaves to dry on a cloth. Finely chop them in several batches. If using fresh spinach or chard, rinse, remove stems, and chop leaves.

Skim excess fat from measured broth in saucepan. Bring broth to a simmer. Add greens and return to a simmer. Cook, uncovered, over medium heat for 3 to 5 minutes, or until just tender.

Heat butter in small skillet, add garlic, and cook over low heat until very light brown, about 1 minute. Add coriander and a pinch of salt and stir over low heat for 15 seconds to blend. Add to *meloukhiya* and cook, uncovered, over medium-low heat for 2 minutes. Taste and adjust seasoning.

Serve chicken pieces in a little chicken broth in shallow soup bowls. Serve *meloukhiya* in deep individual bowls or large serving bowl, for spooning over the chicken and blending into the broth. Accompany with rice, for adding to soup, and with lemon wedges.

Spinach and Dried Meloukhiya Soup

Make soup with ½ pound fresh or ¼ pound frozen spinach. Finely crumble ⅓ cup dried *meloukhiya* leaves. Cook with spinach in measured broth, as above.

Sweet-and-Sour Turkey Soup with Dried Fruit

ash-e torsh

The Persians prepare a great variety of savory soups, both meaty and meatless, with sweet-and-sour flavors from dried and fresh fruit like apples, quinces, plums, or tart cherries. Lemon juice, vinegar, pomegranate juice, or grape juice made from unripe grapes are used for sour flavoring, while the fruits' sweetness might be reinforced with sugar or honey.

Many fruit combinations are a pleasant discovery to nonnatives and open new avenues to soup making. A meatball soup might include chickpeas, walnuts, dried apricots, rice, and mint. Beef or lamb soup might be made with split peas and sour cherries.

This colorful soup has an intriguing flavor combination of dried apricots, turkey, and split peas accented with cinnamon and mint. I like to prepare the soup after Thanksgiving, using stock made from the bones of the roast turkey (see "Basics," page 376) and some of the meat. For more richness you can sauté the onion in oil or butter. Serve the soup with fresh lavash or other flatbread.

- ◆ MAKES 6 FIRST-COURSE OR 3 OR
  4 MAIN-COURSE SERVINGS.

2 tablespoons vegetable oil or butter (optional)

1 large onion, halved and sliced

¾ cup split peas, preferably yellow, sorted, rinsed, and drained

6 cups turkey or chicken stock or broth, or mixed stock and water

4 ounces dried apricots, pitted prunes, or a mixture of both

½ teaspoon ground cinnamon

2 cups diced cooked turkey or chicken, either roasted or poached

2 tablespoons sugar or to taste

2 tablespoons vinegar or to taste

3 tablespoons chopped fresh mint, or 1 tablespoon dried mint

Salt and freshly ground black pepper

If you want to sauté the onion, heat oil or butter in saucepan, add half the sliced onion, and sauté over medium heat about 7 minutes, or until tender and golden brown. Remove from pan and reserve.

Add split peas, stock, and remaining onion slices (or all of them, if you haven't sautéed any) to pan and bring to a simmer. Cover and cook over low heat for 45 minutes, or until peas are tender but not falling apart.

Add apricots and cinnamon and simmer for 10 minutes, or until apricots are tender. Add cooked turkey, sugar, and vinegar. Stir and simmer for 2 minutes, or until sugar dissolves and soup is hot. Add mint and reserved sautéed onion. Season to taste with salt and pepper and more sugar or vinegar, if needed.

Aromatic Beef Soup with Bulgur Wheat

chorbet burgul

Meat soups with wheat are winter staples in the Mideast. The wheat might be bulgur wheat, whole wheat berries, or the grilled green wheat called *fereek* or *farikeh* (see "The Mideast Pantry," page 19).

Another version of wheat used in soups is *kishk*, a sort of ancient instant soup mix that is a blend of powdered bulgur and dried yogurt used in Lebanon, Jordan, and Palestine. For the simplest version, it's blended with water and heated for a few minutes but most people like to add a little meat or at least some chopped onions for flavor.

The best bulgur wheat to use in soups is the larger, most coarsely ground kind, as it gives the soup better texture, but you can use medium bulgur, which is more widely available. Bulgur wheat is sometimes known as cracked wheat, but true bulgur has been pre-cooked and therefore cooks quickly, whereas cracked wheat might be raw. Like rice and barley, bulgur thickens soups.

In the Mideast this soup is made with chicken or beef. Instead of adding meat, you can prepare a faster, lighter version with just beef or chicken stock or broth, simmering the ingredients for only 20 minutes.

◆ MAKES 6 TO 8 FIRST-COURSE OR 3 OR 4 MAIN-COURSE SERVINGS.

1 pound beef stew meat, excess fat removed

1 or 2 tablespoons vegetable oil

1 large onion, chopped

About 6 cups water

Salt and freshly ground black pepper to taste

½ teaspoon ground allspice

¼ teaspoon ground cinnamon

4 large garlic cloves, minced

¾ cup bulgur wheat, preferably large

1 carrot, diced

2 zucchini or Middle Eastern squashes (pale green zucchini), diced

3 tablespoons chopped Italian parsley

Cut beef in 1-inch cubes. Heat oil in large saucepan. Add onion and sauté over medium heat for 5 minutes. Add beef and sauté for 5 minutes, stirring. Add water and bring to a boil, skimming foam. Add salt, pepper, allspice, cinnamon, and garlic. Cover and simmer over low heat for 1½ to 2 hours, or until beef is very tender. Skim off excess fat.

Add bulgur, carrot, and zucchini to soup and simmer for 20 minutes, or until bulgur is tender. Add parsley, taste, and adjust seasoning. Serve hot.

Beef and Winter Vegetable Soup with Rosemary and Cardamom

shorbet lahm bel khodar

Rosemary is native to the Mediterranean and grows freely in many Mideast countries. Sprigs were even found in early Egyptian tombs. I've often found it springing up along Jerusalem sidewalks. Rosemary is primarily matched with meat, poultry, or fish, and it is used less frequently than in Italy or France. Although putting all the ingredients in the pot at the same time is the old-fashioned way to prepare soups like this, I add the vegetables later so they are tender but not mushy.

◆ MAKES 4 OR 5 FIRST-COURSE OR 2 OR 3 MAIN-COURSE SERVINGS.

12 ounces beef stew meat, excess fat removed
1 or 2 tablespoons vegetable oil or butter
1 large onion, chopped
About 5 cups water
Salt and freshly ground black pepper to taste
2 cardamom pods, crushed, or ¼ to ½ teaspoon ground cardamom
3 or 4 boiling potatoes
1 large carrot, diced
1 turnip, peeled and diced
2 celery ribs, sliced
2 teaspoons chopped fresh rosemary, or ¾ teaspoon minced dried rosemary
3 tablespoons chopped Italian parsley

Cut beef in ¾-inch cubes. Heat oil in large saucepan. Add beef and sauté over medium heat for 5 minutes, or until just beginning to brown. Add onion and enough water to just cover the ingredients. Bring to a boil, skimming foam. Add salt, pepper, and cardamom. Cover and simmer over low heat for 1 to 1¼ hours, or until beef is tender. Skim off excess fat.

Peel and dice potatoes and add to soup. Add carrot, turnip, and celery. Add half of the fresh or all of dried rosemary. Simmer for 20 minutes, or until potatoes are tender. Discard cardamom pods. Add remaining fresh rosemary and parsley. Taste and adjust seasoning. Serve hot.

Yemenite Beef Soup with Curry Spices and Potatoes

marak basar teimani

This warming, main-course soup is the centerpiece of the traditional Yemenite diet. My mother-in-law, Rachel Levy, who was born in Yemen, made it just about every week, and her sister Mazal Cohen continues to do so.

Yemenite cooks use any cut of meat that requires long simmering and include plenty of bones. Some cooks make the soup from oxtail and other cuts rarely used in Western cuisines. In our markets chuck and brisket are good choices. My favorite is beef shank slices, the same cut used for veal osso buco; best of all are slices with marrow in the bone.

The secret to the soup's aroma is the spice blend. Some people buy it from spice shops, where it's made to order, but my mother-in-law blended her own. She and I used to pound the cumin seeds in her copper mortar and pestle as we sat on the floor, which turned out to be a comfortable way to do this. We then mixed them with turmeric and black pepper. She always spiced her soup with a liberal hand.

The soup is simple to make and does not require many ingredients; it's the slow simmering that imparts its good, homey taste. Although its cooking time is long, it simmers unattended and is a pleasure to make on a cold weekend. I often make enough for a few days, as Rachel did. To shorten the cooking time, you can use prepared broth instead of soup bones and cut the beef in small pieces or substitute chicken (see Notes). Many leave the fat in the broth but I skim much of it off. Some thicken their soup with a slurry of flour and water.

The Yemenite way to serve the soup is with the hot relish called *zehug* (page 307) on the side and with plenty of fairly thick pita bread for dunking in the soup.

◆ MAKES 4 TO 6 MAIN-COURSE SERVINGS.

1 pound beef soup bones, such as knuckle bones

About 2 quarts water

2½ to 3 pounds beef shank slices, or 1½ to 1¾ pounds chuck, brisket, or beef for stew

2 tablespoons ground cumin

2 teaspoons turmeric

½ teaspoon ground black pepper, or more to taste

Salt to taste

1 large onion, peeled, whole

3 large ripe tomatoes, whole

6 small or medium-size boiling potatoes

2 tablespoons all-purpose flour (optional)

For beef broth, put bones in large heavy saucepan or soup pot and add 1 quart water or enough to cover. Bring to a simmer. Skim off the foam from the surface of the soup. Cover and cook over very low heat for 2 hours. Remove bones, reserving them, and pour broth into bowl.

If using chuck or brisket, cut it into 2-inch chunks. Mix cumin, turmeric, and black pepper. Put beef in saucepan and sprinkle with salt and spice mixture on all sides. Heat over low heat for 7 minutes, turning pieces occasionally so pieces are well coated with spices.

Return bones to pan and add onion and tomatoes. Slowly pour in hot broth near side of pan so most of spice stays on the meat. Add more hot water to cover ingredients. Bring to a boil. Skim foam from surface. Cover and cook over low heat for 1 hour.

Peel potatoes and add to pan. Simmer over very low heat for 1½ to 2 hours, or until meat is very tender and soup is well flavored. Skim off excess fat. Remove onion and tomatoes, chop, and return to soup; or discard them.

To thicken soup, mix flour with ¼ cup water in small bowl until smooth. Slowly pour it into soup, with pan over low heat, stirring constantly. Return soup to a simmer, stirring constantly to prevent lumps. Simmer for 5 minutes.

Taste and adjust seasoning. Serve hot, in shallow bowls.

NOTES To shorten cooking time, omit soup bones and first paragraph of recipe. Use beef chuck cut into 1-inch pieces and quarter potatoes. After heating beef with spices, simmer it in 2 cups canned beef broth and 4 or 5 cups water for a total of 1½ to 2 hours, adding potatoes after 1 hour.

Chicken soup

To make soup with chicken, omit soup bones and substitute 3½ pounds chicken pieces for beef. After heating chicken pieces with spices, simmer in 6 or 7 cups water for a total of 1 to 1½ hours, adding potatoes after 30 minutes.

Veal soup

To make soup with veal shank slices, cook for a total of 2 hours.

Meatball Soup with Orzo, Mint, and Dill

chorbet ima

Meatball soup is an economical staple on family tables in Egypt, Lebanon, and Iran, and often the broth is made simply from the water in which the meatballs simmered. Some cook the meatballs in beef broth for deeper flavor, and others sauté them for extra richness before adding liquid. To make the soup more substantial, cooks might add lentils, split peas, chickpeas, rice, or pasta.

Most often the meatballs are made of lamb or beef, onions, garlic, and seasonings. Another favorite is meat mixed with bulgur wheat to form kibbe balls, which are poached in the soup. In this recipe the soup is seasoned with cinnamon, mint, and dill, in the style of the Levant.

◆ MAKES 4 FIRST-COURSE OR 2 TO
3 MAIN-COURSE SERVINGS.

8 ounces lean ground beef

1 small onion, minced

2 garlic cloves, minced

2 tablespoons minced fresh mint or Italian parsley

1 tablespoon snipped fresh dill

½ teaspoon salt

¼ teaspoon ground black pepper

Ground cinnamon to taste

2 tablespoons vegetable oil (optional)

6 cups beef broth, or mixture beef broth and water

1 leek, white and green parts, split, cleaned, and sliced, or 4 green onions, chopped

⅓ cup orzo or riso (barley- or rice-shaped pasta), or ½ cup very fine egg noodles (soup noodles)

Thoroughly mix beef with onion, garlic, 1 tablespoon mint, 1½ teaspoons dill, salt, pepper, and a pinch of cinnamon. Form walnut-size balls, using about 1 tablespoon mixture for each. Transfer to plate. Refrigerate for 5 minutes.

If you would like to brown the meatballs, heat oil in heavy medium saucepan. Add meatballs in batches and sauté over medium heat for 5 minutes, or until brown. Remove from pan.

Add broth to saucepan and bring to a boil. Add meatballs and a pinch of cinnamon. Cover and simmer over low heat for 15 minutes. Add leek (but not green onions) and orzo. Cover and simmer for 10 minutes, or until pasta and meatballs are

tender, adding green onions, if using, after 5 minutes. Add remaining mint and dill. Taste and adjust seasoning. Serve hot.

Spiced Lamb and Spinach Soup with Rice

shourbet sbaanegh

Thick, satisfying whole-meal soups of meat, greens, and rice are popular in much of the region, especially in Turkey, Egypt, and Lebanon. In this version garlic and cilantro add a fresh touch to enliven the hearty soup. For festive occasions, in addition to the chunks of meat, the soup might be enhanced with kibbe balls of seasoned ground meat and bulgur.

If you prefer, you can substitute beef or chicken for the lamb. For a faster, lighter first-course soup, omit the meat and simply use 6 cups chicken or vegetable stock. You can use brown rice, which tastes good with the meat and greens, for a nontraditional variation; add it to the soup after the meat has cooked for 45 minutes.

♦ MAKES 8 FIRST-COURSE OR 4 TO 6 MAIN-COURSE SERVINGS.

2 to 2½ pounds lamb shanks or lamb shoulder, including bones

3 to 4 tablespoons vegetable oil, butter,
   or ghee

About 2 quarts water

1 bay leaf

Salt and freshly ground black pepper

1 large onion, finely chopped

6 large garlic cloves, chopped

½ cup chopped cilantro

1 teaspoon ground cumin

⅔ cup long-grain white rice

¼ to ½ teaspoon red pepper flakes,
   or cayenne pepper to taste (optional)

12-ounce bunch or 10-ounce bag spinach,
   rinsed, any large stems removed,
   chopped

Cut meat from bones in bite-size pieces, re-serving bones. If you would like to brown meat, heat half the oil in heavy soup pot or stewing pan, add meat in batches, and sauté until brown. Drain excess fat from pan.

Return meat to pan. Add bones and 2 quarts water or enough to just cover. Bring to a boil. Skim foam from surface. Add bay leaf, salt, and pepper. Cover and cook over low heat for 1½ hours, or until meat is tender. Discard bones and bay leaf. Skim excess fat from soup.

In skillet, heat remaining oil, add onion, and sauté over medium heat for 7 minutes, or until soft and golden brown. Add garlic, cilantro, and cumin and sauté, stirring, for 1 minute. Remove from heat.

Return soup to a simmer, add rice and pepper flakes, and stir once. Cover and cook for 10 minutes. Add onion mixture and chopped spinach and simmer for 5 to 10 minutes, or until rice is tender. Taste and adjust seasoning. Serve hot.

Lebanese Fish Soup
with Linguine

chorbet samak

Along the eastern Mediterranean you'll find fish simmering in soup pots with onions, garlic, aromatic herbs, and, sometimes, tomatoes and saffron. Basil is not as popular as it is in Italy but it grows abundantly in the region and occasionally perfumes Lebanese dishes, such as this light main course.

Making soup is one of the most eco-nomical ways to enjoy the fruits of the sea, as a relatively small amount of fish is needed for each portion. Because fish cooks rapidly, fish soups cook faster than most main-course soups. In addition, they can be fairly low in fat; just a little olive oil is needed to sauté the vegetables and flavor the broth.

The most important rule is to choose fish that is fresh. My favorites are those that do not fall apart easily—monkfish or sea bass is an excellent choice, and cod or hal-ibut is good too. To them I occasionally add a small amount of scallops, shrimp, or both;

they require little preparation and add a festive touch.

Use fish stock to give the soup a superior flavor; make your own or buy it frozen at a fine supermarket or fish store. An alternative is bottled clam juice mixed with an equal amount of water. You can freeze the soup base if you make it ahead. Then all you need to do is heat it and add the fish and pasta a few minutes before serving.

- ◆ MAKES 6 FIRST-COURSE OR
  4 MAIN-COURSE SERVINGS.

  2 to 3 tablespoons extra-virgin olive oil

  2 large onions, halved, sliced thin

  12 ounces ripe tomatoes, peeled, seeded, and chopped, or one 14-ounce can tomatoes, drained and chopped (optional)

  6 large garlic cloves, chopped

  5 cups Fish Stock (page 377) or stock mixed with water, or more if needed

  ¼ teaspoon lightly crushed saffron threads

  Salt and freshly ground black pepper to taste

  4 ounces linguine, whole or broken in short pieces, or very fine egg noodles for soup

  8 ounces sea bass or halibut fillet, cut in ¾-inch dice

  8 ounces medium shrimp, shelled, or additional fish

  3 to 4 tablespoons coarsely chopped fresh basil

Heat oil in large, wide casserole. Add onions and cook over medium-low heat for 10 minutes, or until soft but not brown. Add tomatoes and garlic and heat for 1 minute. Add stock, saffron, salt, and pepper.

Bring to a boil. Cook, uncovered, over low heat for 20 minutes.

Cook pasta, uncovered, in large pan of boiling salted water over high heat until tender but firm to the bite; linguine needs about 8 minutes and fine soup noodles about 3 minutes. Drain well.

Bring soup to simmer. Add fish and simmer, uncovered, for 2 minutes. Add shrimp and simmer for 3 minutes, or until all seafood is just tender. Add linguine. If soup is too thick, stir in a little more stock or water. Add basil. Taste and adjust seasoning. Serve hot.

Mideast Minestrone

shurbat al-khudar

In the Middle East hearty minestrone-like soups appear on family tables during the cooler months. Like Italian minestrone, they are composed of vegetables, legumes, and either noodles or rice, and may be meat-based or vegetarian. Yet in color and flavor the Mideastern ones are strikingly different. Instead of a pesto of basil and Parmesan, the minestrone is likely to be fragrant with cilantro, mint, cumin, turmeric, or cinnamon. Some top their soups with thick, rich yogurt, while others like a tangy squeeze of lemon juice.

Chickpeas and lentils are the favorite

legumes, but white beans are used as well, or mung beans in Persian homes. Spinach, chard, or other greens figure frequently and there are always onions and often garlic. Other candidates for the minestrone pot include carrots, leeks, zucchini, celery, green beans, tomatoes, potatoes, and turnips. If you like, fry an extra onion for garnish, as is customary in many homes, or stir in some Egyptian *takliah* (see page 47).

It's not surprising that this main-course soup became a staple in so many regions. It is balanced nutritionally, providing vegetarian protein from the beans, vitamins and minerals from the greens, and filling carbohydrates from the pasta or rice. It thickens on standing, so add a little water when reheating if necessary.

◆ MAKES 6 FIRST-COURSE OR 3 OR
4 MAIN-COURSE SERVINGS.

1 to 2 tablespoons olive oil or vegetable oil

1 onion, chopped

1 large leek, split, cleaned, and sliced,
    or 1 additional onion

½ cup chopped Italian parsley

1¾ cups vegetable or chicken broth,
    or one 14½-ounce can, or a mixture of
    broth and water

1 large carrot, diced

1 large boiling potato, peeled and diced
    (optional)

1 teaspoon ground cumin

¼ teaspoon turmeric

3 or 4 small Middle Eastern pale green
    squash or zucchini (about 1 pound), diced

4 to 5 ounces spinach, turnip greens,
    or other greens, rinsed, large stems
    removed, or half of one 10-ounce bag
    leaves of spinach or other greens,
    chopped (about 4 cups)

3 ounces vermicelli, spaghettini, or extra-fine
    egg noodles, broken in 3- to 4-inch
    lengths (about 1 cup)

1½ cups cooked chickpeas (garbanzo
    beans) or white beans, or one 15-ounce
    can chickpeas or white beans, drained

Salt and freshly ground black pepper

Cayenne pepper to taste

Heat oil in large saucepan. Add onion, leek, and half of parsley and cook over medium-low heat for 10 minutes, or until onion is soft and light golden. Add broth, 1 quart water, carrot, potato, cumin, and turmeric and bring to a boil. If using a potato, add an additional cup of water. Cover and simmer over low heat for 12 to 15 minutes, or until vegetables are tender.

Add squash and spinach and bring to a boil. Add pasta and simmer, uncovered, over medium-low heat for 3 minutes. Add chickpeas and simmer for 5 to 8 minutes, or until pasta and vegetables are tender. Stir in remaining parsley. Season to taste with salt, pepper, and cayenne. Serve hot.

Spicy Lentil Soup with Dill and Cumin

shorbet addss balady

In kitchens everywhere in the Mideast, you find bubbling pots of lentil soup. Cooks prepare simple ones composed of only lentils, onions, and garlic or add tomatoes, carrots, or summer squash. They may spice their soup with cumin, coriander, or sumac. My sister-in-law, Mati Kahn, who was born in India and whose family is from Iraq, makes a variety of lentil soups and finds that a squeeze of fresh lemon does wonders to wake up their flavor.

For heartier soups, chicken or meat simmers with the lentils or, in Turkey, a lemon and egg sauce is added. Persians even serve pureed lentil soup for breakfast, flavoring it simply with salt and oregano and enjoying it with a pat of butter and a sprinkling of sugar.

Lentils are filling and produce a flavorful broth at little cost. These soups are convenient too, as they keep well for a few days in the refrigerator.

Red lentils, which are actually orange and turn golden when cooked, are favorites, as they naturally fall apart in the pot and cook to a puree; you can find them at Middle Eastern and Indian grocery stores. Soups are also made from common brown lentils, which retain their shape, as do the French green lentils. Serve this soup with flatbread, Pita Crisps (page 332), or croutons. If you like, reserve half the sautéed onion and garlic and add them to the finished soup for richness.

◆ MAKES 4 FIRST-COURSE SERVINGS.

1½ cups lentils, any kind

2 or 3 tablespoons olive oil or vegetable oil

1 large onion, chopped

4 large garlic cloves, chopped

1 teaspoon ground cumin

2 celery ribs, sliced (optional)

1 carrot, diced (optional)

4 to 6 cups water

2 zucchini or pale-green Middle Eastern squash, diced (optional)

Salt and freshly ground black pepper

2 tablespoons snipped or chopped fresh dill, or 2 teaspoons dried dill

Middle Eastern red pepper or cayenne pepper to taste (optional)

Lemon wedges (for accompaniment)

Spread lentils on a plate. Pick through them carefully, discarding any stones; rinse and drain lentils.

Heat oil in medium saucepan. Add onion and sauté over medium-low heat for 7 minutes, or until golden. Add garlic and cumin and sauté for 1 minute. Add lentils, celery, carrot, and 4 cups water. Bring to a boil. Cover and simmer over low heat for 30 minutes, adding more water if soup becomes too thick. Add zucchini, salt, and pepper and simmer for 10 minutes, or until lentils are very tender.

Leave the soup chunky, or puree all or part of it in a blender or food processor, as you like. Add dill. Taste and adjust seasoning, adding plenty of black pepper and a pinch of red pepper. Serve with lemon wedges.

Lebanese Lentil and Chard Soup

chorbet adass bi hamod

Lentil soup with greens such as chard and spinach is loved not only in Lebanon, but in Israel, Palestine, Jordan, and Egypt as well. Some like a substantial soup and cook the lentils with potatoes, noodles, or bulgur wheat. Others relish the spicy flavors of cumin, cilantro, and cayenne. As with many lentil dishes, fried onions are a favorite finishing touch, and so is lemon juice.

◆ MAKES 4 FIRST-COURSE SERVINGS.

1½ cups brown or green lentils

2 tablespoons olive oil

1 large onion, chopped

3 large garlic cloves, chopped

4 to 6 cups water, or vegetable broth mixed with water

12 to 16 ounces chard, rinsed and chopped

Salt and freshly ground black pepper

1 teaspoon ground cumin (optional)

¼ cup chopped cilantro

Lemon wedges (for accompaniment)

Spread lentils on a plate. Pick through them carefully, discarding any stones; rinse and drain lentils.

Heat oil in medium saucepan. Add onion and sauté over medium-low heat for 7 minutes, or until golden. Add garlic and sauté for 1 minute. Remove half of mixture from pan. Add lentils and 4 cups water to pan. Bring to a boil. Cover and simmer over low heat for 30 minutes, adding more water if soup becomes too thick. Add chard, salt, pepper, and cumin and simmer for 10 minutes, or until lentils and chard are tender.

Return sautéed onions to pan. Add cilantro. Taste and adjust seasoning. Serve with lemon wedges.

White Bean Soup with Garlic and Hot Pepper

shouraba lubee

Bean soups are popular on many Mideast tables, in both meaty and vegetarian versions, usually flavored with onions and garlic and often with tomatoes. Stirring sautéed garlic into the finished soup is a widespread technique for boosting the flavor.

You can also make this soup with dried

black-eyed peas, another regional favorite; simmer them for 45 minutes before adding the tomatoes. For faster cooking, use frozen black-eyed peas; simmer them for 10 minutes before adding the tomatoes.

◆ MAKES 6 FIRST-COURSE SERVINGS.

1 pound dried white beans (about 2½ cups), such as Great Northern

3 tablespoons olive oil or vegetable oil

2 large onions, chopped

6 large garlic cloves, minced

3 to 4 cups water

3 cups beef, chicken, or vegetable broth, or additional water

1 pound ripe tomatoes, peeled and chopped, or one 14-ounce can diced tomatoes, with their liquid

2 tablespoons tomato paste

Salt and freshly ground black pepper

1 teaspoon paprika (optional)

½ teaspoon Middle Eastern red pepper, or ¼ teaspoon cayenne pepper, or to taste

¼ cup chopped Italian parsley or cilantro

Sort beans, discarding any stones, and rinse them. Heat 2 tablespoons oil in large saucepan. Add onions and sauté over medium heat for 10 minutes, or until light golden. Add half the garlic, sauté a few seconds, and add beans, 3 cups water, and the broth. Bring to a boil, cover, and cook over low heat for 1 hour.

Add tomatoes, tomato paste, salt, pepper, and paprika, if using, and cook for 30 minutes, or until beans are very tender, adding hot water from time to time if soup becomes too thick. Stir in red pepper and half the parsley.

Heat remaining tablespoon oil in small skillet. Add remaining garlic and cook over medium-low heat for 1 minute, or until fragrant but not brown. Add to soup. Taste soup and adjust seasoning. Serve garnished with remaining parsley.

Split Pea Soup with Vegetables, Rice, and Mint

ash-e lapeh

Split pea soups are especially prized in the lands around the Persian Gulf. Rather than cooking the peas on their own as European and American cooks do, those in the Mideast frequently add a variety of vegetables, as well as rice, noodles, or bulgur wheat. Curry is a popular flavoring in Iraq, and turmeric, mint, and cinnamon in Iran. The soups might be vegetarian or might include beef, lamb, chicken, or meatballs.

Fast-cooking yellow split peas are the type favored by Persians, but you can use green ones. Like lentils, all split peas cook quickly.

◆ MAKES 4 TO 6 FIRST-COURSE SERVINGS.

1 cup split peas, yellow or green

3 cups beef, chicken, or vegetable broth
mixed with 3 cups water

2 large onions, halved and sliced thin

8 ounces winter squash, or 2 large carrots,
peeled and diced

2 celery ribs, sliced

1/3 cup chopped Italian parsley

1/2 cup white rice (medium or long grain) or
bulgur wheat

Salt and freshly ground black pepper

1 teaspoon turmeric or curry powder

2 tablespoons fresh-squeezed lemon juice,
or to taste

2 tablespoons vegetable oil or butter

2 tablespoons chopped fresh mint,
or 2 teaspoons dried

Sort peas and rinse them with water. Combine peas with broth and half the onion slices in large saucepan. Bring to a boil. Cover and simmer for 20 minutes if using yellow split peas or 45 minutes if using green ones. Add squash, celery, parsley, rice, salt, pepper, and turmeric and cook for 15 minutes, or until split peas and rice are tender. Add lemon juice.

Heat oil in skillet. Add remaining onion and sauté over medium heat for 7 minutes, or until golden brown. Stir in mint. Remove from heat and pour over soup for garnish.

Tomato Barley Soup with Peppers

hasa'a al-habea

To make soups more satisfying, barley is a common addition in the region. Pearl barley is the most widely available form of the grain, but in Middle Eastern shops you can also find whole barley. It takes longer to cook but has the nutritional benefits of the entire grain. Barley thickens soups considerably as it stands. If you're making the soup ahead, add water when you reheat it to get the consistency you like. Peppers and dill lend a delicate aroma and taste to this colorful vegetable soup.

◆ MAKES 4 TO 6 FIRST-COURSE SERVINGS.

2 tablespoons olive oil, vegetable oil, or butter

1 large onion, diced

2 carrots, diced

2 celery ribs, diced

1 pound ripe tomatoes, diced, or one
14-ounce can diced tomatoes

1 quart beef, chicken, or vegetable broth,
or water

1/2 cup pearl barley

Salt and freshly ground black pepper

2 green peppers, halved, seeded, and diced

1 1/2 cups green beans, cut in thirds,
or 1 cup green peas

2 zucchini, diced

1/2 teaspoon ground allspice (optional)

1 to 2 tablespoons chopped fresh dill,
or 1 to 2 teaspoons dried dill

Heat oil in large saucepan. Add onion and sauté over medium heat for 7 minutes, or until light golden. Add carrots and celery and sauté for 2 minutes. Add tomatoes, broth, and 2 cups water and bring to a boil. Reduce heat to low. Add barley, salt, and pepper. Cover and cook for 30 minutes.

If soup is too thick, add I cup hot water. Add peppers, green beans, zucchini, and, if you like, allspice and cook for 15 more minutes, or until barley and vegetables are tender. Stir in dill. Taste and adjust seasoning. Serve hot.

Hot-and-Sour Summer Squash Soup

maradj kar'a hamiz

Squash appears frequently in mixed vegetable and meat soups, especially zucchini's pale green Mideastern cousin, called Middle Eastern squash, Clarita squash, and by other regional names. In southern California they're often called Mexican squash or white squash, and in Detroit I've seen them as cousa squash. They're slightly sweeter than zucchini and their pastel hue is attractive in this soup.

In this light, simple soup the squash is the star. It's flavored in the Iraqi style with hot red pepper, tomatoes, and lemon. Armenians also like zucchini and tomato soup and flavor theirs with garlic, basil, and a sprinkling of olive oil. For a more substantial soup, cook a little rice in the soup or serve it with croutons. You can puree the soup if you want it to be smooth. In warm weather the soup is good cold.

◆ MAKES 4 OR 5 FIRST-COURSE SERVINGS.

2 to 3 tablespoons extra-virgin olive oil, or 1 to 2 tablespoons vegetable oil

3 large garlic cloves, minced (optional)

1 pound ripe tomatoes, chopped, or one 14-ounce can diced tomatoes with their juice

¼ to ½ teaspoon hot red pepper flakes, or cayenne pepper to taste

Salt and freshly ground black pepper

1½ pounds pale green Middle Eastern squash or zucchini, diced

3 cups chicken, beef, or vegetable broth, water, or a mixture of broth and water

3 tablespoons white rice (optional)

2 tablespoons strained fresh-squeezed lemon juice, or to taste

¼ teaspoon sugar, or to taste

Heat I or 2 tablespoons oil in saucepan. Add garlic, if using, and cook over medium-low heat, stirring, for 30 seconds. Add tomatoes, pepper flakes, salt, and pepper and stir well. Sauté over medium heat for 5 minutes. Add squash, broth, and, if you like, rice and bring to a boil. Cover and cook over low heat for 15 minutes, or until rice and squash are very tender. Add lemon juice and sugar. Taste and adjust seasoning, adding more salt, pepper, lemon juice, or sugar if needed. Serve hot, cold, or at room temperature, drizzled, if you like, with 1 tablespoon olive oil.

Wintertime Wheat and Lentil Soup with Turnips and Garlic

masheh b'shargomeh

This hearty vegetarian soup is popular among the Kurds and the Persians. Usually it features a combination of legumes such as split peas, lentils, or mung beans and grains such as wheat or rice. Meaty versions are made with lamb or beef. To enliven the soup's flavor, cooks mostly use celery or herbs, notably mint, dill, parsley, or cilantro, and occasionally spices like cinnamon or turmeric. I add carrots to make the soup more colorful.

◆ MAKES 3 MAIN-COURSE OR 4 TO 6 FIRST-COURSE SERVINGS.

1 cup brown or green lentils, sorted and rinsed

2 to 3 tablespoons vegetable oil

1 large onion, chopped

12 large garlic cloves, chopped

1 pound turnips, peeled and diced

2 large carrots, diced

6 cups water, or 3 cups broth (beef, chicken, or vegetable) mixed with 3 cups water

2/3 cup bulgur wheat, preferably large

4 celery ribs, sliced thin

Salt and freshly ground black pepper

2 tablespoons chopped cilantro or parsley

Spread lentils on a plate. Pick through them carefully, discarding any stones; rinse and drain lentils.

Heat 1 or 2 tablespoons oil in large saucepan. Add onion and sauté over medium-low heat for 7 minutes, or until golden. Add half the garlic and sauté for 1 minute. Add lentils, turnips, carrots, and water. Bring to a boil. Cover and simmer over low heat for 25 minutes, adding more water if soup becomes too thick. Add bulgur wheat, celery, salt, and pepper and simmer for 15 minutes, or until lentils and bulgur are tender.

Heat remaining tablespoon oil in small skillet. Add remaining garlic and sauté over low heat for 1 minute, or until aromatic. Add to soup and mix well. Taste and adjust seasoning. Serve sprinkled with cilantro.

Cool Pumpkin Borani Soup

mast-o-kadu zard

Borani are salads of yogurt and cooked vegetables, such as greens, eggplant, and beets (page 257). For a super-simple, no-cook starter, I make a *borani* in soup form with canned pumpkin. Although fresh pumpkin is not a summer ingredient, I find it convenient to keep a few cans of pumpkin around to make cold soups when the weather makes it too hot to cook.

This refreshing, pale orange pumpkin soup is ready in seconds. A sprinkling of chives or garlic chives adds a pleasant, attractive accent. If you like, add small cubes of peeled cucumber for additional garnish. Depending on how tangy your yogurt is, you may like to squeeze in a little lime or lemon juice to balance the pumpkin's delicate sweetness.

◆ MAKES 4 FIRST-COURSE SERVINGS.

1 cup canned pumpkin

2 cups plain yogurt

1 to 1½ cups cold water, or to taste

Salt and freshly ground black pepper to taste

Hot sauce to taste

1 to 2 tablespoons strained fresh-squeezed lime or lemon juice, or to taste (optional)

½ cup finely diced peeled cucumber (optional)

4 teaspoons chopped chives or garlic chives

Stir pumpkin with yogurt in bowl until smooth and blended. Gradually stir in water, adding just enough to dilute the mixture to the soup consistency you like. Season to taste with salt, pepper, and hot sauce, adding enough so soup won't be bland. Add lime juice if you like. Cover and refrigerate until ready to serve. Serve cold. Garnish the center of each bowl with diced cucumber, if desired, and a pinch of chives.

Brunch, Lunch, and Supper Foods, for Menus in Minutes

Cauliflower Pepper Shakshuka with Tomatoes • *Shakshuka im Kruvit*

Cheesy Eggs with Tomatoes and Peppers • *Mfarraket Beid*

Scallion Scrambled Eggs with Cumin • *M'farrake Bassal*

Scrambled Eggs with Spinach and Leeks • *M'farrake Sabanegh*

Middle Eastern Herb Omelette • *Ijjit Bayd wa Baqdounis*

Flat Tomato Omelette • *Ijjit Bayd wa Banadoura*

Garlic Fried Eggs with Mint and Sumac • *Beid bi Sumac*

Baked Eggs with Zucchini, Garlic, and Kashkaval Cheese • *Bayd bi Koussa*

Pastrami with Eggs and Eggplant • *Pastirmali Yumurta*

Slow-cooked Brown Eggs • *Beitzim Humot*

Onion Omelette Sandwich with Mushrooms • *Havita im Batzal b'Pita*

Portobello and Peppers in a Pita • *Pitriyot v'Pilpelim b'Pita*

Eggplant and Egg Sandwich with Olive Hummus • *Sabich*

Avocado Vegetable Wrap with Feta • *Avocado Viyrakot b'Laffa*

Broiled Vegetable Sandwich with Tomato Basil Tahini •
Sandvich Yirakot Kluyim im T'hina

Halloumi Cheese Sandwich with Capers and Parsley • *Sandvich Halloumi im Tzlafim*

Thick Yogurt and Yogurt Cheese • *Labneh*

Dairy foods and eggs are customary on the Mideast menu for breakfast and supper. Following the traditional diet of the region, many people prefer a light menu in the evening, having had their substantial repast at midday. This custom has changed in many cities, however, due to modern work schedules. Whichever way you like to structure your eating pattern, Mideastern light-meal specialties make terrific items for brunch, lunch, or supper.

Cheese, yogurt, and *labneh* (kefir cheese) often appear on the table for supper. Occasionally feta and other crumbly cheeses embellish salads of fresh vegetables. Any kind of cheese might simply be served on its own with fresh bread or accompanied by herb sprigs, a few cut vegetables, or olives.

A variety of regional cheeses, from soft, spreadable ones to semisoft, slicing cheeses to firm types for crumbling or grating, are also turned into savory fillings and toppings. They enhance appetizer pastries such as *beurreks* and pizzalike flatbreads, which disappear rapidly at parties and at festive suppers. (For more on Middle Eastern cheeses, see "The Mideast Pantry," page 18.)

A frequent supper choice is an omelette. As in most Mediterranean countries, it is almost always flat, not folded. Omelettes may include a generous amount of vegetables. Onions, greens, zucchini, eggplant, and even beans are all regular additions. Sometimes ingredients end up in the omelette pan that to us seem unusual, such as saffron and tart dried berries in Iran or olives in Egypt. Many families enjoy their omelettes rather thick, like the tortillas of Spain (which are completely different from the Mexican flatbreads of the same name). Unlike the French, people in the Mideast usually prefer their eggs well cooked and don't go for runny omelettes.

For quick suppers many cooks start with a vegetable sauté or quick stew and add eggs to it. Either they poach or bake the eggs in the sauce from the vegetables or scramble them with the medley to make a dish known in Arabic as *shakshuka*. Sometimes people slip such egg dishes or omelettes into a pita to make a tasty sandwich, a popular item both at home and at casual eateries. A favorite of mine is Onion Omelette Sandwich with Mushrooms (page 119), which gains a lively taste from cumin, thyme, and Italian parsley.

Indeed, when it comes to light meals, sandwiches are king. Many of the region's most-loved sandwiches are meatless. Falafel is the most famous Mideast sandwich, but hummus, creamy sesame dip, and fried eggplant slices are enjoyed in sandwiches almost as often, on their own or matched with diced salad, hot pickles, and, sometimes, cold sliced meats or spicy sausages. I find grilled meaty vegetables like mushrooms and peppers also make delicious sandwiches when paired with one of the signature Middle Eastern dips, such as Broiled Vegetable Sandwich with Tomato Basil Tahini (page 123) or Eggplant and Egg Sandwich with Olive Hummus (page 121).

On the meat side of the menu, kabobs and meat patties are likely to be wrapped in flatbreads for a fast lunch, often with the same partners as falafel sandwiches. In fact, at restaurants, if you order grilled meats or sausages, you're usually asked whether you want it on a plate or in a pita.

Just about any cooked food might find its way into a sandwich. I smiled when I saw lentil and rice stew featured as a sandwich on some Mideast restaurant menus in Detroit. The idea reminded me of a starchy British sandwich—spaghetti on toast!

Cauliflower Pepper Shakshuka with Tomatoes

shakshuka im kruvit

Shakshuka is a popular, savory combination of eggs and vegetables. My mother-in-law, who was from Yemen, often prepared *shakshuka* for supper, and her sister still does. Scrambling the ingredients together was her favorite technique, but some cooks add a few extra tomatoes to the cooked vegetable mixture and bake or poach the eggs in it instead.

I like to add cauliflower to the version she made of tomatoes, onions, and peppers. In winter people often substitute white or green onions or leeks for the other vegetables, for another tasty variation.

In our family we enjoy *shakshuka* the traditional way, with a salad of diced vegetables, fresh pita, and *zehug* (page 307) on the side. For this fast, casual dish we don't peel the tomatoes, but you can if the skins bother you, or use one 14-ounce can of diced tomatoes.

◆ MAKES 3 OR 4 SERVINGS.

2 cups small cauliflower florets

3 tablespoons vegetable oil or olive oil

1 medium onion, chopped

1 mild chili, such as Anaheim,
    or ½ green bell pepper, halved, cored,
    seeded, and diced small

2 large garlic cloves, chopped

3 ripe, medium tomatoes, diced
    (total ¾ pound)

Salt and freshly ground black pepper

1 teaspoon ground cumin

¼ teaspoon turmeric

¼ teaspoon cayenne pepper or hot sauce,
    or to taste

6 eggs, or 3 whole eggs and 5 egg whites,
    beaten

2 tablespoons chopped cilantro
    (optional)

Cook cauliflower in saucepan of boiling salted water for 3 minutes, or until nearly tender but still crisp. Drain well.

Heat oil in large skillet. Add onion and chili and sauté over medium heat for 7 minutes, or until onion is light golden, stirring occasionally. Add cauliflower and sauté for 2 minutes, or until tender. Stir in garlic, then tomatoes, salt, pepper, cumin, turmeric, and cayenne. Cook for 2 minutes, stirring often.

Add beaten eggs and 1 tablespoon cilantro to hot mixture in skillet. Scramble over low heat for 2 minutes, or until thoroughly set. Taste and adjust seasoning. Serve immediately, topped with remaining cilantro.

YOGURT

It's fitting that our English word *yogurt* came from the Turkish language, as people there, and throughout the Mideast, are so fond of it. Even with yogurt so easy to find at the store, many people from the Mideast continue the tradition of making their own.

Of course, the health benefits of yogurt are well known. It is a terrific source of calcium and of vitamin B_{12}. Its protein content makes it satisfying and it is low in calories.

Although Middle Eastern people like yogurt with fruit and use it to make cakes and other desserts, they don't ordinarily sweeten their yogurt, as they appreciate its tangy taste. For very simple suppers, diners eat flavorful yogurt on its own or spoon it over salads or dishes of cooked vegetables, legumes, or grains.

Cooks display amazing versatility in their use of yogurt. They pair it with raw or cooked vegetables to come up with salads, dips, and refreshing soups. They use it as the basis of hot and cold sauces to accompany many foods, from vegetables to meat to grains, or heat yogurt gently in soups to enrich them and give them zing.

Cheesy Eggs with Tomatoes and Peppers

mfarraket beid

Lebanese cooks make a tasty variation of *shakshuka* using flavorful *kashkaval* cheese, and butter for cooking the eggs. You can find the cheese at Middle Eastern and Eastern European markets, or substitute feta, Swiss, Gruyère, or ¼ cup Parmesan or Pecorino Romano. Serve the eggs with pita or crusty French or Italian bread.

◆ MAKES 2 SERVINGS.

2 to 3 tablespoons butter

1 small onion, chopped (about ½ cup)

½ green or red bell pepper, cored, seeded, and diced

2 ripe, medium tomatoes, diced small

2 large garlic cloves, chopped

3 or 4 eggs, beaten

Salt and freshly ground black pepper

½ teaspoon paprika (optional)

Cayenne pepper to taste (optional)

½ cup grated *kashkaval* cheese

Melt butter in medium skillet. Add onion and bell pepper and sauté over medium heat for 5 minutes, or until softened. Add tomatoes and garlic and continue cooking for

5 minutes, or until mixture is thick. Add eggs, salt, pepper, and, if you like, paprika and cayenne, and scramble over medium-low heat until set. Stir in cheese. Taste and adjust seasoning. Serve immediately.

Scallion Scrambled Eggs with Cumin

m'farrake bassal

This savory scramble is ready in minutes. It's the fresh green onions and spice that make it so tasty. If you prefer a milder taste, instead of using raw onions, sauté them in the oil for 1 or 2 minutes before adding the eggs. For the freshest-tasting spice, grind whole cumin seeds in a spice grinder, as many Middle Eastern cooks do. Some people serve the cumin separately, raw or toasted (see "Basics," page 370), for sprinkling.

In Iran some flavor the eggs with saffron and cilantro rather than cumin. Instead of green onions, some Lebanese cooks scramble the eggs with the cloves of several heads of garlic. They tame the garlic, however, by blanching the cloves before mixing them with the eggs. A faster variation is to use roasted garlic cloves if you have some on hand, or buy them in a jar.

You can make the egg mixture into a flat omelette instead of scrambling it, following the second and third paragraphs of Middle Eastern Herb Omelette (page 114). With either version, tomatoes and black olives make a tasty, attractive topping.

◆ MAKES 3 TO 6 SERVINGS.

6 to 8 green onions, white and green parts

6 eggs, or 4 eggs combined with 2 or 3 egg whites

1 teaspoon ground cumin

Salt and freshly ground black pepper

2 garlic cloves, finely minced (optional)

2 tablespoons olive oil

1 plum tomato, halved and thinly sliced (optional)

6 black olives, such as kalamata, pitted and sliced (optional)

Chop dark green part of green onion. Halve thicker white and light green part lengthwise and slice very thin. Beat eggs with cumin, salt, and pepper in bowl. Stir in green onions and garlic.

Heat oil in heavy nonstick skillet. Add egg mixture and cook over low heat until eggs are set to your taste, stirring often. Serve immediately, topped with tomato and olive slices if you like.

Scrambled Eggs with Spinach and Leeks

m'farrake sabanegh

Greens of all sorts are paired with eggs in the Mideast. For this recipe you can use mustard greens, Swiss chard, or other cooking greens at your market. Cook them like the spinach, allowing a few extra minutes if necessary, so they are tender before you combine them with the eggs. Favorite accompaniments for this dish are olives, pickles, and potatoes, either boiled or fried. I also like it with feta cheese or a sprinkling of Parmesan.

◆ MAKES 2 TO 4 SERVINGS.

    1 bunch spinach (about 1 pound), stems
        discarded and leaves rinsed well, or one
        10-ounce bag spinach leaves
    2 or 3 tablespoons olive oil or butter
    1 large leek, white and light green parts,
        cleaned and chopped
    Salt and freshly ground black pepper
    4 eggs

Add spinach to saucepan of boiling salted water and boil, uncovered, over high heat for 2 minutes, or until just tender. Drain in colander, rinse with cold water, and drain well. Squeeze spinach by handfuls to remove as much liquid as possible. Chop spinach fine with knife.

Heat oil in heavy nonstick skillet. Add leek, salt, and pepper and cook over medium-low heat for 5 to 7 minutes, or until tender, stirring often. Add spinach and heat through. Taste and adjust seasoning.

Beat eggs with salt and pepper in a bowl. Add egg mixture to skillet and scramble over low heat until set. Serve immediately.

Middle Eastern Herb Omelette

ijjit bayd wa baqdounis

Around the Middle East people flavor omelettes with generous amounts of fresh herbs. The parsley-loving Lebanese use this herb in omelettes, often combined with mint. The Kurds like parsley as well or substitute the leaves and tender ribs of celery. Thyme is popular in Egypt and much of the eastern Mediterranean. Persians use a profusion of herbs and for their omelettes might mix parsley, cilantro, and, for a slightly bitter accent, a little fresh fenugreek. No matter what herb is selected, a member of the onion family is usually also present. Adding a few chopped green olives to the herb and onion mix makes a tasty variation.

This recipe is inspired by an omelette that my husband's aunt makes from either green or white onions or leeks. If she is using leeks, she sautés them until softened but with onions this isn't necessary. Most people serve omelettes like these in small portions for a light meal. Popular accompaniments are sliced tomatoes, or a salad of cucumbers and yogurt. Fresh bread is on the table, and usually so is a plate of olives or pickles.

◆ MAKES 2 TO 4 SERVINGS.

4 eggs

Salt and freshly ground black pepper

½ cup chopped Italian parsley

2 tablespoons chopped cilantro or mint (optional)

½ cup chopped green onions or grated white onions

2 or 3 tablespoons olive oil, vegetable oil, or butter

Beat eggs with salt and pepper in bowl. Stir in parsley, cilantro, and onions.

Heat oil in large heavy skillet, preferably nonstick. Swirl pan slightly so oil coats sides as well. Add egg mixture and cook over medium heat without stirring, occasionally lifting edge of omelette and tipping skillet so that uncooked part of egg mixture runs to edge of pan.

When top of omelette is just set, slide omelette onto a plate, turn it over onto another plate, and slide it back into pan. Cook second side over medium-low heat for 30 seconds, or until just set. Serve hot or warm.

Flat Tomato Omelette

ijjit bayd wa banadoura

Garlic gives this omelette plenty of punch. Use less if you like, or cook it with the onions to mellow it before adding it to the eggs. Serve the omelette with olives, pickles, and radishes or with a green salad. This fresh tomato omelette also makes a tasty sandwich.

◆ MAKES 2 SERVINGS.

2 or 3 tablespoons vegetable oil, or equal amounts oil and butter

1 medium onion, minced

4 eggs, or 2 eggs combined with 2 or 3 egg whites

Salt and freshly ground black pepper

6 large garlic cloves, minced

2 medium tomatoes, diced small

Heat 1 or 2 tablespoons oil in heavy skillet that can go into the broiler; a nonstick skillet is best. Add onion and cook over medium heat about 5 minutes, or until softened, stirring occasionally.

Thoroughly beat eggs with salt and pepper. Stir in garlic and tomatoes. Add remaining oil to skillet and heat over medium heat. Swirl pan slightly so oil coats sides. Add egg mixture. Cook, without stirring, occasionally lifting edge of omelette and tipping skillet so uncooked part of egg mixture runs to edge of pan.

When top of omelette is nearly set, place pan in broiler. Broil briefly, just until top is set and lightly browned. Serve immediately.

Garlic Fried Eggs with Mint and Sumac

---

beid bi sumac

Sumac's tart flavor balances the powerful punch of the garlic and the richness of this dish. If you don't have this purple spice, omit it or substitute 1 teaspoon vinegar if you like. Some flavor this dish with sour pomegranate juice instead of sumac. Adding these purple ingredients to eggs won't seem strange to you if you have enjoyed the Burgundian specialty, poached eggs in red wine. Fried potatoes are a popular partner for the eggs, as is fresh bread.

◆ MAKES 2 SERVINGS.

4 to 8 garlic cloves, to taste, finely minced

1 teaspoon sumac powder

2 to 3 tablespoons olive oil

4 large eggs

½ teaspoon dried mint

Salt and freshly ground black pepper

Combine garlic, sumac powder, and 2 tablespoons water in small bowl.

Heat 2 tablespoons oil in medium-size nonstick skillet. Gently break 2 eggs into a cup, then slide them into skillet. Repeat with 2 remaining eggs. Cover and cook over medium-low heat for 1 minute. Carefully spoon garlic mixture over and around eggs, standing back in case oil splatters, and sprinkle with mint, salt, and pepper. Cover and cook for 3 minutes, or until eggs are done to taste. Serve immediately.

Baked Eggs with Zucchini, Garlic, and Kashkaval Cheese

---

bayd bi koussa

For this eastern Mediterranean brunch or supper dish, you can prepare the zucchini in its quick, thyme-accented tomato sauce in advance, then heat it before adding the eggs. Cooking the eggs thoroughly is the tradition, but I like them soft. Some prepare these eggs as a thick flat omelette resembling a frittata instead of baking them. Be sure to accompany this savory dish with good-quality pita or crusty bread and with a plate of olives, pickles, and 2-inch pieces of fresh green onions.

◆ MAKES 4 SERVINGS.

6 tablespoons butter, or 4 tablespoons
   olive oil

1 pound zucchini or other summer squash,
   diced small

3 garlic cloves, minced

1 pound ripe tomatoes, peeled, seeded,
   and chopped, or one 14-ounce can
   tomatoes, drained and chopped

½ teaspoon dried thyme

Salt and freshly ground black pepper

4 eggs

6 tablespoons grated *kashkaval*, Parmesan,
   or Pecorino Romano cheese

Preheat oven to 425°F. Heat 2 tablespoons butter or olive oil in a large, heavy skillet. Add zucchini and garlic. Cover and cook over low heat for 3 minutes, or until zucchini softens, stirring occasionally. Add tomatoes, thyme, salt, and pepper. Bring to a boil. Cook, uncovered, over medium heat for 10 minutes, or until tomatoes soften, stirring often. Taste and adjust seasoning.

Butter four individual 6-inch shallow baking dishes or a shallow 5-cup baking dish. Melt remaining butter, if using. Reheat zucchini mixture if necessary. Divide hot mixture among dishes. With spoon, make a hollow in center of mixture in each small dish, or make 4 hollows in large dish, each large enough to contain 1 egg. Break an egg carefully into each hollow. Spoon 1 tablespoon melted butter or ½ tablespoon olive oil over each egg and sprinkle egg whites evenly with grated cheese.

Bake eggs about 7 to 9 minutes, until

whites are just set and yolks are still soft, or until they are done to your taste. Set individual baking dishes on plates and serve immediately.

Pastrami with Eggs and Eggplant

---

pastirmali yumurta

For a hearty breakfast, eggs with sausages and other spiced cured meats are common in various parts of the Mideast, and so are eggs with ground meat sautéed with onions. The meat and eggs might be scrambled, made into a flat omelette, or the meat might be used as a bed for poaching the eggs or a topping for fried eggs. I like to include plenty of vegetables, such as zucchini, green beans, fava beans, peppers, or eggplant. They improve not only the nutritional value but the taste of these egg-and-meat dishes, making them lighter and not too salty.

A favorite partner for eggs is *basterma*, the spicy Armenian-Lebanese cured beef that many say is the ancestor of pastrami. You can find it in Middle Eastern and Eastern European markets and delis, but American pastrami works fine too. The brands of *basterma* I have tried are leaner than pastrami and so I add *basterma* directly to the eggs instead of cooking it first. You can also use thin slices of *soujouk*, a beef sausage seasoned like *basterma*. Serve the eggs with pickles and fresh pita or lavash.

◆ MAKES 2 TO 4 SERVINGS.

2 to 4 slices pastrami, *basterma,* or *soujouk,*
　　cut in thin strips

1 to 2 tablespoons vegetable oil or butter

1 onion, chopped

1 fairly small eggplant (½ to ¾ pound),
　　cut in small dice

Salt and freshly ground black pepper

2 garlic cloves, chopped (optional)

1 large tomato, cut in small dice

½ teaspoon dried thyme

4 eggs

If using pastrami, heat it in sauté pan just until the fat runs. Remove with slotted spoon. Add oil to pan and heat over medium heat. Add onion and sauté for 5 minutes, or until beginning to brown. Add eggplant, salt, and pepper. Cover and cook for 8 to 10 minutes. Stir in garlic, if using, tomato, and thyme. Cover and cook for 5 minutes, or until eggplant is tender. Taste and adjust seasoning.

Make four depressions in vegetable mixture. Break each egg into a cup and slide it into a depression. Sprinkle eggs lightly with salt and pepper. Cover and cook for 2 minutes. Sprinkle meat strips around eggs. Cover and cook for 2 more minutes, or until eggs are done to taste. Serve hot.

Slow-cooked Brown Eggs

beitzim humot

These eggs acquire a creamy texture and a pale brown hue from long simmering, while their shells turn a brownish red wine color from cooking with onion peels. I've seen plenty of cooks saving onion skins to prepare eggs this way. Others use different tricks, like cooking the eggs with turnips, beans, coffee, or tea, like the Chinese tea eggs. The eggs are served warm at breakfast with fresh tomato puree or with hot beans. At other meals the eggs are used in sandwiches and to garnish salads.

The eggs also make a tasty accompaniment for savory pastries. A favorite supper of mine in Old Jaffa was cheese *bourekas* (phyllo pastries) accompanied by eggs like these. Sometimes my husband and I got off the bus at our favorite stop on our long ride home from work, in front of Sami's Turkish Bourekas, to enjoy this wonderful treat.

◆ MAKES 6 TO 12 SERVINGS.

12 eggs, rinsed

Skins of 8 to 10 brown onions
　　(about 4 to 5 cups)

1 teaspoon salt

½ teaspoon freshly ground black pepper

½ teaspoon ground cumin

2½ quarts water

1 tablespoon vegetable oil

Fresh Peppery Tomato Puree (page 309)

Check the eggs to be sure they have no cracks. Put half the onion skins in heavy medium saucepan. Top gently with the eggs, then with remaining onion skins. Add salt, pepper, and cumin. Add enough water to cover eggs. Add oil. Bring just to a boil. Reduce heat to very low, cover, and cook eggs for 5 hours, adding boiling water occasionally if too much evaporates.

Serve the eggs warm, in their shells so they keep warm, or peeled, with the cool puree.

Onion Omelette Sandwich with Mushrooms

havita im batzal b'pita

When I lived in the Mideast, I often enjoyed sandwiches of an omelette slipped into a fresh pita. We made them at home for brunch or, sometimes, my husband and I ordered them at a tiny, very casual café in Tel Aviv where people could sit in the shade of a large tree enjoying a quiet coffee break. At the café they put fried potato or eggplant slices in the pita along with the omelette if you wanted them.

Although any flat omelette is good in a sandwich, my favorites are this onion and parsley omelette or a Flat Tomato Omelette (page 115). To accompany it, I like to insert cumin-scented mushrooms into the pita pocket and, sometimes, also cheese, like diced feta or thin slices of *halloumi* or of braided Armenian string cheese. Serve the sandwich with diced salad, pickles, olives, and Hedva's Hot Pepper Relish (page 307) or other hot sauce.

◆ MAKES 2 OR 3 SERVINGS.

> 3 or 4 tablespoons olive oil, or half butter and half oil
>
> 6 to 8 ounces small mushrooms, thickly sliced
>
> Salt and freshly ground black pepper
>
> ½ teaspoon ground cumin
>
> 1 teaspoon chopped fresh thyme, or ½ teaspoon dried thyme
>
> 1 medium onion, minced
>
> 4 eggs, or 2 eggs combined with 2 or 3 egg whites
>
> 3 tablespoons chopped Italian parsley
>
> 2 or 3 fresh pita breads, halved

Heat 1 tablespoon oil in heavy medium skillet, preferably nonstick. Add mushrooms, salt, pepper, cumin, and thyme and sauté over medium-high heat for 3 minutes, or until just tender and lightly browned, stirring occasionally. Remove to plate.

Heat 1 or 2 tablespoons oil in skillet. Add onion and cook over medium heat for 5 minutes, or until tender and beginning to turn golden, stirring occasionally. Leave onions in skillet.

Thoroughly beat eggs with salt, pepper,

and parsley. Add remaining tablespoon oil to skillet and heat over medium heat. Swirl pan slightly so oil coats sides as well. Add egg mixture. Cook, without stirring, occasionally lifting edge of omelette and tipping skillet so uncooked part of egg mixture runs to edge of pan.

When top of omelette is nearly set, slide omelette onto a plate, turn it over onto another plate, and slide it back into pan. Sauté second side over medium-low heat for 30 to 60 seconds, or until just set. Cut omelette in four or six wedges and put them in pita breads. Add mushrooms and serve.

Portobello and Peppers in a Pita

pitriyot v'pilpelim b'pita

This is a vegetarian variation of a supper sandwich I often enjoyed when I lived in the Mideast. My standard sandwich was eggplant dip with garlic mayonnaise topped with smoked turkey, or sometimes kashkaval cheese. Today I make it with grilled mushrooms and peppers and occasionally I stray even farther from tradition by using soy salami. Instead of the eggplant mayonnaise dip, I sometimes spread the pita with tahini eggplant, hummus, parsley tahini (see recipes

in "Appetizers," page 33) or *labneh*, depending on what I have on hand.

Grilled portobello mushrooms are convenient because of their size, but you can substitute thick slices of large white mushrooms. Either grill them on a stovetop grill or sauté them as in Onion Omelette Sandwich with Mushrooms (page 119).

◆ MAKES 4 SERVINGS.

4 large portobello mushrooms, cleaned with a damp towel

2 to 3 teaspoons extra-virgin olive oil

Salt and freshly ground black pepper

2 red bell peppers, grilled and peeled (see "Basics," page 370), or 4 roasted pepper halves from a jar

4 fresh or slightly warmed pita breads

¼ to ½ cup Israeli Eggplant Dip with Garlic Mayonnaise (page 41), or more to taste

Heat a ridged stove-top grill pan over medium-high heat. Rub mushrooms with oil and sprinkle with salt and pepper on both sides. Set mushrooms on hot grill. Grill about 3 minutes per side, or until browned and done to your taste. Cut mushrooms in thick slices.

Cut peppers in thick strips. Cut each pita bread in half and spread with eggplant dip. Put mushroom slices and pepper strips inside pita halves. Serve more eggplant dip on the side.

Eggplant and Egg Sandwich with Olive Hummus

sabich

This is my take on a fairly new item at some falafel stands in Israel—a savory sandwich of fried eggplant, hard-boiled eggs, and hummus. I first enjoyed it at Oved's Place in Givatayim, a tiny, wildly popular hole-in-the-wall that specializes in this tasty sandwich and adds Middle Eastern diced salad and hot sauce. The sandwich is based on a traditional breakfast and brunch favorite of Iraq that combines the eggplant with slow-cooked brown eggs and boiled potatoes. The bread is spread with hummus, tahini, or both, and the sandwich is enlivened with spicy pickles or hot mango chutney, which you can find at Indian markets. You can layer the ingredients in a fresh roll, wrap them in a large, thin flatbread, or tuck them in a fresh pita.

Black olive hummus is popping up in natural foods markets and is a tasty creation. It's easy to make your own by stirring diced olives into hummus. Use flavorful Mediterranean olives such as kalamata. For an even quicker version, stir in a little olive paste, which you'll find at Greek and Middle Eastern markets, or French tapenade, which has capers and anchovies added to the olives and can be found at many supermarkets. Use any pickles you like, as long as they are not sweet. The sandwich is best when the vegetables are warm.

♦ MAKES ABOUT 4 SERVINGS.

1 small eggplant (about ½ pound), cut in slices ¼ inch thick

About 2 or 3 teaspoons olive oil, or a little oil spray

Salt and freshly ground black pepper

2 tablespoons diced pitted black olives

½ cup Classic Hummus (page 34) or packaged hummus

4 long crusty French or sourdough rolls

3 or 4 Slow-cooked Brown Eggs (page 118) or hard-boiled eggs, sliced

2 small warm boiled potatoes, sliced (optional)

1 to 2 tablespoons chopped cilantro

4 to 8 slices spicy pickles or hot mango chutney

Arrange eggplant on a foil-lined baking sheet or broiler pan. Brush or spray lightly with oil and sprinkle with salt and pepper. Broil about 8 minutes. Turn over and broil about 7 minutes, or until tender. Cover and keep warm.

Stir olives into hummus. Taste and adjust seasoning. Split rolls lengthwise and spread olive hummus on each half. On bottom half, layer slices of broiled eggplant, egg, and, if you like, potato, sprinkling each with salt and pepper. Sprinkle top layer with chopped cilantro. Add pickle slices and cover with top half of roll.

Avocado Vegetable Wrap with Feta

avocado viyrakot b'laffa

Sandwiches of grilled meats or vegetables rolled up in flatbread are a staple at Middle Eastern restaurants and lunch counters. I love to combine my grilled vegetables with a delicate avocado spread and a tangy sheep's-milk feta or with slices of *ackawi, halloumi,* Syrian white cheese, or mild string cheese with nigella seeds. If you wish, add a few good-quality olives. For a completely non-traditional variation, I sometimes make this sandwich with thin slices of lox instead of cheese; it tastes very good with avocado.

I especially like whole-wheat lavash for this sandwich. Keep the lavash wrapped until ready to use it, so it won't dry out. You can also make this sandwich with plain or flavored flour tortillas. Serve extra hot relish at the table.

♦ MAKES 4 SERVINGS.

2 onions, peeled and cut in rounds ¼ to ⅜ inch thick

About 2 tablespoons extra-virgin olive oil

1 red and 1 green pepper, halved, cored, seeded, and quartered lengthwise

1 tablespoon fresh-squeezed lemon juice, or to taste

2 ripe avocados, preferably Hass

Salt and freshly ground black pepper

2 teaspoons Hedva's Hot Pepper Relish (page 307), or ½ teaspoon hot pepper sauce, or to taste

4 pieces soft, fresh lavash, 8 or 9 inches square

1 cup shredded lettuce, preferably green-leaf or romaine (optional)

4 plum tomatoes, sliced thin

½ to 1 cup crumbled feta cheese, plain or herb flavored

Preheat broiler with rack about 4 inches from heat, or heat stove-top grill on medium-high heat. Brush onion slices with oil. Broil or grill them about 5 minutes per side, or until done to your taste. Remove onions. Add peppers, skin side facing heat source, and grill about 5 minutes, or until lightly charred but still crunchy. Leave peel on. If you prefer to peel peppers, first put them in a bag, close bag, and let them stand for 5 to 10 minutes, them remove peel. Cut each pepper piece in half lengthwise.

Combine onion and pepper pieces with I tablespoon olive oil and I teaspoon lemon juice and toss lightly.

Halve avocado and remove pit by hitting it with the heel of a chef's knife, using just enough force so that knife sticks in pit. Remove avocado flesh and mash with a fork. Add 2 teaspoons lemon juice, salt, pepper, and hot pepper relish. Taste, adjust seasoning, and add more lemon juice if you like.

To make each sandwich, spread ¼ of avocado spread along one edge of each lavash, leaving a ½-inch border at the ends. Top with lettuce, tomato slices, and grilled onions and peppers. Scatter feta cheese over vegetables. Roll up tightly and serve.

Broiled Vegetable Sandwich with Tomato Basil Tahini

sandvich yirakot kluyim im t'hina

A tasty sandwich of grilled vegetables with parsley tahini sauce at one of my favorite falafel places, Pita Pockets in Northridge, California, gave me the idea for this recipe. The Palestinian owners wrap the filling in their just-baked lavash but it's also good in pita or on baguette or French rolls.

I like to accent the vegetables with Mediterranean olives, capers, or both. If you're not using them, season the grilled vegetables generously so they won't be bland. For extra zip, substitute a broiled peeled poblano chili for the bell pepper (see "Basics," page 370).

Broiling is a convenient way to cook the vegetables. You can use a stove-top grill or barbecue instead, or use grilled vegetables from a previous meal or from a deli. You can spread the pita with *labneh* instead of tahini or, for a light, low-fat sandwich, substitute Classic Cucumber Salad with Yogurt, Garlic, and Mint (page 68). Serve the sandwich with lemon wedges, pickles, and hot sauce.

◆ MAKES 4 SERVINGS.

1 small eggplant (about ½ pound) sliced
⅜ inch thick

1 to 2 tablespoons olive oil, or a little oil
spray

Salt and freshly ground black pepper

1 zucchini, sliced lengthwise about
⅜ inch thick

1 large onion, peeled and cut in rounds
¼ to ⅜ inch thick

1 red or green bell pepper, halved,
cored, seeded, and quartered
lengthwise

4 fresh pita breads or crusty French rolls

About ½ cup Tomato Basil Tahini
(page 34), or more to taste

4 teaspoons capers, drained
(optional)

12 Mediterranean olives, black or green,
pitted and halved (optional)

Preheat broiler. Arrange eggplant in a single layer on foil-lined baking sheet or broiler pan. Brush or spray lightly with oil and sprinkle with salt and pepper. Broil about 8 minutes. Turn over and broil about 7 minutes, or until tender. Transfer to plate. Lightly oil baking sheet and add zucchini slices. Brush or spray them lightly with oil, sprinkle with salt and pepper, and broil them 3 or 4 minutes per side, or until crisp-tender. Transfer to plate.

Brush onion slices with oil and add to pan. Broil about 5 minutes per side, or until done to your taste. Remove onions with slotted spoon. Add pepper pieces, skin side facing heat source, and broil about 5 minutes, or until lightly charred but still crunchy.

Cut a small piece off one end of each pita bread to form a pocket you can fill, or cut each pita bread in half. Cut vegetables in pieces that fit conveniently in the pita and sprinkle them lightly with salt and pepper. Fill pita with slices of broiled vegetables, spoon a little tahini sauce into each one, and add capers and olives. Serve more of the sauce separately.

Halloumi Cheese Sandwich with Capers and Parsley

sandvich halloumi im tzlafim

Halloumi is a springy, semifirm cheese that turns golden when panfried. (For more on *halloumi*, see page 18.) You can also broil the cheese directly on a slice of bread or an opened-up pita. Hot or cold, the cheese is also a favorite in salads.

For this open sandwich, serve the arugula salad on the bread or spoon it separately onto the plate. You can substitute other sliceable cheeses like Mexican *panela* or a mild feta cheese that's not too crumbly. Flour these cheeses first and sauté them very briefly.

◆ MAKES 4 SERVINGS.

  3 to 4 tablespoons extra-virgin olive oil
  1 tablespoon fresh-squeezed lemon juice
  Small pinch salt and freshly ground black
    pepper to taste

  1 cup coarsely chopped arugula
  4 slices country French or Italian bread,
    or 2 pita breads
  8 slices *halloumi* cheese, about ¼ inch thick
  2 plum tomatoes, sliced thin
  1 to 2 tablespoons finely chopped Italian
    parsley
  2 teaspoons capers, drained
  Lemon wedges

Whisk 2 tablespoons oil with lemon juice, salt, and pepper in small bowl. Toss with arugula. If using pita breads, halve them, then split each half carefully so it lies flat.

Heat 2 teaspoons oil in skillet. Add cheese slices and sauté over medium-low heat about 2 minutes, or until light golden. Turn carefully and brown second side.

Top bread with arugula salad, then with tomato slices. Set warm cheese slices on top. Sprinkle with parsley, capers, and a little more oil. Serve with lemon wedges, for squeezing on the cheese.

Thick Yogurt and Yogurt Cheese

labneh

Labneh is a luscious, creamy form of yogurt or soft yogurt cheese served at breakfast or supper or as an appetizer. Instead of buying it, many people make it at home, simply by draining yogurt. The longer you drain it, the thicker it becomes. After a couple of hours, use it as thick yogurt, for enriching soups or for mixing with herbs, spices, or vegetables to make salads, dips, and sauces. If you let it drain overnight or longer, it becomes yogurt cheese, which you can spread on bread for sandwiches, the way you might use cream cheese. Or use it to make Yogurt Cheese Balls in Herb Oil (page 52).

The traditional way to drain yogurt is to wrap it in two or three layers of cheesecloth or muslin and hang it from the faucet, so the whey drips into the sink. You can also drain it in a strainer lined with cheesecloth or with a coffee filter or in a plastic yogurt funnel. If your kitchen is warm, let the yogurt drain in the refrigerator, although it will thicken faster at room temperature.

The result depends on the yogurt you use. You can use whole milk, low-fat, or nonfat yogurt and obviously your choice will affect the richness of the final *labneh*. For best results, use yogurt without gelatin or starch, and, if possible, without pectin. Yogurt containing these thickeners will drain only

slightly. They can be used for making thick yogurt or very soft yogurt cheese to serve as an appetizer with a garnish of mint and olives as below, but not to make cheese balls.

Other popular accompaniments for yogurt cheese are tomato wedges, cucumber sticks, radishes, green onions, zahtar for sprinkling (page 13), and toasted peanuts, pistachios, and pine nuts.

- ◆ MAKES ABOUT 2½ TO 3 CUPS THICK YOGURT OR 1½ TO 2 CUPS YOGURT CHEESE, OR 4 TO 6 BREAKFAST OR APPETIZER SERVINGS.

4 cups plain yogurt
Salt to taste

FOR SERVING FOR BREAKFAST OR AS AN APPETIZER

4 to 6 teaspoons extra-virgin olive oil, or to taste
12 to 18 fresh mint leaves
Good-quality olives
Fresh pita bread

Pour off any liquid from the top of the yogurt. Mix yogurt with a small pinch of salt. Line strainer with large coffee filter or two layers of cheesecloth. Set strainer over bowl so it doesn't touch bottom of bowl. Spoon yogurt into lined strainer. Cover with a paper towel and refrigerate.

Thick Yogurt

Check yogurt after 2 hours. If it is about as thick as sour cream, it's ready. Depending on the type of yogurt, it might take up to overnight. After you've made it a few times, you'll get to know how long the yogurt you use takes to thicken.

Yogurt Cheese

Drain yogurt until it is nearly as thick as soft cream cheese. This can take 12 to 24 hours. To get it thick enough to make Yogurt Cheese Balls in Herb Oil (page 52), it may take even longer. Transfer to bowl or container.

To serve yogurt cheese on its own, taste and add a little more salt if needed. Spread yogurt in a thick layer on small plates and make a depression in center with back of spoon. Pour a little olive oil into depression. Garnish edge of cheese with a few fresh mint leaves. Serve with olives and fresh pita.

Seafood, Favorites from Fresh and Salt Waters

Baked Fish in Chili Cilantro Sauce • *Kouzbariate Samak*

Sea Bass with Peppers in Saffron Onion Sauce • *Yakhnet Samak*

Jalapeño Sea Bass with Tomatoes, Potatoes, and Garlic • *Tagane Samak Belbatatesse*

Halibut Steaks with Tomatoes, Ginger, and Cumin • *Samak bil Bandoura*

Cumin Marinated Fish with Tomato Onion Sauce and Yogurt Mint Dressing •
Kamouniate Samak

Foil-baked Trout with Red Pepper and Garlic • *Samak bel Kari*

Savory Sole with Creamy Walnut Lemon Sauce • *Samak Ma'at Taratur*

Persian New Year Fish • *Sabzi Polo va Mahi*

Roasted Salmon with Garlic, Lemon, and Coriander • *Samke bil Fourn*

Sharm al-Sheikh Sesame Salmon • *Samke bil Fourn bi T'Hineh*

Salmon and Bulgur Salad with Green Peas, Cucumbers, and Toasted Nuts •
Salat Salmon im Burgul

Grilled Fish in Tomato Curry Sauce • *Samak Misguf*

Fish Baked with Cumin Rice • *Sayadiyeh*

Saffron Shrimp and Pine Nut Pilaf • *Karidesli Pilav*

Herbed Seafood Patties with Green Sauce and Capers • *Kibbet Samak*

Shrimp Balls in Spicy Tamarind Tomato Sauce • *Chebeh Rubyan*

Crab and Couscous Salad with Asparagus, Mint, and Pine Nuts •
Salatet Kaboreyah ma Couscous

Since long before the time of the seafaring Phoenicians, the peoples of the Mideast have profited from the Mediterranean and its fruits. Those living near seacoasts, lakes, and rivers, such as the banks of the Nile and the shores of the Red Sea, the Arabian Sea, the Caspian Sea, the Black Sea, and the Sea of Galilee, enthusiastically feast on fish. In seaside cities like Istanbul and Jaffa, diners flock to neighborhoods known for their seafood restaurants.

Until transportation improved in recent years, the inhabitants of regions removed from the sea simply did not eat seafood. In many parts of the Mideast a distinct difference remains between coastal and inland tastes.

On the whole, seafood in the Mideast is cooked simply, as it is in the Mediterranean region. Many people prefer whole fish, feeling that it is most moist and flavorful when cooked with its bones. Large whole fish are usually roasted or grilled, while small or medium ones are fried. Favorite techniques for cooking fillets are grilling them as kabobs or frying them. Fish steaks are frequently braised.

The seasoning secrets of the Middle East can easily brighten our own fish and shellfish menus. Wonderful marinades redolent of garlic, lemon, and cilantro enliven grilled skewered seafood, while spice and pepper perk up crunchy fried fish and simple sautés. When sauce is used, it tends to be quick and easy to prepare, as in Baked Fish in Chili Cilantro Sauce. A much-loved entrée in many areas is Fish Baked with Cumin Rice, which features a tasty sauce of sautéed onions, parsley, and pine nuts.

Coastal cooks have also created a repertoire of fish adaptations of popular meat dishes. Some seafood lovers used their time-honored meatball recipes to make shrimp balls. Others take the idea of *kofta*, or Turkish meat patties, to make fish or shellfish cakes, such as Herbed Seafood Patties with Green Sauce and Capers (page 145).

Baked Fish in Chili Cilantro Sauce

kouzbariate samak

Like the Moroccans, cooks in Egypt make tagines, or savory casseroles of meat or fish. This one is redolent of the fresh flavor of cilantro leaves as well as its seed, coriander. If you like, use fresh dill instead of or in addition to the cilantro, as many Egyptians do. Serve the fish with Rice Pilaf (page 263) or flatbread.

♦ MAKES 4 SERVINGS.

1½ pounds cod, halibut, or other firm lean
    fish, about 1 inch thick, cut in 4 pieces,
    rinsed, and patted dry
1 tablespoon fresh-squeezed lemon juice
3 tablespoons chopped cilantro
3 tablespoons olive oil or vegetable oil,
    or 1 tablespoon oil and
    2 tablespoons butter
Salt and freshly ground pepper to taste
1 medium onion, chopped
1 mild green chili, such as Anaheim,
    or ½ green bell pepper, halved, cored,
    seeded, and diced
2 jalapeño peppers, seeded if desired,
    minced, or ¼ teaspoon hot red
    pepper flakes, or to taste
2 large garlic cloves, minced
1 teaspoon ground coriander
½ teaspoon ground cumin
2 fresh ripe or canned plum tomatoes,
    pureed in a food processor
2 tablespoons tomato paste
⅓ cup water
Cilantro sprigs, for garnish

Put fish steaks in tray in a single layer. Mix lemon juice with 1 tablespoon cilantro, 1 tablespoon oil, and a pinch of salt and pepper. Pour over fish and turn to coat both sides. Let stand while preparing sauce.

Preheat oven to 400°F. Heat remaining oil or butter in skillet. Add onion and cook over medium-low heat about 5 minutes, or until soft but not brown. Add mild chili, jalapeño peppers, and garlic and cook for 1 minute. Stir in ground coriander, cumin, pureed tomatoes, and tomato paste and cook for 2 minutes. Stir in water and bring to a simmer. Add remaining cilantro. Taste and adjust seasoning.

Lightly oil a baking dish large enough to hold fish in a single layer. Spoon about one-third of sauce into dish. Top with fish and sprinkle lightly with salt and pepper. Top with remaining sauce. Cover and bake for 18 to 20 minutes, or until fish can just be flaked with a fork in its thickest part. Serve garnished with cilantro sprigs.

Sea Bass with Peppers in Saffron Onion Sauce

yakhnet samak

You can use any type of fish fillets or steaks in this colorful, Lebanese-inspired dish. Other tasty choices in addition to sea bass are halibut, cod, and scrod. Serve this festive entrée with Rice Pilaf with Toasted Almonds (page 263).

◆ MAKES 4 SERVINGS.

¼ teaspoon saffron threads

4 or 5 tablespoons extra-virgin olive oil

2 large onions, halved and sliced thin

1 large red bell pepper, halved, cored, seeded, and cut in thin strips

5 large garlic cloves, chopped

2 to 4 tablespoons fresh-squeezed lemon juice

Salt and freshly ground black pepper

Cayenne pepper to taste

2 pounds sea bass steaks or fillets, about ½ to ¾ inch thick, cut into 8 pieces, rinsed, and patted dry

1 tablespoon chopped parsley (optional)

SEAFOOD PILAFS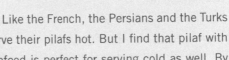

I first learned to prepare seafood and rice pilafs in Paris. In France many chefs consider the Persians the princes of pilaf and the originators of the specialty, while others bow to the Turks as the pashas of pilaf because of the lavish renditions they perfected during the Ottoman Empire.

Both these cuisines have developed wonderful entrées of rice paired with fruits of the sea. Persians layer sautéed fish or shellfish with cilantro or curry-spiced rice. Turkish anchovy rice, made with fresh anchovies, is seasoned with dill, allspice, and a hint of cinnamon and studded with hazelnuts and raisins. Cooks in Turkey also stuff mussels with a similar pilaf, sans anchovies, and enjoy shrimp in saffron pilaf with tomatoes (page 144).

Like the French, the Persians and the Turks serve their pilafs hot. But I find that pilaf with seafood is perfect for serving cold as well. By using olive oil or vegetable oil rather than butter to sauté the rice and vegetables, I have an entrée that is good at any temperature. Unlike butter, oil doesn't stiffen the pilaf much when it cools.

When I want to save time, I opt for quick-cooking, easy-to-prepare seafood like shrimp, mussels, or fish fillets or, for luxurious meals, cooked lobster or crab. I add vegetables to turn my pilaf into a one-pot meal or I accompany it with a green salad. It makes a delicious, easy, and convenient entrée. For a festive final touch in the Turkish fashion, I garnish my pilaf with toasted nuts.

Preheat oven to 400°F. Pour ½ cup hot water over saffron threads in bowl and let stand while sautéing vegetables. Heat 2 or 3 tablespoons olive oil in large ovenproof skillet. Add onions and cook over medium heat for 10 minutes, or until golden, then remove from pan. Add 1 tablespoon oil to skillet and heat it. Add pepper strips and sauté for 7 minutes, or until softened. Add garlic and cook ½ minute.

Return onions to skillet. Add saffron liquid, 2 tablespoons lemon juice, salt, pepper, and cayenne and bring to a simmer. Remove from heat.

If skillet isn't large enough for fish to form a single layer, divide sauce among two skillets. Set fish on sauce mixture and baste it with some of the liquid. Sprinkle fish with remaining tablespoon oil, then with salt, pepper, and cayenne. Cover with foil and bake for 15 minutes, or until fish can just be flaked but is not falling apart. Taste sauce, adjust seasoning, and add more lemon juice if you like. Serve fish and sauce sprinkled with parsley.

Jalapeño Sea Bass with Tomatoes, Potatoes, and Garlic

tagane samak belbatatesse

Give gusto to your fish dishes with a flavorful seasoning paste of garlic, hot pepper, and olive oil, as in this casserole, which is perfect for easy entertaining. Entrées of fish layered with potatoes, onions, and tomatoes are popular along the southern and eastern Mediterranean shores. Garlic and olive oil are the favorite aromatic accents, and other flavorings vary. Cypriots like a gentle tomato sauce cooked with carrot, bay leaves, and oregano, while cooks in Egypt spike their casseroles with hot pepper and a pinch of cinnamon.

You can get this one-pot dish on the table fastest if you have cooked potatoes on hand. If you haven't cooked potatoes ahead, you can microwave them to save time. The seasoning paste is easiest to make in a small food processor.

◆ MAKES 4 OR 5 SERVINGS.

4 large garlic cloves, peeled

¼ cup Italian parsley sprigs, plus 1 tablespoon chopped parsley for sprinkling

1 or 2 jalapeño peppers, seeded if desired, cut in pieces, or ½ teaspoon crushed red pepper (hot pepper flakes)

3 to 4 tablespoons extra-virgin olive oil

1 pound boiling potatoes, cooked (see Note), sliced about ½ inch thick

Salt and freshly ground black pepper

2 red, green, or yellow bell peppers, halved, cored, seeded, and cut in thin strips

1½ pounds ripe tomatoes, sliced ¼ inch thick

2 pounds fish steaks or fillets, such as halibut, cod, or sea bass, 1 inch thick, rinsed and patted dry

Pinch cinnamon (optional)

½ onion, cut in thin slices

Preheat oven to 375°F. Combine garlic, parsley sprigs, and jalapeño peppers in food processor. Process to chop. Add I tablespoon oil and process until blended to a paste.

Oil a shallow 2-quart casserole and arrange the potato slices inside in a single layer. Sprinkle with salt and pepper. Top with bell pepper strips, then with half the tomato slices in one layer. Sprinkle lightly with salt and pepper. Top with fish in a single layer and spread spice paste evenly over it. Sprinkle fish with salt, pepper, and, if you like, cinnamon. Top fish with onion slices, then with remaining tomatoes. Pour remaining oil evenly over top.

Cover and bake for 25 minutes, or until fish can just be flaked with a fork but is not falling apart. Sprinkle with parsley and serve from the casserole.

NOTE To cook potatoes: For fastest cooking, choose small potatoes, either white- or red-skinned or Yukon Gold potatoes. Scrub potatoes and peel if you like. If using medium or large ones, halve or quarter them.

On the stove top: Put the prepared potatoes in a saucepan, cover with water by about ½ inch, and add salt. Bring to a boil. Cover and simmer over medium-low heat about 20 minutes, or until a knife can pierce center of largest piece easily.

In the microwave: Put the prepared potatoes in a microwavable container just large enough to hold them in one layer. Add 3 tablespoons water. Cover and microwave on high for 7 minutes, or until tender.

Halibut Steaks with Tomatoes, Ginger, and Cumin

samak bil bandoura

The ginger in this sauce points to its origin in the easternmost part of the Middle East. Cooks along the Persian Gulf coasts of the Arabian Peninsula use it in all sorts of dishes, combining it with fresh hot peppers and currylike spice blends. Together with cumin and cilantro, the fresh gingerroot lends a lively flavor to this savory tomato sauce, which is a good match for any fish. Rice pilaf and steamed rice are my favorite partners for the fish.

If you don't mind the texture of tomato skins, you can skip the step of peeling them, as do many Mideastern home cooks.

◆ MAKES 4 SERVINGS.

2 to 3 tablespoons vegetable oil

1 medium onion, chopped

1 tablespoon minced peeled gingerroot

5 medium garlic cloves, minced

1 or 2 jalapeño peppers, seeded if desired, minced

2 teaspoons ground coriander

2 teaspoons ground cumin

½ teaspoon turmeric

⅛ teaspoon cayenne

2 teaspoons tomato paste

1 pound ripe tomatoes, peeled, seeded, and coarsely chopped, or one 28-ounce can plum tomatoes, drained and chopped

1½ pounds halibut or salmon steaks, about 1 inch thick, rinsed and patted dry

Salt and freshly ground black pepper to taste

¼ cup chopped cilantro

Heat oil in large sauté pan. Add onion and gingerroot and cook over low heat for 7 minutes, or until onion is soft but not brown. Add garlic, jalapeño peppers, ground coriander, cumin, turmeric, and cayenne, and cook, stirring, 1 minute. Stir in tomato paste, then tomatoes, and bring to a boil. Cover and simmer for 10 minutes.

Sprinkle fish lightly on both sides with salt and pepper. Add fish to sauce, cover, and cook over low heat 7 minutes. Turn over and cook 3 to 5 more minutes, or until it can just be flaked. Stir in half the cilantro. Serve fish sprinkled with remaining cilantro.

Cumin Marinated Fish with Tomato Sauce and Yogurt Mint Dressing

kamouniate samak

Egyptians are fond of fish dishes flavored abundantly with garlic, cumin, and fresh-squeezed lemon juice, in both marinades and sauces. A festive way to present this fish is with two sauces: Serve the fish in the tomato sauce, with the yogurt mint dressing on the side, for spooning over each portion. To echo the dressing's flavor, I put mint in the tomato sauce too.

◆ MAKES 4 SERVINGS.

1½ pounds halibut, cod, or other lean fish steaks, about 1 inch thick, rinsed and patted dry

2 tablespoons fresh-squeezed lemon juice

3 tablespoons olive oil

2 garlic cloves, minced

1 teaspoon ground cumin

Salt and freshly ground black pepper

Pinch cayenne pepper (optional)

FRESH MINT YOGURT DRESSING (OPTIONAL):

½ cup plain yogurt

1½ teaspoons chopped fresh mint

½ small garlic clove, finely minced

TOMATO MINT SAUCE:

1 tablespoon olive oil

2 large garlic cloves, minced

1 teaspoon ground cumin

1½ pounds ripe tomatoes, peeled, seeded, and chopped, or one 28-ounce can tomatoes, drained and chopped

Salt and freshly ground black pepper

1 tablespoon tomato paste

1 to 2 tablespoons chopped fresh mint

Mint sprigs, for garnish

Put fish steaks in tray in single layer. For marinade, mix lemon juice with oil, garlic, cumin, salt, pepper, and, if you like, cayenne. Pour over fish and turn to coat both sides. Cover and marinate in refrigerator 30 to 60 minutes, turning steaks occasionally.

To make Fresh Mint Yogurt Dressing, if you like: Mix yogurt with mint and garlic. Season to taste with salt and pepper. Bring to room temperature for serving.

To make Tomato Mint Sauce: Heat oil in large deep skillet. Add garlic and sauté over medium heat, stirring, for about ½ minute. Add cumin, tomatoes, salt, and pepper. Cook, uncovered, over medium heat until juice begins to come out of tomatoes. Raise heat to medium-high and cook about 5 minutes, or until tomatoes are soft and sauce is thick, stirring often. Add tomato paste.

Add fish steaks to sauce with their marinade and a pinch of salt. Reduce heat to low, cover, and simmer for 10 minutes, or until fish can just be flaked with a fork, basting fish occasionally. Stir in mint. Taste and adjust seasoning.

Serve fish hot, cold, or at room temperature in its tomato sauce, garnished with fresh mint sprigs. Serve yogurt dressing on the side.

Foil-baked Trout with Red Pepper and Garlic

samak bel kari

Hot peppers, garlic, and a hint of curry wake up the trout in this recipe, flavored in the style of the Persian Gulf States. I like to add red bell peppers for their color and sweetness. Baking the fish in foil packets keeps in the juices and aroma and is easy—there's no baking dish to clean afterward.

Use pink-fleshed trout or other small whole fish. Choose fresh trout with bright eyes, shiny skin, glistening firm flesh, and a clean aroma. Some people find fish more flavorful when it cooks with its bones, but for easy eating buy butterflied trout. Store the trout in the coldest part of the refrigerator and try to use them within a day or two.

◆ MAKES 4 SERVINGS.

3 tablespoons vegetable oil or olive oil

½ teaspoon curry powder

4 large garlic cloves, minced

Pinch cayenne pepper

4 trout, butterflied, rinsed, and patted dry

Salt and freshly ground black pepper

2 jalapeño peppers, halved, seeded, and very thinly sliced

1 red bell pepper, halved, cored, seeded, and cut in thin strips

2 plum tomatoes, diced

About ½ lemon (for seasoning) and additional lemon wedges

Mix oil with curry powder in small bowl. Let stand at room temperature for 15 minutes, stirring occasionally. Add garlic and cayenne and mix well.

If trout still has fins, snip them with sturdy scissors and trim tails straight. Rinse fish inside and out, removing any scales by scraping lightly with the back of a knife, and pat dry.

Put trout on large tray. Sprinkle trout inside and out with salt and pepper. Put trout skin side down. Spoon about half the garlic-curry mixture over the trout, dividing it equally among them. Fold each trout in half, reforming it. Set each trout on a piece of foil large enough to wrap it. Spoon remaining garlic mixture over trout and rub it in lightly. Sprinkle each trout with one-fourth of the jalapeño slices, bell pepper strips, tomato dice, and a squeeze of lemon juice. Wrap each trout tightly in foil. Set wrapped trout in a roasting pan.

Preheat oven to 400°F. Bake trout for about 20 minutes, or until a cake tester or thin skewer inserted into thickest part of fish comes out hot to touch. Serve the trout in their foil cases, with lemon wedges, on large plates. At the table cut open each package with scissors and pull it out from under the fish.

Savory Sole with Creamy Walnut Lemon Sauce

samak ma'at taratur

The luscious walnut sauce in this recipe is typical of nut sauces popular with fish in several coastal regions of the Mideast. It somewhat reminds me of a traditional walnut sauce I enjoyed in southern France, but is more lemony and more spicy, with cayenne, black pepper, and a hint of cinnamon. Grinding the walnuts gives the sauce a creamy texture without the need for any cream. Be sure the nuts are very fresh.

In the Mideast, nut sauces like this one are also made from hazelnuts, pine nuts, or a mixture of nuts. Occasionally they are enhanced with a touch of olive oil or tahini. Most people serve the sauce separately, but some thin the sauce with a little water and pour it over the fish before baking.

In this recipe the fish gains zip from a stuffing of garlic and cilantro, which also flavors the sauce. Generally such a stuffing is used for whole fish but it's also delicious with fillets. I spread the stuffing on sole or flounder fillets and fold them in half before baking. You can substitute any thin, white fish fillets that are fresh at your market. Serve the fish hot or at room temperature. If you like, make the sauce ahead and refrigerate it, but bring it to room temperature before serving.

◆ MAKES 4 SERVINGS.

4 large garlic cloves, peeled

½ cup cilantro sprigs

1¼ to 1½ pounds sole or flounder fillets

Salt and freshly ground black pepper

½ cup fish stock, vegetable broth,
   or water seasoned with salt

⅔ cup walnuts

⅓ cup cold water, or more if needed

2 to 3 tablespoons strained fresh-squeezed
   lemon juice, or more to taste

⅛ teaspoon ground cinnamon (optional)

A few pinches Aleppo pepper or cayenne
   to taste

Lemon wedges

Preheat oven to 400°F. Chop garlic in food processor. Add cilantro sprigs and chop together until fine. Remove mixture, reserving half to spread on fish and rest to flavor sauce.

Run your fingers over sole fillets and carefully pull out any bones with your fingers or with the aid of tweezers, a pastry crimper, or a sharp paring knife. Sprinkle sole on both sides with salt and pepper. Spread garlic mixture over fillets and fold each fillet in half.

Oil large baking dish and set folded fillets inside. Pour stock around, not over, fish. Bake for 12 minutes, or until fish is opaque inside; check with point of small knife.

While the fish bakes, prepare the sauce: In food processor, combine walnuts and ⅓ cup water and grind to a smooth paste. Add reserved garlic-cilantro mixture, salt, pepper, and 2 tablespoons lemon juice and

process to a thick sauce. If sauce is too thick, gradually add a little more water. Transfer sauce to bowl. Add cinnamon, if desired, and Aleppo pepper to taste. Taste, adjust seasoning, and more lemon juice if you like.

With slotted spatula, transfer fish to a platter. Serve it with a little sauce spooned on top; or serve sauce separately. Accompany with lemon wedges.

Persian New Year Fish

---

sabzi polo va mahi

The Persians celebrate the New Year at the spring equinox, and the holiday customs honor this season. Traditionally, fruits, sprouts, garlic, sumac, and other items are displayed in homes. Fish plays an important symbolic role, representing life and the end of the astral year, which is associated with the constellation Pisces. Each person sets out a bowl of goldfish as part of the festivities, and fish is always on the menu.

For the holiday, fish is often cooked whole and served with Persian springtime rice, which is studded with fresh green fava beans and flavored with dill. This recipe is a simplified interpretation of this specialty. I use salmon, as it's beautiful with the rice and easy to get whole. You can cook any whole fish following the method below. If you'd rather roast the fish indoors instead of bar-becuing it, put the fish in an oiled roasting pan and bake it at 450°F the same way. If fava beans are not available or if you want a quicker dish, substitute frozen lima beans or green soy beans (edamame).

◆ MAKES ABOUT 6 SERVINGS.

One 4-pound whole salmon, fins and tails trimmed

Salt and freshly ground black pepper

6 fresh tarragon sprigs

6 fresh thyme sprigs

4 limes

2 pounds fresh fava beans, shelled, or 10 to 12 ounces frozen fava or lima beans

¼ teaspoon saffron (optional)

1½ cups basmati rice, rinsed well

2 tablespoons vegetable oil, butter, or ghee

1 medium onion, minced

⅓ cup chopped fresh dill

Clean barbecue well and preheat it. If it has a thermometer, heat it to 450°F.

Rinse fish inside and out, removing any scales by scraping lightly with the back of a knife, and pat it dry. Put it on large tray. Sprinkle fish inside and out with salt and pepper. Put tarragon and thyme sprigs in the cavity of the fish. Slice 1 lime and put the slices inside the fish. Measure thickest point of fish in inches and calculate the grilling time of 9 or 10 minutes per inch. If the fish is 2½ inches thick, it will take

about 22 to 25 minutes. Set fish aside while preparing beans and rice.

Put fresh or frozen beans in medium saucepan of boiling salted water and cook, uncovered, over high heat for 3 to 5 minutes, or until just tender. Drain the beans, rinse with cold water, and drain well. If using fresh or unpeeled frozen fava beans, peel off and discard the tough outer skins.

Soak saffron, if using, in 2 tablespoons warm water in small bowl for about 15 minutes.

Bring 6 cups water to a boil in large heavy saucepan. Add rice and cook it over high heat for 12 minutes, or until rice is nearly tender. Drain, rinse with lukewarm water, and drain well.

Lightly oil barbecue. Put fish on barbecue on its side. Grill for about half the calculated time.

Meanwhile, finish rice: Heat oil in saucepan used to cook rice. Add onion and cook over medium-low heat for 7 minutes, or until soft but not brown. Add beans, salt, and pepper, and toss 1 or 2 minutes over heat. Add rice and toss very gently. Add saffron in its liquid. Cover tightly and cook over low heat, without stirring, for 7 minutes, or until rice is tender. Add dill and salt and pepper to taste. Let stand, covered, until ready to serve.

Turn fish over and grill for the remaining time. Check if fish is done by inserting a skewer into its thickest part (the skewer should come out hot) or cut into the thickest part of the fish and check its color, which should be lighter pink. Remove thyme and tarragon sprigs and lime slices. Halve or quarter the remaining limes.

To serve fish, slit skin along backbone. Use a broad spatula to remove portions of fish, putting spatula under a piece of fillet and lifting the piece off the bones. Fluff rice gently with a fork and mound it on a platter. Serve fish with the limes and rice.

Roasted Salmon with Garlic, Lemon, and Coriander

samke bil fourn

This light and easy entrée is typical of the Mideast way of treating fish. Just a few seasonings, along with olive oil, salt, and pepper, are needed to highlight its delicate flavor. In addition to the garlic, coriander, and lemon juice in this recipe, people often sprinkle the fish with cumin, paprika, hot red pepper, zahtar sesame-herb blend, thyme, or oregano. For more flavor, marinate the fish with the seasonings for 15 minutes before you roast it. It's a good idea to roast extra fish for eating cold or for turning into a colorful salad, such as Salmon and Bulgur Salad with Green Peas, Cucumbers, and Toasted Nuts (page 141).

You need only a little oil to keep the salmon moist. A fruity extra-virgin olive oil is best. If you want to substitute a leaner fish like halibut or cod, increase the amount of oil to 3 tablespoons. If you buy the tail half of the salmon fillet, there will be almost no bones, but the head half is thicker and more meaty.

A fresh fish tastes so delicious when roasted that a sauce is not necessary. If you'd like one, serve Fresh Tomato Sauce (page 305), Lemon Egg Sauce (page 306), Green Tahini (page 34), or Tomato Basil Tahini (page 34). Rice pilaf is a standard accompaniment, as is a colorful salad of diced vegetables.

♦ MAKES 4 SERVINGS.

2 tablespoons strained fresh-squeezed lemon juice

2 tablespoons extra-virgin olive oil

1 or 2 garlic cloves, very finely minced

1½ teaspoons ground coriander

½ teaspoon ground cumin

½ teaspoon zahtar, oregano, or thyme (optional)

1¼ pounds salmon fillet, preferably tail section, about 1 inch thick

Salt and freshly ground black pepper

Italian parsley sprigs (optional)

Lemon wedges

Preheat oven to 450°F. Lightly oil heavy roasting pan or line pan with foil and lightly oil foil. Combine lemon juice, oil, garlic, coriander, cumin, and zahtar in bowl and mix well. Pour mixture over fish and lightly rub it into fish flesh. Let fish marinate for 15 to 20 minutes.

Set fish in roasting pan, skin side down, and sprinkle with salt and pepper. Roast fish in oven about 10 minutes; it should just flake and have changed color in thickest part. If you've lined the pan with foil, slide spatula just under meat so that skin stays stuck to foil, and lift meat out. If serving fish on platter, you might like to surround it with parsley sprigs. Serve fish with lemon wedges.

Sharm al-Sheikh Sesame Salmon

samke bil fourn bi t'hineh

When we took a trip to Sharm al-Sheikh at the tip of the Sinai Peninsula thirty years ago, it was a sleepy area known for its natural beauty. We brought our tent and caught our fish for dinner. Today visitors who come to this Egyptian resort to enjoy the beautiful beaches and the Red Sea's warm waters and coral reefs will find a variety of new luxury hotels and elegant restaurants. There are simple eateries as well, where fresh fish and shrimp are served with tahini sauce and diced salad.

Tahini is a favorite pairing with fish among Lebanese cooks as well. They serve tahini alongside charcoal-grilled whole fish,

use it to sauce cold baked fish instead of mayonnaise, or bake fish in it for a casserole resembling a gratin, as in this recipe.

For serving with fish, make the tahini with more lemon juice than usual. In this version the lemony sesame sauce is enhanced with sautéed onions. Popular accompaniments are cooked rice and tabbouleh salad.

◆ MAKES 4 SERVINGS.

1¼ pounds salmon fillet, preferably tail section, about 1 inch thick

Salt and freshly ground black pepper

½ cup tahini paste

2 large garlic cloves, minced (2 teaspoons)

4 or 5 tablespoons strained fresh-squeezed lemon juice, more if needed

3 or 4 tablespoons water, more if needed

2 tablespoons olive oil

2 large onions, halved and sliced thin

Lemon wedges

Italian parsley sprigs (optional)

Preheat oven to 400°F. Lightly oil a heavy roasting pan; or line it with foil and lightly oil the foil. Sprinkle salmon with salt and pepper.

Stir tahini to blend in its oil in medium bowl. Stir in garlic, 4 tablespoons lemon juice, 3 tablespoons water, and salt and pepper to taste.

Heat oil in sauté pan. Add onions and cook over medium heat about 10 minutes, or until golden, stirring often. Reduce heat to low. Stir in tahini sauce and heat for 1 to 2 minutes, stirring. Remove from heat. Taste for seasoning, and add more lemon juice for sharper flavor, or more water for milder one.

Set fish in roasting pan, skin side down. Sprinkle fish with salt and pepper. Bake for 10 minutes. Remove from oven. Reduce heat to 350°F.

Spread sesame sauce over fish. Bake for 10 minutes, or until fish just flakes and has changed color in its thickest part. If you've lined the pan with foil, slide spatula just under the meat so that the skin stays stuck to the foil. Serve fish with lemon wedges and, if you like, parsley sprigs.

Salmon and Bulgur Salad with Green Peas, Cucumbers, and Toasted Nuts

salat salmon im burgul

Flavored the eastern Mediterranean way with coriander, cumin, green onions, and dill, this salad makes a perfect summertime lunch or supper. I particularly like it with toasted pecans, but it's also delicious with the area's native nut—the pistachio—or with hazelnuts or walnuts.

If you have extra Roasted Salmon with Garlic, Lemon, and Coriander (page 139), it's ideal for this salad but salmon cooked any way is good. You can also substitute cooked shrimp, canned red salmon, or tuna

in olive oil. Bulgur is a good choice for summer because it cooks so quickly, but if you have cooked white or brown rice, barley, or orzo (barley- or rice-shaped pasta) on hand (about 3½ to 4 cups), use them instead.

◆ MAKES ABOUT 6 SERVINGS.

3 or 4 tablespoons extra-virgin olive oil or vegetable oil

1 onion, chopped

2 garlic cloves, minced

1¼ cups medium bulgur wheat

1½ teaspoons ground coriander

1 teaspoon ground cumin

2½ cups vegetable broth, water, or a mixture of both

Salt and freshly ground black pepper

1½ to 2 tablespoons white-wine vinegar or fresh-squeezed lemon juice

⅓ cup chopped green onions (white and green parts)

1 to 1½ cups fresh shelled or frozen peas, cooked

1 to 1½ cups diced cucumbers

3 to 4 cups cooked salmon (see Note), flaked gently in bite-size cubes

2 tablespoons chopped fresh dill

⅓ cup toasted pecans

Cayenne pepper to taste

Heat 2 tablespoons oil in heavy medium saucepan. Add onion and cook over medium heat for 5 minutes, or until softened, stirring often. Add garlic and cook for 1 minute. Add bulgur wheat, coriander, and cumin and sauté, stirring, for 2 minutes to lightly toast the bulgur and the spices. Add broth, salt, and pepper and bring to a boil. Cover and cook over low heat for 15 minutes, or until bulgur is tender and liquid is absorbed.

Fluff bulgur gently with a large fork. Transfer very gently to large bowl and let cool.

In small bowl, whisk remaining oil with vinegar and fold into salad. Add green onions, peas, cucumbers, salmon, 1 tablespoon dill, and half the pecans and fold them in gently. Adjust seasoning, adding cayenne to taste. Serve cold, topped with remaining dill and remaining pecans.

NOTE For a fast way to cook salmon, sprinkle 1½ to 1¾ pounds salmon fillet, about 1 inch thick, with salt, pepper, and olive oil. Set salmon in foil-lined roasting pan and bake it in a preheated 450°F oven for about 10 minutes, or until it just flakes.

Grilled Fish in Tomato Curry Sauce

samak misguf

Curry spices are popular among the Assyrians and Chaldeans living in North America, as part of their culinary heritage from the eastern part of the Mideast. Many came here from Iraq, where these spice blends are liked with fish. Fish might be seasoned with the spices before being grilled, or dipped in curry powder mixed with flour before being fried to give it a lovely golden color and great aroma. The spice mixture also seasons sauces like this one, which gains good flavor from liberal amounts of sautéed onions and plenty of tomato.

♦ MAKES 4 SERVINGS.

2 or 3 tablespoons vegetable oil or butter, plus 1 tablespoon oil for grilling fish

2 large onions, chopped

6 large garlic cloves, minced

1 tablespoon minced peeled gingerroot, or 1 teaspoon ground ginger

2 to 3 teaspoons curry powder, to taste

2 tablespoons tomato paste

One 14-ounce can diced tomatoes, with their liquid

⅓ cup plus 1 tablespoon water

Salt and freshly ground black pepper

2 to 3 tablespoons fresh-squeezed lemon juice

1½ pounds red snapper, sea bass, halibut, or haddock fillets, in 4 pieces

Lemon wedges

Heat 2 or 3 tablespoons oil in sauté pan. Add onions and cook over medium-low heat for 10 minutes, or until beginning to turn golden. Add garlic and ginger and sauté for 1 minute. Add 1½ to 2½ teaspoons curry powder and 1 tablespoon tomato paste, and cook, stirring, 1 minute. Add tomatoes, ⅓ cup water, salt, pepper, and 2 tablespoons lemon juice and cook over medium heat about 10 minutes, or until sauce is thick, stirring often. Taste, adjust seasoning, and add more lemon juice if you like.

Run your fingers over fish and carefully pull out any bones with aid of tweezers, pastry crimper, or sharp paring knife. Pat fish dry.

If using grill, brush or spray it lightly with oil to prevent sticking. Preheat grill or broiler. Mix remaining tablespoon tomato paste with 1 tablespoon water, ½ teaspoon curry powder, and pinch each salt and pepper. Brush fillets with remaining tablespoon oil and season lightly with salt and pepper. Arrange fish on grill or broiler pan. Broil or grill fish for 3 or 4 minutes on each side. Spread tomato paste mixture over fish. Broil or grill, without turning fish, for 1 more minute, or just until fish turns opaque. Watch carefully so topping doesn't burn.

Spoon some of sauce around fish and garnish with lemon wedges. Serve remaining sauce separately.

Fish Baked with Cumin Rice

sayadiyeh

Combining fish with rice pilaf is a favored formula, called *sayadiyeh* in Arabic, and is enjoyed in countless versions. Some people poach the fish, some fry it in butter or olive oil; some serve it hot, others prefer it cold.

Iraq's spice-loving cooks add hot red pepper as well as tomatoes. Lebanese renditions tend to be the fanciest. The dish might be served as a molded cake and often includes hazelnuts, pine nuts, and saffron.

I learned the most basic versions from my husband's cousin Yigal Cohen and his girlfriend Tal Ben-David, who spent some time living among coastal Sinai Bedouins and found their *sayadiyeh* delicious. The desert nomads cooked whole fish in water with only salt and pepper, then removed it and cooked rice in the cooking liquid. They served the fish on top of the rice. The freshness of the just-caught seafood made all the difference.

The Bedouins didn't use many spices because storing ingredients in tents and contending with the sand and the desert winds made this difficult. For my *sayadiyeh* I like to combine the fish and rice with sautéed onions and cumin for extra flavor.

◆ MAKES 4 SERVINGS.

3 tablespoons olive oil

2 medium onions, chopped

2½ cups fish or vegetable broth or water, or more if needed

1¼ pounds fish steaks, such as salmon or halibut, rinsed and patted dry

Salt and freshly ground black pepper

1 to 1½ teaspoons ground cumin, to taste

1¼ cups long-grain rice

1 tablespoon chopped Italian parsley

¼ cup pine nuts or slivered almonds, toasted

Lemon wedges

Preheat oven to 350°F. Heat 2 tablespoons oil in deep sauté pan or large saucepan. Add onions and sauté over medium heat for 7 minutes, or until they begin to turn golden. Remove onions and reserve.

Add 2 cups broth to skillet and bring to a simmer. Add fish, salt, and pepper and return to a simmer. Cover and simmer for 5 minutes; fish will not be cooked through. Remove fish with a slotted spoon. Pour broth into a measuring cup and add additional broth or water to make 2½ cups.

Dry pan and add 1 tablespoon oil. Return onions to pan and heat them until sizzling. Stir in cumin and rice and sauté, stirring, for 3 minutes, or until rice is coated with onion and spices. Add measured broth, salt, and pepper. Stir once and bring to a boil over high heat. Cover and cook over low heat, without stirring, for 17 minutes, or until rice is barely tender. Taste and adjust seasoning.

Fluff rice with a fork. Gently transfer rice to an oiled 2-quart casserole. Discard skin and bones from fish and cut fish in large chunks. Arrange them on top of rice and sprinkle lightly with salt and pepper. Cover and bake for 20 minutes, or until fish is tender. Garnish with parsley and toasted pine nuts; serve with lemon wedges.

Saffron Shrimp and Pine Nut Pilaf

karidesli pilav

Saffron gives a golden hue and an exotic aroma to this Turkish-style entrée without overpowering the shrimp's natural taste. I usually shell and cook the shrimp for the freshest flavor, and if I have a chance, I simmer the shells for 10 minutes to have a light stock to use as the pilaf's cooking liquid. When I'm in a rush, I buy the shrimp cooked and shelled and add it to the pilaf at the last minute.

Sometimes I make this pilaf with salmon, sole, sea bass, or other fish fillets instead of shrimp. For such a pilaf I find that just about any fish cooking technique works fine. For the richest flavor, I sauté the fillets. When I want a leaner dish, I poach, steam, grill, or bake them. When I have extra cooked fish from another meal, adding it to pilaf is a wonderful way to use it.

Summer squash is a quick-cooking vegetable I often use but you can substitute green or red bell pepper strips, sliced mushrooms, or lightly cooked green beans or asparagus pieces. If you are serving this dish cool, see the variation.

◆ MAKES 2 OR 3 MAIN-COURSE SERVINGS.

¼ teaspoon crushed saffron threads
    (2 pinches)
2½ cups boiling water
3 to 5 tablespoons olive oil

1 pound medium shrimp, shelled

Salt and freshly ground black pepper to taste

2 small yellow squash or zucchini,
  cut in ½-inch dice

1 onion, finely chopped

2 garlic cloves, finely chopped

1¼ cups long-grain white rice

1 bay leaf

1 large thyme sprig, or ½ teaspoon dried
  thyme, crumbled

4 plum tomatoes, diced small
  (about ⅜-inch dice)

2 tablespoons chopped Italian parsley,
  cilantro, or basil

¼ to ⅓ cup pine nuts, lightly toasted
  (see "Basics," page 369)

Add saffron to 1 cup boiling water; cover and let stand while you prepare remaining ingredients. Heat 2 tablespoons oil in large sauté pan, large wide saucepan, or deep skillet. Add shrimp, salt, and pepper and sauté over medium-high heat about 2 minutes, tossing often. Remove with slotted spoon. Add squash, salt, and pepper to pan and sauté about 2 minutes. Remove with slotted spoon.

Add 1 tablespoon oil to pan. Add onion and cook over medium heat about 5 minutes, or until soft but not brown. Add garlic and rice and sauté, stirring, about 3 minutes, or until grains begin to turn white.

Pour saffron and its liquid and remaining 1½ cups boiling water over rice and stir once. Add bay leaf, thyme, salt, and pepper. Bring to a boil over high heat. Reduce heat to low, cover tightly, and simmer, without stirring, 15 minutes. Scatter shrimp and squash over top. Cover and simmer for 3 minutes, or until rice is tender and liquid is absorbed. Discard bay leaf and thyme sprig.

Fluff rice with a large fork. Gently stir in diced tomatoes, parsley, and half the pine nuts. Taste and adjust seasoning. Serve topped with remaining pine nuts.

Cool Shrimp Pilaf

To finished pilaf add 1 to 2 tablespoons more olive oil if you like and 1 to 2 tablespoons fresh-squeezed lemon juice, or to taste. Remove the pilaf from the refrigerator about 15 minutes before serving and adjust the seasoning again. Serve garnished with lemon quarters. For a festive presentation, you can use the cool pilaf to fill ripe tomatoes from which you've scooped out the seeds, or cucumber halves hollowed to make boat shapes.

Herbed Seafood Patties with Green Sauce and Capers

kibbet samak

To make fish cakes, cooks in the Mideast usually mix ground fish with bread, mashed potatoes, or rice, which help stretch the amount of fish, give the patties a creamy texture, and enable them to hold together well during sautéing. Herbs, cinnamon, and cumin are popular flavorings. Salting and rinsing the onions is a good way to soften their bite.

You can make these versatile patties from shrimp, salmon, a white-fleshed fish such as halibut, or a combination of seafood. They make a welcome summer entrée topped with a light, mint-flavored green sauce. I like them with a colorful Turkish Shepherd's Salad (page 61), even though it's unlikely that the shepherds who first came up with the salad ages ago served it with fish!

◆ MAKES ABOUT 4 SERVINGS.

1 large onion, minced

1 teaspoon salt

4 slices stale white bread

8 ounces fish fillets, such as halibut, cod, or sole

8 ounces medium shrimp, shelled

2 large eggs

2 large garlic cloves, chopped

3 tablespoons chopped cilantro

2 tablespoons chopped Italian parsley

1 teaspoon dried leaf oregano, crumbled

1 teaspoon dried thyme

½ teaspoon ground cinnamon (optional)

¼ teaspoon freshly ground black pepper

¼ teaspoon cayenne, or to taste

3 to 5 tablespoons olive oil

Minty Green Sauce (page 311)

2 teaspoons capers, drained

Lemon wedges

Put onion in strainer and sprinkle with ½ teaspoon salt. Let stand about 5 minutes. Rinse onions in strainer. Dip each bread slice in a bowl of water to moisten. Add soaked bread to onions and squeeze both dry.

Remove any skin from fish. Grind fish and shrimp in food processor until very fine. Add eggs, onion, garlic, cilantro, parsley, oregano, thyme, cinnamon, remaining salt, pepper, and cayenne. Transfer to bowl. Broil or microwave a teaspoon of mixture and taste it for seasoning. Shape mixture in patties, using about ⅓ cup mixture for each, and flatten them.

Heat 3 tablespoons oil in large heavy skillet. Add enough patties to make a single layer without crowding. Sauté over medium heat for 3 or 4 minutes per side, or until golden brown and cooked through; use two slotted spatulas to turn them carefully. Transfer to paper towels to drain. Keep finished patties warm on a baking sheet in a 250°F oven. Sauté remaining patties in same way, adding oil to skillet if necessary and heating it before adding more patties.

Serve hot or warm, topped with a spoonful of green sauce and a sprinkling of capers, with lemon wedges on the side.

Shrimp Balls in Spicy Tamarind Tomato Sauce

chebeh rubyan

Cooks in the Persian Gulf states prepare many sauces reminiscent of those of India. Often they use ghee (clarified butter) for frying and enjoy the tangy taste of tamarind, the heat of chilies, and blends of aromatic spices such as cinnamon, nutmeg, and cumin. Living near the sea, they enjoy a wealth of seafood and often stew it in currylike sauces enhanced with these flavors.

For special occasions they prepare seafood as intricate stuffed spheres resembling meat kibbe. These shrimp balls are a simplified version. You can use the same sauce for shelled shrimp, lobster, or other seafood. Saffron-seasoned basmati rice is the accompaniment of choice. For more on ghee and tamarind, see "The Mideast Pantry," pages 16 and 17.

◆ MAKES 4 SERVINGS.

1 large onion, chopped

SHRIMP BALLS:

1 pound shelled shrimp

Salt and freshly ground black pepper

4 tablespoons coarsely chopped cilantro

1 large egg

1 large egg white

2 slices day-old white bread, crust removed, ground to fine crumbs

TAMARIND TOMATO SAUCE:

1¼ pounds ripe tomatoes, or one 28-ounce can whole tomatoes

1 or 2 tablespoons ghee, butter, or vegetable oil

2 large garlic cloves, minced

1 jalapeño pepper, seeded if desired, chopped, or cayenne pepper to taste

½ teaspoon ground cumin

1 teaspoon ground coriander

Pinch ground cinnamon

¼ teaspoon ground cardamom (optional)

Pinch freshly grated nutmeg

2 to 3 teaspoons tamarind paste

½ teaspoon sugar (optional)

Mince enough of the onion to make ⅓ cup, to use in shrimp balls. Reserve rest for sauce.

To make shrimp balls: Chop shrimp finely in food processor with pulsing motion. Add ½ teaspoon salt, ¼ teaspoon pepper, 2 tablespoons cilantro (reserving rest for sauce), egg, egg white, and bread crumbs. Process until blended. Add minced onion and pulse a few times just until blended. Transfer to bowl. Form mixture into small balls, using about 2 tablespoons mixture for each, and roll them between your palms until smooth. Put them on plate.

To make sauce: Peel and seed fresh tomatoes, reserving juice; if using canned tomatoes, drain and reserve juice. Coarsely chop tomatoes. Heat ghee in medium saucepan, add remaining minced onion, and sauté over medium-low heat for 7 minutes. Add garlic, jalapeño pepper, tomatoes, salt, pepper, cumin, coriander, cinnamon, cardamom, if you like, and nutmeg. Stir in tamarind paste. Bring to a boil. Cover and cook over low heat for 10 minutes. Transfer sauce to sauté pan.

Measure reserved tomato juice and add enough water to make 1 cup. Add to sauce. Bring to a simmer.

Gently add half the shrimp balls to the sauce. Cover and cook, without stirring, for 20 minutes, or until they are firm. Carefully remove them with slotted spoon. Cook remaining shrimp balls in the same way. Taste sauce, adjust seasoning, and add sugar if you like. Return shrimp balls to sauce. Add remaining cilantro. Serve hot.

Crab and Couscous Salad with Asparagus, Mint, and Pine Nuts

salatet kaboreyah ma couscous

Couscous becomes a delectable warm-weather entrée when tossed with seafood, lemon juice, and a drizzle of extra-virgin olive oil. The salad is perfect for a busy day because it's ready in no time. The couscous needs only five minutes to steep in hot water while you cook the asparagus. When I have very fresh, pencil-thin asparagus, sometimes I skip the cooking; I cut each piece in two thin diagonal slices and add them to the salad raw. You can prepare the salad a day ahead and refrigerate it in a closed container.

For a light but festive springtime lunch, serve colorful Middle Eastern Diced Salad (page 58) as an accompaniment, and a simple dessert of mixed summer berries with sorbet.

If fresh crabmeat is not available, you can use frozen or canned crab. You can also use imitation crab (surimi), which is made of ground fish with crab extract and is easy to find at the supermarket. Or substitute just about any cooked seafood—lobster, shrimp, cooked or canned salmon or tuna, smoked fish, or barbecued cod.

◆ MAKES 4 SERVINGS.

¾ pound thin asparagus

Salt and freshly ground black pepper

1 cup couscous

2 to 3 tablespoons strained fresh-squeezed lemon juice

3 tablespoons extra-virgin olive oil, or to taste

12 ounces crabmeat, picked over, any shell and cartilage discarded

¼ cup minced fresh mint

Cayenne pepper or Aleppo pepper to taste

¼ cup pine nuts or slivered almonds, toasted (page 369)

Trim about 1 inch of asparagus bases and discard. Rinse asparagus well. Cut each spear in three pieces. Pour enough water to easily cover asparagus into sauté pan, add salt, and bring to a boil. Add asparagus and boil about 2 minutes, or until just tender when pierced with a sharp knife. Drain in colander, or remove with slotted spoon and use the cooking liquid as the boiling water for the couscous.

Put couscous in medium saucepan. Shake pan to spread couscous in an even layer. Pour 1½ cups boiling water evenly over mix-ture and return to boil over high heat. Immediately cover pan tightly and let stand for 5 minutes. Transfer mixture to bowl. Fluff with fork. Let cool.

Whisk 2 tablespoons lemon juice with oil in small bowl. Add salt and pepper to taste. Drizzle dressing over couscous and mix gently with a fork. Add crab, asparagus, mint, and cayenne pepper and toss salad gently. Taste and adjust seasoning, adding more lemon juice or oil if you like. Serve sprinkled with pine nuts.

Poultry, a Holiday Tradition

Grilled Whole Chicken with Yemeni Spice Rub • *Farrouj Mechwi*

Grilled Chicken and Eggplant in Tomato Cilantro Sauce • *Oturtma*

Garlic Lovers' Grilled Chicken with Green Salad • *Djaj Mishwi, Toum biz-Zayt*

Saffron Chicken Kabobs • *Chich Tawouk*

Chicken with Aromatic Garlic and Toasted Pita Stuffing • *Djej Mechi*

Roast Chicken with Fennel, Olives, and Bulgur Wheat • *Djej bil Fourn*

Chicken and Chickpea Stew in Tomato Pepper Sauce • *Djej bil Banadoura ma Hommos*

Onion-Braised Chicken with Butternut Squash and Lemon • *Djej ma Arh*

Chicken in Persian Pomegranate Walnut Sauce • *Khoresh Fesanjan*

Chicken with Eastern Mediterranean Couscous, Peppers, and Green Beans • *Mugrabiyeh*

Braised Chicken Breasts with Fava Beans and Yellow Squash • *Feerakh bel Fool*

Chicken Breast Sauté with Curry Spices • *Feerakh bel Curry*

Falafel-crusted Chicken • *Of Bitzipui Falafel*

Chicken Patties in Garlicky Mushroom Tomato Sauce • *Kofta Tavuk*

Turkish Turkey with Hazelnut Currant Rice • *Hindi Dolmasi*

Turkey Thighs with Cumin and Tomatoes • *Hindi Yahni*

Cumin Turkey Burgers with Yogurt Garlic Sauce • *Kofta Hindi*

Sesame Chicken Salad with Barley and Fava Beans • *Salat Of im Zahtar v'Grissim*

Turkey and Rice Salad with Raisins and Pistachios • *Salat Hodu im Orez v'Tzimukim*

Roast Turkey Laffa with Hot Pepper Hummus • *Laffa Hodu im Hummus*

People in the Mideast relish poultry and serve it as the centerpiece of feasts. Chicken braised with allspice and onions may be the choice in Lebanese kitchens, with dill added in Turkish homes and garlic in Palestinian ones, while chicken stewed with chickpeas in peppery tomato sauce will grace Kurdish tables. To create sumptuous meals from chicken or duck, Iranians opt for sauces made with dried fruit or pomegranate juice and nuts.

Roast birds of all kinds, from turkey to quail, often come with stuffings, and those are usually made of grains rather than of bread. Rice is the top choice for stuffings, as in Turkish Turkey with Hazelnut Currant Rice (page 170). Cooks also make stuffings of wheat, especially in the form of bulgur pilaf, like the one in Roast Chicken with Fennel, Olives, and Bulgur Wheat (page 159).

Aromatic chicken soups with vegetables are a staple of family midday meals. For faster entrées, cooks sauté cakes of ground chicken, and then heat in a simple sauce, as in Chicken Patties in Garlicky Mushroom Tomato Sauce (page 168). Small patties might be presented for festive occasions as appetizers, like Chicken Pecan Bulgur Cakes with Cilantro Pesto (page 48).

Grilled poultry is also a popular pick, especially for celebrating warm-weather holidays with the family. Kabobs, or small pieces of skewer-grilled chicken, often cooked with chunks of peppers, onions, or other vegetables, is among the best-known Middle Eastern dishes worldwide. The sizzling morsels are the all-time favorite all over the Mideast, whether people prefer to scoop them into a pita to enjoy every bit of the savory juices, or to eat them with salad, or on a bed of rice pilaf.

A special treat for dining out in kabob restaurants, like those in Tel Aviv's Hatikvah Quarter, is foie gras, the rich liver of fattened geese or ducks. The meat is skewered, grilled briefly, and rolled up in a fresh flatbread. The ancient Egyptians are said to have originated foie gras, which today is best known in the pâté form served in fancy French eateries.

When I'm barbecuing chicken, I follow the Middle Eastern mode and opt for meat on the bone, whether the chicken is in parts or whole. Barbecued this way, the meat is moist and flavorful. For a summertime dinner, I love to serve chicken the Lebanese way, with an assertive garlic sauce and fresh herbs or greens (see Garlic Lovers' Grilled Chicken with Green Salad, page 156). If I'm in a rush and I want to grill boneless chicken without threading it on skewers, I cook it on a stove-top grill instead.

For fine flavor and good hygiene, carefully grilling or roasting chicken is important. Overcooked chicken, especially white meat, is dry but chicken must be served well done. The USDA recommends cooking whole chickens to 180°F and breasts to 170°F. Digital thermometers are sensitive at ½ inch or less but the common instant-read dial type needs 2 inches for an accurate reading and must be inserted sideways for small pieces. Many cooks rely instead on time-honored tests. Color is the easiest; cut into the meat's thickest part—it should not have the pink hue of raw meat, and should be white. Or check the juices: pierce the thigh's thickest part with a skewer—the juices running out should be clear, not pink. Always transfer the cooked chicken to a clean platter, not one that held the raw meat.

Grilled Whole Chicken with Yemeni Spice Rub

farrouj mechwi

For festive dinners I like to grill whole chickens. With little trouble, they become an impressive entrée. Even the most finicky eaters are enthusiastic about the chicken's intense, appetizing aroma, succulent meat, and beautifully browned skin. While the barbecue is heating, we rub the chicken with the traditional spice blend that gives it a wonderful flavor. If you're not planning to eat the skin, lift it gently above the breast meat and rub a little of the spice under the skin, without tearing it.

While you have the grill going, put a selection of vegetables on it too. We like whole eggplants, peppers, thick onion slices, and ears of corn. They are any barbecued chicken's ideal companions. Quarter and season the grilled eggplants with salt, pepper, olive oil, and lemon juice or turn them into Grilled Eggplant Sesame Dip (page 40). A diced salad of tomatoes, cucumbers and onions and some rice pilaf, followed by a refreshing Summer Melon Medley with Mint and Rose Water (page 352) complete the feast.

◆ MAKES 4 SERVINGS.

One 3½-pound chicken, giblets removed, rinsed, and patted dry
1½ teaspoons ground cumin
½ teaspoon turmeric
½ teaspoon freshly ground black pepper, or more to taste
1 teaspoon ground coriander, or ½ teaspoon ground cardamom (optional)
½ teaspoon salt, or to taste
1 tablespoon vegetable oil or olive oil

Put chicken on plate. Combine cumin, turmeric, pepper, coriander, and salt in small bowl and mix. Rub oil, then spice mixture into chicken, both inside and out. Wash your hands immediately so the turmeric won't stain your fingers.

Preheat covered gas grill for indirect heat, according to manufacturer's instructions, and set at medium (350°F to 375°F). If using a charcoal grill, heat the coals until they are covered with gray ash and have only a hint of red; then move the coals to the edge of the grill and put a drip pan in the grill's center so it will be under the chicken. If the grill grate is adjustable, set it about 6 inches above the coals.

Brush grill rack lightly with oil. Set chicken on the rack, in an area that is not directly over heat source, with breast of chicken facing up. Cover and grill about 45 to 60 minutes. To check if chicken is done, pierce the thickest part of a thigh near the bone; the juices that run from the meat should be clear, and the meat should no longer be pink. Transfer to a clean platter. Let chicken stand for 10 minutes before carving.

Grilled Chicken and Eggplant in Tomato Cilantro Sauce

oturtma

This dish updates the traditional Middle Eastern beef-and-eggplant stew to make it lighter, faster, and fresher tasting. Instead of beef, I use boneless chicken thighs, and I grill the meat and the eggplant instead of frying them. They need only brief braising to absorb flavor from the savory tomato sauce accented with garlic and allspice. Substitute dill or parsley for the cilantro if you prefer.

♦ MAKES 4 SERVINGS.

1 to 2 tablespoons olive oil, plus a little more for grilling eggplant and chicken

1 large onion, chopped

2 pounds ripe tomatoes, peeled, or one 28-ounce can tomatoes with their juice

6 large garlic cloves, chopped

Salt and freshly ground black pepper

½ to 1 teaspoon ground allspice, or to taste, plus a little more for sprinkling

1 cup chicken broth

1¼ to 1½ pounds eggplant (1 large or 2 medium), cut in crosswise slices about ⅜ inch thick

1¼ to 1½ pounds boneless, skinless chicken thighs or breasts

2 to 3 teaspoons fresh-squeezed lemon juice (optional)

Cayenne pepper to taste (optional)

4 tablespoons chopped cilantro

Heat oil in stew pan. Add onion and sauté over medium heat for 7 minutes, or until golden. Chop fresh or canned tomatoes and add to pan. Add garlic, salt, pepper, and ½ teaspoon allspice and bring to a boil, stirring often. Stir in broth. Cover and cook over medium heat for 20 minutes or until thickened, stirring often.

Prepare a grill or heat broiler with rack about 4 inches from heat source; or heat a ridged stove-top grill pan over medium-high heat. Brush grill rack lightly with oil. Brush eggplant with oil and sprinkle with salt and pepper. Add enough slices to make a single layer in grill without crowding. Grill or broil for 3 or 4 minutes on each side, or until nearly tender.

Rub chicken with oil. Sprinkle with salt, pepper, and allspice on both sides. Grill or broil chicken about 5 minutes per side, until nearly tender. Remove chicken skin if you like. Cut each chicken piece in 3 or 4 pieces. Quarter eggplant slices.

Taste sauce for seasoning, and add lemon juice, cayenne, and more allspice if you like. Stir in 3 tablespoons cilantro. Add chicken and eggplant to stew pan and spoon sauce over them. Bring to a boil. Cover and simmer for 5 minutes, or until done, occasionally stirring gently. (See Note to bake them instead.) Eggplant should be tender when pierced with a fork. Cut into a thick chicken piece; its color should be white, not pink. If sauce is too thin, remove eggplant and chicken with slotted spoon and simmer sauce until thickened. Serve eggplant and chicken in sauce, sprinkled with remaining cilantro.

NOTE To bake chicken and eggplant: Preheat oven to 375°F. Spoon a little sauce into a baking dish, top with eggplant, then with chicken, and spoon remaining sauce over it. Cover and bake for 10 to 15 minutes, or until tender; uncover after 7 minutes if sauce is too thin.

Garlic Lovers' Grilled Chicken with Green Salad

---

djaj mishwi, toum biz-zayt

Aficionados of Lebanese restaurants are wild about grilled chicken with garlic sauce. The golden, crisp chicken skin and the creamy sauce, which resembles an extra-garlicky version of Provençal aioli, make it a favorite entrée. Cooks spread the sauce on pita for a grilled chicken sandwich, use it as a dipping sauce with chicken drummettes as an appetizer, or serve it with chicken pieces or kabobs and a salad, as in this recipe. I add

asparagus spears and toasted pine nuts to the salad for a festive touch.

◆ MAKES 4 SERVINGS.

2 garlic cloves, peeled

Salt

4 tablespoons strained fresh-squeezed lemon juice

4 to 5 tablespoons extra-virgin olive oil

¼ teaspoon ground cinnamon (optional)

½ teaspoon freshly ground black pepper, or ¼ teaspoon cayenne pepper

2 teaspoons chopped fresh thyme, or 1 teaspoon dried

2½ to 3 pounds chicken thighs, drumsticks, or breast pieces, with skin and bones

Freshly ground black pepper

Garlic Sauce (page 309)

4 to 5 cups mixed baby lettuces or bite-size pieces romaine

4 to 6 cooked asparagus spears, each cut in 3 pieces

3 tablespoons pine nuts or slivered almonds, lightly toasted (see "Basics," page 369)

Lemon wedges

Fresh pita bread

Mince garlic cloves, mash them with pinch of salt, and put in bowl. Add 2 tablespoons lemon juice, 2 tablespoons oil, the cinnamon, if you like, pepper, and half the thyme. Put chicken pieces in shallow dish and pour mixture over. Let stand while heating grill; or cover and marinate in refrigerator for 2 to 6 hours, turning pieces occasionally.

In small bowl, whisk remaining oil with remaining lemon juice and remaining thyme. Season with salt and pepper. Cover and reserve as dressing for greens. Prepare Garlic Sauce.

Preheat covered gas grill for indirect heat, according to manufacturer's instructions, and set at medium (350°F to 375°F). If using a charcoal grill, heat the coals until they are covered with gray ash and have only a hint of red; then move the coals to the edge of the grill. If the grill grate is adjustable, set it about 6 inches above the coals.

Brush grill rack lightly with oil. Sprinkle chicken pieces with salt and set them on the rack. Cover and grill about 20 minutes for breasts or 30 to 35 minutes for thighs or drumsticks, turning pieces over halfway through cooking time. To check if chicken is done, pierce thickest part of thigh near bone; juices that run from meat should be clear and meat should no longer be pink. At thickest part of breast, meat should not be pink. Transfer to clean platter.

Toss lettuce and asparagus with dressing in serving bowl. Taste and adjust seasoning. Sprinkle with pine nuts. Serve hot chicken with salad, garlic sauce, lemon wedges, and pita bread.

Saffron Chicken Kabobs

chich tawouk

I learned to prepare chicken kabobs this way at the first Assyrian Food Festival in Los Angeles. Saffron is the seasoning of choice of Persians as well, who call this dish *jujeh kabab,* for the good flavor and warm, yellow hue it gives the chicken. For marinating the chicken, the saffron is usually combined with grated onion and lemon or lime juice or yogurt. Some people substitute inexpensive turmeric for saffron; the chicken tastes good that way too.

Such savory chunks of skewered chicken appear at special occasions as well as casual ones. At the festival the kabobs were set on flatbreads and came with spicy pickled vegetables and fresh basil sprigs. At dinners they might be served with hot basmati rice, as well as a plate of radishes and several fresh herbs, including chives and marjoram. Other good accompaniments are Tomato Basil Tahini (page 34) and spicy Red Pepper Walnut Dip (page 39).

Thin, flat metal skewers are the favorite kind to use for kabobs in the Middle East but if you are using bamboo skewers, soak them in cold water for 30 minutes before grilling so they won't burn, and cover their ends with foil.

♦ MAKES 4 SERVINGS.

Pinch saffron (⅛ to ¼ teaspoon), crushed

2 or 3 onions

3 tablespoons strained fresh-squeezed lemon juice or lime juice

1½ pounds boneless, skinless chicken breasts or thighs, cut in 1¼-inch pieces

1 or 2 green bell peppers, halved, cored, and seeded

Salt and freshly ground black pepper

8 large cherry or small plum tomatoes

2 tablespoons vegetable oil or melted butter

Basil sprigs, chives, and other fresh herbs

Fresh pita bread

Put saffron in small cup and pour 2 tablespoons hot water over it. Let stand for 5 minutes. Reserve 1 tablespoon liquid saffron for basting chicken. Pour remaining saffron into bowl large enough to contain chicken. Finely grate ½ onion and add to bowl. Add 2 tablespoons lemon juice and mix well.

Add chicken pieces to bowl and mix well. Cover and marinate for 2 to 6 hours in refrigerator.

Cut peppers in 1¼-inch squares. Quarter remaining onions. Remove chicken from marinade, brushing off bits of onion and discarding marinade. Sprinkle chicken with salt and pepper. Thread chicken on skewers, alternating with pepper pieces, onions, and tomatoes.

Heat barbecue, stove-top grill, or broiler and lightly oil rack. Combine remaining liquid saffron with oil and 1 tablespoon lemon juice. Brush this basting liquid over chicken.

Put kabobs on barbecue. Grill or broil about 10 minutes, until chicken is just cooked through but is still succulent, turning kabobs often and brushing them occasionally with basting liquid. To check, cut into a chunk—chicken should not be pink inside. Serve hot with herbs and fresh pita.

Chicken with Aromatic Garlic and Toasted Pita Stuffing

djej mechi

Garlic and cumin are popular Middle Eastern seasonings for poultry stuffings of all types, whether they're based on rice, bulgur, wheat berries, or bread. Many cooks add sautéed chicken liver to the stuffing as well. Almonds lend a festive note to this dish. You can bake them in the stuffing or sprinkle them on top at serving time so they keep their crunchy texture. Serve with baked sweet potatoes or butternut squash.

◆ MAKES 4 SERVINGS.

4 cups diced pita bread

4 to 5 tablespoons olive oil

1 large onion, finely chopped

Liver from chicken (optional)

Salt and freshly ground black pepper

3 teaspoons ground cumin

½ cup chopped celery

½ teaspoon dried thyme, crumbled

6 large garlic cloves, minced

⅓ cup chopped Italian parsley, and a few
sprigs for garnish

1 egg, beaten (optional)

2 to 4 tablespoons chicken broth

One 3½- to 4-pound chicken, excess fat
removed

½ cup blanched almonds, lightly toasted,
whole or coarsely chopped (optional)

Preheat oven to 275°F. Put pita cubes on large baking sheet and bake for 10 minutes or until crisp and dry, stirring occasionally. Transfer to large bowl.

Heat 3 tablespoons oil in large skillet. Add onion, liver from chicken, salt, pepper, and ½ teaspoon cumin. Sauté over medium heat for 3 minutes, or until liver browns lightly on all sides. Remove liver and let cool. Add celery, thyme, and 1½ teaspoons cumin to onions in skillet. Sauté over medium heat for 7 minutes, or until onion begins to turn golden, stirring occasionally. Remove from heat and add garlic and parsley.

Dice liver and add to onion mixture. Add mixture to pita cubes and toss lightly until blended. Taste and adjust seasoning. Add egg, if you like, and toss again. Gradually add broth, tossing lightly. Stuffing may appear dry but will become moister from juices in the bird. Refrigerate stuffing in a covered container if you're making it ahead. Stuff chicken just before roasting it.

Preheat oven to 375°F. Rub chicken lightly with olive oil and sprinkle it with salt, pepper, and remaining teaspoon cumin. Rub spices into skin. Spoon stuffing lightly into chicken. Fold skin over stuffing; truss or skewer closed, if desired. Set chicken in roasting pan. Add a little more broth, if necessary, to extra stuffing to moisten bread, and spoon into lightly oiled baking dish.

Roast chicken for 45 minutes. Spoon 1 or 2 teaspoons chicken pan juices or olive oil over stuffing in baking dish. Cover and bake alongside chicken for 45 minutes, or until chicken is tender. To check, pierce thickest part of thigh with a skewer; the juices should be clear. Insert a skewer into the stuffing inside chicken; it should be hot.

Put parsley sprigs on a platter for garnish. Carve chicken and arrange on the platter with stuffing. Sprinkle stuffing with almonds and serve hot.

Roast Chicken with Fennel, Olives, and Bulgur Wheat

djej bil fourn

Like mint, fennel imparts a refreshing taste to chicken salads, stews, and stuffings and is a favorite in the eastern Mediterranean as well as the Balkan countries. In this recipe the fennel combines with the region's beloved olives to flavor both the sauce and the stuffing.

◆ MAKES 4 SERVINGS.

2 medium fennel bulbs (total about 1¼ pounds) trimmed of stalks and any browned outer leaves

3 tablespoons olive oil

Salt and freshly ground black pepper

2 red bell peppers, cored, seeded, and cut in thin strips

½ medium onion, minced

1 cup medium bulgur wheat

2¼ cups chicken broth, preferably unsalted or low-salt, or water

⅔ to 1 cup pitted olives, black, green, or a mixture, drained well

One 3½- to 4-pound chicken

1 tablespoon tomato paste

½ teaspoon dried oregano

Quarter fennel bulbs. Cut off and discard core from each piece. Holding layers together, cut each piece in ¼-inch slices lengthwise, to obtain long strips. Heat 2 tablespoons oil in large skillet. Add fennel, salt, and pepper and stir. Cover and cook over low heat for 15 minutes, stirring occasionally. Add peppers, cover, and cook for 5 minutes, or until nearly tender.

Heat 1 tablespoon oil in heavy medium saucepan. Add onion and cook over medium heat for 5 minutes, or until beginning to turn golden, stirring often. Add bulgur and sauté, stirring, for 2 minutes. Add

1½ cups broth, salt, and pepper and bring to boil. Reduce heat to low, cover, and cook for 10 minutes, or until bulgur is nearly tender. Stir in half the fennel mixture. Dice ⅓ cup olives and add to bulgur. Taste and adjust seasoning. Let cool completely before stuffing chicken.

Preheat oven to 400°F. Spoon stuffing lightly into chicken; reserve any extra stuffing in a small baking dish and cover. Sprinkle chicken with salt and pepper and set it in a small, heavy roasting pan. Roast for 1 hour, adding dish of extra stuffing after 30 minutes if desired. Chicken is done when its juices come out clear when a skewer is inserted into thickest part of thigh. If juices are pink, continue roasting chicken a few more minutes. Stuffing inside chicken should be hot. Transfer chicken to a carving board, cover, and let stand for 5 to 10 minutes.

Reheat vegetables, adding 1 tablespoon of chicken's pan juices if you like. Skim as much fat as possible from juices in roasting pan. Heat juices, add remaining broth, and return to a boil, stirring and scraping brown bits from pan. Strain juices into small saucepan. Skim off fat. Bring juices to a simmer and whisk in tomato paste. Simmer for 1 minute to slightly thicken. Add oregano and remaining olives and heat through. Add pepper; taste before adding salt.

Carve chicken and set on platter with vegetables. Spoon olive sauce over chicken or serve separately.

Chicken and Chickpea Stew in Tomato Pepper Sauce

djej bil banadoura ma hommos

Following a healthful custom in the Middle East, this traditional entrée has a high proportion of chickpeas to meat, with the legume providing virtually fat-free protein and good flavor. The stew is usually made with lamb, but today many prepare it with chicken. To make this time-honored dish colorful and easy to serve, I add green and yellow squash and carrots. Serve it with rice pilaf or in the Kurdish fashion, with Basic Bulgur Pilaf (page 275) seasoned liberally with pepper.

◆ MAKES 4 TO 6 SERVINGS.

1½ cups dried chickpeas (garbanzo beans), rinsed and sorted, or two 15-ounce cans chickpeas, drained

1½ to 2 pounds chicken pieces

Salt and freshly ground black pepper

1½ to 2 tablespoons olive oil

2 large onions, chopped

2 large garlic cloves, minced

1 pound ripe tomatoes, peeled, seeded, and chopped, or one 14-ounce can tomatoes, drained and chopped

1 teaspoon ground cumin

2 teaspoons paprika

1½ to 2 cups chicken broth or water

1 large thyme sprig, or 1 teaspoon dried thyme

1 green pepper, halved, cored, seeded, and cut in 1-inch dice

8 ounces carrots, diagonally sliced about ½ inch thick

8 ounces zucchini, halved lengthwise, sliced ½ inch thick

8 ounces yellow zucchini or yellow crookneck squash, halved lengthwise, sliced ½ inch thick

1 tablespoon tomato paste (optional)

Cayenne pepper to taste

Put chickpeas in large saucepan and add 5 cups fresh water. Bring to a boil. Cover and simmer over low heat about 1 hour and 15 minutes, or until tender.

Sprinkle chicken with salt and pepper. Heat oil in shallow stew pan. Add chicken pieces and brown them lightly over medium-low heat for about 5 minutes; remove from pan.

Add onions to pan and cook over medium heat about 7 minutes, or until golden. Stir in garlic, then tomatoes, cumin, and paprika. Return chicken pieces to pan and heat until tomatoes are bubbling. Add 1½ cups broth and thyme and bring to a boil. Cover and cook over low heat for 15 minutes.

Add green pepper and carrots to pan of chicken, cover, and cook for 15 minutes, adding broth if sauce becomes too thick. Add green and yellow squash and chickpeas. Cover and cook for 10 to 15 minutes, or until chicken and vegetables are tender. Discard thyme sprig. Stir in tomato paste if you like and return to a simmer. Season to taste with salt, pepper, and cayenne. Serve hot.

Onion-Braised Chicken with Butternut Squash and Lemon

djej ma arh

Throughout the Mideast lemon and onions are favorite flavorings for chicken. In the eastern Mediterranean, nutmeg is sometimes used too. I like to combine these flavorings with butternut squash in this savory dish, in which the delicate sweetness of the stewed onions and the squash balance the lemon's tartness. Freshen the flavor with an extra squeeze of lemon juice at serving time.

◆ MAKES 4 SERVINGS.

2½ pounds chicken pieces

Salt and freshly ground black pepper

2 tablespoons olive oil

3 large onions, halved and sliced thin

2 large garlic cloves, chopped

1 cup chicken broth

2 to 2½ cups diced butternut squash (about 1-inch cubes)

Freshly grated nutmeg to taste

1 tablespoon fresh-squeezed lemon juice, or to taste

1 tablespoon chopped Italian parsley (optional)

Lemon wedges

Sprinkle chicken pieces with salt and pepper on both sides. Heat oil in stew pan. Lightly brown chicken pieces in two batches in skillet over medium heat. Remove with tongs to plate. Add onions and cook over medium-low heat for 10 minutes, or until softened. Return chicken to pan and add any juices from plate. Add garlic and broth. Cover and simmer for 10 minutes. Add squash, sprinkle it with nutmeg, and bring to a simmer. Cover and cook for 20 to 25 minutes, or until chicken and squash are tender, turning chicken pieces once or twice.

Remove chicken and squash pieces from pan but leave in onion. Skim fat from cooking liquid. Stir in lemon juice and add a little more nutmeg. Taste sauce and adjust seasoning. Return chicken and squash to pan. Cover and warm over low heat for about 3 minutes. Sprinkle with parsley if you like and serve hot, with lemon wedges.

POULTRY AND POMEGRANATES—
A PRIZED PERSIAN PAIR

Chicken or duck braised in a sauce of pomegranates and walnuts is a signature dish of the Persian kitchen. The classic stew reminds me somewhat of a French specialty, coq au vin, as the pomegranate juice gives the chicken a color and flavor that recalls red wine. Like wine, pomegranate juice varies in its balance of tartness and sweetness, depending on the type of pomegranate, and as with wine, the taste preference is regional. A friend of mine from northern Iran, Sharouz Zandi, loves juice and paste made from sour pomegranates and has to have visiting relatives bring them because he finds American pomegranates are sweet.

Most often the stew features poultry but cooks also prepare it with beef cubes, meatballs, and even fish. The balance of pomegranate and walnuts determines the taste, texture, and hue of the sauce. I first learned to make this dish from an Iranian student in a French cooking class that I was teaching. She used a generous amount of walnuts and the sauce was rich, creamy, and wonderful. I find the nuts enrich the pomegranate juice the way that butter can enrich a red wine sauce. In both cases, the color is deeper red and more attractive when the sauce is less rich.

I like to make plenty of the sauce so I have it for serving with a variety of foods. When I dined at Reza, a Persian restaurant in Chicago, they served the sauce not only as part of a stew but as a separate dipping sauce that you could order with chicken, lamb, or vegetable kabobs. Try it with Cumin Turkey Burgers (page 172) instead of the yogurt sauce, or even with veggie burgers or simply steamed vegetables and rice. At Persian stores you can buy the sauce prepared in jars but it's so much better when you make your own.

Chicken in Persian Pomegranate Walnut Sauce

khoresh fesanjan

This dish is one of the glories of the Persian kitchen. (See page 163.) Its charm stems from the luxurious sauce in which the chicken gently cooks, served in generous amounts. Although its exotic flavor and slightly chunky texture are different from the usual American and European sauces, it is easy to love.

The stew's time-honored partner is basmati rice, and some add vegetables like eggplant or zucchini to the sauce. I like to accompany the ragout with bright green vegetables, like steamed broccoli or green beans, and lightly cooked carrots.

If you prefer a smoother sauce, add the optional flour in the recipe. Like some cooks, I usually add tomato paste for better color; others consider this heresy. You can add broth for a deeper chicken flavor, or if you're serving the sauce with grilled foods and won't be simmering the chicken in it. For extra color, garnish the chicken with pomegranate seeds when the fresh fruit is in season, or with chopped parsley and a few toasted walnuts.

You can use pomegranate juice or the concentrated form of pomegranate paste, also called pomegranate molasses, which you can find at Mediterranean and Middle Eastern markets and gourmet shops. Substitute cranberry juice if you can't find pomegranate.

◆ MAKES 4 SERVINGS.

2 tablespoons vegetable oil, or 1 tablespoon oil and 1 tablespoon butter

2½ pounds chicken pieces, rinsed and patted dry

1 large onion, chopped

1½ to 2 cups walnuts

1 tablespoon all-purpose flour (optional)

1½ to 2 cups pomegranate juice, or ⅓ to ½ cup pomegranate paste

½ cup water or chicken broth (if using pomegranate juice), or 1½ cups water or broth (if using paste)

Salt and freshly ground black pepper

1 to 2 tablespoons tomato paste, or 3 to 4 tablespoons tomato sauce (optional)

1 teaspoon ground cardamom, or ½ teaspoon cinnamon, or to taste

1 tablespoon fresh-squeezed lemon juice, or to taste

1 to 2 teaspoons sugar, or to taste

⅓ to ½ cup pomegranate seeds (optional)

1 tablespoon chopped Italian parsley (optional)

A few toasted walnuts (optional)

Heat oil in heavy wide casserole or Dutch oven. Add chicken in batches and sauté over medium-high heat until brown. Remove chicken to plate. Discard fat from pan, leaving 1 to 2 tablespoons.

Add onion to pan and sauté over medium heat for 7 minutes, or until golden. Meanwhile, finely chop walnuts with pulsing motion of food processor. Reduce heat under onion pan to low. Stir in flour, then walnuts, and cook over low heat, stirring, for I minute. Stir in pomegranate juice and ½ cup water, or pomegranate paste and 1½ cups water, and bring to a simmer, stirring.

Add chicken and any juices on plate to pan. Sprinkle chicken with salt and pepper. Cover and cook over low heat about 35 minutes for breast pieces or 40 to 45 minutes for leg and thigh pieces, or until chicken is tender, turning occasionally. Remove chicken from pan. Add tomato paste, if you like, and cardamom to sauce and simmer until thickened to your taste. Taste, adjust seasoning, and add lemon juice and sugar if needed. If you like, whisk in a few more teaspoons pomegranate juice or paste. Return chicken to sauce and heat through. Serve hot, garnished if you like with pomegranate seeds, parsley, or walnuts, or all three.

Chicken with Eastern Mediterranean Couscous, Peppers, and Green Beans

mugrabiyeh

Eastern Mediterranean couscous is larger than the Moroccan type and resembles small tapioca. Often it accompanies braised chicken, as in this recipe. You can find the Lebanese version of couscous in Middle Eastern markets in packages labeled *mugrabiyeh*. In gourmet shops it's often sold as Israeli couscous, although in Israel both this ball-shaped type and the tiny Moroccan kind are popular. In this colorful one-pot meal, you can substitute orzo or riso (barley- or rice-shaped pasta).

◆ MAKES 4 SERVINGS.

One 3½-pound chicken, cut in 8 serving pieces

Salt and freshly ground black pepper

½ teaspoon turmeric (optional)

1½ teaspoons ground cumin

2 tablespoons olive oil or vegetable oil

1 large onion, thinly sliced

1 green bell pepper, halved, cored, seeded, and cut in strips

1 red bell pepper, halved, cored, seeded, and cut in strips

3 large garlic cloves, minced

2 ripe or canned tomatoes, chopped

1½ cups chicken stock or water

1½ pounds green beans, ends removed, halved (see Note)

1 cup Israeli couscous

3 tablespoons chopped fresh dill, or 2 to 2½ teaspoons dried dill (optional)

Sprinkle chicken on both sides with salt, pepper, turmeric, if you like, and I teaspoon cumin. Rub seasonings into chicken. Heat oil in shallow stew pan. Add chicken leg and thigh pieces and brown them on all sides over medium-low heat for about 15 minutes. Remove them and brown remaining chicken pieces for 5 minutes; remove.

Add onion to pan and cook over low heat until soft but not browned. Stir in peppers and garlic and cook about 5 minutes, stirring often. Add tomatoes and remaining cumin. Set chicken pieces on top, putting in leg and thigh pieces first to be sure they are close to base of pan.

Add stock and bring to a boil. Cover and cook over low heat for 20 minutes. Add green beans, cover, and cook over low heat for 25 minutes, or until chicken and beans are tender.

Remove chicken, beans, and peppers. Cover and keep warm. Measure sauce and add enough water to make 2½ cups. Bring to a boil. Add couscous and simmer uncovered for 10 to 15 minutes, or until just tender, occasionally stirring gently and adding a few tablespoons hot water if necessary. Return chicken and vegetables to pan and add dill if you like. Heat briefly to blend flavors. Taste and adjust seasoning.

NOTE The green beans become very tender and flavorful when cooked slowly in the Middle Eastern fashion as above. If you prefer beans that are bright green, cook them separately in boiling salted water for 5 minutes and heat them in the casserole before serving.

Braised Chicken Breasts with Fava Beans and Yellow Squash

feerakh bel fool

Simmering meat with fava beans in a tomato sauce has long been a favorite culinary custom in the Mideast. This version is seasoned the Egyptian way, with allspice and cilantro. Choose fairly small chicken breast halves so they will be convenient to serve. If you don't have fava beans, use frozen lima beans, cooked for 5 minutes, or until tender.

◆ MAKES 4 SERVINGS.

1 tablespoon olive oil

1 large sweet onion, quartered and sliced

½ red bell pepper, cored, seeded, and cut in thin strips

2 pounds small chicken breast halves, bone in

1½ cups tomato sauce, preferably home-made (page 305)

1 large sprig fresh thyme

½ to 1 teaspoon ground allspice

Salt and freshly ground black pepper

2 pounds fava beans, shelled (about 2 cups)

3 small yellow squash or zucchini, diced

2 to 3 tablespoons chopped cilantro

Heat oil in large sauté pan. Add onion and sauté for 3 minutes. Add pepper and sauté for 3 minutes. Add chicken, tomato sauce, and thyme. Sprinkle chicken with allspice, salt, and pepper. Cover and cook for 30 minutes, or until chicken is tender, turning pieces over after 15 minutes.

Meanwhile, boil the fava beans for 4 to 5 minutes, or until just tender. Drain beans, let them cool until they can be handled, and peel off and discard the tough outer skins.

Remove chicken pieces from sauté pan. Discard thyme. Add squash to sauce, cover, and cook about 5 minutes, or until it is just tender. Taste and adjust seasoning. Discard chicken skin. Stir fava beans and cilantro into sauce. Return chicken to pan, cover, and heat through. Serve hot.

Chicken Breast Sauté with Curry Spices

feerakh bel curry

In the Mideast, curry blends are most loved in Yemen, Saudi Arabia, Iraq, and the United Arab Emirates, although Israeli and Egyptian cooks use them too. The seasoning mixture in this easy chicken sauté is typical of the Persian Gulf States. For a richer dish, use boneless chicken thighs instead of breasts. Serve this entrée with white basmati rice and green beans.

◆ MAKES 4 SERVINGS.

1½ teaspoons ground cumin

1 teaspoon fennel seeds, crushed or ground (optional)

1½ teaspoons ground coriander

¼ teaspoon cayenne pepper

½ teaspoon turmeric

¼ teaspoon ground cinnamon (optional)

Salt and freshly ground black pepper

4 boneless chicken breasts (about 1½ pounds), skin removed if desired, patted dry

2 to 3 tablespoons vegetable oil

1 large onion, chopped

2 large garlic cloves, chopped (optional)

¾ cup chicken broth

Combine spices, ½ teaspoon salt, and ½ teaspoon ground black pepper in small bowl and mix well. Reserve 2 teaspoons of mixture for sauce. Sprinkle remaining spice mixture over both sides of chicken and rub thoroughly into meat.

Heat oil in large skillet. Add chicken and sauté over medium heat, pressing on it occasionally with spatula to flatten it, for 5 minutes on each side, or until no longer pink inside when you cut into its thickest part. Remove with slotted spatula.

Add onion to pan and sauté for 7 minutes, or until softened. Add garlic if you like and reserved spice mixture and sauté for ½ minute. Stir in broth and bring to a boil. Simmer over low heat for 2 minutes. Return chicken to sauce, cover, and heat gently about 3 minutes, turning once. Taste sauce and adjust seasoning. Serve hot.

Falafel-crusted Chicken

of bitzipui falafel

This three-ingredient dish is one of the fastest, easiest entrées I know. I got the idea from a friend, Faye Waldman, who coated veal chops with falafel mix, panfried them, and was pleased with the results. I find falafel mix a perfect match for the lighter-textured meat of chicken. The seasoned chickpea flour blend gives the meat a spicy, crunchy coating. You don't even need salt and pepper; there's enough in the mix. Naturally, the taste varies according to the brand.

Instead of sautéing the chicken pieces as in this recipe, you can drizzle them with oil and bake them in a hot oven until done, or cut the chicken in finger shapes and deep-fry them to make crusty hors d'oeuvres. You can use boneless chicken thighs instead of breasts, or substitute turkey breast slices or even fish fillets.

Serve the chicken with a salad of hearty greens or Middle Eastern Diced Salad (page 58), as well as Yemenite hot sauce or your favorite salsa. Tahini (page 33) or Classic Cucumber Salad with Yogurt, Garlic, and Mint (page 68) is also a good partner for the chicken.

◆ MAKES 4 SERVINGS.

4 boneless chicken breast halves
  (about 1¼ pounds), skin removed
⅓ to ½ cup dry falafel mix
3 tablespoons vegetable oil or olive oil

Hedva's Hot Pepper Relish (optional,
  page 307)
Lemon wedges (optional)

Trim chicken breast halves of fat, cartilage, and tendons. Spread falafel mix on a plate. Coat chicken pieces with falafel mix on both sides. Tap them to remove excess mix and arrange them side by side on plate.

Heat oil in large heavy skillet. Add coated chicken, in two batches if necessary to avoid crowding them. Sauté chicken over medium heat, pressing on it occasionally with flat spatula, about 6 minutes per side, or until meat changes color from pink to white throughout; cut into thickest part to check. If pan juices start to brown during sautéing, reduce heat to medium low. Transfer to plates. If cooking in batches, keep first batch warm, uncovered, in low oven while sautéing second batch. Serve hot, with hot sauce or lemon wedges if you like.

Chicken Patties in Garlicky Mushroom Tomato Sauce

kofta tavuk

Home and restaurant cooks throughout the Mideast make a variety of cakes like these from meat or chicken. Although they began as measures of frugality, these patties, often called *kofta*, are now prized.

Following the custom in the region, you can serve these chicken cakes in two basic ways. You can simply sauté the patties without making the sauce, and slip them in a pita for a tasty lunch, or serve them topped with a dab of Cilantro Pesto (page 310) or with a spoonful of tahini alongside and a generous mound of salad. For a more substantial entrée, you can briefly braise the patties in the sauce and spoon them onto a plate of pilaf. A convenient way to enjoy these easy-to-make patties is to prepare a double batch and serve them sautéed one day, and heated in the tomato sauce the next day.

◆ MAKES 4 SERVINGS.

4 slices stale white bread

1 pound ground chicken

2 medium onions, minced

4 tablespoons chopped Italian parsley

1½ teaspoons ground coriander

1 teaspoon paprika

1 teaspoon dried thyme

Salt and freshly ground black pepper

6 large garlic cloves, chopped

2 large eggs

3 to 5 tablespoons olive oil

8 ounces mushrooms, sliced

1½ cups Basic Tomato Sauce (page 305) or bottled sauce

Dip each bread slice in bowl of water to moisten; squeeze dry. Mix bread with chicken, onions, 3 tablespoons parsley, co-

riander, paprika, thyme, 1 to 1¼ teaspoons salt, ½ teaspoon pepper, and half the garlic. Add eggs. Mix lightly but thoroughly. Broil or microwave a teaspoon of mixture and taste it for seasoning. Shape mixture in patties, using about ⅓ cup mixture for each, and flatten them.

Heat 3 tablespoons oil in large heavy skillet. Add enough patties to make one layer without crowding. Sauté over medium-low heat for 4 or 5 minutes per side; use two slotted spatulas to turn them carefully. If you're serving them simply sautéed, be sure they are cooked through; if you will be braising them in sauce, they need only be browned at this point. Sauté remaining patties in same way, adding oil to skillet if necessary and heating it before adding more patties. Drain patties on paper towels. You can serve them at this point or braise them in sauce.

To make sauce for braising patties, reheat oil in skillet, add mushrooms, and sauté over medium heat for 2 minutes. Add remaining garlic and cook ½ minute, stirring. Add tomato sauce and ¼ cup water, cover, and heat over low heat. Add a little more water if sauce is too thick. If you are braising the chicken cakes, return them to the skillet, cover, and cook over low heat for 5 minutes, or until hot and cooked through. Taste sauce and adjust seasoning. Serve sprinkled with remaining parsley.

Turkish Turkey with Hazelnut Currant Rice

hindi dolmasi

Turkey's hazelnuts are exported around the world and naturally are used in the country's own cuisine as well. As for turkeys, we all know they don't come from Turkey, but from the New World—the Europeans and Middle Easterners simply named the unfamiliar bird for an exotic place. In French it's *dinde*, in Turkish it's *hindi*, and in Hebrew it's *tarnegol hodu*, all of which mean India bird.

Although turkey is not as common in the Mideast as in North America, people enjoy the bird and prepare it with a variety of techniques. Egyptians make it into *kofte* (patties), or burgers, or braise small whole turkeys with vegetables. Turkey shawarma is popular in Israel.

For festive occasions some Persians and Turks roast whole turkeys. A favorite Turkish stuffing is rice pilaf embellished with nuts and fruit. If you'd like the rice grains to remain firm, prepare the stuffing separately instead of baking it in the bird. The bird will also roast faster this way.

◆ MAKES 6 TO 8 SERVINGS.

7¾ to 8 cups turkey or chicken stock, or a mixture of stock and water

3 tablespoons vegetable oil or butter

1 medium onion, minced

2 cups long-grain rice

Salt

¼ to ½ cup currants

1¼ teaspoons ground allspice, or more to taste

½ teaspoon ground cinnamon

Freshly grated nutmeg to taste

Freshly ground black pepper

½ cup hazelnuts, toasted and peeled (page 369)

One 10-pound turkey

3 to 4 tablespoons vegetable oil or melted butter

4 teaspoons cornstarch dissolved in 3 tablespoons water

Italian parsley sprigs

To make stuffing: Heat 3½ cups stock, cover, and keep warm. Heat oil in large saucepan. Add onion and cook over medium-low heat for 5 minutes, or until soft but not brown. Add rice and sauté over medium heat, stirring, for 2 minutes. Add hot stock and salt and bring to a boil. Cover and cook over low heat for 10 minutes. Add ¼ cup currants, cover, and cook for 2 minutes; rice should not quite be tender. Stir in ¾ teaspoon allspice or more to taste, ¼ teaspoon cinnamon, nutmeg, pepper, and hazelnuts. Taste and adjust seasoning. Let cool completely before stuffing turkey.

Remove the oven's top rack and preheat to 425°F. Sprinkle inside of turkey with salt and pepper. Fold neck skin under body and fasten with a skewer. Pack body cavity loosely with stuffing, if you like, and cover opening with crumpled foil. If you have stuffed the turkey, truss it with a trussing string and needle or close it with skewers. Set aside extra stuffing.

Rub turkey with oil or melted butter and set it, breast side up, on rack in large roasting pan. Sprinkle with salt and pepper. Roast for 30 minutes, basting twice. Reduce oven temperature to 350°F. Roast turkey for 1½ hours, basting with pan juices every 30 minutes. Turkeys vary in the amount of juices they produce as they roast, but there should be at least a thin layer of roasting juices in pan so the drippings won't burn; if pan becomes nearly dry, add ¼ to ½ cup chicken stock.

Spoon reserved stuffing or all of the stuffing (if you have not stuffed the turkey) into an oiled baking dish. Add ¼ cup stock if you have only a little stuffing, or ½ cup stock if you are baking all the stuffing separately. Baste stuffing lightly with turkey pan juices. Cover and bake for 30 minutes, or until rice is tender. Meanwhile, cover turkey with foil and roast it for about 10 more minutes (if it is not stuffed) or 20 to 35 more minutes (if it is stuffed). An instant-read thermometer inserted in stuffing baking inside bird should register 165°F, and when inserted into the thickest part of turkey thigh should register 170–180°F. Transfer turkey carefully to platter or large cutting board. Discard strings or skewers.

Skim excess fat from pan juices. Add 1 cup stock and bring to a boil, stirring and scraping to dissolve any brown bits in pan. Strain into saucepan. Add 2½ cups more stock and bring to a boil. Reduce heat to medium. Whisk cornstarch mixture into sauce and return to boil, whisking. Add remaining ¼ cup currants if you like. Add ½ teaspoon allspice or more to taste, remaining cinnamon, nutmeg, and pepper. Simmer sauce until thick enough to lightly coat a spoon. Taste and adjust seasoning.

Carve turkey, arrange on platter, garnish with parsley, and serve with stuffing. Reheat sauce and serve separately.

Turkey Thighs with Cumin and Tomatoes

hindi yahni

If you like Mexican food, the flavors here will be familiar to you. Cooks in the Mideast love cumin, cilantro, and garlic, which are native to their land, even more than Mexicans do, and are also fond of Mexico's chilies.

In fact, the stew's main ingredients reflect food exchanges that took place centuries ago between the two regions. Cilantro and cumin, both enjoyed in the Mideast since biblical times, were brought by the Spanish to Mexico. They probably brought garlic too, as it is indigenous to Asia and has been widely cultivated in the Mediterranean area. Spanish explorers of Latin America took chilies, tomatoes, and turkey back to the Old World.

Turkey thighs give a wonderful taste to the sauce in this stew. I partially cook them, then remove the skin, bones, and cartilage to make them easier to eat. I also make use of a popular Mideast technique of flavoring a soup or stew with dried chilies, then removing them.

This dish makes a delicious winter entrée with rice, potatoes, or beans. You might also like to serve steamed broccoli or spinach, and a brightly flavored salad such as Mediterranean Mexican Diced Salad (page 61).

◆ MAKES 8 OR 9 SERVINGS.

4½ pounds turkey thighs (3 thighs)

6 cups water

6 small dried chilies, such as *chiles de arbol* or *chiles japones*

Salt and freshly ground black pepper

2 to 3 tablespoons olive oil

1 large onion, chopped

8 large garlic cloves, peeled

1 tablespoon ground cumin

Two 28-ounce cans tomatoes, drained and chopped

1 teaspoon paprika

1½ teaspoons dried oregano or thyme

3 tablespoons chopped cilantro

In heavy stew pan, combine turkey, water, chilies, salt, and pepper. Bring to a boil. Cover and simmer over low heat for 1 hour.

Remove turkey from broth. Discard skin, bones, cartilage, and visible fat adhering to the meat. Pour broth from pan and reserve it, including the chilies. Skim fat from broth.

Heat oil in pan. Add onion and sauté over medium heat for 7 minutes, or until beginning to turn golden. Add garlic and cumin and sauté 1 minute, stirring. Add tomatoes and bring to a boil.

Return turkey to pan and add 2 cups broth and the reserved chilies. Add paprika and oregano. Cover and simmer over low heat for 1 hour, or until turkey is very tender, adding more broth if sauce becomes too thick. Discard chilies. Taste and adjust seasoning. Serve sprinkled with cilantro.

Cumin Turkey Burgers with Yogurt Garlic Sauce

kofta hindi

Lamb or beef is the usual choice for grilled patties in the Mideast but these flavorful turkey burgers are much lighter. For a more luxurious version, add ¼ cup pine nuts or coarsely chopped blanched almonds to the burger mixture. Instead of grilling the burgers, you can panfry them in a nonstick skillet. Serve them with grilled tomatoes and chilies, as in this recipe, or with a green salad or Mideast-California Diced Salad (page 60). In the Mideast, burgers are served either on a plate, on a flatbread, or inside a pita's pocket. Yogurt sauce is a popular partner for them in Turkey and Lebanon.

◆ MAKES 4 SERVINGS.

1¼ to 1⅓ pounds ground turkey or chicken (2⅔ to 3 cups)

1 medium onion, grated

1 teaspoon ground cumin

½ teaspoon salt

½ teaspoon freshly ground black pepper

¼ teaspoon cayenne pepper, or to taste

4 plum tomatoes, halved (optional)

4 mild green chilies, such as Anaheim (optional)

Yogurt Garlic Sauce (page 311), at room temperature

Aleppo pepper or paprika (for sprinkling)

Olive oil, for brushing on burgers

Combine turkey with onion, cumin, salt, pepper, and cayenne. Mix lightly with your hands until well blended. Shape in 4 patties.

Prepare grill with rack about 6 inches above glowing coals and brush with oil. Or lightly oil broiler rack and position it about 4 inches from heat source and heat broiler. Or heat stove-top grill. If serving tomatoes and chilies, grill them about 7 minutes, or just until lightly charred. Remove from grill.

If you want to peel chilies, put them in a bag and close it; let stand 5 minutes, then peel chilies.

Spoon yogurt sauce into bowl and sprinkle lightly with Aleppo pepper. Brush turkey patties with oil. Broil or grill patties about 6 or 7 minutes, or until they are springy when pressed, turning once. Cut one in center to be sure color has changed and it is cooked through. Serve immediately, accompanied by yogurt sauce.

Sesame Chicken Salad with Barley and Fava Beans

salat of im zahtar v'grissim

Zahtar, the popular eastern Mediterranean herb and toasted sesame seed blend (page 14), is delicious in chicken and turkey salads like this one. If you don't have any zahtar in your pantry, it's easy to improvise a similar herbaceous flavor (see Note). To make the salad more quickly, use fast-cooking barley, which you can find in natural food stores, and substitute frozen lima beans for the fava beans. If you'd like to include green beans in this salad, you can cook them in the saucepan with the other beans.

◆ MAKES 4 TO 6 SERVINGS.

1 cup pearl barley

¾ to 1 cup shelled fresh or frozen fava beans or lima beans

12 ounces green beans, cut in thirds (optional)

3 cups diced cooked chicken or turkey

1 or 2 roasted red peppers (see "Basics," page 370, or from a jar), cut in strips

3 green onions, chopped

2 to 4 tablespoons extra-virgin olive oil

1 to 3 tablespoons strained fresh-squeezed lemon juice

Salt and freshly ground black pepper

4 teaspoons zahtar or substitute (see Note)

Lettuce or spinach leaves (optional)

Bring 3 cups water to boil in large heavy saucepan and add a pinch of salt. Add barley and return to a boil. Cover and simmer over low heat for 35 to 40 minutes, or until barley is tender. Rinse barley briefly and drain well. Transfer to large bowl and let cool.

Cook fava or lima beans in saucepan of boiling salted water, uncovered, over medium-high heat until just tender; fresh lima beans take about 15 minutes, fava beans and frozen lima beans, about 5 to 7 minutes. If using green beans, add them during the last 5 minutes of the other beans' cooking time. Drain beans, rinse with cold water, and drain well; if using fava beans, peel off thick skins.

Add green beans, fava beans, chicken, pepper strips, and green onions to bowl of barley. Fold together gently.

Whisk oil, lemon juice, salt, and pepper

in small bowl. Add to salad. Taste and adjust seasoning. Just before serving, fold in all but 1 teaspoon of the zahtar. Sprinkle remaining zahtar on top. If you like, serve salad on a bed of lettuce or spinach leaves.

NOTE If you don't have zahtar, mix 1 tablespoon chopped fresh marjoram or thyme (or 1 teaspoon dried) with 1 teaspoon dried oregano and 1 tablespoon toasted sesame seeds (see "Basics," page 369).

Turkey and Rice Salad with Raisins and Pistachios

salat hodu im orez v'tzimukim

Serve this savory-sweet summer salad as a delicious lunch entrée or as a colorful buffet dish. It is composed of rice pilaf gently spiced with coriander and cumin, accented with vegetables and plenty of fresh chives. If you have roasted or grilled duck, you can use it in this salad, as it goes well with the spices and raisins. In early autumn garnish the salad with pomegranate seeds instead of raisins for a beautiful variation.

◆ MAKES ABOUT 8 SERVINGS.

5 to 6 tablespoons vegetable oil or olive oil

1 zucchini, cut in ½-inch dice

Salt and freshly ground black pepper to taste

1 onion, chopped

1½ cups long-grain white rice

1½ teaspoons ground coriander

1 teaspoon ground cumin

3 cups hot water

1 large carrot, peeled and diced

Pinch cayenne pepper

¼ to ⅓ cup raisins

2 to 3 tablespoons white-wine vinegar or
　　lemon juice

½ to ¾ cup cooked chickpeas
　　(garbanzo beans) or corn, or one
　　8- to 9-ounce can of either, drained

3 to 4 cups diced cooked turkey or chicken,
　　cooked any way you like

1 cup diced cucumber

⅓ cup chopped fresh chives

⅓ cup pistachios, toasted

Heat 1 tablespoon oil in large sauté pan or stew pan. Add zucchini, salt, and pepper and sauté over medium heat for 2 minutes, stirring often. Remove with slotted spoon.

Add 2 tablespoons oil to pan. Add onion and cook over medium heat for 5 minutes, or until soft but not brown. Add rice, coriander, and cumin and sauté, stirring, about 2 minutes or until grains begin to turn opaque.

Pour hot water over rice and stir once. Add diced carrot, 1 teaspoon salt, pinch of pepper, and cayenne. Bring to a boil over high heat. Reduce heat to low, cover tightly, and simmer, without stirring, for 17 minutes. Scatter zucchini over top. Cover and

simmer for 3 minutes, or until rice is tender and liquid is absorbed.

Fluff rice gently with large fork. Transfer very gently to large bowl. Add raisins and fold in gently. Let cool.

In a small bowl, whisk remaining oil with vinegar and gently fold into salad. When mixture is cooled, fold in chickpeas or corn, turkey, cucumber, half the chives, and half the pistachios. Taste and adjust seasoning. Serve topped with remaining chives and pistachios.

Roast Turkey Laffa with Hot Pepper Hummus

laffa hodu im hummus

A laffa is a wrapped sandwich for which the ingredients are rolled up in lavash or other thin flatbread. You can either roll the lavash as one sandwich and cut it in pieces, or cut it first and roll each one individually. Of course, you can spoon the filling into a pita as well, or layer the elements on a halved roll.

The Hot Pepper Hummus dip is a terrific alternative to mayonnaise in turkey or chicken sandwiches. Tahini, on its own or mixed with hummus, is also a good match for the turkey, and so is Garlic Sauce (page

309). For a lighter option that's quick and easy, spoon in Yogurt Garlic Sauce (page 311), but be sure it's thick enough so it won't drip out of the sandwich. Serve the sandwich with pickles or flavorful olives.

◆ MAKES 4 SERVINGS.

2 cups thin strips roast turkey or chicken

⅓ cup chopped green onion

⅓ cup chopped celery (optional)

1 red or green bell pepper, cored, seeded, and diced small, or 1 roasted peeled green or red bell pepper (see "Basics," page 370; or from a jar), cut in thin strips

1 to 2 tablespoons extra-virgin olive oil

2 to 3 teaspoons strained fresh-squeezed lemon juice

Salt and freshly ground black pepper to taste

½ cup Hot Pepper Hummus (page 36), or more to taste

4 pieces lavash, about 8 or 9 inches square

1¼ to 1½ cups shredded lettuce, preferably romaine

2 small ripe tomatoes, cut in thin slices or half slices (optional)

Combine turkey with green onion, celery, if you like, roasted or fresh bell pepper, olive oil, and lemon juice. Season to taste with salt and pepper.

To make each sandwich, spread Hot Pepper Hummus on one end of each lavash, leaving a ½-inch border at the ends. Top with lettuce, turkey salad, and tomato slices. Roll up tightly and serve.

Meat, the Centerpiece of Celebrations

Yakir's Spiced Steak with Mushrooms and Asparagus • *Steak M'tubbal im Pitriyot v'Asperagus*

Curry-spiced Beef with Green Beans and Potatoes • *Murraq*

Grilled Steak Salad with Cilantro Pesto • *Salat Steak im Kuzbarah*

Middle Eastern Beef Cassoulet • *Etli Kuru Fasulye*

Yahalom's Hawaijj Hamburgers • *Hamburger im Hawaijj*

Persian Chickpea Beef Patties • *Kabob Shami*

Turkish Meatballs in Green Pepper Tomato Sauce • *Izmir Köftesi*

Middle Eastern Meat Loaf with Almonds • *Kibbe Seneyyah*

Spicy Beef-stuffed Cabbage in Pepper Sauce • *Malfouf Ablama*

Sweet-and-Savory Stuffed Peppers with Meat, Nuts, and Currants • *Etli Büber Dolmasi*

Eggplant Macaroni Moussaka • *Moussaka*

Lamb or Beef Kabobs with Onion-Herb Marinade • *Kabob*

Lamb Steak Sandwich • *Shawarma*

Grilled Lamb Chops with Garlic Cumin Tomato Salsa • *Kastaletta Mechwie*

Okra and Lamb Stew with Tart Tomato Sauce • *Bamia bel Lahm*

Prince-pleaser Ragout with Cheesy Eggplant Puree • *Hunkar Begendi*

Lamb and Rice Pilaf with Yogurt Sauce • *Mansaf*

Crunchy Lamb Kibbe with Cinnamon and Cloves • *Kibbi Makliya*

Eggplant with Lamb and Almond Stuffing • *Batenjane Mehchi*

Osso Buco, Middle Eastern Style • *Lahm Beatello bel Salsa Tamatem*

Throughout the ages, meat appeared on the Mideast table mostly for feast days and special family gatherings. This custom still holds in many kitchens. Wonderful meat-stuffed vegetables are highlights of holiday spreads. For weekday meals a small portion of meat might be stewed with a generous amount of vegetables. The meat lends richness and savor to these dishes.

Lamb is the meat of choice in most of the region. From ancient times, sheep and shepherds have been part of the area's landscape and history. In the Bible, shepherds are frequently mentioned, notably in the stories of Abraham, Moses, and King David. The Prophet Muhammad worked as a shepherd as a boy. Shepherds figure in the culinary culture as well. Turkish Shepherd's Salad is said to have originally been composed of greens shepherds found in the wild. Now it is a favorite partner for all sorts of meat dishes (see page 61).

Anyone who has glanced at a restaurant menu from a Middle Eastern country notices the numerous kinds of grilled meats. Any size piece is a candidate for the barbecue, from cubes threaded on skewers for kabobs to impressive cone-shaped shawarma, or doner (see page 196), to whole lambs prepared for the most festive of celebrations. Top picks throughout the region are lamb and beef, but those who eat pork turn it into kabobs also, while some use veal, organ meats, or the old-fashioned choices of goat and mutton.

Rather than brushing their meat with barbecue sauce, cooks tend to opt for a very simple marinade or spice rub. The finest meats, such as lamb chops, beef fillet, and rib eye steaks, might be sprinkled only with a little salt and pepper, perhaps mixed with a little olive oil, lemon juice, or fresh thyme. Spicier marinades include cumin, cinnamon, or garlic. Even the grill itself might be flavored. Many

of my Middle Eastern friends clean their barbecue before putting the meat on by dipping half an onion in a little oil and rubbing it vigorously on the grill bars.

The traditional preference in the region is for well-done meats, but obviously you should cook them to your taste. Simple presentations are the norm. Small succulent morsels might be served on a bed of lettuce as part of the meze, and accompanied with sumac for sprinkling or with lemon or lime wedges and often with whole green onions or thin slices of fresh large onions. Small whole radishes and pickles are on the table as well, and Assyrians and Iranians set out sprigs of herbs such as basil or mint.

As an entrée, grilled meat comes with rice, fried potatoes, or pita bread and with Middle Eastern Diced Salad (page 58). Some like hot sauce on the side, while others prefer a cooling yogurt or refreshing Borani Salad (page 257). A pungent Garlic Sauce (page 309) or smooth, rich Tahini (page 33) might also accompany the meat.

Hearty main courses of meat and beans, reminiscent of Provençal cassoulet (see Middle Eastern Beef Cassoulet, page 184), are winter staples. Summertime meals might include Okra and Lamb Stew with Tart Tomato Sauce (page 199), made with plenty of okra and a small amount of lamb to create a savory sauce.

Ground meat is a favorite and is used in countless ways. For quick meals, there are meat patties called *kofta* in Arabic and Turkish. Unlike American hamburgers, which are often sprinkled with salt and pepper after they are cooked, Middle Eastern cooks mix the meat with seasonings before shaping it. In our family we enhance our burgers with the Yemenite spice blend, Hawaijj (see Yahalom's Hawaijj Hamburgers, page 185). Similar meat patty mixtures are turned into kabobs by being shaped into long sausages around flat skewers, or made into meatballs that are simmered in soups or braised in sauces. These ground meat mixtures are also combined with bulgur wheat to make kibbe, a Middle Eastern specialty that is wildly popular fried or baked as an appetizer or entrée.

Yakir's Spiced Steak with Mushrooms and Asparagus

steak m'tubbal im pitriyot v'asperagus

In our household combining steak and vegetables as a meal-in-a-skillet is a favorite technique for making dinners that are festive but quick. We find that cutting a thick steak in cubes and sautéing it briefly can be even faster than grilling or broiling the meat. My Middle East–born husband often prepares steak sautés this way and spices the meat with the seasonings he grew up with—cumin, turmeric, and plenty of black pepper.

In addition to tenderloin, this recipe works well with other tender steaks, such as rib eye, porterhouse, and T-bone. Mushrooms of any type are perfect partners for the beef. For a colorful sauté, we add asparagus, green beans, baby carrots, green peas, or sugar snap peas. Tossed with the beef cubes, the vegetables form an attractive medley, somewhat like a stew, but with a much fresher look and character. Couscous with Pine Nuts and Bell Peppers (page 293) or Turkish Tomato Pilaf (page 264) makes a tasty accompaniment.

◆ MAKES 2 SERVINGS.

10 to 12 ounces thin asparagus spears (1 small bunch), each trimmed and cut in 3 pieces

Salt and freshly ground black pepper

1 to 2 tablespoons vegetable oil

2 small beef tenderloin steaks (about 10 ounces total), fat trimmed, meat cut in 1-inch dice

¾ teaspoon ground cumin

¼ teaspoon turmeric

1½ cups sliced mushrooms

⅔ cup beef or chicken broth

1 sprig fresh thyme, or ½ teaspoon dried thyme

1 to 2 tablespoons butter, cut in 2 to 4 small pieces (optional)

Pour enough water into deep skillet or sauté pan to easily cover asparagus, add salt, and bring to a boil. Add asparagus pieces and boil, uncovered, for 2 minutes, or until barely tender when pierced with sharp knife. Drain, rinse with cold water, and drain.

Heat oil in large heavy nonstick skillet or sauté pan. Add beef cubes and sprinkle with salt and pepper. Sauté beef over high heat for 2 minutes, shaking pan often. Sprinkle with cumin and turmeric and sauté over medium-high heat for 1 minute, or until beef is brown but still medium-rare inside, stirring often; cut a cube to check. Remove meat to plate with slotted spoon.

Add mushrooms to pan and sauté over medium heat about 2 minutes, or until lightly browned. With slotted spoon, transfer about half of mushrooms to plate of beef, leaving remaining mushrooms in pan to flavor the sauce. Add broth and thyme to pan and bring to a boil. Boil for 2 minutes, or until only about 3 or 4 tablespoons of liquid remain. Return asparagus to skillet. Add beef and mushrooms with any juices on the plate. Warm over medium-low flame until heated through. Discard thyme sprig. If you like, add butter and stir just until it blends in. Taste and adjust seasoning. Serve hot.

Curry-spiced Beef with Green Beans and Potatoes

murraq

If you've tasted the northern Indian dishes called curries in the West, the tastes in this Persian Gulf dish will be familiar. Garam masala, which is sprinkled on the stew at the last minute for extra zip, is an Indian spice blend that you can find at many supermarkets. Typically, this dish is served with white basmati rice and accompanied by a cooling dish of Yogurt Garlic Sauce (page 311).

◆ MAKES 4 TO 6 SERVINGS.

2 tablespoons vegetable oil

2 large onions, halved and sliced thin

2 tablespoons finely chopped peeled gingerroot

4 large garlic cloves, chopped

2 jalapeño or 4 serrano peppers, or more if desired, seeded and chopped

1 tablespoon ground coriander

1½ teaspoons ground cumin

½ teaspoon turmeric

½ teaspoon dried red chili flakes, or to taste

Pinch ground cloves

2 black cardamom pods, pounded lightly (optional)

One 3-inch cinnamon stick

2 pounds beef chuck (shoulder), trimmed of excess fat and cut in 1-inch cubes

Salt and freshly ground black pepper

1 green bell pepper, halved, cored, seeded, and cut in strips

4 ripe or canned tomatoes, diced

2 tablespoons tomato paste

1½ cups water

1 pound small or medium-size boiling potatoes

1 pound green beans, ends removed, halved

4 tablespoons chopped cilantro

Cayenne pepper (optional)

1 teaspoon garam masala (optional, for sprinkling)

Heat oil in large stew pan. Add onions and sauté over medium heat about 10 minutes, or until brown. Add ginger, garlic, jalapeño peppers, coriander, cumin, turmeric, chili flakes, cloves, cardamom, and cinnamon and stir over low heat for 1 minute. Add beef, salt, pepper, and green pepper and cook over medium heat for 5 minutes, stirring often. Stir in tomatoes, tomato paste, and water and bring to a boil. Cover and cook over low heat for 1½ hours.

Peel potatoes if you like, and cut in 1-inch

chunks. Add to stew. If stew appears dry, add ½ cup water. Cover and cook for 35 minutes, or until potatoes are nearly tender.

Cook green beans in saucepan of boiling salted water for 5 minutes, or until crisp-tender. Rinse with cold water. Add beans and 3 tablespoons cilantro to stew and cook for 5 minutes, or until potatoes and beans are tender. Taste, adjust seasoning, and add cayenne to taste. Serve sprinkled with remaining cilantro and garam masala.

Grilled Steak Salad with Cilantro Pesto

salat steak im kuzbarah

Grilled meat with salad has long been a favorite combination in the Middle East, whether presented on a plate or enclosed in a pita. Salads of raw vegetables like *Fattoush* (page 63), green salad, or diced salad are popular options, but so are medleys of grilled vegetables. Choose any or all of the vegetables listed below and, if you like, include grilled or broiled eggplant slices too (see "Basics," page 372).

Often chopped cilantro is served with grilled steaks but sometimes it's made into a simple sauce, like the Cilantro Pesto (page 310) used in this recipe, which flavors the salad dressing and accompanies the steaks.

If you don't have time to prepare Cilantro Pesto, improvise by adding 2 tablespoons chopped cilantro to ½ cup of purchased basil pesto.

Serve the salad with fresh bread and hot sauce. To turn it into a sandwich, spread Cilantro Pesto inside cut pita breads or on split crusty rolls before adding the sliced steak and grilled vegetables. Put a little of the dressed greens in the sandwich or serve them separately.

◆ MAKES 4 SERVINGS.

> 3 cups romaine in bite-size pieces
> 3 cups mixed baby greens
> 2 green onions, sliced
> 2 tablespoons coarsely chopped cilantro (optional)
> 2 tablespoons strained fresh-squeezed lemon juice
> 2 to 3 tablespoons extra-virgin olive oil, plus a little extra for brushing on vegetables
> Cilantro Pesto (page 310)
> Salt and freshly ground black pepper
> 2 green or red bell peppers, grilled (see "Basics," page 370), or 4 roasted pepper halves from a jar
> 1 large onion, cut in thick slices
> 6 large mushrooms, halved
> 2 medium zucchini, sliced diagonally about ⅜ inch thick
> 1½ pounds tender steaks, such as rib eye, top loin (New York), or tenderloin, about 1 inch thick
> 12 to 16 cherry tomatoes or other small red, yellow, and orange tomatoes

Prepare grill with rack about 4 inches above coals or heat source, or heat a ridged stove-top grill or broiler.

In bowl, toss lettuce with baby greens, green onions, and chopped cilantro. In small bowl, whisk lemon juice with oil and 2 tablespoons Cilantro Pesto. Season to taste with salt and pepper. Cut grilled pepper pieces in wide strips.

Lightly brush onion, mushrooms, and zucchini with olive oil and sprinkle them with salt and pepper. Grill or broil them about 3 to 5 minutes on each side, or until slightly softened but not dry. Cut onion and zucchini slices in thirds.

Sprinkle steaks with salt and plenty of freshly ground pepper. Grill steaks until done to your taste; for medium-rare, allow about 4 minutes per side on an outdoor grill, or about 3 minutes per side in broiler or on a stove-top grill. Check for doneness by pressing on meat: rare meat gives little resistance, while medium-rare resists slightly. Transfer steaks to clean plate and let stand for a few minutes.

Pour dressing over salad and toss lightly. Taste and adjust seasoning. Divide among 4 plates. Top each salad with grilled vegetables and cherry tomatoes. Slice steaks on the diagonal and set slices in center of salads. Serve remaining Cilantro Pesto separately.

Middle Eastern Beef Cassoulet

etli kuru fasulye

Along the Mediterranean coast, meaty bean casseroles like this, enlivened with tomatoes, garlic, and olive oil, are very popular. This one is seasoned in the style of Turkish, Lebanese, and Israeli dishes, with fresh dill and a touch of hot pepper. Add dried chilies if you like for a little extra heat. You can make this entrée with beef, lamb, or chicken.

If you are familiar with French cooking, this entrée somewhat recalls cassoulet but is much simpler. Some finish it in the oven, as the people in southwest France often do with their famous specialty. If you'd like to bake the stew so the beans get a little crusty, see the Note at the end of the recipe.

◆ MAKES 4 TO 6 SERVINGS.

1 pound dried white beans, such as Great Northern

1 bay leaf

Salt

2 tablespoons olive oil

2 pounds beef chuck, excess fat trimmed and cut in 1-inch cubes

1 large onion, chopped

6 large garlic cloves, chopped

2 pounds ripe tomatoes, diced, or one 28-ounce can tomatoes, drained and diced

4 tiny dried chilies, such as *chiles de arbol*
  (optional)

Freshly ground black pepper

1 or 2 green bell peppers, cored, seeded,
  and cut in strips (optional)

1 teaspoon Aleppo pepper, or ¾ teaspoon
  paprika and ¼ teaspoon cayenne pepper,
  or to taste

1 tablespoon chopped fresh dill,
  or 2 tablespoons chopped parsley

Sort beans, discarding any broken ones and any stones. Put them in saucepan with I quart water and bay leaf and bring to a boil. Cover and cook over low heat for I hour. Add a pinch of salt and cook about ½ hour longer, or until just tender. Discard bay leaf.

Heat oil in heavy wide casserole. Add beef cubes to pan in batches and brown them on all sides over medium-high heat. Remove beef. Add onion and cook over medium-low heat for 5 minutes, or until lightly browned. Add garlic and cook ½ minute. Stir in tomatoes and cook for 2 minutes.

Return meat to pan. Add I½ cups water, chilies, salt, and pepper and bring to a boil. Cover and simmer for 2 hours, adding a few tablespoons of hot water occasionally if sauce looks dry. Add green peppers if you like and simmer for 30 more minutes, or until beef is very tender. Skim off excess fat. Discard chilies.

Drain beans, reserving their cooking liquid, and add them to stew. Add Aleppo pepper and simmer for 5 to 10 minutes to blend flavors. If stew is too soupy, cook un-covered for 5 more minutes. If stew is too thick, add a few tablespoons bean cooking liquid and simmer over low heat for 2 minutes. Add dill. Taste and adjust seasoning. Serve hot.

NOTE To bake the stew, moisten it with ½ cup extra bean liquid. After adding the beans and Aleppo pepper, add the dill and spoon the finished stew into a large gratin dish or other baking dish. Bake, uncovered, at 400°F for 20 to 30 minutes.

Yahalom's Hawaijj Hamburgers

hamburger im hawaijj

My brother-in-law Yahalom Levy loves *hawaijj*, the Yemenite soup spice blend, and came up with these burgers. To keep it a family recipe, we serve it with Yahalom's sister Hedva's jalapeño garlic hot sauce, but it's also good with Middle Eastern Tomato Salsa (see Grilled Lamb Chops with Garlic Cumin Tomato Salsa, page 198) or with Turkish Tomato and Onion Dip (page 38). Serve the burgers in a pita or on a hamburger bun. On the side, serve Eastern Mediterranean Potato Salad (page 71) and Tangy Two-way Coleslaw (page 69).

If you like, substitute ground chicken or

turkey for the beef. If using poultry, brush the burgers lightly with oil before grilling and cook them until well done.

◆ MAKES 4 SERVINGS.

1 teaspoon ground cumin

¼ teaspoon turmeric

Salt and freshly ground black pepper

2 garlic cloves, finely minced (optional)

1⅓ to 1½ pounds ground beef, preferably chuck (3 to 3⅓ cups)

2 to 4 pita breads or sesame hamburger rolls

1 sweet or red onion, halved and sliced thin (optional)

Hedva's Hot Pepper Relish (page 307) or Middle Eastern Tomato Salsa (page 198)

Prepare grill with rack about 4 to 6 inches above heat source or heat a ridged stove-top grill. Lightly oil grill rack.

Mix cumin with turmeric, ¼ teaspoon pepper, and garlic. Combine meat with spice mixture in a bowl, handling meat as gently as possible. Lightly shape meat in four patties ¾ to 1 inch thick. If using hamburger rolls, split them and toast them lightly.

Sprinkle patties with salt and pepper and set them on grill rack above glowing coals or on stove-top grill. Grill them until done to your taste; for medium-rare, allow about 5 minutes per side on a charcoal grill, or about 3 or 4 minutes per side on a stove-top grill. To check, make a small cut in the center of a burger to see its color.

If using pita bread, heat it very briefly on the grill, just a few seconds on each side, making sure the bread stays soft. Quickly cut each pita bread in two, or to fill whole ones, cut a small piece off one end of each pita bread to form a pocket you can fill. Transfer hamburgers to pita or buns and serve with onion slices and relish or salsa.

Persian Chickpea Beef Patties

kabob shami

These tasty little burgers gain their character from ground chickpeas added to the meat. Usually they're sautéed but you can grill them on a stove-top grill or broil them instead. Make them any size you like and serve them on their own or with a sauce. Small ones make tempting hors d'oeuvres with Middle Eastern Cilantro Pesto (page 310) as a dipping sauce. Although many Persians don't go for hot and spicy food, I find Red Pepper Walnut Dip (page 39) a tasty partner too. You can also serve these little cakes as an appetizer topped with Minty Green Sauce (page 311).

As a main course, I like these Persian patties with Pomegranate Walnut Sauce (page 164) or Turkish Tomato Pepper Sauce (page 38). You can heat the sauce to spoon over the patties, or simmer the patties directly in the sauce for a flavor exchange. My favorite accompaniment for these entrées is a mound of basmati rice. For a simpler supper, serve the patties with a quick salad or slip them into a pita.

◆ MAKES 8 APPETIZER OR 4 MAIN-COURSE SERVINGS.

⅓ cup Italian parsley sprigs

One 15-ounce can chickpeas, drained and rinsed, or 1½ cups cooked chickpeas (see Note)

½ large onion, cut in chunks

1 pound lean ground beef

¾ teaspoon salt

½ teaspoon freshly ground black pepper

¼ teaspoon turmeric

3 tablespoons vegetable oil, or more if needed

Italian parsley sprigs

Mince parsley in food processor. Add chickpeas to food processor, chop them fine, and remove mixture. Mince onion in processor. Mix ground beef with salt, pepper, turmeric, and onions. Add chickpea mixture and mix well. If you like, cook a teaspoonful of mixture in the broiler or microwave; taste it and adjust seasoning of patty mixture.

Take 1 or 2 tablespoons of mixture and roll it in your palms so it is compact and smooth. Shape in a patty. Refrigerate until ready to sauté.

Heat oil in large skillet over medium heat. Fry meat patties in batches about 4 minutes per side, or until golden brown and cooked through, adding more oil to the skillet as necessary and heating it before adding more patties. Drain on paper towels. Serve garnished with parsley.

NOTE   For a crunchier texture, substitute ⅔ cup raw chickpeas for the cooked ones. Soak them for 8 hours and drain them before adding them to mixture. Be sure patties are cooked through.

Turkish Meatballs in Green Pepper Tomato Sauce

izmir köftesi

In Middle Eastern households meatballs are served with a variety of sauces and soups. Instead of tomato sauce, you can simmer them in meat or chicken stock, then turn the cooking liquid into Lemon Egg Sauce (page 306) to accompany the meatballs.

For spicy meatballs, substitute 2 teaspoons ground cumin for the cinnamon and add ¼ to ½ teaspoon ground cayenne pepper. Serve the meatballs with spaghetti, orzo, rice pilaf, or fried potatoes, with a plate of diced salad or green salad on the side.

◆ MAKES 4 OR 5 SERVINGS.

2 slices bread

1 pound lean ground beef

1 egg

⅓ cup finely minced onion

2 large garlic cloves, minced

¾ teaspoon salt

½ teaspoon freshly ground black pepper

½ teaspoon ground cinnamon

1 teaspoon paprika

2 tablespoons olive oil, or more if needed

Turkish Tomato Pepper Sauce (page 306)

Soak bread in water, squeeze dry, and break apart into small pieces. Combine bread with beef, egg, onion, garlic, salt, pepper, cinnamon, and paprika. Knead until thoroughly mixed. With moistened hands, shape mixture into balls, using 1 or 2 tablespoons for each. Roll them between your palms until they are smooth.

Heat oil in heavy sauté pan or large saucepan. Add meatballs in batches and brown them on all sides over medium-high heat, adding more oil to the pan as necessary and heating it before adding more meatballs. Transfer to paper towels with a slotted spoon. Discard fat from skillet.

Add Turkish Tomato Pepper Sauce to pan and bring to a simmer. Add meatballs, cover, and simmer over low heat for 10 to 15 minutes, or until cooked through, adding a little hot water if sauce becomes too thick. Taste and adjust seasoning. Serve hot.

Middle Eastern Meat Loaf with Almonds

kibbe seneyyah

Baked kibbe, a popular entrée in the Mideast, is actually a form of meat loaf. Its components are similar to those of fried kibbe (page 204)—a meaty bulgur wheat dough and a meat filling enhanced with nuts. The dough and the filling are layered in a shallow pan and baked. Some make it with beef, others opt for lamb and, as with American meat loaf, some prefer a mixture of beef, lamb, and veal. The meat loaf is served cut in squares or diamond shapes.

Obviously baked kibbe is much faster to assemble and easier to cook than the fried version. To prevent the meat loaf from drying in the oven, many grind lamb fat with the meat. A more healthful solution is to brush the loaf with olive oil and to drain the excess fat from the baking dish before serving. As a main course, baked kibbe is served with one or several salads and often with rice pilaf. It's also served in smaller portions as an appetizer. Either way, there's a bowl of tahini or yogurt on the side for moistening it. I especially like it with Green Tahini (page 34).

◆ MAKES 4 OR 5 SERVINGS.

BULGUR-BEEF DOUGH

⅔ cup bulgur wheat, finest grind

½ onion, coarsely chopped

12 ounces ground beef (about 1½ cups)

1 teaspoon salt

¼ to ½ teaspoon freshly ground black pepper

1 teaspoon ground coriander

½ teaspoon ground cumin

3 tablespoons cold water

BEEF AND ALMOND FILLING

2 tablespoons olive oil or vegetable oil, plus 4 to 5 tablespoons for brushing over loaf

1 medium onion, chopped

½ cup slivered almonds

12 ounces ground beef (about 1½ cups)

Salt and freshly ground black pepper

1 teaspoon ground coriander

½ teaspoon ground cumin

¼ teaspoon cayenne pepper, or to taste (optional)

To make dough: Pour 3 cups cold water over bulgur wheat. Refrigerate and let soak for 10 minutes. Drain in strainer and squeeze out excess liquid. Put in large bowl. Finely chop onion in food processor. Add beef, salt, pepper, coriander, and cumin and process to a paste. Add cold water and process briefly. Transfer to bowl of bulgur wheat and mix very well with your hands. Return half of mixture to food processor and blend well. Repeat with remaining mixture. Mixture should make a slightly sticky dough. Broil or microwave a teaspoon of mixture and taste it for seasoning. Put mixture in a bowl and refrigerate for 30 minutes.

To make filling: Heat oil in heavy medium skillet. Add onion and sauté over medium heat about 7 minutes, or until golden brown. Add almonds and sauté for 1 minute. Add beef, salt, pepper, coriander, and cumin. Sauté about 5 minutes, or until it browns lightly, stirring often to crumble meat. Pour mixture into strainer to drain excess fat. Transfer mixture to bowl. Add cayenne pepper; taste and adjust seasoning. Let cool completely.

Preheat oven to 375°F. Oil a 9-inch square baking dish. Divide dough in half. Press half of dough in baking dish in an even thin layer. Top with filling. Divide remaining dough in 4 pieces. With moistened hands, flatten each piece on a plate until about ¼ inch thick. Set dough pieces on filling. Moisten your fingers and press dough pieces together to seal them in one layer. With the point of a sharp knife, score top in lines to make diamonds or squares, cutting through to bottom.

Brush top generously with oil. Cover with foil and bake for 10 minutes. Uncover, brush again with oil, and bake for 20 more minutes, or until cooked through and browned. Serve with slotted spatula to leave excess oil in the pan, or drain servings briefly on paper towels before putting on the plate.

Spicy Beef-stuffed Cabbage in Pepper Sauce

malfouf ablama

Although we tend to associate stuffed cabbage with the colder climates of northern Europe, people in the Mideast frequently enjoy cabbage, especially in winter. Wrapping the leaves around a stuffing, generally of meat and rice, is one of the most popular uses. Chard leaves are stuffed in the same way.

The stuffing and sauce might be spicy or mild, but cooks are careful to season the stuffing well with salt and pepper so the cabbage rolls won't be bland. In this version the flavor accents in the sweet-and-hot-pepper sauce echo those of the filling.

These cabbage rolls keep well and reheat beautifully. For a leaner dish, substitute ground chicken or turkey for the beef, or make the stuffing vegetarian with soy ground meat.

◆ MAKES 6 SERVINGS.

½ cup white rice, either short, medium, or long grain

3 to 4 tablespoons olive oil

2 large onions, minced

2 large garlic cloves, minced

1 teaspoon paprika

2 teaspoons ground cumin

1 teaspoon dried thyme

½ to 1 teaspoon hot red pepper flakes

8 ounces lean ground beef

2 tablespoons tomato paste

Salt and freshly ground black pepper

1 head green cabbage (3 pounds), cored

2 to 4 jalapeño peppers, chopped

1 green and 1 yellow bell pepper, or 2 green peppers, halved, cored, seeded, and diced

1 cup Basic Tomato Sauce (page 305), or one 8-ounce can tomato sauce

2 tablespoons chopped Italian parsley (optional)

Boil rice, uncovered, in saucepan of 3 cups boiling salted water for 10 minutes; it should be partially cooked. Rinse with cold water and drain well. Transfer to bowl.

Heat half of oil in skillet. Add half of minced onion and cook over medium heat for 5 minutes, or until golden brown, stirring often. Add garlic, paprika, 1 teaspoon cumin, ½ teaspoon thyme, and ¼ to ½ teaspoon pepper flakes and cook, stirring, for 12 minutes. Transfer mixture to bowl of rice and let cool completely. Add beef, 2 teaspoons tomato paste, ¾ teaspoon salt, and ½ teaspoon pepper. Knead by hand to blend ingredients thoroughly. If you like, cook a teaspoonful of mixture in the microwave; taste it, and adjust seasoning of stuffing. Refrigerate in a covered container until ready to use.

Carefully remove 12 to 16 large outer cabbage leaves by cutting them from core of cabbage. Put leaves in large pot of boiling water and boil for 5 minutes to make them flexible enough to roll. Transfer them carefully to a colander and rinse gently with cold water. Pat dry with a towel. Reserve remaining cabbage for other uses.

Heat remaining oil in large stew pan. Add remaining onion and sauté over medium heat 5 minutes, or until golden, stirring often. Stir in remaining cumin, remaining pepper flakes, jalapeño peppers, and bell peppers and remove from heat.

Slightly trim thick ribs of each cabbage leaf so you can bend leaf easily. Put 2 tablespoons stuffing on stem end of a leaf and fold stem end over it. Fold sides over stuffing to enclose it. Beginning at stem end, roll up leaf to a neat package. If any leaves are torn, add a piece of another leaf. Continue with remaining leaves and stuffing. Arrange stuffed cabbage rolls tightly, with seam ends facing down, side by side in the pan containing the onions.

Finely chop any remaining blanched leaves and add to pan. Add tomato sauce, 2 cups water, remaining ½ teaspoon thyme, salt, and pepper. Mix remaining 4 teaspoons tomato paste with ¼ cup water until blended and add to pan. Bring to a simmer. Cover and simmer over low heat for 1 hour and 15 minutes, or until cabbage is very tender and meat is cooked through. Add 1 tablespoon parsley if you like. Taste and adjust seasoning. Serve stuffed cabbage in deep dishes with sauce, sprinkled with remaining parsley.

Sweet-and-Savory Stuffed Peppers with Meat, Nuts, and Currants

etli büber dolmasi

In the Mideast most people prefer their filling-packed peppers whole, as they make such an appetizing serving. Select fairly small peppers that are not tapered so they will stand up straight. Depending on their size, the stuffing will fill four to six peppers. Mint, allspice, and a touch of tomato flavor the filling in this festive, Turkish-inspired recipe. Substitute ground chicken for the meat if you prefer.

◆ MAKES 4 OR 5 SERVINGS.

½ cup white rice, short, medium, or long grain

2 to 3 tablespoons olive oil

1 large onion, finely chopped

8 ounces lean ground beef or lamb

½ teaspoon ground allspice

2 tablespoons chopped fresh mint, or 2 teaspoons dried mint

⅓ cup chopped Italian parsley

Salt and freshly ground black pepper

3 tablespoons slivered almonds

2 tablespoons pine nuts

2 tablespoons currants or raisins (optional)

4 to 6 green bell peppers

2 plum tomatoes, chopped

Lemon wedges (optional)

Add rice to 3 cups boiling salted water in medium saucepan and cook about 10 minutes, until not quite tender. Rinse with cold running water and drain well.

Heat 1 or 2 tablespoons oil in skillet. Add onion and sauté over medium-low heat about 5 minutes, until softened. Let cool.

Put beef in bowl and mix with allspice, mint, parsley, ½ teaspoon salt, and ¼ to ½ teaspoon pepper. Add sautéed onions, almonds, pine nuts, and currants if you like and mix well. Lightly mix in rice.

Preheat oven to 350°F. Cut off stem end of peppers and reserve the slice, leaving stem on; remove core and seeds from each pepper. Spoon stuffing into peppers and cover with reserved tops. Stand them in baking dish in which they just fit. Add 1½ cups hot water to dish. Sprinkle peppers with remaining oil. Cover and bake for 1 hour, or until peppers are very tender and stuffing is hot. Serve hot or warm, with lemon wedges if you like.

DEMYSTIFYING MOUSSAKA

If you frequent Greek eateries, you're familiar with this cuisine's most celebrated specialty, moussaka. In restaurants it's generally an elaborate composition of fried eggplant slices and ground meat filling covered with béchamel, a classic cream sauce. The sauce is enriched with egg and grated *kefalotiri*, a savory sheep's-milk cheese.

But moussaka might have been born farther east. The eggplant was brought to Greece from the Middle East and the word moussaka came to Greek via Turkish and colloquial Egyptian Arabic.

People in the Land of the Pharaohs certainly value this casserole. In *Egyptian Cuisine*, author Nagwa E. Khalil comments that "the most popular eggplant dish is moussaka'ah. . . . It is generally made with fried eggplant and meat stuffing." That's saying a lot in an area where eggplant is the best-loved vegetable. A review in the foremost Egyptian daily *Al Ahram* of a downtown Aswan restaurant named Al-Masri ("The Egyptian") mentioned moussaka first among the menu's items and noted that it is a standard in every home kitchen.

With the exception of Turkey, moussaka in the Middle East is generally cheeseless. Cooks in the region are not keen on cream sauces or cheese toppings. Instead, they crown their moussaka with sliced tomatoes or moisten it with broth or diluted tomato paste. Some Israeli cooks make their moussaka dairy-free because the dish would not be kosher if it intermixed meat and milk products.

Greek cooking expert Aglaia Kremezi writes that "moussaka was, in fact, probably the invention of some educated Turkish chef inspired to use béchamel—a well-known French sauce—as the topping for an eggplant and meat casserole."

Without the white sauce, Mideast-style moussaka is more practical for cooks in a hurry. It's a better option for health-conscious people too, since it does not contain the butterfat and cholesterol in the dairy products. Home cooks in the region tend also to use a high proportion of vegetables to meat in this dish.

Some Egyptian experts feel that moussaka is the busy cook's substitute for another regional favorite—stuffed eggplant. Instead of taking the trouble to hollow out individual eggplants, you simply sandwich the stuffing between layers of eggplant slices.

Families are so fond of moussaka that they enjoy it made with other vegetables too. Eastern Mediterranean cooks sometimes combine potatoes or zucchini with the eggplant or use them instead. Egyptians boast an array of unusual moussaka variations, including cauliflower, Jerusalem artichoke, rutabaga, and even rhubarb. Armenians might replace the eggplant with pumpkin.

Most moussaka aficionados opt for lamb but many substitute beef or combine both. Sautéed onions enhance the meat mixture and often so do tomatoes, green peppers, garlic, and flat-leaf parsley. Extra accent might come from dill, mint, cinnamon, or allspice.

Eggplant Macaroni Moussaka

moussaka

Moussaka is a wonderful option for easy entertaining and is convenient, as it reheats beautifully. This version is quicker to prepare than most.

Moussaka somewhat resembles lasagna, with layers of meat filling alternating with eggplant rather than with noodles. Instead of frying eggplant, I bake it to make the dish lighter. Like some Middle Eastern cooks, I occasionally combine eggplant with sautéed potatoes. When I need to prepare the casserole quickly, I replace the potatoes with pasta. Both play a similar role: They absorb some of the liquid, thus helping to thicken the filling, shorten the baking time, and make serving simple. Instead of an hour-long sojourn in the oven, my moussaka needs only 20 to 25 minutes.

For a festive touch I learned from an Egyptian friend, I put almonds in the filling.

You can toast more almonds and use them for garnish. Some eastern Mediterranean cooks enhance the meat-and-tomato filling with a splash of wine. If you want a firmer casserole, stir 1 or 2 beaten eggs into the macaroni-meat mixture before layering it with the eggplant.

If you prefer a cheesy crust, sprinkle the baked moussaka with ½ cup grated *kashkaval* cheese, as some Lebanese cooks do, or use kasseri, *kefalotiri,* or Parmesan; then brown the top briefly in the broiler.

◆ MAKES 6 TO 8 SERVINGS.

1 large eggplant (about 1½ pounds), unpeeled and sliced crosswise about ¼ inch thick

About 4 tablespoons olive oil

Salt and freshly ground black pepper to taste

1 large onion, minced

1 green bell pepper, halved, cored, seeded, and diced

1 pound lean ground beef, lamb, or chicken

½ teaspoon ground allspice or cinnamon

Freshly grated nutmeg to taste

8 large garlic cloves, minced

⅓ cup dry white wine or meat or chicken broth

One 28-ounce can tomatoes, drained and chopped

4 tablespoons tomato paste

⅓ to ½ cup slivered almonds

1 pound large elbow macaroni, penne, or pasta shells, cooked

½ cup beef or chicken broth

1 tablespoon chopped Italian parsley

Preheat the oven to 450°F. Arrange eggplant slices in a single layer in a shallow, lightly greased baking pan. Brush eggplant lightly with oil and sprinkle with salt and pepper. Bake for 8 minutes per side, or until just tender.

Meanwhile, heat 2 tablespoons oil in large skillet. Add onion and diced peppers and sauté over medium-high heat for 3 minutes. Add meat, allspice, nutmeg, and half the garlic and cook, stirring, for 5 minutes, or until meat browns lightly. Add wine and bring to a simmer. Add tomatoes, 2 tablespoons tomato paste, almonds, salt, and pepper and cook for 3 minutes, or until mixture is thick. In large bowl, combine meat mixture with cooked pasta and mix well. Taste and adjust seasoning.

Reduce oven temperature to 375°F. Grease a 13-by-9-by-2-inch baking dish. Beginning with eggplant, alternate three layers of eggplant with two layers of pasta-meat mixture in dish. Spoon remaining tomato paste into a cup and whisk in ½ cup broth. Add a pinch of salt and pepper and remaining garlic. Pour sauce over moussaka. Drizzle lightly with oil. Bake, uncovered, for 20 to 25 minutes, or until hot and bubbling.

Let stand for 5 to 10 minutes before serving. Serve sprinkled with parsley.

Lamb or Beef Kabobs with Onion-Herb Marinade

kabob

Kabobs take the prize as the most-loved entrée in the Middle East. People often prepare them at home but love to order them when dining out. Most menus of Middle Eastern restaurants feature them prominently. There are numerous eateries devoted solely to these tender meat morsels grilled on skewers, and in some areas, whole streets of such kabob houses. Some credit the Turks with coming up with the idea, as the term *shish kebab* comes from their language, and indeed they boast dozens of kinds. Others claim they were an Armenian invention.

Kabobs are made with lamb, beef, and, in Eastern Christian communities, with pork as well. In some regions goat and mutton are also used. The meat may be cut in strips and threaded on the skewers, or it may be cubed or ground. Some alternate vegetables with the meat, but many grill them separately since their cooking times are different. Marinades are oil-based and usually include lemon juice and may be seasoned with herbs, cinnamon, nutmeg, or saffron and either onion, garlic, or both.

From Lebanon to Afghanistan, people like kabobs with tart purple sumac powder. It is sprinkled directly over the grilled kabobs or tossed with accompanying fresh onion slices. The kabobs are commonly presented as starters on a bed of lettuce or with fresh mint leaves, as sandwiches in pita bread, or as entrées with diced salad and rice pilaf. Hot sauce, tahini sauce, or yogurt garlic sauce are served on the side. Other popular partners are Hummus (page 34), Eggplant Sesame Dip (page 40), Fattoush (page 63), and Tabbouleh (page 77).

Some aficionados insist that the best way to enjoy kabobs is to roll the pieces in flatbread as soon as they come off the grill to absorb all of the tasty juices, and to add the grilled vegetables to the wrapped meat. Certain diners hold the end of the skewer (if it's not too hot), and use the flatbread to grab the meat morsels and slide them off the skewer.

For best results, many cooks prefer flat skewers so the pieces of meat don't roll around when you turn them. If you are using bamboo skewers, soak them in cold water for 30 minutes before grilling so they won't burn, and cover their ends with foil.

◆ MAKES 4 SERVINGS.

   2 pounds boneless leg of lamb or beef tenderloin or rib eye steak, well trimmed
   2 tablespoons strained fresh-squeezed lemon juice
   3 tablespoons extra-virgin olive oil
   2 large garlic cloves, crushed (optional)
   2 bay leaves
   1 teaspoon dried oregano, crumbled

½ teaspoon freshly ground black pepper

A few shakes cayenne pepper (optional)

2 or 3 medium onions, or 1 medium onion and 8 pearl onions, peeled

Salt and freshly ground black pepper

2 green bell peppers (optional), cored, seeded, and cut in 1-inch squares

8 small tomatoes (optional)

Sumac powder or lemon wedges

Fresh pita bread or rice pilaf

Cut meat in 1-inch cubes. In shallow dish large enough to hold meat, combine lemon juice, olive oil, garlic, bay leaves, oregano, pepper, and cayenne. Halve 1 onion and grate it into dish, adding all of onion juices. Add meat cubes and mix well. Cover and marinate in refrigerator for 2 hours or overnight.

Quarter remaining medium onions for grilling, or slice them for serving raw; or see Note below. Remove meat from marinade, brushing off bits of onion and discarding marinade. Sprinkle meat with salt and pepper. Thread meat on skewers, alternating with pepper pieces, quartered or peeled onions, and tomatoes if you like.

Heat barbecue or broiler with rack about 4 inches from heat source; or heat ridged stove-top grill. Put kabobs on barbecue. Grill or broil about 6 minutes for medium rare, or until meat is cooked to your taste, turning kabobs often. Serve hot, with sumac powder and with pita or pilaf.

NOTE If you prefer grilled onions in thinner pieces so they taste more cooked, quarter the onions and separate each quarter in layers. Thread the layers on the skewers in pairs, alternating with the meat pieces and other vegetables.

Lamb Steak Sandwich

shawarma

A large cone-shaped hunk of meat rotating slowly on a vertical rotisserie is an impressive sight and its aroma never fails to draw a crowd. Called shawarma in many areas of the Mideast and *doner kebab* in Turkey, this style of grilling meat is popular around the region and is similar to Greek gyros. Although it looks like a slab of meat, it is composed of layers of meat that are compressed to hold together as a piece as it cooks.

Shawarma rivals falafel as the most popular sandwich in the Middle East. The vendor carves thin slices of the meat and slips them into a pita, often with a few onion slices and sometimes hot sauce or tahini, diced raw vegetables, and French fries. People grab these hot, satisfying sandwiches on the run. You can easily find shawarma at many Middle Eastern restaurants in America. There it is often served as a plated entrée accompanied by diced salad, pickles, and rice pilaf or fried potatoes. Tahini is the usual sauce, but some offer garlic sauce instead.

Shawarma is classically made of lamb but many use beef or a combination of both meats and some substitute veal or turkey. To prepare it, professionals stack large round slices of marinated meat on the rotisserie skewer to form a cylinder, alternating every few meat layers with a slice of fat, generally lamb fat. At home people simulate shawarma by slowly barbecuing a boneless roast on a rotisserie or by pressing together round lamb slices on a skewer, but the effect is not the same because the layers of fat in shawarma continuously enrich the meat.

The charm of shawarma is the crispy brown bits that continuously form on the meat. After the outer layer of meat is sliced, the meat below it continues to rotate and gets a grilled crust. For a quick and easy home version of the sandwich, I grill a lamb steak so it has plenty of tasty crust and is succulent inside. Lamb steaks are made from boneless leg of lamb. If your market doesn't carry them, grill lamb chops instead and cut them off the bone.

◆ MAKES 4 SERVINGS.

1½ pounds lamb steaks, or 8 rib lamb chops

2 onions

1 bay leaf

1 teaspoon fresh thyme leaves, or ½ teaspoon dried thyme

Salt and freshly ground black pepper

Pinch freshly grated nutmeg

Pinch ground cloves (optional)

Pinch ground cinnamon (optional)

¼ cup fresh-squeezed lemon juice or vinegar

1 to 2 tablespoons olive oil

Tahini Sauce (page 33) or Garlic Sauce (page 309)

4 fresh pita breads

Hot sauce (for serving)

To marinate the meat, slice 1 onion and put it in a broad, deep dish large enough to contain the meat. Add bay leaf, thyme, ½ teaspoon pepper, nutmeg, cloves, cinnamon, and lemon juice. If using lamb steaks, add 2 tablespoons olive oil; with lamb chops, add 1 tablespoon. Add meat to marinade and turn to coat it. Cover and refrigerate for 4 hours or overnight. Prepare Tahini Sauce or Garlic Sauce.

Heat barbecue or stove-top grill; or preheat broiler with rack about 3 inches from heat source. Cut remaining onion in thick slices for grilling, or halve it and slice it thin for serving raw.

Remove meat from marinade and discard marinade. Sprinkle lamb with salt and pepper and put on grill. If you'd like to grill the onion, put the thick slices on the grill. Grill or broil lamb until it is done to your taste, turning once, and grill onions until lightly charred. Lamb steaks usually take 3 to 5 minutes per side, depending on thickness, while chops take 5 to 7 minutes per side.

Check for doneness by pressing on the meat; rare lamb gives little resistance, medium-rare lamb resists slightly, and well-done lamb is firm. Or make a small cut in meat's thickest part to check the color; medium-rare meat will be pink.

Split pita breads in half. Set lamb on a cutting board and let rest for a minute or two. If using lamb chops, cut meat from bone. With a sharp knife, cut meat in long, thin slices on the diagonal. Serve hot in pita bread, with grilled or raw onion. Serve Tahini Sauce and hot sauce on the side.

Grilled Lamb Chops with Garlic Cumin Tomato Salsa

kastaletta mechwie

This is one of the most delicious ways to prepare lamb chops. If you have Lebanese Seven Spices blend (see "The Mideast Pantry," page 13) or Middle Eastern *baharat,* you can use 2 teaspoons of the blend instead of the spices below. As accompaniments I like to serve Garlic Marinated Eggplant (page 44) or grilled vegetables, along with rice pilaf, thin slices of sweet onion, and Green Salad with Herbs and Radishes (page 67).

The garlicky hot pepper salsa that ac-companies the lamb packs quite a punch. It's also great with steaks, burgers, chicken, and eggs and makes a fresh and zesty alternative to ketchup. Either make it chunky by dicing the tomatoes or prepare a smooth version in a flash by pureeing the ingredients in a blender.

◆ MAKES 6 SERVINGS.

MIDDLE EASTERN TOMATO SALSA

¼ cup garlic cloves, peeled

2 to 4 jalapeño or 4 to 6 serrano or other hot peppers (see Note)

¼ cup small sprigs of cilantro

¼ teaspoon salt, or to taste

1½ teaspoons ground cumin, preferably roasted (page 370)

1 pound ripe plum tomatoes

Freshly ground black pepper

SPICED LAMB CHOPS

12 loin or rib lamb chops, about 1½ inches thick

1 tablespoon olive oil

Pinch salt

2 teaspoons ground cumin

¼ teaspoon ground cinnamon

Pinch freshly grated nutmeg

Pinch ground cloves

½ teaspoon ground black pepper, or ¼ teaspoon cayenne, or to taste

To make salsa: Combine garlic and peppers in blender or mini food processor and process them until finely chopped. If necessary, add 1 or 1½ tablespoons water, just enough to enable the mixture to be chopped. Add cilantro and process until blended. Add salt and cumin. Transfer to bowl.

Dice tomatoes in fine pieces or puree them in blender or food processor. Combine with garlic mixture and add pepper to taste. Taste, and add more salt if you like.

To make spiced lamb: Trim excess fat from chops, brush both sides with oil, and sprinkle lightly with salt. Mix cumin, cinnamon, nutmeg, cloves, and pepper and sprinkle on both sides of lamb. Let stand while grill is heating. Prepare the grill with rack about 4 inches above coals or heat source; or heat a ridged stove-top grill.

Grill lamb above glowing coals or on heated stove-top grill until done to your taste; for medium-rare, allow about 7 minutes per side on an outdoor grill, or about 5 or 6 minutes per side on a stove-top grill. Check for doneness by pressing on the chops; rare lamb gives little resistance, medium-rare lamb resists slightly, and well-done lamb is firm. Or make a small cut in the meat near the bone to check the color; meat will be pink when medium-rare. Serve hot, with salsa.

NOTE Many jalapeño peppers at the market are not so hot, so taste a bit of yours or smell them when you cut them to judge their potency. If you prefer your salsa less hot, remove the seeds and ribs. Wear gloves when handling peppers if your skin is sensitive.

Okra and Lamb Stew with Tart Tomato Sauce

bamia bel lahm

Although the meat tends to receive top billing in entrées, in this one the okra is the star. This stew is so well loved that numerous Mideastern peoples claim it as their own. Quite a few insist that it's Egyptian because in that country okra is used so often, but the stew is also a favorite in Turkey and throughout the Fertile Crescent. Lamb is the favorite, but many cook beef with the okra and its savory sauce instead.

This recipe, with its peppery lemony tomato sauce flavored generously with garlic, is inspired by a version of the stew that I enjoyed at Al Rayan, a Syrian restaurant in Anaheim, California. There it was served with a generous mound of Rice Pilaf with Toasted Almonds (page 263). In addition to lemon, some like to finish the dish with fresh cilantro and to give the sauce extra tang by stirring in sour pomegranate juice.

◆ MAKES 4 OR 5 SERVINGS.

3 tablespoons olive oil, or 2 tablespoons olive oil and 1 tablespoon butter

1 large onion, chopped

1½ to 2 pounds lamb shoulder, trimmed of excess fat and cut in 1-inch cubes

2 pounds tomatoes, peeled, seeded, and chopped, or one 28-ounce can tomatoes, drained and chopped

Salt and freshly ground black pepper

1 cup water

8 large garlic cloves, chopped

2 teaspoons ground coriander

1 pound small tender okra, rinsed lightly and patted dry

2 tablespoons strained fresh-squeezed lemon juice, or to taste

Cayenne pepper to taste

Heat 1 tablespoon oil in heavy stew pan. Add onion and cook over medium heat for 5 minutes, or until beginning to turn golden. Add lamb and sauté until the meat browns lightly, stirring often. Add tomatoes, salt, pepper, and water and bring to a boil, stirring often. Cover and simmer over low heat for 1 hour or until lamb is tender, stirring occasionally, adding a few tablespoons water if pan becomes dry. Stir in garlic and coriander.

Cut caps off okra without piercing the rest of the pod. Heat 2 tablespoons oil or 1 tablespoon each oil and butter in large sauté pan. Add okra and cook over medium heat for 5 minutes, stirring often.

Add okra to stew and bring to a simmer. Cover and simmer without stirring for 20 minutes, or until okra is just tender. Add lemon juice and cayenne and heat for 1 minute. Taste and adjust seasoning. Serve hot.

Prince-pleaser Ragout with Cheesy Eggplant Puree

hunkar begendi

A legacy of the Ottoman Empire, the Turkish name of this lamb entrée is usually translated as "the Sultan's preferred dish" or "the sovereign appreciates." The secret behind the entrée's royal reputation is the creamy, cheese-accented eggplant that accompanies the meat. When I tasted the dish at Istanbul's Konyali restaurant in the magnificent Topkapi Palace overlooking the Bosphorus, I was sure the sultans who resided in the palace, where the dish probably originated, enjoyed it as much as I did.

For this delicate ragout, the meat is lightly browned in butter and simmered in a simple onion tomato sauce, which might be flavored with a little garlic or bell pepper. Most cooks add a little water or broth, as in this recipe, but some insist the meat should cook in its own juices with only a few diced tomatoes and liquid added only as necessary.

Some prefer the leaner leg of lamb to the shoulder. If you use it, reduce the lamb's cooking time to about 25 to 30 minutes. Many prepare the stew with beef, veal, or chicken instead of lamb, which also give delicious results. Veal takes about as long as lamb to simmer. If you'd like to substitute beef, cook it for about 2½ hours, gradually adding more liquid as needed; chicken pieces need about 45 to 50 minutes. For a fresh take on this time-honored entrée, I add sugar snap peas, which liven it up with their bright color and crisp-tender texture.

You can refrigerate the eggplant puree but add the grated cheese to the hot puree just before serving. Use a sheep's-milk cheese like Greek kasseri, which resembles the cheese used in Turkey.

◆ MAKES 4 SERVINGS.

1½ to 2 pounds lamb shoulder, excess fat removed

2 to 3 tablespoons butter or olive oil, or 1 to 2 tablespoons butter and 1 tablespoon oil

1 large onion, chopped

Salt and freshly ground black pepper

1½ pounds ripe tomatoes, peeled, or one 28-ounce can whole tomatoes, drained

1 cup meat or vegetable broth or water

2 large garlic cloves, chopped (optional)

1 sprig fresh thyme, or ½ teaspoon dried thyme

1 green or yellow bell pepper, halved, cored, seeded, and diced (optional)

CHEESY EGGPLANT PUREE:

2 large eggplants (total about 2 to 2½ pounds), grilled or broiled (see "Cooking Eggplants Whole," page 371)

Salt and freshly ground black pepper

2 to 3 teaspoons fresh-squeezed lemon juice (optional)

2 tablespoons butter

2 tablespoons all-purpose flour

1¼ cups milk

½ cup grated kasseri, *kashkaval,* or Gruyère cheese

TO FINISH STEW:

1 pound sugar snap peas, ends trimmed

1 or 2 tablespoons chopped Italian parsley (optional)

Cut lamb in 1-inch cubes. Heat butter in heavy stew pan. Add onion and cook over medium heat for 5 minutes, or until beginning to turn golden. Add lamb, sprinkle with salt and pepper, and sauté until meat browns lightly.

Chop fresh or canned tomatoes and add to pan. Add broth, garlic, and thyme and bring to a simmer. Cover and simmer over low heat for 30 minutes, stirring occasionally. Add bell pepper and simmer for 30 more minutes, or until lamb is tender, adding a little hot water if needed to keep meat moist. If sauce is too thin, remove lamb and simmer sauce uncovered until thick enough to lightly coat meat; return meat to pan and heat through. Discard thyme sprig.

To make eggplant puree: Cut grilled eggplants in half and scoop flesh from skin. Chop eggplant with a knife to a smooth puree. Put in bowl and season with salt, pepper, and lemon juice if you like.

In heavy saucepan, melt butter over low heat. Add flour and cook about 2 minutes, or until foaming but not browned, whisking constantly. Remove from heat and gradually whisk in milk. Bring to a boil over medium-high heat, whisking. Add a pinch of salt and pepper. Reduce heat to low and cook for 2 minutes, whisking often. Stir in eggplant puree. Cook, stirring, until mixture is hot and thick. If necessary, simmer for 2 or 3 minutes, stirring, to thicken. Stir in cheese. Taste and adjust seasoning. Serve hot.

Cook sugar snap peas, uncovered, in a saucepan of boiling salted water for 2 minutes, or until crisp-tender. Drain well. Reserve a few for garnish and stir remaining peas lightly into sauce. Taste and adjust seasoning.

To serve, spoon lamb alongside eggplant puree or in the center of the puree on a platter or on plates. Garnish with reserved sugar snap peas, and sprinkle with chopped parsley if you like.

NOTE Puree can be served alone, as a side dish or hot appetizer.

Lamb and Rice Pilaf with Yogurt Sauce

mansaf

The first time I tasted this classic dish was at a Bedouin feast years ago in Israel, which my husband, Yakir, and I attended with his brothers and sister and their spouses. At the time I didn't realize that this entrée of hum-

ble Bedouin origin has become the national dish of Jordan, served at the royal palace for important state dinners. Indeed, it is one of only two dishes presented on the Jordanian King's Web site (the other was a whole stuffed baby lamb). Jordanians and Palestinians serve *mansaf* at weddings and important family gatherings.

Essentially a simple dish, *mansaf* is composed of lamb stew with yogurt sauce sitting atop rice pilaf on a bed of pita bread. Usually it is embellished with fried or toasted pine nuts and some make it with chicken instead of lamb. Its charm is the combination of the tangy sauce that flavors the bread and the rice and contrasts with the richness of the meat and the pleasing crunch of the nuts.

In the Mideast a special ingredient called *jameed* is used to make the sauce. *Jameed* is sheep's-milk yogurt that has been dried in chunks. When I found some at a Middle Eastern market in Anaheim, they resembled white rocks. To make them into sauce, they are soaked overnight in water and pureed. Before blenders were available, this was a lot of work because the *jameed* had to be pounded to a smooth sauce. At another market I discovered a modern "convenience food" *jameed*, that had already been diluted with water and was ready to use in a shelf-stable package. The liquefied *jameed* is made into sauce the same way as yogurt, which is the standard substitute when *jameed* is not available. When the sauce is made with *jameed*, its flavor reminds me of Roquefort cream sauce. This isn't so far-fetched; after all, Roquefort is a sheep's-milk cheese.

Bread preferences for the bottom layer vary, some opting for very fine, almost pancakelike breads, while others like thicker types of flatbread. At a neighborhood market, when Yakir happened to strike up a conversation about *mansaf* with a Jordanian chef, he showed me his favorite bread to use. It was a particularly thin, fresh, delicate form of lavash. To season the *mansaf*, sweet spices are the rule, especially cinnamon and cardamom. The chef we met recommends Lebanese Seven Spice blend (see page 13).

◆ MAKES 4 TO 6 SERVINGS.

3 to 6 tablespoons *samnah* (page 17), ghee, or butter, or equal parts butter and margarine or butter and vegetable oil

1 large onion, chopped

1½ to 2 pounds lamb shoulder, trimmed of excess fat and cut in 1-inch cubes

Salt and freshly ground black pepper to taste

6 cups water

2 teaspoons Seven Spices blend, or 1 teaspoon ground allspice, ½ teaspoon ground cinnamon, and a pinch ground cardamom

1½ cups long-grain white rice

3 cups hot chicken, beef, or vegetable broth or water

½ cup slivered almonds or pine nuts, or ¼ cup of each

Creamy Hot Yogurt Sauce (page 312), made with 1½ cups of the lamb broth

4 to 6 portion-size pieces fine, fresh lavash, or 4 to 6 fresh pita breads

Heat 1 to 2 tablespoons *samnah* in heavy stew pan. Add onion and cook over medium heat for 5 minutes, or until beginning to turn golden. Add lamb and sauté until meat browns lightly, stirring often. Add salt, pepper, water, and spices and bring to a boil, stirring often. Cover and simmer over low heat for 1 hour or until lamb is tender, stirring occasionally.

Remove meat with slotted spoon and measure broth. Return the lamb to the pan, add 1 cup broth, cover, and keep it hot. Reserve 1½ cups of the broth to make the yogurt sauce. Measure remaining broth and add enough water to make 3 cups.

To prepare the pilaf, heat the 3 cups liquid in saucepan or in the microwave until hot, and reserve. Heat 2 or 3 tablespoons *samnah* in large saucepan. Add rice and cook, stirring, for 2 minutes or until the grains turn milky white. Add hot broth, salt, and pepper. Bring to a boil. Cover and cook over low heat, without stirring, for 18 minutes, or until rice is tender and liquid is absorbed. Remove from heat. Let rice stand, covered, for 10 to 15 minutes.

To toast the almonds, see "Basics," page 369. If you prefer to sauté them, heat 2 to 3 teaspoons oil or butter in a small heavy skillet. Add almonds and sauté over medium-low heat until lightly browned, stirring often; be careful not to let them burn. Remove from pan immediately and put them on a plate.

Reheat the lamb if necessary. Prepare the yogurt sauce, using the reserved broth.

To serve, fluff rice gently with a fork. Taste and adjust seasoning. Spread a layer of lavash on large heated platter or plates; if using pita, split each in 2 rounds and put on platter, crust side down. Spoon a little yogurt sauce over it to moisten it. Mound half the rice on top and moisten the rice with a few spoonfuls of the sauce. Top it with half of the lamb chunks and sprinkle with part of the almonds. Spoon the remaining rice into a separate bowl and sprinkle it with the remaining nuts. Serve the remaining lamb and sauce separately.

Crunchy Lamb Kibbe with Cinnamon and Cloves

kibbi makliya

A star on Middle Eastern tables, the filled croquettes called kibbe, or kibbeh, are made with only a few ingredients. Classically their main components are lamb, bulgur wheat, and pine nuts, accented with onion and a little spice. Usually there is meat in the dough as well as the stuffing.

Kibbe's appeal lies in its rich flavor and variety of textures. It can be poached, baked, or fried. When fried the traditional way, it is crunchy on the outside and tender inside,

and features a smooth meat crust and a coarsely ground meat filling. To make kibbe, use the finely ground bulgur wheat at Middle Eastern markets ordinarily labeled Bulgur Number One. Instead of the spice mixture below, you can use Lebanese Seven Spices blend or *baharat* ("The Mideast Pantry," page 13).

In the Mideast many pound the meat and bulgur in a mortar and pestle to form the crust, but it's much easier to blend them in a food processor. Suzanne Elmaleh, the Lebanese woman who taught me to make kibbe, advised me "to be patient and allow enough time to shape them carefully." She pointed out that forming kibbe in its customary football shape demands practice but even when it's not perfect, it's always delicious. For an easy way to shape kibbe into flat cakes, see the Note following the recipe. If you'd rather bake the kibbe cakes, see the variation, or bake it in layers as in Middle Eastern Meat Loaf with Almonds (page 188).

Cooks also prepare the meaty dough without filling it and form it into crunchy cakes; see Chicken Pecan Bulgur Cakes with Cilantro Pesto (page 48). This is also a favorite way to use up extra dough.

Serve kibbe as an appetizer, on its own, or with white Tahini or Green Tahini (page 33). Kibbe also makes a tasty entrée. The usual partners are white rice pilaf and a generous bowl of Middle Eastern Diced Salad (page 58). I also like kibbe with Green Salad

with Herbs and Radishes (page 67) or
Cucumber Salad with Green Olives (page
68).

◆ MAKES 6 TO 8 APPETIZER SERVINGS
OR 3 OR 4 MAIN COURSE.

KIBBE DOUGH:
  1 cup bulgur wheat, finest grind
  ½ onion, coarsely chopped
  12 ounces ground lamb (about 1½ cups)
  1¼ teaspoons salt
  ¼ to ½ teaspoon freshly ground black
      pepper
  ½ teaspoon ground allspice
  ½ teaspoon ground cinnamon
  Pinch ground cloves
  ¼ cup cold water

MEAT AND PINE NUT FILLING:
  2 tablespoons olive oil or butter
  1 medium onion, chopped
  3 or 4 tablespoons pine nuts
  6 ounces very lean ground lamb
      (about ¾ cup)
  Salt and freshly ground black pepper
  ½ teaspoon ground allspice
  ¼ teaspoon ground cinnamon
  Pinch ground cloves
  2 tablespoons water

  Oil for deep frying

To make dough: Pour 3 cups cold water
over bulgur wheat. Refrigerate and let soak
for 10 minutes. Drain in strainer and

squeeze out excess liquid. Put in large bowl.

Finely chop onion in food processor.
Add lamb, salt, pepper, allspice, cinnamon,
and cloves and process to a paste. Add cold
water and process briefly. Transfer to bowl
of bulgur wheat and mix very well with your
hands. Return half of mixture to food
processor and blend well. Repeat with remaining mixture. Mixture should make a
slightly sticky dough. Broil or microwave a
teaspoon of mixture and taste it for seasoning. Put mixture in bowl and refrigerate for
30 minutes.

To make filling: Heat oil in heavy
medium skillet. Add onion and sauté over
medium heat about 7 minutes, or until
golden brown. Add pine nuts and sauté for
1 minute. Add lamb, salt, pepper, allspice,
cinnamon, and cloves. Sauté about 5 minutes, or until it browns lightly, stirring often
to crumble meat. Add water and cook for 5
minutes, or until meat is cooked through.
Pour mixture into strainer to drain excess
fat. Transfer mixture to bowl. Taste and adjust seasoning. Let cool completely.

Take about 2 tablespoons of dough and
press into an egg shape, rolling it between
your palms until smooth. Set ball of dough
on a plate. Repeat with remaining dough.

Fill a bowl with cold water. Line baking
sheet with waxed paper. Moisten the palm
of your left hand and the index finger of
your right hand (if you're right-handed).
Put a ball of dough in your left palm. With
your right index finger, make a hole in ball

of dough and gradually push it to elongate it and to form a cone-shaped cavity that is wide at the top, at the same time squeezing and turning the dough around your finger with your left hand. Try to form a thin, even shell without any cracks. If cracks form, close them with moistened fingers or shape the dough into a ball and start again. Put in about 1½ teaspoons filling, or enough to fill cavity by about two-thirds, with your fingers. Wet your right thumb and index finger and pinch end of dough closed, completely enclosing filling. Leave kibbe in an egg shape or shape it like a long football. Set on prepared baking sheet. Continue with remaining dough and remaining filling. Refrigerate, uncovered, for 1 hour or up to overnight.

Heat oil in a deep fryer to 350°F. Fry kibbe in small batches for 5 to 10 minutes, or until deep golden brown; reduce heat if they brown too fast. Stand back while frying, as oil tends to spatter. Drain well on several layers of paper towels. Serve hot or warm.

Flat Kibbe Cakes

Prepare balls of dough as above. With moistened hands, flatten each ball of dough to a disk. Press one disk to flatten further in your palm. Cup your palm so there is a depression in the middle of the dough. Put about 1½ teaspoons filling inside. Bring dough around it and press to join edges to completely enclose filling. Pat again to a disk. Fry as directed above.

Baked Kibbe Cakes

Instead of frying kibbe cakes, set them on an oiled baking sheet and brush them generously with olive oil. Preheat oven to 375°F. Bake kibbe for 30 minutes, or until tops brown.

Eggplant with Lamb and Almond Stuffing

batenjane mehchi

Among the grand variety of stuffings for eggplant in the region, the most prized ones include meat, preferably lamb, usually mixed with onions and rice. Some combine the meat with raw rice to make the stuffing but I parboil it first, as it cooks more evenly this way. Frugal cooks sauté the flesh removed from the hollowed-out eggplant and add it to the stuffing. You can prepare stuffed Middle Eastern squash or zucchini the same way, either whole or halved, following the variation.

Generally, the stuffed eggplant or zucchini finishes cooking in tomato sauce. For special occasions it might simmer in a lamb stew instead. Another alternative favored by eastern Mediterranean cooks is to simmer or bake them with broth and serve them with Creamy Hot Yogurt Sauce (page 312).

◆ MAKES 4 TO 6 SERVINGS.

2 to 2½ pounds small or medium eggplants, stems removed

3 to 4 tablespoons olive oil, plus a little for sprinkling

Salt and freshly ground black pepper

½ cup long-grain rice, rinsed and drained

1 large onion, finely chopped

4 large garlic cloves, chopped

2 tablespoons tomato paste

8 ounces lean ground lamb or beef

⅓ cup slivered almonds, lightly toasted

1¼ pounds ripe tomatoes, diced, or one 15-ounce can diced tomatoes with their juice

Preheat oven to 425°F. Halve eggplants lengthwise. Scoop out centers with a sharp spoon, leaving boat-shaped shells. Reserve centers and chop them to add to stuffing if you like. Put eggplant shells in baking dish. Sprinkle lightly with oil and salt. Bake, uncovered, for 10 minutes. Let cool.

Boil rice, uncovered, in a saucepan of 3 cups boiling salted water for 10 minutes; it should not yet be tender. Rinse with cold water and drain well. Transfer to large bowl.

Heat 2 tablespoons oil in skillet. Add onion and sauté over medium heat for 5 minutes. Add half the garlic. Remove from skillet and let cool. Add 1 or 2 tablespoons oil to skillet, add chopped eggplant, and sprinkle with salt and pepper. Sauté over medium-low heat for 5 minutes, stirring often. Mix 1 tablespoon tomato paste with 2 tablespoons water and add to mixture.

Cook for 5 more minutes, or until eggplant is tender. Let cool.

In large bowl, mix lamb with rice, ½ teaspoon salt, and ½ teaspoon pepper. Add onion mixture, sautéed eggplant, and almonds and mix well. If you like, cook a teaspoonful of mixture in the microwave; taste it, and adjust seasoning of stuffing.

Fill eggplant shells lightly with stuffing. Mix tomatoes with remaining garlic, remaining tomato paste, 1 cup water, salt, and pepper. Pour mixture over eggplant. Cover and bake 15 minutes. Reduce oven temperature to 350°F and bake 15 more minutes. Uncover and bake, basting occasionally, for 30 minutes, or until eggplant is very tender and stuffing is hot; an instant-read thermometer inserted in stuffing should register 160°F. Serve hot, with sauce.

Stuffed Summer Squash or Zucchini: To stuff them whole, buy small pale green Middle Eastern squash (also called Mexican squash or Clarita squash). Cut off the stems and remove the centers with a squash-hollowing tool, or use an apple corer or a vegetable peeler. If you have larger squash or zucchini, halve them lengthwise and scoop out their centers with a spoon. Fill squash with stuffing. If you have stuffed them whole, heat 1 tablespoon oil in skillet, add stuffed squash, and sauté briefly on all sides. Transfer whole or halved stuffed zucchini to baking dish and bake as directed above.

Osso Buco, Middle Eastern Style

lahm beatello bel salsa tamatem

Lamb and beef shanks are popular cuts in the Mideast. Veal is less common but is available in some larger cities. In Europe and North America, Middle Easterners prepare veal as they would lamb. Veal is also featured on the menus of Middle Eastern restaurants in the West for people who prefer its delicate flavor.

This sumptuous entrée of succulent veal shanks is flavored with fresh dill and Lebanese Seven Spices blend. It has plenty of richly flavored sauce and is wonderful served with festive Sweet and Savory Saffron Rice Stuffing with Cranberries (page 272) or with couscous or orzo.

♦ MAKES 4 SERVINGS.

4 crosscut 2-inch slices osso buco, from meaty part of veal shanks, preferably from hind shanks (about 3 pounds total)

Salt and freshly ground black pepper to taste

1 teaspoon Seven Spices blend (see "The Mideast Pantry," page 13), *baharat,* or ground allspice, or to taste

¼ cup all-purpose flour

1½ pounds ripe tomatoes, peeled, or one 28-ounce can tomatoes

2 tablespoons olive oil

2 tablespoons butter or additional oil

1 large onion, chopped

1 medium carrot, finely diced

1 medium celery stalk, finely chopped (optional)

2 cups chicken or meat broth

6 medium garlic cloves, minced

3 fresh thyme sprigs, or 1 teaspoon dried thyme

1 bay leaf

¼ to ½ teaspoon red pepper flakes

1 tablespoon tomato paste

Cayenne pepper to taste (optional)

2 tablespoons chopped fresh dill

Preheat oven to 350°F. Choose large sauté pan or heavy stew pan that can hold veal slices in a single layer. Pat veal dry. Sprinkle veal slices on both cut sides with salt, pepper, and about ½ teaspoon spice mix. Spread flour on a plate. Seed and chop tomatoes, reserving their juice. Strain juice.

Heat oil and butter in sauté pan or stew pan over medium-high heat. Meanwhile, dredge veal pieces on both cut sides in flour. Pat off excess flour. Add veal to hot fat and brown on both cut sides, in two batches if necessary, taking 3 to 4 minutes per side. Regulate heat so fat does not burn. Transfer meat to large plate in a single layer.

With pan over low heat, add onion, carrot, and celery if you like, and scrape in brown juices. Cook for 7 minutes or until vegetables soften, stirring often. Add ½ cup broth, garlic, thyme, bay leaf, and pepper flakes and bring to a simmer, stirring. Return veal pieces to pan with bone standing up. Spoon tomatoes around meat and add their juice. Pour remaining broth into pan and bring to a boil. Push down herbs to immerse them in liquid. Cover and braise veal in oven about 1½ hours, or until tender when pierced with point of a thin-bladed knife but slices are not falling apart.

Transfer veal carefully to platter with slotted skimmer or slotted spatula. Discard thyme sprigs and bay leaf. Stir tomato paste into sauce. Bring to a boil, stirring. Boil until sauce lightly coats a spoon, stirring often. Add ½ teaspoon spice mix, cayenne, salt, and pepper. Return veal shanks to pan of sauce and spoon sauce over to coat them. Bring to a simmer before serving. Stir 1½ tablespoons dill into sauce. Serve sprinkled with remaining dill.

Legumes, Dishes for Today Inherited from Antiquity

Red Beans and Yellow Rice with Carrots and Raisins • *Havij Polo*

Summer Squash Stew with Beans • *Khoresh-e Kadoo*

Aromatic White and Green Bean Stew • *Fasulye Pilaki*

Yellow Split Pea Stew with Mushrooms and Tomatoes • *Khoresh-e Quemen*

Split Peas with Chicken and Tarragon • *Qeymeh*

Fresh Fava Bean Stew with Chicken and Chard • *Foul bel Salq*

Spicy Yemenite Baked Beans with Beef • *Hamin*

Garlicky Chili with Coriander and Cilantro • *Fassoulia bil Kosbarah*

Chickpea and Bulgur Wheat Casserole with Lamb Steaks • *Burghul Bid-Dfin*

The Middle East has a rich legume legacy.

Indeed, legumes are the basis for the best known of the area's dishes—crunchy falafel and creamy hummus. A visit to a Mideast grocery stores reveals an impressive array of these healthful, versatile ingredients.

The love for lentils in the region is legendary. Genesis tells us how Esau sold his birthright to his younger brother, Jacob, in exchange for his lentil pottage. If only the Bible had given us Jacob's recipe for his irresistible thick lentil soup! To this day lentil soup holds a place of honor on family tables as well as restaurant menus and may be the most treasured soup in the region's repertoire. Equally popular are lentils with rice and fried onions, served as a savory side dish for chicken or meat or as a main course with cucumber-yogurt salad. The Koran also speaks of lentils, onions, garlic, herbs, and cucumbers—as foods that Musa (Moses) was asked to pray for.

There is evidence that lentils have been on the Middle Eastern menu for nearly nine millennia. A friend of mine who visited an archaeological dig in the area where the Dead Sea Scrolls were discovered was amazed to learn that lentils were found in that site still strewn around the relics of ancient bowls. This certainly proves they keep well.

Chickpeas have also been known since prehistoric times in this part of the world. Originating in southwest Asia, they became world travelers thanks to their appealing taste and portability. Long ago they were brought to the Mediterranean and to Europe. You may be more familiar with their Spanish name, garbanzos, because Latin American bean fanciers got them from the Spaniards. As a result of the Hispanic influence on American culture, packages

of chickpeas are labeled garbanzo beans in many U.S. markets. With their nutty flavor and somewhat meaty texture, chickpeas rival lentils as the best-liked legume in the Middle East. They are such an important staple and are used in so many ways that I consider them the soybeans of the Mideast.

Inhabitants of the region are such avid legume lovers that they serve them at any meal, including breakfast, and for just about any course, including dessert. Egyptians might begin the day with a sustaining bowl of fava beans spiked with garlic and lemon and topped with fresh vegetables. When I insisted on ordering them with lunch at Al Berdouni restaurant in Dearborn, Michigan, the Egyptian waitress was concerned I wouldn't enjoy them because it wasn't breakfast time. Chickpeas with butter and bits of pita are also on the Middle Eastern breakfast menu.

At any time of day, roasted chickpeas are enjoyed as snacks like peanuts and are often on the table as part of the meze. My father-in-law, who lived his entire life in the Mideast, always had a provision of those satisfying snacks with him. I follow his example and take a little bag of them with me when I'm on a trip. For a sweet treat on its own or with coffee, Armenians and Persians munch on candied chickpeas. You can buy both kinds at Middle Eastern grocery stores.

Fava beans have also been favored in the eastern Mediterranean for ages. In the United States they are less familiar than lentils and chickpeas, even though the British, who call them broad beans, use them often. You can find fresh fava beans at well-stocked supermarkets, Middle Eastern stores, and farmers' markets, where their large green pods make a prominent display. You can also buy them dried at many ethnic groceries.

Persians may take the prize for being the greatest legume aficionados of all. In addition to the Old World selection of fava beans, chickpeas, and lentils, they have enthusiastically adopted New World red and white beans. They use split peas and mung beans too (see Split Peas with Chicken and Tarragon, flavored with cinnamon and mint, page 229) and exuberantly combine three or four kinds of legumes in their hearty entrées.

Along the shores of the Mediterranean, people like to add legumes to stews and soups, both meaty and vegetarian. If you like chicken soup, turn yours into a hearty, tasty main course in the Mideastern fashion by adding chickpeas and a dash of cumin. Cooks in the region braise lamb shanks with lentils or other legumes, or make an easy entrée of lentils mixed with tomato sauce, sautéed onions, and leftover cooked meat or chicken. With a flavorful soup or sauce base, either purchased or homemade, and a can of beans, you've got a satisfying supper in no time.

Another celebrated dish is *hamin*, or cholent, one of the most popular specialties of Jewish cooking prepared in Israel by people of both Middle Eastern and European origin. Although it is not quick, it is convenient, as the ingredients are simply combined and stewed slowly overnight. Because a great variety of beans and seasonings are used, the cherished one-pot meal comes out different in each home. The substantial bean-and-meat casserole is made so faithfully, almost religiously every Sabbath in many observant Jewish homes, that some might even think that the recipe came straight from the scriptures.

My Father-in-law's Falafel

falafel/taamiah

Falafel may be the Middle East's most celebrated sandwich but slipping it into a pita is not the only way it is served. Many prefer it as a party hors d'oeuvre with tahini sauce for dipping, or as an appetizer on a plate with other salads and dips. For more on falafel, see "My Family's Falafel," page 217.

My husband's Yemenite parents made falafel together for many years. I think the secret to their tasty recipe is the generous amount of garlic and cumin they used. Most falafel makers agree that these two are primary flavors. Other seasonings vary. Most add black pepper, cayenne, or both. Egyptians use plenty of cilantro, parsley, and often dill and leeks as well, giving the bean cakes a green tinge. Falafel vendors generally form the mixture into small flat cakes with a tool that resembles an ice-cream scoop. At home many shape them into balls with their hands.

My brother-in-law, Yahalom, soaks dried chickpeas and grinds them in a meat grinder for his falafel, like his parents used to do. I find a food processor is faster and easier; it also gives the falafel a slightly smoother texture. The chickpeas are soaked but not boiled; frying the falafel cooks them through. Canned chickpeas, which are already cooked, are not a good substitute for the dried ones, as a falafel mixture made with them would be too soft.

◆ MAKES ABOUT 12 APPETIZER SERVINGS.

1 pound dried chickpeas (garbanzo beans) (about 2⅔ cups)

2 slices stale white bread, crusts removed

25 garlic cloves, peeled

⅓ cup small cilantro sprigs

¼ cup small Italian parsley sprigs

1 small onion, minced

2 tablespoons plus 2 teaspoons ground cumin

1 tablespoon salt

2 teaspoons freshly ground black pepper

¼ teaspoon cayenne pepper, or more to taste

⅓ cup all-purpose flour

1 teaspoon baking powder

About 6 cups vegetable oil (for frying)

Soak chickpeas for 8 hours or overnight in cool water to generously cover; drain in colander and rinse. Soak the bread in about ⅓ cup water for 5 minutes and squeeze dry.

Mince garlic in food processor. Remove garlic and grind chickpeas and bread in processor in batches, adding part of the cilantro, parsley, and onion to each batch. Transfer to bowl. Add garlic, cumin, salt, pepper, cayenne, flour, and baking powder and mix well. Knead thoroughly with your hands so mixture is well blended.

To shape the falafel, take 1 tablespoon of the mixture and squeeze to compact it, then press it into a ball. Roll lightly between your palms to give it a smooth round shape.

In deep fryer or heavy saucepan, heat oil to about 350°F. Gently slip in enough falafel balls to make a single layer, without crowding them. To avoid splashing the hot oil, do not drop them into the oil. Fry for 2 minutes, or until falafel balls are deep golden brown and crisp. Drain on paper towels. Keep warm in a low oven while frying the rest of the mixture. Serve hot.

NOTE To be at its best, falafel should be freshly fried and still hot, and put in a good-quality pita. Serve with refreshing, crisp vegetables and with just enough smooth tahini (sesame) sauce to moisten the sandwich without dripping out of the pita. Hot sauce is a terrific addition but, as I learned from personal experience, it's best to let each person add his or her own to taste.

Fast Falafel Burgers on the Grill

falafel bagril

For falafel flavor without frying, try these burgers. They make a tasty vegetarian entrée and are easier to prepare than deep-fried falafel. There's no need to soak the chick-peas; simply use canned ones. You can cook them on a stove-top grill or an outdoor barbecue. If you prefer, sauté them instead in 2 tablespoons oil in a skillet.

Like falafel, you can serve these grilled patties on a plate or in a pita with tahini sauce and diced salad. They also make a good meatless main course, served on a bun with sliced tomatoes, onions, and the usual hamburger condiments. If you're having a falafel burger barbecue, you might like to stay in the Mideast mood and, instead of ketchup, serve Turkish Tomato and Onion Dip (page 38).

◆ MAKES 3 OR 4 SERVINGS.

8 large garlic cloves, peeled

⅓ cup small cilantro sprigs

Two 15-ounce cans chickpeas (garbanzo beans), drained

1 small onion, chopped

2 teaspoons ground coriander

1½ teaspoons ground cumin

½ teaspoon salt

¼ teaspoon freshly ground black pepper

¼ teaspoon cayenne pepper, or to taste

2 tablespoons bread crumbs

1 egg

1 tablespoon vegetable oil, plus a little more for brushing

Mince garlic and cilantro in food processor. Add chickpeas, onion, ground coriander, cumin, salt, pepper, cayenne pepper, and bread crumbs. Process with on/off pulses to a slightly chunky puree, scraping down occasionally. Add egg and oil and process until blended. Transfer to bowl. Mix well.

Shape mixture in 6 to 8 smooth patties. Pack mixture firmly when shaping so that burgers hold together.

Heat grill and oil grill. Brush burgers lightly with oil and grill them over medium heat for 5 minutes per side, or until slightly firm on top. Turn them over carefully with two spatulas. Serve hot.

MY FAMILY'S FALAFEL

Falafel, the famous chickpea fritter, was my first taste of the Middle East. I was seventeen, on a trip with other teenagers in Jerusalem, when I tried my first falafel. It was love at first bite, though that hesitant taste sent me running for a glass of water. I didn't know that inside the pita with the innocent-looking diced vegetables, there was hot pepper sauce that the vendor had spooned over them. The experience certainly didn't deter me and I have been an avid falafel eater ever since.

When I met my husband-to-be that same year, I was interested to hear that his parents, Zechariah and Rachel Levy, had a falafel café in Givatayim, a suburb of Tel Aviv. Every day Yakir's father ground the soaked chickpeas in a meat grinder, and his mother seasoned, shaped, and fried them. For Independence Day, they also set up a falafel stand in the town's main square where the celebrations were being held.

Falafel is the name of both the chickpea balls and the sandwich. It's not always made of chickpeas, though, and not always called falafel. Egyptians make the balls with dried fava beans (broad beans) and call them *ta'miya* or *ta'amiya*. Quite a few Lebanese chefs I have talked to say a mixture of nutty chickpeas and earthy fava beans gives the best flavor. Others insist that frugality is the only reason to use fava beans, as they cost less than chickpeas. The tasty fritters are either tucked into a pita's pocket or wrapped in a flatbread.

Instead of sticking to the standard, some are reinterpreting the falafel, accompanying it with pesto or other sauces instead of the classic tahini. There is a new falafel burger restaurant in Egypt, where the falafel is shaped like a hamburger, fried as usual and served in a bun. A few inventive falafel makers are serving spicy red falafels with red peppers, orange falafel with sweet potatoes, and falafel with goat cheese and sun-dried tomatoes. But I saw the most outlandish version at a deli takeout in Los Angeles—falafel sushi, with a falafel ball instead of fish inside the sushi rice!

Curried Chickpeas with Spinach and Zucchini

siserov sbanakh

Chickpeas and spinach are a favorite Middle Eastern combination in soups and stews, seasoned with just salt and pepper or enhanced by a few spices. Serve the medley as a hot entrée with bulgur wheat, rice, or fresh pita bread, as a cold salad with a squeeze of lemon juice, or as a partner for lamb, beef, or chicken. You can substitute 2 to 3 teaspoons curry powder for the spices if you like.

◆ MAKES 4 TO 6 SERVINGS.

One 10-ounce package rinsed spinach, or 12–16-ounce bunch, large stems removed and leaves rinsed

2 to 3 tablespoons olive oil

1 large onion, chopped

2 large garlic cloves, chopped

1 teaspoon ground coriander

1 teaspoon ground cumin

½ teaspoon turmeric

3 cups cooked chickpeas (garbanzo beans) with ⅓ cup cooking liquid (page 374), or two 15-ounce cans chickpeas, drained

⅓ cup vegetable broth or water (optional)

8 ounces zucchini, halved and sliced ½ inch thick

Salt and freshly ground black pepper

½ to 1 teaspoon Aleppo pepper, or a pinch cayenne pepper

Coarsely chop spinach. Heat 1 to 2 tablespoons oil in large saucepan. Add onion and sauté over medium heat for 7 minutes, or until golden. Add garlic, coriander, cumin, and turmeric and sauté ½ minute. Stir in chickpeas and ⅓ cup chickpea cooking liquid or vegetable broth. Add zucchini and bring to a boil.

Reduce heat to low and add spinach in three batches, covering briefly after each addition so spinach wilts. After adding all of spinach, simmer, uncovered, for 3 minutes, or until zucchini is tender. Season to taste with salt, pepper, and Aleppo pepper.

Lentils with Rice and Caramelized Onions

majadra; medardara

When I lived in the Mideast, I discovered the popular lentil and rice specialty called *majadra*. A very simple dish, it's loved throughout the region. In many homes it is seasoned only with salt, and perhaps a little pepper and a touch of cumin. Essential to its good taste is a generous topping of deeply browned onions. They are fried or sautéed in oil or butter until their sugar caramelizes, giving them a complex savory-sweet flavor.

Spices creep in as you travel eastward from the Mediterranean. An Iraqi version calls for plenty of garlic, cumin, and tomato paste. Persians embellish the dish further, adding meat, saffron, raisins, and dates. Cooks disagree on which rice is best, some choosing round, risotto-type rice, others opting for long-grain basmati. Some like the lentils to keep their shape, others prefer a puree, still others make both versions, each with a different name.

You don't need special lentils; the common brown ones from the supermarket are fine. A Lebanese friend told me that classically the lentil rice casserole is made with twice as much rice as lentils but that modern cooks often prefer equal proportions or even more lentils than rice to boost the protein content, especially when serving the dish as a vegetarian main course.

Serve alongside chicken, beef, or lamb, or accompanied by a refreshing tomato-cucumber-parsley salad or a cool yogurt mint sauce for a healthful meatless entrée.

◆ MAKES 4 SERVINGS.

1⅓ cups lentils

3 cups water

1 cup long-grain white rice, preferably basmati

¼ cup extra-virgin olive oil or vegetable oil, or 2 tablespoons oil and 2 tablespoons butter

2 large onions, chopped

4 large garlic cloves, chopped (optional)

1 teaspoon ground cumin (optional)

¼ to ½ teaspoon hot red pepper flakes (optional)

Salt and freshly ground black pepper

3 tablespoons chopped Italian parsley

Combine lentils and 3 cups water in medium saucepan. Bring to a boil. Cover and cook over medium heat for 15 minutes, or until lentils are nearly tender. Drain liquid into a measuring cup and add enough water to make 2 cups; reserve. Rinse and drain rice.

Heat oil in large heavy skillet. Add onions and sauté over medium heat for 15 minutes, or until they are deeply browned, stirring occasionally. Reduce heat if necessary so they become tender but do not burn. With slotted spoon, remove half the onions and reserve.

Add remaining onions with their oil to pan of lentils. Add garlic and cumin and pepper flakes if you like, and stir over medium heat for ½ minute. Add measured liquid and bring to a boil. Add salt, pepper, and rice and return to a boil. Cover and cook over low heat, without stirring, for 15 minutes, or until rice is just tender.

Let stand off heat for 5 to 10 minutes. Fluff very gently with a fork, blending in 2 tablespoons parsley. Taste and adjust seasoning. Serve hot, warm, or cold, topped with reserved onions and remaining parsley.

Red Lentil Puree

majadra

For people in Eastern Mediterranean countries, this lentil puree is pure comfort food, like mashed potatoes are for Americans. It's smooth and mildly seasoned to enhance the savory flavor of the lentils.

Red or orange lentils are sometimes called Egyptian lentils. They cook more rapidly than other varieties and fall apart when they're tender. Cooks take advantage of this tendency and serve these lentils in this simple dish or as a soup. Although the lentils turn into a puree on their own, many people mash or blend them further so they will have a velvety texture.

Usually the lentils are cooked with a small amount of rice to give the dish more body, but you can omit the rice if you like and simply stir the sautéed onions into the puree. To make the lentils more luscious, many finish them with fine olive oil or with butter. Often the puree is served cold or at room temperature, but in some households the onion is sautéed with diced meat and then the dish is served hot.

As an appetizer, the puree is nice served with a fresh vegetable salad, such as Mideast-California Diced Salad (page 60). It also makes a tasty accompaniment for cold sliced meats, roast turkey, or vegetable entrées such as Spicy Stewed Eggplant (page 243).

◆ MAKES 4 SERVINGS.

1½ cups red lentils

4 cups water

⅓ cup long-grain white rice

3 to 4 tablespoons extra-virgin olive oil

1 large onion, chopped

1 teaspoon ground cumin (optional)

Salt and freshly ground black pepper

1 tablespoon finely chopped Italian parsley, chives, or cilantro (optional)

Combine lentils and 4 cups water in medium saucepan. Bring to a boil. Cover and cook over low heat for 10 minutes, or until lentils are tender and falling apart. Drain liquid and reserve.

Return lentils to pan or, for a smooth puree, process them in blender or food processor, adding a few tablespoons of the cooking liquid if necessary. Return puree to saucepan. Rinse and drain rice.

Heat 2 tablespoons oil in heavy skillet. Add onion and sauté over medium heat about 7 minutes, or until deep golden brown, stirring occasionally. Add to pan of lentil puree. Add cumin, if you like, salt, pepper, and 1 cup of reserved lentil cooking liquid. Bring to a boil. Add rice and return to a boil. Cover and cook over low heat for 15 minutes, or until rice is tender. Add a few more tablespoons lentil liquid if puree is too thick. Stir in remaining olive oil and, if you like, parsley. Taste and adjust seasoning. Serve hot, warm, or cold.

Lemony Lebanese Lentils

adass salata

This versatile dish features lentils flavored with sautéed onions, garlic, mint, and parsley and finished with fine olive oil. Prepare it ahead and marinate the lentils in their sauce if you like. Served hot, cold, or at room temperature, it makes a tasty salad, a vegetarian main course with fresh bread, rice, or pasta, or an accompaniment for grilled meat or chicken. To present it as part of a meze buffet, mound it on a bed of lettuce or garnish it with tomato and cucumber slices. Be sure to include fresh lemon wedges for each person to squeeze and perk up his or her portion.

◆ MAKES 4 SERVINGS.

1 cup lentils, sorted and rinsed (see Note)

2 cups water

2 tablespoons vegetable oil

2 onions, chopped

3 garlic cloves, minced

1 teaspoon dried mint

1 to 2 tablespoons extra-virgin olive oil

2 tablespoons fresh-squeezed lemon juice, or to taste

Salt and freshly ground black pepper

3 tablespoons chopped Italian parsley

Lemon wedges

Combine lentils and 2 cups water in medium saucepan. Bring to a boil. Cover and cook over medium heat about 20 minutes, or until lentils are just tender but still firm.

Heat vegetable oil in heavy skillet. Add onions and sauté over medium heat about 10 minutes, until they are golden brown, stirring occasionally. Add to lentils. Stir in garlic, mint, olive oil, lemon juice, and 2 tablespoons parsley. Season to taste with salt and pepper. Serve sprinkled with remaining parsley and accompanied by lemon wedges.

NOTE If you're in a hurry, you can make this dish from canned lentils and skip boiling the lentils.

Black-eyed Peas with Braised Eggplant, Rosemary, and Chili-Garlic Paste

dickeyat loubeyah bel bittingan

The first time I saw fresh black-eyed peas, during my college years in Jerusalem, I was enthusiastic about cooking but didn't have experience or books. I thought they were some kind of green bean and I cooked them whole. The beans inside were delicious but the pods were inedible. I found out the hard way that they have to be shelled.

Occasionally I come across the fresh peas at my neighborhood Mediterranean markets. I love them but it takes time to shell enough of the small pods to feed several people. Dried and frozen black-eyed peas are much easier to find and faster to prepare.

Eggplant is frequently cooked with chickpeas in the eastern Mediterranean, and with yellow split peas in Persia, but I find that black-eyed peas are also a good choice for stews like this one because they too have a satisfying, meaty texture. Finishing the dish with a sautéed onion and fresh chili-garlic paste heightens the flavor of the dish. Serve it with a refreshing cucumber yogurt salad and with white rice, couscous, or fresh flatbread.

◆ MAKES 4 SERVINGS.

8 ounces dried black-eyed peas, sorted and rinsed, or 3 to 3½ cups frozen black-eyed peas

5½ cups water

1 medium eggplant, unpeeled (about 1 pound)

3 or 4 tablespoons olive oil

2 medium onions, chopped

1 tablespoon minced peeled gingerroot (optional)

1 tablespoon ground coriander

2 teaspoons ground cumin

½ teaspoon turmeric

½ teaspoon hot red pepper flakes, or cayenne pepper to taste

Salt and freshly ground black pepper to taste

One 28-ounce can diced tomatoes, drained

2 tablespoons tomato paste

2 green or red jalapeño peppers, or 4 serrano peppers or other chilies

6 large garlic cloves, peeled

2 teaspoons minced fresh rosemary

2 tablespoons chopped Italian parsley

Put dried black-eyed peas in a medium saucepan and add 5 cups water. Bring to a simmer. Cover and cook over low heat for 1½ hours, or until tender. (Cook frozen ones according to package directions.)

Cut eggplant in ¾-inch dice. In heavy wide casserole, heat half of the oil, add half of the onion, and cook over medium heat for 7 minutes, or until beginning to turn golden. Add ginger, coriander, cumin, turmeric, and pepper flakes. Cook, stirring, for 1 minute. Add eggplant and salt and stir over low heat until eggplant is coated with spices. Add tomatoes and bring to a boil over high heat. Mix tomato paste with ½ cup water and stir into mixture. Cover and simmer over low heat for 25 minutes, stirring often.

Meanwhile, halve chilies; discard ribs and seeds if you want less heat. Grind chilies and garlic to a paste in small food processor or blender.

Drain peas, reserving their cooking liquid. Add peas, salt, pepper, and ⅓ cup of their cooking liquid to eggplant.

In skillet, heat remaining oil, add remaining onion, and sauté over medium heat for 7 minutes, or until golden. Add chili-garlic paste and stir over low heat for 3 minutes. Add 1 tablespoon water. Add mixture to black-eyed pea-and-eggplant stew. Stir in rosemary. Cover and simmer for 5 minutes, or until eggplant is very tender and stew is well flavored. Add 1 tablespoon parsley. Taste and adjust seasoning. Serve hot, sprinkled with remaining parsley.

Egyptian Breakfast Beans

---

foul medammes

People in Egypt start their day with a dish of fava beans, often mixed with a small amount of lentils. Depending on the cook's preference and the size and age of the beans, cooking times vary from 3 to 10 hours. Some soak the beans for hours or even days before cooking, while others just rinse them before cooking them over the lowest flame or in a very low oven.

Eggs are a popular accompaniment. Many serve hard-boiled eggs, but certain cooks slip eggs in their shells into the pot to cook along with the beans. When you cook the beans ahead and refrigerate them, you can leave the eggs in the container with the beans. Before serving, reheat them together in a covered saucepan over low heat, leaving the eggs still in their shells and adding a little hot water if necessary so the beans won't become dry. If you're heating a small amount of beans, you can shell the eggs and heat them briefly in the already-warm beans.

Serve the beans very hot, with a variety of additions on small plates. At the table each person slightly mashes the beans with the flavorings he or she likes. Serve with fresh pita bread and, if you like, with Middle Eastern Diced Salad (page 58), radishes, green onions, or sour or hot pickles.

These days people in a hurry use canned fava beans, which are available at Middle Eastern markets. They simply heat the beans and serve them with the seasonings and with hard-boiled eggs.

♦ MAKES 6 TO 8 SERVINGS.

1 pound small dried fava beans
 (2¼ to 2½ cups), sorted and rinsed
¼ cup red lentils (optional), sorted and
 rinsed
6 to 8 eggs in shells, rinsed (optional)
About 10 cups water
Salt
Aleppo pepper or cayenne pepper
Black pepper
½ cup extra-virgin olive oil, vegetable oil,
 or melted butter
3 or 4 lemons, halved
4 green onions, sliced thin, or 2 medium
 onions, coarsely grated
3 or 4 tomatoes, diced small
½ cup chopped Italian parsley (optional)
3 garlic cloves, minced very fine

Soak fava beans in bowl of cold water to cover overnight. Drain beans and put them in heavy saucepan with lentils.

Check eggs to be sure they have no

cracks. Add to beans. Add about 10 cups water, or enough to cover ingredients by about 2 inches. Bring to a boil. Reduce heat as low as possible. Cover and cook for 4 or 5 hours, or until beans are very tender, adding hot water occasionally if too much evaporates. When beans are cooked, if they are very soupy, remove eggs and cook beans, uncovered, over medium-high heat until liquid reduces slightly, stirring occasionally to prevent sticking; the beans should not be dry.

Set out small dishes of salt and Aleppo pepper, black pepper in a grinder, a bowl or cruet of oil or a sauceboat of melted butter, lemon halves for squeezing, and bowls of green onions, diced tomatoes, parsley if you like, and garlic. Serve the eggs on a plate. Serve beans very hot, spooned into bowls with several spoonfuls of their cooking liquid. To eat them, use a fork to slightly mash the beans with seasonings, oil, and lemon juice, then add the eggs and other ingredients to your taste.

Old World Bean Wrap

foul medammes b'laffa

This savory sandwich combines the two original, time-honored beans of the Mideast—chickpeas and fava beans, which are often served together in Jerusalem and in Beirut. I mash some of the beans to spread on the bread, and flavor the sandwich with feta cheese, cumin, garlic, and zahtar.

Instead of rolling the bean medley in flatbread, you can turn this combination into a salad by not mashing the beans. To flavor your salad the Lebanese way, substitute black olives for the cheese and add fresh mint and a few sliced radishes.

For a casual dish like this, I use cooked beans that I have on hand or canned ones. If you're cooking fava beans, the split yellow ones cook faster than the whole beans. These tender beans are perfect for this recipe. To cook them, see Egyptian Fava Bean Dip with Garlic and Coriander (page 36).

◆ MAKES 4 SERVINGS.

1½ cups cooked fava beans, or one 15-ounce can fava beans, drained and liquid reserved

1½ cups cooked chickpeas (garbanzo beans) (see "Basics," page 374), or one 15-ounce can chickpeas, drained and liquid reserved

½ teaspoon ground cumin

2 garlic cloves, minced

2 to 3 tablespoons extra-virgin olive oil

2 to 3 tablespoons fresh-squeezed lemon juice

Salt and freshly ground black pepper

3 green onions, chopped

4 plum tomatoes, diced small

1 cup finely diced peeled cucumber

⅓ cup chopped parsley

1 to 2 teaspoons zahtar (see "The Mideast Pantry," page 14) or chopped fresh thyme, or ½ teaspoon dried thyme

½ teaspoon hot pepper sauce, or to taste

4 pieces soft lavash, 8 or 9 inches square, or 4 pita breads

½ cup crumbled feta cheese

Put ½ cup fava beans, ½ cup chickpeas, and 2 tablespoons of each of their cooking liquid in bowl or food processor. Coarsely mash beans with potato masher; or chop them in food processor, pulsing. If mixture is very thick, add a little more liquid. Transfer mixture to bowl. Add cumin, half the garlic, I tablespoon olive oil, I tablespoon lemon juice, and salt and pepper to taste, and stir until blended.

In another bowl, combine remaining beans with remaining garlic, olive oil, and lemon juice and mix well. Add green onions, tomatoes, cucumbers, parsley, and zahtar and mix well. Season to taste with salt, pepper, and hot sauce.

To make each sandwich, spread one-fourth of bean spread on one side of each lavash, leaving a ½-inch border. Top with bean and vegetable mixture. Scatter feta cheese over the top. Roll up tightly and serve. If using pita, spread bean spread inside and add bean and vegetable mixture and feta.

Red Beans and Yellow Rice with Carrots and Raisins

havij polo

You may be familiar with red beans and rice as a specialty of the Caribbean and the American South. The Persians have their own take on this combination, stewing the beans with a variety of herbs and flavoring them with lime or lemon before spooning them over the rice. Sometimes they go in a sweet direction instead, studding bean and rice dishes with carrots, raisins, or dates and accenting them with cinnamon and a touch of turmeric.

This recipe is inspired by these traditional dishes but is lighter and easier to make. You can make a black bean variation with golden raisins or dried cranberries. For a two-bean dish, use half black beans and half red ones. Serve this colorful accompaniment with roast chicken or meat stews. When the weather is warm, it's good cold with a selection of raw vegetable salads. It also makes an easy, convenient potluck dish.

◆ MAKES 6 SERVINGS.

2 tablespoons vegetable oil

1 large onion, finely chopped

1¼ cups long-grain white rice

½ teaspoon ground coriander

½ teaspoon ground cinnamon

¼ teaspoon turmeric

3 cups hot water

1 teaspoon salt, or to taste

½ teaspoon freshly ground black pepper,
   or to taste

2 large carrots, sliced

1½ to 2 cups cooked red beans, or one
   15-ounce can, drained and rinsed

⅓ cup raisins, dark or golden

¼ cup chopped Italian parsley

Heat oil in large sauté pan or large wide saucepan over medium heat. Add onion and cook over medium heat for 5 minutes, or until soft but not brown. Add rice and cook, stirring, over medium-low heat for 3 minutes, or until grains turn white. Stir in coriander, cinnamon, and turmeric.

Pour 2½ cups hot water over rice and stir once. Add salt and pepper. Bring to a boil. Reduce heat to very low, cover tightly, and simmer for 5 minutes. Scatter carrot slices over the top, without stirring, and pour remaining hot water over them. Cook, covered, for 10 minutes. Scatter beans and raisins over the top of the rice, cover, and cook for 2 to 3 minutes, or until rice is just tender and liquid is absorbed. Let stand, covered, for 5 minutes.

Fluff rice with large fork, gently stirring in parsley. Taste and adjust seasoning. Serve hot or cold.

Summer Squash Stew with Beans

khoresh-e kadoo

This meatless entrée is a light rendition of a hearty Persian stew. Normally, the long-cooking *khoresh* casseroles are made with lamb, beef, or chicken, but I substitute beans for the meat to create an easy vegetarian version. Lime juice and cinnamon, the traditional flavorings, perk up the vegetables and their simple tomato sauce. The caramelized onions and cinnamon contribute a sweetness that balances the tartness of the citrus.

Khoresh is usually served hot with white rice. When the weather is warm, I like this quick and easy dish cool or at room temperature as a salad.

◆ MAKES 6 TO 8 SERVINGS.

2 to 3 tablespoons vegetable oil

2 large onions, halved and thinly sliced

1½ pounds pale green or yellow summer
   squash or zucchini, cut in ¾-inch dice

Salt and freshly ground black pepper to taste

¾ cup water

⅔ cup canned crushed tomatoes

1½ to 2 cups cooked pinto beans
   (see "Basics," page 374), or one
   15-ounce can pinto beans, drained

1½ to 2 cups cooked chickpeas (garbanzo
   beans) (see "Basics," page 374),
   or one 15-ounce can chickpeas, drained

¾ to 1 teaspoon ground cinnamon

½ teaspoon turmeric

2 to 3 tablespoons fresh-squeezed lime juice

Heat oil in large deep sauté pan. Add onions and sauté over medium heat for 15 minutes, or until tender and well browned, stirring occasionally and reducing heat if they brown too fast. Add squash, salt, and pepper and sauté for 1 minute. Add ¾ cup water and bring to a simmer. Cover and simmer over medium heat for 2 minutes.

Add tomatoes, pinto beans, chickpeas, cinnamon, and turmeric. Return to a simmer. Cover and cook over medium heat for 5 minutes, then over low heat for 5 to 10 minutes, or until squash is very tender, adding more water by tablespoons if sauce becomes too thick. Add 2 tablespoons lime juice and cook for 1 minute. Taste and add more lime juice if you like. Season well with salt and pepper to balance the flavor of the lime juice. Serve hot or at room temperature.

Aromatic White and Green Bean Stew

fasulye pilaki

For this dish I add green beans to a simple Middle Eastern white bean stew. In appearance, the result reminds me of a French dish I like, a combination of green and dried beans called *haricots panachés* that often accompanies

roast lamb. The French usually boil white beans or pale green dried flageolets, mix them with blanched green beans, and heat them with butter. In this Middle Eastern dish the flavorings are completely different—cumin, coriander, and lots of onions browned thoroughly in olive oil. You can substitute flageolets for the white beans for a tasty variation, as Lebanese people living in France do.

Some people cook their beans with cubed or ground beef or lamb. Others add a few thin slices of smoked sausage, such as the garlicky Armenian *soujouk*. Turkish cooks might flavor their beans with sliced cured meat like *basterma*, the spicy Armenian-Lebanese pastrami. You can find these meats in Middle Eastern markets, or use pastrami or any spicy or garlicky sausage you like. Simply heat the cooked meat or sausage in the finished stew, or serve the stew as a meatless entrée with rice.

◆ MAKES 6 TO 8 SERVINGS.

7 cups water

1 pound dried white beans, such as Great Northern (2¼ to 2½ cups), sorted and rinsed

1½ pounds green beans, ends removed, broken in half

3 to 4 tablespoons tomato paste

2 to 3 teaspoons ground cumin

2 to 3 teaspoons ground coriander

Salt and freshly ground black pepper

Cayenne pepper to taste (optional)

6 to 7 tablespoons olive oil

3 large onions, chopped

Bring 7 cups water to a boil in large pot. Add white beans. Cover and cook over low heat about 1 to 1½ hours, or until beans are tender.

Add green beans to large saucepan of boiling salted water and boil, uncovered, over high heat 6 minutes, or until crisp-tender. Drain, rinse with cold water, and drain well.

Drain white beans, reserving cooking liquid. Return white beans to pot. Mix tomato paste with 1 cup bean cooking liquid and add to pot. Add cumin, coriander, salt, pepper, and cayenne pepper. Bring to a simmer and keep warm.

Heat oil in large heavy skillet. Add onions and sauté over medium heat for 15 minutes, or until deeply browned, stirring often. Add to pot of white beans. Cover and heat gently for 5 minutes. Add green beans and heat through, uncovered. Taste and adjust seasonings. Serve hot.

Yellow Split Pea Stew with Mushrooms and Tomatoes

khoresh-e quemen

Persians love yellow split peas and turn them into a variety of soups, stews, and legume-and-grain medleys. Often they cook the peas with beef or lamb, and some-times with eggplant, and flavor the stew with tomatoes and either turmeric or cinnamon. For an easy meatless variation, I make this tangy stew with mushrooms. If you don't have yellow split peas, substitute the green type, which are more widely available; they will take about 1 to 1¼ hours to cook and will need about 4 cups liquid. This type of stew is usually served with rice or flatbread.

◆ MAKES 4 SERVINGS.

1 cup yellow split peas, sorted and rinsed

3 cups chicken or vegetable broth or water

2 tablespoons vegetable oil or olive oil

1 large onion, halved and sliced

1 pound mushrooms, quartered

Salt and freshly ground black pepper to taste

1 teaspoon turmeric

2 large tomatoes, peeled, seeded, and diced, or one 14-ounce can diced tomatoes, drained

2 tablespoons tomato paste

1 to 2 tablespoons fresh-squeezed lemon juice, or to taste

Combine split peas and broth in large saucepan and bring to a boil. Cover and simmer for 20 minutes, or until peas are just tender, adding water if mixture becomes too thick.

Heat oil in large skillet. Add onion and sauté over medium heat for 5 minutes, or until soft but not brown. Add mushrooms, salt, and pepper and sauté over medium heat for 7 minutes, or until browned, stirring often. Add turmeric and tomatoes and cook for 5 to 10 minutes, or until mixture is thick.

Mix tomato paste with ¼ cup water and stir into split peas. Add mushroom-tomato mixture. Simmer for 5 to 10 minutes, or until peas are well flavored. Stir in lemon juice. Taste and adjust seasoning. Serve hot.

Split Peas with Chicken and Tarragon

qeymeh

This stew, flavored with cinnamon and herbs in the Iranian fashion, is often made with lamb but I substitute chicken and add zucchini to make a one-pot entrée. It is quick and easy to make because the peas and the boneless chicken cook rapidly. Serve it with basmati rice or with soft lavash or other flatbreads, and a big bowl of Green Salad with Herbs and Radishes (page 67).

♦ MAKES 4 SERVINGS.

¾ cup yellow split peas, sorted and rinsed (see Note)

About 3½ cups chicken broth, water, or a mixture of both

2 tablespoons vegetable oil

1 large onion, sliced

1 pound boneless, skinless chicken breasts or thighs, cut in 1-inch dice

Salt and freshly ground black pepper

½ teaspoon turmeric

½ teaspoon ground cinnamon

2 zucchini, diced

2 tablespoons chopped fresh tarragon, or 2 teaspoons dried

1 tablespoon chopped fresh mint, or 1 teaspoon dried

Combine split peas and 2½ cups broth in large saucepan and bring to a boil. Cover and simmer for 20 minutes, or until peas are just tender, adding water if mixture becomes too thick.

Heat oil in large saucepan. Add onion and sauté over medium heat for 10 minutes, or until golden brown. Add chicken, salt, pepper, turmeric, and cinnamon and sauté until chicken's color lightens. Add remaining cup of broth and bring to a simmer. Cover and cook over low heat for 7 minutes. Add zucchini and cook for 5 to 8 minutes, or until chicken and zucchini are tender. Add cooked split pea mixture and a little more liquid if stew is too thick. Lightly stir in tarragon and mint and simmer for 2 minutes. Taste and adjust seasoning. Serve hot.

NOTE If you are using green split peas instead of yellow ones, cook them for about 1 to 1¼ hours, or until tender, adding broth or water as needed.

Fresh Fava Bean Stew with Chicken and Chard

foul bel salq

Cooks in Egypt often pair beans with greens. For this entrée, which is flavored with diced chicken and lightly thickened with rice, use either green or red chard, or substitute spinach or other greens. Sautéed garlic and a generous amount of dill give it a fresh flavor, but you can substitute mint, cilantro, or a combination of these herbs.

You can find fresh fava beans and often frozen ones at Mediterranean and Latino markets. In the Mideast, people sometimes can get very small, tender fava beans and cook them in their pods, but in American markets I've never found fava beans young enough to cook whole. If you prefer more tender beans with a bright green color, remove their thick skins after cooking them, following the note at the end of the recipe. Some people prefer them with their skins.

◆ MAKES 4 SERVINGS.

2 pounds fresh fava beans, shelled, or 10 to 12 ounces frozen fava or lima beans

2 to 3 tablespoons olive oil

1 large onion, chopped

1 pound boneless chicken breasts or thighs, cut in 1-inch cubes

Salt and freshly ground black pepper

1½ to 1¾ cups chicken stock, broth, or water

¼ cup short- or long-grain rice

6 large garlic cloves, chopped

1½ cups coarsely chopped trimmed Swiss chard leaves

⅓ cup chopped fresh dill

Cayenne pepper to taste

If you want to peel the fava beans so they will be bright green, cook them according to the Note at the end of the recipe.

Heat I to 2 tablespoons oil in stew pan. Add onion and sauté over medium heat for 5 minutes, or until they begin to turn golden. Add chicken, salt, and pepper and sauté until its color lightens. Add I½ cups stock and bring to a boil. Cover and simmer for 10 minutes.

If using fresh or frozen unpeeled fava beans (but not lima beans), add them and return to a boil. Cover and cook for 5 minutes. Add rice, cover, and cook over low heat for 10 minutes. If using lima beans or peeled fava beans, add them now and return to a simmer. Cover and cook for 5 minutes, or until chicken is cooked through and rice and beans are barely tender.

Heat remaining tablespoon oil in heavy skillet. Stir in garlic, then chard, and sauté, stirring, over medium heat for 3 minutes. Transfer mixture to bowl and mash with potato masher; or puree in food processor. Add chard mixture to chicken and beans and stir gently. If stew is too thick, stir in remaining stock. Add dill and cayenne. Cook, uncovered, over medium heat for 2 minutes, or until chicken, beans, chard, and rice are tender. Taste and adjust seasoning. Serve hot.

ΝΟΤΣ For bright green fava beans, blanch them and peel them: Put shelled fresh or frozen beans in large saucepan of boiling salted water and cook, uncovered, over high heat for 5 to 7 minutes, or until barely tender. Drain well and peel off the thick skins.

Spicy Yemenite Baked Beans with Beef

hamin

In many Israeli homes some variation of this entrée is on the menu every week as a hearty Saturday lunch. It usually contains either beef or chicken and is also delicious when made with turkey legs, thighs, or wings. In addition to beans, this economical, slow-cooked casserole often has potatoes, wheat, barley, rice, or a combination of these ingredients. Some people make vegetarian versions by simply omitting the meat. Tradition dictates cooking this casserole overnight on a heating plate or in a very low oven, and many find the flavor is best that way. For a "faster" version, I bake the stew in a fairly low oven for 5 hours.

This recipe, spiced with cumin, turmeric, onions, and plenty of garlic, is based on my mother-in-law's, which remains our family's favorite. Like Egyptian Breakfast Beans (page 223), this bean stew often cooks with eggs in their shells, which are served as a garnish.

Many serve this hearty casserole on its own, but I like to set out a selection of fresh salads, such as Tangy Two-way Coleslaw (page 69) and Middle Eastern Diced Salad (page 58).

◆ MAKES ABOUT 8 SERVINGS.

2 cups dried medium lima beans or other white beans, picked over and rinsed

1½ cups dried chickpeas (garbanzo beans), picked over and rinsed

2 pounds beef chuck, excess fat trimmed, cut in 1½-inch pieces

1½ pounds small whole boiling potatoes, peeled if desired

3 large onions, cut in thick slices

10 garlic cloves, coarsely chopped

2 teaspoons salt

1 to 1½ teaspoons freshly ground black pepper

2 tablespoons ground cumin

4 teaspoons turmeric

8 eggs in shells, rinsed

2 tablespoons chopped Italian parsley (optional)

Preheat oven to 250°F.

In large heavy casserole, combine lima beans, chickpeas, beef, potatoes, onions, and garlic. Sprinkle with salt, pepper, cumin, and turmeric and mix well. Add 2 quarts water or enough to cover the ingredients. Bring to a boil. Simmer, uncovered, for 20 minutes. Remove from heat. Set eggs gently on top and push them slightly into liquid.

Cover tightly and bake mixture, without stirring, for 5 hours, or until beef is very tender and beans are well flavored. During baking, check amount of liquid two or three times; if mixture appears to be getting dry, add ½ cup hot water.

If stew is too soupy and you would like it to be thicker, uncover and bake for 30 to 45 more minutes. Serve stew from the casserole or a deep serving dish. Shell and halve eggs and set them on top for garnish. Serve hot, sprinkled with parsley if you like.

Garlicky Chili with Coriander and Cilantro

fassoulia bil kosbarah

Like American chili, this dish has countless regional variations. In Egypt it might be a cilantro-flavored lentil-and-lamb chili, or one of beef and fava beans garnished with olives. Armenians often opt for beef with chickpeas and dill, while multibean combinations are favored in Iran. Basically, cooks use the seasonings they like with whatever beans and meat they have.

To make this dish colorful, I combine white and lima beans with the meaty sauce. Saving part of the golden onions and garlic to add to the finished stew makes their flavors more pronounced and gives the chili more punch. Many prefer to dice the meat, but ground meat works well and is quicker. Make it with chicken or turkey for a lighter version, or use soy ground meat.

Like tortillas alongside American chili, flatbread is a favorite Mideast partner for these types of dishes. This chili is also delicious spooned as a thick sauce over rice or spaghetti.

◆ MAKES ABOUT 6 SERVINGS.

2 to 3 tablespoons olive oil or vegetable oil

2 large onions, chopped

8 large garlic cloves, minced

1 green bell pepper, halved, cored, seeded, and diced

¾ to 1 pound extra-lean ground beef

2 teaspoons ground coriander

1 teaspoon ground cumin

1½ cups tomato sauce

1 cup beef or chicken broth or water

Salt and freshly ground black pepper to taste

1½ cups frozen lima beans, cooked according to package directions

1½ to 2 cups cooked white beans, or one 15-ounce can white beans, drained

⅓ cup chopped cilantro, dill, or a combination of both

Cayenne pepper to taste

Pitted black or green olives

Heat oil in heavy sauté pan. Add onions and sauté over medium heat for 10 minutes, or until tender and golden, stirring often. Add garlic and sauté for ½ minute. Remove half of mixture and reserve in bowl.

To onion-garlic mixture in pan, add green pepper, beef, coriander, and cumin and cook over medium-low heat for 7 minutes, or until meat browns lightly, stirring often. Add tomato sauce, broth, salt, and pepper. Bring to a simmer. Cover and cook over low heat for 10 minutes, or until meat is cooked through.

Add lima and white beans. If chili is too thick, add ¼ cup water or more if needed. Cover and cook over low heat for 5 minutes, or until stew is thick and well flavored. Add reserved onion-garlic mixture, 3 tablespoons cilantro, and cayenne pepper. Cover and heat through. Taste and adjust seasoning. Serve garnished with remaining cilantro and olives.

Chickpea and Bulgur Wheat Casserole with Lamb Steaks

---

burghul bid-dfin

A popular stew in Lebanon and Syria combines chickpeas with a small amount of meat flavored with cinnamon. Traditionally, it's prepared by simmering the beans with beef or lamb shanks or stew meat. I turn the bean, bulgur, and meat trio into a quick and easy entrée by simply dicing leg of lamb steaks or lamb chops from which I've removed the bones and using canned or already cooked chickpeas. If you prefer beef, use a thick steak, such as sirloin or porterhouse.

◆ MAKES 4 TO 6 SERVINGS.

> 12 ounces lamb steaks, 8 lamb loin or rib chops, or 12 ounces beef sirloin or other steak
>
> 2 tablespoons olive oil or vegetable oil
>
> Salt and freshly ground black pepper
>
> ½ teaspoon ground cinnamon
>
> 8 ounces yellow crookneck squash or zucchini, diced
>
> 1 large onion, halved and sliced
>
> 1 small red bell pepper, halved, cored, seeded, and diced
>
> 1 cup medium bulgur wheat
>
> 2 cups meat, chicken, or vegetable broth, chickpea cooking liquid, or water
>
> 3 cups cooked chickpeas (garbanzo beans) (page 374), or two 15-ounce cans chickpeas, drained
>
> 2 to 3 teaspoons chopped fresh thyme, or 1 teaspoon dried thyme
>
> 2 to 3 tablespoons chopped Italian parsley

Trim excess fat from meat. Heat 1 tablespoon oil in large heavy saucepan or deep sauté pan. Add steaks or chops and sprinkle with salt, pepper, and cinnamon. Sauté over medium-high heat for 1½ to 2 minutes per side, or until browned but not cooked through. Remove meat to plate with slotted spoon. Add squash to hot pan, sauté for 1 minute, and remove.

Heat remaining tablespoon oil in pan. Add onion and red pepper and sauté over medium heat for 5 minutes, stirring often. Stir in bulgur wheat, broth, chickpeas, and thyme and bring to a boil. Cover and cook over low heat for 12 minutes.

Meanwhile, cut meat in ¾- to 1-inch cubes, discarding lamb chop bones. Add meat to bulgur-and-chickpea stew with any juices on plate. Add squash. Cover and cook over low heat for 3 minutes, or until bulgur wheat is tender. Taste and adjust seasoning. Lightly stir in parsley. Serve hot.

Vegetables, from Ancient Favorites to Modern Menu Highlights

Artichokes with Peas, Pearl Onions, and Dill · *Zeytinyağli Enginar*

Easy Baked Eggplant with Olive Oil and Tomato-Garlic Topping · *Imam Bayildi*

Spicy Stewed Eggplant · *Mnazlit al-Batinjan*

Eggplant with Browned Onions, Mild Chilies, and Yogurt-Garlic Sauce · *Mast-e Badenjan*

Armenian Green Beans · *Loligov Ganatch Loopya*

Okra in Tangy Jalapeño Tomato Sauce · *Bamie Ateh*

Spicy Yemenite Peas · *Afunah b'Nosah Teimani*

Savory Stewed Onions, Middle Eastern Style · *Bassal bi-Zayt*

Turkish Braised Leeks with Carrots · *Zeytinyağli Pirasa*

Easy Stuffed Peppers with Rice, Chickpeas, and Olives · *Zeytinyağli Büber Dolmasi*

Wild Mushrooms with Tomatoes, Basil, and Bulgur Wheat • *Mantarli Pilav*

Two-way Summer Squash Stew with Sweet Peppers • *M'tabbaq Koussa*

Lebanese Vegetable Stew with Chickpeas • *Musaka*

Carrots, Beans, and Mushrooms in Savory Tomato Sauce • *Gallaba*

Spinach and Summer Squash Borani with Red Peppers • *Boorani-ye Esfena*

Beet Borani Salad • *Boorani-ye Laboo*

Climate and religion ensure the centrality of vegetables in the culinary culture of the Mideast. Depending on the weather and the calendar, braised, stewed, or stuffed vegetables might be prepared with or without meat. Part of the reason vegetables play such a key role in Middle Eastern menus is frugality. In most areas meat was and remains expensive, and for everyday meals it is used mostly to flavor vegetable and grain dishes. Some experts claim the vegetarian tradition stems from the numerous meat-free days on the Greek Orthodox, Coptic, and Eastern Christian calendars. These guidelines undoubtedly influence the meals in observant households, but most cooks, no matter what their religion, serve these dishes because their families enjoy them.

As a result of trade between the Old World and the New, the selection of vegetables on the region's tables changed drastically. Middle Eastern people got tomatoes, peppers, and potatoes, while North and South Americans received in exchange artichokes, eggplant, figs, cilantro, and saffron. Historically speaking, these new produce items are relatively recent additions to recipes on both sides of the Atlantic. Cooks in the sunny Middle East certainly made up for lost time, integrating tomatoes and peppers so thoroughly into their cuisine that it's hard to imagine their food without them.

Onion and garlic are used generously and with gusto in the region to flavor an enormous range of dishes. Both are loved raw and cooked. Deeply browned onions flavor numerous sauces and top many dishes, especially those of grains and beans. These aromatic vegetables may be the region's all-time favorite flavorings to enhance other foods. Indeed, the ancient Israelites wandering in the Sinai desert complained about missing Egyptian onions. To some, freedom was apparently not worth the price of meals without onions!

Eggplant is king in the Mideast and is loved in all parts of the region. Its uses are practically infinite. Certainly the Ottomans loved it, judging by the stories of sultans who inspired such dishes as *Hunkar Begendi* (page 200), a meat ragout accompanied by a princely puree of grilled eggplant with cheese.

Living in the Mideast awakened me to the myriad possibilities of the region's signature vegetable. I found an astounding array of eggplant creations, from dips to salads to sides to entrées. Local cooks flavor eggplant with garlic, olive oil, tahini, onions, tomatoes, sweet peppers, chilies, herbs, lemon juice, and countless spices. They fry it, grill it, stew it, bake it, stuff it, and even make it into jam.

Before I moved to Israel I had never cooked or even tasted eggplant. Growing up in America, my only childhood memory of the vegetable is asking my mother whether it tasted like eggs, which I loved, and why she didn't use it. She muttered something like "it's not very good" but I doubt she was familiar with it. Since moving to Jerusalem, she has become fond of eggplant and cooks with it often.

The French and British acknowledge the Mideast preeminence in eggplant preparation. Even their word for the vegetable, aubergine, is derived from Arabic and Persian. Classic recipes in European chefs' kitchens often bear testament to their inspiration, with names like eggplant à l'egyptienne and eggplant à la turque.

The importance of tomatoes was made clear to me during a trip to Israel some years ago. I arrived at Tel Aviv airport at the same time as President Clinton, who had come for the signing of the peace agreement between Israel and Jordan. Only a few days after the historic event, instead of political news, an-

other story dominated the airwaves—the sudden scarcity and high price of tomatoes. Politicians were interviewed about the shortage and were asked how people would have their festive end-of-the-week dinners without their favorite vegetable. To relieve the tomato crunch, there was talk of a possible import of Jordanian tomatoes. What better way could there be to reap the first fruits of peaceful relations!

When it comes to green vegetables, there is a definite difference between Mediterranean and Mideastern kitchens and those of North America and northern Europe. In my culinary schooling in Paris I learned that restaurant chefs prefer cooking peas and slim green beans in what they considered the "natural" way, adding few ingredients so their intrinsic character remained evident. Generally they boiled the vegetables briefly in salted water so they stayed bright green, then tossed them with butter. They call such dishes cooking "à l'anglaise"—in the English fashion, to indicate how plain they are.

In contrast, people in the Middle East and around the Mediterranean like their vegetables thoroughly cooked so the flavor of the sauce permeates them. In fact, even in the West, brief cooking is a modern practice and many country favorites feature slow-cooked veggies. When you're preparing Middle Eastern recipes, if you prefer firmer-textured, bright green vegetables, cook fresh ones in boiling water until they are barely tender, and simply warm them in the sauce.

Long, slow cooking is not a rigid rule in the region. Very young vegetables, such as artichokes and fava beans, are sometimes served raw in the Mideast, whereas in our country they are not served this way because few of us can get them small enough.

*E*xchanging recipes with neighbors is friendly and fun. But as a newlywed novice at the stove, I quickly found out that it could lead to unexpected results. When I lived in Bat Yam in metropolitan Tel Aviv, my next-door neighbor's advice on how to make a tasty spread led to a messy outcome—an eggplant explosion.

It all started when my Middle Eastern mother-in-law cited the local proverb that a woman must know 101 ways to prepare eggplant in order to be fit for marriage. To prove myself, I was determined to learn to cook the dark purple fruit. I started with the dips I liked, the three favorites in Israel—eggplant with tahini, eggplant with mayonnaise, and eggplant with oil and lemon. My neighbor made them well and when I asked how she cooked the eggplant, she said, "Nothing could be simpler. Just place your whole eggplant in a very hot oven. You can set it directly on the oven rack—you don't even need a pan."

I put a large eggplant in my oven and went to the living room to study for a college exam. After ten minutes, I heard a loud bang. First I thought there had been a blast in the neigh-borhood. Then I realized it had come from my kitchen. I hesitantly opened the oven and to my surprise, it was empty. On closer inspec-tion I noticed bits of eggplant stuck to the oven's roof and walls. My eggplant had burst into smithereens.

Consulting with another friend, I discov-ered what my error had been. Before you roast the eggplant, she told me, you have to pierce it a few times with a fork. Otherwise the steam that builds up inside the eggplant as it bakes can cause it to blow up. After that memorable experience, I never forgot this step. Since then, as an added precaution, I have always baked or broiled my eggplants in a pan. Soon this traditional trio of Israeli eggplant starters, which can be considered spreads, salads, or dips, became standards in my kitchen.

Which kind of eggplant to use for these sal-ads is a matter of preference. People from the Mideast tend to be partial to the common, fairly large eggplants for their more dominant character. Smaller Asian eggplants cook faster but there are more of them to peel, so there is a trade-off in time. I use whichever I have on hand.

Artichokes with Peas, Pearl Onions, and Dill

zeytinyağli enginar

Cooking artichokes with another spring vegetable is a common practice among Mideast cooks, who share this custom with others around the Mediterranean. Peas and fava beans are the top choice. Sometimes new carrots, pearl onions, and baby potatoes are added. Seasonings are delicate so the fresh flavors of the vegetables stand out. This dish is usually an appetizer but some like it as a light supper with yogurt.

◆ MAKES 4 OR 5 SERVINGS.

1 lemon

4 medium artichokes, preferably with stems

8 to 12 ounces pearl onions, unpeeled

2 to 4 tablespoons extra-virgin olive oil

1 onion, finely chopped

1½ cups water

1 tablespoon fresh-squeezed lemon juice, or more to taste

3 tablespoons chopped fresh dill

Salt and freshly ground black pepper

1½ to 2 cups fresh shelled or frozen green peas

½ teaspoon sugar (optional)

Lemon wedges (optional)

Prepare artichoke hearts: Squeeze juice of ½ lemon into bowl of cold water. Leave stems on artichokes. Pull off bottom leaves of an artichoke. Snap back side leaves to remove tough parts and trim sides of artichoke so it is smooth. Pare stem with paring knife, removing all of the stringy part. Halve artichokes and trim top leaves so they are only ½ inch long. Halve each piece again. Using a spoon, scrape out hairlike choke from each quarter and pull out small, central purple-tipped leaves. Rub each piece with cut lemon; put in lemon water. Continue with remaining artichokes.

Put pearl onions in saucepan, cover with water, and bring to a boil. Cook 1 minute. Rinse under cold water, drain well, and peel.

Heat 2 or 3 tablespoons oil in sauté pan. Add onion and sauté over medium heat for 5 minutes, or until soft but not brown. Add artichokes and sauté for 1 or 2 minutes. Add water, 1 tablespoon lemon juice, 1 tablespoon dill, salt, and pepper. Bring to a boil; lower heat and cover. Cook over low heat for 10 minutes. Add pearl onions and simmer for 5 minutes. Add peas, stir, and bring to a boil. Cover and cook over low heat, adding a few tablespoons water if necessary, for 5 to 7 minutes, or until artichokes, onions, and peas are tender.

If too much liquid remains, remove vegetables with slotted spoon and boil liquid uncovered for 2 or 3 minutes to thicken it slightly. Return vegetables to liquid. Add sugar and more lemon juice if you like, and remaining dill and olive oil. Taste and adjust seasoning. Serve hot, warm, or cold, with lemon wedges if you like.

Easy Baked Eggplant with Olive Oil and Tomato-Garlic Topping

imam bayildi

This aromatic dish, Turkey's most famous specialty, is redolent of garlic and olive oil. To explain its Turkish name, which means "the imam fainted," some say the frugal man was horrified at the cost of the liberal amount of olive oil used, while others insist he swooned from delight at the dish's wonderful fragrance.

When I prepare it, I often choose Japanese or Chinese eggplants. They bake quickly and I enjoy their mild flavor. To cut the time further, you can grill or broil small eggplant halves before adding the topping instead of baking them. Watch them to prevent burning and turn them two or three times for even cooking.

This dish keeps well and tastes even better the next day. Traditionally the dish is seasoned only with generous amounts of salt and pepper. Lemon wedges are a popular garnish, as the fresh juice enlivens the flavors. At serving time you can top it with black olives, parsley, and diced fresh tomatoes. You can also serve hot sauce on the side, or spicy Turkish Tomato and Onion Dip (page 38).

Serve the eggplant as an appetizer, side dish, or as a meatless entrée with rice or couscous, a green salad, feta cheese, and crusty bread or good-quality pita.

◆ MAKES 4 SERVINGS.

2 pounds Japanese, Chinese, or small Italian eggplants, peeled in strips or unpeeled

3 to 5 tablespoons extra-virgin olive oil

Salt and freshly ground black pepper

2 medium onions, halved and sliced thin

4 large garlic cloves, minced

1½ pounds ripe tomatoes, diced, or one 28-ounce can diced tomatoes, drained, juice reserved

¼ cup chopped Italian parsley

Preheat oven to 450°F. Lightly oil roasting pan or shallow baking dish. Remove green caps and halve eggplants lengthwise. Place eggplants cut side up, side by side, in prepared pan. Sprinkle or brush them with 2 tablespoons oil, then season generously with salt and pepper. Bake about 15 minutes, or until eggplants are tender when pierced with a knife.

Heat 1 or 2 tablespoons oil in a large skillet; use a nonstick skillet if you want to keep the oil to a minimum. Add onions and sauté over medium heat 3 minutes, stirring often. Cover and cook over low heat 5 minutes, stirring often, adding 1 or 2 tablespoons water if pan becomes dry or if onions turn too dark. Stir in garlic and sauté for a few seconds. Add tomatoes, salt, and pepper. Cook, uncovered, over medium-high heat for 10 minutes, or until mixture is thick, stirring often. Remove from heat and add parsley. Taste and adjust seasoning; it should be generously seasoned.

Spoon topping over eggplant halves. If you like, drizzle with 1 tablespoon oil. Spoon any extra topping into baking dish and thin it with 3 or 4 tablespoons water or reserved tomato juice. Bake for 5 to 7 minutes to flavor eggplant. Serve hot, cold, or at room temperature.

Spicy Stewed Eggplant

mnazlit al-batinjan

This savory dish gains its flavor from my mother-in-law's Yemenite seasonings. For extra zip, she always put some of her super-hot homemade *zehug* (garlic-pepper relish) on the table so people could stir some into their stew. The eggplant makes a delicious vegetarian entrée with rice and is also a good accompaniment for chicken, lamb, or beef. As an easy variation, you can substitute 1 tablespoon curry powder for the spices.

◆ MAKES 4 SERVINGS.

1¼ pounds eggplant

2 to 3 tablespoons vegetable or olive oil

1 medium onion, chopped

6 large garlic cloves, minced

1½ teaspoons ground cumin

1 teaspoon ground coriander (optional)

½ teaspoon turmeric

Salt and freshly ground black pepper

1½ pounds ripe tomatoes, diced,
    or one 28-ounce can diced tomatoes,
    juice reserved

1 tablespoon tomato paste (optional)

1 to 2 teaspoons Hedva's Hot Pepper Relish
    (page 307), or hot sauce to taste

Cut eggplant in ¾- or 1-inch dice. Heat oil in heavy stew pan. Add onion and sauté over medium heat for 7 minutes, or until golden brown. Stir in garlic. Add diced eggplant, cumin, coriander, if you like, turmeric, salt, and ½ teaspoon pepper and stir over medium-low heat until eggplant is coated with onion mixture.

Add tomatoes with their juice and cook over high heat, stirring, until bubbling. Cover and simmer over medium-low heat for 30 minutes, or until eggplant is tender, stirring often. If using tomato paste, mix with 2 tablespoons water, add to stew, and simmer, uncovered, for 2 minutes, or until thickened to taste. Add hot pepper relish; taste and adjust seasoning. Serve hot or at room temperature.

Eggplant with Browned Onions, Mild Chilies, and Yogurt-Garlic Sauce

mast-e badenjan

This appetizer of eggplant braised with chilies and tomatoes is popular among Persians and Afghanis. Traditionally it is made with fried eggplant but today many cooks, especially those who have moved to Western countries, broil the eggplant to make it lighter, as in this version. (If you prefer to fry the eggplant, see page 372.) For the best flavor, brown the onions thoroughly, as they impart a delicate sweetness to the eggplant and contrast pleasantly with the yogurt. If you like, serve this dish as a light entrée with fresh flatbread or basmati rice.

◆ MAKES 4 APPETIZER SERVINGS.

1 cup plain yogurt, drained of any liquid

1 medium garlic clove, very finely minced

½ teaspoon dried mint

Salt and freshly ground black pepper

2 slender eggplants or 1 large eggplant (1¼ to 1½ pounds total), cut in ¼-inch-thick slices

2 tablespoons vegetable oil (for onions) plus nonstick cooking spray, or 5 to 6 teaspoons oil (for eggplant)

2 large onions, halved and thinly sliced

2 mild green chilies, such as Anaheim, or 1 small green pepper, halved, cored, seeded, and thinly sliced

1 large ripe tomato, halved and sliced thin

¼ teaspoon hot red pepper flakes, or cayenne pepper to taste

Mix yogurt with garlic, mint, and salt to taste. Reserve at room temperature.

Preheat broiler. Line baking sheet or broiler pan with foil. Arrange eggplant in a single layer on prepared pan. Spray eggplant with nonstick cooking spray or brush lightly with oil. Sprinkle with salt and pepper. Broil for 5 minutes. Turn slices over, spray or brush with oil again, and broil for 4 to 5 minutes, or until just tender. Set aside.

Heat 2 tablespoons oil in deep sauté pan. Add onions and sauté over medium heat for 12 minutes, or until well browned, stirring often. Remove half of onions. Add half of green chilies and half of tomato slices to pan. Top with all of eggplant and sprinkle with pepper flakes. Add remaining chilies and tomato slices. Top with remaining sautéed onion. Pour ½ cup water into pan and bring to a simmer. Cover and simmer over medium-low heat for 7 minutes, then over low heat for 10 minutes, or until vegetables are tender. Serve hot or warm, with the yogurt sauce at room temperature.

Armenian Green Beans

loligov ganatch loopya

Armenians flavor their green beans with four key ingredients—onions, garlic, peppers, and tomatoes—and often finish them with fresh parsley or mint. (See "Middle Eastern Marketing," page 22.)

Traditional cooks simmer the beans at length in the sauce, sometimes for over an hour, so they absorb its flavor and become very tender. Cooked this way, they don't remain vivid green. If you prefer bright-colored beans, follow the Note. Serve the beans at room temperature or hot.

◆ MAKES 4 SERVINGS.

2 or 3 tablespoons extra-virgin olive oil

1 medium onion, halved and sliced

1½ pounds green beans, ends removed, broken in 2 pieces

1 cup water

1 small green, red, or yellow bell pepper, cored, seeded, and cut in thin strips

4 large garlic cloves, chopped

One 14-ounce can diced tomatoes, drained, juice reserved

Salt and freshly ground black pepper

1 tablespoon tomato paste (optional)

Cayenne pepper to taste (optional)

Pinch sugar (optional)

2 tablespoons chopped fresh mint or Italian parsley, or 2 teaspoons dried mint (optional)

Heat oil in large wide saucepan or deep sauté pan. Add onion and sauté over medium heat for 7 minutes, or until it begins to turn golden. Add beans and 1 cup water. Bring to a boil, cover, and cook over medium heat for 5 minutes.

Add green pepper, garlic, tomatoes, salt, and pepper. Return to a boil. Cover and cook over medium-low heat for 5 to 10 minutes, or until beans are tender. If using tomato paste, mix with 2 tablespoons reserved tomato juice or hot water and stir into sauce. Cook, uncovered, over medium heat for 2 minutes, or until thickened to your taste, stirring often. Add cayenne, if you like; taste and adjust seasoning. Add a pinch of sugar if needed. Stir in mint. Serve hot, cold, or at room temperature.

NOTE For quicker, brighter green beans, boil beans in large saucepan of boiling salted water for about 5 minutes, or until crisp-tender. Drain in colander or strainer, rinse under cold running water until cool, and drain thoroughly.

Make sauce using ½ cup water instead of 1 cup. Add beans to finished sauce and heat through.

Okra in Tangy Jalapeño Tomato Sauce

bamie ateh

One of the most valued vegetables in the Mideast, okra is delicious when cooked carefully so it does not become sticky. It is best flavored with garlic, cilantro, coriander seed, and a tomato sauce made tangy with lemon juice and pomegranate paste or sometimes with tamarind. Cooks also braise the vegetable with meat (see Okra and Lamb Stew with Tart Tomato Sauce, page 199), and some like dill and mint rather than cilantro.

Be sure to choose small okra pods so they will be tender. They should be firm and dark green. Serve this okra as an appetizer or a partner for roasted or stewed meats and rice pilaf.

◆ MAKES 4 SERVINGS.

1 pound okra, preferably under 3 inches long, rinsed lightly and patted dry

1 or 2 red or green jalapeño peppers

3 to 4 tablespoons extra-virgin olive oil

1 onion, chopped

4 medium garlic cloves, minced

⅓ cup chopped cilantro

1 pound ripe tomatoes, peeled and diced, or one 14-ounce can tomatoes, diced, juice reserved

1 teaspoon ground coriander

½ teaspoon ground allspice

Salt and freshly ground black pepper

1 tablespoon pomegranate paste (optional)

1 to 2 tablespoons fresh-squeezed lemon juice

Cut off okra stems without cutting into seed part of pods. Remove membranes and seeds from jalapeño peppers if you like less heat; chop peppers.

Heat 2 tablespoons oil in deep skillet or sauté pan. Add okra and sauté over medium heat for 2 minutes, stirring often. Remove from pan with slotted spoon.

Heat 1 tablespoon oil in sauté pan. Add onion and sauté over medium heat for 5 minutes, or until it begins to turn golden, stirring often. Add garlic and jalapeño peppers and sauté for 30 seconds. Stir in 3 tablespoons cilantro, tomatoes, tomato juice, coriander, allspice, salt, and pepper. Bring to a boil. Return okra to pan. Cover and cook over medium-low heat for 20 minutes, or until okra is tender.

Uncover and cook for 5 minutes if sauce is too thin. Lightly stir in pomegranate paste, if you like, and lemon juice, being careful not to break up okra, and heat through. Remove from heat and stir in remaining oil and remaining cilantro. Taste and adjust seasoning. Serve hot, lukewarm, or cold.

Spicy Yemenite Peas

atunah b'nosah teimani

Many Western cooks boil peas briefly in water so they stay bright green. My husband's aunt Mazal, who was born in Yemen, cooks peas in a completely different manner, with tomatoes, garlic, cumin, turmeric, and plenty of pepper. The result resembles an Indian vegetable stew. With their savory sauce, her spicy peas make an excellent meatless entrée spooned over rice or bulgur wheat. They also are a tasty accompaniment for chicken, turkey, or lamb.

Others in the region braise their peas in a sauce flavored with ground beef and spiced with cinnamon, paprika, and cayenne pepper.

◆ MAKES 4 SIDE-DISH OR 2 MAIN-COURSE SERVINGS.

1½ pounds ripe tomatoes, or one 28-ounce can whole tomatoes

1 or 2 tablespoons vegetable oil

1 onion, chopped

1 teaspoon ground cumin

½ teaspoon turmeric

½ teaspoon paprika

Salt and freshly ground black pepper

1 tablespoon tomato paste (optional)

2 to 4 tablespoons water

4 garlic cloves, chopped

2 pounds fresh peas, shelled and rinsed (about 2 cups shelled), or 2 cups frozen peas

2 tablespoons chopped cilantro (optional)

Grate fresh tomatoes on the large holes of a grater, or puree them in a food processor. If using canned tomatoes, drain and puree in food processor.

Heat oil in large saucepan or sauté pan. Add onion and sauté over medium heat for 7 minutes, or until light brown. Add cumin, turmeric, paprika, pureed tomatoes, salt, and pepper to onions. Bring to a boil. Cover and cook over low heat for 10 minutes, stirring occasionally. If you'd like sauce to be redder or thicker, add tomato paste. Add water, garlic, and peas. Cover and cook for 10 to 20 minutes, or until peas are done to your taste. Stir in cilantro, if you like. Taste and adjust seasoning; season generously with pepper.

Savory Stewed Onions, Middle Eastern Style

bassal bi-zayt

Slowly stewing onions is one way that cooks in the Mideast enhance their sweetness. Often they enjoy them simply with olive oil, tomatoes, and herbs, as in this recipe, or add about half their weight in finely diced or ground lamb or beef for extra flavor.

Served hot, these delicate onions make a tasty relish for grilled meat or chicken, a bed for baking eggs, and a good sandwich partner for spicy garlic sausages like *soujouk* (see "The Mideast Pantry," page 10). Some serve them cold as a meze item, topped with yogurt, sour cream, or a little tahini, or as a companion for grilled eggplant salad or hummus. They also make a change-of-pace pizza topping or a savory-sweet onion sauce for pasta. If you like, substitute well rinsed, sliced leeks for the onions. You'll need to cook them only 10 minutes before adding the tomatoes.

◆ MAKES 4 SERVINGS.

1½ pounds onions, peeled (3 large)
3 to 4 tablespoons extra-virgin olive oil
Salt
1 pound ripe tomatoes, peeled, seeded, and
    chopped, or one 14-ounce can whole
    tomatoes, drained and chopped
1 tablespoon chopped fresh dill,
    or 3 tablespoons chopped Italian parsley
Freshly ground black pepper
Cayenne pepper (optional)

Halve onions and cut them in thin slices lengthwise, so the stew will be slightly chunky. Heat oil in heavy stew pan. Add onions and salt and sauté over medium heat for 10 minutes, stirring often. Cover and cook over low heat for 10 minutes, or until onions are tender and beginning to brown, stirring often.

Stir in tomatoes and cook, uncovered, over medium heat for 10 minutes, or until mixture is thick. Stir in most of the dill or parsley, reserving a little for garnish. Season

to taste with salt and pepper, and cayenne pepper if you like. Serve hot, warm, at room temperature, or cold, sprinkled with remaining dill or parsley.

Turkish Braised Leeks with Carrots

zeytinyağli pirasa

This recipe is inspired by a wonderful version made by Turkish chef Esin Denktas, who braises the leeks with a little onion and a few diced tomatoes. The delicate flavor reminds me of a buttery Parisian leek compote that is a favorite of mine, but in the Turkish classic the richness comes from extra-virgin olive oil. A squeeze of lemon juice balances the subtle sweetness of the leeks and carrots, and a small amount of rice lightly thickens the sauce.

Traditionally these leeks are served as a cold appetizer or salad. I also love them as a savory accompaniment for poached or baked salmon. Some cooks omit the carrots and cook the leeks in a cayenne-spiced tomato sauce, for serving hot with meat. Others thicken the sauce with Lemon Egg Sauce (page 306).

◆ MAKES 4 TO 6 SERVINGS.

2 pounds leeks
3 or 4 tablespoons extra-virgin olive oil

1 medium onion, chopped

2 carrots, sliced thin

Salt and freshly ground black pepper

3 tablespoons long-grain rice

2 ripe tomatoes, peeled, seeded, and diced,
or 2 canned tomatoes, diced and
drained

1½ to 2 cups water

½ to 1 teaspoon sugar, or to taste

1 to 2 tablespoons fresh-squeezed lemon
juice, or to taste

1 tablespoon finely chopped parsley
(optional)

Lemon wedges (optional, for garnish)

Split leeks lengthwise twice by cutting them with a sharp knife, beginning about 1 inch from root end and cutting toward green end, leaving root end attached. Dip leeks repeatedly in a sinkful of cold water. Check the layers to be sure they are clean. If soil remains, soak the leeks in cold water for several minutes. Then separate the leaves under running water to rinse away any clinging soil. Cut off root ends. Cut leeks in thin slices, removing the top 2 or 3 inches, where they are very dark green. (You can save them for adding to stock.)

Heat oil in a large heavy sauté pan or stew pan. Add onion and cook over medium-low heat for 5 minutes, or until slightly softened but not brown, stirring often. Add leeks, carrots, salt, and pepper. Cover and cook over low heat for 5 minutes, stirring occasionally. Add rice, tomatoes, 1½ cups water, and ½ teaspoon sugar and bring to a boil.

Cover and cook over low heat for 20 minutes or until vegetables and rice are tender, stirring often and adding hot water by quarter-cupfuls as needed; be careful not to let them burn. Add lemon juice to taste, and more sugar, salt, and pepper if needed. Serve garnished with chopped parsley and lemon wedges, if you like.

Easy Stuffed Peppers with Rice, Chickpeas, and Olives

zeytinyağli büber dolmasi

This fast way to stuff peppers fits the bill when you want a tasty, attractive appetizer or light summer entrée but have little time. The filling is subtly scented with cumin and allspice and enlivened with capers. When I have chives, garlic chives, tarragon, or thyme in my garden, I stir some in. Cilantro and basil are good too.

Instead of baking the stuffed peppers, you can microwave them for about 5 to 7 minutes to soften them slightly or to heat them if you want to serve them hot. If you're really pressed for time, simply spoon the stuffing into the boiled peppers without cooking them further and serve them cold. They'll be a bit firm but will provide a pleasing textural contrast to the tender stuffing.

Serving it this way is great on warm days—the dish becomes a salad in a pepper. Nice accompaniments are lemon wedges or Yogurt Garlic Sauce (page 311).

◆ MAKES 4 APPETIZER OR 8 LIGHT
    MAIN-COURSE SERVINGS.

3 to 4 tablespoons olive oil

2 medium onions, finely chopped

1 cup long-grain white rice

¾ teaspoon ground cumin

¼ teaspoon ground allspice

Salt and freshly ground black pepper

2 cups hot water

2 tablespoons tomato paste

¾ cup canned chickpeas (garbanzo beans),
    drained (about half of one 15-ounce can)

4 to 6 tablespoons diced pitted olives,
    green or black

1 tablespoon capers, drained

4 tablespoons chopped green onions or
    Italian parsley, or 2 tablespoons chopped
    fresh mint or dill, plus a little extra for
    garnish

4 large red or green bell peppers, halved
    lengthwise, seeded, and cored

Preheat oven to 375°F. Lightly oil one or two shallow baking dishes. Prepare stuffing: Heat 3 tablespoons oil in large sauté pan. Add onions and sauté over medium-low heat for 5 minutes, or until they begin to turn light golden. Add rice, cumin, and allspice and stir over low heat for 2 minutes. Add ½ teaspoon salt, pepper to taste, and 1¾ cups hot water and bring to a boil. Cover tightly and cook over low heat, with-

out stirring, for 12 minutes. Mix ¼ cup hot water with 1 tablespoon tomato paste and pour over rice without stirring. Cover and cook for 6 more minutes, or until rice is tender and liquid is absorbed. Let cool slightly. With fork, fluff rice gently and mix in chickpeas, olives, capers, and half the green onions or herbs. Taste and adjust amounts of salt, pepper, and allspice.

While rice is cooking, prepare peppers: Cook pepper halves in large saucepan of boiling water for 4 minutes. Drain in colander and rinse briefly. Set peppers in prepared baking dishes.

Divide stuffing among pepper halves, mounding it high. (See Note below.) Mix remaining tablespoon tomato paste with ½ cup water, salt, pepper, and remaining green onions or herbs. Spoon a little sauce over the peppers and pour the rest into the baking dish. If you like, drizzle 1 tablespoon oil over peppers. Cover and bake for 15 minutes, or until peppers are nearly tender, or a few minutes longer if you want them softer. Serve hot, cold, or at room temperature, garnished with a sprinkling of fresh herbs.

NOTE The amount of stuffing needed varies with the size of the peppers. If you have extra, serve it hot or cold as a side dish or salad.

Rice and Mushroom Stuffing
Sauté 4 to 8 ounces diced mushrooms with the onions.

Rice and Meat Stuffing

Stir 1 to 2 cups chopped cooked meat or chicken into the cooked rice.

Rice Stuffing with Pine Nuts and Currants

Sauté ¼ cup pine nuts with the rice and add 2 to 3 tablespoons currants or raisins with the water. Substitute ½ teaspoon ground cinnamon and freshly grated nutmeg to taste for the cumin and allspice.

Wild Mushrooms with Tomatoes, Basil, and Bulgur Wheat

mantarli pilav

Ripe tomatoes and fresh basil give this mushroom medley a wonderful, bright flavor. It is inspired by a recipe for a bulgur pilaf with woodland mushrooms and basil in *Istanbul la Magnifique,* by Artun and Beyhan Unsal. The tasty mushroom juices enrich the bulgur, and the result recalls a mushroom risotto. With risotto in mind, I like to pass around a bowl of freshly grated *kashkaval,* Parmesan, or Pecorino Romano cheese when I'm serving it. If you don't have wild mushrooms, substitute button mushrooms and cut them in thick slices.

This mushroom medley is delicious as an appetizer, a light entrée, or a delicate accompaniment for grilled fish or chicken breasts.

◆ MAKES 4 SERVINGS.

> 8 to 12 ounces fresh wild mushrooms, such as chanterelles or shiitake
>
> 4 tablespoons extra-virgin olive oil or butter
>
> 1 small green or red bell pepper, halved, cored, seeded, and diced
>
> 1 large onion, minced
>
> ¾ cup medium bulgur wheat
>
> 1½ cups water
>
> Salt and freshly ground black pepper
>
> 1 or 2 large ripe tomatoes, diced
>
> 2 green onions, chopped
>
> 4 to 5 tablespoons chopped fresh basil

Clean mushrooms very gently with damp paper towel. If using shiitake mushrooms, cut off the stems, which are tough. If mushrooms are large, cut in bite-size pieces.

Heat 2 tablespoons oil in a heavy medium saucepan. Add green pepper and half of the onion and cook over medium-low heat for 6 minutes, or until they soften, stirring often. Add bulgur and sauté over medium heat, stirring for 2 minutes. Add water, ½ teaspoon salt, and pepper to taste and bring to a boil. Cover and cook over low heat for 15 minutes, or until water is absorbed.

Heat remaining 2 tablespoons oil in large skillet. Add remaining onion and sauté over medium heat for 3 minutes. Add mushrooms, salt, and pepper. Sauté over medium-high heat about 3 to 5 minutes, or until mushrooms are tender and any liquid in skillet has evaporated, stirring often.

Add tomato, green onions, half of basil, and mushrooms to pilaf and fold them in lightly with a fork. Cover and let stand for 5 minutes. Taste and adjust seasoning. Serve sprinkled with remaining basil.

Two-way Summer Squash Stew with Sweet Peppers

m'tabbaq koussa

A child growing up in the Middle East quickly learns that cooked vegetables arrive on the table in one of two ways: cooked with meat or with oil. Both of these quick stews are based on the same technique. To make them meaty, you simmer the vegetables in a light meat-and-tomato sauce accented with sweet spices, golden onions, and garlic. Ground beef and lamb are favorites, as they produce the most flavorful sauce, but you can substitute chicken or turkey if you want a leaner dish.

To enhance the vegetarian version (see the variation), people often choose their finest olive oil and pour it with a liberal hand. An easy way to turn it into a more sat-isfying entrée is to add a 15-ounce can of chickpeas, as many Lebanese cooks do, or other beans such as white or pinto beans.

For a colorful medley, choose yellow bell peppers if you're using zucchini, or green or red bell peppers if you have yellow or pale green summer squash. The stew is good with fresh pita or crusty bread and cool Classic Cucumber Salad with Yogurt, Garlic, and Mint (page 68). For a heartier supper, serve it with Rice Pilaf with Toasted Almonds (page 263), or with a simple dish of Basic Bulgur Pilaf (page 275).

◆ MAKES 3 OR 4 LIGHT-ENTRÉE SERVINGS.

3 tablespoons olive oil, vegetable oil, or butter, or more if needed

1¼ to 1½ pounds zucchini, pale-green squash, or yellow squash, halved and cut in ⅜ inch slices

Salt and freshly ground black pepper

1 large onion, chopped

1 yellow, red, or green bell pepper, halved, cored, seeded, and cut in strips

3 large garlic cloves, minced

8 ounces lean ground beef or lamb

½ teaspoon ground allspice

¼ teaspoon ground cinnamon

1½ pounds ripe tomatoes, peeled, seeded, and chopped; or one 28-ounce can whole tomatoes, drained and chopped

1 to 2 tablespoons tomato paste mixed with ¼ cup water (optional)

4 tablespoons chopped Italian parsley

1 tablespoon fresh-squeezed lemon juice (optional)

Heat 2 tablespoons oil in large heavy sauté pan or stew pan. Add zucchini, salt, and pepper and sauté over medium heat for 2 minutes, or until not quite tender, stirring often. Remove to plate with slotted spoon.

Heat 1 tablespoon oil in sauté pan. Add onion and bell pepper and sauté over medium heat for 5 minutes, or until onion begins to turn golden; if pan becomes dry, add a little more oil or 1 tablespoon water to prevent burning. Add garlic, beef, all-spice, and cinnamon and sauté for 5 minutes, or until meat browns lightly, stirring often. Add tomatoes, tomato paste mixture if you like, salt, and pepper and stir well. Bring to a boil, stirring. Cook, uncovered, over medium-low heat for 10 minutes, or until sauce becomes thick and chunky and beef is tender, stirring occasionally; if sauce becomes too thick, stir in a few tablespoons hot water.

Add sautéed zucchini to pan and simmer for 5 minutes, or until it is done to your taste. Stir in 3 tablespoons parsley. Taste and adjust seasoning, adding lemon juice if you like. Serve hot, sprinkled with remaining parsley.

Meatless Squash Stew

Omit beef. Just before serving, stir in 1 or 2 more tablespoons extra-virgin olive oil if you like. Serve cold or at room temperature.

Lebanese Vegetable Stew with Chickpeas

musaka

This traditional vegetarian dish appears on tables in Lebanon, Syria, Palestine, and Egypt and is completely different from the layered meat-and-eggplant moussaka. Usually it's a simple, gently seasoned stew of eggplant, zucchini, or a combination of both in savory tomato sauce flavored with extra-virgin olive oil. Some Egyptian cooks deep-fry their eggplant until very rich and tender before heating it in the sauce. (If you'd like to fry the eggplant, see "Basics," page 372.) Season the eggplant well so it won't be bland.

This version is inspired by the one I enjoyed at Oasis Restaurant in Walled Lake, Michigan, near Detroit. Lebanese chef/owner Mohammed Hachem enhanced his eggplant stew with chickpeas and freshened it with plenty of parsley. I use a combination of eggplant and summer squash. Serve it as a hot entrée with rice pilaf or as a cold appetizer.

For festive occasions, use a generous splash of extra-virgin olive oil to sauté the vegetables and to finish the dish. If you want to make it very low in fat, cover the onion when you sauté it so it partly steams.

♦ MAKES 4 TO 6 APPETIZER OR SIDE-DISH OR 2 TO 3 MAIN-COURSE SERVINGS.

1 eggplant (about 1 pound)

1 to 5 tablespoons extra-virgin olive oil

1 large onion, chopped

Salt and freshly ground black pepper

12 ounces pale green skinned zucchini
(Clarita squash, cousa squash, white
squash, or Mexican squash), cut in
¾-inch dice

1 cup tomato sauce, homemade (page 305)
or packaged

2 to 4 garlic cloves, chopped (optional)

½ teaspoon ground allspice (optional)

1½ to 2 cups cooked chickpeas (garbanzo
beans), or one 15-ounce can chickpeas,
drained

⅓ cup chopped Italian parsley

If eggplant skin is not tough, you can leave eggplant unpeeled. Cut eggplant in small dice of about ¾ inch.

Heat I to 3 tablespoons oil in sauté pan. Add onion and sauté over medium heat for 7 minutes, or until beginning to turn golden; if using a small amount of oil, cover pan and add I tablespoon water if necessary to prevent burning. Add eggplant, salt, and pepper. Cover and cook over low heat for 5 minutes, stirring occasionally. Add squash, cover, and cook for 3 minutes.

Added tomato sauce, garlic, allspice, ½ cup water, and chickpeas. Bring to a boil. Cover and cook over low heat for 25 minutes, or until eggplant is tender. Add half of parsley and simmer for ½ minute. Taste and adjust seasoning. If you like, add I or 2 tablespoons oil to enrich the dish. Stir in remaining parsley. Serve hot, lukewarm, or cold.

Carrots, Beans, and Mushrooms in Savory Tomato Sauce

gallaba

Middle Eastern cooks prepare this vegetable casserole frequently, varying it according to the seasons and sometimes sautéing some of the vegetables. Tomatoes simmered with tomato paste give the sauce a deep, mellow flavor. In addition to sautéed onions and garlic, this savory stew might be accented with ground coriander, allspice, cilantro, parsley, or mint. For additional richness, you can drizzle it with an extra tablespoon of olive oil when you remove it from the heat. Serve the vegetables warm or at room temperature as an appetizer, or hot as a side dish or as an entrée with rice pilaf.

This casserole is also made into a one-pot meal with the addition of 1½ to 2 cups cooked beans, chicken, turkey, beef, lamb, or shrimp. For this simple version, I cook the vegetables separately to shorten their cooking time and keep their bright color and crisp-tender texture. To prepare it the more traditional way so the vegetables are soft and absorb more of the sauce's flavor, see the Note following the recipe.

◆ MAKES 4 SERVINGS.

4 medium carrots, sliced on the bias about
⅜ inch thick

8 ounces green beans, ends removed,
broken in 2 pieces

8 ounces large mushrooms, quartered,
  or medium mushrooms, halved

3 tablespoons extra-virgin olive oil

1 medium onion, chopped

2 large garlic cloves, chopped

One 14½-ounce can diced tomatoes,
  drained, juice reserved

Salt and freshly ground black pepper

1 teaspoon ground coriander

1 to 2 tablespoons tomato paste

Put carrots in saucepan, cover with water, add a pinch of salt, and bring to a simmer. Cover and cook for 5 minutes. Add green beans and mushrooms and return to a boil. Cook for 5 more minutes, or until the vegetables are just tender. Drain vegetables, reserving cooking liquid.

Heat oil in deep sauté pan. Add onion and sauté over medium heat for 7 minutes, or until golden. Add garlic and sauté for 30 seconds. Add tomatoes, salt, pepper, coriander, and ½ cup cooking liquid from the vegetables or water. Bring to a boil. Cook, uncovered, over medium heat for 5 minutes, or until thickened.

Mix tomato paste with 2 tablespoons reserved tomato juice and 2 tablespoons vegetable cooking liquid or hot water; stir into sauce. Add cooked vegetables. Cook, uncovered, over medium heat for 2 minutes, or until vegetables are heated through and sauce thickens to your taste, stirring often. Taste and adjust seasoning. Serve hot or at room temperature.

Vegetables in Savory Tomato Sauce, the Traditional Way:

Cook the carrots as above for only 3 minutes, then add them with the other vegetables directly to the sauce. Cover and cook over low heat for 30 to 60 minutes, or until the vegetables are very tender, adding water as needed so the sauce doesn't become dry.

Spinach and Summer Squash Borani with Red Peppers

boorani-ye esfenaj

This version of the cooling summer vegetable and yogurt dish known as *borani* (page 256) is flavored with sautéed onions and garlic and embellished with walnuts. For a pungent accent, you can add a bit of finely mashed or crumbled feta cheese.

You can make the *borani* up to two days ahead and keep it in a covered container in the refrigerator. It's delicious as a side dish with kabobs or cold meat or with legume and rice entrées such as Garlic Cumin Chickpeas with Rice (page 269). As an appetizer, serve it with fresh pita or with Persian or soft Armenian flatbread.

◆ MAKES 4 OR 5 SERVINGS.

HOT WEATHER CALLS FOR A COOLING BOWL OF *BORANI*

When Middle Eastern cooks crave a refreshing appetizer or accompaniment, they will often whip up a batch of *borani*, a blend of yogurt and vegetables, usually cooked ones. The formula is as simple as can be: steam, boil, sauté, fry, or grill a vegetable and combine it with yogurt. You can season it with just salt and pepper, but *borani* often includes garlic or golden-brown onion. When made with a quick-cooking vegetable, *borani* is ready in no time.

The Persians are especially fond of these creamy, cooling salads. Najmieh Batmanglij, author of *A New Food for Life: Ancient Persian and Modern Iranian Cooking and Ceremonies*, writes that they were named *pourani* for a yogurt-loving ancient Persian queen, Pourandokht, whose chef came up with many yogurt and vegetable dishes for her. Eventually such mixtures were called *boranis* in much of the Mideast and bordering countries. Spinach, beets (see pages 257 and 258), and eggplant are classic partners for the yogurt. In some Persian households, mushrooms are used, as are artichokes, cardoons, and lentils, and a pinch of turmeric or cinnamon might lend a gentle hint of spice. Afghans might add tomato sauce to their eggplant *borani*.

Throughout the yogurt-loving regions of the world, families relish these appetizers, especially on hot summer days. Some Turks turn grilled hot chilies into *borani* so the yogurt will tame their fire. Armenians fold eggplant or zucchini cubes into yogurt, sometimes combined with fried red and green peppers. Green bean *borani* made with sautéed onions and a fresh herb like tarragon, basil, or sage is popular in Georgia. On Bulgarian tables beet *borani* comes flavored with dill. Others in the Caucasus region, which was influenced by Turkish culture, prefer cauliflower or okra.

For garnish there might be a drizzle of olive oil, a sprinkling of mint or dill, a dusting of paprika or cayenne, or a streak of liquid saffron, made by soaking saffron threads in hot water. Some Middle Easterners like more substantial toppings, such as chopped walnuts or sliced hard-boiled eggs.

In some regions *borani* is made with sheep's- or goat's-milk yogurt. Whichever yogurt you choose, it should be thick. Traditional cooks drain their yogurt for a few hours before making their *borani;* to do this, see Thick Yogurt and Yogurt Cheese (page 125). For quick preparation, I don't bother with this step. If you like, you can buy thick yogurt from a Mediterranean market. Using it will make your *borani* more luscious, but you'll have good results with any plain yogurt.

1½ pounds fresh spinach (including stems), or one 10-ounce bag of cleaned spinach leaves

2 to 3 tablespoons vegetable oil, olive oil, or butter

1 large onion, halved and thinly sliced

2 small yellow crookneck squash or green or yellow zucchini, diced small

2 or 3 large garlic cloves, chopped

¼ teaspoon ground cinnamon or turmeric, or to taste (optional)

Salt and freshly ground black pepper

1 red bell pepper, grilled and peeled (page 370), or from a jar

1½ to 2 cups plain yogurt, any kind

2 to 3 tablespoons chopped walnuts (optional)

Discard spinach stems, rinse leaves well, and coarsely chop them. Add spinach to large sauté pan with the water clinging to its leaves. Cover and cook over medium heat for 3 to 5 minutes, or until wilted, stirring often. Drain in colander and rinse briefly with cold water. Squeeze gently to remove excess water.

Dry the pan used to cook spinach. Heat oil in pan. Add onion and sauté over medium heat for 5 minutes, until tender. Add squash and sauté for 3 minutes, or until just tender, stirring occasionally, covering pan if necessary so the oil won't burn. Add garlic and cinnamon and sauté for ½ minute. Stir in spinach, sprinkle with salt and pepper, and cook for 2 or 3 minutes to evaporate excess moisture. Transfer mixture to bowl and cool.

Cut red pepper in strips and mix lightly with vegetables. Stir yogurt until smooth. Stir into vegetable mixture. Taste and adjust seasoning. Serve cold, sprinkled with walnuts if you like.

Beet Borani Salad

boorani-ye laboo

Borani is a simple, refreshing medley of vegetables and yogurt most popular among Persian cooks (see box, page 256). I find tangy yogurt a wonderful complement to the delicate sweetness of beets. Rich yogurt is traditional but I also like this salad with low-fat or even nonfat yogurt. You can save the beet greens, cook them like spinach, then chop them and make them into *borani* on another day.

For a pink salad, stir the beets thoroughly with the yogurt. If you prefer a striped effect, fold them in partially at the last minute. Special varieties like yellow or striped beets make an attractive variation. If you have them, use some of the slices for garnish. I prefer steamed beets in this salad for their delicate flavor but you can use boiled beets or, when you're in a rush, canned sliced beets. For an Egyptian variation, stir in diced cucumbers and tomatoes.

◆ MAKES 4 SERVINGS.

6 medium beets, about 1½ to 2 inches in
    diameter

3 cups plain yogurt

3 tablespoons chopped fresh mint,
    or 2 to 3 teaspoons dried mint, crumbled

Salt and freshly ground black pepper

Fresh mint leaves or a little dried mint for
    garnish

Trim bottoms of beets and cut off greens, taking care not to pierce beet skins; reserve greens for other uses. Rinse beets and put them in a steamer rack above boiling water. Cover tightly and steam 50 to 60 minutes, or until tender, adding boiling water occasionally if it evaporates. Let cool. Run beets under cold water and slip off the skins. Halve beets and slice them.

Mix yogurt with mint, salt, and pepper to taste. Reserve a few beet slices for garnish. Add remaining beets to yogurt and fold them in lightly so that yogurt is streaked with pink and some beet slices still show. Spoon into shallow serving bowl or individual bowls. Garnish with mint leaves or a light dusting of dried mint. Serve cold.

Grains, Gifts from the Mideast to the Western World

Rice Pilaf with Toasted Almonds • *Riz bil Lowz*

Turkish Tomato Pilaf • *Domatesli Pilav*

Almond Apricot Basmati Rice • *Riz bil Lowz wa Mishmish*

Red Rice with Yellow Vegetables and Raisins • *Riza Smokah bit Kashmisheh*

Summertime Tarragon-Chive Rice with Vegetables • *Sabzi Polo*

Aromatic Golden Rice with Pistachios • *Riz bil Zaafarane*

Garlic Cumin Chickpeas with Rice • *Nohutlu Pilav*

Rice Pilaf with Chard, Pine Nuts, and Pomegranate Seeds • *Riz bi Silk*

Holiday Rice Stuffing with Toasted Nuts and Spiced Lamb • *Riz bi Titbika*

Sweet and Savory Saffron Rice Stuffing with Cranberries • *Shirin Polo*

Layered Rice and Chicken Casserole with Green Vegetables and Allspice • *Maklubah*

Assyrian Brown Rice and Bean Casserole with Mushrooms • *Riz Beryani*

Basic Bulgur Pilaf • *Bulgur Pilavi*

Bulgur Wheat with Eggplant, Tomatoes, and Mint • *Bourghol bil Batenjane*

Armenian Bulgur Wheat and Lentils with Sweet Peppers • *Vospov Kheemah*

Wheat Berries with Chickpeas and Chicken • *Haleem*

Curry-scented Barley Casserole with Peppers and Spinach • *Habea Matboukha*

Breakfast Barley Stew with Beef • *Keshkek*

Kamut with Raisins, Almonds, and Peanuts • *Fereek bel Zbeeb*

Middle Easterners have held grains in such high regard that these glorious foods inspired them to originate agriculture. Besides making bread, in all parts of the region people use grains creatively, from the sumptuous rice pilafs of Persia and Turkey to the savory salads and sides of bulgur wheat to the hearty casseroles of barley, wheat berries, and kamut.

Semolina appears in dumplings, pastries, and cakes. One of the oldest forms of fast food is bulgur, also called cracked or crushed wheat. Because it is steamed before being dried, bulgur cooks very quickly. People use different sizes of bulgur for different purposes. Well known in the West as the basis for tabbouleh, in its area of origin bulgur is also made into soups, entrées, accompaniments, and crunchy filled croquettes called kibbe. Another age-old convenience food found in some Middle Eastern markets is *kishk,* a blend of powdered bulgur wheat or flour and dried yogurt. When Lebanese, Jordanian, and Palestinian cooks need to get a meal on the table in a hurry, they turn their *kishk* into speedy soups.

Whole wheat berries are used in savory casseroles and in desserts similar to rice pudding. So is kamut, a nonhybridized form of wheat that originated in Egypt and now is valued by shoppers at natural foods markets in North America. Young wheat or green wheat, called *fereek* or *farikeh,* which is harvested while still slightly green and grilled before being packaged, is used to make festive side dishes and stuffings for quail and other birds and for lamb. It is cooked like Basic Bulgur Pilaf (page 275) and is often garnished with fried or toasted almonds or pine nuts.

Rice, however, is clearly the king of grains. It is the favorite partner for just about every major food—meat, poultry, fish, vegetables, and legumes. Rice is the basis of stuffings for vegetables as well as for poultry. Cooks prepare it in many ways but the preferred method is pilaf. One of the best-traveled of recipes, pilaf originated in Persia and spread to the eastern Mediterranean. The rice gains a toasty flavor from being sautéed, often with onions. It may then be stained yellow with saffron or red with tomato. Cooks simmer the rice with seafood, chicken, or vegetables to make a main-course pilaf. For savory meatless entrées, greens such as chard or spinach are steamed with rice pilaf, then garnished with roasted nuts.

Barley is often used by Assyrian, Iranian, and Israeli cooks in soups, meat stews, and vegetarian entrées. In many Mideastern countries, an old-fashioned comfort food is barley cooked at length into porridge with beef or chicken and served with cinnamon and sugar (see Breakfast Barley Stew with Beef, page 280).

Rice Pilaf with Toasted Almonds

riz bil lowz

Rice pilaf is the region's most popular partner for main courses, whether grilled or sauced, meaty or vegetarian. To give the rice pizzazz, it is often crowned with toasted or sautéed nuts. At some Middle Eastern eateries, a generous mound of this rich, buttery rice topped with plenty of toasted slivered almonds accompanies every stew, and it is definitely welcome with the flavorful sauces.

Golden noodles strewed throughout white grains of rice are, like nuts, a common addition in most Middle Eastern countries, to make a dish known as *riz bi chairie.* (See the first variation.) Turkish, Armenian, Lebanese, Palestinian, Egyptian, and Persian cooks enjoy the flavor, texture, and attractive appearance of the pasta in the pilaf.

In this pilaf you can use basmati rice if you sauté it lightly for only 1 minute and handle it gently once it is cooked. Many cooks do not sauté basmati rice but combine the delicate grains directly with liquid to make sure they remain whole. Brown rice is not traditional in the Mideast but makes a tasty pilaf, as in the second variation. You can prepare pilaf in a shallow saucepan, sauté pan, or skillet, as long as it has a tight-fitting lid. Letting the rice rest improves its texture. For other tips, see Note.

◆ MAKES 4 TO 6 SERVINGS.

2 to 4 tablespoons extra-virgin olive oil, vegetable oil, ghee, or butter
1 onion, minced
1½ cups long-grain white rice
3 cups hot chicken, beef, or vegetable broth or water
Salt and freshly ground black pepper
⅓ to ½ cup slivered almonds

Heat 2 or 3 tablespoons oil or butter in large saucepan. Add onion and cook over medium-low heat for 5 minutes, or until soft but not brown, stirring occasionally. Add rice and cook, stirring, for 2 minutes, or until the grains turn milky white.

Add broth, salt, and pepper. Bring to a boil. Cover and cook over low heat, without stirring, for 18 minutes, or until rice is tender and liquid is absorbed. Remove from heat. Let rice stand, covered, for 10 to 15 minutes.

Toast almonds (see page 369); or sauté them: Heat 2 to 3 teaspoons oil or butter in a small heavy skillet. Add almonds and sauté over medium-low heat until lightly browned, stirring often; do not let them burn. Remove from pan immediately.

Fluff rice gently with a fork. Taste and adjust seasoning. Mound on a platter, garnish with almonds and serve hot.

NOTE For fluffier pilaf, after adding the liquid, some people cover their rice with a round of buttered parchment paper with a hole cut in its center before putting the lid on. Others cover the cooked rice with a cloth, then the lid, and let it rest briefly before serving.

Toasted Noodle and Rice Pilaf

You can make this pilaf with or without almonds. Omit the onion. Heat 3 tablespoons oil or butter in large sauté pan. Add ½ to ¾ cup very fine egg noodles or vermicelli broken in 1- or 2-inch pieces and sauté over medium heat for 4 minutes, or until light golden, stirring constantly. Add rice and continue as in recipe above, cooking pilaf until rice and noodles are tender.

Brown Rice Pilaf

Follow recipe, allowing 40 to 45 minutes to simmer the rice.

Turkish Tomato Pilaf

domatesli pilav

Tomatoes contribute their sweet-tangy taste to this pilaf and tint it reddish orange. Cooks in Turkey give the pilaf additional flavor by simmering the rice in rich meat or chicken broth and often use a generous amount of fresh or clarified butter (ghee) to sauté the onion. I love it with homemade chicken stock or, after Thanksgiving, with turkey stock made from the bones of the roasted birds.

Tomato pilaf is a favorite partner for kabobs and stews. For a light supper, it's served simply with yogurt or with Classic Cucumber Salad with Yogurt, Garlic, and Mint (page 68).

◆ MAKES 6 SERVINGS.

2 tablespoons vegetable oil,
    or 2 to 4 tablespoons butter

1 small onion, chopped (¾ cup)

2 garlic cloves, chopped

One 15-ounce can diced tomatoes, drained,
    liquid reserved

Salt and freshly ground black pepper

1½ cups long-grain rice

3 cups chicken or vegetable broth or water,
    or a mixture of broth and water

Heat oil or 2 tablespoons butter in heavy saucepan. If you'd like to enrich the pilaf later with additional butter, bring it to room temperature.

Add onion to saucepan and cook over medium-low heat for 5 minutes, or until soft but not brown. Add garlic, then tomatoes, salt, and pepper. Heat until sizzling. Cook over medium heat for 10 minutes or until thick, crushing any large tomato dice with wooden spoon.

Add rice, stir over medium-low heat until coated with tomato mixture, and cook for 2 minutes, stirring. Add broth, liquid from tomatoes, 1 teaspoon salt, and pepper to taste. Stir once or twice and bring to a boil. Cover and simmer over very low heat for 18 to 20 minutes, or until rice is just tender. Add remaining butter in a few pieces if you like. Let pilaf stand, covered, for 10 minutes. Fluff rice lightly with fork. Taste and adjust seasoning.

Almond Apricot Basmati Rice

riz bil lowz wa mishmish

Fruit-garnished rice with toasted nuts is loved around the Mideast and is especially prized by the Persians. For the finest flavor and aroma, prepare this simple dish with the aromatic, extra-long grain basmati rice, the most esteemed variety throughout the region. It's easy to find basmati rice in Indian and Middle Eastern groceries and in many supermarkets. Handle the rice gently during cooking and serving to avoid bruising its fine, long grains.

Serve this holiday rice with roast chicken or turkey or with grilled lamb chops. For a more delicate version, omit the sautéed onion and the oil, and add 1 to 3 tablespoons butter when you remove the rice from the heat. Use white pepper if you want to keep the rice white.

♦ MAKES 4 TO 6 SERVINGS.

   8 to 12 whole dried apricots, plus ½ cup diced dried apricots

   2 to 3 tablespoons butter, or 2 tablespoons vegetable oil

   1 onion, minced

   1½ cups white basmati rice, rinsed and drained

   2½ cups hot water

   Salt and freshly ground black pepper

   1 tablespoon sugar

   ½ cup slivered or whole blanched almonds, toasted (see "Basics," page 369)

Put whole apricots in bowl and cover with water. Leave them to soak while rice cooks.

To cook rice, heat 2 tablespoons butter or oil in large saucepan. Add onion and cook over low heat for 7 minutes, or until soft but not brown, stirring occasionally. Add rice, diced apricots, 2½ cups hot water, salt, and pepper and bring to a boil over high heat. Cover and cook over low heat, without stirring, for 18 minutes, or until rice is just tender and liquid is absorbed. Remove from heat. To enrich with butter, add it now, without stirring. Cover rice and let it stand for 10 to 15 minutes.

Meanwhile, transfer apricot soaking liquid to very small saucepan. Add sugar and stir to blend. Cut the whole apricots in two if they are large and add to saucepan. Add enough water to barely cover the apricots. Bring to a simmer. Cover and cook over low heat for 3 minutes, or until apricots are just tender.

Fluff rice very gently with a fork, lightly blending in butter. Mound on a platter and garnish with toasted almonds. Remove poached apricots from liquid with a slotted spoon and set them on rice. Serve hot.

Variation

To use brown basmati rice, cook it as above, allowing about 40 minutes' cooking time.

Red Rice with Yellow Vegetables and Raisins

riza smokah bit kashmisheh

Flavored with well-caramelized onions and tomato sauce, red rice is particularly pretty when mixed with light-colored vegetables. It's often enhanced with chickpeas or mushrooms by cooks of Chaldean, Kurdish, and Iraqi origin. A diced yellow pepper is another tasty addition.

For special occasions, cooks stud the rice with golden raisins and toasted almonds, as in this version. Purchase toasted almonds to save time, or use toasted cashews or pine nuts instead.

◆ MAKES 6 SERVINGS.

6 to 8 ounces mushrooms, sliced (optional)

3 to 4 tablespoons vegetable oil

Salt and freshly ground black pepper to taste

2 medium onions, halved and cut in thin slices

1½ cups long-grain rice

½ teaspoon paprika

1½ cups cooked chickpeas (garbanzo beans), or one 15-ounce can chickpeas, drained, or ¾ cup chickpeas and ¾ cup corn kernels

3 cups hot water

¼ teaspoon cayenne pepper, or to taste

½ cup tomato sauce

1 large tomato, diced (¾ cup)

1 yellow bell pepper, halved, cored, seeded, and diced (optional)

⅓ cup golden raisins, rinsed and drained

⅓ to ½ cup almonds, toasted (see "Basics," page 369)

If using mushrooms, heat I tablespoon oil in large, deep sauté pan or shallow stew pan. Add mushrooms and sauté over medium-high heat for 3 minutes, or until lightly browned. Sprinkle with salt and pepper. Transfer to bowl.

Add remaining oil to pan and heat it. Add onions and sauté over medium heat for 12 to 15 minutes, or until tender and deep brown. Remove half of onion mixture and reserve.

Add rice and paprika to pan and sauté, stirring, for 2 minutes or until rice turns white. Add chickpeas, 2¾ cups hot water, I teaspoon salt, pepper to taste, and cayenne pepper. Stir once and bring to a boil over high heat. Cover and cook over low heat, without stirring, for 10 minutes. Mix tomato sauce with diced tomato and remaining ¼ cup water. Add tomato mixture and yellow pepper to pan without stirring. Cook, covered, over very low heat for 8 to 10 minutes, or until rice is just tender. Add reserved onion mixture, mushrooms, and raisins without stirring. Cover rice and let stand off heat for 5 to 10 minutes.

Fluff rice lightly with a fork. Taste and adjust seasoning. Serve topped with almonds.

Summertime Tarragon-Chive Rice with Vegetables

sabzi polo

Persians share with the French a fondness for herbs like tarragon and chives. Unlike French pilafs, this colorful dish is scented with cinnamon and golden-brown onions. When the weather is warm, I turn herb-scented rice into a colorful meal-in-one-pot by combining it with diced ripe tomatoes and an assortment of lightly cooked vegetables, such as green beans, corn, summer squash, sugar snap peas, green peas, asparagus, sweet red peppers, and broccoli. I often add legumes as well, which augment the protein, as the Persians do in their herb-accented rice classic known as *sabzi polo.* The pilaf also makes a good partner for simple meat and fish dishes.

◆ MAKES 6 TO 8 SIDE-DISH OR
4 OR 5 MAIN-COURSE SERVINGS.

3 cups water
Salt and freshly ground black pepper to taste
1½ cups green beans, cut in 2-inch pieces, or small broccoli florets
3 tablespoons vegetable oil or olive oil
2 pale-green Middle Eastern or Mexican squash (¾ pound), zucchini, yellow squash, or other soft-skinned squash, cut in ½-inch to ¾-inch dice
¾ cup cooked corn kernels

¾ cup cooked or canned red, white, or black beans or chickpeas, drained and rinsed (optional)
1 tablespoon chopped fresh tarragon, or more to taste
2 teaspoons chopped fresh thyme, or 1 teaspoon dried thyme
1 large onion, chopped
1½ cups long-grain white rice
1 large carrot, cut in ½-inch slices on the diagonal
½ teaspoon ground cinnamon
1 or 2 large ripe tomatoes, diced
¼ cup sliced fresh chives

Bring 3 cups water to a boil with pinch of salt in small saucepan. Add green beans or broccoli and cook, uncovered, for 3 or 4 minutes, or until barely tender. Remove with slotted spoon, reserving liquid; rinse vegetable with cold water and drain well. Add enough hot water to cooking liquid to make 3 cups; return it to pan and cover to keep it warm.

Heat I tablespoon oil in large sauté pan or stew pan. Add squash, salt, and pepper and sauté over medium heat for 2 minutes, or until not quite tender, stirring often. Transfer to bowl and add corn, red beans, green beans, half of tarragon and half of thyme. Toss lightly. Season to taste with salt and pepper.

Add 2 tablespoons oil to pan. Add onion and cook over medium heat for 7 minutes, or until light golden. Add rice and sauté for 2 minutes, or until grains turn white, stirring often.

Pour reserved vegetable cooking liquid over rice and stir once. Add carrot, cinnamon, I teaspoon salt, and ½ teaspoon pepper or to taste. Bring to a boil over high heat. Reduce heat to low, cover tightly, and simmer, without stirring, for 15 minutes. Lightly scatter vegetable mixture over top without stirring. Cover and cook for 3 minutes, or until rice is tender and liquid is absorbed.

Fluff rice with fork. Gently fold in diced tomatoes, remaining tarragon and thyme, and 2 tablespoons chives. Taste and adjust seasoning. Serve hot, room temperature, or cold, sprinkled with remaining chives.

Aromatic Golden Rice with Pistachios

riz bil zaafarane

Rice colored yellow with saffron is one of the most popular side dishes in the Mideast, particularly for celebrations. In most areas, the entire dish of rice is flavored with saffron, but Persian and Indian cooks often go for a two-tone effect. Here is my Iranian friend Treaty Zartoshty's trick for doing this: She blends a little liquid saffron with part of her cooked basmati rice, scatters the golden rice over the remaining white rice at serving time, and fluffs the grains delicately to partially mix them, so that the white grains are strewn with yellow-orange ones. For garnishing golden rice, pistachios or pine nuts are favorites, the luxurious nuts seen as fitting partners to the costly spice.

Many cooks use turmeric to prepare yellow rice and often combine it with cumin to enhance the flavor. Some look down on turmeric as a cheap saffron substitute, as the flavor of this cousin of ginger is completely different, but in fact this type of yellow rice is delicious too. To make it, see the Note following the recipe. I also like this type of golden rice in salads, such as Yellow Rice Salad with Red Peppers, Beans, and Dill (page 80).

◆ MAKES 4 TO 6 SERVINGS.

¼ teaspoon crushed saffron threads (2 pinches)

3 cups hot chicken or vegetable broth or water

2 to 3 tablespoons olive oil, vegetable oil, or butter

1 onion, minced

1½ cups long-grain white rice

Salt and freshly ground black pepper

½ cup shelled pistachios, toasted

Combine saffron and ¼ cup hot broth in small cup. Cover and let stand while sautéing onion.

Heat 2 to 3 tablespoons oil or 2 tablespoons butter in large saucepan. Add onion and cook over medium-low heat for 5 minutes or until soft but not brown, stirring occasionally. Add rice and cook, stirring, for 2 minutes, or until the grains turn milky white.

Add 2¾ cups broth, saffron broth, salt, and pepper. Bring to a boil. Cover and cook over low heat, without stirring, for 18 minutes, or until rice is tender and liquid is absorbed. Remove from heat. To enrich rice, add remaining tablespoon butter now, without stirring. Cover rice and let it stand for 10 to 15 minutes.

Fluff rice gently with fork, blending in butter. Taste and adjust seasoning. Mound on a platter, garnish with pistachios, and serve hot.

Turmeric Yellow Rice

Omit the saffron and skip the first step in the recipe. After sautéing the rice, add the 3 cups broth, ¼ teaspoon turmeric and, if you like, I teaspoon ground cumin.

Garlic Cumin Chickpeas with Rice

nohutlu pilav

Chickpeas and rice are a beloved duo in the Mideast. In a version I enjoyed in Turkey, the cooked chickpeas were heated in a little olive oil or butter, then added to Turkish Tomato Pilaf (page 264). Lebanese cooks stew chickpeas with lamb and rice.

I like to bring this easy dish to potluck dinners, as it never fails to please. The spiced chickpeas are sautéed with garlic and olive oil, then combined with white rice pilaf. Use plain or aromatic long-grain rice. Flat-leaf parsley is the herb that's commonly added, but I sometimes accent the pilaf with garlic chives from my garden. The rice makes a tasty accompaniment for kabobs, grilled chicken, or eggplant stew.

◆ MAKES 6 SERVINGS.

2 to 3 tablespoons extra-virgin olive oil

1 large onion, finely chopped

1½ cups long-grain white rice

4 large garlic cloves, minced

3 cups hot chicken, meat, or vegetable broth or water

Salt and freshly ground black pepper

1 teaspoon ground cumin

1½ to 2 cups cooked chickpeas (garbanzo beans), with 2 tablespoons cooking liquid (see "Basics," page 374), or one 15-ounce can chickpeas, drained

⅛ to ¼ teaspoon cayenne pepper, or to taste

3 tablespoons chopped Italian parsley, or 1 tablespoon chopped garlic chives

Heat 1½ to 2 tablespoons oil in heavy shallow stew pan or large sauté pan. Add onion and cook over medium-low heat for 8 minutes, or until soft but not brown, stirring often. Add rice and half the garlic and sauté, stirring, about 2 minutes, or until the grains turn milky white.

Add broth, salt to taste, ¼ teaspoon pepper, and ½ teaspoon cumin. Stir once and bring to a boil. Cover and cook over low heat, without stirring, for 18 minutes. Taste rice; if it is not yet tender, simmer 2 more minutes. Taste and adjust seasoning. Cover and let stand for 10 minutes, or until ready to serve.

Heat remaining ½ to 1 tablespoon oil in saucepan. Add remaining garlic and cook over low heat for ½ minute, or until fragrant. Add chickpeas, ½ teaspoon cumin, 2 tablespoons chickpea cooking liquid or water, salt, pepper, and ⅛ teaspoon cayenne. Cover and heat over medium heat for 2 minutes, or until heated through, stirring once or twice.

Gently fluff rice with a fork. Fold in chickpea mixture and 2 tablespoons parsley or 2 teaspoons garlic chives. Taste and adjust seasoning, adding more salt, pepper, or cayenne if needed. Serve hot, sprinkled with remaining herb.

Rice Pilaf with Chard, Pine Nuts, and Pomegranate Seeds

riz bi silk

In the Mideast, rice is cooked with all sorts of greens, and chard is especially popular. You can use either the green or the red variety of chard or substitute spinach. In the early autumn, fresh pomegranate seeds make a beautiful garnish. For an easy technique for removing seeds from a pomegranate, see "Basics," page 374. In other seasons you can substitute dried cranberries.

◆ MAKES 4 TO 6 SERVINGS.

1¼ to 1½ pounds chard
3 or 4 tablespoons olive oil
1 large onion, chopped
Salt and freshly ground black pepper
3 large garlic cloves, chopped
1½ cups long-grain white rice
3 cups hot water
¼ cup pine nuts, toasted (page 369)
¼ to ½ cup pomegranate seeds

Rinse chard thoroughly. Peel stems if they are stringy and cut them in ½-inch dice. Chop leaves and keep them separate from stems.

Heat 2 or 3 tablespoons oil in large heavy sauté pan or shallow stew pan. Add onion and sauté over medium heat for 5 minutes, or until soft but not brown, stirring often. Add chard stems and sauté for 2 minutes. Add leaves and sprinkle with salt and pepper. Cover and cook over low heat for 5 minutes, or until wilted, stirring occasionally. Transfer mixture to bowl.

Add remaining tablespoon oil to pan and heat it. Add garlic and rice and sauté over medium heat, stirring, until rice begins to turn white. Return chard mixture to pan. Add water, 1 teaspoon salt, and a pinch of pepper and stir once. Cover and cook over low heat, without stirring, for 18 minutes, or until rice is tender.

Taste rice and adjust seasoning. Serve pilaf on a platter, sprinkled with toasted pine nuts and pomegranate seeds.

Holiday Rice Stuffing with Toasted Nuts and Spiced Lamb

riz bi titbika

In the Mideast this sumptuous pilaf is the most popular stuffing for all sorts of poultry, from quail to turkey, and even for whole roasted lamb. When it's not used as a stuffing, it's served as a bed for roasted poultry or meat or as a main course. Most often it's flavored with sautéed ground lamb or beef but chicken giblets are another option, like in a Louisiana specialty known as dirty rice. I particularly enjoyed a rich rendition I tasted in Turkey as an accompaniment for a braised whole chicken, where the rice was enriched with just a bit of lamb and with plenty of pine nuts and currants. Butter-roasted almonds, walnuts, hazelnuts, or pistachios might also embellish this creation, and the most festive versions include several kinds of nuts as well as dried fruit.

If you have Seven Spices or *baharat* spice blend (see "The Mideast Pantry," page 13), you can substitute 1 to 1½ teaspoons of it for the allspice and cinnamon in this recipe.

You can fry the nuts the traditional way following the directions in Rice Pilaf with Toasted Almonds (page 263), but I toast them instead.

♦ MAKES 4 OR 5 SERVINGS OR ABOUT 5 TO 5½ CUPS, ENOUGH TO STUFF A CHICKEN WITH EXTRA TO SERVE SEPARATELY.

2 to 3 tablespoons vegetable oil,
    or 2 to 4 tablespoons butter
1 onion, chopped
8 to 12 ounces lean ground lamb or beef
½ to 1 teaspoon ground allspice
½ teaspoon ground cinnamon
1½ cups long-grain white rice
3 cups hot meat or chicken broth or water
Salt and freshly ground black pepper
½ cup pine nuts, toasted
½ cup slivered almonds, toasted
    (see "Basics," page 369)
½ cup shelled pistachios, toasted

Heat 2 to 3 tablespoons oil or butter in deep sauté pan or stew pan. Add onion and sauté over medium heat for 5 minutes, or until softened. Add meat, allspice, and cinnamon and sauté until it browns lightly, stirring to separate meat into small pieces. Add rice and sauté, stirring, for 2 minutes. Add broth, salt, and pepper. Stir once and bring to a boil. Cover and cook over low heat, without stirring, for 18 minutes, or until rice is just tender. Dot with remaining tablespoon butter. Cover and let stand for 10 minutes, or until ready to serve.

Gently fluff rice with fork. Taste and adjust seasoning. Lightly fold in two-thirds of the toasted nuts. Serve hot, topped with remaining nuts.

Sweet and Savory Saffron Rice Stuffing with Cranberries

shirin polo

Studded with nuts and fruit and flavored with carrots and orange zest, this colorful, easy pilaf is inspired by an elaborate Iranian casserole of rice and chicken. Traditionally the rice is flavored with orange zest and tart, reddish barberries that somewhat resemble cranberries. Some Persian cooks candy the orange zest to enhance the sweetness of the dish.

Ghee (clarified butter) is the traditional choice to enrich the rice, but today many use fresh butter, margarine, or vegetable oil. You can bake the rice inside a chicken or Cornish hen or serve it as a colorful pilaf alongside poultry or meat kabobs. It also makes a lovely partner for a Thanksgiving turkey or a roast duck.

◆ MAKES ABOUT 4 SERVINGS OR 5 CUPS STUFFING, ENOUGH TO STUFF A CHICKEN WITH EXTRA TO SERVE SEPARATELY.

3½ cups chicken broth mixed with water, about equal parts of each

¼ teaspoon saffron threads (2 pinches), lightly crushed

3 tablespoons vegetable oil, butter, or ghee

1 medium onion, minced

1¾ cups long-grain white rice

Salt and freshly ground black pepper

1 cup coarsely grated carrot

1 teaspoon finely grated orange zest

⅓ cup dried cranberries

⅔ cup slivered almonds or shelled pistachios, or ⅓ cup of each, lightly toasted

Heat broth and water to a simmer in small saucepan, or heat them in a large measuring cup in microwave. Add saffron, cover, and let steep while you sauté onions.

Heat oil in large sauté pan, wide stew pan, or deep skillet. Add onion and cook over medium heat for 5 minutes, or until soft but not brown. Add rice and cook for 3 minutes, or until grains begin to turn white, stirring gently.

Pour saffron broth over rice, add a little salt and pepper, and stir once. Bring to a boil over high heat. Reduce heat to low, cover tightly, and simmer, without stirring, for 12 minutes. Scatter carrots, orange zest, and cranberries over top. Cover and simmer for 5 minutes, or until rice is tender and liquid is absorbed.

Sprinkle rice with half the nuts. Fluff rice with a fork, gently stirring to evenly distribute the ingredients. Taste and adjust seasoning. If using as stuffing, cool completely before using.

Serve hot, topped with remaining nuts.

Layered Rice and Chicken Casserole with Green Vegetables and Allspice

---

maklubah

This is a light and easy interpretation of a traditional Palestinian dish. Known as *maklubah*, which means "upside down," it's a casserole that's turned out after being cooked so the meat and vegetables come out on top of the rice. Layered casseroles of meat or chicken combined with vegetables and rice are also popular in Iran.

Maklubah is classically made with stewed red meat flavored with sautéed onions, garlic, and, sometimes, sweet spices. The vegetables most commonly used are eggplant and cauliflower, which are fried before being layered with the other ingredients. For this lighter version, I substitute chicken for the meat and add lightly blanched green beans and zucchini. Although it's far from the custom, I also like it with salmon and, for a vegetarian version, with sautéed mushrooms.

To keep presentation simple, I serve the casserole directly from its baking dish. If you'd like to turn it out, assemble it in a round, fairly shallow casserole with straight sides or in a cake pan; spoon all of the chicken onion mixture on the bottom and the rice on top. After baking it, let it stand for 10 or 15 minutes, then turn it over onto a large platter.

♦ MAKES 4 OR 5 SERVINGS.

4 to 5 tablespoons extra-virgin olive oil

2 large onions, sliced

4 large garlic cloves, chopped

2½ to 3 cups shredded cooked chicken, preferably dark meat

Salt and freshly ground black pepper

½ teaspoon ground allspice

¼ to ½ teaspoon ground cinnamon, or to taste (optional)

1½ cups long-grain rice

½ pound green beans, ends removed, cut in 1-inch pieces

1 zucchini, diced

1 cup frozen green peas (optional)

2 medium tomatoes, fresh or canned, diced

⅔ cup chicken broth, heated

1 tablespoon chopped Italian parsley

Preheat oven to 350°F. Heat 2 or 3 tablespoons oil in large saucepan. Add onions and sauté over medium heat for 7 minutes, or until beginning to brown, stirring often. Add garlic and sauté for a few seconds, then add chicken, salt, pepper, allspice, and cinnamon. Cook for about 1 minute. Remove from pan.

In same pan, bring 7 cups water to a boil with a pinch of salt. Add rice and boil, uncovered, for 5 minutes. Add green beans and boil, uncovered, for 2 minutes. Add zucchini and peas, if you like, and boil for 2 more minutes. Drain rice and vegetables, rinse with cold water, and drain well. Rice will be partially cooked.

In bowl, gently mix rice mixture with tomatoes and with salt and pepper to taste.

Spoon half of chicken mixture into a 2-quart casserole. Top with half the rice mixture. Repeat layers. Spoon remaining 2 tablespoons oil over top. Pour hot broth around the edge of the casserole. Bake uncovered for 45 minutes, or until rice is tender and broth is absorbed. Serve sprinkled with chopped parsley.

Assyrian Brown Rice and Bean Casserole with Mushrooms

riz beryani

Hearty entrées of bulgur wheat or rice combined with beans often appear on Assyrian tables. Usually they contain lamb or beef, but Assyrian cooks have a strong vegetarian tradition and often create meatless varia-

tions. Following their example, I make this layered casserole with mushrooms. Its lively flavor comes from fresh thyme, cilantro, hot peppers, garlic, and a savory cheese topping.

◆ MAKES 4 TO 6 SERVINGS.

3 tablespoons olive oil

2 large onions, chopped

12 to 16 ounces mushrooms, cut in thick slices

Salt and freshly ground black pepper

1 or 2 jalapeño or other hot peppers, seeded if desired, chopped

3 garlic cloves, chopped

1½ cups long-grain brown rice

2½ cups hot vegetable or chicken broth or water

One 14-ounce can tomatoes, chopped, with their liquid

1 large thyme sprig, or 1 teaspoon dried thyme

One 10-ounce package frozen lima beans, or 2 cups frozen black-eyed peas, cooked according to package directions

¼ cup chopped cilantro or Italian parsley (optional)

Cayenne pepper to taste

⅓ to ½ cup grated *kashkaval*, Parmesan, or Pecorino Romano cheese, or ⅓ cup bread crumbs and 1 tablespoon olive oil

Heat 2 tablespoons oil in stew pan or deep sauté pan. Add onions and sauté over medium heat for 12 minutes, or until golden brown, stirring occasionally. Remove with slotted spoon. Add remaining oil to pan and heat it. Add mushrooms, salt, and pepper and sauté over medium-high heat for 3 minutes, or until lightly browned, stirring occasionally. Transfer about two-thirds of mushrooms to plate, leaving remaining mushrooms in pan. Return one-third of onions to pan.

Heat onions and mushrooms briefly. Add jalapeño peppers, garlic, and rice and cook over medium-low heat, stirring, for 3 minutes, or until rice is evenly coated and lightly toasted. Add broth, tomatoes with their liquid, thyme, salt, and pepper. Stir once and bring to boil. Cover and cook over low heat, without stirring, for 35 minutes, or until rice is just tender.

Meanwhile, preheat oven to 400°F. Lightly oil a 2-quart casserole. Fluff rice with a fork, discarding thyme sprig. Add lima beans, cilantro, and cayenne pepper. Taste and adjust seasoning.

Transfer half of rice mixture to casserole. Top with half of reserved mushrooms and onions. Spoon remaining rice mixture over them, then add remaining mushrooms and onions. Sprinkle with grated cheese or with bread crumbs and oil. Bake for 15 minutes, or until topping browns lightly.

Basic Bulgur Pilaf

bulgur pilavi

Bulgur, an ancient convenience food, is wheat that has been steamed before it is dried and therefore needs only brief cooking or simply rehydrating in water. Note that natural food shops also carry packages of cracked wheat that has not been precooked and requires simmering for about 45 minutes. If you find a package of cracked wheat that is not labeled bulgur, check the cooking directions to see which you have, and adjust the cooking time if necessary.

A staple in the Middle East, bulgur is used to make pilaf nearly as often as for tabbouleh. To make pilaf, the bulgur is lightly sautéed to enhance the wheat's nutty taste. Flavor the pilaf with onion, as in the recipe below, or with minced garlic. For fat-free bulgur, toast the grains in a dry pan instead of sautéing them; omit the onion or add it with the broth.

If you find grilled green wheat (*fereek* or *farikeh*) at a Middle Eastern market, use it, following the variation, for a particularly pleasing pilaf.

♦ MAKES 4 TO 6 SERVINGS.

1 to 3 tablespoons olive oil, vegetable oil, or butter

1 small onion, finely chopped

1½ cups medium bulgur wheat

3 cups meat, vegetable, or chicken broth or water

Salt and freshly ground black pepper

Heat oil in heavy saucepan. Add onion and sauté over medium heat for 5 minutes, or until it begins to turn golden. Add bulgur wheat and sauté, stirring, for 1 minute, or until bulgur grains are coated with the onion mixture and lightly toasted. Add broth, salt, and pepper and bring to a boil. Cover and cook over low heat for 15 minutes, or until bulgur is tender and water is absorbed. Taste and adjust seasoning. Serve hot.

Fereek Pilaf

Substitute green wheat for the bulgur wheat. Rinse it and prepare as above, using broth (not water) and cook it for about 25 minutes.

Bulgur Wheat with Eggplant, Tomatoes, and Mint

---

bourghol bil batenjane

Turkish cooks like to make eggplant and rice pilaf, while those in neighboring Lebanon sometimes cook the vegetable with bulgur wheat. Made either way, the dish is served cold or at room temperature as an appetizer. I also like it hot as a partner for grilled meat or as a vegetarian entrée. Many deep-fry the eggplant before combining it with the bulgur wheat, but for an easier, lighter dish I braise it in the sauce instead.

◆ MAKES 4 SERVINGS.

1 medium eggplant (¾ to 1 pound)

3 to 4 tablespoons extra-virgin olive oil

1 large onion, chopped

Salt and freshly ground black pepper

One 14-ounce can diced tomatoes

2 large garlic cloves, chopped

½ to 1 teaspoon ground allspice

2 cups chicken, meat, or vegetable broth or water

1 cup large or medium-grain bulgur

1 tablespoon chopped mint, or 1 teaspoon dried mint

2 tablespoons chopped Italian parsley

Peel eggplant if skin is tough and cut it in ¾-inch dice. Heat 3 tablespoons oil in large, deep sauté pan or stew pan. Add onion and sauté over medium heat for 5 minutes, or until softened. Add eggplant, salt, and pepper and sauté over medium heat for 5 minutes, stirring often. Add tomatoes with their juice, garlic, and allspice and cook over high heat, stirring, until bubbling. Cover and cook over medium-low heat for 15 minutes, or until eggplant is nearly tender, stirring often, adding a few tablespoons water if pan becomes dry.

Add broth and bring to a boil. Add bulgur wheat. Cover and cook over low heat for 15 to 20 minutes, or until bulgur wheat is just tender. Fluff with a fork, lightly blending in remaining oil if you like. Add mint and half of parsley. Taste and adjust seasoning. Serve hot, cold, or at room temperature, sprinkled with remaining parsley.

Armenian Bulgur Wheat and Lentils with Sweet Peppers

vospov kheemah

Bulgur and lentil stew is nearly as popular as its rice-and-lentils cousin, and on some menus the bulgur version sometimes goes by the same name as the rice one, *majadra*. Usually bulgur with lentils is plain, simple comfort food seasoned mainly with fried onions. To make it fresh-tasting and colorful, add red and green peppers and spice it with Aleppo pepper. It's good warm or at room temperature, as a meatless main course or a hearty appetizer. If you're serving it as a first course, you can spoon it onto a bed of lettuce and garnish it with olives and cherry tomatoes.

◆ MAKES 4 TO 6 SERVINGS.

1 cup lentils, sorted

2 cups chicken, meat, or vegetable broth or water

4 to 5 tablespoons extra-virgin olive oil

1 red bell pepper, halved, cored, seeded, and finely diced (about ⅜-inch dice)

1 green bell pepper, halved, cored, seeded, and finely diced

2 medium onions, chopped

1 cup bulgur wheat, large or medium grain

Salt and freshly ground black pepper

1 teaspoon Aleppo pepper, or ¾ teaspoon paprika and ¼ teaspoon cayenne pepper, or to taste

¼ cup chopped green onions

⅓ to ½ cup chopped Italian parsley

Lemon wedges

Combine lentils and 2 cups broth in saucepan. Bring to a boil. Cover and cook over medium heat about 20 minutes, or until lentils are just tender. Drain liquid into a measuring cup and add enough water to make 2 cups; reserve. Keep lentils in the pan.

Heat 1 tablespoon oil in heavy skillet. Add red and green peppers and sauté over medium heat for 10 minutes, or until tender but not brown, stirring often. Remove from pan. Add 2 or 3 tablespoons oil to pan and heat it. Add onion and sauté over medium heat for 12 minutes, or until well browned, stirring occasionally.

Add half of browned onions to pan of lentils. Add measured liquid and bring to a boil. Add bulgur wheat and salt and return to a boil. Cover and cook over low heat for 15 to 20 minutes, or until bulgur wheat is just tender.

Add peppers and remaining browned onions to pan of lentils without stirring. Cover and let stand for 5 or 10 minutes. Fluff with a fork, lightly blending in vegetables. Add black and Aleppo pepper, green onions, and parsley and toss lightly. Taste and adjust seasoning, adding remaining tablespoon oil if you like. Serve at room temperature or hot, with lemon wedges.

Wheat Berries with Chickpeas and Chicken

haleem

This one-pot meal is an easy version of an old-fashioned Middle Eastern stew. Wheat berries and chickpeas are its main components, while the chicken serves mostly to flavor them. Eastern Mediterranean cooks often flavor the stew with a touch of cinnamon, Persians like turmeric, and Armenians opt for paprika or cumin. I find that cumin, turmeric, and red pepper flakes give the stew a wonderful taste.

You can put this stove-top casserole together in a short time, then leave it to simmer practically unattended. (For a faster version, see Note.) To reduce the fat, you can pull the skin off the chicken before putting it in the pan. You can also omit the oil and simply add the chopped onions to the other ingredients.

Wheat berries are available at natural food stores. If you've never tried them, you'll find they retain a pleasing, slightly chewy texture when cooked. I like this casse-

role with Turkish Shepherd's Salad (page 61) or with Green Salad with Herbs and Radishes (page 67) and a simple cooked vegetable such as green beans or broccoli.

◆ MAKES 5 OR 6 SERVINGS.

> 2 tablespoons olive oil or vegetable oil
> 2 large onions, coarsely chopped
> 1 teaspoon paprika
> 1 teaspoon ground cumin
> ¼ teaspoon turmeric
> 1½ to 2 pounds chicken thighs, with or without skin
> Salt and freshly ground black pepper to taste
> 1½ cups wheat berries, rinsed
> 1 cup dried chickpeas (garbanzo beans), sorted and rinsed
> ½ teaspoon hot red pepper flakes, or to taste
> 7 to 8 cups water (more if necessary)
> One 14-ounce can tomatoes, coarsely chopped

Heat oil in stew pan. Add onions and sauté over medium heat for 12 minutes, or until golden brown, stirring occasionally. Add paprika, cumin, and turmeric and stir briefly over low heat. Add chicken to onions, sprinkle it lightly with salt and pepper, and turn it over to lightly coat it with spice on both sides.

Add wheat berries, chickpeas, pepper flakes, and 7 to 8 cups water, or enough to generously cover ingredients. Bring to a boil. Cover and cook over very low heat for 45 to 60 minutes, or until chicken is tender. Remove chicken. Add tomatoes to casserole. Cover pan and continue cooking, adding hot water ⅓ cup at a time if necessary, for 30 to 60 more minutes, or until wheat berries and chickpeas are tender. Skim excess fat from sauce.

If casserole is too soupy, remove wheat berries and chickpeas with slotted spoon and boil sauce until it thickens. Remove chicken from bones, cut it in strips, and return it to pan. Taste and adjust seasoning. Serve hot.

ΝΟΤΣ To cut down on the simmering time, substitute brown rice for the wheat berries and 2 to 2½ cups canned chickpeas for the dried ones. Add the rice to the pan with the chicken and 6 cups water, but do not add the chickpeas yet. After removing the chicken, add the chickpeas with the tomatoes and cook for 10 minutes.

Curry-scented Barley Casserole with Peppers and Spinach

habea matboukha

One of the grains mentioned in the Bible, barley has been used in the region since time immemorial. It often appears in meat soups but is also loved in vegetable medleys, often enhanced with split peas or chickpeas. This casserole gains flavor from browned onions, curry, and tomato sauce. Serve this meal-in-one-dish with Classic Cucumber Salad with Yogurt, Garlic, and Mint (page 68) or Middle Eastern Diced Salad (page 58). In smaller portions, it also makes a good accompaniment for simple entrées of chicken or meat.

◆ MAKES 4 TO 6 SERVINGS.

2 to 4 tablespoons olive oil or butter,
    or 2 to 3 tablespoons vegetable oil

2 large onions, sliced

1 green pepper, halved, cored, seeded,
    and cut in strips

1 red bell pepper, halved, cored, seeded,
    and cut in strips

1 teaspoon curry powder

1 cup medium pearl barley, rinsed and
    drained

⅓ cup tomato sauce

3 cups hot vegetable or chicken broth
    or water

One 12-ounce bunch spinach,
    or one 10-ounce bag spinach leaves,
    rinsed and chopped

½ cup sliced celery

One 15-ounce can chickpeas, drained
    (optional)

Salt and freshly ground black pepper

Lemon wedges

Preheat oven to 350°F. Heat 2 to 3 tablespoons oil or butter in large skillet. Add onions and sauté over medium heat for 12 minutes, or until golden. Remove half of onions. Add green and red peppers to skillet and sauté for 5 minutes, or until they begin to soften. Stir in curry powder and barley and sauté for 1 minute. Remove from heat.

Oil a 2-quart casserole. Transfer barley mixture to casserole, reserving skillet. Pour tomato sauce and 2 cups hot broth over barley mixture. Add spinach, celery, chickpeas, salt, and pepper. Add remaining cup of broth to skillet and bring to a boil, stirring. Pour over barley. Cover and bake for 1¼ hours, or until barley is tender, stirring 3 or 4 times.

Fluff with fork, gently blending in reserved sautéed onions and adding more olive oil or butter if you like. Taste and adjust seasoning. Serve hot, with lemon wedges.

Breakfast Barley Stew with Beef

keshkek

This stew is inspired by an ancient dish of grains and meat that appears around the Mideast, from Lebanon to Persia, and is made with either barley or wheat. It's so popular in Iran that certain restaurants specialize in making it.

Cooks disagree about which meat is the best, some opting for beef and others for lamb, venison, duck, goose, turkey, or chicken. Traditionally the grain cooks for hours with a little meat or a few soup bones for flavor. The meat is then shredded and cooked again with the grain and the mixture is beaten to a mush. It is served as a very filling bowl of breakfast cereal or a warming wintertime lunch. Eating this dish during Ramadan to break the daily fast is said to have been the custom of the Prophet Muhammad, and many Saudis, who call the dish *tirbiyali*, do the same.

Often people cook the meat and wheat with hardly any seasoning. On its own the result is very bland, but the toppings make the dish—melted butter and a choice of cinnamon and sugar, coarsely ground coriander, or cumin for sprinkling.

When we ate it at Istanbul's Borsa restaurant, where it was called *keshkek*, it was made with superb lamb, which gave the soft wheat an excellent flavor. The stew makes pleasing comfort food, is easy to prepare, and tastes even better when made a day ahead; it also thickens considerably on standing.

When people make this dish with wheat, they generally choose pale wheat berries labeled "peeled wheat" available at Middle Eastern groceries, but some substitute faster-cooking bulgur wheat. Pearl barley is a good choice because it's easy to find at any supermarket and has a soft texture.

You might like to accompany the stew with a simple cooked vegetable, such as green beans, broccoli, or sautéed zucchini. Some serve it with yogurt instead of butter, while others like it with fresh bread and pickles, or, for a hearty meal, with lentil stew.

◆ MAKES 4 TO 6 SERVINGS.

1½ pounds beef with bones, such as beef shank

About 8 cups water

1 cinnamon stick, or ½ teaspoon ground cinnamon

1 medium onion, whole or chopped

Salt and freshly ground black pepper

1 cup pearl barley

Ground cinnamon (for sprinkling)

Sugar (for sprinkling)

Coarsely ground coriander or cumin (for sprinkling)

4 to 6 tablespoons butter (optional)

Put beef in large stew pan. Add 4 or 5 cups water or enough to cover and bring to a boil. Skim off excess foam. Add cinnamon stick, onion, salt, and pepper. Cover and simmer over low heat for 30 minutes. Add barley and 3 cups hot water. Bring to a simmer. Cover and cook over low heat for 1½ hours, or until beef is very tender, stirring occasionally.

Remove beef from pan. Skim off excess fat from stew and discard cinnamon stick and whole onion. Remove meat from bones and shred meat in thin strips. Return beef to pan and mix well. (If bones have marrow, you can return them to pan too; it's not traditional but the marrow is delicious.) If you

would like stew to be thicker, cook it uncovered over low heat until it thickens, stirring frequently. If it is too thick, add hot water. Taste and adjust seasonings.

At serving time, put out small dishes of cinnamon, sugar, and coriander or cumin for sprinkling. If you like, melt butter in small skillet or saucepan. Ladle hot stew into bowls and spoon a little butter over each one.

Kamut with Raisins, Almonds, and Peanuts

fereek bel zbeeb

Kamut is an ancient Egyptian variety of wheat. It was rediscovered by Westerners in the twentieth century and is a popular grain at natural food stores. Sometimes called Egyptian wheat, kamut is available whole or made into pasta. It expands into larger-size grains than other wheat berries and it has a pleasing nutty flavor. You can use it as you would wheat berries, or you can substitute them for the kamut in this casserole, which is flavored with sweet spices and a touch of mint. Kamut is good tossed with legumes, such as lentils or beans, and with other grains, such as cooked white or brown rice.

In the Mideast, grain entrées are often

served with yogurt-based dishes. A good choice with this one is Spinach and Summer Squash Borani with Red Peppers (page 255). The casserole is also good with hot vegetables, like Aromatic White and Green Bean Stew (page 227) and makes a satisfying accompaniment for braised or sautéed chicken breasts.

◆ MAKES 4 TO 6 SERVINGS.

6 cups water

1½ cups kamut berries, rinsed (see Note)

Salt and freshly ground black pepper to taste

2 tablespoons olive oil, vegetable oil, or butter

2 large onions, coarsely chopped

½ teaspoon ground cinnamon

½ teaspoon ground allspice

2 carrots, diced

1¼ cups vegetable broth or water

1 cup fresh or frozen corn kernels

Freshly grated nutmeg to taste (optional)

⅓ to ½ cup raisins

1 tablespoon chopped fresh mint, or 1 teaspoon dried mint

¼ cup almonds, toasted

¼ cup peanuts, toasted

Boil 6 cups water in stew pan and add salt. Add kamut and return to a boil. Cover and cook over low heat for 1½ to 2 hours, or until tender but a little chewy. Drain kamut and remove from pan.

Heat oil in pan. Add onions and sauté over medium heat for 12 minutes, or until golden brown, stirring occasionally. Reduce heat to low, add cinnamon and allspice, and stir briefly. Add carrots and broth and bring to a boil. Add corn, return to a boil, and simmer for 5 minutes. Add kamut, salt, pepper, nutmeg, and raisins and return to a boil. Cover and cook for 2 to 3 minutes, or until carrots are tender and raisins are plumped, adding broth or water if mixture becomes dry.

Add mint. Taste and adjust seasoning. Serve hot, topped with toasted almonds and peanuts.

ИΟΤΣ If you prefer, soak kamut overnight in water to cover, then drain and cook as above. The cooking time will be about 50 to 60 minutes.

Pasta, a Popular Use of an Age-Old Staple

Spicy Pasta Spirals with Chicken Saffron Sauce • *Macarona bel Dajaj*

Layered Couscous Chicken Casserole with Almonds and Herb Sauce • *Maftul*

Linguine with Lamb, Pistachios, and Zucchini • *Macarona bil Lahm*

Pearl Pasta with Baked Lamb and Tomato Sauce • *Mugrabiyeh*

Fusilli with Shrimp in Cilantro Tomato Sauce • *Macarona bil Kreidess*

Noodles with Goat Cheese and Egyptian Coriander Chard Sauce • *Macarona bil Gibna wa Salq*

Couscous with Pine Nuts and Bell Peppers • *Couscous bel Snoober wal Felfel*

Orzo Pilaf with Saffron, Peas, and Pecans • *Markarna Pilavi*

Spaghetti with Spinach, Garlic, and Lentils • *Rachta bi Sabanikh wa Adass*

Angel Hair Pasta with Peppery Walnut Sauce • *Shariya bil Mohammarah*

Egyptian Pasta and Lentil Casserole with Chili Tomato Sauce ◆ *Koshari*

Persian Toasted Noodles with Leek Sauce and Beans ◆ *Ash-e Reshteh*

Sautéed Vermicelli with Hazelnuts and Raisins ◆ *Sha'riya*

Pasta with Pumpkin and Cranberries ◆ *Ash-e Kadu*

The earliest remains of wheat were found by archaeologists on sites in the Middle East dating from the seventh millennium B.C. With their long history of eating wheat, people in the area have found plenty of ways to make use of it. In addition to cooking the whole and cracked grains and making flour into bread, they also make pasta. Depending on regional preferences, they opt for spaghetti like strands or for Persian toasted noodles. Some cook with orzo and other small pastas that resemble barley or rice, and others prepare meat-stuffed pastas that resemble ravioli.

Couscous, or tiny pasta made of semolina, was originally a specialty of the Maghreb countries of Morocco, Tunisia, and Algeria, but it spread eastward and is a favorite of many in the eastern Mediterranean. Cooks use it exuberantly, matching it with meatballs or hearty stews. It's also perfect for making quick, light dishes, like Couscous with Pine Nuts and Bell Peppers (page 293), accented with herb and sesame zahtar.

Special forms of couscous, different from the North African ones, have developed in some areas. In Turkey there is a couscouslike pasta known as *tarhana*, which is also made in Greece. Lebanese cooks prefer a larger type of couscous resembling tapioca balls, used in such dishes as Pearl Pasta with Baked Lamb and Tomato Sauce (page 290). These small spheres of pasta are common in Israel too, and in North America are best known as Israeli couscous. Because of its pleasing texture, this couscous has become à la mode on the menus of contemporary American chefs.

Middle Eastern sauces of meats and vegetables make good companions for pasta, especially twisted types that catch the bits of sauce. Families in the

Mideast have long been fond of Italian pasta preparations too. "After all," an Egyptian chef told me when I was curious about the spaghetti Bolognese on his menu, "we have had a connection with Italy since the days of Cleopatra." But he and his compatriots adapt such specialties to their national tastes. He flavors the ground meat sauce for his spaghetti with such seasonings as cumin and cilantro, or tosses pasta with chard and lentils.

In many homes pasta, like grains, is embellished with nuts or fruit for festive occasions. I find this custom a pleasing way to vary my own pasta dishes. Spaghetti sauce gains glamour with such a garnish, as in Linguine with Lamb, Pistachios, and Zucchini (page 289). Dried cranberries give orecchiette paired with pumpkin a delicate, appealing sweetness when flavored gently with cinnamon, mint, and sautéed onions, and is a perfect partner for roast chicken or kabobs.

Sautéing pasta is a widespread technique in the Mideast. The golden pasta is then simmered with rice as part of pilaf or made into a dish on its own. Sautéed Vermicelli with Hazelnuts and Raisins (page 299), for example, makes a tasty accompaniment for grilled meat, or doubles as a winter dessert when sweetened and moistened with warm milk.

Pasta is used to make other sweet courses as well. On Egyptian tables a simple bowl of couscous sprinkled with sugar, raisins, and toasted nuts is a beloved children's dessert. Persians serve an unusual rose-water scented sorbet studded with fine white noodles for contrasting texture. You can find this refreshing sorbet in markets that cater to Iranian customers.

Spicy Pasta Spirals with Chicken Saffron Sauce

macarona bel dajaj

Cinnamon, cardamom, chilies, and cumin, along with the saffron, give this sauce an exotic character loved south of the Persian Gulf. The pasta finishes cooking in the sauce, so it absorbs flavor and becomes slightly golden from the saffron. In the kitchens of the Emirates and Saudi Arabia, cooks use dried limes to give the sauce a tangy taste, but I add a squeeze of lime or lemon juice. Instead of the traditional lamb, I make this lighter version of the aromatic sauce with chicken.

♦ MAKES 4 OR 5 SERVINGS.

2 tablespoons vegetable oil

2 onions, chopped

2 jalapeño peppers, seeded if desired, chopped

12 ounces ground chicken

½ teaspoon ground cumin

½ teaspoon ground cardamom

¼ teaspoon ground cinnamon

One 28-ounce can diced tomatoes, with their juice

1 cup chicken broth or water

¼ teaspoon saffron threads, crushed

Salt and freshly ground black pepper to taste

12 to 16 ounces pasta spirals or shells

1 tablespoon fresh-squeezed lime juice, or to taste

1 tablespoon chopped Italian parsley

Heat oil in large sauté pan. Add onions and sauté over medium heat for 10 minutes, or until they begin to turn golden. Add jalapeño peppers, chicken, cumin, cardamom, and cinnamon and sauté for 5 minutes, or until chicken's color lightens, stirring often. Add tomatoes with their juice, ½ cup broth, saffron, salt, and pepper and bring to a simmer. Cover and cook for 10 minutes, or until chicken is cooked through and sauce is well flavored. Taste and adjust seasoning.

Cook pasta in large pot of boiling salted water over high heat for 5 minutes, or until nearly tender but still firm to the bite, separating strands occasionally with a fork. Drain well and add to spaghetti sauce. Add ½ cup broth. Cook, uncovered, over medium heat for 2 minutes or until pasta is just tender, tossing often. Add lime juice. Taste and adjust seasoning. Serve hot, sprinkled with parsley.

Layered Couscous Chicken Casserole with Almonds and Herb Sauce

maftul

Around the Mideast people often compose casseroles by layering rice with chicken or meat braised in a savory sauce. For a more nutritious, faster alternative, I use whole-wheat couscous and pair it with a fresh green sauce of garlic, mint, and cilantro. You can find the couscous at natural food stores, or use plain couscous if you prefer.

For a vegetarian version of this dish, substitute diced firm tofu for the chicken. Serve this dish with olives and pickles and with Turkish Shepherd's Salad (page 61) or Mideast-California Diced Salad (page 60).

♦ MAKES 4 SERVINGS.

3½ cups chicken or vegetable broth, or broth mixed with water

2 large carrots, sliced ½ inch thick

1 cup fresh shelled or frozen peas

1 large yellow crookneck squash or zucchini, sliced ½ inch thick

3 to 4 tablespoons extra-virgin olive oil

One 10-ounce package whole-wheat couscous (1²⁄₃ cups)

Salt and freshly ground black pepper

4 large garlic cloves

½ cup small Italian parsley sprigs

⅓ cup small cilantro sprigs

2 to 3 tablespoons fresh mint leaves, or 2 teaspoons dried mint

½ teaspoon Aleppo pepper or paprika

Cayenne pepper to taste

2 cups shredded cooked chicken

⅓ cup slivered almonds

Preheat over to 350°F. Bring broth and carrots to a boil in medium saucepan. Cover and cook over low heat for 7 minutes. Add peas and squash and return to a boil. Cover and cook over low heat for 5 minutes, or until vegetables are just tender. Remove vegetables with slotted spoon.

Add 1 tablespoon oil to broth in saucepan and return to a boil. Stir in couscous. Cover pan and remove from heat. Let stand for 5 minutes. Season to taste with salt and pepper.

Finely chop garlic in food processor. Add parsley, cilantro, and mint and chop fine. Transfer to bowl. Add 2 tablespoons oil, salt, pepper, Aleppo pepper, and cayenne pepper and mix well. Mix lightly with chicken. Taste and adjust seasoning.

Oil an 8- to 10-cup baking dish. Spoon half the couscous into the dish. Top with the chicken mixture, then with the cooked vegetables. Top with the remaining couscous and mound it in a smooth layer. Sprinkle with remaining oil if you like, then with almonds. Bake, uncovered, for 25 minutes, or until almonds are browned and casserole is hot.

Linguine with Lamb, Pistachios, and Zucchini

macarona bil lahm

With fresh mint or cilantro, allspice, and a hint of cinnamon, as well as a festive topping of toasted pistachios, spaghetti sauce gains new dimensions of flavor. Instead of linguine, you can toss the sauce with other long thin pastas like vermicelli, spaghettini, or fusilli, or serve it in a bowl for spooning over orzo, couscous, rice, or bulgur wheat.

◆ MAKES 4 TO 6 SERVINGS.

  2 tablespoons olive oil, vegetable oil,
      or butter

  1 large onion, chopped

  12 ounces ground lean lamb

  4 large garlic cloves, minced

  ½ teaspoon ground allspice

  ⅛ teaspoon ground cinnamon

  1½ pounds ripe tomatoes, peeled,
      seeded, and chopped, or one 28-ounce
      can plum tomatoes, drained and
      chopped

  Salt and freshly ground black pepper
      to taste

  2 tablespoons tomato paste

  ¼ cup chopped fresh mint or cilantro

  1 pound linguine

  8 ounces zucchini, sliced lengthwise,
      then cut in strips

  ½ to ⅔ cup shelled pistachios, roasted

Heat oil in large sauté pan. Add onion and sauté over medium heat for 7 minutes, or until it begins to turn golden. Add lamb, garlic, allspice, and cinnamon and sauté for 5 minutes, or until meat browns lightly, stirring often. Add tomatoes, salt, and pepper, cover and cook for 5 minutes. Add tomato paste, stir until blended, and cook, uncovered, for 5 minutes, or until sauce is thick. Add mint. Taste and adjust seasoning. Remove half of sauce to a bowl, cover, and keep warm.

Cook pasta in large pot of boiling salted water over high heat for 6 minutes, separating strands occasionally with a fork. Add zucchini and cook together for 2 minutes, or until pasta is just tender but still firm to the bite. Drain well and add to sauce in sauté pan. Toss gently over low heat for 1 or 2 minutes so pasta absorbs flavor from sauce. Taste and adjust seasoning.

Transfer pasta to serving dish. Spoon remaining sauce in a ribbon across the top of pasta and sprinkle with pistachios.

Pearl Pasta with Baked Lamb and Tomato Sauce

mugrabiyeh

Pasta shaped like tapioca, which is sold at gourmet shops as Israeli couscous and at Middle Eastern groceries as *mugrabiya* (Lebanese couscous), is delicious when baked in the savory juices of braised lamb. If you don't have this pasta, use orzo or very fine noodles instead, as Turkish cooks do for a similar dish. Some people make this casserole with rice, bulgur wheat, or a combination of bulgur and noodles.

Usually this pasta and lamb entrée is flavored simply, with only sautéed onions, tomato sauce, salt, and pepper, although some add mushrooms or a topping of fried onions. Serve it with a plate of fresh green onions, cucumbers, radishes, and sweet peppers, or with Green Salad with Herbs and Radishes (page 67). Yogurt Garlic Sauce (page 311) is also a popular accompaniment.

♦ MAKES 6 SERVINGS.

2 to 2½ pounds lamb shoulder chops
    (1 to 1¼ inches thick), trimmed of skin
    and excess fat, or leg of lamb steaks
3 tablespoons olive oil, or 2 tablespoons
    butter and 1 tablespoon oil
Salt and freshly ground black pepper to taste
2 large onions, chopped
2 large garlic cloves, chopped (optional)
3 cups meat or chicken broth or water
½ teaspoon ground cinnamon (optional)
1 cup tomato sauce
1 tablespoon chopped fresh thyme,
    or 1 teaspoon dried thyme
1 pound pearl-shaped pasta
    (Israeli couscous or *mugrabiya*)
2 tablespoons chopped Italian parsley
    (optional)

Preheat oven to 450°F. Put lamb in a 10-cup gratin dish or other large baking dish. Sprinkle lamb with 1 tablespoon oil and with salt and pepper on both sides. Bake for 10 minutes, turning once.

Meanwhile, heat remaining oil or butter in large skillet. Add onions and sauté over medium heat for 7 minutes, or until golden. Reserve skillet.

Reduce oven temperature to 350°F. Add sautéed onions, garlic, broth, and cinnamon, if you like, to lamb. Bake for 10 to 15 minutes, or until meat is nearly done; when cut, it should be pink, not red.

Cut meat from bones, keeping meat in large pieces and reserving bones. Reserve meat on a plate and cover. Return bones to baking dish and stir. Bake for 15 minutes, or until onions are very tender. Discard bones.

Add remaining broth to the skillet and bring to a boil. Pour into baking dish and add tomato sauce, thyme, salt, and pepper. Add pasta and stir once. Bake, uncovered, for 20 minutes. Set meat pieces on top in one layer, pressing gently into mixture.

Return to oven and bake for 10 minutes, or until couscous is tender but firm to the bite and meat is done to your taste; if pasta absorbs all of liquid before it becomes tender, add ⅓ cup boiling water, bake for 3 to 5 more minutes and check again. Taste and adjust seasoning. Sprinkle with parsley if you like and serve hot.

Fusilli with Shrimp in Cilantro Tomato Sauce

macarona bil kreidess

Many in the eastern Mediterranean area use this lively tomato sauce flavored with garlic, cilantro, and hot pepper for all sorts of foods, from vegetables to meat. It gives shrimp a robust flavor, making them a superb match for pasta. Substitute basil or Italian parsley for the cilantro if you prefer. If you don't have time to marinate the shrimp in the garlic, cilantro, and olive oil, simply toss them in the mixture and cook them right away.

♦ MAKES 4 SERVINGS.

⅓ cup cilantro sprigs, packed, plus
   1 tablespoon chopped cilantro leaves
4 large garlic cloves, peeled
1 to 2 teaspoons ground coriander or
   cumin

Salt and freshly ground black pepper
   to taste
3 to 5 tablespoons extra-virgin olive oil
1 pound large shrimp (about 30 to 35),
   shelled
One 28-ounce and one 14-ounce can
   tomatoes, drained and coarsely
   chopped
¼ to ½ teaspoon hot red pepper flakes,
   or pinch of cayenne pepper, or more
   to taste
8 ounces fusilli
1 or 2 teaspoons fresh-squeezed
   lemon juice (optional)
Lemon wedges

Reserve 1 tablespoon chopped cilantro leaves for garnish. Chop garlic in food processor. Remove about half of garlic and reserve for sauce. Add cilantro sprigs, ground coriander, salt, pepper, and 2 or 3 tablespoons oil to food processor. Process until blended. Transfer to bowl, add shrimp, and toss to combine. Let stand to marinate while you prepare sauce, or cover and refrigerate up to 2 hours.

Heat 1 tablespoon oil in large sauté pan. Stir in reserved chopped garlic, followed by tomatoes, salt, pepper, and pepper flakes. Bring to a boil. Cook, uncovered, over medium heat for 10 minutes, or until sauce is thick, stirring occasionally.

Cook fusilli in large pot of boiling salted water, uncovered, over high heat for 7 minutes, or until tender but firm to the bite, stirring occasionally.

Meanwhile, bring tomato sauce to a simmer. Add shrimp with its seasoning mixture and sprinkle with salt and pepper. Cover and cook over medium-low heat for 3 minutes, or until shrimp are cooked, stirring occasionally. To check, cut through a thick end of a shrimp; it should be white throughout. Taste and adjust seasoning, adding lemon juice if you like.

Drain pasta, reserving ½ cup of its cooking liquid. Toss pasta gently with shrimp and sauce in sauté pan or in large shallow bowl, adding a few tablespoons pasta cooking liquid if mixture is too thick. Taste again for seasoning. Serve hot, drizzled with remaining olive oil. Set a few of the shrimp on top for garnish, sprinkle with reserved cilantro, and serve with lemon wedges.

Noodles with Goat Cheese and Egyptian Coriander Chard Sauce

macarona bil gibna wa salq

I like the Egyptian technique of making sauces from pureed greens. Traditionally these sauces are paired with poultry, meat, or legumes but they also adapt well to pasta dishes. Goat cheese is popular in the Middle East, where often it is firm enough to slice neatly rather than creamy soft or crumbly; use any type of goat cheese in this dish. If

you want the pasta to accompany a chicken, fish, or meat dish, omit the cheese.

◆ MAKES 4 SERVINGS.

1½ pounds Swiss chard (about 2 bunches), rinsed thoroughly

3 to 5 tablespoons extra-virgin olive oil

8 to 12 ounces white or brown mushrooms, cut in thick slices (optional)

Salt and freshly ground black pepper

6 large garlic cloves, chopped

1 to 1½ teaspoons ground coriander

12 ounces fettuccine, tagliatelle, or medium-width noodles

1 to 2 tablespoons chopped cilantro

6 ounces goat cheese, crumbled or diced

Cut chard leaves from stems. Peel stems if they are stringy. Cut them in thin strips. Pile chard leaves and chop them. Keep them separate from stems. In saucepan of boiling salted water, cook stems, uncovered, for 5 minutes. Drain and add to leaves.

Heat 1 tablespoon oil in large, heavy sauté pan. Add mushrooms, salt, and pepper and sauté over medium-high heat for 3 or 4 minutes, or until light brown. Transfer to bowl.

Add 1 or 2 tablespoons oil to pan and heat it. Add garlic and sauté for 15 seconds. Add half of chard, ½ teaspoon ground coriander, and a sprinkling of salt and pepper. Sauté over medium heat, stirring, for 3 minutes. Transfer to bowl. Add 1 tablespoon oil to pan and heat it. Add remaining chard, salt, pepper, and ½ teaspoon ground coriander and sauté for 3 minutes. Transfer to bowl. Puree chard mixture in food processor, in batches if necessary, until smooth. Return to pan.

Cook noodles, uncovered, in large pot of boiling salted water over high heat for 6 to 9 minutes, or until tender but firm to the bite, stirring occasionally. Drain, reserving ½ cup of cooking liquid. Add to chard sauce in pan. If sauce is too thick, add a few tablespoons pasta cooking liquid. Add mushrooms. Heat gently, tossing with tongs, for 1 to 2 minutes to blend flavors. Add cilantro, three-quarters of goat cheese, and remaining oil. Taste and adjust seasoning, adding more ground coriander if you like. Serve hot, topped with remaining cheese.

Couscous with Pine Nuts and Bell Peppers

---

couscous bel snoober wal felfel

The savory sesame herb blend called zahtar, together with fresh herbs, perks up this couscous medley. To give the couscous a little extra flavor, I sauté the grains as for rice pilaf before adding the water.

Serve this colorful, fast, and easy dish as a light summer accompaniment for grilled fish or chicken. To make it even more quickly, use roasted peppers from a jar or from a deli. If you'd like the couscous cold, spoon it onto the center of a bed of baby lettuces and serve it as an appetizer.

♦ MAKES 4 SERVINGS.

  2 to 4 tablespoons extra-virgin olive oil
  1⅔ cups or one 10-ounce package couscous
  Salt and freshly ground black pepper
  2 cups hot water
  1 red or orange bell pepper, grilled and peeled (see "Basics," page 370)
  1 green bell pepper, grilled and peeled (see "Basics," page 370)
  ½ cup finely chopped red onions or sweet onions
  ¼ cup chopped Italian parsley
  2 to 3 teaspoons fresh-squeezed lemon juice
  ⅓ cup pine nuts, toasted (see "Basics," page 369)
  3 tablespoons chopped cilantro or shredded basil
  2 teaspoons zahtar or chopped fresh thyme

Heat 1 tablespoon oil in large saucepan. Add couscous and pinch of salt and pepper and stir mixture with a fork over low heat until blended. Pour 2 cups hot water evenly over couscous, return to a boil, and remove from heat. Cover and let stand for 5 minutes. Meanwhile, cut peppers in thin strips.

Fluff couscous with a fork. Add onions, parsley, 2 teaspoons lemon juice, and 1 tablespoon olive oil. Reserve a few pepper strips, 2 tablespoons pine nuts, and 1 tablespoon cilantro or basil for garnish and add remaining peppers, nuts, and cilantro to couscous.

Add I teaspoon zahtar. Toss mixture lightly with fork; taste, adjust seasoning, and add more lemon juice or olive oil if needed. Transfer to serving dish, sprinkle with remaining zahtar and garnish with reserved pepper strips, pine nuts, and fresh herbs. Serve hot or at room temperature.

Orzo Pilaf with Saffron, Peas, and Pecans

markarna pilavi

In Turkey, as in Greece, orzo is made into pilaf the same way as rice. Prepared this way, the orzo is much more flavorful than if boiled in water like other types of pasta. This recipe is an orzo variation of a sumptuous Turkish rice pilaf, in which the grains gain a rich taste from chicken stock and a golden hue from saffron. Traditionally the pilaf is studded with poached chicken, sautéed chicken livers, peas, and toasted nuts. I have simplified the recipe by omitting the chicken and livers but if you have I or 2 cups of cooked chicken or turkey, shred it and add it to the orzo for the last 2 minutes of its cooking time. Serve the orzo as a festive accompaniment for roasted meats.

◆ MAKES 4 TO 6 SERVINGS.

¼ teaspoon crushed saffron threads (2 pinches)

3⅓ cups hot chicken stock, preferably homemade (see "Basics," page 376)

3 to 4 tablespoons olive oil

1 large onion, finely chopped

1½ cups orzo or riso (rice-shaped pasta) (about 12 ounces)

Salt and freshly ground black pepper

1 cup fresh shelled or frozen peas

⅓ to ½ cup toasted pecans (see "Basics," page 369) or toasted pumpkin seeds (pepitas)

Combine saffron and ⅓ cup hot stock in small cup. Cover and let stand while sautéing onion.

Heat oil in medium saucepan. Add onion and sauté over medium heat for 7 minutes, or until it begins to turn golden, stirring often. Add orzo and cook over low heat, stirring, for 3 minutes. Add remaining stock, saffron liquid, and a little salt and pepper and bring to a boil. Cover and cook over low heat for 7 minutes. Add peas and return to a boil. Cover and cook for 8 more minutes, or until orzo and peas are just tender.

Fluff orzo with a fork. Coarsely chop half the pecans, add to the orzo, and toss lightly to combine. Taste and adjust seasoning. Serve hot, garnished with whole pecans.

Spaghetti with Spinach, Garlic, and Lentils

rachta bi sabanikh wa adass

Start with the classic Italian *spaghetti a l'aglio e olio* (with garlic and olive oil), throw in some chopped spinach and lentils, then give it some zip with a sprinkling of mint and a squeeze of lemon juice. The result is a refreshing dish favored in Lebanon. It's good hot as an entrée or cool as a salad.

For a novel presentation, you can make the dish with spinach noodles instead of spaghetti. If you like, substitute cooked or canned red or black beans, yellow split peas, or other legumes for the lentils. To make it easy, some people cook the lentils, spaghetti, and spinach together, but I find the pasta cooks more evenly on its own.

◆ MAKES 4 SERVINGS.

One 12-ounce bunch spinach, rinsed thoroughly and trimmed, or one 10-ounce bag spinach leaves

4 to 5 tablespoons extra-virgin olive oil

Salt and freshly ground black pepper to taste

2 onions, chopped

6 large garlic cloves, peeled

1 cup cooked or canned lentils, drained, liquid reserved (see Note)

8 ounces spaghetti

1 teaspoon dried mint

Lemon wedges

Coarsely chop the spinach. Heat 1 tablespoon oil in large sauté pan. Add half of spinach and pinch of salt and pepper. Cook for 3 minutes, or until spinach wilts, stirring often. Transfer to bowl with slotted spoon. Add remaining spinach to skillet and cook it in same way. Pour contents of skillet into bowl of spinach.

Add 3 tablespoons oil to pan and heat it. Add onions and sauté over medium heat for 15 minutes, or until well browned, stirring often. Add garlic and sauté for 1 minute. Add lentils and heat through. Return spinach mixture to pan and toss with lentil mixture. Taste and adjust seasoning.

Cook spaghetti, uncovered, in large pot of boiling salted water over high heat for 6 to 9 minutes, or until tender but firm to the bite, separating strands occasionally with a fork. Drain spaghetti, reserving ½ cup cooking liquid. Add spaghetti to spinach mixture in pan. If mixture is dry, add a few tablespoons lentil or pasta cooking liquid. Heat gently, tossing with tongs, for 1 to 2 minutes to blend flavors; or, if the pasta doesn't fit in the pan, toss it in a heated bowl. Add mint and remaining oil. Taste and adjust seasoning. Serve hot or at room temperature, with lemon wedges.

NOTE If you don't have cooked lentils on hand, sort ½ cup raw lentils and put them in a saucepan with 1½ cups water. Bring to a boil. Cover and cook over medium-low heat for 20 to 30 minutes, or until tender.

Angel Hair Pasta with Peppery Walnut Sauce

shariya bil mohammarah

I find the spicy walnut dip called *mohammara* to be a wonderful sauce for pasta, grains, vegetables, and fish. For serving with pasta, I augment the heat with fresh hot peppers. Sweet peppers and green onions give this pasta dish a fresh look and taste.

◆ MAKES 4 TO 6 SERVINGS.

Red Pepper Walnut Dip (page 39)

2 red or green jalapeño peppers

2 or 3 tablespoons extra-virgin olive oil

1 red bell pepper, halved, cored, seeded, and cut in thin strips

1 yellow or green bell pepper, halved, cored, seeded, and cut in thin strips

Salt and freshly ground black pepper to taste

1 medium tomato, diced

8 to 12 ounces angel-hair pasta or capellini

⅓ cup chopped green onion, white and green parts

Prepare Red Pepper Walnut Dip. Remove seeds and ribs from jalapeño peppers if you want them less hot. Mince peppers in small food processor or with knife.

Heat oil in large heavy skillet. Add red and yellow bell peppers, salt, and pepper. Cook over medium heat about 8 minutes, or until peppers soften but remain slightly crisp, stirring often. Add jalapeño peppers and cook for 1 minute. Remove from heat and stir in diced tomato.

Cook pasta, uncovered, in large pan of boiling salted water over high heat for 2 to 5 minutes, or until just tender but still slightly firm to the bite, separating strands occasionally with a fork.

Drain pasta well and transfer to shallow bowl. Add walnut dip and toss until well combined. Add pepper mixture and green onions and toss lightly. Taste and adjust seasoning. Serve hot or at room temperature.

Egyptian Pasta and Lentil Casserole with Chili Tomato Sauce

koshari

There are as many variations of this popular dish as there are cooks. People enjoy the savory casserole at home, in restaurants, and on the street, where vendors sell it from carts. In its most basic version, it is made of seasoned lentils mixed with pasta or with rice but the favorite way to prepare it is to combine all three and to moisten them with a flavorful hot pepper tomato sauce. Some serve an additional sauce, either garlic and vinegar or Fresh Chili Vinaigrette (page 308). Most cooks opt for the usual greenish brown lentils but some prefer the fast-cooking orange variety. Still others add chickpeas.

Usually *koshari* is a vegetarian dish but in some households, it comes with a meaty tomato sauce or a layer of sautéed ground meat spooned over the pasta. The components can be heated as a stove-top casserole, baked in the oven as in this recipe, or simply layered on the plate at serving time.

♦ MAKES 5 OR 6 SERVINGS.

5 cups water

1 cup long-grain rice

Salt and freshly ground black pepper

6 ounces medium pasta shells or orecchiette (pasta disks) (2¼ to 2½ cups dry)

1½ to 2 cups cooked or canned lentils (see Notes)

4 or 5 tablespoons extra-virgin olive oil

2 large onions, halved and sliced thin

1 to 2 teaspoons vinegar

2 cups Spicy Tomato Sauce (page 305 or see Notes)

Cayenne pepper to taste

Bring 5 cups water to a boil in large saucepan and add salt. Add rice and boil, uncovered, over high heat for 12 to 14 minutes, or until just tender. Drain well. Cook pasta, uncovered, in large pot of boiling salted water over high heat, about 5 to 8 minutes for shells or 10 minutes for orecchiette, or until tender but firm to the bite. Drain well. Combine rice, lentils, and pasta in large bowl.

Heat 3 tablespoons oil in heavy skillet. Add onions and sauté over medium heat for 15 minutes, or until they are deeply browned, stirring occasionally. Reduce heat if necessary so they become tender but do not burn. With slotted spoon, remove half the onions and reserve. Add remaining onions and their oil to the pasta mixture.

Mix vinegar into tomato sauce. Add ½ cup sauce to pasta mixture and toss lightly. Add remaining oil, salt, pepper, and cayenne pepper to taste.

Preheat oven to 350°F. Oil a shallow baking dish. Spoon ¼ cup tomato sauce into dish. Top with pasta mixture, then with remaining sauce. Cover and bake for 15 minutes, or until hot. Uncover and bake for 10 minutes. Top with reserved browned onions and bake for 5 more minutes. Serve hot.

NOTES

Cooked lentils

If you don't have cooked lentils on hand, sort ¾ to 1 cup raw lentils and put them in a saucepan with 3 cups water. Bring to a boil. Cover and cook over medium-low heat for 20 to 30 minutes, or until tender.

Spicy Tomato Sauce

If you don't have time to make tomato sauce, mix 2 cups canned or bottled tomato sauce with 1 teaspoon ground cumin and with ¼ to ½ teaspoon hot red pepper flakes or cayenne pepper to taste.

Persian Toasted Noodles with Leek Sauce and Beans

ash-e reshteh

Persians are so fond of toasted noodles that they package them pretoasted. These pale brown noodles are easy to spot at Middle Eastern grocery stores. In appearance they resemble whole-wheat noodles, which I find are a good substitute because they have a similar nutty flavor. You can also prepare this recipe with toasted vermicelli, following the recipe below.

When prepared the traditional way, the noodles are boiled with leeks, spinach, herbs, and a variety of legumes to make a thick soup, then garnished with sautéed onions and fried mint. For a fresher tasting and brighter colored version, I cook the vegetables briefly to make a sauce for the noodles. Serve the dish with the flavorful Persian liquefied whey called *kashk* (see "The Mideast Pantry," page 17) or with rich yogurt.

♦ MAKES 3 OR 4 SERVINGS.

3 medium leeks, split, rinsed thoroughly

3 to 6 tablespoons vegetable oil or butter

1 medium onion, halved and sliced (optional)

Salt and freshly ground black pepper to taste

3 to 3½ cups hot vegetable broth or water

8 ounces toasted noodles, vermicelli, or whole-wheat spaghetti or linguine

1½ to 2 cups cooked or one 15-ounce can red, white, or pinto beans or chickpeas

1½ to 2 cups chopped spinach

⅓ cup chopped Italian parsley

¼ cup *kashk* (liquefied dried whey), or ½ cup yogurt or Thick Yogurt (page 125)

1 tablespoon chopped fresh mint, or 1 teaspoon dried mint

Discard dark green part of leeks or save them for making broth. Cut light green and white parts of leeks in thin slices.

Heat 1½ to 2 tablespoons oil in large deep skillet or sauté pan. Add onion and sauté over medium heat for 7 to 10 minutes, or until golden brown. Remove from skillet and reserve for garnish.

Add 1½ to 2 tablespoons oil to skillet and heat it. Add leeks and pinch of salt and pepper. Cover and cook over low heat for 7 minutes, or until tender but not brown, stirring occasionally. Add 1 cup broth and reserve.

Break noodles into 2-inch lengths. If using vermicelli, toast it if you like: Heat 2 tablespoons oil in large heavy sauté pan over medium heat. Add vermicelli and sauté for 7 minutes, or until golden, stirring it constantly and turning it over from time to time. Add 2 cups broth and bring to a boil. If using Persian toasted noodles or whole-wheat spaghetti, add it now. Cook, uncovered, over medium-heat for 10 minutes, or until pasta is just tender, stirring occasionally and gradually adding more broth as needed.

When pasta is nearly ready, bring leek sauce to a boil. Add beans and spinach and cook over medium heat for 3 minutes, or until spinach wilts, stirring often. Combine with pasta in one pan. Add parsley and toss over low heat for 2 to 3 minutes to blend flavors. Taste and adjust seasoning. Serve garnished with a dollop of *kashk* or yogurt, sautéed onions, and mint.

Sautéed Vermicelli with Hazelnuts and Raisins

sha'riya

Cooks in the Mideast like to sauté thin noodles before cooking them to give them an attractive golden hue. Often the browned noodles become part of Rice Pilaf with Toasted Almonds (page 263) but they're also popular as a pasta dish. The sautéed noodles are cooked directly in their sauce, enabling them to absorb more flavor and eliminating the need for a big pot of boiling water. You can make the dish using vermicelli, capellini (angel hair pasta), very fine egg noodles used for soups, or Spanish coiled fideos.

Serve these savory-sweet noodles with roast chicken or lamb. You can vary the fruit, substituting dried cherries, cranberries, or blueberries to your taste. Instead of hazelnuts, toasted almonds make a congenial match with the vermicelli and the fruit, as does a mixture of nuts.

In some households the noodles are served with warm milk for a holiday breakfast or brunch. To prepare them this way, omit the onion and parsley and cook the noodles in water instead of broth. Sometimes this sweet version is turned into a dessert, with the addition of fresh fruit, such as sliced strawberries or bananas.

♦ MAKES 4 OR 5 SERVINGS.

8 ounces very thin egg noodles for soup (4 cups) or vermicelli

5 tablespoons butter, oil, or a mixture of both

1 large onion, finely chopped

2 cups hot chicken broth, or broth mixed with water

¼ cup dark raisins

½ cup hazelnuts, toasted and peeled (see "Basics," page 369)

3 tablespoons chopped Italian parsley

Salt and freshly ground black pepper

If using long pasta, break it in 2-inch pieces. Heat 3 tablespoons butter in large heavy deep skillet or sauté pan over medium heat. Add noodles and sauté for 7 minutes, or until golden, stirring constantly and turning them over from time to time. Transfer to bowl.

Add remaining 2 tablespoons butter to pan. Add onion and cook over medium heat for 5 minutes, or until softened and beginning to turn golden, stirring often. Return pasta to pan. Add 1½ cups broth and bring to a boil. Cover and cook over low heat for 10 minutes, or until pasta is tender and has absorbed the broth, stirring occasionally. If the pan becomes dry before pasta is tender, add more broth, ¼ cup at a time, and continue cooking.

Meanwhile, pour enough hot water over raisins to cover them. Let stand for 5 minutes to plump, then drain well. Coarsely chop most of the hazelnuts, reserving a few whole ones for garnish.

When pasta is ready, add parsley, half of raisins, and half of chopped hazelnuts. Season to taste with salt and pepper. Serve pasta topped with remaining raisins and chopped and whole nuts.

Pasta with Pumpkin and Cranberries

---

ash-e kadu

Pumpkin simmered with grains is popular on Turkish, Armenian, Kurdish, and Persian tables. Some cooks highlight the pumpkin's sweetness with lots of sugar and raisins, while others add a touch of cinnamon or go for a sweet-and-sour effect with both sugar and lemon. Rice is the pumpkin's usual partner, but I also pair it with pasta, as

in this dish. Serve it with roasted chicken, kabobs, lamb chops, or steak.

I especially like to use sweet pumpkin like the Japanese kabocha, the Latino calabaza, or the familiar butternut squash. If you're using acorn squash, which tends to be less sweet, sprinkle it with a little more sugar. Disk-shaped pasta called orecchiette ("little ears") is tasty and attractive with the pumpkin, but any small shape that's easy to mix with the pumpkin will work fine.

◆ MAKES 4 OR 5 SERVINGS.

1½ to 2 pounds butternut or other winter squash, peeled, seeds removed

2 to 3 tablespoons vegetable oil or butter

1 medium onion, chopped

½ teaspoon ground cinnamon

½ teaspoon ground ginger (optional)

Salt and freshly ground black pepper

¾ cup vegetable broth or water

3 to 4 tablespoons dried cranberries or raisins

2 to 6 teaspoons sugar, or to taste

1 to 3 teaspoons fresh-squeezed lemon juice (optional)

8 to 12 ounces orecchiette or medium pasta shells

1 to 2 teaspoons dried mint (optional)

Cut squash in ¾-inch dice. Heat 2 tablespoons oil in large heavy saucepan or stew pan, add onion, and sauté over medium heat for 5 minutes, or until beginning to turn golden. Add squash, cinnamon, ginger, if you like, salt, and pepper. Cover and cook over low heat for 5 minutes, stirring occasionally. Add broth and bring to a simmer. Cover and cook over low heat for 25 minutes, or until squash is barely tender, occasionally stirring gently and adding a few tablespoons water if necessary so that juices do not burn. Add cranberries, 2 teaspoons sugar, and I teaspoon lemon juice if desired and cook for 5 minutes, or until squash is just tender.

Cook pasta, uncovered, in large pot of boiling salted water over high heat, stirring occasionally, about 10 minutes for orecchiette or 5 to 8 minutes for shells, or until tender but firm to the bite. Drain, reserving ½ cup pasta cooking liquid. Add pasta and mint to pan of squash and toss over low heat for I to 2 minutes to blend flavors, adding a few tablespoons pasta liquid if mixture is too dry. Season to taste with salt and pepper and add more sugar, lemon juice, or oil if you like. Serve hot.

Sauces and Relishes

Most Middle Eastern sauces, unlike those in classic European cuisines, are not elaborate, yet they are equally important for people's enjoyment of their meals. In each country cooks use the foods at hand to create sauces, relishes, and condiments, from hot chutneys based on fresh or dried chilies to rich, mild sauces made from nuts.

Savory tomato sauce is central to the cuisines of the region, both as a component of a variety of stews and as an accompaniment for fish, meats, and stuffed vegetables. Tomato sauces might be thick or thin, mild or peppery, perfumed with herbs, or seasoned with spices, sautéed onions, or garlic.

Blends of herbs and garlic similar to the green sauces of Italy and southern France are popular partners for crunchy appetizers, like Chicken Pecan Bulgur Cakes with Cilantro Pesto (page 48). Some sauces, such as cold mixtures of yogurt and herbs, double as dips, appearing on the table at the beginning of a meal, to be enjoyed as an appetizer or added to whatever foods the diner chooses.

Every area has its own most-loved hot sauce, which accents many foods for those who crave zip. On the tables of my Yemenite in-laws, for example, a fiery medley of chilies and garlic known as *zehug* (see Hedva's Hot Pepper Relish, page 307) is a must.

In much of the Mideast, nut-based sauces are loved with seafood, chicken, and vegetables, as their richness enhances lean, delicate foods. One reason is availability—in some areas dairy products are not plentiful but there is an abundance of almonds, hazelnuts, pistachios, pine nuts, or walnuts. The nuts are ground to a creamy sauce, as in the celebrated Chicken in Walnut Garlic Sauce (page 49), a highlight of the Turkish table.

Bright colored pickles and a great selection of olives are also staples on Mideast tables. Whether someone is serving a grand assortment of meze or snacking on a quick sandwich, these prepared flavor enhancers are likely to be included. Pickles might be hot, salty, or sour but are rarely sweet. Cucumbers are pickled with garlic and hot pepper, with dill, or, Persian style, with tarragon vinegar. Several vegetables, like carrots, cucumbers, sweet peppers, and chilies, might be pickled together to make a lively medley.

To make pickles, pale vegetables are frequently combined with colorful ingredients to make them more attractive. Cauliflower becomes golden when pickled with turmeric. Cooks make turnips red by pickling them with slices of beets. These popular pickles of a bright fuchsia hue appear everywhere, from falafel stands to elegant restaurants to family tables.

Since ancient times, olives have flourished in the Middle East and olive trees have been treasured. One of the area's signature ingredients, olives are prized as appetizers, as accompaniments for other starters and as additions to salads. They garnish smooth, creamy foods like *labneh* (kefir cheese) and hummus (chickpea dip), as well as crunchy Middle Eastern diced salads. Wrinkled salt-cured black olives and flavorful kalamata olives are favorites, as are shatta olives, very hot green olives flavored with hot red pepper sauce; pickled green olives; and a variety of marinated green olives. Some have a rich texture from an olive oil marinade with herbs and lemon wedges, while others are very hot from marinating with chilies. Often green olives are labeled cracked, which doesn't mean they are damaged, but rather, they are slitted on one side to help the marinade penetrate; it also makes them easier to pit.

Basic Tomato Sauce

salsat tamatem

Tomato sauce is the most popular cooked sauce in the Mideast for vegetables, meats, and fish. Even when tomatoes are not available, people make a simple version from tomato paste, water, and sautéed onions and garlic. You can make it peppery, tangy with lemon, or delicately sweet with a pinch of sugar. To make a spicy version that's great with pasta dishes like *Koshari* (page 296) and with rice, vegetables, or chicken, flavor it generously with chilies and with cumin, allspice, coriander seed, or all three (see variation).

For a completely smooth sauce instead of a slightly chunky one, puree the finished sauce in a food processor or blender. You can keep the sauce for two days in the refrigerator, or you can freeze it.

◆ MAKES ABOUT 2 CUPS.

2 or 3 tablespoons extra-virgin olive oil, vegetable oil, or butter

1 onion, finely chopped

3 large garlic cloves, minced (optional)

2½ to 3 pounds ripe tomatoes, peeled, seeded, and finely chopped, or two 28-ounce cans tomatoes, drained and chopped

1 large sprig of thyme, or ½ teaspoon dried thyme (optional)

1 bay leaf (optional)

Salt and freshly ground black pepper

1 tablespoon tomato paste (optional)

½ to 1 teaspoon sugar (optional)

1 tablespoon fresh-squeezed lemon juice (optional)

3 tablespoons chopped Italian parsley or cilantro (optional)

Heat oil in large sauté pan, stew pan, or shallow saucepan. Add onion and sauté over medium heat until soft but not brown. Stir in garlic if you like and sauté for ½ minute. Stir in tomatoes, thyme, bay leaf if desired, salt, and pepper. Cook, uncovered, over medium-high heat for 10 to 20 minutes, or until tomatoes are soft and sauce is thick, stirring often. Add tomato paste if using and simmer for 5 more minutes. Discard bay leaf. Taste and adjust seasoning, adding sugar or lemon juice if you like. Sauce can be kept for two days in refrigerator, or can be frozen. Stir in any fresh herbs after reheating.

Spicy Tomato Sauce

Omit thyme, bay leaf, sugar, and lemon juice. Chop 2 to 3 jalapeño or serrano chilies or other small fresh hot peppers, removing ribs and seeds if you want less heat. Add chilies to pan with garlic. Add 1 teaspoon ground cumin and, if you like, 1 teaspoon ground coriander and/or ½ teaspoon ground allspice with tomatoes.

Turkish Tomato Pepper Sauce

domates buberli salcasi

Serve this savory, quick, easy-to-make sauce with Turkish Meatballs in Green Pepper Tomato Sauce (page 187), Persian Chickpea Beef Patties (page 186), or as an accompaniment for grilled or broiled chicken. For a meatless meal, I also like it with broiled eggplant slices, veggie burgers, or even tofu, with brown basmati rice or whole-wheat couscous.

◆ MAKES 4 OR 5 SERVINGS.

1½ pounds ripe tomatoes, peeled, seeded, and chopped, or one 28-ounce can tomatoes, drained and chopped

2 large garlic cloves, chopped

1 green or yellow bell pepper, halved, cored, seeded, and diced

1 cup water

Salt and freshly ground black pepper

1 tablespoon extra-virgin olive oil (optional)

2 to 3 teaspoons tomato paste (optional)

½ teaspoon sugar (optional)

Combine tomatoes, garlic, bell pepper, and water in saucepan or sauté pan and bring to a boil. Add salt and pepper and simmer, uncovered, over medium heat for 15 minutes, or until thickened, stirring occasionally. Add oil, tomato paste, and sugar if desired, for a richer flavor. Continue simmering over low heat until sauce thickens to your taste. Taste and adjust seasoning. Serve hot or warm.

Lemon Egg Sauce

terbiye

This tangy sauce is loved in Turkey and in other eastern Mediterranean cuisines. The classic version of the sauce curdles easily because the eggs are very sensitive to heat. To get around this problem, some cooks stabilize the eggs by whisking them with flour. The flour also helps thicken the sauce so that you can use fewer eggs. An even tastier solution that I learned from cooking teacher Pandora Randall is to make a quick roux of butter and flour to thicken the broth, and then to add the eggs to the sauce, as in this recipe. You can make the sauce base ahead and reheat it, and all you need to do before serving is heat the eggs and lemon juice in the sauce for a minute or two.

The sauce is sometimes flavored with garlic and accompanies fish, meat, vegetables, and stuffed grape leaves. Often it's used as a finishing touch for stews and soups of meat, fish, or vegetables, and then it is made from the cooking liquid.

◆ MAKES 4 TO 6 SERVINGS.

2 tablespoons butter

1 garlic clove, minced (optional)

2 tablespoons all-purpose flour

1½ cups chicken, meat, fish, or vegetable broth

Salt and freshly ground white or black pepper to taste

2 or 3 egg yolks, or 2 eggs

2 to 3 tablespoons fresh-squeezed lemon juice, or to taste

Melt butter in small heavy saucepan. Add garlic and stir over low heat for a few seconds. Add flour and cook over low heat, whisking, for 2 minutes, or until mixture is foamy but not brown. Remove from heat. Gradually whisk in broth. Bring to a boil over medium-high heat, whisking. Add salt and pepper and cook over low heat for 5 minutes, or until the sauce is thick enough to coat a spoon, whisking often. Remove from heat.

Whisk egg yolks or eggs in a bowl. Gradually whisk in about ½ cup of the sauce. Add 1 to 2 tablespoons lemon juice. Slowly pour mixture into pan of sauce, whisking constantly. Set pan over low heat and bring just to a simmer, whisking constantly. Taste, adjust seasoning, and add more lemon juice if you like. Serve hot.

Hedva's Hot Pepper Relish

zehug

For many people of Yemenite heritage, a meal is incomplete without *zehug*. Most often, *zehug* is simply put on the table before a meal and diners sample a little on bread to wake up their appetites for the soup that often follows. Many also stir a little *zehug* into their bowl of soup.

Unlike bottled hot sauces, *zehug* is a thick pepper puree, somewhat like Indonesian *sambal oelek* in texture. My sister-in-law Hedva Cohen got the recipe from her aunt Mazal Cohen, who was born in Yemen and spent her girlhood there. Hedva has taken over her mother's tradition of being the family's *zehug*-maker, providing jars for relatives who need some.

Zehug is also used to flavor fresh tomato puree served as a cold sauce. Some stir the hot relish into salads, or serve it alongside hummus for those who want extra zip. Hedva finds that a little *zehug* does wonders for plain yogurt as a snack or salad dressing.

Like Mexican hot sauces, *zehug* comes in red or green. The red type is usually made with fresh red chilies, while the green one includes cilantro and often green chilies. Hedva prefers dried chilies, which are red, for their flavor and convenience, and in this recipe the green *zehug* is dotted with red.

When making *zehug*, people always leave the seeds in the chilies. Cilantro, cumin, and garlic complement the chilies' heat. Some cooks also add ground cardamom, coriander, or cloves.

You can buy *zehug* in jars in the refrigerator case in Mideastern grocery stores, yet many Yemenite cooks prefer to make their own. It's easy to prepare in the blender, although Hedva finds it's even better when she makes it in a mortar with a pestle (see Note). Some people make *zehug* in large amounts, refrigerate enough for a few weeks' use, and freeze the rest.

◆ MAKES ABOUT I CUP, ABOUT
   8 TO 12 SERVINGS.

   6 to 7 dried small hot red peppers,
      such as chiles de arbol
   1 cup cilantro sprigs
   4 large garlic cloves, peeled
   1 tablespoon whole cumin seeds, freshly
      ground, or ground cumin
   2 or 3 tablespoons water, or more if needed
   ½ teaspoon salt, or to taste
   ¼ teaspoon freshly ground black pepper,
      or to taste

Soak hot peppers in lukewarm water for 10 minutes. Remove them and discard water. Remove caps from chilies but leave seeds inside.

Put chilies in blender or food processor with cilantro, garlic, and cumin. Add just enough water to allow you to blend the ingredients. Process until they become a paste. Season to taste with salt and pepper. Spoon into a clean jar, cover, and refrigerate.

Zehug in a mortar

Crush whole cumin seeds in the mortar to release their flavor. Add the garlic to the mortar and crush it. Add the remaining ingredients and continue working them in the mortar until they form a paste.

Fresh Chili Vinaigrette

khall bel filfil

Serve this peppery dressing with meat and poultry salads and legume dishes, like Egyptian Pasta and Lentil Casserole with Chili Tomato Sauce (page 296). It's also delicious with vegetables, such as steamed or boiled broccoli or green beans.

If you don't have fresh chilies, make a quick chili dressing by adding hot sauce or hot pepper relish such as *zehug* (above) to taste.

◆ MAKES ABOUT ½ CUP, ABOUT
   4 TO 8 SERVINGS.

   1 or 2 fresh jalapeño, serrano, or other fresh
      chilies, green or red, chopped
   1 large garlic clove, chopped
   ⅓ cup extra-virgin olive oil
   3 or 4 tablespoons fresh-squeezed lemon
      juice
   Salt and freshly ground black pepper to taste
   2 tablespoons finely chopped cilantro or
      Italian parsley

In blender or mini food processor, combine chilies and garlic and mince finely. Add oil, lemon juice, salt, and pepper and puree until dressing is well blended. Transfer to bowl and stir in cilantro. Taste and adjust seasoning. Serve at room temperature.

Fresh Peppery Tomato Puree

resek agvaniot harif

If you have made garlicky Yemenite hot pepper relish (zehug), it's perfect for flavoring purees of fresh tomatoes. Otherwise, substitute any hot sauce you like. If your hot sauce does not contain garlic or if you want more, add fresh minced garlic to the puree. Serve this puree with fried or baked eggplant, egg dishes, vegetables, as a dip with fresh pita, or any way that you would use salsa.

◆ MAKES ABOUT 12 SERVINGS.

    4 large, very ripe tomatoes,
       or 1½ to 2 pounds plum tomatoes
    2 to 4 tablespoons Hedva's Hot Pepper
       Relish (page 307), or hot sauce to taste
    2 garlic cloves, finely minced (optional)
    Salt to taste

Puree tomatoes in blender until very smooth, or grate them on the large holes of a grater. Transfer to bowl. Slowly stir in rel-

ish, tasting to see how hot you would like it. If you want, add garlic. Season with salt. Serve cold or at room temperature.

Garlic Sauce

toum biz-zayt

This is a favorite Lebanese sauce for grilled chicken or lamb. It's also delicious as a dip for raw vegetables and for flavoring cooked ones.

    The secret, according to some experts, is to pound the garlic in a mortar with a pestle and to add the olive oil drop by drop. Still, the fastest, easiest, and most practical way to make the tasty garlic sauce at home is to puree the ingredients in a blender, so the sauce resembles a thick vinaigrette. You can also make the sauce in a bowl with a whisk. If you'd like the sauce to be thicker and creamy, stir in a little mayonnaise, as directed below. Be sure to use very fresh garlic.

◆ MAKES ABOUT ¾ CUP.

    3 to 5 large garlic cloves, minced
    2 to 3 tablespoons mayonnaise (optional)
    ½ cup extra-virgin olive oil
    ¼ cup fresh-squeezed lemon juice
    Salt to taste

To make sauce in bowl: Mix garlic with mayonnaise, then gradually whisk in olive oil and lemon juice.

To make sauce in blender: Puree garlic with pinch of salt in blender, add mayonnaise, and blend briefly. With motor running, gradually add olive oil and lemon juice. Transfer to bowl.

Taste sauce and adjust seasoning. Refrigerate the sauce if making it ahead. Serve at room temperature.

Cilantro Pesto

salsa bel kizbarah

Garlic and cilantro often are used together in Middle Eastern marinades and sauces as well as in hot salsa-type relishes. To accompany grilled meats, some cooks set out a mixture of chopped garlic and cilantro for sprinkling over the meat. I like to combine the two in this pesto, which is savory but not hot, and serve it as a partner for grilled meats and fish. Like its basil cousin, this dairy-free pesto is delicious as a sandwich spread and for tossing with pasta, grains, and cooked vegetables. I serve the pecan pesto variation with Chicken Pecan Bulgur Cakes (page 48).

◆ MAKES ¾ CUP, ABOUT 8 SERVINGS.

6 to 8 medium garlic cloves

4 to 6 tablespoons pine nuts or walnuts

2 cups small cilantro sprigs, loosely packed

1 cup small Italian parsley sprigs, loosely packed

⅔ cup extra-virgin olive oil

1 teaspoon paprika

Salt and freshly ground black pepper to taste

Pinch cayenne pepper (optional)

Finely chop garlic in food processor. Add half the nuts, half the cilantro, and half the parsley and process until herbs are chopped. Remove mixture and chop remaining nuts, cilantro, and parsley. Return first mixture to processor. With blade turning, add olive oil. Scrape down sides and process until mixture is well blended. Transfer to bowl. Add paprika, salt, pepper, and cayenne to taste if you like; mix well.

Pecan Pesto

Substitute pecans for the other nuts.

Minty Green Sauce

Green sauce is made in many Mediterranean countries from whatever fresh herbs people have on hand, usually combined with olive oil and an onion, and often lemon juice as well. It might be embellished with a small amount of chopped olives, capers, pickles, or nuts. One of its customary uses is to brighten chicken or meat that was cooked in soup. This light, refreshing sauce adds a lively note to grilled or poached fish or chicken, and is excellent with fish cakes, like Herbed Seafood Patties (page 145). I also like to toss it with diced vegetables as a salad or combine it with grilled vegetables and chicken for a tasty sandwich filling.

◆ MAKES ABOUT 1 CUP, ABOUT 4 TO
   6 SERVINGS.

   2 medium garlic cloves, peeled
   ⅓ cup mint sprigs
   ⅓ cup small Italian parsley sprigs
   ½ cup diced mild onion
   4 or 5 tablespoons extra-virgin olive oil
   2 or 3 tablespoons fresh-squeezed
      lemon juice
   6 to 8 pitted green olives, diced (optional)
   Salt and freshly ground black pepper to taste

In food processor, chop garlic, add mint and parsley, and chop together finely. Add onion and pulse until chopped. Transfer to bowl.

Stir in 4 tablespoons oil, 2 tablespoons lemon juice, olives, salt, and pepper. Taste, and add more oil and lemon juice if needed.

Yogurt Garlic Sauce

In the Mideast and Afghanistan, people love yogurt seasoned with garlic and dried mint. It is popular with meat dishes, pasta, and vegetables, especially eggplant and squash. It tastes best if you use thick, creamy yogurt, but I like it made with low-fat and nonfat yogurt too. For authentic flavor, try making it with yogurt from a Greek or Middle Eastern market. When the yogurt sauce accompanies hot dishes, it is served at room temperature.

◆ MAKES 2 CUPS, 4 TO 6 SERVINGS

   2 cups plain yogurt, drained of any liquid
   2 medium-size, very fresh garlic cloves,
      very finely minced
   1 teaspoon dried mint
   Salt to taste

Mix yogurt with garlic, mint, and salt to taste. Serve cold or at room temperature.

Creamy Hot Yogurt Sauce

salsat al-laban

Yogurt gives sauces and soups a creamy texture and tangy flavor. To make sauces, cooks blend the yogurt with cornstarch so it won't separate during heating, then heat the mixture with flavorful broth. Armenian and Turkish cooks use the same technique to make soup.

People of the eastern Mediterranean, especially Palestinians and Jordanians, love this tangy sauce with vegetables and with chicken and lamb stews, using the sauce to enrich the cooking broths. A version of this sauce is used in the famous Jordanian specialty, *Mansaf* (page 202), which is made with liquefied dried yogurt called *jameed* for its distinctive flavor, although regular yogurt is often used as a substitute. If you're making the sauce with *jameed*, you probably won't need to add any salt.

The sauce is popular with stuffed zucchini and eggplant, but I find that it is also good with lightly cooked carrots, peas, or broccoli. Traditionally the sauce is made with rich, whole-milk yogurt, but you can also use a low-fat variety.

◆ MAKES 6 SERVINGS.

1½ cups plain yogurt, at room temperature, or liquefied *jameed*

1 tablespoon plus 1½ teaspoons cornstarch

1½ cups chicken, meat, or vegetable broth or stew's cooking liquid

1 tablespoon butter or vegetable oil

3 garlic cloves, minced

Salt and freshly ground black pepper to taste

Mix yogurt with cornstarch until blended. Slowly stir in broth.

Heat butter in heavy saucepan. Add garlic and cook over medium-low heat for about ½ minute, or until aromatic. Remove from heat. Stir in yogurt mixture and mix very well. Return to medium-low heat and cook until sauce is hot but not boiling, stirring constantly. Cook over low heat for 3 to 5 minutes, stirring, until sauce is smooth and thickened to your taste. Season to taste with salt and pepper. Serve hot.

Beet-red Turnip Pickles

lift makboos or torshy lift

In the Mideast, pickles, often called *torshy*, are a standard on the table, at home, and at restaurants. Pickle shops in the region are enticing places, with beautiful jars of pickles of many different colors. Especially striking in pickle shops in Turkey are the pickled whole red peppers stuffed with other pickled vegetables. One of the most popular pickles is made of turnips, which gain an attractive beet-red hue from sitting in the pickling solution with beets or with a little beet cooking liquid. (The beets used for this purpose are not usually served, although Middle Eastern cooks do pickle beets on their own.) The turnips might be simply brined with salted water, peppery from chilies, garlic-flavored, or tart from vinegar.

◆ MAKES ONE 6- TO 8-CUP JAR OF PICKLES.

1½ pounds turnips, preferably small

1 small beet, raw or cooked

2 garlic cloves (optional)

3 cups water

2 tablespoons salt

2 tablespoons white vinegar or white-wine vinegar

Scrub turnips well. Peel only if their peel is very tough. Cut turnips in ¼-inch slices or in sticks. Peel and slice beet. Alternate turnip and beet slices in a sterilized 6- to 8-cup jar. Add garlic cloves, if desired. Mix water and salt until salt is dissolved (see Note). Add vinegar. Pour enough of the liquid into jar to cover vegetables and to fill jar. If necessary, add more salted water, allowing 2 teaspoons salt for every cup. Cover tightly and let stand at room temperature. Taste to check if turnips are flavorful enough; they'll take at least 4 days or up to 2 weeks. Once pickles are ready, refrigerate them; they'll keep up to 3 weeks.

NOTE   For faster pickles, bring water and salt to a boil in small saucepan. Remove from heat and add vinegar.

Breads and Savory Pastries

Pita Bread   ◆   *Pita; Khoubz*

Whole-Wheat Pita   ◆   *Pita; Khoubz*

Sesame Herb Bread   ◆   *Manakeesh bi Zahtar*

Yemenite Layered Flatbreads   ◆   *Malawah*

Lebanese Meat and Pine Nut Pizzas   ◆   *Lahmajune or Lahm bi Ajine*

Onion Pizza with Soft Cheese   ◆   *Fatayer bi Jibne*

Fast Pita Pizzas with Peppers and Mushrooms   ◆   *Pizza Meheera*

Individual Spinach Pies with Walnuts   ◆   *Fatayers bi Sbaneck*

Calzone with Meat, Almonds, and Raisins   ◆   *Sambousek*

Feta Phyllo Turnovers with Chard   ◆   *Peynirli Pazili Böreği*

Savory Cheese Phyllo Fingers   ◆   *Peynirli Sigara Böreği*

Sesame Pita Crisps   ◆   *Pitot Prihot im Sumsum*

Since ancient times wheat has been revered in the Mideast and has long been used to make bread. Yeast was first used by Egyptian bakers to leaven bread more than 5,000 years ago.

Many of the region's breads are flatbreads, of which pocket pita is the best known. Pita bread is a staple on the Middle Eastern table and accompanies appetizers like hummus, tahini, and eggplant spreads as well as main courses. You'll find the best pita breads at Mediterranean or Middle Eastern markets or bakeries. Baking your own is another way to ensure freshness and to vary the flavors, as you can spice the breads with seeds or herbs. Pita is made from dough resembling pizza dough and is quick and easy to shape and bake.

A flatbread that's increasingly easy to find in many supermarkets is lavash or lavosh, a large thin bread that's wonderful for wrapping around such foods as grilled chicken and fresh vegetables to make a light, tasty sandwich. You'll likely find an assortment of lavash, including whole-wheat and seed-studded ones, in Armenian, Persian, and other Middle Eastern grocery stores. Use the soft, flexible lavash to make sandwiches, not the crisp lavash cracker bread.

A variety of thicker flatbreads without pockets are also popular in the Mideast, from Egypt and Turkey to Iran. You'll find some of them in North America as well, depending on the origin of the local Middle Eastern population. For examples, see page 4.

Flatbreads with a variety of pizzalike toppings are a favorite regional treat for appetizers, snacks, and quick meals. Yeast-risen dough is also made into turnovers filled with meat or vegetables. Meat fillings are sometimes spicy, sometimes sweetly accented with raisins and almonds, while meatless ones may

be enriched with cheese. Both kinds of filling might also be spiked with the tart flavors of pomegranate paste, sumac powder, or lemon juice.

When I lived in the Mideast, I became acquainted with delectable, savory filled pastries made of phyllo dough, which is believed to have been invented in Turkey. These scrumptious turnovers, known in Turkey as *beurreks* and in Israel as *bourekas*, could be considered the empanadas of the eastern Mediterranean. You can buy them at bakeries, in cafés, at restaurants, and at eateries that specialize in these pastries. Cheese, spinach, beef, or potato are the traditional fillings, but you can also find mushroom or eggplant *beurreks*, or even pizzalike mixtures of tomato and Parmesan cheese.

For many home cooks, *beurreks* are a popular choice for festive hors d'oeuvres, especially on holidays. The pastry forms luscious layers as it bakes, making these warm, aromatic, tempting treats the first items to disappear at parties. Phyllo dough is convenient because it comes ready-made, so you need only to prepare a filling. To shape *beurreks*, you simply cut phyllo sheets to the size you need, brush the dough with melted butter or olive oil, and fold it around the filling, then keep the pastries in the refrigerator or freezer, ready to bake when you need them. For tips on handling phyllo, see "Basics," page 375.

You can make phyllo appetizers in different shapes, such as strudels, fingers, snails, and wreaths. Triangles are the most practical shape for *beurreks* because they are easy to form and to serve; each makes an individual portion, so no cutting is required at serving time. People tell me the shaping technique is the same as in flag folding. If I ever need to fold a flag, I guess I'll know how to do it from folding my phyllo!

Pita Bread

pita; khoubz

In many homes in the Mideast, pita, also known as *khoubz*, appears on the table at just about every meal. Since freshness is a must for good pita, people buy it daily from bakeries that turn out the loaves in ovens resembling pizza ovens. To keep it even for one day, many put it in the freezer or they let extra pita dry to make salads like Fattoush (page 63). Because the dough is easy to mix and bakes rapidly, it's quick and simple to bake at home.

Some pita comes without pockets and is used for wrapping or for folding rather than for filling. This recipe makes pocket bread but if a pocket doesn't form in some of them, it will still be a pita and will taste good.

For a delicious accent, add nigella seeds, sometimes called black caraway, to the dough. My mother-in-law often did this and I love the taste and aroma they impart to the dough. You can find them at Middle Eastern markets. If you'd like to make sesame pita, dip each ball of dough in sesame seeds before rolling them into thin rounds.

Yeast dough develops better flavor if it rises slowly but if you need to speed up the rising, use two envelopes of yeast. Although classic pita does not contain oil, you can add a little for a slightly richer dough. The dough is simple to make by hand. For a faster method, use a food processor, following the first note at the end of the recipe.

◆ MAKES 8 PITA BREADS.

> 4 cups bread flour or all-purpose flour
> 1⅓ cups lukewarm water (105°F to 115°F)
> One ¼-ounce envelope active dry yeast,
>   or 2½ teaspoons active dry yeast,
>   or one ⅗-ounce cake fresh yeast
> 2 teaspoons salt
> 1 to 2 teaspoons vegetable oil (optional)
> 1 tablespoon nigella seeds (black caraway)
>   (optional)

Sift flour into bowl and make a well in center. Pour ½ cup lukewarm water into well. Sprinkle the dried yeast or crumble the fresh yeast over the water. If using fresh yeast, stir to blend. Let the yeast mixture stand for 10 minutes.

Stir to dissolve yeast. Add remaining water, salt, and oil and mix with ingredients in middle of well. Stir in flour and mix well, to obtain a fairly soft dough. When dough becomes difficult to mix with wooden spoon, mix in remaining flour by hand. Add nigella seeds. If dough is dry, add 1 tablespoon water. Knead dough by slapping it vigorously on a lightly floured work surface until dough is very smooth and elastic. If it is very sticky, flour it occasionally while kneading.

Transfer dough to large oiled bowl and turn dough over to oil its entire surface. Cover with a damp towel or plastic wrap and let rise in a warm place for 1½ hours, or until doubled in volume.

Knead dough again briefly on floured surface until smooth. Roll it to a thick log. With a floured knife, cut dough in 8 equal pieces. With cupped palms, roll each to a smooth ball on an unfloured surface; flour only if dough begins to stick. Put on floured board or other surface. Cover and let rise for about 20 minutes. Meanwhile, preheat oven to 500°F.

Lightly flour two baking sheets. Using floured rolling pin, roll 4 balls of dough on a lightly floured surface to 6-inch rounds, about ¼ inch thick. Try to keep them round, but do not worry if they are a little uneven. Transfer two rounds to each prepared baking sheet.

Bake for 3 minutes, or until just beginning to brown. Turn over and continue baking 2 to 3 minutes, until just firm but not brown. Repeat with remaining dough. If not serving pita immediately, let cool on racks and keep loaves wrapped tightly in plastic wrap or plastic bags; freeze those that will not be used within 2 days.

NOTE To make dough in a food processor: Sprinkle yeast over ½ cup lukewarm water in a bowl and leave for 10 minutes. Stir to dissolve yeast. In food processor, blend flour and salt briefly to mix them. Add remaining water and oil to yeast mixture. With blades of processor turning, gradually pour in yeast-liquid mixture. If dough is too dry to come together, add 1 tablespoon water and process again. Process for 1 minute to knead dough. Remove to work surface, sprin-kle with nigella seeds, and knead dough until they are blended in.

Baking on a pizza stone: If you have a pizza stone or oven tiles, you can heat them thoroughly in the oven and use them for baking the pita breads, following the method you use for pizza.

Whole-Wheat Pita

pita; khoubz

Flatbreads made from whole-wheat flour are common in several Mideastern countries. For baking at home, the dough is easiest to handle if you use half whole-wheat and half white flour. This recipe makes substantial flatbreads without pockets. If you prefer, you can shape and bake them the same way as white pita breads (see recipe above) to make pocket pitas.

◆ MAKES 8 PITA BREADS.

2 cups whole-wheat flour

2 cups bread flour or all-purpose flour

Two ¼-ounce envelopes active dry yeast (5 teaspoons)

1¼ to 1½ cups lukewarm water (105°F to 115°F)

½ teaspoon sugar (optional)

2 teaspoons vegetable oil

2 teaspoons salt

Sift whole-wheat flour and bread flour into large bowl and make a well in center. Sprinkle yeast into well. Pour ½ cup water over yeast and sprinkle with sugar if desired. Let stand for 10 minutes. Stir to dissolve yeast. Add ¾ cup water, oil, and salt to well and mix briefly. Stir in flour, to obtain a fairly soft dough. When dough becomes difficult to mix with a wooden spoon, mix in remaining flour by hand. If dough is dry, add more water by tablespoons. Knead dough by slapping it vigorously on a lightly floured working surface until dough is very smooth and elastic. If it is very sticky, flour it occasionally while kneading.

Transfer dough to an oiled bowl and turn dough over to oil its entire surface. Cover with a damp towel or plastic wrap and let rise in a warm place for 1½ hours, or until doubled in volume.

Knead dough again briefly on a floured surface until smooth. Roll it to a thick log. With a floured knife, cut dough in 8 equal pieces. With cupped palms, roll each piece to a smooth ball, flouring only if dough begins to stick. Put balls of dough on a floured board or other surface. Cover and let rise for 20 minutes. Preheat oven to 450°F.

Lightly flour two baking sheets. With a floured rolling pin, roll 4 balls of dough on a lightly floured surface to 6-inch rounds, about ⅜ inch thick. Transfer two rounds to each prepared baking sheet. Prick lightly with a fork.

Bake for 5 minutes, or until just beginning to brown. Turn over and continue baking for 3 or 4 minutes, until just firm but not brown. Repeat with remaining dough. If not serving pita immediately, cool on racks and wrap tightly in plastic wrap or in plastic bags; freeze those that will not be used within two days.

Sesame Herb Bread

manakeesh bi zahtar

Zahtar bread, a flatbread with a savory sesame-and-herb topping, is a favorite Middle Eastern snack and is also loved for breakfast with olives and *labneh* (kefir cheese). One of the best examples I've had came from an Arab bakery called Abulafia in Jaffa, where the bread had many little depressions in its top to hold plenty of zahtar and olive oil.

Bake zahtar into pizza dough for this irresistible flatbread (see below), or sprinkle it on the tomatoes when making your favorite pizza. Make a simple version of zahtar, following the recipe below; for baking it on the bread, there's no need to toast the sesame seeds. You can also use 3 tablespoons zahtar mix from a Middle Eastern store or of homemade zahtar, if you've already made some for your pantry (see "The Mideast Pantry," page 14). For a fancier zahtar, add 1 tablespoon finely chopped pistachios to any version of the blend.

This dough is a snap to prepare in the food processor but it doesn't take long to make by hand either. Another popular way to make zahtar bread when time is very short is to start with purchased pita or other flatbread. Simply mix zahtar with olive oil to taste, spread it on the bread, and toast it lightly for a tempting treat.

♦ MAKES 4 SERVINGS.

PIZZA DOUGH:

> One ¼-ounce envelope active dry yeast, or 1 cake fresh yeast
>
> ¾ cup lukewarm water (105°F to 115°F)
>
> 2 cups bread flour or all-purpose flour, preferably unbleached
>
> 1 teaspoon salt
>
> 1½ tablespoons olive oil

TOPPING:

> 2 tablespoons sesame seeds
>
> 2 teaspoons dried thyme
>
> ½ teaspoon salt
>
> ½ teaspoon freshly ground black pepper, or to taste
>
> 2 tablespoons extra-virgin olive oil
>
> ½ teaspoon fresh-squeezed lemon juice (optional)

To make dough in food processor: Sprinkle dry yeast or crumble fresh yeast over ¼ cup lukewarm water in a cup and let stand for 10 minutes. Stir until smooth. In food processor, process flour and salt briefly to mix them.

Add remaining ½ cup water and oil to yeast mixture. With blades of processor turning, gradually pour yeast-liquid mixture into flour mixture. Process until mixture becomes a dough. If dough is too dry to come together, add 1 tablespoon water and process again. Process about 1 minute to knead dough.

To make dough by hand: Sift flour into a bowl and make a well in center. Sprinkle dry yeast or crumble fresh yeast into well. Pour ¼ cup water over yeast and let stand for 10 minutes. Stir until smooth. Add remaining ½ cup water, oil, and salt and mix with ingredients in middle of well. Stir in flour and mix well to obtain a fairly soft dough. If dough is dry, add 1 tablespoon water. Knead dough, slapping it on work surface, until it is smooth and elastic. If it is very sticky, flour it occasionally while kneading.

Lightly oil a medium bowl. Add dough; turn to coat entire surface. Cover with plastic wrap or a lightly dampened towel. Let dough rise in a warm draft-free area about 1 hour, or until doubled in volume.

To make topping: Mix sesame seeds with thyme, salt, and pepper. Combine zahtar with olive oil and lemon juice and mix well.

Preheat oven to 450°F. Lightly oil two baking sheets. Divide dough in 4 pieces. Roll each to a 7- or 8-inch round slightly over ⅛ inch thick. Put on prepared baking sheets. Spread 1 tablespoon plus 1 teaspoon topping evenly over each pizza, leaving a ½-inch border. Let breads rise for about 15 minutes.

Bake breads for 8 minutes, or until dough is golden brown and firm. Serve warm. If not serving breads immediately, cool them on racks. Wrap them tightly in plastic wrap or plastic bags.

NOTE The dough makes enough for 4 individual pizzas or 1 larger pizza. To make pizza dough for 6 to 8 servings, follow recipe above, using these proportions:

- One ¼-ounce envelope active dry yeast, or 1 cake fresh yeast
- 1 cup plus 2 tablespoons lukewarm water
- 3 cups bread flour or all-purpose flour
- 1½ teaspoons salt
- 2 tablespoons olive oil

Yemenite Layered Flatbreads

malawah

When he was growing up in the Middle East, my husband loved his mother's delicious *malawah*, which frequently appeared on the supper table. The increasing popularity of *malawah* in restaurants is yet another testimony to America's growing fondness for Middle Eastern food. The Yemenite specialty is now available in some Middle Eastern and Jewish stores frozen and ready to be baked.

Malawah is a flatbread that acquires a flaky texture from a special technique for preparing the dough. Traditionally, it is a simple, unleavened flour and water dough folded with *samnah* (clarified butter or ghee) and panfried. Today some lighten the dough with baking powder, enrich it with egg, or substitute margarine or butter for the *samnah*. Yakir always liked his *malawah* topped with sugar, honey, or jam, but many prefer a savory partner, like Middle Eastern cheese or a fried egg. His brother Prachya prefers *malawah* served the traditional way, with Fresh Peppery Tomato Puree (page 309) and Slow-cooked Brown Eggs (page 118).

Malawah resembles rich versions of an Indian flatbread, paratha. In Turkey I found a similar skillet bread flavored with tahini called *tahinli katmer.*

Note that you need to make the dough ahead and keep it overnight before panfrying it. You can freeze the shaped dough and thaw it before sautéing it. *Malawah* are best when fresh from the frying pan but if you've cooked some ahead, you can wrap and refrigerate them, and reheat them uncovered in a 350°F oven for 10 or 15 minutes.

♦ MAKES 6 TO 8 GENEROUS SERVINGS.

- ¾ cup homemade *samnah* (see "The Mideast Pantry," page 17), ghee, butter, or margarine (for making dough), plus about 2 tablespoons (for panfrying)
- 4¼ cups all-purpose flour, plus a few tablespoons if needed
- 1 teaspoon baking powder
- 1¾ teaspoons salt
- 1 tablespoon vegetable oil
- 1 large egg (optional)
- 1½ to 1¾ cups water

If making your own *samnah*, make it several hours or a day ahead so it is well chilled. Combine flour, baking powder, and salt in food processor and process to blend. Add oil, egg, if using, and 1¼ cups water; if you're not adding an egg, use 1½ cups water. Process with on/off turns to mix. With motor running, gradually add enough of remaining water so mixture comes together to a smooth, fairly stiff dough. It will be sticky. If it is very sticky, add a few more tablespoons flour and process briefly to blend it in.

Remove dough from processor. Knead dough well by slapping it vigorously on a work surface and removing it from surface with rubber spatula. Divide in 6 or 8 pieces, depending on how large you want your *malawah*. Knead each one with a slapping motion until smooth. Roll each in your palm to a ball. Put on an oiled plate or tray, cover, and refrigerate for 4 hours or up to overnight.

Oil work surface and rolling pin. Let ¾ cup samnah stand at room temperature until very soft but not melted. Roll out 1 ball of dough as thin as possible, so you can almost see through it, to about a 10- to 12-inch square. If dough tears, simply press it together. Spread dough with 1½ tablespoons samnah (if you've made 8 portions), or 2 tablespoons (if you've made 6). Roll as for a jelly roll. Flatten the roll slightly with your knuckles and roll this flattened rope in a snail shape, like a thin cinnamon roll. Put it on a plate. Continue with remaining dough. Cover these dough spirals and refrigerate overnight or up to 2 days.

To panfry the *malawah*, use a heavy 8-inch skillet for smaller ones or a 9-inch skillet for larger ones. Set a spiral of dough on a lightly oiled plate. Oil your hands lightly and flatten it to a round as large as the skillet. Heat 1 teaspoon ghee in skillet and add round of dough. Cover and fry over medium-high heat for 30 seconds, then over medium-low heat for about 5 minutes per side or until brown on both sides and cooked through. If you want to serve all the *malawah* at the same time, keep them warm on a baking sheet in a low oven while panfrying the rest. Serve hot.

Lebanese Meat and Pine Nut Pizzas

lahmajune *or* lahm bi ajine

Ground lamb is the topping of choice for these pizzas, but you can use beef or substitute chicken or turkey to make the pizza lighter. In its simplest form, the topping is a mixture of meat, onions, salt, and pepper. Other favorite flavors are garlic, parsley, nutmeg, cinnamon, allspice, or blends of sweet and sometimes hot spices.

Some bakers make the base from pie dough instead of yeast-leavened pizza dough.

If you want to make your own pizza dough but need to bake the pizzas in a short time, use fast-rising yeast and let the dough rise while you prepare the topping ingredients. Since this is a thin-crust pizza, the dough will still be fine even if it does not double in volume. For a quicker option, you can use prepared pizza dough or bread dough or a ready-made pizza shell. Serve these individual pizzas as a main course or party snack or in wedges as an appetizer.

◆ MAKES 4 SERVINGS.

Pizza Dough (page 320)

8 ounces lean ground lamb (1 cup)

1 tablespoon tomato paste

1 medium onion, minced

3 large garlic cloves, minced

½ teaspoon salt, or to taste

½ teaspoon freshly ground black pepper, or to taste

½ teaspoon Seven Spices blend (page 13) or ground allspice, or to taste

½ teaspoon Aleppo pepper or pinch cayenne (optional)

8 ounces ripe tomatoes, peeled, seeded, and finely chopped, or one 8-ounce can diced tomatoes, drained and chopped smaller

⅓ cup finely chopped Italian parsley

⅓ cup pine nuts

1 to 2 tablespoons extra-virgin olive oil

Make dough and let rise in bowl for 1 hour.

To make topping: In bowl, thoroughly mix meat with tomato paste, onion, garlic, ½ teaspoon salt, ½ teaspoon black pepper, spice blend, and Aleppo pepper if you like. Add tomatoes, parsley, and pine nuts and mix well. Broil a teaspoon of the mixture on a piece of foil until cooked through and taste it for seasoning. Add more salt, pepper, and spice to mixture if needed.

Lightly oil two baking sheets. Divide dough in 4 pieces. Roll each to a 7- or 8-inch round slightly more than ⅛ inch thick. Put on prepared baking sheets. Spread topping evenly but gently over pizza with back of spoon, leaving a ½-inch border. Press lightly so topping adheres and sprinkle it with oil.

Preheat oven to 400°F. Let pizzas rise for about 15 minutes. Bake for 18 minutes, or until dough is golden brown and firm and meat is cooked through. Serve hot.

Onion Pizza with Soft Cheese

fatayer bi jibne

You can often find an array of Lebanese and Armenian pizzas at Middle Eastern markets but the best ones are those baked fresh. At a small Israeli-Arab bakery called Bishtawi Bakery in Akko I was impressed by the selection of scrumptious pizzas. Many people from the neighborhood brought their own toppings of cheese or vegetables, shaped their pizzas using the bakery's dough and baked it in its wood-fired oven. This recipe is inspired by a pizza made with *baladi* cheese that I enjoyed there.

The pizza features slowly stewed onions paired with tender, delicate cheese and a sprinkling of herbs. Traditionally soft or semisoft cheeses are used. Usually they melt just a little during baking, without becoming runny. I add the cheese when the pizza is nearly ready, so it comes out warm but not dry.

A very mild feta, such as French feta, marries well with the onions but there are plenty of other options. Middle Eastern chefs often use *ackawi*, a soft but sliceable cheese that tends to be less salty than feta. Depending on its flavor, some cooks soak thick slices of the cheese in water overnight to remove the excess salt. Another popular option is a milder cheese called "sweet cheese" sold at some Middle Eastern markets; it's flavored with a little salt, not sugar. Some good substitutes for these cheeses are thin slices of fresh mozzarella, fresh goat cheese, or *panela*, a tasty, semisoft, white Mexican cheese that's available at many supermarkets. For a delicate pizza, gently spread a thin layer of ricotta on the dough just before topping it with one of the salty cheeses.

♦ MAKES 2 PIZZAS, 6 TO 8 SERVINGS.

4 to 6 ounces mild cheese, such as *ackawi, panela,* mild feta, fresh goat cheese, or fresh mozzarella

Pizza dough for 6 to 8 servings (page 320, variation of recipe)

4 to 5 tablespoons extra-virgin olive oil

3 large onions, halved and cut in thin slices

Salt and freshly ground black pepper

1 to 2 teaspoons zahtar (see "The Mideast Pantry," page 13), dried thyme, or dried oregano

If using *ackawi* cheese, taste it; if it's too salty, cut it in I-inch slices and soak in a bowl of cold water for 4 hours or up to overnight.

Make dough. While dough is rising in bowl, prepare topping: Heat 3 tablespoons oil in skillet over low heat. Add onions, salt, and pepper. Cover and cook over medium-low heat about 20 minutes, or until very tender, stirring occasionally.

Lightly oil two baking sheets. Knead dough briefly, divide in two pieces, and put each on a prepared baking sheet. With oiled hands, pat each portion of dough into a 10-inch circle, with rims slightly higher than centers.

Preheat oven to 425°F. Meanwhile, let pizzas rise for about 15 minutes. Brush dough lightly with oil. Bake for 10 minutes.

While pizza is baking, cut cheese in strips about ¼ inch wide; if it doesn't slice neatly, crumble or mash it finely instead. Set cheese slices on dough or crumble it over top. Gently and evenly spoon onion mixture over cheese, leaving a ½-inch border. Sprinkle lightly with zahtar and drizzle with a little more oil. Bake for 7 more minutes, or until dough is golden brown and just firm. Serve hot or warm.

Fast Pita Pizzas with Peppers and Mushrooms

pizza meheera

Friends of mine in the Mideast prepare this as a family supper dish, as it's very easy to make and especially popular with children. You can use pita that's no longer fresh. Heating it in the oven with a savory topping gives it new life.

Any pizza topping is good, as long as you don't use too much of any wet ingredient, which would make the pita soggy and might leak through it. Spread tomato sauce in a thin layer and if you use fresh tomatoes, top your pizza with only a few thin slices, preferably of a meaty kind like plum tomatoes. Because these pizzas bake very briefly, just to warm the ingredients, it's best to sauté most

PIZZA, MIDDLE EASTERN STYLE

When I'm looking for tasty ways to vary my pizzas, I turn to the cuisine of the Middle East. Lebanese, Turkish, and Armenian bakeries proudly present their *lahmajune* or *lahm bi ajine*, with meat toppings. People in the region don't call their flatbreads with savory toppings pizzas, and they don't taste like Italian pizza, but they are made by the same principle. You can purchase them at Middle Eastern markets and bakeries but they are easy to prepare at home from a simple bread dough that you can make quickly in a food processor (page 320).

Unlike American pizzas, the toppings have a concentrated flavor and thus are spread on the dough in a thin layer. This allows the pizza to bake quickly and prevents the crust from becoming soggy. Health-conscious diners prefer the lighter toppings because often they produce a leaner pizza.

Lebanese pizza toppings generally do not contain cheese. Often the dough is simply spread with a blend of olive oil and the herb-sesame blend zahtar. When cheese is included, it's generally feta or goat cheese combined with olive oil and onions, like in Onion Pizza with Soft Cheese (page 323).

Another traditional topping is ground lamb or beef flavored with onions, garlic, tomatoes, and plenty of flat-leaf parsley. Some enrich the filling with butter, *samnah* (Middle Eastern ghee or clarified butter), or tahini or accent it with lemon juice, vinegar, yogurt, or sour pomegranate syrup as well as sweet spices. Lebanese bakers like to add pine nuts, which contribute a lovely flavor (see recipe, page 322).

vegetables like onions, peppers, mushrooms, eggplant, or zucchini, before putting them on the pita. Naturally, if you have grilled or sautéed vegetables on hand, you'll get this pizza on the table even more quickly.

MAKES 4 SERVINGS.

2½ to 3 tablespoons extra-virgin olive oil

1 small yellow, green, or red bell pepper, halved, cored, seeded, and cut in strips

6 ounces mushrooms, sliced

1 teaspoon dried thyme or zahtar

Salt and freshly ground black pepper

¾ cup thick tomato sauce

2 garlic cloves, minced

¼ teaspoon hot red pepper flakes, or to taste

4 pita breads

3 to 4 tablespoons grated Parmesan or *kashkaval* cheese, or ⅓ cup finely diced feta or *halloumi* cheese

Preheat oven to 400°F. Heat 2 tablespoons oil in skillet. Add bell pepper and sauté for 5 minutes over medium heat. Add mushrooms and thyme. Sauté over medium-high heat about 2 minutes, or until vegetables are nearly tender, stirring occasionally. Season to taste with salt and pepper. Mix tomato sauce with garlic and hot pepper flakes in bowl. Taste sauce and adjust seasoning.

Carefully split each pita bread in two rounds. Set them on baking sheets in a single layer, crust side down. Spread each with 3 tablespoons tomato sauce. Top with pepper-mushroom mixture. Sprinkle with cheese, then with a little oil. Bake for about 10 minutes, or until hot and Parmesan or *kashkaval* cheese melts; feta and *halloumi* will soften. Serve hot or warm.

Individual Spinach Pies with Walnuts

fatayers bi sbaneck

Like Italian calzone, these filled pastries are usually made with yeast dough, although sometimes a pastry resembling pie dough is used instead. Like Jewish hamantaschen, they are often shaped like three-corner turnovers, but a faster, easier way to shape them is to fold them in half-moons.

You'll find the dough easiest to roll and shape if you make it a day ahead and refrigerate it. There's no need to let the shaped pastries rise before baking them.

The filling usually has tart flavorings—lemon juice, sumac, pomegranate seeds or paste, or some combination of these. Richer fillings include chopped walnuts or pine nuts. Besides spinach, people make fillings from other greens like kale or cabbage, from potatoes, or from ground beef or lamb mixed with onions.

MAKES ABOUT 24 PASTRIES.

YEAST DOUGH:

¾ cup lukewarm water (105°F to 115°F), or more if needed

One ¼-ounce envelope active dry yeast (2½ teaspoons)

1 tablespoon sugar

About 3¼ cups all-purpose flour

1½ teaspoons salt

⅓ cup vegetable oil

2 large eggs

SPINACH WALNUT FILLING:

One 12- to 16-ounce bunch spinach, stems removed, or one 10-ounce bag spinach leaves, rinsed and patted dry

¼ cup vegetable oil

1 onion, preferably sweet, finely chopped

1 teaspoon salt, or to taste

Freshly ground black pepper to taste

1 to 2 tablespoons fresh-squeezed lemon juice, or to taste

1 teaspoon sumac, or to taste (optional)

⅓ to ½ cup walnuts, finely chopped

To make dough: Pour ¼ cup lukewarm water into small bowl. Sprinkle with yeast and 1 teaspoon sugar. Let mixture stand for 10 minutes, or until foamy.

Mix 3 cups flour with salt in large bowl or in bowl of mixer with dough hook. Make a well in center of flour mixture and to it add yeast mixture, remaining ½ cup water, oil, eggs, and remaining 2 teaspoons sugar. Mix ingredients with dough hook or with your hands until they come together to a soft dough, adding more water by tablespoons if

needed. If using mixer, beat dough at medium speed until very smooth, adding more flour as necessary if dough is too sticky.

If making dough by hand, knead dough on lightly floured surface, adding flour as necessary to keep it from sticking, until smooth.

Form dough into a ball, put it in an oiled bowl, and turn to coat it with oil. Cover with plastic wrap. Let rise in a warm place for 1 hour, or until double in bulk. If you like, refrigerate dough overnight before shaping pastries.

To make the filling: Chop spinach very fine. Heat 2 tablespoons oil in large sauté pan. Add onion and sauté over medium-low heat for 3 minutes to soften slightly. Add spinach, salt, and pepper and cook over medium heat for 3 minutes, or until spinach is just wilted, stirring often. Transfer to bowl and let cool. Add lemon juice, sumac if you like, walnuts, and remaining oil. Taste and adjust seasoning.

Lightly grease two or three baking sheets. Cut dough in 4 equal parts; return 3 parts to refrigerator. Shape fourth part in a ball. Roll it on a lightly floured surface until it is about ⅛ inch thick. Cut in 4-inch rounds, reserving scraps.

Put 2 or 3 teaspoons filling in center of one round. To make three-corner pastries, bring up dough from three sides of round and pinch it above filling to form a triangle, leaving the very top, where the three parts meet, slightly open so the filling is visible, if you like. Alternatively, fold the round in half around filling, pinching edges together to form a half-moon. Repeat with remaining dough and filling. Fill and fold each round before shaping more, to prevent the moist filling from leaking out. Put pastries on prepared baking sheets, spacing them about 1½ inches apart.

Preheat oven to 400°F. Bake for 20 minutes, or until bottoms of pastries are golden brown. If top isn't brown enough, broil briefly.

If you like, prepare more pastries from dough scraps. Serve warm or at room temperature.

Calzone with Meat, Almonds, and Raisins

sambousek

When I lived in the Mideast I was glad to discover these tasty turnovers. They are related to the samosas of India, although they also resemble Russian piroshki, Latin American empanadas, and Italian calzone. These pastries are a specialty of Iraq, but Egyptian, Lebanese, and Israeli cooks are also aficionados of these savory snacks.

Fillings of meat and of cheese are the most popular. The choice meat is lamb but many use beef or a mixture of both, while some in Lebanon use pork. Cooks brown the ground meat with onions and sometimes add sweet or pungent spices. The filling in this recipe is seasoned lightly with hot spices and accented with the sweetness of raisins and almonds.

Cheese fillings generally feature feta, grated *kashkaval,* or Parmesan cheese mixed with a mild ricotta-like cheese. Creative cooks have also come up with fillings made of fish, eggplant, spinach, and fruit-studded rice, as well as sweet fillings for dessert *sambouseks.*

Bread dough or an enriched yeast dough forms the envelope, although many opt for simple pie dough instead. My friend Lior Moore, an Israeli native whose husband is of Iraqi origin, makes hers from puff pastry and a fried-onion-enhanced filling of chicken, chickpeas, or mashed potatoes.

As with numerous traditional pastries, the time-honored way to cook *sambouseks* is to deep-fry them. Today many people bake them instead for an easier-to-make, lighter pastry. These make terrific party treats or hearty appetizers, or they can be served as a main course with a salad of diced vegetables.

◆ MAKES 35 TO 40 TURNOVERS.

YEAST DOUGH:
    ¼ cup lukewarm water (105°F to 115°F)
    One ¼-ounce envelope active dry yeast
       (2½ teaspoons)
    2 teaspoons sugar
    About 3¼ cups all-purpose flour
    1½ teaspoons salt
    ¾ cup lukewarm milk or water, or more if
       needed

6 tablespoons melted butter or vegetable oil

1 large egg

1 egg, beaten with a pinch of salt, for glaze

FILLING:

2 tablespoons vegetable oil

2 large onions, minced

8 ounces lean ground beef

½ teaspoon ground allspice

½ teaspoon ground cumin

½ teaspoon curry powder

¼ teaspoon cayenne pepper, or to taste

Salt and freshly ground black pepper

⅓ cup raisins

⅓ cup slivered almonds, coarsely chopped

To make dough: Pour ¼ cup lukewarm water into small bowl. Sprinkle with yeast and 1 teaspoon sugar. Let mixture stand for 10 minutes, or until it is foamy.

Mix 3 cups flour with salt in large bowl or in bowl of mixer with dough hook. Make a well in center of flour mixture and add yeast mixture, ¾ cup milk, butter, egg, and remaining teaspoon sugar. Mix ingredients with dough hook, wooden spoon, or with your hands until they come together to a fairly soft dough, adding more milk or water by tablespoons if needed.

If using mixer, beat dough at medium speed for 10 minutes, or until smooth, adding more flour as necessary if dough is too sticky. If making dough by hand, knead it on a lightly floured surface, adding more flour as necessary to keep it from sticking, for 10 minutes, or until smooth.

Form dough into a ball, put it in an oiled bowl, and turn to coat it with oil. Cover with plastic wrap. Let rise in a warm place for 1 to 1½ hours, or until it doubles in bulk. Knead it again lightly. Cover and refrigerate overnight.

To make filling: Heat oil in heavy medium skillet. Add onions and sauté over medium heat for 10 minutes, or until golden brown. Add beef, allspice, cumin, curry powder, cayenne, salt, and pepper. Sauté about 10 minutes, or until beef browns lightly and is cooked through, stirring often. Add raisins and almonds. Transfer to bowl. Taste and adjust seasoning. Cool, cover, and refrigerate until ready to use.

Lightly grease two or three baking sheets. Cut dough in 4 equal parts; return 3 parts to refrigerator. Shape fourth part in a ball. Roll it on a lightly floured surface until it is about ⅛ inch thick. With a 3-inch cutter, stamp out rounds; reserve scraps.

Brush each round of dough lightly with water. Place 1½ teaspoons filling in center of each round. Fold in half to enclose filling. Pinch edges together well. Arrange turnovers 1½ inches apart on prepared baking sheets. Cover with a lightly dampened towel and let rise in a warm place for 15 minutes. Continue with remaining dough and filling. Knead dough scraps together and use to shape more turnovers.

Preheat oven to 400°F. Brush turnovers with egg glaze. Bake for 15 minutes, or until golden brown. Serve hot or warm.

Feta Phyllo Turnovers with Chard

peynirli pazili böreği

Beurreks, Turkish pastries filled with greens, cheeses, or meats, are loved around the Mideast. Greens are used on their own or enriched with cheese—either a mild creamy one, a pungent feta type, or a mixture of both, as in this recipe. If you prefer, make the filling with Gruyère or Swiss cheese instead of feta, or substitute ⅓ cup Parmesan.

Beurreks come in rounds, half-moons, finger shapes, and triangles. The filling might be folded into phyllo dough or enclosed in pastry resembling pie dough and baked. Some cooks roll the filling inside a simple dough resembling egg-roll wrappers and fry their *beurreks* instead.

These *beurreks* are convenient for entertaining because you can assemble them ahead and bake them when you need them. Cover them tightly with plastic wrap and refrigerate them on baking sheets or on plates for one or two days; or freeze them, tightly covered, on baking sheets.

◆ MAKES ABOUT 25 PASTRIES,
  OR 8 APPETIZER SERVINGS.

¾ pound phyllo sheets (about 15 sheets)

12 to 16 ounces chard, stems discarded, leaves rinsed

2 tablespoons extra-virgin olive oil

½ cup minced onion

Salt and freshly ground black pepper

3 ounces feta cheese, finely crumbled (about ¾ cup)

¼ cup ricotta cheese or farmer cheese

1 large egg

½ to ⅔ cup melted butter, olive oil, or a mixture of both (for brushing dough)

About 2 teaspoons sesame seeds (optional, for sprinkling)

If phyllo sheets are frozen, thaw them in refrigerator 8 hours or overnight. Remove sheets from refrigerator 2 hours before using; leave them in their package.

Cut chard leaves in 3 or 4 pieces. Cook them in large saucepan of boiling salted water, uncovered, over medium-high heat for 3 to 4 minutes, or until wilted, stirring occasionally. Drain, rinse with cold water, and squeeze to remove as much liquid as possible. Chop chard finely with a knife.

Heat 2 tablespoons oil in saucepan. Add onion and cook over medium-low heat for 5 minutes, or until soft but not brown, stirring occasionally. Add chard, salt, and pepper and heat, stirring, for 2 minutes to blend flavors. Transfer to bowl and let cool. Add feta and ricotta cheeses, egg, and salt and pepper to taste.

Remove phyllo sheets from their package and spread them on a dry towel. With a sharp knife, cut stack in half lengthwise to form two stacks of sheets of about 16 by 7 inches. Immediately cover phyllo with plastic wrap. Work with only one sheet at a time, keeping remaining sheets covered so they do not dry out.

Remove one pastry sheet. Brush it lightly with butter and fold it in half lengthwise, so it measures about 16 by 3½ inches. Dab it lightly with melted butter. Place about 2 teaspoons filling at one end of strip. Fold end of strip diagonally over filling to form a triangle and dab it lightly with butter. Continue folding it over and over, keeping it in a neat triangular shape after each fold, until you reach end of strip. Brush sheet lightly with butter before last fold to stick triangle together. Set pastry on lightly oiled baking sheet. Shape more triangles with remaining filling. Brush tops lightly with butter.

Preheat oven to 350°F. If you like, brush pastries again with butter. Sprinkle with sesame seeds if using. Bake for 15 to 18 minutes, or until golden brown. Serve warm (not hot) or at room temperature.

Savory Cheese Phyllo Fingers

peynirli sigara böreği

The charm of these popular pastries is their rich, layered dough and flavorful, cheesy filling. Cigar- or finger-shaped pastries are one of the most popular forms of cheese-filled *beurreks*, both at home and at Turkish restaurants. Another attractive way to make cheese *beurreks* is to roll the filling in a larger piece of phyllo into a thin strudel or rope shape, then wind this phyllo rope around itself into a spiral-shaped pastry, like a loosely rolled cinnamon roll.

Cigar-shaped *beurreks* can be baked, pan-fried, or deep-fried. Some like their phyllo buttery, while others prefer mild olive oil or margarine. For frying the fingers as crisp hors d'oeuvres, the dough is not brushed with oil; instead, cooks brush a little water at the end of the filled pastry to seal it.

The filling is easy to make. Choose the balance of cheeses according to your taste— pungent or mild. In the Mideast the most popular cheese for fillings is a feta type or a semisoft, sliceable cheese like *ackawi*, although some also use grating cheeses similar to Swiss or Gruyère. Make your own fillings out of any of the cheeses described in Onion Pizza with Soft Cheese (page 323), or combine feta with a bland cheese like farmer cheese or ricotta, as in this recipe.

You can shape these pastries and freeze them, then bake them without thawing. Allow about 5 extra minutes for them to heat through.

♦ MAKES ABOUT 15 TO 18 PASTRIES.

½ pound phyllo dough (about 8 to 10 sheets)

¼ cup farmer cheese or ricotta cheese

¾ cup finely crumbled feta cheese or grated Gruyère, Swiss, or *kashkaval* cheese, or half feta and half grated cheese

1 large egg, beaten lightly

1 tablespoon chopped fresh dill, or 1 teaspoon dried dill

1 to 2 tablespoons chopped Italian parsley (optional)

Salt (optional) and freshly ground black pepper to taste

⅓ to ½ cup melted butter, mild olive oil, or mixture of butter and oil, for brushing dough

If phyllo sheets are frozen, thaw them in the refrigerator 8 hours or overnight. Let phyllo sheets stand at room temperature, still in their package, for 2 hours before using.

To make filling: Mash farmer cheese with feta cheese in bowl and stir until blended. Add egg, dill, parsley, pepper, and salt if needed. Mix until smooth.

Line two baking sheets with parchment paper or butter them. Unwrap phyllo sheets and unroll them on a dry towel. With sharp knife, cut stack in half lengthwise. Immediately cover phyllo with plastic wrap. Work with only one sheet at a time, keeping remaining sheets covered so they do not dry out.

Remove one phyllo strip from pile. Brush it lightly with melted butter. Spoon 1 to 1½ tablespoons filling in a strip near the end of phyllo closest to you, arranging it to extend nearly to the edge. Fold bottom edge of phyllo over filling. Fold the two sides of the phyllo, to your left and right, inward slightly over filling, then roll up tightly in a finger shape, brushing dough with more butter halfway through rolling if you like. Set pastry seam side down on baking sheet. Brush lightly with butter. Shape more fingers with remaining phyllo and filling.

Preheat oven to 350°F. Bake pastries for 15 minutes, or until very light golden. Cool slightly on a wire rack before serving. Serve warm, not hot, or at room temperature.

Sesame Pita Crisps

pitot prihot im sumsum

Preparing pita crisps or pita chips is a good way to make use of stale pita. They are used in salads like *Fattoush* (page 63) and are a good, crunchy accompaniment for soups or dips. Instead of sesame seeds, you can use caraway, nigella, cumin, or poppy seeds or a mixture of seeds. Since you need only a little oil to stick the seeds to the pita, they are much lower in fat than most packaged chips.

◆ MAKES 32 TO 40 CRISPS.

2 pita breads
Olive oil or oil spray
2 to 3 teaspoons sesame seeds

Preheat oven to 325°F. Tear each pita in half crosswise. Split each pita half gently with a serrated knife to separate the two layers, so they will be even, without thick edges. Put pita quarters on baking sheet. Brush lightly with oil or spray with oil spray, then sprinkle with sesame seeds. Pat lightly to stick the seeds to the pita.

Bake for 10 minutes, or until dry and light golden. Break each piece in 4 or 5 rough wedges while they are still warm. Cool on racks. Store in airtight containers.

Cakes, Cookies, and Desserts, for Holidays and Special Occasions

Queen of Sheba Chocolate Cake • *Malikate Saba'a*

Citrus Yogurt Cake with Honey and Walnuts • *Kecat Zabady*

Semolina Squares with Orange Syrup and Almonds • *Namura*

Middle Eastern Shortbread Cookies with Toasted Nuts • *Graybeh; Korabiye*

Aromatic Pistachio-filled Cookies • *Ma'amoul*

Date Pinwheel Cookies • *Qrass bi Tamr*

Pecan-Cinnamon Baklava Fingers • *Assabeh Baklawa*

Marzipan Chocolate-Chip Phyllo Triangles with Pine Nuts • *Baklawa Mossalassat*

Nut-filled Baklava • *Baklava*

Fruit Salad with Honey and Toasted Almonds • *Khoushaf*

Summer Melon Medley with Mint and Rose Water • *Khoushaf Shaahd*

Citrus and Spice-scented Quinces with Cranberries   •   *Ayva Kompostosu*

Pomegranate Poached Pears   •   *Khoushaf Injas*

Figs in Fennel Syrup   •   *Khoushaf Teen*

Date-Nut Halvah Balls   •   *Halawate Bellouze*

Yemenite-spiced Rice Pudding with Mango   •   *Pudding Orez im Mango*

Sweet Couscous with Hazelnuts, Apricots, and Raisins   •   *Couscous bel Bondock*

Wheat Berry Pudding with Walnuts, Dried Fruit, Milk, and Honey—Noah's Pudding   •   *Asure*

Mocha Pudding with Spiced Whipped Cream   •   *Pudding Mocha*

Creamy Rose Water Pudding with Pistachios and Strawberries   •   *Muhallebi; Mallabi*

Creamy Orchid Root Drink   •   *Salep; Sahlab*

Turkish Coffee   •   *Qahwah*

Phyllo pastries such as baklava are the most famous items in the Middle Eastern repertoire of sweets and of pastry appetizers. *Phyllo* means "leaf" in Greek, and indeed the sheets are very thin. When baked, the pastry is light, delicate, and flaky. Around the world, many people consider these rich, tender pastries simply irresistible.

You can find them at many bakeries, but they're one of the most popular desserts to make at home. Convenience is part of the reason. You can shape the pastries ahead and keep them in the refrigerator or freezer, so you can have freshly baked pastries when you want them. Best of all, there is no need to make pastry dough or use a rolling pin. Phyllo sheets of fine quality are easy to find in the frozen-foods section of the supermarket. At Mediterranean and Middle Eastern specialty stores you can find more brands and often fresh phyllo dough as well.

Nutty, sweet baklava is famous worldwide, but there is a great variety of other Mideast desserts that deserve to be better known. Over the ages cooks have developed an enormous range of sweets from grains, fruits, and even some vegetables. With the ancient spice route running through the region, they've had centuries of experience using sweet spices like cinnamon, ginger, cardamom, and cloves. Special flavorings, such as orange flower water, mastic, and even saffron, give their desserts a unique character. Nuts of all types are lavishly used to accent desserts, as are dates, figs, dried apricots, and raisins.

This great selection of sweets is not surprising. It was people from the Mideast who first made cane sugar and taught the Europeans how to produce it.

Honey is treasured, as are syrups made from dates, carob, and grapes, as well as molasses from sugarcane. These may sound like items from the shelves of health food stores, and in the West they often are, but in the Middle East they are traditional favorites.

Creamy desserts tend to be less obvious in the display cases of typical Middle Eastern pastry shops but people prize luscious puddings, cakes, and pastries. Cooks use milk, yogurt, cream, and butter, both raw and clarified, to enhance their sweet treats.

A very rich clotted cream used mostly to accompany desserts and sometimes in fillings is called *eshta* in most of the region and kaymak in Turkey. Amazingly, kaymak is so thick that it occasionally comes rolled in sheets. In some areas, it is traditionally made from water-buffalo milk, which has particularly rich and delicious cream. Today kaymak is most often made from cow's milk, and the water-buffalo type is not easy to find. When we found it on the Asian side of Istanbul, we savored this rare treat slowly. In Mideast markets in North America you rarely find fresh kaymak, though it's available in cans. Certain Middle Eastern pastry shops make their own to flavor their desserts. If you ever come across a recipe that calls for it, you can substitute crème fraîche, English clotted cream, or even Italian mascarpone cheese. When it's called for as an accompaniment, some cooks simply use whipped heavy cream instead.

Still, butter and cream figure less prominently in Middle Eastern desserts than in those of the West. Cooks achieve rich results in other ways. Almonds and pistachios have been popular in the area since biblical times. They and other

nuts are the basis of many scrumptious sweets, from phyllo fingers to creamy puddings to fillings for cookies like Aromatic Pistachio-filled Cookies, or *ma'amoul* (page 345).

Sesame appears in several forms on the dessert table. The seeds are used for sprinkling, but they are also ground with sugar to make sesame halvah, a delightful treat served on its own, spread on bread, or made into desserts. I also use it on sundaes, by pouring carob syrup over vanilla ice cream and sprinkling crumbled halvah on top. Sesame paste, or tahini, has sweet roles as well. Like peanut butter, it enriches cakes and cookies. Mixed with date syrup or grape syrup, it becomes a spread for bread or can be turned into a fudgelike sauce.

Coffee originated in this region, and syrupy pastries are the perfect complement to this beloved beverage. Indeed, if you were surprised, as I was, by the sweetness of certain Middle Eastern pastries when you first tasted them, remember that the best way to enjoy them is with black coffee or tea, as they are traditionally served.

In the Mideast, syrups provide a finishing touch to doughnuts, often called *lokma*. At a *lokma* shop in Turkey I saw them being made freshly and in several different shapes—balls, small and large rings, and ridged. They all got a brief bath of syrup as soon as they were cooked. Syrups are used to moisten cakes as well, like Semolina Squares with Orange Syrup and Almonds (page 342). Middle Easterners are not the only ones to enjoy such treats. The French have popularized their syrup-moistened cakes—baba and savarin—around the world.

Indeed, one of the most popular cakes in Tel Aviv bakeries is *sabrina*, a Mideast take on savarin.

Rich desserts are usually reserved for holidays, celebrations, and special feasts. For daily menus, fruit is the usual finale to a meal. Many fruits are native to the Mideast and a great variety of fruits from other lands flourish there as well. Naturally, the refreshing quality of fresh fruit and just-squeezed fruit juices makes them most welcome in the region's warm climate. People also love fruit in salads or poached in an aromatic syrup with cinnamon, cloves, and citrus. A selection of dried fruits and nuts is a popular dessert and snack that seems to always appear on the table when friends and family members get together.

In Turkey, Lebanon, Egypt, and Iran many people perfume their desserts with rose water or orange-flower water. These essences lend a pleasing aroma that is inviting and exotic. Another floral flavoring is *sahlap*, which could be considered the vanilla of the Middle East. Like vanilla, it comes from an orchid. It is used mostly to make warm creamy drinks and occasionally to flavor ice cream.

Queen of Sheba Chocolate Cake

malikate saba'a

This rich chocolate dessert was created to celebrate a legendary royal romance. The Queen of Sheba, according to I Kings 10:2, "came to Jerusalem with a very great train, with camels that bare spices, and very much gold, and precious stones." Certainly she didn't bring any chocolate with her, since this tempting ingredient is native to the New World, which was not yet discovered. But she might have carried another stimulating offering, indigenous to her region—coffee.

Because she is imagined as a dark, rich beauty, chefs thought of her when creating this sumptuous chocolate dessert flavored with coffee or spices. Queen of Sheba Chocolate Cake is popular in France as well as in the Middle East, where it is sometimes sweetened with honey.

This version is a luscious, brownielike cake with a rich chocolate flavor accented with coffee and almonds. It is best baked for a relatively short time so it remains moist inside. With chocolate truffle frosting and a garnish of pistachios, it makes a beautiful, ultrarich treat. Unfrosted and wrapped, it keeps for four days in the refrigerator. With frosting, it keeps for two days.

♦ MAKES 8 SERVINGS.

4 ounces bittersweet or semisweet chocolate, coarsely chopped

¾ cup blanched almonds (3½ ounces)

¼ cup all-purpose flour

½ teaspoon instant-coffee powder

Pinch salt

½ cup (1 stick) unsalted butter, at room temperature

3 large eggs, separated, plus 1 additional egg white

⅔ cup granulated sugar

Confectioners' sugar (optional)

CHOCOLATE TRUFFLE FROSTING AND GARNISH (OPTIONAL):

⅓ cup heavy cream, half-and-half, or milk

4 ounces bittersweet or semisweet chocolate, chopped

¼ cup (½ stick) unsalted butter, at room temperature

2 to 3 tablespoons chopped pistachios, toasted, or 8 to 10 toasted blanched almonds, chocolate coffee beans, or thin slices of crystallized ginger

Preheat oven to 350°F. Butter an 8- or 9-inch round cake pan, about 1½ inches deep. Line base of pan with foil or parchment paper; butter foil or paper and flour the lined pan.

Melt chocolate in small saucepan above hot water over low heat, stirring until smooth. Remove chocolate from water and let cool. In nut grinder or food processor, process almonds with a pulsing motion to a fine powder. Sift flour and mix it with almond powder, coffee, and salt.

mixer until very soft. Beat
...ate. Beat in 3 egg yolks, one
...en ⅓ cup sugar. Beat until

...ip 4 egg whites until soft peaks
...m. Gradually beat in remaining ⅓ cup
sugar. Beat at high speed until whites are
stiff and shiny but not dry. Fold about ¼
of whites into chocolate mixture, then
quickly spoon remaining whites on top.
Sprinkle almond mixture over whites and
fold together lightly and quickly, just until
blended.

Transfer immediately to prepared pan.
Bake for 25 to 35 minutes, or until a cake
tester or toothpick inserted into cake about
halfway between edge and center of pan
comes out dry; the cake's center should still
be slightly soft.

Cool cake in pan about 5 minutes. Slide a
thin knife carefully around side of cake.
Turn out onto wire rack, carefully remove
paper, and let cake cool completely. (Cake
can be kept, covered, in refrigerator for four
days; or it can be frozen.) Serve it at room
temperature. If you're not making frosting,
serve cake sprinkled with confectioners'
sugar if you like.

To make frosting: Bring cream to a boil
in small saucepan. Remove from heat and
immediately add chopped chocolate. Stir
quickly with a whisk until mixture is
smooth. Let cool completely but do not let
it harden. Beat mixture with mixer at high
speed for about 3 minutes, or until its color
lightens.

Cream butter in large bowl until very...
and smooth. Gradually beat in choco...
mixture until frosting is smooth.

Spread frosting on side and top of cake
and smooth with a long metal spatula. If
desired, swirl the frosting on top. Garnish
center with pistachios or edge with almonds. Refrigerate for 2 hours before serving. Serve at room temperature.

Citrus Yogurt Cake with Honey and Walnuts

kecat zabady

Bakers in the Mideast often make cake
batter with yogurt, as its tangy taste complements the cake's sweetness, and soak
such cakes in syrup or in light honey. I like
to mix honey with citrus juices and serve
it as a sauce with this cake, which resembles American sour cream coffee cake in
texture.

Instead of the honey sauce, you can pour
Orange Syrup (page 343) over the cake or
serve it as a sauce. Spoon fresh fruit, such as
berries, orange segments, or sliced peaches,
mangoes or bananas, around each serving
for a perfect flavor complement and pretty
presentation.

◆ MAKES ABOUT 10 SERVINGS.

1¾ cups all-purpose flour

1¼ teaspoons baking powder

½ teaspoon baking soda

1¼ cups plain yogurt

¼ cup fresh-squeezed orange juice

½ cup (1 stick) unsalted butter,
    at room temperature

1 cup sugar

3 large eggs

½ cup chopped walnuts

1½ teaspoons grated lemon zest

1 teaspoon grated orange zest

1 teaspoon vanilla extract

HONEY CITRUS SAUCE AND GARNISH:

½ cup orange blossom or other honey

2 or 3 tablespoons fresh-squeezed orange
    juice

1 to 2 tablespoons fresh-squeezed lemon
    juice

¼ cup toasted chopped walnuts, almonds,
    or pistachios (optional, for garnish)

Position rack in center of oven and preheat to 350°F. Butter a 9- or 10-inch round cake pan 2½ to 3 inches deep, such as a spring-form pan. Sift flour, baking powder, and baking soda into bowl. In another bowl, mix yogurt with ¼ cup orange juice.

Cream butter in large bowl until light. Add sugar and beat until smooth and fluffy. Beat in eggs, one at a time. At low speed, stir in flour mixture alternately with yogurt mixture, each in two portions. Stir in walnuts, lemon and orange zests, and vanilla.

Pour batter into prepared pan and it smooth. Bake for 45 minutes, or until toothpick inserted in cake comes out clean. Cool in pan for 10 minutes.

To make sauce: Warm honey gently. Gradually stir in enough orange and lemon juices for the taste and thickness you prefer. Brush a little sauce over the cake and, if you like, sprinkle it with toasted walnuts. Serve remaining sauce separately.

Semolina Squares with Orange Syrup and Almonds

namura

Part cake, part pudding, syrup-moistened semolina desserts like this one are loved around the Mideast. You can find them at Mideast bakeries and restaurants by their Egyptian name, *basbousa,* by their Syrian and Lebanese one, *namura,* and sometimes by the name *harissa.* They are easy to spot, as they are scored in squares or diamond shapes, with an almond in the center of each. Some make the batter with milk, while others prefer yogurt.

The dessert might be flavored with coconut, sesame, or walnuts and accented with citrus, sweet spices, vanilla, or rose water. The most surprising version I ever tasted was at Al Najah Sweets inside the walls of Jerusalem's Old City where it was flavored with fenugreek seeds—it was delicious!

This recipe features the fresh touch of orange syrup. Once the dessert is baked, you spoon the syrup over it—either cold syrup over the hot cake or hot syrup over the cooled cake. To encourage the cake to absorb more syrup, some cooks prick it with a skewer before pouring syrup over it. Make the dessert at least a day ahead so it absorbs the syrup well. Popular garnishes at serving time are berries or other fresh fruit and thick or whipped cream.

♦ MAKES 6 TO 8 SERVINGS.

ORANGE SYRUP:

    1 cup sugar

    ½ cup water

    6 pared strips of orange zest

    3 to 4 tablespoons fresh-squeezed orange juice

    1 to 2 teaspoons orange-flower water (optional) or Grand Marnier

SEMOLINA CAKE:

    1½ cups semolina

    1 teaspoon baking powder

    ¼ teaspoon baking soda

    Pinch salt

    6 tablespoons (¾ stick) butter, at room temperature

    ¾ cup sugar

    1 large egg

    ½ cup milk or water

    1 teaspoon grated orange zest or vanilla extract

    ½ cup plain yogurt

    4 to 5 tablespoons blanched almonds

To make syrup: Combine sugar, water, and orange zest in a small heavy saucepan. Cook over low heat until sugar dissolves, stirring gently to avoid splashing syrup on side of pan. Once sugar has dissolved, stop stirring. Bring syrup to a boil over high heat. Reduce heat to medium-low and simmer, uncovered, for 5 minutes without stirring. Remove orange zest strips with a slotted spoon. Stir in orange juice and orange-flower water or Grand Marnier. Let cool.

To make semolina cake: Preheat oven to 350°F. Generously butter an 8- or 9-inch square cake pan. Sift semolina with baking powder, baking soda, and salt.

Cream the butter in bowl until smooth. Add sugar and beat until mixture is well blended. Add egg and beat until blended. Beat in milk. Stir in orange zest or vanilla. With a wooden spoon, stir in semolina mixture alternately with yogurt, each in three portions.

Spoon batter into prepared pan. Spread it until smooth. With knife, score batter in small diamond or square shapes, without cutting all the way through. Put an almond in the center of each one. Bake for 30 minutes, or until cake is golden and a toothpick inserted in center comes out clean. Cut shapes the rest of the way through.

Slowly spoon cool syrup over hot cake,

adding enough so cake becomes moist but not soggy. Let cool completely so the syrup is distributed through the cake. Serve warm, cold, or at room temperature. If you have extra syrup, you can serve it separately.

NOTE Orange Syrup is also a good accompaniment for Marzipan Chocolate-Chip Phyllo Triangles with Pine Nuts (page 348) and Pecan-Cinnamon Baklava Fingers (page 347). I like to add a few spoonfuls of the syrup to fruit salads, and to use it for poaching fresh or dried fruit. Grand Marnier is not a classic ingredient in Middle Eastern syrups, but I find it adds a pleasant touch.

Middle Eastern Shortbread Cookies with Toasted Nuts

graybeh; korabiye

One of the best-loved cookies in the Middle East, these delicate, buttery shortbreads are also popular in Morocco and Greece. They are special-occasion treats and in Turkey, for example, they are sometimes called wedding cookies. Each cookie is usually topped with one or two nuts, generally pistachios or almonds, which become gently toasted as the cookies bake. The cookies'

quality depends on careful baking. They must remain pale, almost white, to keep their delicious taste and tender, appealing texture.

I received this recipe from my dear friend Ronnie Venezia, cookbook author and baker extraordinaire, who lives in Jerusalem. It is a family treasure, handed down from her mother, Suzanne Elmaleh, from whom I had the pleasure of learning specialties of her native Lebanon. Ronnie finds that *graybeh* have the best taste and texture when made with half butter and half margarine, although her mother made excellent ones solely with margarine. Many other bakers use butter exclusively.

The cookies come in a variety of forms—rounds, crescents, diamonds, or S shapes. Ronnie's resemble rings that are not completely hollow in the center. For faster cookies, you can shape them in rounds as in the variation.

◆ MAKES 30 TO 34 COOKIES.

7 tablespoons butter, at room temperature

7 tablespoons margarine, at room temperature

½ cup confectioners' sugar, sifted

2⅓ cups all-purpose flour, sifted

1 egg white, lightly beaten

Unsalted pistachio halves, preferably raw

Line two baking sheets with parchment paper or nonstick baking paper. In mixer, beat butter and margarine with confectioners' sugar for 10 minutes, or until mixture is light and airy. Gradually add flour and beat at low speed until just blended in.

Shape dough in 1½-inch balls. Roll each ball briefly between your palms until it is smooth and even. Press lightly to flatten. Dip your small finger in flour and, with a gentle circular movement, make a depression in the center of each cookie, not quite to its bottom. Cookies will be almost ring-shaped but centers should not be completely hollow.

Put cookies on prepared baking sheets, spacing them about 1½ inches apart. Brush top of each cookie very lightly with egg white in two spots on opposite sides of depression and press half a pistachio on each brushed spot. Refrigerate sheets of cookies for 30 to 60 minutes.

Preheat oven to 325°F. Bake cookies for 17 to 22 minutes, or until bottoms are very light golden; tops should remain very pale, almost white. Put the baking sheets on wire rack to cool for 2 minutes. Remove cookies with metal spatula to a rack and cool completely. They will firm up when cooling. Store in airtight containers.

Almond Shortbread Cookies
After rolling dough in balls, press lightly to flatten each one. Set half a blanched almond in the center of each one. Bake as directed above.

Aromatic Pistachio-filled Cookies

ma'amoul

One of the highlights of Middle Eastern pastry shops is the fluted cookie called *ma'amoul,* composed of a tender, buttery pastry enclosing a flavorful filling. It comes in several different shapes—thick patties, round or oval mounds, or mountains with peaks. The dough might be made of flour, semolina, or a mixture of both. When *ma'amoul* are baked at home, the cookies' ridges are made with pastry pinchers and serve not only to decorate the pastries but to catch enough confectioners' sugar to sweeten them. At bakeries they often use special *ma'amoul* molds.

Date *ma'amoul* are favorites in the Mideast and those I have tasted, whether baked in Jerusalem or in Jedda, Saudi Arabia, have been wonderful. The most beloved filling is made of pistachios, which are native to the region. Pistachio trees are said to have been planted in the Hanging Gardens of Babylon.

Walnuts are also popular for filling *ma'amoul,* and so are mixtures of nuts. These cookies gain their exotic fragrance and flavor from rose water or orange-flower water added to the pastry and the filling. If you prefer, flavor the filling with 1 teaspoon cinnamon and use orange juice or water to moisten the dough. You can keep these buttery cookies up to three days in airtight containers.

◆ MAKES ABOUT 25 TO 30 COOKIES.

2⅔ cups all-purpose flour
1 cup (2 sticks) cold butter, cut in pieces
5 tablespoons rose water or orange-flower water
2 tablespoons water, or more if needed
2 cups shelled unsalted pistachios
2 tablespoons granulated sugar
Confectioners' sugar (for dredging)

To make the dough: Combine flour and butter in food processor and pulse until mixture resembles fine meal. Add 3 tablespoons rose water and 2 tablespoons water. Process until dough just forms a ball. It should be fairly soft and pliable; if it is dry, add I more tablespoon water and process briefly. Wrap dough and refrigerate for I hour.

To make filling: Pulse pistachios and granulated sugar in food processor, leaving some pieces; do not grind nuts finely. Transfer to bowl and stir in 2 tablespoons rose water.

To shape pastries: Take I tablespoon dough and roll it between your palms to a ball. Holding pastry ball in one hand, poke it with the index finger of your other hand to make a depression. Enlarge this cavity, turning dough around your finger, until you have a thin shell for filling. Gently add enough pistachio mixture to fill the shell.

Pinch dough around filling to enclose it. Press gently to a ball, then press to flatten slightly. Put on an ungreased baking sheet, with side of cookie that was open facing up. Repeat with remaining dough and filling.

Use a pastry pincher to decorate each cookie all around with ridges going from top to bottom of pastry. Pinch firmly, or marks will disappear during baking. Pinch top once or twice with pastry pincher also. If you don't have a pastry pincher, use the tines of a fork to make up-and-down ridges in the cookie. Refrigerate cookies for 30 minutes, or up to several hours; or freeze for I5 minutes.

Preheat oven to 375°F. Bake cookies for 20 to 25 minutes, or until they turn light beige; do not let them brown. While they are still hot, dredge them generously in confectioners' sugar.

Date Pinwheel Cookies

qrass bi tamr

Date palms are an integral part of the Mideastern landscape and their fruit has long been prized. Dates are the fruit of choice for filling cookies because of their luscious texture and sweetness. Home bakers in the region often prepare cookies like these, rolling the filling inside the dough like a jelly roll and then cutting it to make pinwheels. You can also cut the dough in triangles, roll them up, and curve them to form filled crescent cookies.

MAKES ABOUT 24 COOKIES.

  2 cups all-purpose flour
  3 tablespoons confectioners' sugar
  ½ teaspoon baking powder
  ½ teaspoon salt
  ½ cup (1 stick) plus 2 tablespoons cold
      unsalted butter, cut in small pieces
      (5 ounces)
  1 large egg
  3 tablespoons diced walnuts or almonds
  12 ounces pitted dates, cut in pieces
  2 tablespoons water
  ½ teaspoon grated orange zest (optional)
  ½ teaspoon ground cinnamon (optional)

To make dough: Combine flour, confectioners' sugar, baking powder, and salt in food processor. Process briefly to blend. Scatter butter pieces over mixture. Pulse until mixture resembles coarse meal. Beat egg and pour it evenly over mixture. Process with on/off motion, occasionally scraping down the side of bowl, until dough just begins to come together in a ball. If mixture is dry, add water by tablespoons, and process briefly after each addition.

Transfer dough to bowl or work surface. Knead lightly to blend. With rubber spatula, transfer dough to sheet of plastic wrap, wrap it, and shape it into a disk. Refrigerate at least 1 hour or overnight.

To make filling: Chop nuts finely in food processor and remove. Puree dates in processor. Add chopped nuts and water and process to blend. Transfer date-nut mixture to bowl. Stir in orange zest and cinnamon if you like.

Lightly grease two baking sheets. Divide dough in two pieces. Roll one to a rectangle about ⅛ inch thick. Spread with half the filling, leaving a ½-inch border. Beginning at a long side, roll up tightly. Cut a slice ½ inch thick and set it on prepared baking sheet with side that you just cut facing down. Continue with remaining slices. Refrigerate slices. Repeat with remaining dough and filling. Refrigerate cookies at least 30 minutes or overnight.

Preheat oven to 375°F. Bake cookies for 12 minutes, or until they are light golden at edges. Cool on racks. Store them in an airtight tin.

Pecan-Cinnamon Baklava Fingers

assabeh baklawa

Like baklava, these elegant, buttery treats are made of phyllo dough and a nut filling, but unlike their diamond-shaped cousins, these phyllo fingers are not soaked in syrup. As a result, they are light, delicately crisp, and have only a touch of sweetness. Instead of sprinkling them with confectioners' sugar, you can accompany them with Orange Syrup (page 343) for drizzling lightly on top. You can fill them with any nuts that you like. Some bakers prefer a mixture, such as almonds, walnuts, and pine nuts.

If you like, you can shape the pastries one day ahead, cover them tightly with plastic wrap, and refrigerate them on baking sheets; or you can freeze them, ready to be baked. Once baked, store them in an airtight container at room temperature for a day or two, or freeze them.

◆ MAKES ABOUT 30 PASTRIES.

½ pound phyllo dough (½ package)

1¾ cups pecans

1 teaspoon ground cinnamon

2 to 3 tablespoons confectioners' sugar, plus more for sprinkling

½ cup (1 stick) butter, melted

If phyllo sheets are frozen, thaw them in refrigerator 8 hours or overnight. Let phyllo sheets stand at room temperature, still in their package, for 2 hours before using.

Chop pecans with pulsing motion in food processor, leaving some pieces; do not grind nuts finely. Transfer to bowl and stir in cinnamon and confectioners' sugar.

Preheat oven to 350°F. Line two baking sheets with parchment paper or grease them. Unwrap phyllo sheets and unroll them on a dry towel. With sharp knife, cut stack in half lengthwise, then in half crosswise to make

squares. Cover phyllo immediately with plastic wrap. Work with only one sheet at a time, keeping remaining sheets covered so they don't dry out.

Remove one phyllo square from pile. Brush it lightly with melted butter. Spoon about 2 teaspoons filling on the side closest to you, arranging it to extend nearly to the edge. Fold bottom edge of phyllo square over filling. Fold the two sides of the square, to your left and right, in slightly over filling, then roll up tightly to form a thin finger. Transfer to prepared baking sheet. Shape more fingers with remaining phyllo and filling. If you like, brush each one very lightly with more melted butter.

Bake pastries for 15 minutes, or until very light golden. Cool on wire rack. Before serving, sprinkle generously with confectioners' sugar.

Marzipan Chocolate-Chip Phyllo Triangles with Pine Nuts

baklawa mossalassat

Chocolate is becoming popular in Mideast phyllo desserts. Chocolate phyllo dough is now available at some Mediterranean and Middle Eastern markets, but for these flaky pastries, I use plain phyllo dough to wrap a rich chocolate-studded almond filling. You can serve them with Orange Syrup (page 343) for a touch of extra sweetness. If you like, you can shape the pastries one day ahead; keep them refrigerated on baking sheets, and cover them tightly with plastic wrap.

♦ MAKES ABOUT 36 PASTRIES.

    1 pound phyllo sheets (about 20 sheets)

    ¾ cup whole blanched almonds

    6 tablespoons sugar

    1 large egg, beaten

    ¼ cup pine nuts

    3 ounces bittersweet or semisweet chocolate, finely chopped

    2 teaspoons orange-flower water, rose water, or vanilla extract

    2 tablespoons fresh-squeezed orange juice or water (optional)

    About 1 cup (2 sticks) unsalted butter, melted, or more if needed

    About 2 teaspoons sesame seeds (optional)

If phyllo dough is frozen, thaw in refrigerator for 8 hours or overnight. Let phyllo sheets stand at room temperature, still in their package, for 2 hours before using.

Grind almonds with 2 tablespoons sugar in food processor to a fine powder. Add remaining 4 tablespoons sugar and egg and process until blended. Transfer to bowl and stir in pine nuts, chocolate, and orange-flower water. If mixture is too dry to hold together, stir in orange juice or water.

Preheat oven to 350°F. Butter two baking sheets. Remove phyllo sheets from their package and spread them out on a dry towel. Using sharp knife, cut stack in half lengthwise to form two stacks of sheets, about 16 by 7 inches. Immediately cover phyllo with plastic wrap. Work with only one sheet at a time, keeping remaining sheets covered so they do not dry out.

Carefully remove one filo sheet from pile. Brush lightly with melted butter; fold in half lengthwise so its dimensions are about 16 by 3½ inches. Place about 1½ teaspoons filling at one end of strip. Fold end of strip diagonally over filling to form a triangle. Fold it over and over, keeping it in a triangular shape after each fold, until you reach the end of the strip. Brush sheet lightly with butter before last fold to seal the triangle. Set triangle on prepared baking sheet and brush lightly with butter. Cover with plastic wrap. Repeat with remaining phyllo sheets and filling.

Just before baking, brush pastries lightly with melted butter. Sprinkle with sesame seeds if you like. Bake for 25 minutes, or until light golden brown. If baking on two racks, switch their positions halfway through baking time. Serve warm or at room temperature.

Nut-filled Baklava

baklava

Fine, fresh baklava is a magical sweet of luscious layers of buttery flaky phyllo and rich nut filling. The first records we have of baklava come from Syria near the Turkish border, although it is thought to be based on ancient Assyrian cakes made of bread dough layered with nuts and dried fruit. The sweet was adopted by the Turks, who spread it to other parts of the Mediterranean during the epoch of the Ottoman Empire. Yet even the Turks acknowledge that the Syrians are the baklava experts. Indeed, miniature baklava and other pastries from Sweets Alsaddik in Damascus were among the most exquisite examples of these phyllo sweets that I had ever tasted.

Fillings can be made of pastry cream, but nuts are by far the most popular. In Turkey pistachios are the top choice, but almonds, walnuts, and mixtures of nuts are also used. The filling might be flavored with cinnamon or cloves, or in Persian homes, with cardamom. Syrup scented with the same spices used in the filling, or with lemon juice, honey, rose water or orange-blossom water, is spooned over the baklava to sweeten it and infuse it with more flavor.

Using syrup is practical, as it helps keep the desserts moist, but it should be added judiciously so the pastry is not saturated and remains flaky. Although you can buy baklava at bakeries, when you make it at home you can use as much or as little syrup as you please, and serve more on the side for anyone who wants to drizzle a bit more over his or her portion.

How the pastry is layered depends on the baker's preference. Some like the filling in the center, with half the phyllo on top and half on the bottom. Others alternate every few pastry sheets with filling. Still others prefer more pastry on top, since the upper layers come out the flakiest. You can keep baklava, covered, for several days at room temperature. Some people serve baklava with whipped cream.

◆ MAKES ABOUT 16 TO 24 PIECES.

1 pound phyllo sheets

3 cups pistachios or blanched almonds, or 1½ cups of each

4 to 6 tablespoons sugar

1 to 2 teaspoons ground cinnamon

1 cup (2 sticks) unsalted butter, melted

SYRUP:

1½ cups sugar

1 cup water

2 teaspoons fresh-squeezed lemon juice

1 to 2 tablespoons rose water or orange-flower water (optional)

If phyllo sheets are frozen, thaw them in refrigerator 8 hours or overnight. Let phyllo sheets stand at room temperature, still in their package, for 2 hours before using.

To make filling: Chop nuts in batches by pulsing them in food processor, leaving some pieces; do not grind them to a powder. Transfer to bowl and stir in sugar and cinnamon.

Preheat oven to 350°F. Brush a 13-by-9-inch cake pan with melted butter. Unwrap phyllo sheets and unroll them. With sharp knife, trim stack of sheets to fit pan. Cover phyllo immediately with plastic wrap. Work with only one sheet at a time, keeping remaining sheets covered so they don't dry out.

Put one cut phyllo sheet in pan and brush it lightly and evenly with butter. Top it with five more sheets, brushing each one lightly with butter before adding the next one. Evenly cover it with 1½ cups of the nut mixture. Cover with another sheet of phyllo, brush it with butter, and top it with five more sheets, buttering each one. Evenly cover it with remaining filling. Cover with remaining phyllo sheets, lightly buttering each one. Brush top layer with butter.

With very sharp knife, cut pastry in square- or diamond-shaped pieces 1½ to 2 inches wide or smaller, cutting all the way to the pan. Bake for 30 minutes. Cover loosely with foil, reduce heat to 300°F, and bake for 20 more minutes, or until golden brown.

While baklava is baking, make syrup: Combine sugar and water in heavy saucepan. Cook over low heat until sugar dissolves, stirring gently to avoid splashing syrup on side of pan. Once sugar has dissolved, stop stirring. Bring syrup to a boil over high heat. Reduce heat to medium-low and simmer, uncovered, without stirring, for 5 minutes. Add lemon juice and simmer for 2 more minutes. Remove from heat and let cool. Stir in rose water if you like.

When baklava is done, remove from oven and slowly and evenly ladle cooled syrup over top, using all or half the syrup, as you prefer. Let stand for 3 or 4 hours before serving. You can keep baklava, covered, for several days at room temperature. If necessary, cut pieces again before serving. If you've used only half the syrup, serve the rest on the side.

Fruit Salad with Honey and Toasted Almonds

khoushaf

In late summer, when our fig trees yield their luscious fruit, we usually run to the garden, eat them on the spot, and feel like we're in the Garden of Eden. Chefs often use fresh figs in elegant menus, and you can find them in gourmet shops, but this fruit is not a trendy item. It has been loved in Mediterranean countries from time immemorial and in season it can always be found in ethnic shops.

I add late-season peaches or pears and

bananas to the traditional combination of figs, dates, almonds, and honey. Before sprinkling the salad with toasted almonds, you can add a creamy topping to each portion—a dollop of crème fraîche, softly whipped cream, sour cream, or rich yogurt. *Labneh* (kefir cheese) is good too; if it's very thick, stir in a few teaspoonfuls cold water.

◆ MAKES 4 SERVINGS.

    1 to 2 tablespoons honey
    1 to 1½ tablespoons fresh-squeezed lime
        or lemon juice
    1 tablespoon water
    1 banana
    2 peaches or ripe pears
    2 cups halved or quartered fresh figs
    1 cup plump, good-quality dates,
        such as Medjool or very soft fresh Barhi
    1 to 2 tablespoons slivered almonds, toasted
        (see "Basics," page 369)

Mix I tablespoon honey with I tablespoon lime juice and water in serving bowl. Peel and slice banana; add to bowl. Cut peaches or pears in wedges and add them. Add figs and dates. Mix gently. Add remaining honey and lime juice if you like. Refrigerate until ready to serve. Serve topped with almonds.

Summer Melon Medley with Mint and Rose Water

khoushaf shaahd

Rose water and citrus are popular Middle Eastern accents for fruit salads and fruit desserts of all kinds. This easy dessert is most delicious when made with homemade mint-scented melon sorbet, but it's also good on its own or with lemon or orange sorbet, vanilla ice cream, or frozen yogurt. For a colorful variation, add balls of seedless red and yellow watermelon.

◆ MAKES 4 SERVINGS.

MINT-SCENTED MELON SORBET:
    1½ cups sugar
    1 cup water
    1 cup fresh mint leaves
    3 to 3½ pounds ripe cantaloupe or
        honeydew melon
    2 tablespoons fresh-squeezed lemon
        or lime juice, or to taste

MELON MEDLEY:
    2 to 3 teaspoons rose water
    1 teaspoon sugar
    1 teaspoon fresh-squeezed lemon
        or lime juice
    ½ teaspoon finely chopped mint
    16 to 20 cantaloupe balls
    16 to 20 honeydew balls
    Mint sprigs, for garnish

To make sorbet: Combine sugar and water in heavy medium saucepan. Heat over low heat until sugar dissolves completely, stirring gently. Stop stirring. Bring to a full boil over medium-high heat. Add mint and return to a boil. Cover and let stand off heat 15 minutes. Strain into medium bowl, pressing on leaves, and cool completely. Cover and refrigerate for 1 hour.

Halve melon and remove seeds. Cut off rind and discard. Cut flesh in cubes. Puree melon in food processor until very smooth. Pour puree into large bowl. Add 1 cup syrup (for honeydew) or 1¼ cups syrup (for cantaloupe) and mix thoroughly. Stir in lemon juice. Taste, and add more syrup or lemon juice if needed. Mixture should taste slightly too sweet.

Chill medium-sized metal bowl or airtight container in freezer. Transfer sorbet mixture to ice-cream machine and process until mixture has consistency of soft ice cream; it should not be runny but will not become very firm. Transfer sorbet as quickly as possible to chilled bowl; it melts very quickly. Cover tightly and freeze until ready to serve. If keeping sorbet longer than 3 hours, transfer it when firm to the airtight container, pack it down well, and cover tightly.

To make melon medley: Mix rose water, sugar, lemon juice, and chopped mint in medium bowl. Add melon balls and toss. Cover and refrigerate until ready to serve.

Before serving, chill 4 dessert dishes or glasses so that sorbet won't melt too quickly. To serve, add a scoop or a heaping spoonful of sorbet to each dish. Spoon melon balls around sorbet. Garnish with mint and serve immediately.

NOTE The sorbet makes 6 to 8 servings (about 3 to 4 cups). It tastes best on the day it was made but can be kept for 4 or 5 days. If you have kept it for a few days and it is frozen solid, soften it in food processor before serving. First chill food processor bowl and blade in refrigerator. Puree sorbet, about 2 cups at a time, in food processor for just a few seconds. You can then return softened sorbet to chilled container in the freezer and it will remain soft for 1 or 2 hours.

Citrus and Spice-scented Quinces with Cranberries

ayva kompostosu

Around the Mideast quinces are made into jams, and syrup-poached quinces are a favorite fall dessert. If you have never prepared them, try this easy recipe of sweet quinces fragrant with cinnamon, cloves, orange, and lemon. They are tasty hot or cold and turn an attractive pink.

For an American twist, I add dried cranberries, a beautiful garnish that complements the sweet syrup and makes this autumn dessert perfect for Thanksgiving. The quinces are delicious on their own, spooned over vanilla ice cream, or as a partner for rice pudding, sweet couscous, or simple cakes. You might like to try them the Turkish way, topped with blanched almonds and accompanied by rich cream; the Turks use *kaymak* (see "The Mideast Pantry," page 17), but you can use crème fraîche, clotted cream (Devonshire cream), or sour cream.

♦ MAKES 6 SERVINGS.

4 large quinces (about 2½ pounds total)

2 cinnamon sticks, or 2½ teaspoons ground cinnamon

2 whole cloves, or ¼ teaspoon ground cloves

Zest of ½ lemon, pared in thin strips, yellow part only, bitter white pith removed

Zest of ½ orange, pared in thin strips, orange part only

1⅓ cups sugar

3 to 5 tablespoons strained fresh-squeezed lemon juice

½ cup dried cranberries

½ cup whole blanched almonds (for serving)

Sour cream (optional, for serving)

Peel quinces, cut them in eighths, and cut out core and seed section from each piece. Put quinces in large heavy saucepan with cinnamon sticks and whole cloves (but not ground spices). Add lemon and orange zest strips.

Add water just to cover and bring to a boil. Cook, uncovered, over medium heat, carefully turning quince slices over from time to time, for 50 minutes, or until tender when pierced with a fork; cooking time varies with size and ripeness of quinces. At this point the water should have reduced by about half. Discard citrus zest strips and cloves.

Add sugar, ground cinnamon, ground cloves, and 3 tablespoons lemon juice to pan. Swirl pan to dissolve sugar, but avoid stirring quinces so they don't fall apart. Cook over medium heat for 5 minutes, then over low heat, basting occasionally, for 25 minutes, or until quinces are glazed and very tender and syrup is concentrated. Add cranberries and cook for 5 minutes, or until they soften. Add remaining lemon juice if you like. Serve quinces and cranberries with a few tablespoons syrup in deep dishes. Top with blanched almonds. Serve warm or cold, with sour cream if you like.

Pomegranate Poached Pears

khoushaf injas

Like red wine, pomegranate juice makes a tasty syrup for poaching fruit. You can buy it at Middle Eastern groceries or use diluted pomegranate paste. If you don't have either, you can poach the pears in lightly sweetened cranberry juice instead. When fresh pomegranates are in season, the seeds make a lovely garnish. (For more on pomegranate juice and paste, see Chicken in Persian Pomegranate Walnut Sauce, page 164.)

Anjou, Bosc, and Bartlett are my favorite pears for poaching. You can use pears that are still firm and not juicy enough to eat fresh, but they should not be rock hard. Ripen pears at room temperature, not in the refrigerator.

Serve these pears warm, cold, or at room temperature. As a variation, you might like to add 8 to 12 pitted prunes along with the pears. They cook in the same time and complement the taste of the pears and the syrup.

◆ MAKES 4 SERVINGS.

1 cup pomegranate juice,
    or 3 to 4 tablespoons pomegranate paste

¼ cup sugar, or more if needed

One 3-inch cinnamon stick, or ½ teaspoon
    ground cinnamon, or 1 vanilla bean

2 whole cloves

½ to 1¼ cups water

4 ripe but firm, medium-size pears
    (total about 1½ pounds)

1 tablespoon fresh-squeezed lime juice
    (optional)

½ cup pomegranate seeds (optional)

Combine juice with sugar, cinnamon, and cloves in medium saucepan. Add ½ cup water if using pomegranate juice, or 1¼ cups water if using paste. Peel pears if desired. Halve and core pears. Cut each half in 3 lengthwise slices.

Bring pomegranate mixture to a simmer, stirring. Add pears and return to simmer. Cover and cook over low heat for 10 to 15 minutes, or until pears are just tender.

Taste syrup. If you prefer a thicker, more concentrated syrup, remove pears with slotted spoon and boil syrup over medium-high heat for 3 to 5 minutes, or until thickened slightly. Taste syrup; if it is not sweet enough, add 1 to 2 tablespoons sugar and heat over low heat until sugar dissolves. If it is too sweet, stir in 1 tablespoon lime juice. Pour syrup over pears.

Leave pears in syrup until ready to serve. Serve pears in deep dishes with some of their syrup. Add pomegranate seeds to each dish if you like.

Figs in Fennel Syrup

khoushaf teen

Figs are native to the Middle East and cooks have developed countless ways to use them, both savory and sweet. This easy dessert is inspired by Lebanese fig jam, which contains anise seeds. Instead of making jam, I poach fresh figs in a light syrup with fennel seeds, which give an aroma similar to that of anise and provide a lively accent to the rich-flavored figs.

You can make this easy dessert with purple-skinned or green-skinned figs. For the prettiest result, use some of each. The compote is also good when made with dried figs; in that case, use 1½ cups water.

◆ MAKES 3 TO 4 SERVINGS.

1 cup water

3 tablespoons sugar, or to taste

½ teaspoon fennel seeds

6 to 8 ounces small fresh figs (about 2 cups)

2 teaspoons fresh-squeezed lemon or lime juice, or 1 tablespoon Meyer lemon juice

Mix water with sugar and fennel seeds in heavy saucepan over low heat until sugar dissolves. Bring to a simmer. Add figs. Return to a simmer, cover, and cook over low heat for 7 minutes, or until figs are tender. Remove from heat and add lemon juice. Transfer figs gently to a container. Taste syrup and add more sugar if you like, stirring very gently to dissolve it. Pour syrup with fennel seeds over figs and let cool. Refrigerate at least 1 or 2 hours before serving. Serve cold.

Date-Nut Halvah Balls

---

halawate bellouze

The derivation of the word *halvah* indicates the intriguing route the sweet took to North America. It came to English from Yiddish, before that from Romanian and Turkish. Ultimately, it comes from the Arabic word *halwa*, meaning "sweet confection."

Sesame is the flavor of halvah most familiar to us. In Mideast homes, cooks prepare halvah from a great variety of ingredients, including dried fruit, almond paste, butter-sautéed semolina, and quince puree, and present it as squares or spheres.

This tasty fruit halvah, which is popular in Egypt, is similar to a Sephardic version of *haroset*, a Passover spread that is sometimes served in balls like French chocolate truffles. It is a lovely sweet that's very simple to make and perfect when you need a speedy treat. Health-conscious eaters are glad to hear that its sweetness comes from fruit, not refined sugar, and its richness from nuts, not butter.

◆ MAKES 10 TO 12 SERVINGS.

¼ cup pecans or walnuts

⅓ cup almonds

4 ounces pitted dates

4 ounces dried apricots or figs

½ cup raisins

½ teaspoon ground cinnamon

1 to 2 tablespoons fresh-squeezed orange or lemon juice or water, if needed

1 to 2 teaspoons finely grated lemon zest

1 to 2 tablespoons sugar (optional)

Finely chop pecans and almonds in food processor. Transfer to bowl. Halve dates and remove any pits or pit fragments. Add dates, apricots, raisins, and cinnamon to processor and grind until fairly smooth. Mix with nuts in bowl. If mixture is too dry to come together, gradually add a little juice or water. Stir in grated lemon zest. Usually the dessert is sweet enough, but taste the mixture and add sugar if you like.

Roll fruit mixture between your palms into small balls about ¾ or I inch in diameter. Serve in candy papers.

Yemenite-spiced Rice Pudding with Mango

pudding orez im mango

This creamy dessert gains punch from the spices that Yemenites use in coffee—cinnamon, cardamom, and ginger, which I add in candied form. Others in the region perfume rice pudding at the last moment with a few teaspoons of rose water or orange-blossom water, which make delicious variations. For a fresh touch, I love the pudding topped with ripe mangoes or peaches, or, in winter, with orange segments.

◆ MAKES 5 OR 6 SERVINGS.

6 cups water
1 cup short-grain rice, such as Arborio
4 cups milk

1 cinnamon stick

Pinch salt

6 tablespoons sugar

⅓ cup golden raisins (optional)

½ to 1 teaspoon ground cardamom

2 to 3 tablespoons finely chopped candied ginger

2 or 3 ripe mangoes, or 4 or 5 ripe peaches or nectarines

2 to 3 tablespoons chopped toasted pistachios or almonds (optional)

Choose a large heavy saucepan so the milk will not boil over or scorch. Bring 6 cups of water to a boil in saucepan and add rice. Boil, uncovered, for 7 minutes; drain well.

Bring milk and cinnamon stick to a simmer in same saucepan over medium-high heat, stirring occasionally. Add rice and salt. Reduce heat to medium-low and cook, uncovered, for 15 minutes, or until rice is very soft and absorbs most of the milk, stirring often. Rice should look creamy, not soupy and not dry. Stir in sugar and cook for 1 minute, stirring. Remove from heat and stir in raisins, cardamom, and candied ginger. Remove cinnamon stick.

Serve warm or cold. Before serving, peel and dice mangoes or dice peaches. Top each serving with a generous amount of diced fruit and a sprinkling of pistachios.

Sweet Couscous with Hazelnuts, Apricots, and Raisins

---

couscous bel bondock

When I need a simple dessert that's ready in minutes, this one is perfect. It is inspired by Egyptian couscous desserts that are embellished with dried fruit and toasted nuts, and could be considered a couscous version of rice pudding.

If you like, substitute poached dried figs or dates for the apricots and reduce the sugar in the syrup to ⅓ cup. When fresh peaches, apricots, strawberries, or raspberries are in season, I use them instead of dried fruit and omit the syrup; to sweeten this fresh fruit couscous, I sprinkle the dessert with additional sugar.

Traditional cooks steam the tiny grains of pasta at length above boiling water. I opt instead for the quick technique of soaking the couscous briefly in hot liquid, so that I can have a dessert in no time. Serve the sweet couscous warm or cold. If you're serving it warm, serve it in heated bowls and accompany it with pats of soft butter and a pitcher of hot milk.

◆ MAKES 4 SERVINGS.

½ cup granulated sugar

3 cups water

1 cup dried apricots, cut in bite-size
    pieces

½ cup dark raisins

1 cup milk

One 10-ounce package couscous
    (1⅔ cups)

Pinch salt

Confectioners' sugar (for sprinkling)

⅓ cup hazelnuts, almonds, or pistachios,
    toasted and chopped

Combine granulated sugar and 2 cups water in medium saucepan and bring to a boil, stirring gently. Add apricots and return to a simmer. Cover and poach over low heat for 5 to 10 minutes, or until tender. Add raisins. Remove from heat, cover, and let stand until ready to serve.

Bring milk to a boil in heavy saucepan. Stir in couscous, add a pinch of salt, and return to a simmer. Remove from heat and cover pan. Let stand for 5 minutes, or until couscous softens. Taste and add more salt if needed.

To serve, mound couscous on a platter or spoon it into bowls and sprinkle it with confectioners' sugar. With slotted spoon, garnish it with a few apricots and raisins. Sprinkle with hazelnuts. Serve remaining fruit in its syrup separately.

Wheat Berry Pudding with Walnuts, Dried Fruit, Milk, and Honey

Noah's pudding; asure

You'd think a dessert of grains, beans, and dried fruit was dreamed up by a health nut in the seventies. But Noah's pudding, or *asure* (pronounced *ashureh*), has a long tradition. Indeed, legend takes it back to the beginnings of mankind. When the water from the flood receded and Noah and his family came out of their ark, the story goes that they made a dessert out of whatever staples they still had to celebrate and to express their thanks.

Versions of this hearty dessert appear throughout the Mideast. Usually, it's full of good things—like generous amounts of nuts and fruit. The dessert ranges from a homey, basic, old-fashioned dish of wheat with a few raisins to an extravagant pudding with forty ingredients. It is common in the vast region that was once the Ottoman Empire, especially in Turkey, where Noah's ark is said to have rested on Mount Ararat, near the borders of Armenia and Iran.

This prehistoric pudding is customary at religious occasions. Bulgarians and some Armenians serve it for Christmas. Muslims enjoy it during their calendar month when the deluge is said to have ended. Turkish tradition requires making a big pot of the pudding at this time and sharing it with neighbors. Christiane Dabdoub Nasser notes in *Classic Palestinian Cookery* that the pudding is named *burbara* for the feast of Saint Barbara, and she flavors hers with toasted fennel and anise seeds. The dessert figures prominently in some areas at family celebrations, such as weddings or parties for a baby's first tooth; in some communities it is served after funerals.

In Turkey, Noah's pudding is popular year-round. I saw it everywhere in Istanbul, especially in the pudding shops, where it holds its own against other tempting treats like buttery baklava, caramel flans, and French chocolate profiteroles. The first time I tried it, at Lale's pudding shop, I was surprised by how much I liked it. Theirs had a few white beans peeking out of the pudding, which was crowned with cinnamon, raisins, and hazelnuts.

The basis of the dessert is cooked wheat, barley, or a mixture of wheat and rice. Instead of sugar, the pudding might be sweetened with molasses or grape syrup. In addition to the dried fruit, fresh apples might simmer with the wheat. Rose water is a favorite accent, but some prefer coriander or vanilla. Many include a large number of ingredients, as in a recipe from a sultan's cook that called for wheat, fava beans, white beans, dried peas, chickpeas, three kinds of raisins, dates, pine nuts, toasted hazelnuts, almonds, butter, rice flour, cornstarch, and rose water. In Ottoman palaces such elaborate renditions were served from elegant porcelain dishes called *asurelik*. Others prefer to keep the pudding simple. Dogan Ozcan of Istanbul, a connoisseur of Turkish culture, told me that wheat, raisins, sugar, and cinnamon are the most important components; his wife makes their *asure* with only those elements.

It is the topping that makes this humble comfort food so enticing. Cooks decorate the dessert in fanciful ways, with pomegranate seeds, sesame seeds, nuts, and fruit arranged artfully on each serving. You can sprinkle a mixture of nuts or follow a common presentation in Istanbul—divide the pudding surface in four and place different kinds of nuts in each section. In Egypt, this classic peasant's pudding can become quite luxurious. At Saber's pudding parlors in Alexandria and Cairo it is embellished not only with a variety of nuts but also with *eshta* (see "The Mideast Pantry," page 10) and freshly churned ice cream.

Time-honored Turkish recipes call for cooking whole wheat berries at length with the beans. Many cooks use light-colored peeled wheat berries, which cook faster; you can find them in Middle Eastern and in some Latino markets. To adapt the recipe for quick cooking, I substitute bulgur wheat (see variation).

◆ MAKES ABOUT 6 SERVINGS.

6 cups water
Pinch salt
1½ cups whole wheat berries, rinsed
1 to 1½ cups milk, or more if needed
½ cup sugar

½ cup raisins or diced dried figs or dates
½ cup canned chickpeas (garbanzo beans) or white beans, drained and rinsed (optional)
2 to 4 tablespoons honey, or to taste
2 tablespoons butter (optional)
1 to 2 tablespoons rose water or orange-flower water (optional)
½ cup toasted walnuts, pistachios, almonds, hazelnuts, or a mixture of nuts (see "Basics," page 368)
Ground cinnamon (optional, for sprinkling)

Boil 6 cups water in large saucepan and add salt. Add wheat berries and return to a boil. Cover and cook over low heat for 1½ to 2 hours, or until wheat is tender but a little chewy. Drain well and return to pan. Add 1 cup milk, and bring to a simmer. Cook over medium-low heat until milk is absorbed, stirring often.

Stir in sugar, raisins, chickpeas, and honey and cook over low heat until blended. Pudding should look creamy, not soupy and not dry. If pudding is too thick, slowly stir in more milk and heat through briefly. Stir in butter if you like, rose water, and half the nuts.

Serve pudding warm or cold. To serve, spoon pudding into bowls and sprinkle with cinnamon and with remaining nuts.

Speedy Noah's Pudding

Bring 2¼ cups water and salt to a boil in large, heavy saucepan and add 1½ cups large or medium bulgur wheat. Cover and cook over medium-low heat for 5 minutes, or until water is absorbed. Stir in 3 cups milk and bring to a boil over medium-high heat, stirring often. Cook, uncovered, over medium-low heat for 10 to 15 minutes, or until bulgur is tender and absorbs most of milk, stirring often. Continue from second paragraph of recipe.

Mocha Pudding with Spiced Whipped Cream

pudding mocha

When it comes to sweets, it's not surprising that mocha is at the top of my husband's list of favorite flavors. Yakir's parents and their ancestors were born in Yemen, which many consider the birthplace of coffee. Experts believe that coffee was first cultivated in this area. Long before coffee was introduced to Europe, coffeehouses were common in Yemen and the beverage was popular in other parts of the Middle East.

Originally coffee beans were exported from Mocha, a Yemeni city on the Red Sea that became a coffee port of international importance when Yemen was under Ottoman rule. The town's name became associated with the area's stimulating drink and the beans from which it is brewed. In fact, the words *coffee* and *café* also come from the Arabic word for coffee, *qahwah*.

When coffee arrived in Europe, chefs realized that the deep brown brew was great for flavoring sweets. They named their desserts mocha to evoke the main ingredient's exotic background.

In North America, cooks developed a different style of mocha by combining coffee with chocolate. The rationale for matching these two flavors also goes back to the birthplace of the beans. Coffee aficionados know that the fine beans known as Yemen Mocha produce a dark rich cup of joe with distinctive chocolate undertones. Because mocha beans are rare, some vendors mix chocolate with their coffee to imitate the mocha-java flavor, which should be a blend of Yemeni and Indonesian coffee beans. Purists look down on such practices, but few dispute that pairing coffee with chocolate makes for sensational sweets.

For this satisfying dessert, inspired by Yemeni-style coffee flavored with cinnamon, ginger, and other spices, I top the warm, soufflé-like mocha pudding with coffee-and-spice whipped cream. For garnish you might like to add thin slices of candied ginger, candied coffee beans, or chocolate coffee beans.

MAKES 8 OR 9 SERVINGS.

5 ounces semisweet chocolate, chopped

3 tablespoons water

2½ teaspoons instant-coffee powder or freeze-dried coffee granules

½ teaspoon ground cinnamon

½ cup (1 stick) plus 2 tablespoons unsalted butter, cut in pieces, at room temperature

4 large eggs, separated

¼ teaspoon cream of tartar

½ cup plus 4 tablespoons sugar

5 tablespoons all-purpose flour, sifted

¾ cup heavy cream or whipping cream, well chilled

¼ teaspoon ground ginger

Pinch ground cloves (optional)

Preheat oven to 325°F. Lightly butter an 8-inch square baking pan. Line base with parchment paper or waxed paper. Butter paper and flour lined pan. Melt chocolate with water, 1 teaspoon coffee, and ¼ teaspoon cinnamon in small bowl over nearly simmering water. Stir until smooth. Add butter and stir until blended. Remove from pan of water; let cool.

Beat egg yolks in large bowl. Beat in ½ cup sugar. Whip mixture at high speed for 5 minutes, or until pale and very thick. In another large dry bowl, beat egg whites with cream of tartar to soft peaks. Gradually beat in 2 tablespoons sugar. Whip at high speed until whites are stiff and shiny but not dry.

Gently stir chocolate mixture into yolk mixture with wooden spoon. Sift flour over chocolate mixture; fold in gently with spatula. Gently fold in whites in three batches. Pour batter into prepared pan. Bake for 40 minutes, or until a toothpick inserted in center of pudding comes out clean. Cool pudding in pan on wire rack until lukewarm; the center will settle slightly. Cut pudding in squares in the pan.

A short time before serving, prepare the spiced cream topping: In large chilled bowl, combine cream, 2 tablespoons sugar, 1½ teaspoons coffee powder, ¼ teaspoon cinnamon, ginger, and if you like, cloves. Whip at medium-high speed until cream forms soft peaks. Cover and refrigerate until ready to serve.

Serve the pudding lukewarm or at room temperature. Top each portion with a dollop of the coffee-spiced whipped cream.

Creamy Rose Water Pudding with Pistachios and Strawberries

muhallebi; mallabi

When my husband dreams of the comfort foods of his childhood in the Mideast, he always mentions *mallabi*. The version Yakir grew up with came topped with shredded coconut, chopped peanuts, and a spoonful of red syrup. Like ice cream in the United

States, *mallabi* is sold by street vendors in the Middle East. In Turkey, pudding shops make these sweet, smooth desserts in countless variations, flavored with fruit, nuts, rose water, or cinnamon and topped with toasted nuts or fruit. Some cooks prefer orange-flower water or vanilla extract.

For home cooks, few desserts are faster, easier, and more economical to prepare than this thick, creamy pudding. The basis is sweetened milk or fruit juice thickened with cornstarch, rice flour, or a mixture of both. This pudding base provides a neutral canvas for cooks to flavor as they choose. Some simmer raisins or chopped dried figs or dates in the pudding, others stir in ground nuts. For fancier versions, almonds, pistachios, or other nuts might first be infused in the milk to make nut milk. When a festive presentation is in order, the dessert is topped with whipped cream and toasted pistachios and accompanied by crisp cookies.

Most of the time *mallabi* is served cold but in winter it's enjoyed warm. When I have time, I infuse a vanilla bean in the pudding by heating the milk, adding the bean, and letting it stand for 20 minutes. If you like, you can prepare this pudding with low-fat milk or almond milk. Instead of strawberries, you can top it with sliced bananas, diced mangoes, or orange segments, which are also favorites in the region. I also like it with raspberries or blueberries.

◆ MAKES 4 SERVINGS.

2 to 4 tablespoons unsalted pistachios, toasted

¼ cup cornstarch

3 cups milk

4 to 5 tablespoons sugar

2 teaspoons rose water, orange-flower water, or vanilla extract, or to taste

1½ to 2 cups sliced strawberries

If you'd like to flavor the pudding with pistachios throughout, use 4 tablespoons pistachios. Grind 2 tablespoons of the pistachios very finely and chop the remaining pistachios.

Mix cornstarch with ½ cup cold milk to a smooth paste. Combine remaining milk with sugar in heavy saucepan and bring to a simmer, stirring. Stir cornstarch mixture again until smooth and pour it gradually into the simmering milk, whisking rapidly. Bring to a boil, stirring constantly. Cook for 5 minutes, or until mixture becomes a thick, smooth pudding. Stir in the ground pistachios.

Remove from heat and cool to room temperature, stirring occasionally. Stir in rose water. Transfer to shallow dessert dishes and refrigerate. Sprinkle chopped pistachios in the center of each one and surround nuts with strawberry slices. Serve any remaining strawberries separately.

Creamy Orchid Root Drink

---

salep; sahlab

Salep is used in the Mideast to flavor and thicken drinks and ice cream. It is most widely used to flavor a warm, comforting, creamy beverage that is especially loved in winter. I call salep the vanilla of the Mideast not only because it is used in similar ways but because, like vanilla, salep comes from an orchid. Salep is also the name of the drink, which is said to have been a favorite of the women of the sultan's harem at the time of the Ottoman Empire. On the other hand, my husband associates it with early morning prayers at the Sephardic synagogue in Givatayim, a suburb of Tel Aviv, where he used to go with his family as a child.

You can buy salep powder in Middle Eastern grocery stores. The drink is made like a simple pudding that thickens as it simmers. It's usually served sprinkled with cinnamon, and occasionally with finely chopped pistachios as well. Some people like to sprinkle a mixture of spices similar to Coffee Spice (page 365) or to substitute other toasted nuts or coconut for the pistachios.

◆ MAKES 2 SERVINGS.

2 cups milk

2 to 5 tablespoons sugar, or to taste

1 tablespoon salep powder

Cinnamon (for sprinkling)

1 to 2 teaspoons finely chopped toasted pistachios or almonds (optional, for sprinkling)

Combine milk, 2 tablespoons sugar, and salep powder in small heavy saucepan and mix well. Bring to a simmer, stirring constantly. Cook over low heat for 5 minutes, or until it thickens to taste. Taste, and add more sugar if you like. Pour into mugs and serve hot, sprinkled with cinnamon and pistachios.

Turkish Coffee

---

qahwah

A small cup of strong, thick black coffee is a staple in the Mideast. For many, it is absolutely necessary at the end of the meal and is also served throughout the day at home, at work, and at cafés. People sip the coffee slowly and enjoy it with plenty of sugar or occasionally with a sweet dessert like baklava. It's an acquired taste to the uninitiated but once acquired, it's addictive.

The coffee should be made from beans that are roasted very dark and ground as finely as possible. Home coffee grinders do not usually grind it finely enough. It's best to buy the roasted beans and ask to have them ground for Turkish coffee. To prepare the coffee, you need a special pot, which is small and very narrow at the top. You can buy it at Middle Eastern shops. For serving, use very small cups, such as espresso cups.

Unlike other ways of preparing the brew, for Turkish coffee the coffee is cooked. You bring it nearly to a boil and let it foam up without boiling over. The foam is considered a hallmark of a good cup of coffee, and some people bring the coffee to a boil repeatedly to make sure it's right. Most people add sugar when making the coffee, but you can serve sugar or other sweeteners separately.

When the coffee is flavored with sweet spices such as cardamom, cinnamon, ginger, and cloves, it is called Arabic coffee, or, by Yemenis, Yemeni coffee. All of my Yemenite relatives have a jar of this spice mixture, which they call "coffee spice," in their pantry; they either make it at home or buy the mix freshly ground. The spice is used in minute quantities, generally less than ¼ teaspoon per cup. Instead of the mix, some people infuse cardamom pods in the coffee, then remove them before serving.

◆ MAKES 2 SERVINGS.

⅔ cup water

2 teaspoons finest-grind dark roast coffee

2 to 4 teaspoons sugar, or to taste (optional)

Coffee Spice (optional, see Note)

Combine water, coffee, and sugar in a Turkish coffeepot and mix well. Bring nearly to a boil over medium-high heat, stirring. Be careful not to let it boil over as it foams up. Remove from heat and let stand for 1 or 2 minutes. Bring nearly to a boil again, then pour into 2 espresso cups or other small cups. If you like, set out a small container of coffee spice for people to add to their coffee.

Coffee Spice

Mix 2 tablespoons ground ginger, 1 tablespoon ground cinnamon, 1 tablespoon ground cardamom, and ½ teaspoon ground cloves. Store mixture in tightly covered jar or airtight container in dark cupboard.

Basics

Middle Eastern cooking is simple, casual, and relaxed and thus requires few special techniques. But here are some tips.

Blanching Almonds

You can buy blanched almonds, but they taste better and fresher if you prepare them yourself. Use them in cakes and pastries, or toast them for garnish.

Boil enough water in a saucepan to generously cover almonds. Add almonds and return to a boil. Boil about 10 seconds.

Remove 1 almond with slotted spoon. Press on one end of almond with your thumb and index finger; almond will come out of its skin. If it does not, boil them a few more seconds and try again. When almonds can be peeled easily, drain them and peel the rest.

Spread blanched almonds in a single layer on shallow trays or dishes lined with towels or paper towels to dry, and put towels on top of almonds as well. Pat them dry. Be sure they are thoroughly dried before storing or grinding them.

Toasting Nuts

Toasted nuts are a favorite garnish for rice and other grain dishes, and for pastas, salads, and desserts.

Toast nuts on a baking sheet in a preheated 350°F oven. A toaster oven is convenient for small amounts of nuts. Transfer them to a plate as soon as they're ready.

If you will be chopping or grinding the toasted nuts in a food processor, cool them completely before processing.

Pine Nuts

Toast pine nuts in oven about 3 minutes, or until lightly browned, shaking baking sheet once or twice. Transfer them to a plate.

Instead of using the oven, you can toast them in a dry skillet over medium-low heat for 2 to 3 minutes, tossing them often. Some cooks find a skillet safer than the oven because you can watch it and there's less chance of burning the nuts.

Hazelnuts

Toast hazelnuts about 8 minutes, or until their skins begin to split, shaking baking sheet once or twice. Transfer to a strainer. While nuts are hot, remove most of skins by rubbing nuts energetically with a towel against strainer.

Almonds

Whole with skins or whole blanched: Toast almonds in oven about 7 minutes; blanched almonds should brown lightly.

Slivered or sliced almonds: Toast slivered almonds 4 to 5 minutes, and sliced almonds 2 to 3 minutes, or until browned lightly, shaking baking sheet once or twice.

Walnuts or Pecans

Toast walnuts or pecans about 5 minutes, until aromatic and very lightly browned, shaking baking sheet once or twice.

Toasting Seeds

Sesame Seeds

Toasted sesame seeds are popular sprinkled over salads and in the popular Middle Eastern herb blend, zahtar (page 14).

Preheat oven to 350°F. Put sesame seeds on small baking sheet and toast about 5 minutes, until golden brown, shaking pan occasionally. Transfer immediately to a plate.

To toast a few tablespoons of seeds in a skillet, put seeds in small, heavy skillet over medium-low heat. Toast them about 4 minutes, or until golden brown, shaking pan often. Transfer immediately to a plate.

Cumin Seeds

Toasting cumin seeds is a favorite technique of many Middle Easterners. After they cool, the seeds are ground in a spice grinder or crushed in a mortar with pestle. They make a delicious accent when sprinkled on a variety of foods or used in spicy relishes (page 307).

Toast a few tablespoons of cumin seeds in small heavy skillet over medium heat about 2 to 3 minutes, until seeds are fragrant and turn slightly darker, shaking pan often. Transfer immediately to a plate.

Grilling Peppers

Grilled peppers make a very popular appetizer and garnish element in the Mideast. You can buy them in jars, but they taste even better when you prepare them yourself.

You can grill peppers on an open flame, either on the barbecue or on top of a burner, or you can broil them until their skins blacken. Then you put them in a bag, where the trapped steam loosens their skins. They're easy to peel and the seeds can be easily scraped off with a knife. I never rinse grilled peppers to help remove the skins and seeds. Doing this makes them lose flavor. For easy cleanup when I'm broiling, I put the peppers on a foil-lined broiler rack.

Preheat broiler with rack 2 to 4 inches from heat source, or far enough so peppers just fit; or heat grill. Put whole peppers, with core and stems still on, in broiler or on grill. Broil or grill peppers until their skins are blistered and charred all over but do not let them burn. If you don't want the peppers to soften too much, grill them until only slightly charred but still firm. The approximate cooking times are:

Bell peppers: 15 minutes

Anaheim (California, green or mild) chilies: 10 minutes

Poblano (pasilla), jalapeño, serrano, or other small chilies: 5 minutes

During broiling, turn peppers occasionally with tongs so another side faces flame—bell peppers every 5 minutes, Anaheim chilies every 3 minutes, jalapeño or serrano chiles every minute.

Transfer peppers to bowl and cover; or put them in paper or plastic bag and close bag. Let stand for 10 minutes. If your skin is sensitive, wear gloves when handling hot chilies. Peel peppers using paring knife.

Halve peppers; be careful because they may have hot juice inside. Discard seeds and ribs, and pat dry. Do not rinse. Or, if you would like to keep the peppers whole, gently pull each one open from its side and drain off any liquid inside, then carefully cut or pull out core with seeds.

Cooking Eggplants Whole

Grilling or baking eggplants whole is the easiest method for cooking them. An added bonus—you cook the eggplant without any fat.

Eggplant is best when thoroughly cooked, not al dente. Whether you roast, broil, or grill an eggplant, it should be very tender.

Roasted eggplants are easier to peel than grilled or broiled ones. You can peel eggplants most easily while they are still slightly warm; often you can simply pull the skin off. If they've cooled completely, peel them with the aid of a paring knife; or halve them lengthwise and scoop out the pulp with a spoon.

GRILLING

Prick each eggplant 5 or 6 times with a fork. Set them on barbecue at medium- or medium-high heat. Grill eggplants for 40 minutes, or until they feel soft when you press them, turning them over occasionally. You can use lower heat if your coals are less hot; the eggplant will simply take longer.

Let stand until cool enough to handle. Cut off caps and remove peel with the aid of a paring knife.

Broiling

Prick each eggplant 5 or 6 times with a fork. Set them on broiler rack or broiler pan, lined with foil if you like. Broil eggplants for about 40 minutes, or until they feel soft when you press them, turning them over occasionally.

Let stand until cool enough to handle. Cut off caps and remove peel with the aid of a paring knife. If eggplants appear wet, halve them lengthwise and drain in a colander for about 10 minutes.

Roasting

Preheat oven to 400°F. Prick each eggplant 5 or 6 times with a fork. Set them in a shallow roasting pan, lined with foil if you like. Bake eggplants for 45 to 60 minutes, or until they are very soft when you press them and look collapsed, turning them over once.

Let stand until cool enough to handle. Cut off caps and pull off eggplant peel. Halve eggplant lengthwise and put it in a colander. Leave it for about 10 minutes to drain off any liquid from inside eggplant.

Frying Eggplant Slices

Fried eggplants are a popular appetizer in the Mideast and also accompany a variety of sandwiches and entrées. To serve them as a simple first course, top the slices with tangy Fresh Chili Vinaigrette (page 308) or with Yogurt Garlic Sauce (page 311). They're also delicious with Spicy Tomato Sauce (page 305). For the traditional taste, salt the eggplant slices before frying them.

Cut a large eggplant (about 1¼ pounds) in ⅜-inch slices crosswise or lengthwise. If you like, sprinkle the slices lightly and evenly with salt. Put them on a rack and let stand to drain for about 1 hour, turning slices over after 30 minutes. Thoroughly pat them dry with paper towels.

For 1 eggplant you will need 7 to 10 tablespoons olive or vegetable oil. Heat 2 or 3 tablespoons oil in a large heavy skillet over medium heat. Quickly add enough eggplant slices to make one layer; if slices are added too slowly, the first ones soak up all the oil. Sauté for 3 minutes per side, or until they are tender when pierced with a fork. Transfer to plate with slotted spatula.

Add 2 tablespoons oil to pan, heat oil, and sauté another batch of eggplant in same way. Continue frying remaining eggplant in batches, adding 2 tablespoons oil before each batch and heating oil before adding the eggplant.

Transfer fried eggplant to paper towels and pat them to absorb excess oil. Transfer them to serving plate.

Peeling and Seeding Tomatoes

Many Middle Eastern cooks do not bother to peel tomatoes, but for some sauces it's a good idea to remove their skins so the sauce has a smooth texture. It depends on your personal taste.

To Peel Tomatoes

Cut green cores from tomatoes, turn each tomato over, and slit skin on bottom of tomato in an X shape.

Put a few tomatoes in saucepan of enough boiling water to cover them generously. Boil tomatoes for 10 to 15 seconds, or until their skin begins to pull away from their flesh. Immediately remove tomatoes from water with slotted spoon and put them in bowl of cold water. Leave for a few seconds so they cool.

Remove tomatoes from water and peel their skins with the aid of a paring knife. Continue with remaining tomatoes, in batches.

To Seed Tomatoes

Cut tomatoes in half horizontally. Hold each tomato half over bowl, cut side down. Squeeze tomato to remove seeds and juice. Don't worry if some of the seeds remain.

If you like, strain the juice and refrigerate it for drinking. You can add tomato skins to vegetable or meat stocks.

Slicing Onions

In the Mideast onions are often sliced lengthwise so they will have distinct pieces, especially for making caramelized onions, a popular topping for many dishes. When you want them to soften more and to almost melt to a sauce as they cook, slice them crosswise.

To slice an onion, cut it in half lengthwise, from its stem end through its root end. Put the halves on your board, cut side down, and hold one half lightly with your fingers curved. Holding a chef's knife in your other hand against your curved fingers, slice the onion in half-circles, moving your fingers back on the onion after each slice to guide the knife to cut even slices.

Seeding Pomegranates

Pomegranate seeds are a popular garnish for dips and desserts and are lovely on rice as well. When removing them from the fruit, this method minimizes the mess and helps prevent stains.

Cut a thin slice off the top and bottom of the pomegranate. With a knife, score the rind from the top to the bottom several times, as for cutting the peel from an orange.

Put the pomegranate in large bowl of cold water. Holding the fruit under water, remove rind and break fruit in sections. With your fingers, pull seeds out of membranes. Remove membranes from water, then remove pomegranate seeds from bottom of bowl. Drain them well.

Cooking Chickpeas and Other Dried Legumes

In the Mideast many people soak dried beans before cooking them. I generally soak only soybeans and fava beans to soften their skins. You can soak other beans if it's convenient or if you've had them a long time; doing so will slightly cut their cooking time.

◆ MAKES 5 TO 7 CUPS COOKED BEANS, ABOUT 6 SERVINGS.

1 pound dried chickpeas (garbanzo beans) or white, red, or black beans (2¼ to 2½ cups)

7 cups water, more if needed

Pinch salt

If you'd like to soak beans, put them in bowl and cover generously with cold water. Soak overnight in cool place or, if weather is hot, in refrigerator. Drain before cooking.

Put beans in large pot and add 7 cups water or enough to generously cover. Bring to a boil. Cover and simmer over low heat until tender, about 1¼ to 1½ hours for most beans and about 1½ to 2 hours for chickpeas, adding salt halfway through cooking time and adding hot water occasionally to keep them covered with water. If cooking beans ahead, refrigerate beans in their cooking liquid. Reserve cooking liquid for soups and stews.

Handling Phyllo Dough

Phyllo dough is a Mideastern favorite for savory and sweet pastries. It has an advantage over other pastries in that it does not contain fat. However, the dough must be brushed with some melted butter, margarine, or oil before baking or else it will be too dry. It's up to you to regulate how rich you want the dessert or appetizer to be, by brushing the pastry either lightly or generously with butter.

- Always keep phyllo dough tightly wrapped. If the sheets are frozen, thaw them in refrigerator 8 hours or overnight. Remove phyllo from refrigerator about 2 hours before using, but leave dough in its package until ready to use.
- Clear plenty of space for working with phyllo, as the sheets are large.
- Because phyllo dough contains no fat, it dries quickly and can become brittle and impossible to handle. To prevent this, keep it covered while assembling pastries. When you remove dough from package, cover it with plastic wrap or slightly damp towel. Work with one sheet at a time, keeping remaining sheets covered.
- Handle phyllo dough gently; it tears easily. When making triangles, do not worry about small holes in dough because folds will keep filling in.
- You can shape phyllo pastries one or two days ahead and refrigerate on baking sheets, or freeze for longer storage. Cover tightly with plastic wrap. If you have frozen pastries, thaw them for 30 minutes before baking and increase the baking time slightly.

Chicken Stock

khoulaset feraakh

In the Mideast, chicken broth is often made with whole chickens or meaty chicken pieces and served as soup. Stock is a more economical alternative, made from chicken bones or bony pieces, necks, wing tips, trimmings, and giblets. Both are much more delicious than canned broth and the results show in the dishes you make with them. It's useful to have stock in the freezer when you need a tasty liquid for cooking rice pilaf and other grain dishes or to make sauces and quick stews from boneless chicken pieces or vegetables.

♦ MAKES ABOUT 3 TO 3½ QUARTS.

> 4 pounds chicken wings, bones, backs, necks, and giblets (except livers)
>
> 2 onions, halved
>
> 2 carrots (optional)
>
> 2 celery stalks, with leaves (optional)
>
> 2 or 3 leeks, dark green parts, cleaned (optional)
>
> 2 garlic cloves (optional)
>
> 2 bay leaves, or 4 cardamom pods, cracked (optional)
>
> About 5 quarts water
>
> 2 sprigs fresh thyme, or 1 teaspoon dried thyme (optional)

Combine chicken, onions, carrots, celery, leeks, garlic, and bay leaves if you like in large pot. Add enough water to cover ingredients. Bring to a boil, skimming froth. Add thyme.

Reduce heat to low so that stock bubbles very gently. Partially cover and cook for 2 hours, skimming foam and fat occasionally. Strain stock into large bowls. Cool stock, refrigerate until cold, and skim solidified fat off top.

Turkey Stock

Substitute turkey wings or wing tips, turkey bones, and giblets (except livers). Cook the stock for 3 hours. You can also use bones and carcass of one roast turkey. Chop it into pieces that fit in pot. Cook stock for 2 to 3 hours.

Meat Stock

khoulaset lahm

Meat stock gives great flavor to soups, stews, and rice dishes. People in the region use beef or lamb. Use beef soup bones or any bony cut of beef or lamb, trimming off excess fat first. For a more delicate stock, use veal bones or bony pieces. Home cooks in the Mideast do not usually roast the bones first, as French chefs do.

The stock is easy to make and simmers on its own, needing practically no attention. If you make it in a pressure cooker, it's ready in 2 hours. It keeps well in the freezer.

♦ MAKES ABOUT 2 QUARTS.

5 pounds beef soup bones, chopped in
pieces by the butcher

2 onions, rinsed but not peeled, root end
cut off

2 carrots, scrubbed but not peeled (optional)

2 celery stalks, cut in 3-inch pieces (optional)

2 bay leaves, or 4 cardamom pods, cracked

1 large thyme sprig (optional)

4 large garlic cloves, unpeeled

About 4 quarts water

In stock pot or other large pot, combine all
ingredients. Add enough water to cover.
Bring to a boil, skimming froth. Partially
cover and cook stock over very low heat, so it
bubbles very gently, skimming foam and fat
occasionally. During first 2 hours of cooking, add hot water occasionally to keep ingredients covered. Cook stock for a total of
6 hours. Strain stock. Cool stock, refrigerate
until cold, and skim solidified fat off top.

Fish Stock

khoulaset samak

Mediterranean and Middle Eastern shoppers use the heads and tails of the fish they
buy to make stock, or braise their fish in big
chunks so that the liquid turns into broth
for use as a sauce for the same dish or to use
at another meal.

Since our fish in North America is usually

sold already filleted, it's good to use stock to
intensify the taste of sauces that go with
them. Use heads, tails, and bones of any fish
except strong-flavored ones like tuna and
mackerel. You can ask for these inexpensive
parts at the fish store. An alternative available in some North American markets is rea-
sonably priced "fish pieces for chowder,"
or "fish collars," our equivalent of what's
sold in Mediterranean countries as "fish for
soup," which are usually small, bony whole
fish.

You can simply simmer the bones in
water, or flavor the stock with herbs or an
onion. If you're not using the stock within
two days, freeze it.

♦ MAKES 4½ TO 5 CUPS.

1 pound fish bones or fish pieces for
chowder

1 onion, chopped (optional)

1 tablespoon olive oil or vegetable oil
(optional)

1 large thyme sprig, or 1 teaspoon dried
thyme (optional)

1 bay leaf (optional)

6 cups water

Rinse fish bones thoroughly. If you want to
flavor your stock with sautéed onion, heat
oil in large saucepan, add onion, and cook
over medium heat for 5 minutes, or until
softened but not brown. Instead of sautéing,
you can simply add onion to pan with the
other ingredients. Add fish bones, thyme,
bay leaf, and water to cover. Bring to a boil;

skim off foam. Simmer, uncovered, over low heat for 15 to 20 minutes, skimming occasionally. Strain into bowl.

Vegetable Stock

---

khoulaset khodar

Vegetable stock adds a delicate pleasing flavor to soups, sauces, stews, and grain dishes and is useful to have on hand. In addition to being very economical, fat-free, and almost effortless, homemade stock has an advantage over most packaged versions in that it is not overly salty. When you have parsley stems and trimmings of onions, leeks, carrots, mushrooms, tomatoes, and celery, you can freeze them to add to the pot when you're ready to make stock.

For a very light vegetable broth, I use the cooking liquid from mild vegetables such as carrots, zucchini, and asparagus. Whenever I cook vegetables, I save the liquid in a jar in the refrigerator. Vegetable stock or broth keeps for two or three days.

◆ MAKES ABOUT 6 CUPS.

3 large onions, coarsely chopped

1 or 2 large carrots, cut in large dice (optional)

2 or 3 celery stalks with leafy tops, sliced (optional)

Dark green part of 1 or 2 leeks, rinsed thoroughly and sliced (optional)

1 large soft tomato, halved (optional)

3 sprigs fresh thyme, or 1½ teaspoons dried thyme

10 parsley stems (optional)

4 large garlic cloves, peeled and crushed (optional)

Pinch of salt (optional)

2 quarts water

Combine ingredients in medium saucepan. Bring to a boil. Cover and cook over low heat for 45 minutes to 1 hour. Strain broth, pressing on ingredients in strainer; discard ingredients in strainer. Refrigerate or freeze broth until ready to use.

Menus for Entertaining
and for Every Day

Supper for a Sultan

Warm Carrot Salad with Lemon, Garlic, and Mint

Spicy Beef-Stuffed Cabbage in Pepper Sauce

Saffron Shrimp and Pine Nut Pilaf

Prince-pleaser Ragout with Cheesy Eggplant Puree

Pecan-Cinnamon Baklava Fingers

Dinner from the Land of the Pharaohs

Egyptian Fava Bean Dip with Garlic and Coriander

Middle Eastern Diced Salad

Cumin Marinated Fish with Tomato Onion Sauce and Yogurt Mint Dressing

Rice Pilaf with Chard, Pine Nuts, and Pomegranate Seeds

Date-Nut Halvah Balls

Buffet of Biblical Inspiration

Cucumber Salad with Green Olives

Sesame Chicken Salad with Barley and Fava Beans

Savory Stewed Onions, Middle Eastern Style

Wheat Berry Pudding with Walnuts, Dried Fruit, Milk, and Honey

Queen of Sheba Chocolate Cake

A Favorite Feast of My Middle Eastern Family

Three-Bean Salad with Tomatoes, Olives, and Cilantro

Grilled Whole Chicken with Yemeni Spice Rub

Yahalom's Hawaijj Hamburgers

Hedva's Hot Pepper Relish—*Zehug*

Rice Pilaf with Toasted Almonds

Mocha Pudding with Spiced Whipped Cream

Autumn Harvest Celebration

Feta Phyllo Turnovers with Chard

Israeli Eggplant Dip with Garlic Mayonnaise

Two-way Summer Squash Stew with Sweet Peppers

Sweet-and-Savory Stuffed Peppers with Meat, Nuts, and Currants

Turkish Tomato Pilaf

Citrus and Spice-scented Quinces with Cranberries

Meze Brunch Buffet

Eastern Mediterranean Potato Salad

Herbed Hummus

Tomato Basil Tahini

Sweet-and-Spicy Marinated Grilled Peppers

Chicken Tabbouleh Salad

Marzipan Chocolate-Chip Phyllo Triangles with Pine Nuts

Casual Winter Get-Together

Grated Vegetable Salad with Pistachios, Raisins, and Yogurt

Lebanese Meat and Pine Nut Pizzas

Roast Chicken with Fennel, Olives, and Bulgur Wheat

Pomegranate Poached Pears

Potluck Summertime Supper

Crab and Couscous Salad with Asparagus, Mint, and Pine Nuts

Turkish Shepherd's Salad

Hot Pepper Hummus

Mideast Minestrone

Figs in Fennel Syrup

A Welcome to Spring

Asparagus with Egyptian Takliah Dressing

Green Salad with Herbs and Radishes

Persian New Year Fish

Aromatic Pistachio-filled Cookies

Warm-Weather Vegetarian Luncheon

Diced Vegetable Salad with Garlic-Mint Dressing and Toasted Pita—*Fattoush*

Classic Cucumber Salad with Yogurt, Garlic, and Mint

Avocado Vegetable Wrap with Feta

Armenian Green Beans

Red Beans and Yellow Rice with Carrots and Raisins

Fruit Salad with Honey and Toasted Almonds

BIBLIOGRAPHY

Abdennour, Samia. *Egyptian Cooking: A Practical Guide.* New York: Hippocrene Books, 1998.

Abourezk, Sanaa. *Secrets of Healthy Middle Eastern Cuisine.* New York: Interlink, 2000.

Abu-Ghoch, Nawal. *The Arab-Israeli Cuisine.* Jerusalem: Keter, no publication date. (Hebrew)

Al Hashimi, Miriam. *Traditional Arabic Cooking.* Reading, UK: Garnet, 1993.

Alford, Jeffrey, and Naomi Duguid. *Flatbreads & Flavors: A Baker's Atlas.* New York: Morrow, 1995.

Algar, Ayla Esen. *The Complete Book of Turkish Cooking.* London: Kegan Paul International, 1985.

Almoni, Malka. *Yemenite Cooking.* Jerusalem: The Jerusalem Publishing House, 1983. (Hebrew)

Anthony, Dawn, Elaine, and Selwa. *Lebanese Cookbook.* Sydney, Australia: Lansdowne Press, 1978.

Antreassian, Alice. *The 40 Days of Lent: Selected Armenian Recipes.* New York: Ashod Press, 1985.

Aoun, Fayez. *280 Recettes de Cuisine Familiale Libanaise.* Paris: Jacques Grancher, 1980.

Batmanglij, Najmieh. *New Food for Life: Ancient Persian and Modern Iranian Cooking and Ceremonies.* Washington, D.C.: Mage, 1996.

Boulos-Guillaume, Nouhad. *La Cuisine Libanaise Naturelle.* Paris: Edifra, 1988.

Burum, Linda. *A Guide to Ethnic Food in Los Angeles.* New York: HarperPerennial, 1992.

Corey, Helen. *The Art of Syrian Cookery.* New York: Doubleday, 1962.

Der Haroutunian, Arto. *A Turkish Cookbook.* London: Ebury Press, 1987.

Der Haroutunian, Arto. *Patisserie of the Eastern Mediterranean.* New York: McGraw-Hill, 1989.

Eren, Neset. *The Art of Turkish Cooking.* New York: Hippocrene Books, 1993.

Farah, Madelain. *Lebanese Cuisine.* Portland, Ore.: Madelain Farah, 1981.

Ghanoonparvar, M. R. *Persian Cuisine Books One and Two.* Lexington, Ky.: Mazda, 1982 and 1984.

Gokalp, Emine H. *L'Art Culinaire en Turquie.* Paris: Publisud, 1990.

Gotz, Margrit. *La Cucina Afghana.* Bologna: Calderini, 1986.

Hekmat, Forough. *The Art of Persian Cooking.* New York: Hippocrene Books, 1998.

Khalil, Nagwa E. *Egyptian Cuisine.* Washington, D.C.: Worldwide Graphics, 1980.

Kremezi, Aglaia. *The Foods of Greece.* New York: Stewart, Tabori & Chang, 1993.

Mallos, Tess. *The Complete Middle East Cookbook.* New York: McGraw-Hill, 1979.

Markarian, Gerard. *100 Recettes de Cuisine Traditionnelle Armenienne.* Paris: Jacques Grancher, 1996.

Mazda, Maideh. *In a Persian Kitchen.* Rutland, Vt.: Charles E. Tuttle, 1960.

Mohamed, Salima Ait. *La Cuisine Egyptienne: Des Pharaons a Nos Jours.* Marseilles: Autres Temps, 1997.

Mouzannar, Ibrahim. *La Cuisine Libanaise.* Beirut: Librairie du Liban, 1983.

Najor, Julia. *Babylonian Cuisine: Chaldean Cookbook from the Middle East.* New York: Vantage Press, 1981.

Nasser, Christiane Dabdoub. *Classic Palestinian Cookery.* London: Saqi Books, 2001.

Nicolaou, Nearchos. *Cooking From Cyprus.* Nicosia, Cyprus: Theopress, 1979.

Ozan, Ozcan. *The Sultan's Kitchen: A Turkish Cookbook.* Boston: Periplus, 2001.

Perez-Rubin, Pascale. *Delicacies of Iraq.* Tel Aviv: Modan, 1990. (Hebrew)

Perez-Rubin, Pascale. *Israeli Flavors.* Ramat Gan, Israel: R. Sirkis Publishers, 1987. (Hebrew)

Perry, Charles. "Tabbouleh Town," *Los Angeles Times,* April 24, 2002.

Rayess, George N. *Rayess' Art of Lebanese Cooking.* Beirut: Librairie du Liban, 1991.

Roden, Claudia. *The New Book of Middle Eastern Food.* New York: Knopf, 2000.

Salloum, Habeeb, and James Peters. *From the Lands of Figs and Olives.* New York: Interlink, 1995.

Saberi, Helen. *Afghan Food & Cookery.* New York: Hippocrene Books, 2000.

Shaheer, Jameela. *Arab World Cook Book.* Saudi Arabia: The International Bookshops, 1973.

Shaida, Margaret. *The Legendary Cuisine of Persia.* New York: Interlink, 2002.

Shihab, Aziz. *A Taste of Palestine: Menus and Memories.* San Antonio, Texas: Corona, 1993.

Shilo, Varda. *Kurdistani Cooking.* Jerusalem: Kaneh Publishing, 1986. (Hebrew)

Simmons, Shirin. *Entertaining the Persian Way.* Luton, England: Lennard, 1988.

Unsal, Artun and Beyhan. *Istanbul la Magnifique.* Paris: Laffont, 1991.

Uvezian, Sonia. *The Cuisine of Armenia.* New York: Hippocrene Books, 1998.

Wolfert, Paula. *The Cooking of the Eastern Mediterranean.* New York: HarperCollins, 1994.

Wright, Clifford A. *A Mediterranean Feast.* New York: Morrow, 1999.

Zamir, Levana. *Cooking from the Nile's Land.* Israel: Hakibbutz Hameuchad, 1982. (Hebrew)

Index